The Oxford Illustrated Dictionary
For Children

The Oxford Illustrated Dictionary For Children

Compiled by John Weston
and Alan Spooner

Illustrated by
Henry Barnett

TREASURE PRESS

First published in 1976 by
Oxford University Press under the title
The Oxford Children's Dictionary in colour

This edition published in 1985 by
Treasure Press
59 Grosvenor Street
London W1

© Oxford University Press 1976

ISBN 1 85051 086 5

Printed in Czechoslovakia
50602

We have written this dictionary for young readers who want a real dictionary which is helpfully arranged and easy to understand. We have included all the words they are likely to meet and want to use for themselves. To make spelling quite safe we have included in full all the various forms of the words.

No dictionary is ever written without help. We are particularly grateful to our families and friends who have given us such generous help and encouragement over the years. We have been proud to share in the Oxford tradition and wish to record our gratitude to Miss J. M. Hawkins, Mrs E. J. Pusey, and Mr M. W. Grose, members of the Oxford English Dictionary Department and Mrs W. K. Davin, who retired recently from the Education Department of the Oxford University Press.

JOHN WESTON

October 1975 ALAN SPOONER

Aa

a, an 1. One, any. 2. Each, every. *He earns two pounds an hour.*

aback *Taken aback*, surprised.

abandon (abandons, abandoning, abandoned) 1. To give up. 2. To leave without intending to return. *To abandon ship.*

abattoir (abattoirs) A slaughterhouse, a place where animals are killed for food.

abbess (abbesses) The head of a nunnery.

abbey (abbeys) 1. A group of buildings where monks or nuns live and work. 2. A church which is or was part of an abbey. *Westminster Abbey.*

abbot (abbots) The head of an abbey.

abbreviation (abbreviations) A short way of writing a word.

abdicate (abdicates, abdicating, abdicated) To give up the throne. abdication.

abdomen (abdomens) The part of the body containing the stomach.

abduct (abducts, abducting, abducted) To kidnap, to carry off illegally. abduction.

abhorrent Hateful.

abide (abides, abiding, abode) 1. (old-fashioned) To remain, to stay. *Abide with me.* 2. *I can't abide it!* I can't bear it!

abiding 1. Lasting. 2. Staying.

ability See able [2].

ablaze On fire, burning brightly.

able [1] Having the power or opportunity to do something. *Are you able to come?*

able [2] (abler, ablest) Clever, skilled. ably, ability.

able seaman A fully-trained seaman.

abnormal Not normal, unusual abnormally, abnormality.

Abo (Abos) (Australian informal) An Aboriginal.

aboard On a ship.

abode (abodes) A place where someone lives.

abolish (abolishes, abolishing, abolished) To put an end to something, to do away with something.

abominate (abominates, abominating, abominated) To hate. abominable, abomination.

Aboriginal (Aboriginals) One of the Aborigines.

Aborigines The original inhabitants of a country, especially of Australia.

about 1. In various directions. *Running about.* 2. In various places. *Lying about the room.* 3. Near, near by. *Is anybody about?* 4. In connection with. *I told the police about it. How about it?* What is your opinion? 5. Roughly. *About three metres long.* 6. *While you are about it,* while you are doing it.

above 1. Higher than. 2. Greater than, more than. 3. Too proud to do something. *He thinks he's above playing with us.* 4. *That's above me,* that's too difficult for me. 5. *Above-board,* thoroughly honest.

abrasive Scraping.

abreast Side by side.

abridged Shortened.

abroad In another country.

abrupt Sudden. abruptly.

abscess (abscesses) A sore on the body full of pus.

abscond (absconds, absconding, absconded) To run away secretly.

absence (absences) 1. Being away from somewhere. 2. Lack of something. *The plants died in the absence of water.*

absent 1. Away. *Absent from school.* 2. *Absent-minded,* forgetful, vague.

absolute Complete, not restricted, not limited. absolutely.

absorb (absorbs, absorbing, absorbed) 1. To soak up. absorbent. 2. *To be absorbed,* to be very interested. *Absorbing,* interesting.

abstain (abstains, abstaining, abstained) *To abstain from,* to do without, to refrain from.

abstract Concerned with ideas rather than things. abstraction.

absurd Silly, unreasonable. absurdly, absurdity.

abundant Plentiful, more than enough. abundantly, abundance.

abuse (abuses, abusing, abused) 1. To treat something badly. 2. To say insulting things to someone. abusive, abusively.

abysmal (informal) Very bad.

abyss (abysses) A deep hole in the ground, a bottomless pit.

academic 1. Scholarly. 2. Theoretical, logical, not practical.

academy (academies) 1. A college. 2. A society devoted to learning or art.

accelerate (accelerates, accelerating, accelerated) To increase speed. acceleration.

accelerator (accelerators) One of the pedals in a motor vehicle. When pressed down, it makes the engine run faster.

accent (accents) 1. The way in which a language is pronounced. *Mr. O'Reilly speaks English with an Irish accent.* 2. A mark written above a letter, as in *café.*

accept (accepts, accepting, accepted) 1. To take something which is offered. 2. *The accepted idea,* the generally agreed idea.

acceptable Pleasing.

access Approach.

accessible Easily reached.

accession (accessions) A coming to the throne.

accessory (accessories) An extra part.

accident (accidents) An unexpected event, usually unfortunate. *By accident,* without being planned or intended.

accidental Happening by chance, not intended. accidentally.

accommodate (accommodates, accommodating, accommodated) To provide a room for someone in a hotel or lodging house. accommodation.

accommodating Helpful.

accompany (accompanies, accompanying, accompanied) 1. To go with somebody or something. 2. To happen at the same time as something else. 3. To make music to support a singer or player. accompaniment.

accomplice (accomplices) A helper, a companion in wrongdoing.

accomplish (accomplishes, accomplishing, accomplished) To finish something successfully.

accomplished Skilled.

accomplishment (accomplishments) A skill.

accord Agreement. *Of one's own accord,* without being asked.

according *According to,* 1. On the authority of somebody. 2. In proportion to. 3. Following the order of something.

accordingly 1. Therefore. 2. As the circumstances suggest. *Act accordingly.*

accordion (accordions) A musical instrument with bellows and often with a keyboard.

account[1] (accounts, accounting, accounted) 1. *To account for something,* to explain it. 2. To make a record of how money was spent.

account [2] (accounts) 1. A statement of money received or spent or owing, a bill. 2. A description, a story. 3. *Of no account*, of little value. 4. *On account of*, because of. 5. *On no account*, for no reason. 6. *To take into account*, to consider.

accountant (accountants) An expert in looking after bills and accounts.

accumulate (accumulates, accumulating, accumulated) To pile up, to collect together. **accumulation.**

accumulator (accumulators) A device for storing electricity.

accurate Exact, correct. **accurately, accuracy.**

accursed Cursed, hateful.

accuse (accuses, accusing, accused) To blame somebody, to state that he has done something wrong. **accusation.**

accustomed 1. Usual. *In its accustomed place.* 2. *To be accustomed to something*, to be used to it.

ace (aces) 1. The 'one' on playing-cards. 2. In tennis, a service that the other player cannot return.

ache [1] (aches, aching, ached) To have a pain which lasts a long time, like a headache.

ache [2] (aches) A continuous pain.

achieve (achieves, achieving, achieved) To do something successfully, to reach a certain point. **achievement.**

acid [1] (acids) 1. A sour substance. 2. A chemical containing hydrogen which makes a substance called litmus turn red.

acid [2] Sour, sharp-tasting.

acknowledge (acknowledges, acknowledging, acknowledged) 1. To admit that something is true. 2. To show thanks for something. **acknowledgement.**

acorn (acorns) The seed of an oak tree.

acoustics 1. The science of sound. 2. *A hall with bad acoustics*, a hall where it is hard to hear clearly.

acquaintance (acquaintances) 1. *An acquaintance*, a person one has met but who is not yet a friend. 2. *To make someone's acquaintance*, to get to know someone.

acquainted *To be acquainted with*, to know.

acquire (acquires, acquiring, acquired) To get, to obtain. **acquisition.**

acquit (acquits, acquitting, acquitted) To declare that somebody is not guilty.

acre (acres) A measure of area of land, 4,840 square yards or 4,047 square metres.

acrid Sharp, bitter-smelling.

acrobat (acrobats) A person who does clever and exciting gymnastic exercises. **acrobatic.**

across 1. From one side to the other. *He walked across the bridge.* 2. On the other side. *I live across the street.*

act [1] (acts) 1. An action. 2. A law passed by parliament. 3. Part of a play. 4. A performance or a pretence. *He's only putting on an act.*

act [2] (acts, acting, acted) 1. To do something. 2. To perform in a play or a film. 3. To pretend.

acting Temporary.

action (actions) 1. The doing of something, something done. *An unkind action.* 2. *To take action*, to do something. 3. *Out of action*, not working properly. 4. A battle. *Action stations*, positions taken up before a battle.

active Energetic, able to do things. **actively.**

activity (activities) 1. Liveliness. 2. Something to be done, an occupation.

actor (actors) A performer in a play or a film.

actress (actresses) A female actor.

actual Real. actually.

acute 1. Sharp, keen. acutely. 2. *An acute angle*, an angle smaller than a right angle. 3. *An acute accent*, the mark (´) as used in *café*.

A.D. *Anno Domini*, in the year of our Lord, after the birth of Jesus Christ. *A.D. 1066 is the year of the Battle of Hastings.*

adamant Very firm, determined.

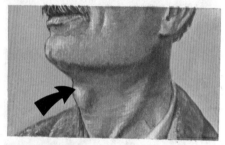

Adam's apple The lump seen in the front of a man's neck.

adapt (adapts, adapting, adapted) To make something suitable for another purpose. adaptable, adapter.

add (adds, adding, added) 1. To join one thing to another. 2. *To add to*, to increase. 3. *To add up*, to find the sum total of several numbers.

adder (adders) A poisonous snake.

addict (addicts) A person who has a harmful habit and cannot give it up. addiction, addicted.

addition (additions) 1. Adding up. 2. Something which has been added. additional.

address (addresses) The details of a place where somebody lives, as written on an envelope.

adenoids A mass of spongy flesh growing at the back of the nose.

adequate Enough, as much as is needed. adequately.

adhere (adheres, adhering, adhered) To stick to something or somebody.

adhesive [1] (adhesives) Glue or paste.

adhesive [2] Sticky. *Adhesive tape.*

adieu Good-bye.

adjacent Lying alongside or near.

adjective (adjectives) A describing word. *Hard, lazy,* and *tall* are adjectives.

adjourn (adjourns, adjourning, adjourned) 1. To break off a meeting until another time. 2. To move to another place.

adjudicate (adjudicates, adjudicating, adjudicated) To judge. adjudicator, adjudication.

adjust (adjusts, adjusting, adjusted) To arrange something, to put it exactly right.

administer (administers, administering, administered) 1. To look after business affairs. 2. To give. *To administer punishment.* administrator, administration.

admiral (admirals) An officer of high rank in the navy.

admire (admires, admiring, admired) 1. To have a high opinion of somebody or something. 2. To look at something with pleasure. *We admired the view.* admirer, admiration, admirable.

admit (admits, admitting, admitted) 1. To let someone in. *He admitted the guests.* 2. To confess. *He admitted that he was guilty.* admission, admittedly.

ado Fuss.

adolescence The time between being a child and being grown up. adolescent.

adopt (adopts, adopting, adopted) To take somebody into one's family and treat him as one's own child. adoption.

adore (adores, adoring, adored) To worship, to love very much. adorable, adoration.

adorn (adorns, adorning, adorned) To decorate. adornment.

adrift Drifting.

adult (adults) A fully grown person.

adultery (adulteries) Unfaithfulness to one's husband or wife. adulterer.

advance [1] (advances, advancing, advanced) To move forward.

advance[2] (advances) A forward movement, progress. *In advance of*, before.

advantage (advantages) 1. Something useful or helpful. 2. Profit, benefit. 3. *To take advantage of something*, to use it profitably. 4. *To take advantage of somebody*, to make unfair use of him.

Advent 1. The coming of Jesus Christ. 2. The period before Christmas.

adventure (adventures) 1. A strange, exciting, or dangerous event or journey. 2. Risk, danger. **adventurous, adventurously, adventurer.**

adversary (adversaries) An enemy.

adverse Hostile, opposing. **adversely.**

adversity (adversities) A trouble or misfortune.

advertise (advertises, advertising, advertised) To make something known to other people in order to encourage sales. **advertiser, advertisement.**

advice An opinion, a suggestion.

advisable Sensible. **advisability.**

advise (advises, advising, advised) To give advice, to recommend. **adviser.**

aerial (aerials) A device of rods and wire used to transmit and receive broadcast radio and television signals.

aerobatics Clever flying of aircraft in an exciting display.

aerodrome (aerodromes) An area of ground where aeroplanes may land and take off.

aeroplane (aeroplanes) A flying machine with wings.

aerosol (aerosols) A device which releases its contents in a fine misty spray.

afar Far off.

affair (affairs) 1. A thing, an event. 2. *Affairs*, business.

affect (affects, affecting, affected) To have an effect on someone or something. *Damp, cold weather affects my health.*

affection (affections) Kindly feeling, love. **affectionate, affectionately.**

affirmative Answering 'yes'.

afflict (afflicts, afflicting, afflicted) To cause someone pain or trouble. **affliction.**

affluent Wealthy, rich. **affluence.**

afford (affords, affording, afforded) To spare money or time for something. *I can't afford a long holiday this year.*

aflame In flames.

afloat 1. Floating. 2. At sea.

afraid 1. Frightened. 2. *I'm afraid I'm late*, I'm sorry I'm late.

afresh Again, in a new way.

African Of Africa.

Afrikaans The language of the Afrikaner in South Africa.

Afrikaner (Afrikaners) A South African of Dutch descent.

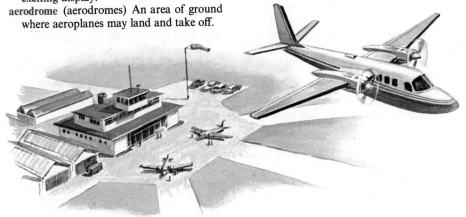

aft Towards the stern of a boat.

after 1. Later than. *After lunch.* 2. Next, following. *He came in after you.* 3. Behind. *Shut it after you, please.* 4. In spite of. *After all she did for him, he never wrote to her.*

afternoon (afternoons) The time between midday and evening.

afterwards Later.

again 1. Once more. *Now and again*, occasionally. 2. As before. *Put it back again!*

against 1. Not on the side of, not in favour of. 2. Touching or hitting. *The waves beat against the cliffs. The ladder was standing against the wall.*

age (ages) 1. The length of time a person has lived or a thing has existed. *Of age*, 18 or over. 2. *Middle age, old age*, stages of life following youth. 3. A period of history. *The Iron Age. The Middle Ages.*

aged Old.

agency (agencies) The office of an agent.

agent (agents) A man who arranges things for other people.

aggravate (aggravates, aggravating, aggravated) 1. To make worse. 2. (informal) To annoy. **aggravation.**

aggressive Liable to attack first, attacking first. **aggressively, aggression, aggressor.**

aghast Shocked, horrified.

agile Quick-moving. **agility.**

agitate (agitates, agitating, agitated) To stir up, to disturb. **agitator, agitation.**

agnostic (agnostics) A person who believes that nothing can be known about God.

ago In the past.

agog Eager.

agony (agonies) Severe pain.

agree (agrees, agreeing, agreed) 1. To consent, to say 'yes'. *I agree to your plan.* 2. To have the same ideas and opinions. *Jack and Jill don't quarrel, they always agree.* 3. *To agree with*, to suit, to be good for the health of. *Fatty foods did not agree with Jack Sprat.* **agreement, agreeable, agreeably.**

agriculture Farming, the cultivation of the soil. **agricultural.**

aground Stranded, touching the bottom in shallow water.

ahead 1. In front. *To stay ahead.* 2. Into the future. *To think ahead.* 3. Forwards. *To go ahead.*

ahoy A cry used by seamen to attract attention.

aid[1] (aids, aiding, aided) To help.

aid[2] 1. Help. 2. (aids) Something which gives help. *A hearing aid.*

ailment (ailments) An illness.

aim (aims, aiming, aimed) 1. To point a gun or other weapon at something. 2. To throw or kick something in a certain direction. *He aimed the ball at the stumps.* 3. To have a particular plan in mind. *We aim at arriving for dinner.* **aimless, aimlessly.**

air[1] (airs) 1. The mixture of gases which surrounds the earth and which people breathe. 2. A tune, a melody.

air[2] (airs, airing, aired) 1. To put something in a warm place to dry. **airing-cupboard.** 2. To let air into a room. 3. To show to others what one knows. *To air one's opinions*, to make them known.

airborne 1. In the air. 2. Carried by air.

air-conditioner (air-conditioners) An apparatus which supplies clean fresh air at a comfortable temperature. **air-conditioning, air-conditioned.**

aircraft (aircraft) A flying machine such as an aeroplane or a helicopter.

aircraft-carrier (aircraft-carriers) A ship with a flat deck on which aircraft may take off or land.

aircrew (aircrews) The crew of an aircraft.

airfield (airfields) An aerodrome.

air force A body of men and aircraft organized for fighting.

air-gun (air-guns) A gun worked by compressed air.

air hostess A woman who looks after passengers and serves meals on an air-liner.

airline (airlines) A company whose business

is to carry passengers or goods by aeroplane.

air-liner (air-liners) A passenger aircraft.

airmail Letters and parcels which are carried by aircraft.

airman (airmen) The pilot or a member of the crew of an aircraft.

airplane (airplanes) The American word for aeroplane.

airport (airports) An aerodrome from or to which aircraft make regular flights carrying passengers or goods.

air raid An attack by aircraft.

airship (airships) A large balloon with engines, designed to carry people or goods.

airstrip (airstrips) A strip of land cleared for aircraft to take off and land.

air-tight Fitting so closely that air cannot get in or out.

airworthy Safe to fly. **airworthiness**.

airy 1. Breezy, with plenty of fresh air. 2. Light-hearted, gay. **airily**.

aisle (aisles) A passage between or beside pews in a church or seats in a theatre or an aeroplane.

ajar Partly open.

akin Related.

alarm[1] (alarms, alarming, alarmed) To warn, to frighten, to disturb. **alarmingly**.

alarm[2] (alarms) A warning. *An alarm clock.*

alas A cry of sorrow.

albatross (albatrosses) A large sea-bird.

albino (albinos) An animal or person with white hair and pink eyes.

album (albums) A book or record containing many items.

alcohol An intoxicating liquid. **alcoholic**.

alcove (alcoves) Part of a room set back into a wall.

alderman (aldermen) A senior member of a city or county council.

ale (ales) Beer. **alehouse**.

alert Watchful, lively. *On the alert*, on guard, ready. **alertly**, **alertness**.

algebra A kind of mathematics in which letters are used to represent numbers.

alias (aliases) A false name.

alibi (alibis) A defence which declares that a person accused of a crime was somewhere else when it was committed.

alien Foreign.

alight Burning, on fire.

alike 1. Like one another. *The twins look alike.* 2. In the same way. *The twins are treated alike.*

alive Living, lively.

all 1. The whole number or the whole amount of something. *All the king's horses.* 2. Everything. *All is lost!* 3. Completely. *He was dressed all in black.*

Allah The Muslim name of God.

allegiance Loyalty.

alleluia (alleluias) 1. Praise God! 2. A song of praise to God.

allergic *To be allergic to something*, to be liable to become ill if one touches or eats it.

alley (alleys) A narrow lane or passage between buildings.

alliance (alliances) An agreement between allies.

alligator (alligators) A kind of crocodile found in America.

allot (allots, allotting, allotted) To distribute, to give out in proper shares.

allotment (allotments) A small area of land for which someone pays rent in order to grow vegetables, fruit, or flowers.

allow (allows, allowing, allowed) 1. To permit. *Smoking is not allowed.* 2. To give, to set aside. *The teacher allowed them an hour for their painting.* **allowable**, **allowance**.

alloy (alloys) A mixture of two or more metals. *Brass is an alloy of copper and zinc.*

all right 1. Well, in good condition. *Are you all right?* **2.** Satisfactory. *The food is all right.* **3.** Yes. *All right, I'm coming.*

all-rounder (all-rounders) A sportsman gifted in various ways.

allude (alludes, alluding, alluded) To refer to something. **allusion.**

alluring Fascinating, charming. **alluringly.**

ally (allies) A person or country that has agreed to support another.

almanac (almanacs) A calendar with notes, an annual book of information.

almighty Having all power. *The Almighty,* God.

almond (almonds) A kind of nut.

almost Nearly.

alms Money and goods given to the poor.

aloft High up in the air or in the rigging of a ship.

alone 1. By oneself. *I like to be alone sometimes.* **2.** And nobody else. *You alone know my secret.* **3.** Untouched. *Leave my model alone.*

along 1. From one end to another of something, on any part of its length. **2.** *Come along!* Hurry up! **3.** *I knew it all along,* I knew it all the time.

alongside Beside.

aloof Distant, unfriendly.

aloud 1. In an ordinary voice, not in a whisper, not silently. *To read aloud.* **2.** In a loud voice.

alp (alps) A high mountain. *The Alps,* the mountains in and around Switzerland. **alpine.**

alphabet (alphabets) The letters of a language arranged in order, the ABC. **alphabetical.**

already By now, before now.

Alsatian (Alsatians) A kind of large dog.

also As well, besides, too.

altar (altars) **1.** The Communion table in a Christian church. **2.** A flat-topped platform used for sacrifices in former times.

alter (alters, altering, altered) To change. **alteration.**

alternative (alternatives) A choice between two or more things.

although Though.

altitude (altitudes) Height, height above sea-level.

altogether 1. Entirely, completely. **2.** On the whole.

aluminium A very light, silvery-white metal.

always 1. All the time, every time. **2.** Often, again and again.

am *See* be.

a.m. *Ante meridiem,* before midday. *10 a.m.*

amalgamate (amalgamates, amalgamating, amalgamated) To join together. **amalgamation.**

amateur (amateurs) A person who does something for the love of it, not for money. *An amateur footballer.*

amaze (amazes, amazing, amazed) To astonish, to surprise. **amazement.**

Amazon (Amazons) One of a legendary race of fierce women warriors.

ambassador (ambassadors) An important official who is sent abroad as a representative of his own government.

amber 1. A hard, clear, yellowish substance used for making ornaments and jewellery. **2.** Its yellowish colour.

ambiguous Not clear in meaning, having more than one possible meaning. **ambiguously, ambiguity.**

ambition (ambitions) **1.** A strong wish to become successful or famous. **2.** The thing a person wants to do more than anything else. *John's ambition is to be an astronaut.* **ambitious, ambitiously.**

amble (ambles, ambling, ambled) To walk along without hurrying.

ambulance (ambulances) A motor vehicle for carrying sick or injured people.

ambush[1] (ambushes, ambushing, ambushed) To lie hidden and attack by surprise.

ambush[2] (ambushes) 1. Troops or bandits concealed for a surprise attack. 2. Their hiding-place.

amen A word used at the end of prayers and hymns.

amend (amends, amending, amended) To correct something, to improve it. **amendment.**

American Of America.

amethyst (amethysts) A precious stone.

amiable Good-natured. **amiably, amiability.**

amicable Friendly. **amicably.**

amidships In the middle of a ship.

ammonia A sharp-smelling gas or liquid.

ammunition Shells and cartridges for guns.

amnesia Loss of memory.

amnesty (amnesties) A pardon, a promise to set prisoners free.

among or **amongst** 1. Surrounded by, in the middle of. *Hiding among trees.* 2. One of. *Among our oldest inhabitants.* 3. Shared between. *He divided his fortune amongst his four sons.*

amount[1] (amounts, amounting, amounted) To add up to, to be equal to. *The bill for the repairs amounted to £47.*

amount[2] (amounts) 1. The total, the whole. *Half that amount would be enough.* 2. A quantity. *A large amount was lost in the fire.*

amphibious Able to go on land or in the water.

ample Quite enough, plentiful, rather generous. **amply.**

amplifier (amplifiers) An apparatus used for increasing the volume of sound. **amplification.**

amputate (amputates, amputating, amputated) To cut off a part of the body such as an arm or a leg. **amputation.**

amuck *To run amuck*, to behave furiously and murderously.

amuse (amuses, amusing, amused) 1. To make time pass pleasantly for somebody. 2. To make somebody laugh or smile. **amusingly.**

amusement (amusements) 1. Something that makes time pass pleasantly, entertainment. 2. Being amused.

anaemic Pale and feeble because of a poor condition of the blood. **anaemia.**

anaesthetic (anaesthetics) A drug or a gas used to make people unconscious so that they will not feel pain.

analyse (analyses, analysing, analysed) To examine something closely to find out what it is made of. **analysis, analyst.**

anarchy Disorder, lack of good government. **anarchist.**

anatomy The scientific study of the structure of the body. **anatomical.**

ancestor (ancestors) A forefather, anybody from whom a person is descended. **ancestry, ancestral.**

anchor[1] (anchors) An iron device with hooks which can be lowered to the bottom of the sea to stop a ship from moving.

anchor[2] (anchors, anchoring, anchored) 1. To moor a ship by means of an anchor. 2. To fix anything firmly. **anchorage.**

ancient 1. Very old. 2. Belonging to times long past.

and A joining word.

anew Again, in a new way.

angel (angels) A messenger from God. **gelic, angelically.**

anger The strong feeling that makes people want to quarrel or fight.

angle (angles) The space between two lines or surfaces that meet.

angler (anglers) A fisherman.

angry (angrier, angriest) Filled with anger. angrily.

anguish Severe suffering.

animal (animals) A living creature that can breathe, feel, and move about. Horses, flies, fish, birds, snakes, and men are all animals.

animation 1. Liveliness. 2. The art of making cartoons, puppets, and models appear to move in cinema and television films. animated.

ankle (ankles) The joint connecting the foot and the leg.

anklet (anklets) An ornament worn round the ankle.

annals Historical records.

annexe (annexes) An extra building.

annihilate (annihilates, annihilating, annihilated) To destroy completely. annihilation.

anniversary (anniversaries) The yearly celebration of the date of an event such as a wedding or a birthday.

announce (announces, announcing, announced) To make something generally known. announcer, announcement.

annoy (annoys, annoying, annoyed) To make someone rather angry. annoyance.

annual¹ Coming every year. annually.

annual² (annuals) 1. A book that is published each year with new contents. 2. A plant which lives only one year.

anonymous (Often shortened to anon.) Without a name. *This poem is anonymous*, the author's name is not known. anonymously.

anorak (anoraks) A weather-proof jacket with a hood.

another A different one, one more of a similar kind.

answer¹ (answers, answering, answered) 1. To say, write, or do something in reply. *To answer a question. To answer a letter. To answer the door-bell.* 2. *To answer back*, to answer rudely. 3. To solve.

answer² (answers) 1. A reply. 2. A solution.

ant (ants) A kind of small insect.

antagonize (antagonizes, antagonizing, antagonized) To make an enemy of someone. antagonist, antagonism.

Antarctic *The Antarctic*, the regions round the South Pole.

antelope (antelopes) An animal like a deer.

antenna 1. (antennae) One of the two feelers on the head of some insects. 2. (antennas) An aerial.

anthem (anthems) A song of praise intended to be sung in church.

anthology (anthologies) A collection of poems or other kinds of writing.

anthracite A kind of coal used in boilers.

anti-aircraft For use against aircraft.

antibiotic (antibiotics) A drug such as penicillin which acts against bacteria.

anticipate (anticipates, anticipating, anticipated) 1. To look forward to something. 2. To do something before the proper time. 3. To do something before someone else does. anticipation.

anticlimax (anticlimaxes) A disappointment after an exciting preparation.

anticyclone (anticyclones) An area in which the pressure of the air is high, generally causing fine weather.

antidote (antidotes) A medicine which acts against the effects of a poison.

anti-freeze A liquid added to water to prevent it from freezing.

antipodes Places on opposite sides of the earth. antipodean.

antiquated Old-fashioned, out of date.

antique (antiques) A valuable object many years old.

antiquities Interesting remains from ancient times.

antiseptic (antiseptics) Something that prevents infection.

antisocial Unpleasant for other people.

antler (antlers) The branching horns of a deer.

anvil (anvils) A heavy block of iron on which heated metal is hammered into shape.

anxiety (anxieties) 1. Worry, uncertainty. 2. Eager desire. anxious, anxiously.

any 1. Some amount of something. *Have you any wool?* 2. No matter which. *Come any day you like.* 3. At all. *Is your father any better?* 4. *In any case, at any rate,* whatever happens.

anybody Any person.

anyhow 1. In any way. *Do it anyhow you like.* 2. Carelessly. *It was written all anyhow.* 3. At any rate, in any case. *It is too late, anyhow.*

anyone Anybody.

anything Any thing.

anywhere In any place, to any place.

apart 1. Away from each other. *The two houses are far apart.* 2. To one side. *He stood apart and watched.* 3. To pieces. *We had to scrap our car: it was falling apart.*

apartment (apartments) A flat.

ape (apes) A tailless monkey, such as a chimpanzee or a gorilla.

apex (apexes) The highest point of something.

apiary (apiaries) A place where bees are kept.

apologize (apologizes, apologizing, apologized) To make an apology.

apology (apologies) A statement that one is sorry for doing something wrong. apologetic, apologetically.

apostle (apostles) One of the twelve men sent out by Jesus to spread his teaching.

apostrophe (apostrophes) A punctuation mark '. It is used where letters have been left out (*don't*, do not) or with 's' to show ownership (*Jean's hat*, the hat owned by Jean).

appal (appals, appalling, appalled) To shock deeply, to dismay, to fill with fear.

apparatus (apparatuses) Machinery, instruments or other equipment put together for a scientific experiment or to do a particular job.

apparent 1. Clearly seen, obvious. 2. Likely to be true. apparently.

apparition (apparitions) A ghost.

appeal (appeals, appealing, appealed) 1. To ask very seriously for something. 2. To ask for a decision of a lawcourt to be reconsidered. 3. To be interesting or attractive. *This picture appeals to me.*

appear (appears, appearing, appeared) 1. To come into sight. 2. To seem. 3. To act in a play or film. appearance.

appease (appeases, appeasing, appeased) To soothe, to calm, to make peace. appeasement.

appendicitis A disease of the appendix in a person's body.

appendix (appendices) 1. A part of the body. 2. A section added at the end of a book.

appetite (appetites) A desire, usually a desire for food. appetizing.

applaud (applauds, applauding, applauded) To give loud approval to something, to clap, to cheer. applause.

apple (apples) A firm, round fruit.

appliance (appliances) An apparatus, a machine.

apply (applies, applying, applied) 1. *To apply for*, to ask for. 2. *To apply to you*, to concern you. 3. *To apply oneself*, to give one's full attention to something. 4. *She applied the plaster to the cut*, she put it on the cut. application, applicable, applicant.

appoint (appoints, appointing, appointed) 1. To arrange something. 2. To select someone for an appointment.

appointment (appointments) 1. A time chosen for a meeting. 2. A position or job. *A good appointment in a business firm.*

appreciably To a noticeable extent.

appreciate (appreciates, appreciating, appreciated) 1. To know the value of something, to enjoy it. 2. To become higher in value. appreciation, appreciative.

apprehensive Anxious, rather frightened. apprehensively.

apprentice (apprentices) A young person learning a trade apprenticeship.

approach¹ (approaches) 1. A way towards something. 2. An advance.

approach² (approaches, approaching, approached) To come near to somebody or something.

appropriate Suitable. appropriately.

approval Approving. *Goods on approval*, goods which may be sent back if they are not satisfactory.

approve (approves, approving, approved) To be in favour of something.

approximate Roughly correct, about right. approximately.

apricot (apricots) A yellow fruit.

April The fourth month of the year.

apron (aprons) A garment worn in front of a person to keep clothes clean.

apt 1. Quick to learn. 2. Suitable. 3. *Apt to*, likely to. aptly.

aptitude A natural gift for doing something well.

aquarium (aquariums) 1. A glass tank for keeping fish in. 2. A building which contains tanks for fish.

aquatic Having to do with water.

aqueduct (aqueducts) A bridge which carries water across a valley.

arable land Land which is ploughed for growing crops.

arbitrary Unreasonable. arbitrarily.

arbitrate (arbitrates, arbitrating, arbitrated) To help the two sides in an argument to settle their differences. arbitration, arbitrator.

arc (arcs) A curved line, part of a circle.

arcade (arcades) A covered walk or pavement.

arch¹ (arches) A curved shape in a bridge, or in any other piece of architecture.

arch² (arches, arching, arched) To make a curved shape like an arch. *The cat arched its back.*

archaeology The digging up and study of ancient remains. archaeologist, archaeological.

archangel (archangels) A chief angel.

archbishop (archbishops) A chief bishop.

archer (archers) A person who shoots with a bow and arrow. archery.

archipelago (archipelagos) A group of islands.

architect (architects) A person who designs buildings.

architecture The art of designing buildings. architectural.

arctic 1. Very cold. 2. *The Arctic*, the regions round the North Pole.

arduous Hard and difficult.

are *See* be. *Are you ready? Yes, we are.*

area (areas) 1. The measurement of a flat surface. *An area of six square metres.* 2. A region of land. *The London area.*

arena (arenas) A space for competitions or fighting.

aren't (informal) Are not.

argue (argues, arguing, argued) 1. To quarrel in words. 2. To discuss. 3. To give reasons for something. *A well-argued case.* argument, argumentative.

aria (arias) A solo in an opera or oratorio.

arid 1. Dry. 2. Barren.

arise (arises, arising, arose, arisen) 1. To get up. 2. To come into being. *A problem has arisen.*

aristocrat (aristocrats) A person of noble birth, a member of a ruling class of nobles. aristocratic, aristocratically, aristocracy.

arithmetic The science of numbers, working with numbers. arithmetical, arithmetically.

Ark *The Ark*, the ship in which Noah escaped the Flood.

arm¹ (arms) 1. One of the two upper limbs of the body. *With open arms*, with enthusiasm. 2. Anything shaped like an arm.

arm² (arms) Usually arms Weapons. *To take up arms, to lay down arms.*

arm³ (arms, arming, armed) To supply somebody with arms, to prepare to fight.

armada (armadas) A fleet. *The Spanish Armada*, the Spanish fleet sent against England in 1588.

armaments Weapons and fighting equipment.

armchair (armchairs) A chair with supports for the arms.

armful (armfuls) As much as can be carried in the arms.

armistice (armistices) An agreement between enemies to stop fighting.

armlet (armlets) A band worn round the arm.

armour A metal covering to protect men, ships, or vehicles in battle. armoured.

armoury (armouries) A place where weapons are kept.

army (armies) A large number of men trained for fighting.

aroma (aromas) A pleasant smell.

arose *See* arise.

around 1. On every side. 2. Here and there. 3. About.

arouse (arouses, arousing, aroused) To awaken, to stir up.

arrange (arranges, arranging, arranged) 1. To put things in their proper place. 2. To make plans for something. *To arrange a party.* arrangement, arranger.

arrest (arrests, arresting, arrested) 1. To take someone prisoner. 2. To stop something.

arrive (arrives, arriving, arrived) 1. To reach the end of a journey. 2. To come in due time. *At last Christmas arrived.* 3. *To arrive at*, to reach. arrival.

arrogant Proud and scornful. arrogantly, arrogance.

arrow (arrows) 1. A thin, straight stick which is shot from a bow. 2. A sign shaped like an arrow.

arsenal (arsenals) A place where weapons or ammunition are made or stored.

arsenic A deadly poison.

arson Deliberately starting a fire to damage someone's property.

art (arts) 1. Skill, cunning. 2. Painting, drawing, modelling, and other ways of making beautiful things.

artery (arteries) A tube carrying blood from the heart around the body.

artesian well A well in which water rises to the surface without pumping.

artful Crafty. **artfully.**

arthritis A disease causing pain in the joints.

article (articles) 1. Any particular thing. 2. A piece of writing published in a newspaper or magazine.

articulated lorry A lorry built in two parts. It can bend at the joint.

artificial 1. Made by man, not found in nature. 2. Unnatural. **artificiality.**

artillery 1. Big guns. 2. The soldiers who fire them.

artist (artists) A person who is skilled in painting or some other art. **artistic, artistically.**

artless Simple, innocent, natural.

as This word has many uses including the following: 1. A word used in making comparisons. *I am as tall as you and can run as fast.* 2. When, while. *I saw him as I was going out.* 3. Because. *As you won't come with me, I'll go alone.* 4. In the same way. *Do as I do.* 5. *I thought as much,* I thought so. 6. *As long as,* provided that. *I'll come, as long as I don't have to do any work.*

asbestos A fire-proof material.

ascend (ascends, ascending, ascended) To go up. **ascent.**

Ascension Day The day (the sixth Thursday after Easter) on which the ascent of Jesus Christ into heaven is remembered.

ash[1] (ashes) 1. The powder which is left after a fire. **ashy.** *An ash tray,* a small bowl for cigarette ash. 2. *The Ashes,* the trophy for which England and Australia play each other at cricket.

ash[2] (ashes) A large kind of tree.

ashamed Feeling shame, upset by one's own behaviour.

ashore To the shore, on the shore.

Ash Wednesday The first day of Lent.

Asian Of Asia.

aside To one side, on one side.

ask (asks, asking, asked) 1. To put a question, to seek information. *We asked what time the bus was due.* 2. To request to be allowed to do something. *He asked to leave.* 3. To invite. *I asked her to my party.*

asleep Sleeping.

asparagus A vegetable cultivated for its tender edible shoots.

aspect (aspects) A way of looking at something.

asphalt A substance like tar. It is mixed with sand and stones for making the surface of roads and playgrounds.

aspire (aspires, aspiring, aspired) *To aspire to something,* to want something which is at present out of reach. **aspiration.**

aspirin (aspirins) A drug, usually in the form of a tablet, taken to reduce pain.

ass (asses) 1. A donkey. 2. A stupid person.

assail (assails, assailing, assailed) To attack.

assassin (assassins) A murderer.

assassinate (assassinates, assassinating, assassinated) To murder a king, a politician, or some other well-known person. **assassination.**

assault (assaults, assaulting, assaulted) To attack suddenly and violently.

assemble (assembles, assembling, assembled) To gather together, to put together.

assembly 1. A gathering, especially at the beginning of the school day. 2. Assembling.

assert (asserts, asserting, asserted) To state something firmly. *To assert oneself*, to stand up for oneself. assertion, assertive.

assess (assesses, assessing, assessed) To put a value on something. assessment, assessor.

assets Property. *A great asset*, something of value.

assignment (assignments) A job somebody is set to do.

assist (assists, assisting, assisted) To help. assistance, assistant.

association (associations) 1. A society. 2. *Association football* (also called *soccer*), the type of football played with a round ball by two teams of eleven a side.

assorted Mixed, of various sorts. assortment.

assume (assumes, assuming, assumed) 1. To accept something as true. 2. *An assumed name*, a false name. assumption.

assure (assures, assuring, assured) To tell someone something definitely. *He assured us that the bridge was safe.* assurance.

assured Confident.

asterisk (asterisks) The mark * .

asteroid (asteroids) A tiny planet.

asthma A disease which causes difficulty in breathing. asthmatic.

astir 1. Busy, doing things. 2. Out of bed.

astonish (astonishes, astonishing, astonished) To give someone a big surprise. astonishment.

astound (astounds, astounding, astounded) To astonish.

astray Away from the right path.

astride With one leg on each side of something. *To sit astride a horse.*

astrology The art of telling how the positions of the stars and planets are supposed to affect our lives. astrologer.

astronaut (astronauts) A space-traveller.

astronomy The scientific study of the sun, moon, planets, and stars. astronomer.

astute Clever, crafty. astutely.

asylum (asylums) 1. A refuge or shelter. 2. An old word for a mental hospital.

asymmetrical Not symmetrical.

at A word which shows the place, direction, time, or manner of something. 1. *We live at home.* 2. *Throw the ball at the stumps!* 3. *We have breakfast at eight.* 4. *She ran at top speed.*

ate *See* eat.

atheist (atheists) Someone who believes that there is no God. atheism.

athletics Competitive sports like running, jumping, or throwing. athletic, athlete.

atishoo The sound of a sneeze.

atlas (atlases) A book of maps.

atmosphere 1. The air which we breathe. 2. A feeling, a vague general impression. *The haunted house had an evil atmosphere.* atmospheric.

atoll (atolls) A coral island.

atom (atoms) A tiny part of a substance. atomic. *An atomic bomb*, a nuclear bomb.

atrocious Very wicked, very bad.

atrocity (atrocities) A violent and cruel crime.

attach (attaches, attaching, attached) 1. To fasten or join something to something else. 2. *To be attached to something*, to be fond of it. attachment.

attack[1] (attacks) 1. A violent attempt to hurt, damage, or defeat somebody. 2. A sudden pain or illness.

attack[2] (attacks, attacking, attacked) To make an attack.

attainment (attainments) An achievement.

attempt (attempts, attempting, attempted) To try.

attend (attends, attending, attended) 1. To give care and thought to something or somebody. 2. To be present somewhere. attendance.

attendant (attendants) A servant, a companion.

attention 1. The action of directing one's thoughts. *Pay attention to what you should be doing.* 2. A kind or polite action. 3. A position in military drill.

attentive Paying attention. attentively.

attic (attics) A room in the roof of a house.

attire Dress.

attitude (attitudes) 1. A way of feeling or behaving. 2. A manner of standing or holding the body.

attorney (attorneys) A person authorized to act for another in business or legal matters.

attract (attracts, attracting, attracted) 1. To pull something with a power that cannot be actually seen. *Magnets attract steel.* 2. To get somebody's attention. attraction.

attractive Pleasant. attractively.

auburn Reddish brown.

auction (auctions) A public sale in which goods are sold to the person who offers the highest price. auctioneer.

audible Loud enough to be heard. audibly, audibility.

audience (audiences) People gathered together to see or hear something.

audio-visual aids Types of apparatus used by teachers, such as projectors and tape-recorders.

audition (auditions) A test taken by a performer hoping to get a job.

August The eighth month of the year.

aunt (aunts) The sister of one's father or mother, or the wife of one's uncle.

aunty (aunties) (informal) An aunt.

au pair (au pairs) A girl who works for a time in somebody's home in another country.

au revoir Good-bye till we meet again.

auspicious Favourable.

Aussie (Aussies) (informal) An Australian person.

austere 1. Strict. 2. Simple and plain. austerely, austerity.

Australian Of Australia.

authentic Genuine, known to be true. authentically, authenticity.

author (authors). The writer of a book, play, or poem. authorship.

authority (authorities) 1. A person or group of people with the power to give orders. 2. The right to give orders. 3. An expert. *An authority on stamp-collecting.*

authorize (authorizes, authorizing, authorized) To give authority or official permission to someone to do something.

autobiography (autobiographies) The story of a person's life written by himself. biographical.

autograph (autographs) A signature, someone's name written in his own handwriting.

automatic[1] 1. Done without thinking. 2. *An automatic machine*, a machine which works on its own and does not need continuous attention. automatically.

automatic[2] (automatics) A kind of pistol.

automation Automatic control of the manufacture of a product through many stages.

automobile (automobiles) A motor car.

autumn (autumns) The season of the year between summer and winter. autumnal.

auxiliary Helping.

available 1. Ready for use, within reach. 2. On sale. availability.

avalanche (avalanches) The sliding down of snow and ice from a steep slope.

avarice Greed for money. avaricious.

avenge (avenges, avenging, avenged) To take

vengeance on somebody for something. **avenger**.

avenue (avenues) 1. A road or pathway lined with trees. 2. A kind of road in towns.

average (averages) 1. Midway between two extremes, usual, normal. 2. *The average*, a mathematical expression. The average of 3, 4, and 5 is 4.

averse Opposed to, feeling dislike.

aversion (aversions) A dislike.

aviary (aviaries) A place to keep birds in.

aviator (aviators) An airman. **aviation**.

avid Eager. **avidly, avidity**.

avoid (avoids, avoiding, avoided) To keep out of the way of something or somebody. **avoidance**.

awake[1] Not sleeping.

awake[2] (awakes, awaking, awoke, awoken, awaked) To cease sleeping, to rouse somebody from sleep.

awaken (awakens, awakening, awakened) To wake.

award[1] (awards) A prize.

award[2] (awards, awarding, awarded) To give. *To award a prize*.

aware *To be aware of*, to know. **awareness**.

awash Under water, flooded.

away 1. At a distance. *Stay away!* 2. From here. *I live far away.* 3. Continuously. *We chatted away for over an hour.* 4. To nothing. *The snow melted away.* 5. *Right away*, at once.

awe Respect combined with fear or reverence. **awe-inspiring**.

awful 1. Fearful, dreadful. 2. (informal) Very bad, very great. **awfully**.

awkward 1. Inconvenient. 2. Clumsy. **awkwardly, awkwardness**.

awning (awnings) A roof or shelter made of canvas.

awoke, awoken *See* **awake**.

axe (axes) A tool for chopping wood.

axle (axles) The rod which passes through the centre of a wheel.

ay or **aye** Yes.

azure Sky-blue.

Bb

babble (babbles, babbling, babbled) To talk in a meaningless way, to make sounds like a baby. **babbler**.

babe (babes) A baby.

baboon (baboons) A large kind of monkey.

baby (babies) A new-born child, a very young child. **babyish, babyishness**.

baby-sitter (baby-sitters) Someone who looks after a child while its parents are out.

bachelor (bachelors) An unmarried man.

back[1] (backs) 1. The rear part of anything, the side opposite to the front. 2. The part of a person's body between his shoulders and his bottom, the top of a four-legged animal's body. 3. A defending player in football and other games.

back[2] (backs, backing, backed) 1. To move backwards. 2. To bet on something. **backer**. 3. *Back me up*, give me your help.

back[3] 1. At the back, furthest from the front. *The back row.* 2. To where one has come from. *Go back!*

backbone (backbones) The spine.

backfire (backfires, backfiring, backfired) To make a loud explosion in a petrol engine.

backside (backsides) A person's bottom.

backstroke A way of swimming on one's back.

backward 1. Towards the back, towards where a person started from. 2. Having made less than normal progress. **backwardness**.

backwards 1. Towards the back. 2. In reverse. *I can say the alphabet backwards.*

bacon Smoked or salted meat from the back or sides of a pig.

bacteria Tiny organisms, some of which cause diseases.

bad (worse, worst) 1. Not good, evil, wicked. 2. Unpleasant, unwelcome. 3. Serious. *A bad mistake.* 4. Incorrect. *Bad spelling.* 5. (informal) Ill. *To feel bad.* 6. *To go bad*, to become unfit to eat. 7. *Bad blood*, hatred. **badness**.

bade *See* bid [2].

badge (badges) A sign worn to show membership of a school or club, a sign of a person's rank or position.

badger (badgers) An animal that burrows in the ground.

badly In a bad way. *Badly off*, poor.

badminton A game like lawn tennis, played with a shuttlecock instead of a ball.

baffle (baffles, baffling, baffled) To puzzle.

bag [1] (bags) A container made of something flexible such as paper or plastic. *A shopping bag. A tool bag.*

bag [2] (bags, bagging, bagged) 1. To put in bags. 2. To seize or capture.

baggage Luggage.

baggy Hanging in loose folds.

bagpipe (bagpipes) A musical instrument with pipes and a wind-bag.

bail [1] A payment or promise of money which allows an accused person to go free until his trial. The money is forfeited if he does not come to court at the proper time.

bail [2] (bails) One of the pieces of wood placed on top of the stumps in cricket.

bail [3] (bails, bailing, bailed) To scoop water out of a boat.

bairn (bairns) (Scottish) A child.

bait [1] Food which is put on a hook or in a trap to catch fish or animals.

bait [2] (baits, baiting, baited) 1. To put bait on a hook or in a trap. 2. To tease, to torment.

bake (bakes, baking, baked) 1. To cook in an oven. 2. To heat something, to make a thing hard by heating. 3. To become very hot.

Bakelite The trade name of a kind of plastic.

baker (bakers) A person whose business is baking bread and cakes. **bakery**.

balance [1] 1. Steadiness. 2. An equal distribution of weight.

balance [2] (balances, balancing, balanced) 1. To make a thing steady. 2. To be steady, to make oneself steady. 3. To distribute weight equally on each side of something.

balance [3] (balances) A device for weighing things.

balcony (balconies) 1. An outside platform which can be reached from an upstairs window. 2. Rows of seats in the upstairs part of a cinema or theatre.

bald (balder, baldest) Without hair. **baldness**.

balderdash Nonsense.

bale [1] (bales) A large bundle of hay, straw, or wool.

bale [2] (bales, baling, baled) *To bale out*, to jump with a parachute from an aircraft.

ball (balls) 1. A round object for playing games, such as a football. 2. A round shape. *A ball of string.* 3. A big party with dancing.

ballad (ballads) A simple song or poem that tells a story.

ballerina (ballerinas) A woman ballet-dancer.

ballet (ballets) A stage entertainment telling a story or expressing an idea in dancing and mime.

balloon (balloons) 1. A large container filled with air or gas, sometimes with a basket beneath to carry passengers. 2. A small bag filled with air or gas and used as a toy.

ballot (ballots) 1. Secret voting on pieces of paper. 2. A piece of paper on which a vote is recorded.

ball-point (ball-points) A kind of pen with a tiny steel ball for a nib.

balmy Peaceful, healing.

balsa A light-weight wood.

bamboo (bamboos) A plant with hollow stems or canes.

ban (bans, banning, banned) To forbid.

banana (bananas) 1. A tropical fruit-plant. 2. Its yellow-skinned fruit.

band (bands) 1. A strip of material in the form of a loop. *A rubber band.* 2. A stripe. 3. A group of people. *A band of robbers.* 4. A group of musicians. **bandsman, bandstand.**

bandage (bandages) A strip of material used to bind a wound.

bandanna (bandannas) A coloured handkerchief.

bandit (bandits) An outlaw, a robber.

bandy (bandies, bandying, bandied) *To bandy words,* to argue.

bandy-legged Having legs curved outward at the knee.

bang (bangs) 1. A heavy blow. 2. A sudden loud noise.

bangle (bangles) An ornament worn round the arm or leg.

banish (banishes, banishing, banished) To punish someone by sending him away from his country.

banisters A handrail with upright supports at the side of stairs.

banjo (banjos) A musical instrument with strings.

bank[1] (banks) 1. Raised or sloping ground. 2. The dry ground at the edge of a pond, river, or canal.

bank[2] (banks) A business which looks after people's money. **banker, bank-note.**

bank[3] (banks, banking, banked) 1. To put money in a bank. 2. *To bank on,* to rely on. 3. *To bank up,* to heap up. 4. To lean over, or lift one side higher than the other, while turning a corner. *The plane banked as it turned in to land.*

bankrupt Unable to pay all one's debts. **bankruptcy.**

banner (banners) A flag carried in procession.

banns An announcement in church that two people are going to be married.

banquet (banquets) A feast.

bantam (bantams) A small kind of chicken.

banter Good-humoured teasing.

baptize (baptizes, baptizing, baptized) To christen. **baptism.**

bar[1] (bars) 1. A long piece of any hard substance. *A bar of chocolate. A metal bar.* 2. A place where drinks are served. 3. A term used in music. *In a waltz you count three beats to the bar.*

bar² (bars, barring, barred) 1. To fasten with a bar. 2. To keep somebody out.

barbarian (barbarians) An uncivilized, savage person. barbaric, barbarous, barbarism.

barbecue (barbecues) 1. A metal framework for cooking meat over a fire. 2. An open-air party where food is cooked on a barbecue.

barbed With jagged hooks or points. *Barbed wire.*

barber (barbers) A men's hairdresser.

bard (bards) A minstrel, a poet.

bare¹ (barer, barest) 1. Uncovered, without protection or decoration. *To lay bare*, to uncover. *Barefaced*, insolent. *Bare-headed*, with no hat. 2. Empty or nearly empty. 3. Just enough. *A bare possibility.* barely.

bare² (bares, baring, bared) To uncover, to reveal.

bargain¹ (bargains) 1. An agreement to buy or sell something. 2. Something bought unusually cheaply.

bargain² (bargains, bargaining, bargained) To argue about the price of something.

barge (barges) A large flat-bottomed boat used especially on canals.

bark¹ (barks) 1. The sound made by a dog or a fox. 2. The outer covering of the trunk of a tree.

bark² (barks, barking, barked) 1. To make the sound of a dog or a fox. 2. To injure oneself by scraping one's skin on something. *I barked my shin.*

bark³ (barks) A kind of sailing ship.

barley 1. A cereal plant. 2. Its seed used for food and in making various drinks. barley-water.

barley-sugar A sweet made of boiled sugar.

barmaid (barmaids) A woman who serves drinks at a bar in a public house. barman.

barn (barns) 1. A storage building on a farm. 2. *A barn dance*, an American country dance.

barnacle (barnacles) A shellfish that sticks to the bottoms of ships.

barometer (barometers) An instrument that measures air pressure, used in studying the weather.

baron (barons) A nobleman.

baroness (baronesses) A noblewoman, a baron's wife.

barracks A building where soldiers live.

barrage (barrages) 1. Heavy gunfire. 2. A dam across a river, a barricade.

barrel (barrels) 1. A container with curved sides and flat ends. 2. The tube through which the shot is fired.

barrel-organ (barrel-organs) A musical instrument which plays tunes when the handle is turned.

barren Unfruitful, not producing anything. *Barren land. A barren tree.*

barricade (barricades) A barrier quickly put together to keep out an enemy.

barrier (barriers) A fence or obstacle.

barrister (barristers) A lawyer with the right to speak and argue in the higher lawcourts.

barrow (barrows) 1. A small cart. 2. A mound of earth made in prehistoric times to cover a grave.

base¹ (bases) 1. The lowest part of anything, the part on which a thing stands. 2. A headquarters, a place where stores and reinforcements are kept.

base² (bases, basing, based) To put on or in a base. *He based his story on fact*, he used something that had really happened as the basis for his story.

base³ (baser, basest) Mean, selfish, cowardly. basely, baseness.

baseball An American game played rather like rounders.

basement (basements) A room or rooms below the ground floor.

bash (bashes, bashing, bashed) (informal) To hit hard.

bashful Shy. **bashfully**.

basic   **basically**.

basin (basins) A deep dish, a bowl, an open container for liquids.

basis (bases) 1. A foundation, a starting-point. 2. The main ingredient of something.

bask (basks, basking, basked) To enjoy warmth and light.

basket (baskets) A kind of container, usually woven from canes, raffia, or similar material.

basket-ball A game in which a ball is thrown into basket-shaped nets which are the goals.

bass (basses) 1. A male singer with the lowest type of voice. 2. The lowest part in a piece of music.

bassoon (bassoons) A woodwind instrument which can produce low notes.

bastard (bastards) An illegitimate child.

bat [1] (bats) A small flying animal. *As blind as a bat*, unable to see clearly.

bat [2] (bats) A wooden implement used to hit the ball in cricket, baseball, and other games.

bat [3] (bats, batting, batted) To use a bat, to hit the ball. **batsman**.

batch (batches) A set of things.

bated *With bated breath*, speaking very quietly or holding one's breath in excitement.

bath (baths) 1. A washing of the whole body. *To have a bath*, to sit in water and wash oneself all over. 2. A large container for water in which to have a bath. **bath-tub**. 3. The water used in having a bath. *Hurry up! Your bath's getting cold.* **bathroom.**

bathe (bathes, bathing, bathed) 1. To go swimming. **bather, bathing-cap, bathing-costume, bathing-suit**. 2. To wash something gently. *Bathe your sore finger.*

baths A swimming-pool.

baton (batons) 1. A stick used to conduct an orchestra. 2. The stick carried by runners in a relay race.

battalion (battalions) A unit of the army.

batten (battens) A strip of wood.

batter [1] (batters, battering, battered) To strike hard and often, to beat out of shape. *A battering-ram*, a post swung to break down walls.

batter [2] A mixture of flour, eggs, and milk used in cooking.

battery (batteries) 1. A portable device for storing and supplying electricity. 2. A number of guns organized together. 3. *Battery hens*, hens kept in small cages.

battle (battles) A fight between armies.

battle-axe (battle-axes) A heavy axe formerly used as a weapon.

battlefield (battlefields) A place where a battle is fought.

battlements The top of a castle wall.

battleship (battleships) A heavy warship.

bawl (bawls, bawling, bawled) To shout or cry out loudly.

bay (bays) 1. A wide inlet, a curved part of the sea-shore. 2. An alcove, or an area between two partitions or dividing walls. 3. The bark of a hound. 4. *To keep at bay*, to fight off.

bayonet (bayonets) A dagger fixed to the end of a rifle.

bay window A window in the bay of a room.

bazaar (bazaars) 1. A market in Eastern countries. 2. A kind of shop. 3. A sale to raise money for charity.

B.C. Before Christ. *Julius Caesar came to Britain in 55 B.C.*

be (am, are, is; being; was, were; been) **1.** To exist, to live. **2.** To become. *What are you going to be when you grow up?* **3.** To happen, to take place. *When will sports day be?* **4.** To remain. *I'll be here all day.* **5.** To go, to visit. *Have you been to school today?*

beach (beaches) A sea-shore covered in sand or pebbles.

beacon (beacons) A light used as a warning signal.

bead (beads) **1.** A small, pretty ball with a hole through it for making necklaces. **2.** A small drop of liquid.

beagle (beagles) A small hound.

beak (beaks) The hard, horny part of a bird's mouth.

beaker (beakers) A large cup or mug.

beam[1] (beams) **1.** A long, thick bar of wood. **2.** Rays of light or radio waves.

beam[2] (beams, beaming, beamed) **1.** To smile happily. **2.** To send out a light or radio beam.

bean (beans) **1.** A kind of plant with seeds growing in pods. **2.** Its seeds or pods used as food. **bean-stalk.**

bear[1] (bears, bearing, bore, borne) **1.** To carry, to support. **2.** To produce. *To bear fruit.* **3.** To suffer, to put up with.

bear[2] (bears, bearing, bore, born) To produce or give birth to offspring.

bear[3] (bears) **1.** A large heavy animal with rough hair. **2.** *The Great Bear, the Little Bear,* two groups of stars in the northern sky.

beard (beards) The hair on the lower part of a man's face.

bearings Where one place is in relation to another. *To lose one's bearings,* to lose one's sense of direction.

beast (beasts) **1.** A four-footed animal. **2.** (informal) A cruel, disgusting, or badly behaved person. **beastly, beastliness.**

beat[1] (beats, beating, beaten) **1.** To hit often, usually with a stick. **2.** To stir up something briskly before cooking it. *To beat eggs.* **beater. 3.** To hammer into shape, to make

metal flat. **4.** To defeat somebody. **5.** (informal) *Dead beat,* tired out. **6.** *To beat time,* to conduct. **7.** *The rain was beating down,* the rain was coming down heavily.

beat[2] (beats) **1.** Regular rhythm. **2.** A repeated stroke. *The beat of a drum.* **3.** The regular route of a policeman.

beauty (beauties) The pleasant quality in something that makes a person admire it and enjoy its loveliness. *The beauty of the sunset.* **beautiful, beautifully.**

beaver (beavers) A fur-covered animal living on land and in water.

becalmed Unable to sail on because the wind has dropped.

became *See* become.

because 1. For the reason that. **2.** *Because of,* on account of.

beckon (beckons, beckoning, beckoned) To make a sign to someone asking him to come.

become (becomes, becoming, became) **1.** To come to be. *It became darker.* **2.** *To become of,* to happen to. *What has become of Jill? We haven't seen her lately.* **3.** To look attractive on someone. *That new dress becomes you.*

becoming Suitable, attractive.

bed (beds) **1.** A place to sleep or rest. *The tramp made a bed of straw.* **2.** A piece of furniture for sleeping on. **bed-clothes, bedroom, bedside, bedtime. 3.** A piece of ground for growing flowers, fruit, or vegetables. **4.** The bottom of the sea or of a river. **5.** A base or foundation.

bedding Things for making a bed.

bedlam Noisy confusion.

bedraggled Wet, dirty, and untidy.

bedridden Unable to get out of bed because of illness.

bedspread (bedspreads) A top cover for a bed.

bedstead (bedsteads) The framework of a bed.

bee (bees) An insect which makes honey.

beech (beeches) A kind of tree.

beef The meat of an ox, bull, or cow.

beefeater (beefeaters) A Yeoman of the Guard, a guard at the Tower of London.

beefy Strong, with large muscles.

beehive (beehives) A box or other container made for bees to live in.

been See be.

beer An alcoholic drink made from malt and hops.

beetle (beetles) An insect with hard, shiny wing-covers.

beetroot A dark-red root vegetable.

befall (befalls, befalling, befell) To happen.

before 1. Earlier than. *Before the week-end.* 2. In front of. *Leg before wicket.* 3. Rather than. *They'd die before giving in.*

beg (begs, begging, begged) 1. To ask for money, food, and other necessities. 2. To ask earnestly and with feeling. *He begged me not to report him.*

began See begin.

beggar (beggars) 1. Somebody who lives by begging. 2. A poor person. beggary.

begin (begins, beginning, began, begun) To start, to come into existence.

beginner (beginners) A learner.

beginning (beginnings) A starting-point.

begrudge (begrudges, begrudging, begrudged) To feel envy and dissatisfaction about something.

begun See begin.

behalf *On my behalf,* on my account, for me.

behave (behaves, behaving, behaved) 1. To act. *The commander behaved badly in the crisis.* 2. To act well. *Do try to behave yourself!* behaviour.

behead (beheads, beheading, beheaded) To cut off somebody's head.

behind[1] 1. At the rear of. *The driver sits behind the wheel.* 2. At or in the rear, after people have gone. *The old man lagged behind. We were left behind when the bus went,* the bus went without us. 3. Not making good progress, late. *He is behind with his rent.*

behind[2] (behinds) (informal) A person's bottom.

behindhand Late.

behold (beholds, beholding, beheld) To see.

beige A sandy colour.

being[1] Existence.

being[2] (beings) A creature. *A human being.*

belated Late, too late. belatedly.

belch (belches, belching, belched) 1. To send out, to erupt. *The dragon belched out smoke and flames.* 2. To let gases from the stomach noisily out through the mouth.

belfry (belfries) A tower in which bells are hung.

belief (beliefs) What a person believes.

believe (believes, believing, believed) 1. To feel sure that something is true. *I believe your story.* 2. To feel sure that someone is telling the truth. *I believe you.* 3. *To believe in,* to trust, to have faith in. 4. *To make believe,* to pretend. believable, believer.

bell (bells) 1. A hollow metal instrument that rings when struck or swung. 2. Any instrument that makes a ringing sound, such as a door-bell or a bicycle bell.

belligerent Warlike.

bellow (bellows, bellowing, bellowed) To roar like a bull, to shout.

bellows A device for blowing air.

belly (bellies) The stomach, the abdomen.

belong (belongs, belonging, belonged) 1. *To*

belong to someone, to be owned by someone. 2. To be in the proper place. *The butter belongs in the fridge.*

belongings Possessions.

beloved Much loved.

below 1. Lower than. 2. At a lower level, to a lower level.

belt (belts) 1. A strip of material worn round the waist. 2. A strip, a band, a long line. *A belt of trees.*

bench (benches) 1. A long, hard seat. 2. A work-table, such as a carpenter's bench. 3. A judge's or magistrate's seat.

bend¹ (bends, bending, bent) 1. To force something into a curved or crooked shape. 2. To become curved or crooked 3. To bow or stoop.

bend² (bends) A curve, a turn. *A bend in the road.*

beneath Below, underneath.

benediction (benedictions) A blessing.

benefactor (benefactors) Someone who has generously given something to another person or to a charity.

benefit (benefits) Help, advantage. **beneficial.**

benevolent Kindly, helpful. **benevolently, benevolence.**

bent¹ *See* bend¹.

bent² (bents) A natural liking for something.

bequest (bequests) A gift left to somebody in a will.

bereaved Left sad because somebody has died. **bereavement.**

bereft Deprived of something. *Bereft of reason*, mad.

beret (berets) A round soft cap.

berry (berries) A small fruit containing seeds.

berserk Suddenly violent.

berth (berths) 1. A sleeping place on a ship or a train. 2. A place where ships tie up in harbour.

beside 1. At the side of. *A spider sat down beside her.* 2. Compared with. *You don't seem tall beside your father.* 3. *Beside himself,* no longer in control of himself.

besides 1. In addition to, as well as. *I have two more besides these.* 2. Moreover, also, anyway. *It's too late to go now. Besides, I don't want to any more.*

besiege (besieges, besieging, besieged) To surround a place and attack it from all sides.

best 1. *See* good¹. 2. *See* well². 3. Excellent things or people. *He's one of the best.* 4. *The best man,* the bridegroom's friend at a wedding.

bet¹ (bets, betting, betted, bet) To risk losing or winning money on the result of a race or some other event.

bet² (bets) Money risked in betting.

betray (betrays, betraying, betrayed) 1. To be false to someone, to give him up to the enemy. 2. To let something become known which should be kept secret. *To betray one's feelings.* **betrayer.**

betrothed Engaged to be married.

better 1. *See* good¹. 2. *See* well². 3. Recovered from an illness. *I had mumps, but I am better now.* 4. *He got the better of me,* he outwitted me. 5. *I thought better of it,* I changed my mind. 6. *You had better not go,* you ought not to go.

between 1. A word showing within which limits something is. *We live between the park and the river. I go to bed between 8 and 9 o'clock. They walked between 3 and 4 miles.* 2. In shares. *We'll divide it between us,* we shall have equal shares. 3. When comparing. *Can't you tell the difference between right and wrong?*

betwixt (old-fashioned) Between. *Betwixt and between,* neither one thing nor the other.

beverage (beverages) A drink.

beware Be careful. *Beware of the dog.*

bewilder (bewilders, bewildering, bewildered) To puzzle, to confuse. **bewilderment.**

bewitch (bewitches, bewitching, bewitched) To put a magic spell on someone.

beyond 1. On the far side of. *We'll be safe when we get beyond the river.* 2. Out of the reach of. *This problem is beyond me*, it is too hard for me to understand. 3. Farther on. *The road goes over a hill, I can't see what lies beyond.*

biased Influenced, probably unfairly. *The referee is biased, his brother is on their side.*

bib (bibs) Something tied under a child's chin during meals.

Bible (Bibles) The holy book of the Christian Church. **biblical.**

bicycle (bicycles) A two-wheeled vehicle.

bid[1] (bids, bidding, bid) To offer a price for something. **bidder.**

bid[2] (bids, bidding, bade, bidden) (old-fashioned) To order or invite someone.

bide (bides, biding, bided) To stay. *To bide one's time*, to wait for a favourable opportunity.

bifocals Spectacles with divided lenses for close reading and general use.

big (bigger, biggest) Of great size or importance. *Big game*, large animals hunted for sport.

bigamy The crime of having two wives or two husbands at a time. **bigamous, bigamist.**

biggish Fairly large.

bike (bikes) (informal) A bicycle.

bikini (bikinis) A two-piece bathing-costume for women.

bilge (bilges) The almost flat part of the bottom of a ship where water tends to collect.

bilious 1. *A bilious attack*, an illness with headache and sickness. 2. Gloomy and peevish.

bill (bills) 1. A bird's beak. 2. An account showing how much money is owing. 3. A poster. 4. A proposed law, to be discussed by Parliament.

billabong (billabongs) (Australian) A branch of a river that comes to a dead end.

billiards An indoor game played with balls and long sticks called cues on a cloth-covered table.

billion (billions) 1. In Britain, one million million (1,000,000,000,000). 2. In U.S.A., one thousand million (1,000,000,000).

billow (billows, billowing, billowed) To swell up, to rise like great waves.

billy (billies) or **billycan** (billycans) A tin used by campers to cook in and eat out of.

billy-goat (billy-goats) A male goat.

bin (bins) A large container, usually with a lid.

binary Consisting of two parts or two units.

bind (binds, binding, bound) 1. To tie up. *The prisoner was bound in chains.* 2. To fasten material round something. *To bind up a wound. To bind the edge of a carpet.* 3. To fasten the pages of a book into a cover. **binder.**

binding (bindings) A book cover.

bingo A gambling game in which each player has a card on which numbers are printed, and covers these when they are called.

binoculars An instrument with lenses looked through with both eyes, for making distant objects look nearer.

biography (biographies) The written story of a person's life.

biology The science of living things.

biplane (biplanes) An aircraft with two pairs of wings, one above the other.

birch (birches) A kind of tree.

bird (birds) An animal with feathers and wings. **bird-cage, bird-seed.**

birth (births) The process of being born. *A birth-mark*, a mark which has been on a person's body since birth. *A birth-place*, the place where a person was born.

birthday (birthdays) The date of a person's birth.

biscuit (biscuits) A flat thin crisp cake.

bishop (bishops) 1. A clergyman of high rank. 2. A piece in chess.

bison (bison) An American buffalo, a wild ox.

bit¹ (bits) A small piece of anything. *Bit by bit*, gradually. *A bit of a hero*, rather a hero.

bit² *See* bite.

bitch (bitches) A female dog.

bite (bites, biting, bit, bitten) 1. To cut into something with the teeth. 2. *To bite the dust*, to be killed. 3. To sting.

bitter (bitterest) 1. Unpleasant-tasting, the opposite of sweet. 2. Filled with envy or hatred. 3. Very cold. *A bitter wind.* bitterly, bitterness.

bitumen Pitch, asphalt.

black¹ The darkest of all colours, the opposite of white.

black² (blacker, blackest) 1. Black in colour. 2. Very dirty. 3. Gloomy, evil, sinister. 4. *Black ice*, dangerous ice on roads. 5. *A black Maria*, a police van. blackly, blackness.

black-beetle (black-beetles) A cockroach.

blackberry (blackberries) A juicy black berry that grows on bushes.

blackbird (blackbirds) A common European song-bird.

blackboard (blackboards) A dark surface for writing on with chalk.

blacken (blackens, blackening, blackened) To make a thing black.

blackfellow (blackfellows) An Australian Aboriginal.

blackguard (blackguards) A rogue, a scoundrel.

blackish Rather black.

blackmail The crime of demanding money from someone in return for keeping quiet about something.

black-out (black-outs) 1. An electric power failure. 2. The switching off of all lights. 3. A temporary period of unconsciousness.

blacksmith (blacksmiths) A person who forges and repairs things made of iron, a person who makes shoes for horses.

bladder (bladders) 1. The part of the body in which waste liquid collects before it is passed out of the body. 2. The rubber bag inside a football.

blade (blades) 1. The sharp part of a knife or any other cutting instrument. 2. Something blade-shaped.

blame (blames, blaming, blamed) 1. To say that someone or something is the cause of what is wrong. *My brother broke the window, but Mum blamed me!* 2. *He was to blame*, it was his fault. blameless.

blancmange (blancmanges) A pudding made with cornflour and milk.

blank¹ (blanker, blankest) 1. Not written or printed on. *Blank paper.* 2. Not showing any expression. *A blank look.* blankly.

blank² (blanks) 1. An empty space. 2. A cartridge which makes a noise but does not fire a bullet.

blanket (blankets) A piece of thick cloth used as a warm covering on a bed.

blare (blares, blaring, blared) To make a loud, harsh noise.

blasphemous Wicked and irreverent. blasphemously, blasphemy.

blast[1] (blasts) 1. A sudden rush of air. 2. A loud noise, such as the sound of a trumpet.

blast[2] (blasts, blasting, blasted) To blow up something with explosives.

blatant Very obvious. **blatantly.**

blaze (blazes, blazing, blazed) 1. To burn with bright flames. 2. To shine brightly. 3. To be full of strong feelings. 4. *To blaze away*, to fire guns continually. 5. *To blaze a trail*, to make cuts on trees to mark a path.

blazer (blazers) A type of jacket.

bleach (bleaches, bleaching, bleached) 1. To become white. 2. To make white.

bleak (bleaker, bleakest) Bare, cold, and miserable. **bleakly.**

bleary-eyed Dull and misty eyed.

bleat (bleats) The cry of a lamb or calf.

bleed (bleeds, bleeding, bled) To lose blood.

bleep (bleeps) The sound produced by an electronic signal.

blemish (blemishes) A mark, a flaw.

blend (blends, blending, blended) To mix together, to mix pleasantly and successfully.

bless (blesses, blessing, blessed) 1. To wish somebody well, to be good to him. 2. To make something holy.

blessing (blessings) 1. A prayer, a grace before meals. 2. Something one is grateful for.

blight (blights) A disease, an evil influence.

blind[1] 1. Unable to see. 2. Unable to understand. 3. Reckless, thoughtless. 4. *A blind alley*, a road which has one end closed. **blindly, blindness.**

blind[2] (blinds, blinding, blinded) To make blind.

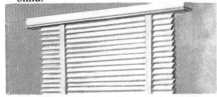

blind[3] (blinds) A kind of screen for windows. *Venetian blinds.*

blindfold With eyes covered up.

blink (blinks, blinking, blinked) To shut and open the eyes rapidly.

bliss Great happiness. **blissful, blissfully.**

blister (blisters) A swelling like a bubble under the skin.

blitz A sudden attack, usually from the air.

blizzard (blizzards) A severe windy snowstorm.

bloated Swollen.

blob (blobs) A drop of liquid, a small round lump of something.

block[1] (blocks) 1. A lump of something. *A block of ice.* 2. A large building or a group of buildings. 3. *Block letters*, capital letters.

block[2] (blocks, blocking, blocked) To stop something up, to bar it. *To block the way.*

blockade (blockades) A kind of siege.

blockage (blockages) Something that blocks the way.

blockhead (blockheads) A slow, foolish person.

bloke (blokes) (informal) A man.

blond or **blonde**[1] Fair-haired. *A blond boy. A blonde girl.*

blonde[2] (blondes) A fair-haired woman.

blood 1. The red liquid that flows through veins and arteries. 2. *In cold blood*, deliberately and cruelly. 3. *He has royal blood*, he has royal ancestors. **bloody, bloodless, blood-stained, blood-thirsty.**

bloodhound (bloodhounds) A large dog with a keen scent.

bloodshed Killing, slaughter.

bloodshot *Bloodshot eyes*, red eyes.

bloom[1] (blooms) A flower. *In bloom*, flowering.

bloom[2] (blooms, blooming, bloomed) 1. To open into flowers. 2. To be strong and healthy.

blossom[1] (blossoms) 1. A flower. 2. A mass of flowers.

blossom[2] (blossoms, blossoming, blossomed) To open into flowers.

blot[1] (blots) 1. A spot of ink. 2. A mark, a flaw.

blot² (blots, blotting, blotted) 1. To make a blot. 2. To dry wet ink-marks by pressing them with a special paper called blotting-paper. 3. *To blot out*, to cover up, to hide.

blotch (blotches) A spot or patch of colour.

blouse (blouses) A type of garment for the top half of the body.

blow¹ (blows, blowing, blew, blown) 1. To make a movement of the air. *A gale is blowing.* 2. To be moved by the wind. *His hat blew away.* 3. To make something move by blowing. *She blew the dust away.* 4. To force air into something. *Blow up this balloon.* 5. To make a sound produced by blowing. *The whistle blew.* 6. To puff, to pant. 7. *To blow up*, to explode, to destroy with explosives. blower.

blow² (blows) 1. A hard knock. 2. An unexpected misfortune.

blubber¹ Fat from a whale.

blubber² (blubbers, blubbering, blubbered) To weep noisily.

blue¹ 1. A colour, the colour of a cloudless sky. 2. *Blues*, a sad song in jazz rhythm.

blue² (bluer, bluest) 1. Blue in colour. 2. Feeling sad, depressed.

bluebell (bluebells) A blue wild flower.

bluebottle (bluebottles) A large fly.

bluff¹ (bluffs, bluffing, bluffed) To try to deceive somebody by pretending to have the power to do something.

bluff² Bluffing.

bluish Rather blue.

blunder¹ (blunders, blundering, blundered) To stumble, to make a clumsy mistake.

blunder² (blunders) A clumsy mistake.

blunderbuss (blunderbusses) An old type of gun firing several bullets at once.

blunt (blunter, bluntest) 1. Not sharp, without a point. 2. Plain-spoken, not very polite. bluntly, bluntness.

blur (blurs, blurring, blurred) 1. To become confused or not clear. 2. To make something confused or not clear.

blurt (blurts, blurting, blurted) To speak suddenly and without thinking.

blush¹ (blushes, blushing, blushed) To become red in the face.

blush² (blushes) A reddening of the face.

blustery Windy.

boa-constrictor (boa-constrictors) A large snake.

boar (boars) 1. A wild pig. 2. Any male pig.

board¹ (boards) 1. A plank. 2. A flat piece of wood or other material. 3. A board made for a special purpose. *A notice-board, a dart-board, a chess-board.* 4. *On board*, on a ship.

board² (boards, boarding, boarded) 1. To go on to a ship or aircraft. 2. To lodge. *A boarding-house*, a lodging house. *A boarding-school*, a school where the children live in. boarder.

boast¹ (boasts, boasting, boasted) 1. To praise oneself, to be proud and puffed up. 2. To take a pride in owning something.

boast² (boasts) Boasting. boastful, boastfully, boastfulness.

boat (boats) 1. A small ship. *A rowing-boat. A motor boat.* 2. A ship of any size. boat-man, boat-house, boat-race.

boathook (boathooks) A hook for handling boats.

boating Going out in a boat.

boatswain (boatswain) A senior seaman.

bob (bobs, bobbing, bobbed) To move up and down like something that floats.

bodice (bodices) The upper part of a woman's dress.

body (bodies) 1. The physical part of a person. *Exercise develops a healthy body.* 2. A dead body, a corpse. 3. The main part of one's body, not the head, arms, or legs.

4. The main part of anything. 5. A collection of things, people, or ideas. 6. *Heavenly bodies*, suns, stars, and planets. **bodily.**

bodyguard (bodyguards) A guard for an important person.

bog (bogs) Wet and spongy ground, marsh. **boggy.**

bogie (bogies) A set of wheels.

bogus False, sham.

bogy (bogies) A goblin, a devil. *The bogy-man.*

boil [1] (boils) An inflamed spot on the skin.

boil [2] (boils, boiling, boiled) 1. To bubble and give off steam. 2. To cook in boiling water. 3. To be very hot.

boiler (boilers) An apparatus for heating water.

boisterous Wild, noisy, and cheerful. **terously.**

bold (bolder, boldest) 1. Fearless. 2. Shameless. 3. Clearly seen. **boldly, boldness.**

bolster (bolsters) A long pillow.

bolt [1] (bolts) 1. A type of fastening for a door. 2. A thick metal pin on which a nut can be threaded. 3. A short, heavy arrow fired from a cross-bow.

bolt [2] (bolts, bolting, bolted) 1. To fasten with a bolt. 2. To run away suddenly. 3. To gulp food down quickly.

bomb [1] (bombs) An explosive device.

bomb [2] (bombs, bombing, bombed) To drop or throw bombs. **bomber.**

bombard (bombards, bombarding, bombarded) 1. To attack with gunfire. 2. To fire questions at someone. **bombardment.**

bomb-shell (bomb-shells) A shattering surprise.

bond (bonds) Something which binds or ties.

bondage Slavery.

bone (bones) One of the parts of a skeleton. *Bone dry*, completely dry. **bony.**

bonfire (bonfires) A large outdoor fire.

bonnet (bonnets) 1. The hinged lid over a car's engine. 2. A kind of hat.

bonus (bonuses) An extra payment.

boo (boos, booing, booed) To show disapproval by shouting 'boo'.

booby (boobies) A silly person. *A booby-trap*, a dangerous device designed to take an enemy by surprise.

book [1] (books) A set of sheets of paper fastened together inside a cover. *An exercise book, a library book. A book-token*, a voucher that can be used to buy books.

book [2] (books, booking, booked) 1. To record something in a book. 2. To reserve seats for a journey or an entertainment. **booking-office.**

bookcase (bookcases) A piece of furniture designed to hold books.

bookie (bookies) (informal) A bookmaker.

booklet (booklets) A small book.

bookmaker (bookmakers) A person whose business is taking bets.

boom [1] (booms, booming, boomed) To make a deep sound like a heavy gun, an organ, or the wind.

boom [2] (booms) A booming sound.

boom [3] (booms) A long pole holding a sail straight at the bottom.

boomerang (boomerangs) A curved throwing-stick, something that returns to the person who threw it.

boost (boosts, boosting, boosted) To give something a push upwards, to increase it in size or value.

booster (boosters) A rocket that launches a space ship.

boot (boots) 1. A shoe that covers the ankle and sometimes also the calf. 2. The luggage space in a car.

bootee (bootees) A tiny knitted boot for a baby.

booty Loot.

booze (informal) Alcoholic drink. **boozy**.

border (borders) **1.** An edge, a boundary, a frontier. **2.** A flower bed.

bore[1] *See* bear[1, 2].

bore[2] (bores, boring, bored) **1.** To make a narrow, round hole. **2.** To make someone weary by being dull and uninteresting.

bore[3] (bores) A dull, uninteresting person or thing. **boredom**.

born, borne *See* bear[1, 2].

borough (boroughs) A town with special privileges.

borrow (borrows, borrowing, borrowed) To use something which belongs to someone else and which must be returned. **borrower**.

Borstal (Borstals) A school for young offenders.

bosom (bosoms) A person's breast.

boss (bosses) The person in control. **bossy**.

botany The scientific study of plants. **botanist, botanical**.

both **1.** The two. *You can have cake or a biscuit, but not both.* **2.** *Both wise and rich,* not only wise but also rich.

bother[1] Trouble, worry. **bothersome**.

bother[2] (bothers, bothering, bothered) **1.** To cause trouble to someone. **2.** To worry. **3.** To take trouble.

bottle[1] (bottles) A narrow-necked container for liquids.

bottle[2] (bottles, bottling, bottled) To put something in a bottle, to keep it in a bottle.

bottle-neck (bottle-necks) A narrow part of a road where traffic jams occur.

bottom (bottoms) **1.** The lowest or farthest part of anything. *The bottom of the garden,* the end of the garden. **2.** The part of the body on which a person sits. **3.** The ground under the water in a river, a lake or the sea. **bottomless**.

bough (boughs) A branch.

bought *See* buy.

boulder (boulders) A large rock worn smooth by water or weather.

bounce (bounces, bouncing, bounced) **1.** To jump back when thrown against some-thing hard. **2.** To move with jumps and jolts. **3.** *A bouncing baby,* a big, healthy baby. **bouncy**.

bound[1] **1.** *See* **bind**. **2.** *To be bound to do something,* to be obliged to do it. **3.** *To be bound for somewhere,* to be ready to go there, to be on the way.

bound[2] (bounds, bounding, bounded) To leap, to bounce.

boundary (boundaries) **1.** A line marking the edge of something **2.** A hit to the edge of a cricket field.

boundless Unlimited.

bounds *Out of bounds,* where certain people are forbidden to go.

bounty (bounties) A generous gift, a payment. **bounteous, bountiful**.

bouquet (bouquets) A bunch of flowers.

bout (bouts) **1.** A contest, a trial of strength. **2.** An attack of an illness.

boutique (boutiques) A fashionable shop.

bow[1] (bows) **1.** A weapon. **2.** The stick used to play the violin or other stringed instru-ments. **3.** A knot made with loops. **bow-tie**.

bow² or bows The front part of a ship.

bow³ (bows, bowing, bowed) To bend politely forward.

bowels 1. The lowest part of the digestive system in the body. 2. The deep inside part of something. *The bowels of the earth.*

bowl¹ (bowls) A basin.

bowl² (bowls, bowling, bowled) To send a ball for the batsman to play in cricket.

bow-legged Having legs curved outward at the knee.

bowler (bowlers) 1. The person bowling in cricket. 2. A man's hard round hat.

bowls A game played by rolling large balls on turf.

bow window A curved bay window.

box¹ (boxes) 1. A container. *A money-box.* 2. A hut or shelter. *A signal box.* 3. *A box-office*, a booking-office at a theatre or cinema. 4. *A box on the ears*, a slap on the side of the face.

box² (boxes, boxing, boxed) To fight with fists. boxer, boxing-gloves.

Boxing Day The first week-day after Christmas Day.

boy (boys) 1. A male child. 2. A son. 3. *A boyfriend*, a young man courting a girl. boyhood, boyish.

boycott¹ (boycotts, boycotting, boycotted) To refuse to have anything to do with somebody or something.

boycott² (boycotts) A refusal to have anything to do with somebody or something. *They put his goods under a boycott.*

bra (bras) A brassière.

brace A pair.

bracelet (bracelets) An ornament worn round the wrist.

braces Straps worn over the shoulders to keep the trousers up.

bracken A kind of fern.

bracket (brackets) 1. A support for something fastened to a wall. 2. *Brackets*, punctuation marks like these ().

brackish Slightly salt.

brag (brags, bragging, bragged) To boast.

braid (braids) A kind of ribbon.

braille A method of writing which blind people read by touch.

brain (brains) 1. The grey matter inside people's or animals' heads. 2. Intelligence. 3. (informal) *A brain wave*, a sudden bright idea. brainy.

brake¹ (brakes) A device for slowing down or stopping a vehicle.

brake² (brakes, braking, braked) To use brakes.

bramble (brambles) A blackberry plant.

bran Husks of wheat or other grain.

branch¹ (branches) 1. Something that sticks out from a main part. *A branch of a tree. A branch railway.* 2. A part of a larger organization. *A branch of Woolworth's.*

branch² (branches, branching, branched) To form a branch.

brand¹ (brands) 1. A mark made by a red-hot iron. 2. A particular kind of goods. *The cheapest brand of butter.*

brand² (brands, branding, branded) To burn with a hot iron.

brandish (brandishes, brandishing, brandished) To wave about.

brand-new Very new.

brandy A strong alcoholic drink.

brass 1. A yellow metal made by mixing copper and other metals. 2. Musical instruments made of brass, such as trumpets and trombones. *A brass band.* brassy.

brassière (brassières) A woman's undergarment.

brat (brats) (informal) A child.

brave¹ (braver, bravest) Courageous, fearless. bravely, bravery.

brave² (braves) A North American Indian warrior.

bravo Hurray! Well done!

brawl (brawls) A noisy quarrel.

brawn 1. Strength, muscle. brawny. 2. A kind of cold meat.

bray (brays, braying, brayed) To make a harsh noise like an ass.

brazen 1. Made of brass 2. Shameless.

brazier (braziers) A metal container for burning coals.

breach (breaches) A gap.

bread Food made by baking flour, water, and yeast. *The breadwinner*, the person whose wages support a family.

breadth Width.

break[1] (breaks, breaking, broke, broken) 1. To divide in pieces, to smash, to snap, to crack, to pull apart. 2. To fail to keep to something. *To break a law, to break a promise.* 3. *To break a record*, to do something better than anyone has done before. 4. *To break down*, to collapse, to stop working properly. 5. *To break in*, to enter a building illegally. 6. *To break off*, to bring to an end. 7. *To break up*, to come to the end of a school term. 8. To change. *The weather has broken. His voice is breaking.* **breaker, breakable, breakage.**

break[2] (breaks) A gap, an interval, an interruption.

breaker (breakers) A wave crashing on the shore.

breakfast (breakfasts) The first meal of the day.

breakneck Dangerous.

breakwater (breakwaters) A wall built out into the sea as a protection against heavy waves.

breast (breasts) 1. A person's or animal's chest. 2. One of the parts of a woman's body where milk is produced. 3. *The breast-stroke*, a way of swimming.

breast-plate (breast-plates) Armour protecting the chest.

breath (breaths) 1. Air taken into and let out of the body. 2. *Out of breath*, panting. 3. *Under one's breath*, in a whisper. **breathless, breathlessly.**

breathe (breathes, breathing, breathed) To take air into the lungs or body and let it out again.

bred *See* breed[1].

breech (breeches) The closed end of the barrel of a gun.

breeches Clothing for the legs, trousers fitting tightly at the knee.

breed[1] (breeds, breeding, bred) 1. To give birth to. 2. To keep animals to produce their young. 3. To bring up, to educate. 4. *Good breeding*, good manners.

breed[2] A particular kind of animal. *What breed of dog is that?*

breeze (breezes) A wind. **breezy.**

brethren (old-fashioned) Brothers.

brew (brews, brewing, brewed) 1. To make tea or beer. 2. *Trouble is brewing*, trouble is coming.

brewery (breweries) A place where beer is brewed.

bribe[1] (bribes) A gift offered to a person to tempt him to do someone a favour.

bribe[2] (bribes, bribing, bribed) To give someone a bribe. **bribery.**

brick (bricks) 1. A block of hard-baked clay used in building. 2. A toy building block.

bricklayer (bricklayers) Someone who builds with bricks.

bride (brides) A woman on her wedding-day. **bridal.**

bridegroom (bridegrooms) A man on his wedding-day.

bridesmaid (bridesmaids) A girl or young woman who helps a bride at her wedding.

bridge (bridges) 1. A structure which allows people to cross from one side of something to the other. 2. The high platform over a ship's deck. 3. The top bony part of the nose. 4. A card game.

bridle (bridles) The part of a horse's harness which goes on its head.

brief (briefer, briefest) Short. briefly.

brigade (brigades) A unit in an army.

brigadier (brigadiers) An army officer in charge of a brigade.

brigand (brigands) A bandit, a robber.

bright (brighter, brightest) 1. Shining, giving a strong light. 2. Cheerful. 3. Clever. brightly, brightness.

brighten (brightens, brightening, brightened) To make brighter, to become brighter.

brilliant Very bright. brilliantly, brilliance.

brim (brims) The edge of something. *The cup was full to the brim.*

brimming Full. *Brimming over*, overflowing.

brimstone Sulphur.

brine Salt water. briny.

bring (brings, bringing, brought) 1. To carry, to fetch, to take with you. *Bring your own sandwiches. 2. To bring something about*, to cause it to happen. 3. *To bring someone round*, to make him conscious again. 4. *To bring up a child*, to look after him and educate him.

brink The edge of a steep or dangerous place.

brisk (brisker) Lively, quick-moving. briskly.

bristle (bristles) A short stiff hair. bristly.

British Of Great Britain.

Briton (Britons) A native of Great Britain.

brittle Hard and easily broken.

broad (broader, broadest) 1. Wide, a long way from side to side. 2. Fully complete. *Broad daylight*. 3. Not detailed. *A broad outline of a story*.

broadcast[1] (broadcasts, broadcasting, broadcast) 1. To send out by radio or television. 2. To take part in a broadcast.

broadcast[2] (broadcasts) A broadcast programme.

broad-minded Not easily shocked.

broadside (broadsides) The firing of all the guns on one side of a ship.

brochure (brochures) A pamphlet, an advertising leaflet.

brogue (brogues) 1. A strong shoe. 2. A way of talking in certain areas.

broke *See* break[1].

broken 1. *See* break[1]. 2. *A broken home*, a home where the parents are separated. 3. *Broken English*, English badly spoken by a foreigner.

bronchitis A disease of the lungs.

bronco (broncos) A wild horse.

bronze 1. A metal, a mixture of copper and tin. 2. A reddish brown colour like bronze. 3. *The Bronze Age*, the period when the best tools and weapons were made of bronze.

brooch (brooches) An ornamental pin.

brood[1] (broods) A family of young birds.

brood[2] (broods, brooding, brooded). 1. To sit on eggs to hatch them. 2. To keep thinking about one's troubles.

brook (brooks) A stream.

broom (brooms) 1. A long-handled brush for sweeping. broomstick. 2. A shrub with yellow, white, or pink flowers.

broth A kind of soup.

brother (brothers) A son of the same parents as the person speaking or being spoken about.

brought *See* bring.

brow (brows) 1. The forehead. 2. An eyebrow. 3. The top of a hill, the edge of a cliff.

brown[1] A colour, the colour of earth.

brown[2] (browner, brownest) Brown in colour.

brownie (brownies) 1. A friendly goblin. 2. *Brownie*, a junior Guide.

bruise[1] (bruises) A dark mark on the skin caused by a blow.

bruise[2] (bruises, bruising, bruised) To cause a bruise, to get a bruise.

brunette (brunettes) A woman with dark hair.

brush[1] (brushes) 1. An instrument for painting, sweeping, or scrubbing. 2. A fox's tail.

brush[2] (brushes, brushing, brushed) 1. To use a brush. 2. *To brush against something*, to touch it lightly. 3. *To brush up*, to revise.

Brussels sprouts A kind of green vegetable.

brutal Cruel, beastly. brutally, brutality.

brute (brutes) 1. An animal. 2. A stupid and cruel person.

bubble [1] (bubbles) 1. A small filmy ball of liquid filled with air. 2. A ball of air or gas in a liquid. **bubbly.**

bubble [2] (bubbles, bubbling, bubbled) To send up bubbles, to make bubbles.

buccaneer (buccaneers) A pirate.

buck [1] (bucks) A male deer, hare, or rabbit.

buck [2] (bucks, bucking, bucked) 1. To jump as if to throw off a rider. 2. (informal) *To buck up*, to hurry.

bucket (buckets) A container for water or other things. **bucketful.**

buckle [1] (buckles) A type of fastener for a belt or strap.

buckle [2] (buckles, buckling, buckled) 1. To fasten with a buckle. 2. To bend.

bud (buds) A flower or leaf before it is fully open.

budding 1. Growing buds. 2. Developing.

budge (budges, budging, budged) To move very slightly. *It won't budge.*

budgerigar (budgerigars) An Australian bird commonly kept as a pet.

budget (budgets) A plan for the wise spending of money.

budgie (budgies) (informal) A budgerigar.

buffalo (buffaloes) A kind of wild ox.

buffer (buffers) A device designed to soften the blow when a railway engine or other vehicle hits something.

buffet (buffets) 1. A refreshment counter. 2. An informal meal.

bug (bugs) 1. An insect. 2. (informal) A germ.

bugle (bugles) A musical instrument like a small trumpet.

build (builds, building, built) To construct, to make something by putting parts together. *To build a house.*

building (buildings) Something built, such as a house, a church, or a block of flats.

bulb (bulbs) 1. An electric lamp. 2. A part of certain plants. *A tulip bulb.*

bulge [1] (bulges) A swelling.

bulge [2] (bulges, bulging, bulged) To swell.

bulk 1. Size, especially large size. 2. *In bulk*, in large quantities. **bulky.**

bull (bulls) A male ox, elephant, or whale.

bulldog (bulldogs) A type of dog.

bulldozer (bulldozers) A heavy tractor used to flatten land.

bullet (bullets) A round or pointed piece of metal shot from a rifle or pistol. *Bulletproof*, able to stop bullets.

bulletin (bulletins) An official news announcement.

bull-fight (bull-fights) A contest between men and bulls.

bullfinch (bullfinches) A small bird.

bullfrog (bullfrogs) A large frog.

bullion Bars of gold or silver.

bullock (bullocks) A young bull.

bull's-eye (bull's-eyes) 1. The centre of a target. 2. A peppermint sweet.

bully [1] (bullies, bullying, bullied) To frighten and hurt a weaker person.

bully [2] (bullies) A person who bullies others.

bumble-bee (bumble-bees) A large kind of bee.

bump [1] (bumps) 1. A knock, a collision. 2. A lump or swelling.

bump [2] (bumps, bumping, bumped) 1. To give or receive a bump. 2. To go along with jerky up and down movements. **bumpy.**

bumper [1] (bumpers) A buffer on a motor vehicle.

bumper [2] Exceptionally large.

bumptious Full of one's own importance. **bumptiously.**

bun (buns) A small, round cake.

bunch (bunches) 1. A cluster, a number of things growing or fastened together. *A bunch of grapes. A bunch of flowers.* 2. (informal) A gang.

bundle [1] (bundles) A collection of things

wrapped or tied together. *A bundle of old clothes.*

bundle² (bundles, bundling, bundled) **1.** To make into a bundle. **2.** To put away carelessly. **3.** *To bundle someone off,* to send him away in a hurry.

bung¹ (bungs) A stopper, a large cork.

bung² (bungs, bunging, bunged) To stop something up, to clog it up.

bungalow (bungalows) A house with only one storey.

bungle (bungles, bungling, bungled) To do a job badly or clumsily. **bungler.**

bunk (bunks) A kind of bed.

bunker (bunkers) **1.** A place for storing fuel. **2.** An underground stronghold.

buoy (buoys) A float used as a marker or as a mooring-place.

burden (burdens) **1.** A load. **2.** Anything hard to bear. **burdensome.**

bureau (bureaux) **1.** A writing-desk with drawers. **2.** An office.

burglar (burglars) Someone who breaks into a house or shop to steal something. **burglary.**

burgle (burgles, burgling, burgled) To break into a house or shop as a burglar.

burial (burials) The burying of a dead person.

burly Big and strong.

Burmese Of Burma.

burn¹ (burns, burning, burned, burnt) **1.** To be in flames, to be destroyed while giving out heat, flames, and smoke. *Asbestos won't burn.* **2.** To use as fuel. *Our boiler burns coke.* **3.** To damage by fire, heat, or acid. *Mind you don't burn the cakes, Alfred.*

burn² (burns) **1.** An injury caused by burning. **2.** The firing of a rocket engine.

burn³ (burns) (Scottish) A stream.

burner (burners) The part of a lamp or stove from which the flame comes.

burning Intense, exciting.

burnished Brightly polished.

burnt *See* burn¹.

burrow¹ (burrows) A hole in the ground, like those made by rabbits.

burrow² (burrows, burrowing, burrowed) To dig a burrow.

burst¹ (bursts) **1.** An explosion. **2.** A violent effort. **3.** A number of shots fired continuously.

burst² (bursts, bursting, burst) **1.** To explode, to break apart, to be forced open. **2.** *To burst in,* to rush in.

bury (buries, burying, buried) To put something in the ground, to hide it away.

bus (buses) A road vehicle for the public to travel in.

bush (bushes) **1.** A shrub. **bushy. 2.** *The bush,* wild land in Africa and Australia.

busily In a busy manner.

business (businesses) **1.** A trade or occupation. *A business man.* **2.** *Business-like,* careful, brisk, and accurate. **3.** *It's none of your business,* it does not concern you. **4.** A matter. *I'm sick of the whole business.*

bust¹ (informal) Broken.

bust² (busts) Bosom.

bustle (bustles, bustling, bustled) To fuss about, to hurry.

busy (busier, busiest) **1.** Having something to do. **2.** Full of activity. *busyness.*

busybody (busybodies) An interfering person.

but 1. On the other hand, however. *I called but he did not answer.* **2.** Except. *We were all there but Peter.* **3.** Only. *He's but a boy.*

butane A kind of gas used as fuel.

butcher (butchers) A person who kills, prepares, and sells the flesh of animals as food.

butler (butlers) A senior male servant.

butt¹ (butts) **1.** A target. **2.** A large barrel.

butt² (butts, butting, butted) **1.** To charge into something head first. **2.** *To butt in,* to interrupt.

butter A fatty food made by churning cream.

buttercup (buttercups) A yellow wild flower.

butterfingers A person who drops things.

butterfly (butterflies) An insect with large wings.

butterscotch A sweet made with butter and sugar.

buttocks The part of the body on which a person sits.

button[1] (buttons) 1. A small disc sewn on clothes as a fastener or for decoration. 2. A small knob.

button[2] (buttons, buttoning, buttoned) To fasten with a button.

button-hole (button-holes) 1. A hole for a button. 2. A flower worn on the lapel of a coat.

buttress (buttresses) A support built against a wall.

buxom Plump and healthy-looking.

buy (buys, buying, bought) To get something by paying for it. buyer.

buzz[1] (buzzes, buzzing, buzzed) 1. To make a rough humming sound like a bee. 2. To annoy another aircraft by flying too close to it. buzzer.

buzz[2] (buzzes) The sound of buzzing.

buzzard (buzzards) A bird of prey.

by 1. Near. *Sit here by me.* 2. Through, along. *We came by the main road.* 3. Past. *Who has just gone by the window?* 4. During. *The sun shines by day and the moon by night.* 5. Not later than. *Let me know by tomorrow.* 6. Through the means of. *We cook by gas.* 7. According to. *It's two o'clock by my watch.* 8. In reserve. *Put the money by, you may need it later.* 9. *By and by,* later, before long.

bye (byes) A run made in cricket when the batsman has not hit the ball.

bygone Belonging to the past.

by-law (by-laws) A law which applies only to a particular town or district.

bypass (bypasses) A main road which goes round a town.

bystander (bystanders) A spectator.

Cc

C 100 in Roman numerals.

cab (cabs) 1. A taxi. 2. A compartment for the driver in a lorry, bus, or railway locomotive.

cabaret (cabarets) An entertainment given in a restaurant.

cabbage (cabbages) A green vegetable.

cabin (cabins) 1. A hut. 2. A room or compartment in a ship or air-liner. 3. *A cabin cruiser,* a large motor boat with a cabin.

cabinet (cabinets) 1. A piece of furniture with shelves or drawers. 2. *The Cabinet,* the ministers chosen by the Prime Minister to be responsible for government affairs.

cable (cables) 1. Thick strong rope, wire, or chain. 2. Heavy insulated wire for electricity or telephones. 3. A telegram.

cache (caches) Hidden treasure or stores.

cackle (cackles) 1. The sound made by a hen. 2. A noisy laugh.

cactus (cacti) A prickly desert plant.

cad (cads) A person who behaves dishonourably.

cadaverous Corpse-like.

cadet (cadets) A young person being trained for service in the army, navy, or air force, or in the police force.

cadge (cadges, cadging, cadged) To beg.

café (cafés) A shop which sells meals or refreshments.

cafeteria (cafeterias) A café where customers serve themselves.

caftan (caftans) A kind of tunic.

cage (cages) A framework of bars in which animals or birds are kept.

cairn (cairns) A pile of stones set up as a landmark or a monument.

cake (cakes) 1. A baked mixture of flour, eggs, butter, and other ingredients. 2. Anything made into a flat bun shape. *A cake of soap*, a piece of soap.

caked Covered with something that dries hard. *Shoes caked with mud.*

calamity (calamities) A disaster. **calamitous.**

calculate (calculates, calculating, calculated) 1. To find out by using mathematics. 2. To make a careful plan, to do something deliberately. *That was no accident, it was calculated.* **calculation, calculator.**

calendar (calendars) A list or arrangement of days, weeks, and months.

calf (calves) 1. A young cow, whale, or elephant. 2. The part of a person's leg behind the shin.

call (calls, calling, called) 1. To shout, to cry, to speak loudly. 2. To summon. *Call the next witness!* 3. To telephone. 4. To wake someone up. *Mum calls me at 7.30 every day.* 5. To name. *What is your dog called?* 6. To describe as. *I would call him a fairly good footballer.* 7. *To call someone names*, to insult him. **caller.**

calling (callings) A profession or trade.

callous Hard, cruel. **callously.**

calm (calmer, calmest) Quiet, windless, untroubled. **calmly.**

calorie (calories) A measure of energy supplied by food.

calves *See* calf.

calypso (calypsos) A West Indian song.

camber (cambers) The slight curve on a road's surface which makes rain-water run to the sides.

came *See* come.

camel (camels) An animal used in desert countries for carrying people and goods.

camera (cameras) An apparatus for taking photographs.

camouflage (camouflages, camouflaging, camouflaged) To disguise the appearance of something.

camp¹ (camps) A place where people live for a time in tents or huts. **camp-bed.**

camp² (camps, camping, camped) To make a camp, to have a holiday in a camp. **camper.**

campaign (campaigns) 1. A series of battles in a particular area. 2. A series of happenings planned for a particular purpose. *A road safety campaign.*

campus (campuses) The grounds of a school, college, or university.

can¹ (could) 1. To be able to do something. *I can play the piano.* 2. To be allowed to do something. *The vicar told me I could practise on the organ.*

can² (cans) A metal container for liquids or foods, a tin.

canal (canals) An artificial waterway for barges and other vessels.

canary (canaries) A yellow song-bird.

cancel (cancels, cancelling, cancelled) 1. To say that something already arranged is not to take place. *He cancelled the party.* 2. To cross something out by drawing a line or using a rubber stamp.

cancer A diseased growth in some part of the body.

candid Open, straightforward, honest. **candidly.**

candidate (candidates) 1. A person offering himself for election. 2. A person taking an examination.

candle (candles) A stick of wax with a wick through the centre used as a light. **candle-light, candlestick.**

candy Sweets.

cane (canes) 1. A stick. 2. A long hollow reed.

canine Like a dog.

canister (canisters) A small container, a metal box.

cannibal (cannibals) 1. A person who eats human flesh. 2. Any creature that eats its own kind. cannibalism.

cannon (cannons *or* cannon) 1. A large heavy gun. 2. The larger size of machine-gun that fires shells.

cannot *I cannot*, I am unable to.

canoe[1] (canoes) A kind of light, narrow boat.

canoe[2] (canoes, canoeing, canoed) To travel by canoe.

canopy (canopies) An overhanging covering or shelter.

can't (informal) Cannot.

canteen (canteens) 1. A restaurant for workers in a factory or offices. 2. A container for food or water. 3. A box holding cutlery.

canter (canters, cantering, cantered) To go at a gentle gallop.

canvas A kind of strong, coarse cloth.

canyon (canyons) A deep valley, usually with a river flowing along it.

cap[1] (caps) 1. A kind of hat. 2. A lid, a top covering. 3. A small explosive device, like those used in toy pistols.

cap[2] (caps, capping, capped) 1. To put a cap on, to cover. *A mountain capped with snow.* 2. To award a cap to a member of a games team.

capable 1. Gifted, able. 2. *Capable of something*, able to do it. capably, capability.

capacious Roomy, able to hold a great deal.

capacity (capacities) 1. *The capacity of a container*, the amount the container will hold. 2. A person's ability. *This is within my capacity*, I am able to do it.

cape (capes) 1. A short cloak. 2. A piece of land jutting into the sea.

capering Leaping happily.

capital (capitals) 1. The chief city or town of an area. 2. The decorative top of a pillar. 3. *Capital letters*, letters of this type: A, B, C, D. 4. *Capital punishment*, punishment by putting to death.

capitulate (capitulates, capitulating, capitulated) To surrender. capitulation.

caprice (caprices) A sudden change of mind for trivial or unknown reasons. capricious.

capsize (capsizes, capsizing, capsized) To overturn a boat in the water.

capsule (capsules) 1. A hollow pill containing medicine. 2. A container for men or instruments fired into space on a rocket.

captain (captains) 1. The leader or commander. 2. An army officer above a lieutenant and below a major. 3. A senior officer in the navy. 4. The pilot of an air-liner.

caption (captions) 1. A headline in a newspaper or magazine. 2. An explanation printed under a picture.

captivating Fascinating, charming.

captive (captives) A prisoner. captivity.

capture (captures, capturing, captured) To seize something, to take somebody prisoner.

car (cars) 1. A motor car. *A car-port*, a shelter for a motor car. 2. *A buffet car*, *a dining car*, a railway carriage where refreshments or meals are served.

caravan (caravans) 1. A covered cart or wagon for living in, a mobile home. 2. A company of people journeying together.

carbon 1. A black chemical found in charcoal. 2. *Carbon paper*, a kind of copying paper.

carburettor (carburettors) Part of a petrol engine.

carcass (carcasses) An animal's dead body.

card (cards) 1. Thick, stiff paper. 2. A piece of card made for a particular purpose. *A postcard. A Christmas card. Playing-cards.*

cardboard Thick card.

cardigan (cardigans) A knitted woollen jacket.

cardinal (cardinals) One of the leading priests in the Roman Catholic Church.

care[1] (cares, caring, cared) 1. To take an interest, to have feelings about something, to feel concerned. 2. *To care for*, to look after.

care[2] (cares) 1. Worry, anxiety. 2. *To take care*, to be careful. 3. *To take care of*, to look after.

career[1] (careers) 1. A job, a profession, a settled way of earning one's living. 2. Progress through life. *You have a bright future —I shall watch your career with interest!*

career[2] (careers, careering, careered) To rush wildly along.

carefree Free from worry.

careful Cautious, not taking risks.

careless 1. Thoughtless. 2. Light-hearted. **carelessly.**

caress (caresses, caressing, caressed) To touch gently and lovingly.

caretaker (caretakers) Someone who is paid to look after a school, a church, or some other building.

careworn Worn out by worry.

cargo (cargoes) Goods carried in a ship or aircraft.

caricature (caricatures) An amusing picture of someone.

carnage Slaughter, killing.

carnation (carnations) A garden flower.

carnival (carnivals) A time for merry-making.

carnivorous Eating meat as food. *A carnivorous animal.*

carol (carols) A kind of song, especially one sung at Christmas.

carp (carp) A freshwater fish.

carpenter (carpenters) A man who makes things with wood. **carpentry.**

carpet (carpets) A large rug used as a floor covering.

carriage (carriages) 1. A horse-drawn vehicle. 2. A wagon with compartments for passengers on a train.

carrier (carriers) 1. A person who carries. 2. A device for carrying. 3. *A carrier-pigeon*, a pigeon trained to carry messages.

carrion Dead and decaying flesh.

carrot (carrots) An orange-coloured vegetable.

carry (carries, carrying, carried) 1. To lift and move something from one place to another. 2. To support. *The whole roof is carried on those two pillars, Samson.* 3. To reach. *The arrows carried easily to the target.* 4. *To carry the day*, to be victorious. 5. *Don't get carried away*, don't get too excited. 6. *To carry out something*, to do what one has planned or been told to do. 7. *Please carry on*, please continue.

cart (carts) A vehicle. **cart-horse, cart-load.**

carton (cartons) A cardboard box.

cartoon (cartoons) 1. An amusing drawing. 2. *A strip cartoon*, a series of drawings which tell a story. 3. A film made by photographing a series of drawings. **cartoonist.**

cartridge (cartridges) 1. The case containing the explosive for a bullet or a shell. **cartridge-belt.** 2. The device for holding the stylus in a record-player. 3. A small container.

cartwheel (cartwheels) A sideways somersault with arms and legs stretched out.

carve (carves, carving, carved) 1. To slice meat. 2. To cut something deliberately or artistically. **carver, carving-knife.**

case (cases) 1. A box, bag, covering, or container. 2. An example or occurrence of

something, an instance. *A case of measles.*
3. A·question to be decided in a lawcourt,
the facts and arguments used on each side.
He has a strong case, he has good evidence
on his side.

casement *A casement window*, a window that
opens on hinges.

cash Coins or bank-notes, ready money.

cashier (cashiers) A person in charge of cash
in a bank, office, or shop.

cashmere A soft, woollen material.

casino (casinos) A public building for
gambling and other entertainments.

cask (casks) A barrel.

casket (caskets) A small box for valuables.

casserole (casseroles) 1. A kind of cooking
dish. 2. Food cooked in a casserole.

cassette (cassettes) A small plastic case containing recording tape.

cassock (cassocks) A long, black robe worn
by some priests.

cast[1] (casts, casting, cast) 1. To throw. 2. To
throw off, to shed. 3. To mould, to shape.
Cast iron.

cast[2] (casts) 1. Something made in a mould.
A plaster cast. 2. All the actors in a play.

castanets A percussion instrument.

castaway (castaways) A shipwrecked person.

castle (castles) 1. A large building with
fortifications. 2. A piece in chess, also
called a rook.

castor (castors) A small wheel on a piece of
furniture.

castor oil An unpleasant-tasting oil used as a
medicine.

casual 1. Accidental, not planned. *A casual
meeting.* 2. Careless, not bothering. 3.
Casual clothes, clothes suitable for holidays.
casually.

casualty (casualties) 1. A person killed or
injured in battle or in an accident. 2. *A
casualty ward*, a hospital ward where
people injured in accidents are looked after.

cat (cats) A small furry domestic animal.

catacombs Underground burial chambers.

catalogue (catalogues) A list.

catamaran (catamarans) A boat with two
hulls.

catapult (catapults) 1. A device for shooting
small stones. 2. An ancient weapon of war.
3. A device to assist the take-off of gliders
or aeroplanes.

cataract (cataracts) 1. A steep waterfall.
2. A disease of the eye.

catarrh An inflammation causing a blocked
or runny nose.

catastrophe (catastrophes) A sudden disaster.

catch[1] (catches, catching, caught) 1. To stop
something and grasp it, to capture it.
Caught in a trap. 2. *To catch a bus or train*,
to be in time for it. 3. To hear, to understand. *I can't quite catch what you're saying.*
4. To hit. *I caught him on the chin.* 5. *To
catch an illness*, to get an illness. 6. *To
catch up with*, to come up and join, to
overtake. 7. *To catch fire*, to begin to burn.
8. *To catch on*, to become popular.

catch[2] (catches) 1. The action of catching.
2. Something that has been caught. 3. A
trick. *There's a catch in it somewhere.*
4. A device for keeping a door shut.

catching Infectious.

catchy Easily learnt and remembered.

catechism (catechisms) A set of questions
and answers about the Christian faith.

category (categories) A class, a group, a set.

caterpillar (caterpillars) 1. The larva of a
butterfly or moth. 2. The endless track of a
tank or a tractor.

cathedral (cathedrals) The chief church of a
diocese.

Catherine-wheel (Catherine-wheels) A kind
of firework.

Catholic 1. Belonging to all Christianity. *The Holy Catholic Church.* 2. Roman Catholic.

catkin (catkins) One of the fluffy flowers of willow, hazel, or some other trees.

cattle Cows, bulls, or bullocks.

catty Sly, spiteful. cattily.

caught *See* catch [1].

cauldron (cauldrons) A large cooking-pot.

cauliflower (cauliflowers) A vegetable with a white flower-head.

cause [1] (causes) 1. A reason why something happens. 2. A purpose. *A good cause.*

cause [2] (causes, causing, caused) To make something happen.

causeway (causeways) A raised path or road across swampy land.

caution [1] 1. Taking care. 2. A warning. *The judge let him off with a caution.*

caution [2] (cautions, cautioning, cautioned) To give somebody a warning.

cautious Careful. cautiously.

cavalcade (cavalcades) A procession of people on horseback.

cavalier (cavaliers) 1. A horseman, a gentleman. 2. A supporter of King Charles I.

cavalry Soldiers who fight on horseback.

cave (caves) A hollow, underground place.

caveman (cavemen) A man who lived in a cave in ancient times.

cavern (caverns) A cave. cavernous.

caviare A very expensive delicacy made from the roe of a fish called sturgeon.

cavity (cavities) A hole, a hollow space.

cease (ceases, ceasing, ceased) To stop.

ceaseless Never stopping, endless. ceaselessly.

cedar (cedars) An evergreen tree.

ceiling (ceilings) The roof of a room.

celandine (celandines) A yellow wild flower.

celebrate (celebrates, celebrating, celebrated) 1. To do something to show that a day or an event is special. *To celebrate one's birthday with a party.* 2. *Celebrated,* famous. celebration.

celebrity (celebrities) A famous person.

celery A vegetable with crisp white stems.

celestial Heavenly.

cell (cells) 1. A small room in a prison or monastery. 2. A hole in a honeycomb. 3. An electrical battery. 4. A microscopic unit of living matter.

cellar (cellars) An underground room.

cello (celli) A bass violin. cellist.

Cellophane The trade name of a material as transparent as glass and as thin as paper.

cellular Woven with many holes or cells. *A cellular shirt.*

celluloid A transparent plastic material.

cement 1. A grey powder used to make mortar and concrete. 2. A strong glue.

cemetery (cemeteries) A place where people are buried.

censor (censors) An official who decides whether something is suitable for the public. censorship.

censure Disapproval.

census An official counting of the inhabitants of a country or district.

cent (cents) 1. A coin. In U.S.A. 100 cents = 1 dollar. 2. *Ten per cent*, ten in every hundred.

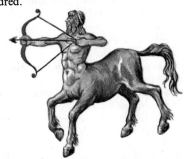

centaur (centaurs) A legendary creature half man and half horse.

centenary (centenaries) The hundredth anniversary of something.

centigrade A scale for measuring temperature with the freezing-point of water at 0 degrees and the boiling-point at 100 degrees.

centimetre (centimetres) A unit of length, one hundredth of a metre.

centipede (centipedes) A small crawling creature.

central At the centre, to do with the centre. **centrally.**

central heating A method of heating a building from one boiler.

centre (centres) 1. The middle of something. 2. A place where there is a great deal going on, a place designed for certain activities. *A youth centre.*

centurion (centurions) A Roman army officer.

century (centuries) 1. A period of 100 years. 2. A score of 100 runs in cricket.

cereal (cereals) 1. Grain crops used as food such as wheat and maize. 2. A breakfast food made from maize or other cereals.

ceremony (ceremonies) A dignified public occasion. **ceremonial, ceremonially, ceremonious.**

certain 1. Sure to happen. *The passengers in the damaged plane faced certain disaster.* 2. Sure. *I'm certain I'm right!* 3. *A certain person,* someone whom we are not going to mention by name. **certainly.**

certainty (certainties) Something which is sure to happen.

certificate (certificates) A piece of paper which gives official proof of something. *A birth certificate.*

cesspool (cesspools) A pit into which drains empty.

chaff Dry husks, chopped straw or hay.

chaffinch (chaffinches) A small bird.

chain[1] (chains) 1. A row of metal rings, called links, passing through one another. 2. A line of people or things.

chain[2] (chains, chaining, chained) To fasten with chains.

chain mail Armour made of iron rings.

chair (chairs) A seat with a back, for one person.

chalet (chalets) A wooden house or cottage.

chalice (chalices) A goblet.

chalk (chalks) 1. Soft, white rock. 2. A stick of a similar substance used for writing and drawing. **chalky.**

challenge (challenges, challenging, challenged) 1. To demand an explanation or a password. *The sentry challenged the stranger.* 2. To invite someone to play a game or fight a duel. **challenger.**

chamber (chambers) A room.

chamber music Music for a small number of players.

champagne A bubbly French wine.

champion (champions) 1. Someone who has beaten all other competitors. 2. Someone who fights for a particular cause. **championship.**

chance (chances) 1. An accident. *By chance.* 2. A possibility, a risk, an opportunity. *There's no chance of that!*

chancel (chancels) The eastern part of a church, containing the altar.

chancellor (chancellors) A chief minister of state.

chancy Risky.

chandelier (chandeliers) A hanging display of candles or electric lights.

change[1] (changes, changing, changed) 1. To put something in place of something else, to take something of equal value for what is given. 2. *To change one's mind,* to alter one's opinion. 3. *To change trains,* to move into another train. 4. To take on another form. *The frog changed back into a handsome prince.*

change[2] (changes) 1. The act of changing. 2. Money in small coins. 3. Money to be given back when too much money is offered in payment.

changeable Liable to change.

channel (channels) 1. A stretch of water joining two seas. *The English Channel.* 2. A way for water to flow along. 3. A radio or television wavelength.

chant (chants) A tune, especially a psalm tune.

chaos Utter disorder, complete confusion. chaotic, chaotically.

chap (chaps) (informal) A person.

chapel (chapels) A place of worship.

chaplain (chaplains) A clergyman. *A hospital chaplain.*

chapped Rough and cracked.

chapter (chapters) A section of a book.

char (chars) (informal) A charwoman.

character (characters) 1. Those qualities that make up the nature of someone or something. 2. A personality. *A well-known character.* 3. A person in a story or a play.

charade (charades) A party game.

charcoal A black substance made by burning wood slowly.

charge[1] (charges) 1. An accusation. 2. A fast and sudden attack. 3. The price asked for something. 4. A quantity of explosive. 5. *To be in charge of something*, to be in command of it, to be responsible for it.

charge[2] (charges, charging, charged) 1. To accuse. 2. To rush forward, to attack. 3. To ask a price for something. 4. To fill something, such as a pipe with tobacco, a gun with powder, or a battery with electric power.

chariot (chariots) A horse-drawn vehicle used in ancient times for racing or fighting. charioteer.

charity[1] Kindness, generosity. charitable.

charity[2] (charities) An organization which gives help to those who are in need.

charm[1] (charms) 1. A magic spell. 2. Something worn or carried for good luck. 3. Attractiveness.

charm[2] (charms, charming, charmed) 1. To bewitch, to put a spell on someone or something. 2. To delight. charmer.

charming Attractive. charmingly.

charred Made black by burning.

chart (charts) 1. A map, especially one used by sailors. 2. A diagram or list with information about prices, sales, or other things.

charter (charters, chartering, chartered) To hire. *A charter flight*, a journey on a chartered aircraft.

charwoman (charwomen) A woman paid to do housework.

chary Cautious.

chase (chases, chasing, chased) 1. To run after, to try to overtake. 2. *To chase away*, to drive away.

chasm (chasms) A deep opening in the ground.

chaste Pure, virtuous. chastely, chastity.

chat[1] (chats, chatting, chatted) To have a friendly talk.

chat[2] (chats) A friendly talk.

château (châteaux) A French castle or mansion.

chatter (chatters, chattering, chattered) To talk quickly and continuously about unimportant things.

chatterbox (chatterboxes) Someone who chatters.

chauffeur (chauffeurs) A person paid to drive someone's motor car.

cheap (cheaper, cheapest) 1. Not expensive, costing little money. 2. Of poor quality. cheaply, cheapness.

cheat[1] (cheats, cheating, cheated) To play or act dishonestly, to trick someone.

cheat[2] (cheats) A person who cheats.

check[1] (checks, checking, checked) 1. To make sure that something is correct. *Check your answers.* 2. To stop something, or make it go slower.

check[2] (checks) 1. A pattern of squares. 2. A term used in chess. checkmate.

cheek (cheeks) 1. The side of the face below the eye. cheek-bone. 2. Saucy behaviour, mild rudeness. cheeky.

cheer[1] (cheers, cheering, cheered) 1. To encourage, to comfort. *To cheer up*, to become happier. 2. To shout joyfully, to urge somebody on.

cheer[2] (cheers) A cry of encouragement or rejoicing. *Three cheers.*

cheerful Happy. cheerfully, cheerfulness.

cheese (cheeses) A solid food made from milk.

cheese-paring Stingy, mean.

cheetah (cheetahs) A kind of leopard.

chef (chefs) A professional cook.

chemical[1] Of chemistry.

chemical[2] (chemicals) A substance used in chemistry, such as an acid.

chemist (chemists) 1. An expert in chemistry. 2. A person who prepares and sells medicines.

chemistry The branch of science dealing with what substances are composed of and how they act upon each other.

cheque (cheques) A written instruction to somebody's bank to pay out money.

cherish (cherishes, cherishing, cherished) To care for, to look after.

cherry (cherries) A small red or white fruit.

cherub (cherubim) A kind of angel.

chess A game played on a board with black and white squares. chess-board.

chest (chests) 1. The upper part of the front of the body. 2. A strong box with a lid. *A treasure chest.* 3. *A chest of drawers*, a piece of furniture with drawers.

chestnut (chestnuts) 1. A large tree which produces shiny brown nuts in spiky green cases. 2. Its nut.

chew (chews, chewing, chewed) To crush food with the teeth by continued motion of the jaw.

chic Fashionable.

chick (chicks) A young bird.

chicken (chickens) A young fowl.

chicken-hearted Cowardly.

chicken-pox A disease causing red spots on the skin.

chief[1] Most important.

chief[2] (chiefs) A leader, a ruler.

chiefly 1. Above all. 2. Mainly. *It's built chiefly of stone.*

chieftain (chieftains) A leader.

chilblain (chilblains) A painful swelling, usually on a hand or foot, occurring in cold weather.

child (children) 1. A young boy or girl. 2. Someone's son or daughter. childhood, childish, childlike.

chill[1] 1. A feeling of coldness. 2. An illness which often causes sickness and shivering.

chill[2] (chills, chilling, chilled) To make a person or thing cold.

chilly (chillier, chilliest) 1. Rather cold. 2. Unfriendly. chilliness.

chime[1] (chimes, chiming, chimed) To make a sound like a bell.

chime[2] (chimes) The sound of a bell.

chimney (chimneys) A part of a building which carries smoke away from a fire. **chimney-pot, chimney-stack.**

chimney-sweep (chimney-sweeps) A person who cleans chimneys.

chimpanzee (chimpanzees) An African ape.

chin (chins) The part of a person's face below the mouth.

china 1. A fine kind of pottery. 2. Cups, saucers, plates, and so on.

Chinese Of China.

chink (chinks) 1. A narrow crack or opening. 2. A sound like that of coins or glasses hitting each other.

chip¹ (chips) 1. A small piece cut or broken off something. 2. *Chips*, pieces of fried potato.

chip² (chips, chipping, chipped) To cut or knock chips off something.

chirp (chirps, chirping, chirped) To make short sharp sounds like a bird.

chirpy Lively.

chisel (chisels) A cutting tool.

chivalry 1. The rules and customs of knights in the Middle Ages. 2. Politeness, loyalty, and bravery. **chivalrous.**

chlorine A chemical used as a disinfectant in water.

chloroform An anaesthetic.

chocolate (chocolates) A kind of sweet made from cocoa powder.

choice (choices) 1. Choosing. 2. The right or opportunity to choose.

choir (choirs) A group of people trained to sing together.

choke¹ (chokes, choking, choked) 1. To be prevented from breathing properly. 2. To block somebody's breathing by squeezing his throat. 3. To block something up.

choke² (chokes) One of the controls in a motor car.

cholera A serious disease.

choose (chooses, choosing, chose, chosen) 1. To select, to pick out. 2. To make a decision.

chop¹ (chops, chopping, chopped) To cut by hitting downwards with an axe or a heavy knife.

chop² (chops) 1. A chopping blow. 2. A thick slice of meat.

chopper (choppers) 1. A small axe. 2. (informal) A helicopter.

chopsticks A pair of sticks to eat with.

choral To do with a choir.

chord (chords) A number of musical notes sounded together.

chore (chores) An everyday job.

chortle (chortles) A chuckle with a gurgle in it.

chorus (choruses) 1. Music for a group of singers. 2. Part of a song which is sung after every verse. 3. A choir.

chose, chosen *See* choose.

christen (christens, christening, christened) To receive a child into the Christian Church and to give it its Christian name.

Christian (Christians) Someone who believes in Jesus Christ. **Christianity.**

Christmas Day December 25th, the day on which the birth of Jesus Christ is celebrated. **Christmas-tree.**

chromatic *A chromatic scale*, a scale using all the black and white notes on a piano.

chromium A bright shiny silvery metal. **chromium-plated.**

chronic Lasting a long time.

chronicle (chronicles) A record of events.

chronometer (chronometers) A specially accurate watch or clock.

chrysalis (chrysalises) The form taken by an insect between the larva or caterpillar stage and the flying stage.

chrysanthemum (chrysanthemums) A garden flower blooming in autumn.

chub (chub) A small river fish.

chubby Plump, rather fat.

chuck (chucks, chucking, chucked) (informal) To throw.

chuckle [1] (chuckles, chuckling, chuckled) To laugh quietly.

chuckle [2] (chuckles) A quiet laugh.

chum (chums) A friend. chummy.

chunk (chunks) A thick lump. chunky.

church (churches) A building for Christian worship.

churchyard (churchyards) The piece of ground round a church, a graveyard.

churn (churns) 1. A machine for making butter. 2. A large can for milk.

chutney A strong-tasting mixture of sweet and sour flavours sometimes eaten with meat.

cider An alcoholic drink made from apples.

cigar (cigars) A fat roll of tobacco leaf for smoking.

cigarette (cigarettes) Tobacco rolled in paper for smoking.

cinder (cinders) A small piece of partly-burnt coal or wood.

cine-camera (cine-cameras) A camera for taking moving pictures.

cinema (cinemas) A theatre where films are shown.

circle [1] (circles) 1. A perfectly round, flat shape. 2. Something shaped like an ◯ circular. 3. A balcony in a cinema or theatre.

circle [2] (circles, circling, circled) To travel in a circle, to go right round something.

circuit (circuits) 1. A circular race-course. 2. A circular journey. 3. The path followed by an electric current.

circulate (circulates, circulating, circulated) To send something round, to go round. circulation.

circumference (circumferences) 1. The boundary of something, especially the outside of a circle. 2. The distance round the edge of something.

circumstance (circumstances) 1. A fact or detail. 2. *Circumstances*, the conditions in which something is done. *You'll understand when you know the circumstances.*

circus (circuses) An entertainment given by clowns, acrobats, trained animals, and other performers.

cistern (cisterns) A water-tank.

citadel (citadels) A fortress.

citizen (citizens) 1. A person who lives in a city or town. 2. A person having full rights in a particular community. citizenship.

citrus *Citrus fruits*, fruits such as oranges, lemons, and grapefruit.

city (cities) An important town.

civic Having to do with the government of a city.

civil 1. Of citizens. *A civil war*, a war between different parties inside one country. 2. *The Civil Service*, government departments. 3. Polite. civilly, civility.

civilian (civilians) A person not in one of the armed services.

civilized Living in an orderly, well-developed state. civilization.

clad Clothed.

claim (claims, claiming, claimed) 1. To demand something because one has a right to it. 2. To declare something as a fact. *He claims that he can cure warts.*

clam (clams) A large shellfish.

clamber (clambers, clambering, clambered) To climb by using the hands to help.

clammy Damp, cold, and sticky.

clamour Shouting, a confused noise.

clamp (clamps) A device for holding things together.

clan (clans) A family group, a tribe.

clang (clangs, clanging, clanged) To make a noisy, ringing sound.

clank (clanks, clanking, clanked) To make the sound of heavy pieces of metal knocked together.

clap¹ (claps, clapping, clapped) To hit the palms of the hands together, especially in showing that one approves of something.

clap² (claps) *A clap of thunder*, the noise of thunder.

clarify (clarifies, clarifying, clarified) To make clear, to become clear. clarification, clarity.

clarinet (clarinets) A woodwind instrument. clarinettist.

clash (clashes, clashing, clashed) 1. To make a noise like the sound of cymbals. 2. To collide, to fight.

clasp¹ (clasps) 1. A device for fastening a necklace, a belt, or some other object. 2. An embrace.

clasp² (clasps, clasping, clasped) 1. To fasten. 2. To hold something firmly.

class (classes) 1. A group of children or students who are taught together. class-room. 2. A group of things or people with something in common. *The working class. The Navy has a new class of destroyers.*

classic (classics) 1. Something, such as a book or piece of music, generally said to be very good of its kind. 2. *Classics*, the study of the ancient Greeks and Romans. classical.

classify (classifies, classifying, classified) To arrange things in sets, groups, or classes. classification.

clatter (clatters, clattering, clattered) To make a confused noise of rattling and knocking.

claustrophobia The fear of being shut in.

claw¹ (claws) One of the curved, pointed nails on the feet of some creatures.

claw² (claws, clawing, clawed) To scratch or tear at something with claws or hands.

clay A stiff, sticky kind of earth. clayey.

clean¹ (cleaner, cleanest) 1. Free from dirt. 2. Fresh, unused. 3. (informal) Completely. *I clean forgot.* cleanly, cleanliness.

clean² (cleans, cleaning, cleaned) To make clean.

cleaner (cleaners) 1. A person who cleans. 2. A thing used for cleaning.

clear¹ (clearer, clearest) 1. Easy to see through. 2. Easy to see, to hear, or to understand. 3. Without any doubt. *A clear memory.* 4. Free from obstacles or difficulties or unwanted things. *The road is clear.* 5. Completely. *The prisoner escaped and got clear away.* 6. Without touching something, at some distance from it. *Keep clear of the gates.* clearance.

clear[2] (clears, clearing, cleared) 1. To make a thing clear. 2. To become clear. 3. To go over or past something without touching it. *The horse just cleared the fence.* 4. (informal) *To clear off,* to go away. 5. *To clear something out,* to empty it. 6. *To clear up,* to make things tidy. 7. *The weather is clearing up,* it is becoming fine again.

clearing (clearings) An open space in wooded country.

clearly Distinctly, without doubt.

clef (clefs) A sign that labels a stave in music.

clematis A flowering climbing plant.

clemency Mercy.

clenched Grasped tightly together.

clergy Clergymen.

clergyman (clergymen) A Christian minister, a person who is authorized to conduct services in the Christian Church.

clerk (clerks) An office worker. clerical.

clever (cleverer, cleverest) Quick to learn, skilful, intelligent. cleverly, cleverness.

click (clicks) A short sharp little sound.

client (clients) A customer, a person who does business with a bank or other firm.

cliff (cliffs) A steep rock face.

climate (climates) The normal weather conditions of a particular area. *A dry climate.*

climax (climaxes) The most important of a series of events.

climb (climbs, climbing, climbed) 1. To go up ,or down something. 2. To grow upwards. 3. To rise. climber.

cling (clings, clinging, clung) To hold tightly to something.

clinic (clinics) A place where people go for medical advice or treatment. clinical.

clink (clinks, clinking, clinked) To make a small ringing sound.

clip[1] (clips) A fastening device. *A paper-clip.*

clip[2] (clips, clipping, clipped) 1. To fasten with a clip. 2. To cut with scissors or shears. *To clip a hedge.* clippers.

clipper (clippers) A fast sailing ship.

cloak (cloaks) An outer garment which hangs loose from the shoulders.

cloak-room (cloak-rooms) 1. A place where coats or luggage may be left. 2. A lavatory.

clock (clocks) An instrument for measuring time.

clockwise Moving round in the same direction as a clock's hands.

clockwork Driven by a spring which has to be wound up. *A clockwork engine.*

clod (clods) A lump of earth.

clog[1] (clogs) A wooden shoe.

clog[2] (clogs, clogging, clogged) To block something up.

cloister (cloisters) A covered pathway along the side of a building such as a cathedral or a monastery.

close[1] (closes, closing, closed) 1. To shut. 2. To end. closure. 3. *To close in,* to move nearer. 4. *The days are closing in,* the days are getting shorter.

close[2] (closer, closest) 1. Near. 2. Careful, thorough. *Pay close attention!* 3. Tight. *A close fit.* 4. Stuffy, uncomfortably warm. *Close weather.* 5. Mean, stingy. *A miser is close with his money.* 6. *A close-up,* a detailed photograph taken at short range.

clot[1] (clots, clotting, clotted) To form soft lumps.

clot[2] (clots) A lump formed when a liquid dries or thickens. *A clot of blood.*

cloth 1. Material woven from wool, cotton, nylon, or other substances. 2. A piece of cloth used for a particular purpose. *A table-cloth. A dish-cloth.*

clothe (clothes, clothing, clothed or clad) To cover, to cover with clothes.

clothes or clothing Garments, things that we can wear.

cloud (clouds) A mass of tiny water-drops, or smoke, or dust, floating in the air. cloudless.

cloud-burst (cloud-bursts) A violent rain-storm.

cloudy (cloudier, cloudiest) 1. Covered with clouds, full of clouds. 2. Not clear, hard to see through.

clout (clouts, clouting, clouted) (informal) To hit.

clove-hitch (clove-hitches) A kind of knot.

clover A small plant.

clown (clowns) The funny man in a circus.

club (clubs) 1. A heavy stick. 2. A stick with a head for use in golf. 3. A society of people who meet together.

clubs A suit of playing-cards.

cluck (clucks, clucking, clucked) To make a noise like a hen.

clue (clues) Something that helps to solve a puzzle or a mystery.

clumsy (clumsier, clumsiest) Awkward. clumsily, clumsiness.

clung See cling.

cluster (clusters) A number of people or things of the same type gathered together.

clutch¹ (clutches, clutching, clutched) To hold something eagerly, to snatch at it.

clutch² (clutches) 1. One of the controls in a motor car. 2. A set of eggs in a nest.

clutter (clutters) An untidy quantity of things.

coach¹ (coaches) 1. A bus. 2. A carriage with four wheels drawn by four horses. 3. A railway passenger carriage. 4. An instructor, especially in athletics or games.

coach² (coaches, coaching, coached) To train people, especially in sports.

coal (coals) A black solid fuel. *A coalfield*, an area where coal is to be found. *A coal-mine*, a place where coal is dug from the earth. *A coal-scuttle*, a bucket for keeping coal by the fireside.

coarse (coarser, coarsest) Rough, common, not smooth or delicate. coarsely, coarseness.

coast¹ (coasts) The sea-shore and the land close to it. coastal.

coast² (coasts, coasting, coasted) To free-wheel down a slope.

coat (coats) 1. A garment with sleeves, a jacket. 2. A covering. 3. A layer of paint.

coating (coatings) A covering.

coax (coaxes, coaxing, coaxed) To persuade very gently.

cobber (cobbers) (Australian informal) A friend.

cobble (cobbles) A round, smooth stone.

cobbled Made with cobbles. *A cobbled street.*

cobbler (cobblers) A person whose business is mending shoes.

cobra (cobras) A poisonous snake.

cobweb (cobwebs) A spider's web.

cock¹ (cocks) 1. A male bird. 2. A male farmyard fowl.

cock² (cocks, cocking, cocked) 1. *To cock a gun*, to make it ready for firing. 2. *An animal cocks its ears*, it raises its ears.

cockatoo (cockatoos) A kind of parrot.

cockerel (cockerels) A male farmyard fowl, a cock.

cockle (cockles) A kind of shellfish.

cockney (cockneys) 1. Someone born in London. 2. A kind of English spoken in London.

cockroach (cockroaches) A dark brown beetle.

cocksure Very certain, too confident.

cocktail (cocktails) A mixed alcoholic drink.

cocky (informal) Conceited, cheeky.

cocoa 1. A kind of hot drink. 2. The powder from which this is made.

coconut (coconuts) A large brown nut which grows on palm-trees.

cocoon (cocoons) The outer covering of a chrysalis.

cod (cod) A large sea fish.

code (codes) 1. A set of rules. *The Highway Code.* 2. A secret language. *The message was in code.* 3. A set of signals used for sending messages. *Morse code.*

coeducation The education of boys and girls together. coeducational.

coffee 1. A kind of hot drink. 2. The roasted beans from which this is made.

coffin (coffins) A box in which dead bodies are buried or cremated.

cog-wheel (cog-wheels) A toothed wheel.

coherent 1. Holding together. 2. Clear and logical. **coherently, coherence.**

coil [1] (coils, coiling, coiled) To twist into a spiral.

coil [2] (coils) Something coiled. *A coil of rope.*

coin (coins) A piece of metal money.

coinage (coinages) A system of money. *Decimal coinage.*

coincide (coincides, coinciding, coincided) To happen at the same time or place as something else. **coincidence.**

coke A solid fuel.

colander (colanders) A bowl with holes in it for draining food.

cold [1] (colder, coldest) 1. Not warm, low in temperature. *Winter days are short and cold.* 2. Unkind, unfeeling. 3. *In cold blood*, deliberately, without excitement. **cold-blooded, cold-bloodedly.** 4. *A cold war*, hostility between nations without actual fighting. **coldly, coldness.**

cold [2] (colds) An illness of the nose and throat.

colic Severe pain in the stomach and bowels.

collaborate (collaborates, collaborating, collaborated) To share work with someone else. **collaboration, collaborator.**

collage (collages) A picture made out of scraps of paper or material.

collapse [1] (collapses, collapsing, collapsed) To fall down or in. *The roof collapsed under the weight of the snow.*

collapse [2] (collapses) The act of collapsing.

collapsible Capable of being folded up.

collar (collars) 1. Part of the clothing that goes round the neck. 2. A band that goes round the neck of an animal.

collect (collects, collecting, collected) 1. To gather together, to bring to a central place. 2. To get specimens of things to study or enjoy them. *David collects stamps.* 3. To come together. *A large crowd collected to admire the elephant.* 4. To fetch. *Jane's father collected her from school.* **collection, collector.**

college (colleges) A place where people go for further study after leaving school.

collide (collides, colliding, collided) To crash together. **collision.**

collie (collies) A Scottish sheep-dog.

collier (colliers) 1. A coal-miner. 2. A ship which carries coal.

colliery (collieries) A coal-mine.

collywobbles (informal) A rumbling stomach.

colon (colons) A punctuation mark : .

colonel (colonels) An army officer in charge of a regiment.

colony (colonies) 1. A land which has been developed by settlers from another country and is not yet independent. **colonist, colonial.** 2. A group of people, animals, or birds living together.

colossal Huge, giant-like.

colour [1] (colours) 1. *Red, yellow,* and *blue* are all colours. **colourful, colourless, colouring.** 2. The flag of a particular ship or regiment.

colour [2] (colours, colouring, coloured) 1. To put paint or crayon on something, to add colour to it. 2. To blush.

colour bar Treating people differently because of the colour of their skin.

colour-blind Unable to see the difference between certain colours.

colt (colts) A young male horse.

column (columns) 1. A pillar. 2. Something which is long and narrow. *A column of smoke. A column of soldiers.*

coma (comas) An unnatural deep sleep.

comb[1] (combs) **1.** An instrument for making one's hair tidy. **2.** The red crest on a chicken's head.

comb[2] (combs, combing, combed) **1.** To tidy hair with a comb. **2.** To search thoroughly.

combat (combats) A fight, a battle. *Mortal combat*, a fight to the death. **combatant.**

combine (combines, combining, combined) To join together. **combination.**

combine-harvester (combine-harvesters) A machine that both cuts and threshes corn.

combustion Burning. *An internal combustion engine*, a petrol or diesel engine.

come (comes, coming, came) **1.** To move towards, to move near. **2.** To arrive. *He came late.* **3.** To happen. *No harm will come to you.* **4.** To go with somebody. *May I come with you?* **5.** To amount to something. *It came to a lot of money.* **6.** To become. *Dreams sometimes come true.*

comedian (comedians) A performer who makes people laugh.

comedy (comedies) An amusing play.

comet (comets) A heavenly body which looks like a star with a tail of light.

comfort (comforts, comforting, comforted) To calm somebody's fear, to ease his pain.

comfortable 1. Easy. *A comfortable chair.* **2.** Free from pain or worry. **comfortably.**

comic[1] Funny. **comical, comically.**

comic[2] (comics) **1.** A paper for children with stories told in pictures. **2.** A comedian.

comma (commas) The punctuation mark **,** .

command[1] (commands) **1.** An order. **2.** *In command*, in authority, in control. **3.** Skill and mastery. *A good command of English.*

command[2] (commands, commanding, commanded) **1.** To order. **commandment. 2.** To be in charge of. **commander, commandant.**

commando (commandos) A soldier trained to take part in dangerous raids.

commence (commences, commencing, commenced) To begin. **commencement.**

commend (commends, commending, commended) To praise. **commendation.**

comment[1] (comments, commenting, commented) To make remarks about something.

comment[2] (comments) A remark.

commentary (commentaries) A description of what is going on.

commentator (commentators) A person giving a commentary.

commerce Trade.

commercial To do with trade. *A commercial traveller*, a person who travels to sell goods.

commit (commits, committing, committed) **1.** To do, to perform. *To commit a crime.* **2.** *To commit oneself*, to promise to do something. **3.** *To commit to memory*, to learn by heart. **commitment.**

committee (committees) A group of people with the job of discussing and organizing something. *The Sports Day Committee.*

common[1] (commoner, commonest) **1.** Belonging to or shared by a lot of people. *Common knowledge.* **2.** Ordinary, found in many places. *Sparrows are common birds.* **3.** Rude, vulgar. *Don't be common!* **4.** *Common sense*, the kind of sensible thinking to be expected of a normal person. **5.** *The Common Market*, a group of European countries which trade freely together. **commonly.**

common[2] (commons) An area of land which anyone can use.

commonplace Ordinary.

commonwealth (commonwealths) A group of countries or states which co-operate and help each other.

commotion (commotions) Confusion, excited movement.

communal Shared by a number of people.

communicate (communicates, communicating, communicated) To pass information, news, or feelings to another person.

communication (communications) 1. A message, something which has been communicated. 2. *Communications*, ways of sending messages or of getting from one place to another.

communicative Ready and willing to talk.

communion Sharing. *Holy Communion*, a service of the Christian Church in which consecrated bread and wine are given to worshippers.

communiqué (communiqués) An official announcement.

communism A set of political beliefs, a political system like that in Russia.

communist (communists) A person who believes in communism. *The Communist Party*, a political party.

community (communities) The people living in one place.

commuter (commuters) A person who travels daily to work.

compact[1] As small as possible. compactly.

compact[2] (compacts) A small container holding face-powder.

companion (companions) Someone who shares a journey, a hardship, or an interest with someone else. companionship.

company[1] 1. Being together with someone else. *To keep someone company. To part company.* 2. (informal) Visitors.

company[2] (companies) 1. A set of people who do things together. *A ship's company.* 2. A unit in the army.

compare (compares, comparing, compared) 1. To judge the similarity of two or more things. 2. To be similar to. *Robinson cannot compare with Jones*, he is not nearly so good. comparable, comparative, comparison.

compartment (compartments) A division in a railway carriage.

compass (compasses) 1. An instrument with a swinging needle that always points north.

2. *A pair of compasses*, an instrument for drawing circles.

compassion Pity, active concern. compassionate, compassionately.

compel (compels, compelling, compelled) To force somebody to do something, to demand obedience.

compensate (compensates, compensating, compensated) To give somebody something to make up for a loss or injury. compensation.

compère (compères) A person who introduces the various performers in a variety show.

compete (competes, competing, competed) 1. To take part in a race or contest. 2. To try to win, to try to do better than other people. competitive, competitor.

competent Properly qualified and quite able to do a particular job. *A competent driver.* competently, competence.

competition (competitions) 1. A game or contest in which people compete with each other. 2. Competing.

compile (compiles, compiling, compiled) To put together. *To compile a magazine.* compiler, compilation.

complacent Self-satisfied, smug. complacently, complacence.

complain (complains, complaining, complained) 1. To say that one is not satisfied with something. *We complained about the food.* 2. To say that one has an illness or pain. *She complained of a cold.* complaint.

complete[1] (completes, completing, completed) 1. To finish. 2. To make whole, to make up the full number. *The arrival of the last guest completed the party.* completion.

complete[2] 1. Finished, completed. 2. Perfect. *A complete success.* completely.

complex Complicated. complexity.

complexion (complexions) The natural colour and appearance of a person's skin.

complicated Made up of many parts, hard to understand.

complication (complications) Something that makes something else complicated or difficult. *All was going well, but now there's a complication.*

compliment (compliment) An admiring remark. *To pay someone a compliment,* to say something nice about him. complimentary.

component (components) A part.

compose (composes, composing, composed) 1. To put together, to make up. *Our class is composed of 15 boys and 18 girls.* 2. To make up music. composer, composition.

compost Manure made of decayed stalks, leaves, and similar stuff. *A compost heap.*

compound (compounds) 1. Something made of several parts or ingredients. 2. A fenced area in which buildings stand.

comprehend (comprehends, comprehending, comprehended) 1. To understand. comprehensible. 2. To include.

comprehension Understanding.

comprehensive Including many kinds or things. *A comprehensive school,* a secondary school providing many kinds of education.

compress (compresses, compressing, compressed) To squeeze together, to get something into a smaller space than it would usually occupy. compression.

comprising Consisting of, including.

compulsion Being compelled. compulsive.

compulsory Having to be done, not voluntary.

compute (computes, computing, computed) To count, to calculate.

computer (computers) A very complicated automatic calculating machine.

comrade (comrades) A good friend or companion. comradeship.

concave Curved like the inside of a ball.

conceal (conceals, concealing, concealed) To hide, to keep secret. concealment.

conceit Vanity, self-satisfaction.

conceited Vain and self-satisfied.

conceive (conceives, conceiving, conceived) 1. To become pregnant. 2. To have an idea or plan in the mind. conceivable, conceivably.

concentrate (concentrates, concentrating, concentrated) 1. To give full attention to

something, to think hard. 2. To gather things together. concentration.

concentric *Concentric circles,* circles having the same centre.

concept (concepts) An idea.

conception Conceiving.

concern[1] (concerns) 1. Something a person is interested in or responsible for. *That's no concern of mine.* 2. A business. *A going concern,* a successful business. 3. Worry, anxiety.

concern[2] (concerns, concerning, concerned) 1. To affect, to be of interest or importance to. 2. *To feel concerned,* to feel anxious.

concerning About.

concert (concerts) A musical performance. *A concert hall.*

concerto (concertos) A musical composition for a solo instrument and orchestra.

concession (concessions) Something allowed as a right or privilege.

concise Brief, using only a few words.

conclude (concludes, concluding, concluded) 1. To finish. 2. To form an opinion. *After waiting 15 minutes, we concluded that we had missed the bus.* conclusion.

conclusive Convincing.

concoct (concocts, concocting, concocted) To invent, to make up. concoction.

concord Agreement, peace, harmony.

concrete A mixture of cement, gravel, sand, and water which sets like rock.

concussion An injury to the brain caused by a hard knock on the head.

condemn (condemns, condemning, condemned) 1. To say that someone has done wrong or that something is wrong. *We condemn cruelty to animals.* 2. *To condemn* a *thief to gaol*, to send him to gaol as a punishment. **condemnation.**

condense (condenses, condensing, condensed) 1. To make smaller or shorter. *Condensed milk*, milk made thicker and sweetened. 2. To turn into water or liquid. *Steam condenses on a cold window-pane.* **condensation.**

condescending Kind in a superior sort of way.

condition (conditions) 1. A state. *In good condition*, in a good state. *Out of condition*, in a bad state. 2. *On condition that*, provided that. 3. *Conditions*, circumstances. *It'll be an exciting match if the conditions are good.*

conduct[1] (pronounced *con*duct) Behaviour.

conduct[2] (pronounced con*duct*) (conducts, conducting, conducted) 1. To guide. *We were conducted round the castle.* 2. To direct, to be in charge of. *To conduct an orchestra.* 3. *To conduct oneself well*, to behave well. 4. To allow electricity to pass. *Copper wire conducts electricity.*

conductor (conductors) 1. A person who sells tickets on a bus or tram. **conductress.** 2. A person who conducts an orchestra. 3. Something which conducts electricity.

cone (cones) 1. An object which is round at one end and pointed at the other. **conical.** 2. The fruit of certain evergreen trees. *Pine cones.*

confectioner (confectioners) A person who keeps a sweet shop. **confectionery.**

confederate (confederates) An ally, a partner.

conference (conferences) A meeting for discussion.

confess (confesses, confessing, confessed) To own up, to admit having done something wrong. **confession.**

confetti Small pieces of paper showered on the bride and bridegroom at weddings.

confide (confides, confiding, confided) To trust someone with a secret.

confidence (confidences) 1. Faith in somebody or something. 2. *In confidence*, as a secret. *I'll take you into my confidence*, I'll tell you my secret. 3. *A confidence trick*, a criminal deception.

confident Trusting, feeling certain. **confidently.**

confidential To be kept secret. **confidentially.**

confine (confines, confining, confined) To imprison, to keep somebody somewhere.

confinement (confinements) 1. Imprisonment. *Solitary confinement.* 2. Giving birth to a child.

confirm (confirms, confirming, confirmed)1. To agree for certain.2. To show the truth of.3. *To be confirmed*, to become a full member of the Christian Church.

confiscate (confiscates, confiscating, confiscated) To take something away from somebody as a punishment. **confiscation.**

conflagration (conflagrations) A big fire.

conflict[1] (pronounced *con*flict) (conflicts) A fight, a struggle, a bitter argument.

conflict[2] (pronounced con*flict*) (conflicts, conflicting, conflicted) To be against or opposed, to disagree.

confounded (informal) Most annoying.

confront (confronts, confronting, confronted) To bring face to face, to meet face to face. **confrontation.**

confuse (confuses, confusing, confused) To mix up, to muddle. **confusion.**

congealed Frozen, stiffened, solid.

congenial Pleasant, agreeable. *Congenial company*.

conger (congers) A large eel.

congested Overcrowded, too full. **congestion.**

congratulate (congratulates, congratulating, congratulated) To tell someone that one is very pleased about some happy event which has happened to him, or about something that he has done. **congratulation.**

congregate (congregates, congregating, congregated) To come together, to make a crowd. **congregation.**

congress (congresses) A meeting.

conical Cone-shaped.

conifer (conifers) A tree on which cones grow, like pine or fir. **coniferous.**

conjecture (conjectures) A guess. **conjectural.**

conjunction (conjunctions) 1. A joining word, such as *and, but.* 2. *In conjunction with,* together with.

conjure (conjures, conjuring, conjured) 1. To do clever tricks which seem magical. 2. *To conjure up,* to make something seem to appear. **conjurer.**

conker (conkers) (informal) A horse-chestnut.

connect (connects, connecting, connected) To join, to link. **connection.**

conning-tower (conning-towers) The observation tower of a submarine.

connoisseur (connoisseurs) An expert at judging matters of taste.

conquer (conquers, conquering, conquered) To defeat, to overcome, to win by battle. **conqueror.**

conquest (conquests) Conquering, victory.

conscience (consciences) The knowledge of right and wrong, the awareness that makes people feel guilty when they have done wrong.

conscientious Careful, honest, dutiful. **conscientiously.**

conscious Awake, aware of what is happening. **consciously, consciousness.**

conscription A system of making people join the armed forces.

consecrate (consecrates, consecrating, consecrated) To make something holy.

consecutive Following regularly one after the other. **consecutively.**

consent[1] (consents, consenting, consented) To agree, to give permission.

consent[2] Agreement, permission. *She gave her consent.*

consequence (consequences) 1. Something that follows as a result of something else. *In consequence of,* as a result of. **consequently.** 2. *Of no consequence,* unimportant.

conservation Preservation and care. **conservationist.**

conservative 1. Being opposed to great and sudden change. 2. *The Conservative Party,* a political party. **conservatism.**

conservatory (conservatories) A greenhouse attached to a house.

consider (considers, considering, considered) 1. To think about something. 2. To hold an opinion.

considerable Important. **considerably.**

considerate Kind and thoughtful. **considerately.**

consideration 1. Thoughtful feelings for other people. 2. Careful thought. 3. Something needing careful thought.

considering Taking something into account.

consignment (consignments) A batch of things sent together.

consist (consists, consisting, consisted) To be made up of something.

consistent 1. Regular. *He is a good and consistent supporter.* 2. In agreement with. *That is not consistent with what you said yesterday.* **consistently, consistency.**

console (consoles, consoling, consoled) To give comfort or sympathy. **consolation.**

consolidate (consolidates, consolidating, consolidated) 1. To strengthen. 2. To combine.

consonant (consonants) Any letter of the alphabet except a, e, i, o, and u.

consort (consorts) The husband or wife of a queen or king.

conspicuous Noticeable, very easily seen.

conspire (conspires, conspiring, conspired) To plot, to get together for some evil purpose. **conspirator, conspiracy.**

constable (constables) A policeman.

constabulary (constabularies) A police force.

constant Faithful, unchanging, continual.

constantly Always, often.

constellation (constellations) A group of stars.

consternation Surprise and dismay.

constipated Unable to empty the bowels easily and regularly. constipation.

constituency (constituencies) A town or district which elects one Member of Parliament.

constitute (constitutes, constituting, constituted) To form, to make up. *These 30 children constitute Class I.*

constitution (constitutions) 1. All the laws and rules according to which a country is governed. 2. General health. *He has a strong constitution*, he is very healthy. constitutional.

construct (constructs, constructing, constructed) To make, to build. constructor, constructive, constructively, construction, constructional.

consul (consuls) An official who lives in a foreign town to help and protect his countrymen there.

consulate (consulates) A consul's office.

consult (consults, consulting, consulted) To go to a person or book for information or advice. *We consulted our dictionary.* consultation.

consume (consumes, consuming, consumed) To eat up, to use up. consumer, consumption.

contact[1] 1. Touching. *In contact with*, in touch with. 2. *Contact lenses*, tiny spectacle lenses worn on the eye itself.

contact[2] (contacts) An electrical connection.

contact[3] (contacts, contacting, contacted) To get in touch with someone.

contagious *A contagious disease*, a disease that is caught by touching infected people or things.

contain (contains, containing, contained) To hold something inside, to include. container.

contaminate (contaminates, contaminating, contaminated) To spoil something by making it dirty or unhealthy. contamination.

contemplate (contemplates, contemplating, contemplated) 1. To look steadily at something. 2. To think deeply. 3. To plan to do something. contemplation.

contemporary 1. Living or existing at the same time as somebody or something else. 2. Up-to-date, modern in style.

contempt Scorn, lack of respect.

contemptible Unworthy of respect.

contemptuous Scornful. contemptuously.

contend (contends, contending, contended) 1. To struggle against somebody for something. 2. To argue. contender, contention.

content 1. Satisfied. 2. Ready and willing to do something. contentment.

contented Satisfied. contentedly.

contents The things contained in something.

contest[1] (pronounced con*test*) (contests, contesting, contested) To argue, to dispute, to contend, to fight. contestant.

contest[2] (pronounced *con*test) (contests) A fight, a competition.

continent (continents) One of the big land masses of the world, such as Africa or Asia. continental.

continual 1. Going on without a break. 2. Very frequent. continually.

continue (continues, continuing, continued) 1. To go on, to go further. 2. To stay, to remain unchanged. 3. To start again after an interruption. continuation.

continuous Going on without a break. continuously, continuity.

contortion (contortions) Twisting into unusual shapes.

contortionist (contortionists) Someone who is clever at twisting his body into strange positions.

contour (contours) 1. An outline. 2. *Contour*

line, a line on a map joining all points at the same height above sea-level.

contraband Smuggled goods.

contraceptive (contraceptives) A device or drug which prevents a woman from becoming pregnant. contraception.

contract [1] (pronounced *con*tract) (contracts) An official agreement.

contract [2] (pronounced con*tract*) (contracts, contracting, contracted) 1. To make a contract. 2. To catch, to get. *To contract an illness*. 3. To make smaller, to become smaller. contraction.

contractor (contractors) A person who undertakes to do certain work after a contract has been made. *A building contractor*.

contradict (contradicts, contradicting, contradicted) To say that something someone has said is not true, to say the opposite of what someone else has said. contradiction, contradictory.

contralto (contraltos) A female singer with a low voice.

contraption (contraptions) A strange-looking device.

contrary 1. Opposite. 2. Obstinate. 3. *A contrary wind*, an unfavourable wind. contrarily, contrariness.

contrast [1] (contrasts, contrasting, contrasted) 1. To point out the differences when comparing things. 2. To be obviously different when compared. *Our red shirts contrasted with the visiting team's blue shirts*.

contrast [2] (contrasts) 1. A very great difference. 2. Something that differs greatly.

contribute (contributes, contributing, contributed) 1. To give money or help to a particular cause. *We contributed to the swimming-pool fund*. 2. To play a part in. *His accurate bowling contributed to his team's victory*. 3. To write a story or article for a magazine or newspaper. contribution, contributor.

contrive (contrives, contriving, contrived) To invent, to find a way of doing something. contrivance.

control [1] (controls, controlling, controlled) To keep in order, to direct, to be in charge of, to hold back. controller.

control [2] (controls) 1. The ability to control people or things. *Our teacher has good control over the class*. 2. *In control*, in charge. 3. *Controls*, the various levers, switches, and instruments by which a machine is controlled.

controversy (controversies) A prolonged argument. controversial.

conundrum (conundrums) A riddle.

conurbation (conurbations) A group of towns joined together.

convalescence Recovery after an illness. convalescent.

convector (convectors) A heater which makes warm air circulate.

convenience (conveniences) 1. Something suitable, handy, and easy to use. 2. *At your convenience*, as it suits you. 3. *A public convenience*, a public lavatory. convenient, conveniently.

convent (convents) A house where nuns live and work.

convention (conventions) A settled way of doing things. conventional.

converge (converges, converging, converged) To come together.

conversation (conversations) Talking. conversational.

convert (converts, converting, converted) 1. To change something, to make it suitable for a new purpose or for new conditions. 2. To make somebody change his beliefs. conversion, converter, convertible.

convertible (convertibles) An open car with a folding hood.

convex Curved like the outside of a ball.

convey (conveys, conveying, conveyed) 1. To carry something. 2. To communicate, to mean. *This message conveys nothing to me*, I do not understand it.

conveyance (conveyances) A vehicle.

conveyor *A conveyor belt*, an endless belt on which goods can be shifted.

convict¹ (pronounced *con*vict) (convicts) A condemned criminal.

convict² (pronounced con*vict*) (convicts, convicting, convicted) To declare someone guilty, to condemn him. conviction.

convince (convinces, convincing, convinced) To persuade someone of the truth of something. conviction.

convoy (convoys) A fleet of ships sailing together for safety.

convulsion (convulsions) A violent disturbance, a fit. convulsive.

coo (coos, cooing, cooed) To make a soft murmuring sound.

cook¹ (cooks, cooking, cooked) To make food ready to eat by boiling, frying, baking, or some other method of heating.

cook² (cooks) Someone who cooks.

cooker (cookers) An oven or some other apparatus for cooking.

cookery Cooking.

cool¹ (cooler, coolest) 1. Fairly cold. 2. Calm. *Keep cool, don't panic!* 3. Not enthusiastic. coolly, coolness.

cool² (cools, cooling, cooled) To become cool, to make cool. cooler.

coop (coops) A kind of cage to keep chickens in.

co-operate (co-operates, co-operating, co-operated) To work helpfully together. co-operation, co-operative.

coot (coots) A water bird.

cope (copes, coping, coped) To manage, to deal with something successfully. *Can you cope with that huge pile of books?*

copious Plentiful. copiously.

copper¹ 1. A reddish-brown metal. 2. *Coppers*, coins made of copper or bronze.

copper² (coppers) (informal) A policeman.

coppice (coppices) or copse (copses) A clump of small trees.

copulate (copulates, copulating, copulated) To mate. copulation.

copy¹ (copies) 1. An imitation, something made to look like something else. 2. Something written out a second time. *I made a neat copy of my poem.* 3. A book. *Where's my copy of 'Treasure Island'?*

copy² (copies, copying, copied) To make a copy, to imitate.

coracle (coracles) A small boat made of skins stretched over a wooden framework.

coral A hard substance built up from the sea bed by small sea-creatures.

cord (cords) A thin rope.

cordial¹ Warm and friendly. cordially, cordiality.

cordial² (cordials) A sweet drink.

cordite A kind of explosive.

cordon (cordons) A line of troops or police acting as guards.

corduroy 1. A thick cloth with raised velvet lines on its surface. 2. *Corduroys*, trousers made of this.

core (cores) The central part of something. *An apple core.*

cork¹ The light, thick bark of a tree called the cork-oak.

cork² (corks) A piece of cork used to stop a bottle.

corkscrew (corkscrews) A tool for removing corks.

cormorant (cormorants) A large shiny black sea-bird.

corn¹ Grain, the seeds of wheat, barley, oats, and rye.

corn² (corns) A small lump of hardened skin on the foot.

corned Salted. *Corned beef.*

corner (corners) 1. The place where two walls, roads, or lines meet. 2. A secret place. 3. A kick taken from a corner of the field in football.

cornered Trapped in a corner.

cornet (cornets) 1. A cone-shaped wafer containing ice-cream. 2. A musical instrument rather like a trumpet.

cornflour A fine flour used in cooking.

cornflower (cornflowers) A blue wild flower.

corny (informal) Heard too often to be interesting.

coronation (coronations) The ceremony of crowning a king or queen.

coroner (coroners) An official who inquires into why people died.

coronet (coronets) A small crown.

corporal[1] (corporals) A rank in the army.

corporal[2] *Corporal punishment*, whipping or beating.

corporation (corporations) A group of people acting together to govern a city or to run a business.

corps A part of an army. *The Royal Army Medical Corps.*

corpse (corpses) A dead body.

corpulent Fat.

corral (corrals) An enclosure for horses or cattle.

correct[1] (corrects, correcting, corrected) 1. To put right. 2. To mark mistakes. **correction.**

correct[2] Right, true, without mistakes. **correctly, correctness.**

correspond (corresponds, corresponding, corresponded) 1. To exchange letters with. *I correspond with a pen-friend in France.* 2. To be similar to, to be equivalent to.

correspondence Letters or written messages.

correspondent (correspondents) 1. Someone who writes letters. 2. Someone who sends news to a newspaper.

corridor (corridors) A long passage with doors leading into many rooms or compartments.

corroboree (corroborees) A dance performed by Australian Aborigines.

corrode (corrodes, corroding, corroded) To destroy gradually, to eat away, to decay. *To be corroded by rust.* **corrosion, corrosive.**

corrugated With wrinkles or folds. *Corrugated iron.*

corrupt[1] Dishonest, taking bribes. **corruptly.**

corrupt[2] (corrupts, corrupting, corrupted) To make a person corrupt. **corruptible, corruption.**

corset (corsets) An undergarment which fits tightly to make the waist and hips look slimmer.

cos A kind of lettuce.

cosmetics Substances used to make someone prettier, such as lipstick and face-powder.

cosmonaut (cosmonauts) A Russian space-traveller.

cosmos The universe. **cosmic.**

cost[1] (costs) 1. The price of something. 2. *At all costs*, whatever the cost may be.

cost[2] (costs, costing, cost) 1. To be bought for a certain price. 2. To cause the loss of. *The mistake cost him his life.*

costermonger (costermongers) A person who sells from a street barrow.

costly Expensive, valuable.

costume (costumes) 1. A way of dressing, a style of clothing. 2. A woman's suit.

cosy (cosier, cosiest) Warm and comfortable. **cosily, cosiness.**

cot (cots) A child's bed with sides to prevent him falling out.

cottage (cottages) A small house.

cotton 1. A soft white substance from the seeds of the cotton plant. *Cotton wool*, clean, fluffy cotton used in nursing. 2. Thread made from this. 3. Cloth made from cotton thread.

couch (couches) A long seat rather like a bed.

cough[1] (coughs) 1. An explosion of air from the lungs. 2. *To have a cough*, to cough frequently.

cough² (coughs, coughing, coughed) To make a cough.

could *See* can¹.

council (councils) A group of people elected to plan and work together. councillor.

council-house (council-houses) A house rented from the local town council.

count¹ (counts, counting, counted) 1. To say the numbers in order. *To count down*, to say the numbers backwards. 2. To add up. 3. To include in the total. *There were five of us not counting the driver*, there were six of us altogether. 4. *To count on*, to rely on.

count² (counts) A nobleman in certain foreign countries.

countenance (countenances) A face, the expression on a face.

counter (counters) 1. A small disc used for keeping count in games. 2. A long, narrow table at which customers are served in a shop, café, or bank.

counter-attack (counter-attacks) An attack in reply to an attack by the enemy.

counter-espionage Spying on an enemy's spies.

counterfeit (counterfeits, counterfeiting, counterfeited) To forge, to copy something unlawfully.

counterpane (counterpanes) A quilt, a top covering for a bed.

countess (countesses) A noblewoman, the wife of an earl or count.

countless Too many to count easily.

country (countries) 1. A land inhabited by a particular nation, such as Australia, England, or Spain. 2. A nation, the people who live in a country. *The whole country is involved in a general election.* 3. An area which is nearly all fields, woods, or open land. countryside. 4. *A country-dance*, a kind of folk-dance.

countryman (countrymen) 1. Someone from one's own nation. *My countrymen.* 2. Someone who lives in the country, not in the town.

county (counties) One of the divisions of Great Britain.

couple¹ (couples) 1. A pair. *A couple of things*, two things. 2. A husband and wife, or a boy-friend and girl-friend.

couple² (couples, coupling, coupled) To join together.

coupling (couplings) A device for joining two things together, especially a link for railway carriages.

coupon (coupons) A ticket, a piece of paper which gives a person the right to do something or to receive something.

courage Bravery. courageous, courageously.

courier (couriers) A person who accompanies and helps holiday parties, especially abroad.

course (courses) 1. The direction taken by something or somebody. *The course of a river, the course of a ship, a course of events.* 2. A race-course. 3. An area set out for playing golf. 4. A series. *A course of lessons.* 5. A part of a meal. *The meat course.* 6. *In the course of*, during. 7. *In due course*, at the proper time. 8. *Of course*, certainly, naturally.

court¹ (courts) 1. A king or queen with his or her family and councillors, the place where these assemble officially. courtly. 2. The place where cases are tried by a judge or magistrate. 3. An area marked out for tennis or other games. 4. *A court card*, a king, queen, or jack in a pack of cards.

court² (courts, courting, courted) To try to win someone's love or support. courtship.

courteous Having good manners, being very polite. courteously, courteousness.

courtesy (courtesies) A polite action.

courtier (courtiers) A person at the royal court.

court martial (courts martial) A court where people in the armed forces who break military laws are tried.

courtyard (courtyards) A space surrounded by buildings or walls.

cousin (cousins) A child of one's uncle or aunt.

cove (coves) A small bay.

cover¹ (covers, covering, covered) 1. To place one thing over another to hide or protect it. 2. *To cover a lot of ground*, to go over a lot of ground. 3. To aim a gun at someone. **coverage.**

cover² (covers) 1. Something that covers, such as a lid, a wrapper, or the binding of a book. 2. A shelter, a hiding-place.

coverlet (coverlets) A bed cover.

covet (covets, coveting, coveted) To want to possess something. **covetous.**

cow (cows) A female animal kept by farmers for its milk.

coward (cowards) A person unable to control his fears. **cowardly, cowardice.**

cowboy (cowboys) A man who looks after cattle in America.

cowed Frightened.

cower (cowers, cowering, cowered) To crouch in fear.

cowslip (cowslips) A yellow wild flower.

cox (coxes) or **coxswain** (coxswains) A sailor or boatman who steers a boat.

coy Pretending to be shy or embarrassed. **coyly, coyness.**

coyote (coyotes) A North American prairie wolf.

crab (crabs) A shellfish with five pairs of legs.

crab-apple (crab-apples) A small, sour kind of apple.

crack¹ (cracks) 1. A narrow gap, a line where something is broken but has not come completely apart. *A crack in a cup.* 2. A sudden sharp noise. *The crack of a pistol shot.* 3. A sudden knock. *A crack on the head.*

crack² (cracks, cracking, cracked) 1. To get or make a crack. 2. *To crack a joke*, to make a joke. 3. *His voice cracked*, his voice became rough and grating.

crack³ (informal) First-rate. *A crack player.*

cracker (crackers) 1. A kind of firework. 2. A Christmas plaything which explodes when pulled apart. 3. A kind of biscuit.

crackle (crackles, crackling, crackled) To make small cracking sounds. *The ice crackled underfoot.*

crackling The crisp skin of roast pork.

cradle (cradles) A kind of cot, a bed for a baby.

craft¹ (crafts) 1. Skill, art, cunning. 2. A job which needs skill in the use of the hands. **craftsman, craftsmanship.**

craft² (craft) A boat, a ship.

crafty Cunning, deceitful. **craftily, craftiness.**

crag (crags) A high, steep, rough rock. **craggy.**

cram (crams, cramming, crammed) To fill to overflowing, to push too much into.

cramp Painful tightening of the muscles, often caused by cold or too much work.

cramped Crowded tightly together, with too little room.

crane¹ (cranes) 1. A large wading bird. 2. A machine for lifting heavy weights.

crane² (cranes, craning, craned) To stretch one's neck.

crane-fly (crane-flies) A daddy-long-legs, a kind of insect.

crank (cranks) 1. A bent rod. 2. (informal) A person with strange ideas. **cranky.**

cranny (crannies) A crack, a narrow opening.

crash [1] (crashes, crashing, crashed) 1. To fall, to strike noisily, to break up on landing. 2. To force a way through something. *The elephant crashed through the undergrowth.*

crash [2] (crashes) 1. The noise of crashing. 2. A violent fall or blow. *A crash-helmet*, a helmet worn to protect the head in a crash. 3. *A crash-landing*, an emergency landing which damages an aircraft.

crate (crates) A wooden packing-case.

crater (craters) 1. The mouth of a volcano. 2. A shell-hole.

cravat (cravats) A broad necktie.

crawl [1] (crawls, crawling, crawled) 1. To move slowly, usually on hands and knees. 2. To be covered with crawling things. *The ground was crawling with ants.*

crawl [2] 1. A crawling movement. 2. A swimming stroke.

crayon (crayons) A coloured drawing pencil.

craze (crazes) A short-lived enthusiasm for something.

crazy Mad. *Crazy paving*, paving stones of odd sizes fitted together. **crazily.**

creak (creaks, creaking, creaked) To make a noise like the sound of a door whose hinges need oiling. **creaky.**

cream 1. The top of the milk. 2. Its colour, between white and yellow. 3. Something that looks like cream. *Face-cream.* **creamy, creaminess.**

crease [1] (creases) 1. A line in a piece of paper or cloth caused by folding or pressing. 2. A line on a cricket pitch to show where the batsman should stand.

crease [2] (creases, creasing, creased) To make a crease in paper or cloth.

create (creates, creating, created) To make, to bring something into existence. **creative, creatively, creation.**

creator (creators) A maker. *The Creator*, God.

creature (creatures) A living thing, especially an animal.

crèche (crèches) A nursery.

credible Believable. **credibly, credibility.**

credit 1. Belief or trust. 2. Good reputation. 3. A person or thing that brings honour. *He was a credit to his parents.* 4. *To buy something on credit*, to be allowed to pay later. 5. *Credits*, a list of people who helped to make a film.

creditable Praiseworthy. **creditably.**

credulous *A credulous person*, someone who will believe anything. **credulity.**

creek (creeks) 1. A narrow inlet of water in a coastline, shaped like the mouth of a river. 2. (Australian) A small stream.

creep (creeps, creeping, crept) 1. To move along close to the ground, to move stealthily. *He crept up on his victim.* 2. To come on gradually. *Sleep crept over him.*

creeper (creepers) A plant that creeps or climbs.

creepy Weird, causing a shudder.

cremate (cremates, cremating, cremated) To burn a dead body. **cremation.**

crematorium (crematoria) A place where bodies are cremated.

creosote An oily liquid used to prevent wood from rotting.

crept See **creep.**

crescendo Becoming louder and louder.

crescent (crescents) A shape like a new moon.

cress A green plant used in salads.

crest (crests) 1. A tuft of feathers, skin, or hair on a creature's head. 2. A plume on a helmet. 3. A badge. 4. The top of a hill, the top of a wave.

crestfallen Disappointed, downcast.

crevasse (crevasses) A deep crack in ice.

crevice (crevices) A crack, a narrow split.

crew (crews) All the people who work on a ship or aircraft.

crib[1] (cribs) 1. A baby's cot. 2. A rack from which animals eat hay.

crib[2] (cribs, cribbing, cribbed) To cheat by copying.

cricket[1] An outdoor game played with a ball, bats, and wickets.

cricket[2] (crickets) An insect like a grasshopper.

cried, crier, cries *See* cry[1,2].

crime (crimes) A serious offence against the law.

criminal (criminals) Someone who has committed a crime.

crimson A deep red colour.

cringe (cringes, cringing, cringed) To cower.

crinkle (crinkles) A small fold, a wrinkle.

cripple[1] (cripples) A lame person.

cripple[2] (cripples, crippling, crippled) To make someone lame, to damage something very badly.

crisis (crises) A time of particular danger, difficulty, or suspense.

crisp[1] (crisper, crispest) 1. Hard, dry and easily broken. 2. *Crisp weather*, dry, frosty weather. 3. Quick, definite, smart. crisply.

crisp[2] (crisps) A crisp slice of fried potato.

criss-cross With crossing lines.

critic (critics) 1. A person who writes about new books, films, plays, music, and other arts. 2. Someone who finds fault with things and people.

critical 1. Criticizing. 2. Very serious. *A critical illness.* critically.

criticize (criticizes, criticizing, criticized) To find fault with. criticism.

croak (croaks, croaking, croaked) To make a hoarse sound like a frog.

crochet A kind of knitting done with a hooked stick called a crochet-hook.

crock (crocks) 1. (informal) A person who cannot work well because of bad health. 2. An old motor car. 3. A piece of crockery.

crockery Plates, cups, saucers, and other pottery dishes.

crocodile (crocodiles) A large river animal. *Crocodile tears*, false tears.

crocus (crocuses) A spring flower.

crony (cronies) A close friend.

crook (crooks) 1. A stick with a rounded hook for shepherds' use. 2. (informal) A person who makes a living by dishonest means, a criminal.

crooked 1. Not straight, bent. 2. Dishonest. crookedly, crookedness.

croon (croons, crooning, crooned) To sing softly. crooner.

crop[1] (crops, cropping, cropped) 1. To cut something short. *Close-cropped hair.* 2. *To crop up*, to arise unexpectedly.

crop[2] (crops) 1. The yearly produce of agriculture, the plants in the field. 2. *A riding-crop*, a kind of small whip.

croquet A garden game played with mallets and balls.

croquette (croquettes) A meat ball, a fish-cake.

cross[1] (crosses) 1. A mark such as + or ×. 2. Anything made in such a shape. 3. *The Cross*, the gallows on which Jesus Christ was crucified. 4. An animal whose parents are of different breeds.

cross[2] (crosses, crossing, crossed) 1. To move from one side of something to the other. 2. *It crossed my mind*, it occurred to me. 3. To make a cross shape with something. *Cross your fingers!* 4. To pass somebody or something going in the opposite direction. 5. To annoy somebody, to spoil his plans. 6. *To cross out*, to draw a line through something.

cross[3] (crosser, crossest) Bad-tempered, annoyed. crossly.

cross-bar (cross-bars) A horizontal bar or beam.

crossbow (crossbows) An ancient weapon for shooting arrows.

cross-country Across the countryside.

cross-examination (cross-examinations) Asking stern and searching questions.

cross-eyed Squinting.

crossfire The paths of bullets coming from several directions.

crossing (crossings) A place where people can cross a road. *A zebra crossing.*

cross-roads A place where two roads cross.

crossword (crosswords) A kind of puzzle in which letters forming words are filled into numbered spaces.

crotchet (crotchets) A note in music. It is written ♩.

crotchety Bad-tempered.

crouch (crouches, crouching, crouched) To stoop, to bend.

croup A disease which causes sharp coughing.

crow [1] (crows) A large black bird.

crow [2] (crows, crowing, crowed) 1. To make a noise like a cock. 2. To boast.

crow-bar (crow-bars) An iron bar used as a lever.

crowd [1] (crowds) 1. A large number of people together in one place. 2. A particular group of people. *We don't have anything to do with that crowd!*

crowd [2] (crowds, crowding, crowded) 1. To make a crowd, to come together as a crowd. 2. To fill a space too full for comfort.

crown [1] (crowns) 1. The golden head-dress worn by a king or queen. 2. *The crown*, royal authority. *This land belongs to the crown,* this land belongs to the king or queen. 3. The top part of anything. *The crown of a hill.* 4. *A crown, a half-crown,* old British coins.

crown [2] (crowns, crowning, crowned) 1. To put a crown on a king or queen. 2. To reward. *His efforts were crowned with success.*

crow's nest A look-out position at the top of a ship's mast.

crucible (crucibles) A pot for melting metals or other substances.

crucifix (crucifixes) An image of Jesus Christ on the cross.

crucify (crucifies, crucifying, crucified) To put someone to death by fastening him to a cross. crucifixion.

crude (cruder, crudest) 1. Raw, in a natural state. *Crude oil.* 2. Rough, clumsy. *A crude carving.* 3. Rude, coarse. *Crude manners.* crudely, crudity.

cruel (crueller, cruellest) 1. Deliberately causing pain or suffering. 2. Pleased by someone else's pain or suffering. cruelly, cruelty.

cruise [1] (cruises, cruising, cruised) 1. To have a holiday on a ship, visiting various places. 2. To travel at a moderate, pleasant speed.

cruise [2] (cruises) A cruising holiday.

cruiser (cruisers) A kind of warship.

crumb (crumbs) A tiny piece of bread or cake. crumby.

crumble (crumbles, crumbling, crumbled) To break into small pieces, to make into crumbs. crumbly.

crumple (crumples, crumpling, crumpled) To crush into folds and creases, to become creased.

crunch (crunches, crunching, crunched) 1. To chew noisily. 2. To crush.

crusade (crusades) A holy war. crusader.

crush [1] (crushes, crushing, crushed) 1. To press and break something. *They were all crushed to death.* 2. To defeat someone. *The rebels were soon crushed.*

crush [2] (crushes) 1. A crowd. 2. A fruit drink.

crust (crusts) 1. The outer covering of a loaf or a pie. 2. Any hard outer covering.

crusty 1. Hard like a crust. 2. Irritable. crustily, crustiness.

crutch (crutches) A walking aid for a crippled person.

cry [1] (cries, crying, cried) 1. To weep. 2. To shout, to yell. crier.

cry² (cries) 1. A loud sound, an excited call. 2. A fit of weeping.

crypt (crypts) An underground room beneath a church.

crystal 1. A glass-like mineral. *A crystal ball*, a glass sphere used in fortune-telling. 2. A small shiny piece. *Crystals of ice.*

crystallize (crystallizes, crystallizing, crystallized) To form crystals.

cub (cubs) A young lion, fox, bear, or other animal. *A Cub Scout*, a junior Scout.

cube (cubes) Something that has six square sides. cubic.

cubicle (cubicles) A small room divided off from another one.

cuckoo (cuckoos) A bird that makes the sound 'cuckoo'.

cucumber (cucumbers) A vegetable used in salads.

cud The food which a cow brings up from its first stomach to chew again.

cuddle (cuddles, cuddling, cuddled) 1. To hold someone closely and lovingly in one's arms. 2. *To cuddle up*, to lie close and comfortably. cuddly, cuddlesome.

cudgel (cudgels) A short, thick stick.

cue (cues) 1. A signal for an actor to say or do something. 2. A long stick used in the game of billiards.

cuff¹ (cuffs, cuffing, cuffed) To slap, to hit with the hand.

cuff² (cuffs) The wrist end of a sleeve.

cuff-links Fastenings for the cuffs of shirts.

culprit (culprits) A person who has done wrong.

cult (cults) A religion.

cultivate (cultivates, cultivating, cultivated) 1. To prepare the soil and grow crops. 2. To try to make something grow or develop. *To cultivate a friendship.* 3. *Cultivated*, having good manners and education. cultivation.

cultivator (cultivators) A machine for digging the ground.

culture Various kinds of learning, art, music, literature, and science. cultural.

cultured Well educated.

cumbersome Clumsy, heavy, and awkward to carry.

cunning Artful, clever at deceiving others.

cup (cups) 1. A bowl with a handle, for drinking from. cupful. 2. A gold or silver bowl given as a prize or trophy.

cupboard (cupboards) A piece of furniture or a part of a room fitted with shelves and doors.

cup-tie (cup-ties) A match to decide which team goes on to the next round in a competition for a cup. cup-final.

cur (curs) A bad-tempered or worthless dog.

curate (curates) A clergyman who helps a vicar or rector.

curator (curators) A person in charge of a museum or art gallery.

curb (curbs, curbing, curbed) To keep something under control. *To curb one's temper.*

curd (curds) 1. A thick liquid formed while making milk into cheese. 2. Any similar foodstuff. *Lemon curd.*

curdle (curdles, curdling, curdled) To form into curds. *To curdle a person's blood*, to horrify him.

cure¹ (cures, curing, cured) 1. To bring somebody back to health, to find a remedy for a trouble. 2. To preserve food by smoking or salting it.

cure² (cures) 1. Curing, being cured. 2. A substance or treatment that cures someone.

curfew (curfews) An order that everybody must be indoors by a certain time.

curious 1. Eager to learn about anything new. 2. Showing too much interest in other people's affairs. 3. Strange, unusual. curiously, curiosity.

curl¹ (curls) Something twisted into pleasant curves.

curl² (curls, curling, curled) 1. To twist into curls. 2. *To curl up*, to make oneself small and comfortable.

curlew (curlews) A wading bird.

curly (curlier, curliest) Having curls. curliness.

currant (currants) 1. A small dried grape.
2. A small juicy fruit.

currency (currencies) Money.

current[1] (currents) 1. A stream of air or water.
2. The flow of electricity through a circuit.

current[2] Happening at the present time.
Current affairs. currently.

curry (curries) A hot-flavoured, spicy food.

curse[1] (curses) Violent language, words calling for destruction or injury to fall on a person or thing.

curse[2] (curses, cursing, cursed) 1. To use violent language, to use a curse against someone or something. 2. *To be cursed with something,* to suffer from it.

cursory Hurried and careless.

curt Short. curtly.

curtail (curtails, curtailing, curtailed) To cut short. curtailment.

curtain (curtains) 1. A piece of cloth hung at a window or door. 2. The cloth screen across the front of a stage.

curtsy[1] (curtsies) Bending the knees, a respectful movement made by women and girls.

curtsy[2] (curtsies, curtsying, curtsied) To make a curtsy.

curve[1] (curves) A line which is not straight and which has no sharp angles.

curve[2] (curves, curving, curved) To move in a curve, to bend into a curve. curvature.

cushion (cushions) A bag filled with soft material for sitting on.

cussedness Obstinacy.

custard A sweet sauce eaten with fruit or puddings. custard-powder.

custodian (custodians) A caretaker or guardian.

custody Keeping safe, guarding.

custom (customs) The usual way of doing things. *It is our custom to give presents on Christmas Day.* customary.

customer (customers) A person who goes into a shop to buy something.

customs 1. Taxes which have to be paid on goods brought into a country. 2. The officers who collect these taxes. *To go through the customs,* to go through the place where these taxes are collected.

cut[1] (cuts, cutting, cut) 1. To use a knife, axe, spade, or any other sharp instrument on something. *To cut string. To cut a slice of bread. To cut the grass.* 2. To make something by cutting. *To cut a channel.* 3. To make something smaller or shorter. *Cut-price,* at a specially low price. 4. *To cut off,* to stop, to interrupt. 5. To divide a pack of cards. 6. *To cut in,* to overtake another car and then drive in front of it suddenly.

cut[2] (cuts) 1. A small wound. 2. The result of cutting, damage caused by cutting. 3. *A short cut,* a quicker way to somewhere. 4. A stroke in cricket.

cute (cuter, cutest) 1. Quick and clever. 2. (informal) Attractive.

cutlass (cutlasses) A short sword with a wide curved blade.

cutlery Knives, forks, and spoons.

cutlet (cutlets) A thick slice of meat.

cutter (cutters) 1. Someone or something that cuts. 2. A kind of sailing ship.

cutting (cuttings) 1. A steep-sided way cut through a hill for a road or railway. 2. Something cut out of a newspaper or magazine.

cycle[1] (cycles) 1. A bicycle. 2. A series of events which keep on coming round in the same order. *The cycle of the seasons.*

cycle[2] (cycles, cycling, cycled) To ride on a bicycle. cyclist.

cyclone (cyclones) A violent wind-storm, a hurricane.

cygnet (cygnets) A young swan.

cylinder (cylinders) 1. A tube-shaped thing. 2. Part of an engine in which a piston moves. cylindrical.

cymbal (cymbals) A musical instrument, one of a pair of brass plates which are struck together.

cynical Not expecting to find good in anything. cynically, cynicism.

cypress (cypresses) An evergreen tree.

Dd

D 500 in Roman numerals.

dab (dabs, dabbing, dabbed) To touch something lightly and quickly.

dabble (dabbles, dabbling, dabbled) To splash something in and out of water.

dachshund (dachshunds) A kind of small dog.

dad (dads) or **daddy** (daddies) (informal) Father.

daddy-long-legs An insect with very long legs.

daffodil (daffodils) A yellow flower.

dagger (daggers) A knife used as a weapon.

dahlia (dahlias) A garden flower.

daily Happening every day, done every day.

dainty (daintier, daintiest) Pretty, neat, and delicate. **daintily, daintiness.**

dairy (dairies) 1. A building where milk is kept and butter and cheese are made. 2. A shop where such things are sold. **dairy-farm, dairymaid, dairyman.**

daisy (daisies) A small flower.

dale (dales) A valley.

dally (dallies, dallying, dallied) To waste time.

Dalmatian (Dalmatians) A kind of spotted dog.

dam [1] (dams) A wall built across a river to hold back the water and make a reservoir.

dam [2] (dams, damming, dammed) To make a dam across a river or a lake.

damage [1] 1. Injury, harm. 2. *Damages*, compensation for injury.

damage [2] (damages, damaging, damaged) To injure, to harm.

dame (dames) 1. (old-fashioned or informal) A woman. 2. *Dame*, a woman's title corresponding to 'Sir'.

damn (damns, damning, damned) 1. To condemn, to say that something is worthless or bad. 2. *Damn!*, a swear word.

damp (damper, dampest) Slightly wet, not quite dry. **dampness.**

dampen (dampens, dampening, dampened) To make a thing damp.

damsel (damsels) (old-fashioned) A girl.

damson (damsons) A small, sour plum.

dance [1] (dances, dancing, danced) 1. To move about to the rhythm of music. 2. To move in a lively way. *He danced for joy!* **dancer.**

dance [2] (dances) 1. A piece of music for dancing. 2. A special pattern of movements for dancing. 3. A party where dancing takes place.

dandelion (dandelions) A yellow wild flower.

dandruff Small flakes of dead skin in the hair.

Dane (Danes) A Danish person.

danger (dangers) 1. The chance of being killed or injured. 2. Something which may cause misfortune or disaster. *The wreck is a danger to other ships.* **dangerous, dangerously.**

dangle (dangles, dangling, dangled) To hang or swing loosely.

Danish Of Denmark.

dank Unpleasantly damp.

dappled Marked with patches of light and shade.

dare (dares, daring, dared) 1. To be brave enough or cheeky enough to do something. 2. To challenge someone to do something. *I dare you to hit me!*

dare-devil (dare-devils) Someone who does foolish and dangerous things.

dark (darker, darkest) 1. With no light, with very little light. *A dark night.* 2. Nearly black. *Dark hair.* 3. Having a deep, strong colour. *Dark red.* 4. Secret. *Keep it dark!* **darkly, darkness.**

darken (darkens, darkening, darkened) 1. To make something dark. 2. To become dark.

darling (darlings) Someone who is loved very much.

darn [1] (darns, darning, darned) To mend a hole in clothing with criss-cross stitches.

darn [2] (darns) A place mended by darning.

dart [1] (darts) A short arrow which is thrown in the game of darts.**dart-board.**

dart [2] (darts, darting, darted) To move quickly and suddenly.

dash [1] (dashes, dashing, dashed) 1. To throw something violently. *The ship was dashed against the rocks.*2. To rush. *The criminal dashed past with the police in pursuit.*

dash [2] 1. A sudden rush, a sprint. *To make a dash for freedom.*2. *A dash of milk*, a little milk.3. The punctuation mark — .

date [1] (dates) 1. The way of naming a particular day of the year. *The date of Alan's birthday is 10th August.* 2. The year in which something happened. *1066 is the date of the Battle of Hastings.*3. A meeting, an engagement to go out with someone. 4. *Out of date*, old-fashioned.5. *Up to date*, modern.

date [2] (dates) The small sweet brown fruit of a tree called the date-palm.

daughter (daughters) Someone's female child.

daunt (daunts, daunting, daunted) To discourage.

dawdle (dawdles, dawdling, dawdled) To be slow.**dawdler.**

dawn [1] (dawns) The first light of day.

dawn [2] (dawns, dawning, dawned) 1. To begin to grow light.2. *It dawned on me*, it occurred to me.

day (days) 1. The period from sunrise to sunset. **daylight, day-time.** 2. A period of 24 hours.3. A period of time. *The present day. The old days.*

day-break Dawn.

day-dream (day-dreams) Idle and pleasant thoughts.

dazed Bewildered.

dazzle (dazzles, dazzling, dazzled) To shine so brightly that people cannot see properly. *Dazzling headlights.*

deacon (deacons) A kind of minister, official of a church.**deaconess.**

dead 1. Not living.2. Numb, without feeling. 3. Completely, suddenly. *To stop dead.* 4. *A dead heat*, the end of a race in which two winners finish exactly together.

deaden (deadens, deadening, deadened) 1. *To deaden a pain*, to make it less severe. 2. *To deaden noise*, to make it less loud.

deadly (deadlier, deadliest) Likely to cause death.

deaf (deafer, deafest) Unable to hear properly.**deafness.**

deafen (deafens, deafening, deafened) To make so much noise that nothing else can be heard clearly.

deal [1] (deals, dealing, dealt) 1. To give out, to distribute. *To deal cards.* 2. *To deal with something*, to be concerned with something, to manage or attend to it.**dealer.**

deal [2] (deals) A business agreement.

deal [3] *A great deal, a good deal*, a large amount.

dean (deans) A cathedral clergyman.

dear (dearer, dearest) 1. Loved.2. The polite way of beginning a letter. *Dear Sir, Dear John.*3. Expensive.4. *Oh dear!*, an exclamation.

dearly 1. At great cost. 2. Very much. *I should dearly like to come.*

death (deaths) The end of life, dying. *To put to death*, to kill.**deathly.**

death-blow (death-blows) A blow which kills.

death's-head (death's-heads) A picture of a skull.

death-trap (death-traps) A very dangerous thing or place.

debate [1] (debates, debating, debated) 1. To have a sensible argument, to discuss something in public. 2. To think something over very carefully. *She debated whether to spend her money or save it.* debatable.

debate [2] (debates) A discussion.

debris Scattered fragments, wreckage.

debt (debts) Money due to be paid to somebody, something owed to somebody. debtor.

decade (decades) A period of ten years.

decapitate (decapitates, decapitating, decapitated) To cut off somebody's head. decapitation.

decay [1] (decays, decaying, decayed) To go bad, to rot.

decay [2] The process of decaying.

deceased Dead.

deceit Deceiving. deceitful, deceitfully, deceitfulness.

deceive (deceives, deceiving, deceived) To mislead someone, to trick him.

December The last month of the year.

decent 1. Modest. 2. (informal) Pleasant. decently, decency.

deception (deceptions) A trick which deceives someone.

deceptive Deceiving, misleading. deceptively.

decide (decides, deciding, decided) To make up one's mind about something.

deciduous Losing its leaves in winter. *A deciduous tree.*

decimal 1. To do with tens or tenths. 2. *Decimal currency*, a system of money in which units are counted by tens. 3. *The decimal point*, the dot in numbers like 2·5.

decipher (deciphers, deciphering, deciphered) To find the meaning of something badly written, or of something written in code.

decision (decisions) 1. Deciding. 2. What is decided.

decisive 1. Deciding. *A decisive battle*, a battle that settles a war. 2. Able to decide. *A decisive person*, someone who is sure of his own wishes. decisively, decisiveness.

deck (decks) One of the floors in a ship or bus.

deck-chair (deck-chairs) A kind of folding chair.

declare (declares, declaring, declared) 1. To make something known officially. *To declare war.* 2. To say something very definitely. 3. In cricket, to close an innings before the batsmen are all out. declaration.

decline (declines, declining, declined) 1. To refuse, to say no to something. 2. To become weaker, to become less.

decode (decodes, decoding, decoded) To work out the meaning of a message in code.

decompose (decomposes, decomposing, decomposed) To decay, to rot.

decorate (decorates, decorating, decorated) 1. To make something look more beautiful or colourful. 2. To smarten a house with new paint or wall-paper. decorator. 3. To give someone a medal. *He was decorated for bravery.* decoration, decorative, decoratively.

decoy [1] (decoys) Something used to tempt a person or an animal into a trap.

decoy [2] (decoys, decoying, decoyed) To use a decoy.

decrease [1] (decreases, decreasing, decreased) 1. To make something smaller or less. 2. To become smaller or less.

decrease [2] (decreases) A decreasing, the amount by which something decreases.

decree [1] (decrees) An official order.

decree [2] (decrees, decreeing, decreed) To make a decree.

decrepit Old and worn out.

dedicated Devoted. dedication.

deduct (deducts, deducting, deducted) To subtract a part of something.

deduction (deductions) 1. Something deducted. 2. Something worked out by reasoning.

deed (deeds) 1. An action, something which has been done. 2. A legal document.

deep (deeper, deepest) 1. Going a long way down from the top. *A deep hole*. 2. Going a long way in from the front. *A deep shelf*. 3. Measuring from top to bottom or from front to back. *One metre deep*. 4. Dark and strong in colour. *Deep purple*. 5. *A deep note*, a low note. deeply.

deer (deer) A kind of wild animal. The male has horns called antlers.

deface (defaces, defacing, defaced) To spoil the surface of something.

defeat [1] (defeats, defeating, defeated) To conquer somebody, to win a victory over him.

defeat [2] (defeats) 1. Defeating someone. 2. Being defeated.

defect [1] (pronounced *defect*) (defects) A fault.

defect [2] (pronounced de*fect*) (defects, defecting, defected) To go over and join the enemy. defector, defection.

defective Faulty. defectively.

defence (defences) 1. Defending. *He rushed to her defence*, he rushed to protect her. 2. A protection, something used for defending. defensive, defensively, defenceless.

defend (defends, defending, defended) To guard, to protect, to make safe.

defendant (defendants) A person accused of something in a court of law.

defer (defers, deferring, deferred) To put something off until later.

defiant Defying. defiantly, defiance.

deficient Lacking. deficiency.

defile [1] (defiles, defiling, defiled) To make a thing dirty. defilement.

defile [2] (defiles) A narrow pass between mountains.

define (defines, defining, defined) To explain exactly what something is, to explain what a word means. definition.

definite Clear, certain. definitely.

deformed Badly shaped, not naturally shaped. deformity.

defraud (defrauds, defrauding, defrauded) To cheat.

deft Clever, skilful. deftly.

defunct Dead.

defy (defies, defying, defied) 1. To resist boldly and openly. 2. To challenge. *I defy you to come any further*.

degenerate (degenerates, degenerating, degenerated) To become worse.

degree (degrees) 1. A unit for measuring angles. *There are 90 degrees (90°) in a right angle*. 2. A unit for measuring temperature. *Water boils at 100 degrees centigrade (100°C)*. 3. An award given by a university to someone who has passed an examination. 4. *By degrees*, by stages, gradually.

dehydrated Dried out, with all the water removed. dehydration.

de-ice (de-ices, de-icing, de-iced) To remove the ice from something.

deity (deities) A god.

dejected Sad, gloomy. dejectedly, dejection.

delay (delays, delaying, delayed) 1. To make someone or something late. 2. To put something off until later.

delete (deletes, deleting, deleted) To cross out. deletion.

deliberate 1. Done on purpose. 2. Slow and careful. deliberately, deliberation.

delicacy (delicacies) 1. Delicate quality. 2. A delicious food.

delicate 1. Soft, tender, fine. *A delicate material*. 2. Easily damaged. *Delicate machinery*. 3. Liable to become ill. *A delicate child*. 4. Needing great skill and care. *Delicate work*. 5. Not strong, subtle. *A delicate flavour*. 6. Tactful. delicately.

delicatessen (delicatessens) A shop which sells unusual foods, especially foreign foods.

delicious Very good to eat. deliciously.

delight [1] (delights, delighting, delighted) 1. To give great pleasure to someone. 2. *To delight in*, to enjoy.

delight [2] (delights) Pleasure, enjoyment. delightful, delightfully.

delinquent (delinquents) Someone who does wrong.delinquency.

delirium 1. A confused state of mind during an illness. 2. Wild excitement. delirious, deliriously.

deliver (delivers, delivering, delivered) 1. To take something to the place where it has to go. *To deliver a letter.*2. *To deliver a lecture*, to give a lecture. 3. *To deliver a baby*, to help a mother at the birth of her child. deliverance, delivery.

delta (deltas) The area between the branches of a river at its mouth.

delude (deludes, deluding, deluded) To deceive.

deluge (deluges) A great flood, violent rainfall.

delusion (delusions) A false idea or belief.

de luxe Luxurious, special.

demand 1 (demands, demanding, demanded) To ask for something, especially in a forceful manner.

demand 2 (demands) 1. The act of demanding. 2. What is demanded.3. *In great demand*, asked for by many people.

demented Mad.dementedly.

demerara A kind of brown sugar.

democracy (democracies) 1. A system of government by the people. 2. A country which is governed in this way. democrat, democratic, democratically.

demolish (demolishes, demolishing, demolished) To knock down.demolition.

demon (demons) A devil.

demonstrate (demonstrates, demonstrating, demonstrated) 1. To show. demonstrable, demonstrative. 2. To hold a demonstration. demonstrator.

demonstration (demonstrations) 1. A showing.2. A public procession, a meeting.

demonstrative Showing one's feelings.

demure Quiet, modest.demurely.

den (dens) 1. The home or hiding-place of a wild animal.2. A private or secret place.

denial (denials) 1. A statement that something is not true.2. A refusal.

denim 1. A kind of cotton cloth.2. *Denims*, trousers or overalls made of this.

denomination (denominations) A branch of the Christian Church.

denounce (denounces, denouncing, denounced) To inform against someone. denunciation.

dense (denser, densest) 1. Thick. *A dense fog.* 2. Packed close together. *A dense crowd.* 3. Stupid. *You are dense today!* densely, density.

dent 1 (dents) A hollow made in a flat surface by hitting or pressing it.

dent 2 (dents, denting, dented) 1. To make a dent.2. To become dented.

dental Of the teeth. *A dental surgeon.*

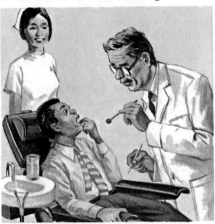

dentist (dentists) A person who fills or removes bad teeth and fits artificial ones.

denture (dentures) A set of false teeth.

deny (denies, denying, denied) 1. To declare that something is not true.2. To refuse.

deodorant (deodorants) Something that removes smells.

depart (departs, departing, departed) To go away, to leave.departure.

department (departments) 1. A part of a big organization.2. *A department store*, a large shop which sells many kinds of goods. departmental.

depend (depends, depending, depended) *To depend on*, 1. To need, to rely on. 2. *It depends on the price*, I shall decide when I know the price. 3. To trust, to be certain about someone or something. *You can depend on John, he's a good goal-keeper.*

dependable Reliable. dependability.

dependant (dependants) A person who depends on another.

dependent Depending. dependence.

depict (depicts, depicting, depicted) 1. To paint, to draw, to show in a picture. 2. To describe.

deplorable Regretable. deplorably.

deport (deports, deporting, deported) To send someone out of the country. deportation.

depose (deposes, deposing, deposed) To remove a monarch from the throne.

deposit¹ (deposits, depositing, deposited) 1. To put something down. 2. To pay money into a bank.

deposit² (deposits) 1. A first payment for something. 2. Money paid into a bank.

depot (depots) A base, a station. *A bus depot.*

depraved Corrupt, bad. depravity.

depress (depresses, depressing, depressed) 1. To make somebody sad. 2. To press something down.

depression (depressions) 1. Low spirits. 2. An area of low air pressure which may bring rain. 3. A shallow hollow in the ground.

deprive (deprives, depriving, deprived) To take something away from somebody.

depth (depths) 1. Measurement from top to bottom or from front to back. 2. *Depth charge*, an underwater bomb for use against submarines.

deputation (deputations) A small group of people representing others.

deputy (deputies) An official substitute for someone, an assistant. *A deputy sheriff.*

derail (derails, derailing, derailed) To cause a train to run off the rails. derailment.

deranged Mad.

derelict Abandoned, broken-down.

derision Scorn. derisive, derisively.

derive (derives, deriving, derived) To obtain something from something else. derivation.

dermatitis A skin complaint.

derrick (derricks) 1. A type of crane. 2. A device used to hold the drill when boring a well.

descant (descants) 1. A tune sung or played above another tune. 2. *A descant recorder*, a small recorder.

descend (descends, descending, descended) To come down, to go down. *They are descended from a French family*, their family has French origins. descendant, descent.

describe (describes, describing, described) To say what somebody or something is like. description, descriptive, descriptively.

desert¹ (pronounced *des*ert) (deserts) 1. A large area of very dry, often sandy, land. 2. *A desert island*, an uninhabited island.

desert² (pronounced de*sert*) (deserts, deserting, deserted) To abandon something or someone. *The soldiers deserted*, they left the army without permission. desertion, deserter.

deserts (pronounced de*serts*) What someone deserves. *To get your just deserts.*

deserve (deserves, deserving, deserved) To have earned something, to be worthy of it.

design¹ (designs) 1. A plan, a drawing which shows how something can be made. 2. A pattern.

design² (designs, designing, designed) To plan, to make a design. designer.

desire[1] (desires, desiring, desired) To want, to long for something. desirable, desirability.

desire[2] (desires) A strong wish.

desk (desks) A piece of furniture for writing or reading at.

desolate Neglected, unhappy. desolately, desolation.

despair[1] Hopelessness.

despair[2] (despairs, despairing, despaired) To lose hope.

desperado (desperadoes) A gangster, a reckless criminal.

desperate 1. Without hope, in despair. 2. Very serious. *A desperate situation.* 3. Violent, dangerous. *A desperate criminal.* desperately, desperation.

despise (despises, despising, despised) To have a very low opinion of someone or something, to regard him as worthless. despicable.

despite In spite of.

despondent Gloomy, unhappy. despondently.

dessert 1. Fruit served at the end of a meal. 2. *A dessert-spoon*, a spoon used for eating pudding.

destination (destinations) The place to which someone or something is going.

destined Intended, fated.

destiny Fate.

destitute Without the necessities of life, very poor.

destroy (destroys, destroying, destroyed) To damage beyond repair. destruction.

destroyer (destroyers) A kind of warship.

destructive Likely to cause damage. destructively, destructiveness.

detach (detaches, detaching, detached) To unfasten and remove something. detachment, detachable.

detached 1. Separated. *A detached house*, one not joined to another. 2. Fair, not taking sides. detachment.

detail (details) A small part of something, an item. *The details of something*, exact particulars about it.

detailed Fully described.

detain (detains, detaining, detained) 1. To keep somebody waiting. 2. To keep somebody somewhere against his will.

detect (detects, detecting, detected) To discover. detection, detector, detectable.

detective (detectives) A policeman who investigates crime.

detention Being kept in, temporary imprisonment.

deter (deters, deterring, deterred) To put somebody off from doing something.

detergent (detergents) A kind of washing powder or liquid.

deteriorate (deteriorates, deteriorating, deteriorated) To get worse. deterioration.

determined Having made up one's mind firmly. determination.

deterrent (deterrents) Something that deters people.

detest (detests, detesting, detested) To hate. detestable, detestation.

dethroned Deposed.

detonate (detonates, detonating, detonated) To set off an explosion. detonator, detonation.

detour (detours) A roundabout route, a diversion.

detrimental Harmful.

devastate (devastates, devastating, devastated) To destroy a place, to make it uninhabitable. devastation.

develop (develops, developing, developed) 1. To become bigger or better or more important. 2. To make something bigger or better or more important. 3. *To develop a cold*, to get a cold. 4. *To develop a film*, to treat film with chemicals so that the pictures can be seen. development.

device (devices) An invention, something made for a particular purpose.

devil (devils) 1. A wicked spirit. 2. *The Devil*, Satan, the enemy of God. devilish, devilry.

devilment Mischief.

devious 1. Indirect. 2. Rather dishonest.

devise (devises, devising, devised) To invent, to plan.

devoted Loyal, loving, enthusiastic.

devotion Strong, deep love or loyalty.

devour (devours, devouring, devoured) To eat hungrily.

devout Religious, sincere. **devoutly.**

dew Tiny drops of water formed on cool surfaces out of doors during the night. **dewy.**

dexterity Skill.

dhow (dhows) An Arab sailing ship.

diabetes A disease in which too much sugar is found in the blood. **diabetic.**

diabolical Devilish. **diabolically.**

diadem (diadems) A crown.

diagnose (diagnoses, diagnosing, diagnosed) To examine a patient and say what is wrong with him. **diagnosis, diagnostic.**

diagonal (diagonals) 1. A straight line across a square or oblong from one corner to the opposite one. 2. *A diagonal line*, a slanting line. **diagonally.**

diagram (diagrams) A sketch or plan made to explain or illustrate something.

dial [1] (dials) 1. The face of a clock or any similar-looking instrument. 2. The circle with numbers on it, attached to a telephone, used when making a call.

dial [2] (dials, dialling, dialled) To make a telephone call by turning the dial.

dialect (dialects) The form of a language used by people living in a particular district. *The Yorkshire dialect.*

dialogue (dialogues) A conversation, a discussion.

diameter (diameters) A line drawn from one side of a circle to the other passing through the centre.

diamond (diamonds) 1. A precious stone. 2. A shape which has four equal sides but which is not a square.

diamonds A suit of playing-cards.

diarrhoea An illness which makes a person go to the lavatory frequently.

diary (diaries) A book in which daily events are written down.

dice (dice) A small cube marked with dots (1 to 6) on the sides, used in various games.

dictate (dictates, dictating, dictated) To speak or read something aloud for somebody else to write down. **dictation.**

dictator (dictators) A ruler with absolute power. **dictatorial, dictatorship.**

dictionary (dictionaries) A book that explains the meanings of words.

did *See* do.

die (dies, dying, died) To cease to live, to come to an end.

diesel (diesels) A kind of oil-burning engine.

diet (diets) 1. The food someone normally eats. 2. The food someone has to eat for medical reasons.

differ (differs, differing, differred) To be different.

difference (differences) 1. Being different. 2. The amount by which something is different. 3. A quarrel.

different Unlike, not the same. **differently.**

difficult 1. Hard to do, not easy. *Difficult work.* 2. Hard to please. *A difficult person.* **difficulty.**

dig (digs, digging, dug) 1. To break up earth with a spade or fork. 2. To make something by removing earth. *To dig a hole.* 3. To poke. *To dig someone in the ribs.* **digger.**

digest (digests, digesting, digested) To soften and change food in the stomach so that the body can absorb its goodness. **digestion, digestible, digestive.**

digit (digits) 1. A finger or a toe. 2. Any of the numbers 0 to 9.

dignified Calm, serious, stately.

dignity Calm and serious behaviour.

dike (dikes) 1. A large ditch. 2. An earth wall, often made to prevent flooding.

dilapidated Broken down.**dilapidation.**

dilemma (dilemmas) *To be in a dilemma*, to have to make a difficult choice.·

diligent Hard-working, careful. **diligently, diligence.**

dilute (dilutes, diluting, diluted) To mix a liquid with water.**dilution.**

dim (dimmer, dimmest) Not bright.**dimly.**

dimension (dimensions) Measurement, size.

diminish (diminishes, diminishing, diminished) 1. To make a thing smaller. 2. To become smaller.

diminutive Tiny.

dimple (dimples) A small hollow in the cheek or chin.

din (dins) A loud noise.

dine (dines, dining, dined) To have dinner. **dining-room.**

ding-dong The sound of a bell.

dinghy (dinghies) A small open boat.

dingo (dingoes) An Australian wild dog.

dingy (dingier, dingiest) Dirty and depressing. **dingily, dinginess.**

dinner (dinners) The main meal of the day.

dinosaur (dinosaurs) A prehistoric animal.

diocese (dioceses) The area looked after by a bishop.**diocesan.**

dip [1] (dips, dipping, dipped) 1. To lower something into a liquid. 2. *To dip into something*, to put a hand or ladle into it to take something out. 3. To make lower. 4. To become lower.5. *To dip into a book*, to read here and there in a book.

dip [2] (dips) 1. Dipping.2. A quick swim.3. A downward slope.

diphtheria A disease of the throat.

diploma (diplomas) A certificate awarded for passing an examination.

diplomat (diplomats) An ambassador or one of his assistants.

diplomatic 1. Having to do with a diplomat. 2. Tactful.**diplomatically, diplomacy.**

dire (direr, direst) Extremely serious.

direct [1] 1. As straight as possible.2. Straightforward, without deception or hesitation. *A direct manner*.**directly, directness.**

direct [2] (directs, directing, directed) 1. To show somebody the way.2. To aim, to turn something or someone a certain way.3. To manage, to control.**direction, director.**

directory (directories) A long list of names. *A telephone directory*, a list of people with their telephone numbers.

dirge (dirges) A mournful song or tune.

dirk (dirks) A dagger.

dirt 1. Mud, dust, anything unclean.2. *A dirt track*, a race track made of cinders.

dirty (dirtier, dirtiest) 1. Not clean, covered with dirt. 2. Unpleasant, unfair. **dirtily, dirtiness.**

disable (disables, disabling, disabled) To make someone unable to do something, to cripple.disability.

disadvantage (disadvantages) A difficulty, something that hinders.

disagree (disagrees, disagreeing, disagreed) 1. To have different opinions about something. 2. To have a bad effect on. *Onions disagree with me.*disagreement.

disagreeable Unpleasant.disagreeably.

disappear (disappears, disappearing, disappeared) To vanish, to go out of sight. disappearance.

disappoint (disappoints, disappointing, disappointed) To make someone sad by not doing what was expected or by not being as good as was hoped. disappointment, disappointingly.

disapprove (disapproves, disapproving, disapproved) To have a low opinion of someone or something.disapproval.

disarm (disarms, disarming, disarmed) 1. To take away someone's weapons. 2. To reduce the size of the armed forces. disarmament. 3. *A disarming smile*, one which makes it hard to be angry.

disaster (disasters) A very serious accident, a great misfortune.disastrous.

disbelieve (disbelieves, disbelieving, disbelieved) Not to believe.disbelief.

disc (discs) 1. Any round flat object. 2. A gramophone record. *A disc jockey*, a person who introduces and plays records.

discard (discards, discarding, discarded) To throw something away.

discern (discerns, discerning, discerned) To see clearly, to understand.discernment.

discharge (discharges, discharging, discharged) 1. To send someone away, to release him from service. 2. To fire a gun. 3. To send out a liquid or gas.

disciple (disciples) A follower. *The disciples of Jesus Christ.*

discipline Good, well-trained behaviour.disciplined.

disclaim (disclaims, disclaiming, disclaimed) *To disclaim responsibility for something*, to say that one is not responsible for it.

disclose (discloses, disclosing, disclosed) To make known, to uncover.disclosure.

disco (discos) (informal) A discothèque.

discolour (discolours, discolouring, discoloured) To stain, to spoil the colour of something.

discomfort Uneasiness, lack of comfort.

disconcert (disconcerts, disconcerting, disconcerted) To upset someone.

disconnect (disconnects, disconnecting, disconnected) To remove a connection.

disconsolate Unhappy.disconsolately.

discontented Not contented.discontentedly.

discontinue (discontinues, discontinuing, discontinued) To stop doing something.

discord (discords) 1. Disagreement. 2. A clash of sounds in music.discordant.

discothèque (discothèques) 1. A place for dancing to popular music played on records. 2. A party with dancing to such music, introduced by a disc jockey.

discount (discounts) An amount by which a price is reduced.

discourage (discourages, discouraging, discouraged) 1. To take away someone's confidence and enthusiasm. 2. To try to persuade someone not to do something. discouragement.

discourteous Rude.discourteously.

discover (discovers, discovering, discovered) To find something out, to make something known for the first time. discovery, discoverer.

discreet Careful and tactful. discreetly, discretion.

discriminate (discriminates, discriminating, discriminated) 1. To be aware of the differences between things. 2. To treat people differently because of their race or sex or religion.discrimination.

discus (discuses) A heavy disk thrown in athletic sports.

discuss (discusses, discussing, discussed) To talk seriously about something.discussion.

disdain (disdains, disdaining, disdained) To scorn.

disease (diseases) Illness, sickness. **diseased.**

disembark (disembarks, disembarking, disembarked) To land goods or people from a ship, to come ashore.

disentangle (disentangles, disentangling, disentangled) To untie, to untwist.

disfigure (disfigures, disfiguring, disfigured) To spoil the beauty of something or someone. **disfigurement.**

disgrace[1] **1.** Shame. *In disgrace*, out of favour, disapproved of. **2.** A person or thing that causes shame.

disgrace[2] (disgraces, disgracing, disgraced) To bring disgrace upon something or someone. **disgraceful, disgracefully.**

disgruntled Bad-tempered.

disguise[1] (disguises, disguising, disguised) To change the appearance of someone or something in order to deceive.

disguise[2] (disguises) Something worn by someone to disguise himself.

disgust[1] A strong feeling of dislike.

disgust[2] (disgusts, disgusting, disgusted) To cause disgust.

dish (dishes) **1.** A plate or bowl from which food is served. **dish-cloth, dish-washer. 2.** The food brought to the table in a dish.

dishearten (disheartens, disheartening, disheartened) To make someone sad.

dishevelled With untidy hair.

dishonest Not honest. **dishonestly, dishonesty.**

dishonour Shame, disgrace. **dishonourable.**

disillusion (disillusions, disillusioning, disillusioned) To make someone aware of the sad truth about something. **disillusionment.**

disinclined Unwilling. **disinclination.**

disinfect (disinfects, disinfecting, disinfected) To make a thing free from germs. **disinfectant.**

disinherit (disinherits, disinheriting, disinherited) To prevent someone from inheriting.

disintegrate (disintegrates, disintegrating, disintegrated) To break up into small pieces. **disintegration.**

disinterested Not biased.

disjointed Broken up into parts.

dislike[1] (dislikes, disliking, disliked) Not to like something or somebody.

dislike[2] A feeling of not liking something or somebody.

dislocate (dislocates, dislocating, dislocated) To put something out of place or out of order. **dislocation.**

dislodge (dislodges, dislodging, dislodged) To move something from its place.

disloyal Not loyal. **disloyalty.**

dismal Sad and gloomy. **dismally.**

dismantle (dismantles, dismantling, dismantled) To take parts off something, to take it to pieces.

dismay[1] A feeling of fear and discouragement.

dismay[2] (dismays, dismaying, dismayed) To fill someone with dismay.

dismembered Torn limb from limb.

dismiss (dismisses, dismissing, dismissed) **1.** To send someone away, to cease to employ him. **2.** To stop thinking about something. *I advise you to dismiss the idea of revenge.* **3.** To get a batsman out in cricket. **dismissal.**

dismount (dismounts, dismounting, dismounted) To get off a bicycle or a horse.

disobey (disobeys, disobeying, disobeyed) To refuse to obey. **disobedience, disobedient, disobediently.**

disorder (disorders) 1. Confusion. 2. Rioting. 3. An illness.

disorderly 1. Untidy. 2. Badly-behaved.

disorganize (disorganizes, disorganizing, disorganized) To upset the order or system, to throw into confusion. **disorganization.**

disown (disowns, disowning, disowned) *To disown something*, to declare it has nothing to do with oneself.

disparaging Uncomplimentary, rude.

dispatch [1] (dispatches, dispatching, dispatched) 1. To send something off somewhere. 2. To kill.

dispatch [2] (dispatches) A message, a report. **dispatch-rider.**

dispensary (dispensaries) A place where medicines are made up and given out.

dispense (dispenses, dispensing, dispensed) 1. To give out, to distribute. **dispenser.** 2. *To dispense with something*, to do without it, to get rid of it.

disperse (disperses, dispersing, dispersed) To scatter in different directions. **dispersal.**

display [1] (displays) An exhibition, a show.

display [2] (displays, displaying, displayed) To show something publicly.

displease (displeases, displeasing, displeased) To annoy. **displeasure.**

disposable Made to be thrown away after use.

disposal 1. Disposing. *A bomb-disposal expert*, someone who knows how to make bombs harmless. 2. *At your disposal*, for you to use.

dispose (disposes, disposing, disposed) 1. *To dispose of*, to get rid of. 2. *Disposed to*, willing to.

disposition (dispositions) Character, state of mind. *A kind disposition.*

disprove (disproves, disproving, disproved) To show that something is false.

dispute (disputes, disputing, disputed) To argue, to quarrel.

disqualify (disqualifies, disqualifying, disqualified) To declare that someone is no longer fit or qualified for something. *Disqualified from driving*. **disqualification.**

disquiet Worry, uneasiness. **disquieting.**

disregard (disregards, disregarding, disregarded) To pay no attention to something.

disreputable Not respectable.

disrespect Rudeness, lack of respect. **disrespectful.**

disrupt (disrupts, disrupting, disrupted) To break up, to obstruct. **disruption.**

dissatisfied Not satisfied. **dissatisfaction.**

dissect (dissects, dissecting, dissected) To cut something into pieces in order to examine it. **dissection.**

dissent Disagreement. **dissention.**

dissimilar Not similar.

dissolve (dissolves, dissolving, dissolved) 1. To mix something with a liquid so that it becomes liquid too. 2. To disappear, to fade away.

dissuade (dissuades, dissuading, dissuaded) To persuade someone not to do something. **dissuasion.**

distance (distances) 1. The amount of space between two places. *The distance between home and school is one kilometre.* 2. *Within walking distance*, near enough to walk to. 3. *In the distance*, far away.

distant Far away. **distantly.**

distaste Dislike. **distasteful.**

distemper 1. A disease of dogs and other animals. 2. A kind of paint.

distended Swollen.

distil (distils, distilling, distilled) To purify a liquid by boiling it and condensing the steam. **distiller, distillation.**

distinct 1. Easily heard or seen. 2. Clearly separate. **distinctly.**

distinction (distinctions) 1. A difference. 2. Excellence, honour. 3. An award for excellence. **distinctive, distinctively.**

distinguish (distinguishes, distinguishing, distinguished) 1. To notice the differences between things. 2. To make out, to recognize. 3. *Distinguished*, famous. *A distinguished poet*. **distinguishable.**

distort (distorts, distorting, distorted) To pull something out of shape. **distortion.**

distract (distracts, distracting, distracted) To take someone's attention away from what he is doing.**distraction.**

distress [1] Severe pain, sorrow, or difficulty.

distress [2] (distresses, distressing, distressed) To cause distress.

distribute (distributes, distributing, distributed) To share out, to give out. **distributor, distribution.**

district (districts) A part of a country, an area.

distrust [1] Lack of trust.

distrust [2] (distrusts, distrusting, distrusted) Not to trust, to be suspicious of someone or something.**distrustful, distrustfully.**

disturb (disturbs, disturbing, disturbed) 1. To spoil someone's rest or quiet.2. To cause worry. 3. To move something from its proper position.**disturbance.**

disused No longer used.

ditch (ditches) A narrow trench or channel.

dither (dithers, dithering, dithered) To fuss about aimlessly.

ditto The same as the thing just mentioned.

ditty (ditties) A short simple song.

divan (divans) A kind of bed.

dive (dives, diving, dived) 1. To go head first into water.2. To move quickly downwards.

diver (divers) A person who works under water in a special suit called a diving-suit.

diverge (diverges, diverging, diverged) To go in different directions.

diverse Varied.**diversity.**

divert (diverts, diverting, diverted) 1. To change the direction of something. *To divert the traffic.*2. To entertain, to amuse. **diversion.**

divide (divides, dividing, divided) 1. To separate into smaller parts. *To divide into teams.*2. To share out. *Divide the sweets between you.*3. In arithmetic, to find out how often one number is contained in another. *36 divided by 3 = 12.*4. To keep things apart, to separate. *A dividing fence.* **division, divisible.**

dividers A mathematical measuring instrument.

divine 1. Belonging to God, from God. 2. Like a god.**divinely, divinity.**

diviner (diviners) Someone who claims to be able to find hidden water or minerals with a stick called a divining rod.

divorce (divorces, divorcing, divorced) To end a marriage legally.

divulge (divulges, divulging, divulged) To make something known to somebody.

dizzy Confused, giddy.**dizzily.**

do (does, doing, did, done) 1. This word is used in questions, and in statements with 'not'. *Do you want this? I do not like it.* 2. To perform an action. *To do a job.* 3. To deal with something. *To do the potatoes.*4. To be suitable for something, to be enough. *That will never do. That's enough, that will do.*5. *This is to do with something,* this is concerned or connected with it. *Have nothing to do with him,* do not work or play with him. 6. (informal) *We could do with this,* we should like to have it. 7. *To do without something,* to manage without it.**doer.**

docile Easily controlled, meek, obedient. **docility.**

dock [1] (docks) 1. A place where ships may be loaded, unloaded, or repaired. 2. *A dry dock,* a dock which can be emptied of water.**docker, dockyard.**

dock [2] (docks, docking, docked) 1. To come into dock. 2. To join two spacecraft together in orbit.

dock [3] A weed with broad leaves.

dock [4] (docks) A place for the prisoner in a criminal court.

doctor (doctors) A person trained to heal sick people.

document (documents) An important paper, an official record. **documentation**.

documentary (documentaries) A film showing people in real life.

dodder (dodders, doddering, doddered) To move unsteadily like a very old person. **dodderer**.

dodge[1] (dodges, dodging, dodged) To move about quickly keeping out of someone's way. **dodger**.

dodge[2] (dodges) (informal) A plan, a trick.

dodo (dodos) An extinct bird.

doe (does) A female deer, rabbit, or hare.

doer, does See **do**.

doesn't (informal) Does not.

dog (dogs) 1. An animal that barks, often kept as a pet. 2. (informal) *Dog-tired*, very tired.

dogged Obstinate, persistent. **doggedly**.

doggerel Bad verse.

dole (informal) Unemployment benefit. *To be on the dole*, to receive money from the government while out of work.

doleful Dreary, sad. **dolefully**.

doll (dolls) A toy baby or person.

dollar (dollars) A unit of money in the U.S.A. and other countries. *100 dollars* is written $100.

dollop (dollops) A shapeless lump of something.

dolphin (dolphins) A sea animal like a small whale.

domain (domains) Lands ruled over by a king or a lord.

dome (domes) A rounded roof.

domestic 1. Connected with the home. 2. *Domestic animals*, tame animals.

domesticated 1. Fond of home. 2. Tamed.

dominant Most important, outstanding, ruling.

dominate (dominates, dominating, dominated) To have a strong influence over people or things, to be dominant. **domination**.

domineering Tyrannical, bossy.

domino (dominoes) A flat, oblong piece of wood or plastic with dots (1 to 6) or a blank space at each end, used in the game of dominoes.

donate (donates, donating, donated) To give. **donation**.

done See **do**.

donkey (donkeys) An animal that brays, also called an ass.

donor (donors) A giver. *A blood donor*.

don't (informal) Do not.

doodle (doodles, doodling, doodled) To scribble absent-mindedly.

doom Ruin, death, fate. **doomed**.

door (doors) 1. A device which opens and closes to let people into and out of a building or room. 2. Any similar device. *A cupboard door*. 3. *Out of doors*, in the open air. 4. *Next door*, the next house. **door-bell, door-mat, doorway**.

dope (dopes) (informal) 1. A drug. 2. A stupid person.

dormant Sleeping.

dormer window An upright window in a sloping roof.

dormitory (dormitories) A room arranged for several people to sleep in.

dormouse (dormice) A small hibernating animal.

dorsal On the back. *A shark has a dorsal fin*.

dose[1] (doses) An amount of medicine taken at one time.

dose[2] (doses, dosing, dosed) To give someone a dose.

dot¹ (dots) A small spot.

dot² (dots, dotting, dotted) To mark with dots. *A dotted line.*

dote (dotes, doting, doted) To love somebody in a silly way.

dotty (dottier, dottiest) (informal) Feeble-minded, slightly mad. dottiness.

double¹ (doubles, doubling, doubled) 1. To make something twice as big. 2. To become twice as big. 3. To bend something over in two. 4. *To double back*, to go back the way one came.

double² 1. Having two of something. double-barrelled, double-edged. 2. Suitable for two. *A double bed.* 3. Twice as much, twice as many. *To see double.*

double³ (doubles) Someone who looks very like someone else.

double-bass (double-basses) A deep-sounding string instrument.

double-cross (double-crosses, double-crossing, doubled-crossed) To cheat and betray someone.

double-decker (double-deckers) A bus with two decks.

doubt¹ (doubts) A feeling of being unsure. doubtful, doubtfully, doubtless.

doubt² (doubts, doubting, doubted) To be unsure about something, to question the truth of it.

dough 1. A thick mixture of flour and water for making bread, buns, or cake. doughy, doughnut. 2. (informal) Money.

dove (doves) A kind of bird that makes a cooing sound.

dovecote (dovecotes) A pigeon-house.

dowdy (dowdier, dowdiest) Shabby, badly dressed. dowdily, dowdiness.

down¹ Soft, fluffy feathers. downy.

down² 1. From a higher part to a lower part of something. *The rain came down heavily. We ran down the hill.* 2. To a position of rest. *He lay down.* 3. Along. *She walked down the street.* 4. *To pay £10 down*, to pay £10 now and the rest later. 5. *To be down on someone*, to treat him unfairly.

downcast Down-hearted.

downfall (downfalls) 1. A shower of rain. 2. Ruin, a cause of ruin. *Over-confidence was his downfall.*

down-hearted Sad, depressed.

downhill Down a slope.

downpour (downpours) A heavy shower of rain.

downs Gentle, grass-covered hills.

downstairs 1. To a lower floor in a building. 2. On a lower floor.

downtrodden Badly treated.

downward or downwards Towards a lower position.

dowry (dowries) Money or property which a father gives to his daughter when she marries.

doze¹ (dozes, dozing, dozed) To sleep lightly, to be half asleep.

doze² (dozes) A light sleep. dozy, doziness.

dozen (dozens) 1. *A dozen*, twelve. *In dozens*, in sets of twelve. 2. *Dozens of things*, a lot of things.

Dr. Doctor.

drab Dull, not colourful. drabness.

drag (drags, dragging, dragged) 1. To pull something along. 2. To move slowly or painfully. 3. To search under water with hooks and nets. *To drag a canal.*

dragon (dragons) A fire-breathing monster.

dragon-fly (dragon-flies) A large flying insect.

drain¹ (drains) A pipe or ditch for taking away water or sewage. drain-pipe, drainage.

drain² (drains, draining, drained) 1. To take away water by means of drains. 2. To empty liquid out of a container. *He drained his glass.* 3. *Put the plates to drain*, leave them so that the water will run off them. draining-board. 4. To exhaust. *Drained of strength.*

drake (drakes) A male duck.

drama (dramas) 1. A play. dramatist. 2. A series of exciting happenings. dramatic, dramatically.

drank See drink¹.

drape (drapes, draping, draped) To hang up cloth in folds over something.

draper (drapers) A shop-keeper selling cloth and clothing.

drapes Curtains, draped material.

drastic Having a violent effect. **drastically.**

draught (draughts) A current of air indoors. **draughty.**

draughts A game played with counters on a chess-board.

draw [1] (draws, drawing, drew, drawn) 1. To use a pencil, a piece of chalk, or something similar, to make a picture, diagram, or pattern. **drawing-board.** 2. To pull. *To draw a boat out of the water. To draw water from a well.* 3. To take out money from a bank account. 4. To attract. *The circus drew large crowds.* 5. To end a game with neither side having won or lost. 6. To move. *To draw near.* 7. *To draw something out*, to make it longer. 8. *To draw up*, to stop. *The taxi drew up at the gate.*

draw [2] (draws) 1. An attraction, a pull. 2. A choice made by drawing lots. 3. A drawn game.

drawback (drawbacks) A disadvantage.

drawbridge (drawbridges) A bridge that can be raised when a castle is attacked.

drawer (drawers) A tray which slides in and out of a piece of furniture.

drawers Knickers.

drawing (drawings) Something drawn with pencil, chalk, or something similar.

drawing-pin (drawing-pins) A short pin with a large flat top.

drawing-room (drawing-rooms) A sitting-room.

dread [1] (dreads, dreading, dreaded) To fear greatly.

dread [2] Great fear. **dreadful, dreadfully.**

dream [1] (dreams) 1. Things a person seems to see while he is asleep. 2. A mental picture. *A dream of wealth and happiness.* **dreamy, dreaminess.**

dream [2] (dreams, dreaming, dreamed) To have a dream.

dreary (drearier, dreariest) Sad, depressing. **drearily, dreariness.**

dredge (dredges, dredging, dredged) To pull things up from the bottom of the sea or a river to keep a channel clear of mud. **dredger.**

dregs The unwanted bits left at the bottom of a bottle or other container.

drench (drenches, drenching, drenched) To make something or somebody thoroughly wet.

dress [1] (dresses) 1. A one-piece garment with a skirt, worn by women and girls. 2. Clothing. **dressmaker.** 3. Costume. *National dress. Fancy dress.* 4. *A dress rehearsal*, the final rehearsal in which actors wear their costumes.

dress [2] (dresses, dressing, dressed) 1. To put clothes on. *To dress up*, to put on special clothes. 2. To prepare something, to get it ready. 3. To attend to a wound and put a dressing on it.

dresser (dressers) A piece of furniture with shelves for plates and dishes.

dressing (dressings) 1. A bandage or some other covering for a wound. 2. A kind of sauce. *Salad dressing.*

dressing-gown (dressing-gowns) A gown which can be worn over night clothes.

dressing-table (dressing-tables) A piece of bedroom furniture.

drew *See* **draw** [1].

dribble (dribbles, dribbling, dribbled) 1. To allow saliva to trickle out of the side of the mouth as babies do. 2. In football, to take the ball forward with very short kicks.

dried, drier *See* **dry** [2].

drier, driest *See* **dry** [1].

drift [1] (drifts) 1. A heap of snow or sand piled up by the wind. 2. The general meaning of something.

drift [2] (drifts, drifting, drifted) 1. To make drifts. *Drifting snow.* 2. To be carried along by gently moving air or water. *A drifting ship.* 3. To move about aimlessly.

drift-wood Wood washed up on the beach.

drill[1] (drills) 1. A tool for boring holes. 2. Marching or other exercises done as part of a soldier's training.

drill[2] (drills, drilling, drilled) 1. To make a hole with a drill. 2. To do marching or other kinds of strict training.

drily *See* dry[1].

drink[1] (drinks, drinking, drank, drunk) 1. To swallow any kind of liquid. 2. *To drink up, to drink in*, to soak up greedily or with pleasure. 3. *He drinks heavily*, he drinks a lot of alcohol. **drinkable, drinker, drinking-water.**

drink[2] (drinks) 1. A liquid for drinking. 2. An alcoholic drink.

drip[1] (drips, dripping, dripped) 1. To fall in drops. 2. To let liquid fall in drops. *A dripping tap.* 3. *Dripping wet*, very wet. 4. *Drip-dry clothes*, clothes which dry quickly and do not need ironing.

drip[2] (drips) A falling drop of liquid.

dripping Fat which comes from roasting meat.

drive[1] (drives, driving, drove, driven) 1. To force someone or something to move in a certain direction. *The wind drove the ship towards the rocks.* 2. To be in control of a moving vehicle. *To drive a car.* 3. To take someone for a ride in a car, to go for a ride in a car or other vehicle. 4. To hit a ball in cricket, golf, or tennis. 5. *Driven by steam*, worked or powered by steam. **driver.**

drive[2] (drives) 1. A journey in a vehicle. 2. A stroke in cricket or golf. 3. A road, a road up to a house. 4. Energy, enthusiasm.

drivel Nonsense.

drizzle[1] Fine misty rain.

drizzle[2] (drizzles, drizzling, drizzled) To rain with fine misty drops.

dromedary (dromedaries) A camel with one hump.

drone[1] (drones) 1. A male bee. 2. A low humming sound.

drone[2] (drones, droning, droned) 1. To make a low humming sound like bees. 2. To talk in a boring voice.

droop (droops, drooping, drooped) To hang down wearily.

drop[1] (drops) 1. A small spot of a liquid, a tiny quantity of something. 2. A kind of sweet. *Acid drops.* 3. A fall. *A drop in prices.*

drop[2] (drops, dropping, dropped) 1. To fall, to let something fall, to make it fall. 2. *To drop in*, to visit.

drought (droughts) A period of continuous dry weather, a water shortage.

drove *See* drive[1].

drown (drowns, drowning, drowned) 1. To die or to kill by suffocation under water. 2. To make such a loud noise that another sound can no longer be heard.

drowsy Sleepy. **drowsily, drowsiness.**

drudgery Hard, boring work.

drug[1] (drugs) 1. A substance which can be used to cure diseases or to kill pain. 2. A substance which can produce effects rather like drunkenness. *A drug addict.*

drug[2] (drugs, drugging, drugged) To give drugs to someone.

druid (druids) A pagan priest in ancient Britain.

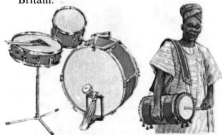

drum[1] (drums) 1. A percussion instrument. **drumstick.** 2. A cylindrical container. *An oil drum.*

drum[2] (drums, drumming, drummed) 1. To play a drum. **drummer.** 2. To tap or thump something.

drunk 1. *See* drink[1]. 2. In a helpless state through drinking too much alcohol.

drunkard (drunkards) A person who is frequently drunk.

drunken *A drunken man*, a man who is drunk, a drunkard. **drunkenness.**

dry¹ (drier, driest) 1. Not wet, without any moisture. 2. (informal) Thirsty. 3. Dull. *A dry book.* 4. *Dry cleaning*, a method of cleaning which does not use water. **drily, dryness.**

dry² (dries, drying, dried) 1. To make something dry. 2. To become dry. **drier.**

dual Double. *A dual carriageway*, a wide road divided down the middle.

dubious Doubtful. **dubiously.**

duchess The wife of a duke.

duck¹ (ducks) 1. A common water-bird. 2. *To make a duck*, to score 0 in cricket.

duck² (ducks, ducking, ducked) 1. To go or push someone suddenly under water. 2. To bend down quickly to avoid being hit or seen.

duckling (ducklings) A baby duck.

dud (informal) Useless.

due 1. Owing, to be paid. *Club subscriptions are now due.* 2. Right, suitable. *You should show due respect to the headmaster.* 3. Expected. *The train is due at 11.30.* 4. *Due to*, caused by. 5. *Due north*, exactly north.

duel (duels) A fight between two people.

duet (duets) A piece of music for two performers.

duffel bag A bag tied at the top with a cord.

duffel coat A coat made of thick, coarse cloth.

dug-out (dug-outs) 1. A canoe made by hollowing out a tree trunk. 2. A rough underground shelter.

duke (dukes) A nobleman of high rank, next below a prince.

dull (duller, dullest) 1. Slow to understand, stupid. *A dull boy.* 2. Uninteresting. *A dull programme.* 3. Not bright, gloomy. *A dull day.* 4. Not sharp. *A dull pain.* **dully, dullness.**

duly Rightly, as expected.

dumb Unable to speak, silent. **dumbly.**

dumbfounded Struck dumb with surprise.

dummy (dummies) 1. An imitation, something made to look like a person or an object. 2. A rubber teat for a baby to suck.

dump¹ (dumps) 1. A place where rubbish or unwanted things may be left. 2. A military stores depot. *An ammunition dump.* 3. (informal) *Down in the dumps*, sad, depressed.

dump² (dumps, dumping, dumped) 1. To put something on a dump. 2. To put something down carelessly and untidily.

dumpling (dumplings) A lump of boiled or baked dough.

dumpy (dumpier, dumpiest) Short and fat.

dunce (dunces) Someone who is slow at learning.

dune (dunes) A low hill of loose sand.

dung Manure.

dungarees Overalls.

dungeon (dungeons) A dark underground prison.

dupe (dupes, duping, duped) To deceive.

duplicate¹ (duplicates) An exact copy.

duplicate² (duplicates, duplicating, duplicated) To make a duplicate. **duplication, duplicator.**

durable Lasting. **durability.**

duration The time something lasts.

during 1. Throughout. *The sun shone during the whole match.* 2. *During the afternoon*, at some moment in the afternoon.

dusk Dim evening light.

dust[1] Finely-powdered dry dirt.

dust[2] (dusts, dusting, dusted) 1. To clean away dust. 2. To sprinkle with dust or powder.

dustbin (dustbins) A container for household rubbish.

dustcart (dustcarts) A kind of lorry into which dustbins are emptied.

duster (dusters) A cloth used for dusting.

dustman (dustmen) A person who empties dustbins.

dusty Covered with dust, like dust.

Dutch 1. Of Holland. **Dutchman, Dutchwoman.** 2. *Double Dutch*, nonsense, meaningless language.

duty (duties) 1. What a person must do, what he ought to do. **dutiful, dutifully.** 2. What a person does as part of his job. 3. A kind of tax. *Customs duty.*

duvet (duvets) A kind of eiderdown.

dwarf[1] (dwarfs) 1. A very small person. 2. Anything much smaller than the usual size.

dwarf[2] (dwarfs, dwarfing, dwarfed) To make something look smaller.

dwell (dwells, dwelling, dwelt) To live somewhere. **dweller.**

dwelling (dwellings) A place to live.

dwindle (dwindles, dwindling, dwindled) To get gradually smaller.

dye[1] (dyes, dyeing, dyed) To colour a material by dipping it in a special liquid.

dye[2] (dyes) A substance used for dyeing material.

dying *See* die.

dynamic Energetic.

dynamite An explosive.

dynamo (dynamos) A machine for generating electricity.

dysentery A painful disease with severe diarrhoea.

Ee

each 1. Every one of a group. *Give one sweet to each child.* 2. Every one. *You may have one sweet each*, every one of you may have one sweet. 3. *Jack and Jill love each other*, he loves her and she loves him.

eager Showing or feeling great desire, keen. **eagerly, eagerness.**

eagle (eagles) A large bird of prey.

ear (ears) 1. The organ of the body with which we hear. **ear-ache, ear-ring.** 2. *An ear of corn*, the cluster of grains at the top of the stalk.

earl (earls) A nobleman of high rank.

early (earlier, earliest) 1. Near the beginning of a period of time. *Early in the day.* 2. Before the usual time, before the right time. *To go to bed early.* **earliness.**

earn (earns, earning, earned) To get something as a reward for something done. *I earn £1 a week delivering papers.*

earnest Serious, determined. *In earnest*, not joking. **earnestly, earnestness.**

earnings Wages, money earned.

ear-phone (ear-phones) A listening device fitting over a person's ear.

earshot Hearing distance. *Within earshot.*

earth 1. The planet we live on. **earthly.** 2. Ground, soil. **earthy.** 3. The hole where a fox or badger lives.

earthenware Dishes made of baked clay.

earthquake (earthquakes) A sudden violent shaking of the earth.

earthworm (earthworms) A worm which lives in the ground.

earwig (earwigs) A kind of insect.

ease¹ 1. Freedom from pain or anxiety. 2. Comfort, rest.

ease² (eases, easing, eased) 1. To give ease to someone. *To ease someone's pain.* 2. To do something gradually and carefully. *The lame man eased himself into a chair.* 3. *To ease off,* to become less severe.

easel (easels) A wooden stand for a painting or a blackboard.

east 1. One of the points of the compass, the direction from which the sun rises. 2. From the east. *The east wind.* easterly. 3. In the east. *The east coast.* eastern. 4. Towards the east. *Sailing east.* eastward, eastwards.

Easter The day on which the resurrection of Jesus Christ is celebrated.

easy (easier, easiest) 1. Able to be done without trouble. 2. Free from pain or anxiety, comfortable. easily, easiness.

eat (eats, eating, ate, eaten) 1. To take food into the mouth and then swallow it. 2. To destroy something. *The river had eaten away the bank.* eater.

eatable Fit to eat.

eaves The overhanging edges of a roof.

eavesdrop (eavesdrops, eavesdropping, eavesdropped) To listen secretly to a conversation. eavesdropper.

ebb¹ The going down of the tide.

ebb² (ebbs, ebbing, ebbed) To go down, to become less.

ebony A hard black wood.

eccentric Behaving oddly. eccentricity.

echo¹ (echoes) A sound which bounces back and is heard again.

echo² (echoes, echoing, echoed) 1. To send back an echo. *The hills echoed the sound.* 2. To cause echoes. *The pistol shot echoed through the caves.*

éclair (éclairs) A small cake with a chocolate top and cream inside.

eclipse¹ (eclipses) 1. *An eclipse of the sun*, a time when the moon gets between the sun and the earth and blocks its light. 2. *An eclipse of the moon*, a time when the earth's shadow falls on the moon.

eclipse² (eclipses, eclipsing, eclipsed) To cause an eclipse.

ecology The science which deals with living creatures in their surroundings. ecologist.

economize (economizes, economizing, economized) To use less money or fewer things than before.

economy (economies) Careful use and control of money and other things, avoiding waste. economical, economically.

ecstasy (ecstasies) An excited feeling of joy. ecstatic.

eddy (eddies) A circular movement of wind or water.

edge¹ (edges) 1. The sharp cutting part of a knife or other tool. 2. The limit or boundary of something. 3. *On edge*, nervous. edgy.

edge² (edges, edging, edged) 1. To move slowly forwards or sideways. 2. To make an edge.

edgeways With the edge forwards or outwards.

edible Fit to be eaten.

edifice (edifices) A building.

edit (edits, editing, edited) To get a newspaper or magazine ready for publication. **editor.**

edition (editions) All the copies of a newspaper, magazine, or book issued at the same time.

editorial (editorials) An article written by the editor of a newspaper or magazine.

educate (educates, educating, educated) To teach, to train, to bring someone up. **education, educational, educator.**

eel (eels) A long, snake-like fish.

eerie Strange, weird, frightening. **eerily.**

effect (effects) 1. A result. *To take effect,* to come into use, to produce results. 2. A general impression. *The decorations made a colourful effect.* **effective, effectively.** 3. *Effects,* goods, property.

effervescent Giving off little bubbles, fizzy. **effervescence.**

efficient Competent, doing work well. **efficiently, efficiency.**

effort (efforts) 1. Hard work, trying hard. 2. An attempt to do something.

egg [1] (eggs) 1. The round or oval object laid by a bird, insect, fish, or reptile in which her young begins its life. 2. A hen's egg used as food. **egg-cup, egg-shell, egg-spoon.**

egg [2] (eggs, egging, egged) (informal) *To egg on,* to encourage.

Egyptian Of Egypt.

eiderdown (eiderdowns) A softly-padded bed covering.

eight (eights) The number 8. **eighth.**

eighteen The number 18. **eighteenth.**

eighty (eighties) The number 80. **eightieth.**

eisteddfod (eisteddfodau) A Welsh musical festival.

either 1. One of two people or things. 2. *At either end,* at both ends.

eject (ejects, ejecting, ejected) To throw out. **ejection, ejector-seat.**

elaborate Carefully planned, complicated, detailed. **elaborately.**

elapse (elapses, elapsing, elapsed) *Time elapses,* time passes.

elastic A material which can be stretched and which goes back to its original size afterwards. *An elastic band.*

elated In high spirits, very pleased. **elation.**

elbow (elbows) The joint in the middle of a person's arm.

elder [1] (eldest) Older.

elder [2] (elders) A small tree with black berries.

elderly Rather old.

elect (elects, electing, elected) To choose.

election (elections) Choosing by voting. **elector.**

electric Worked by electricity. **electrical, electrically.**

electrician (electricians) An expert in dealing with apparatus using electricity.

electricity A form of power or energy used for lighting, heating, and working machinery. It is supplied by batteries or along wires from generators.

electrify (electrifies, electrifying, electrified) 1. To alter something so that it can be worked by electricity. *To electrify a railway.* **electrification.** 2. To excite, to thrill.

electrocute (electrocutes, electrocuting, electrocuted) To kill someone by means of electricity. **electrocution.**

electro-magnet (electro-magnets) An electric magnet.

electronics The science concerned with radio, television, and other similar apparatus.

elegant Graceful, tasteful. **elegantly, elegance.**

element (elements) 1. A substance which cannot be divided into simpler substances. 2. One of the parts of which something is made. 3. *The elements of a subject,* the simplest parts of the subject which are learnt first. 4. *The elements,* the weather, especially bad weather. 5. The coil of wire which gives out heat in an electric fire, kettle, or cooker.

elementary Easy, simple, basic.

elephant (elephants) A large animal with tusks and a trunk.

elevate (elevates, elevating, elevated) To lift up. **elevation, elevator.**

eleven 1. The number 11. **2.** (elevens) A team in cricket, hockey, or association football. **eleventh.**

elf (elves) A small fairy, a mischievous creature. **elfish, elvish, elfin.**

eligible Suitable, qualified. **eligibility.**

eliminate (eliminates, eliminating, eliminated) To remove, to get rid of someone or something. **elimination.**

Elizabethan Belonging to the reign of Queen Elizabeth I.

elk (elks) A large North American deer.

ellipse (ellipses) An oval shape. **elliptical.**

elm (elms) A tall tree with rough bark.

elocution The art of speaking well.

elongated Lengthened.

elope (elopes, eloping, eloped) To run away from home with a lover. **elopement.**

eloquent Speaking fluently and with fine-sounding speech. **eloquence.**

else 1. Besides, as well. *Have you anything else to do?* **2.** Otherwise. *You must hurry, or else you'll be late.*

elsewhere In another place, to another place.

elude (eludes, eluding, eluded) To escape capture, to avoid. **elusive.**

elves *See* **elf.**

emaciated Made thin, wasted away.

emancipate (emancipates, emancipating, emancipated) To set free.

embalm (embalms, embalming, embalmed) To preserve a dead body from decay. **embalmer.**

embankment (embankments) **1.** A wall built to strengthen a river bank. **2.** A bank made for a road or railway.

embark (embarks, embarking, embarked) **1.** To go on a ship, to put something or someone on a ship. **2.** To start a sea voyage or other adventure. **embarkation.**

embarrass (embarrasses, embarrassing, embarrassed) To make someone feel awkward and self-conscious. **embarrassment.**

embassy (embassies) The place where an ambassador lives and works.

embers Small pieces of smouldering material in a dying fire.

embezzle (embezzles, embezzling, embezzled) To steal money while being trusted to look after it. **embezzlement.**

embittered Made to feel bitter.

emblem (emblems) **1.** A symbol. **2.** A badge.

embrace (embraces, embracing, embraced) To hug, to put one's arms lovingly round someone.

embroider (embroiders, embroidering, embroidered) To sew designs or pictures on cloth. embroidery.

embryo (embryos) A young animal before it is born or a bird before it is hatched.

emerald (emeralds) A bright green precious stone.

emerge (emerges, emerging, emerged) To come out, to come into view.

emergency (emergencies) Sudden danger, a crisis.

emery-paper A gritty paper used for polishing metal.

emigrate (emigrates, emigrating, emigrated) To leave one country and settle in another. emigrant, emigration.

eminent Famous, outstanding. eminently, eminence.

emit (emits, emitting, emitted) To give out, to send out. emission.

emotion (emotions) Feeling, excitement. emotional, emotionally.

emperor (emperors) The ruler of an empire.

emphasis (emphases) 1. Saying something with a particular stress or firmness. 2. Drawing attention to the importance of something. emphatic, emphatically.

emphasize (emphasizes, emphasizing, emphasized) To give emphasis to something. *Our teacher always emphasizes the importance of neatness.*

empire (empires) A group of countries under one ruler.

employ (employs, employing, employed) 1. To give work to someone and pay him. 2. To use something. employer.

employee (employees) Someone who works for an employer.

employment (employments) A job or trade.

empress (empresses) 1. The wife of an emperor. 2. A woman who rules an empire.

empty¹ (emptier, emptiest) With nothing inside. emptiness.

empty² (empties, emptying, emptied) To remove the contents of something, to leave nothing inside it.

emu (emus) An Australian bird that cannot fly.

emulsion paint A kind of paint for walls and ceilings.

enable (enables, enabling, enabled) To make something possible for somebody.

enamel (enamels) 1. A coloured glass-like coating on metal. 2. A paint that dries with a hard, shiny surface.

enchant (enchants, enchanting, enchanted) 1. To charm, to delight. 2. To put a spell on somebody.

encircle (encircles, encircling, encircled) To surround.

enclose (encloses, enclosing, enclosed) To shut something up, to put a wall or fence around it. enclosure.

encore 1. *Encore!* Do it again! 2. (encores) An extra performance after the first has been applauded at a concert.

encounter (encounters, encountering, encountered) To meet somebody or something.

encourage (encourages, encouraging, encouraged) To fill somebody with hope or confidence, to urge him on. encouragement.

encumber (encumbers, encumbering, encumbered) To hamper. encumbrance.

encyclopedia (encyclopedias) A book of information on many different subjects.

end¹ (ends) 1. The point at which something finishes or stops. *The end of a journey.* 2. The bit that is left after something has been used. *A cigarette end.* 3. A purpose. *For his own ends,* for his own purposes. 4. *To stand something on end,* to stand it upright. 5. *For days on end,* day after day.

end² (ends, ending, ended) To finish.

endearing Lovable. endearingly.

endeavour (endeavours, endeavouring, endeavoured) To try, to attempt.

endless Without an end. endlessly.

endure (endures, enduring, endured) 1. To suffer. 2. To put up with something. 3. To last, to continue. endurance, endurable.

enemy (enemies) 1. Someone who hates and wishes to harm someone else. 2. *The enemy*, the opposing army or people. 3. Something harmful. *Slugs are enemies to the gardener.*

energy 1. Strength and liveliness. energetic, energetically. 2. The ability of animals and machines to do work. Food provides energy for animals, fuel provides it for machines.

enforce (enforces, enforcing, enforced) To compel people to obey rules or laws. enforcement.

engage (engages, engaging, engaged) 1. To reserve, to employ. 2. *To become engaged*, to agree to get married. 3. *To be engaged in something*, to be busy doing it. 4. *To engage in battle*, to begin fighting a battle.

engagement (engagements) 1. An agreement between a man and woman that they will get married. 2. An arrangement to meet someone or to be in a particular place at a particular time. 3. A battle.

engine (engines) 1. A machine which provides power. *A petrol engine.* 2. A railway locomotive. engine-driver.

engineer (engineers) 1. A person who designs and builds machines, bridges, ships, and so on. 2. A technical expert. *A heating engineer.* 3. A man in charge of a ship's engines.

engineering The job done by an engineer.

English Of England. Englishman, Englishwoman.

engrave (engraves, engraving, engraved) To cut patterns or writing on a metal, wood, or stone surface.

engrossed Interested and absorbed.

engulfed Swallowed up.

enjoy (enjoys, enjoying, enjoyed) To take pleasure and delight in something. *To enjoy oneself*, to have a good time. enjoyable, enjoyment.

enlarge (enlarges, enlarging, enlarged) To make a thing bigger.

enlargement (enlargements) A photograph printed larger than its negative.

enlist (enlists, enlisting, enlisted) To join one of the armed services.

enmity Hatred.

enormous Very large indeed. enormously.

enough As many or as much as required. *Have you enough petrol for the journey?*

enquire (enquires, enquiring, enquired) To ask about something. enquiry.

enrage (enrages, enraging, enraged) To make someone very angry.

enrich (enriches, enriching, enriched) To make someone or something become richer.

enrol (enrols, enrolling, enrolled) To enter a person's name on a list for something. enrolment.

ensemble (ensembles) A group. *A recorder ensemble.*

ensign (ensigns) A flag.

enslave (enslaves, enslaving, enslaved) To make someone a slave.

ensnare (ensnares, ensnaring, ensnared) To catch in a trap.

ensure (ensures, ensuring, ensured) To make certain.

entangle (entangles, entangling, entangled) To tangle up. **entanglement.**

enter (enters, entering, entered) 1. To go in, to come in. 2. To write something in a book. *Enter your names in the register.* 3. To become a competitor in a race, competition, or examination.

enterprise A spirit of adventure, willingness to try something difficult.

enterprising Adventurous, showing enterprise.

entertain (entertains, entertaining, entertained) 1. To amuse someone, to give him enjoyment. 2. To have people as guests and give them food and drink. **entertainment.**

enthusiasm Keenness, a strong and lively interest in something. **enthusiastic, enthusiastically, enthusiast.**

entice (entices, enticing, enticed) To tempt, to attract, to persuade.

entire Whole, complete, not broken. **entirely.**

entitled 1. Called. *I read a book entitled 'Robinson Crusoe'.* 2. *To be entitled to something*, to have a right to it.

entrance[1] (pronounced *en*trance) (entrances) 1. A way in. *Please pay at the entrance.* 2. Coming in. *The crowd cheered the entrance of the home team.*

entrance[2] (pronounced en*trance*) (entrances, entrancing, entranced) To enchant, to give someone great delight as if by magic.

entrant (entrants) Someone who enters a race, competition, or examination.

entreat (entreats, entreating, entreated) To ask very seriously.

entrust (entrusts, entrusting, entrusted) To give something to someone to look after. *I'm entrusting this money to you.*

entry (entries) 1. Entering. 2. A way in, an entrance.

entwine (entwines, entwining, entwined) To twist together.

envelop (envelops, enveloping, enveloped) To wrap something up.

envelope (envelopes) A paper wrapper with a flap such as is used to hold letters.

enviable Liable to cause envy.

environment (environments) Surroundings.

envy[1] A bitter feeling because of someone else's good fortune. **envious, enviously.**

envy[2] (envies, envying, envied) To feel envy.

epic (epics) 1. A heroic story. 2. A grand spectacular film.

epidemic (epidemics) A rapidly-spreading outbreak of illness.

epilepsy A disease causing fits. **epileptic.**

epilogue (epilogues) Words spoken or written at the end of something.

episode (episodes) 1. An incident that is one of a series of events. 2. One programme in a radio or television serial.

epistle (epistles) A letter, a written message. *The Epistles of St. Paul.*

epitaph (epitaphs) The words written on a tomb.

equal[1] 1. The same in number, size or value. 2. *To be equal to a task*, to be fully able to do it. **equally.**

equal[2] (equals, equalling, equalled) To be the same in number, size, or value. **equality.**

equalize (equalizes, equalizing, equalized) 1. To make equal. 2. To score the goal which makes the scores equal. **equalizer.**

equator An imaginary line round the earth half way between the North and South Poles. **equatorial.**

equidistant The same distance apart.

equilateral With sides of equal length.

equilibrium Balance.

equip (equips, equipping, equipped) To provide someone or something with the things needed for a particular purpose.

equipment Things needed for a particular purpose. *Deep-sea diving equipment.*

equivalent Equal in value or meaning. *'Merci' is the French equivalent of 'thank you'.*

era (eras) A period of history, an age.

eradicate (eradicates, eradicating, eradicated) To get rid of something completely.

erase (erases, erasing, erased) To rub out. eraser.

erect [1] (erects, erecting, erected) To build, to raise, to set up. erection.

erect [2] Upright. erectly.

ermine 1. A stoat with its fur turned white in winter. 2. This fur.

erode (erodes, eroding, eroded) To wear away. erosion.

err (errs, erring, erred) To do wrong, to make mistakes.

errand (errands) A small job which a person is sent to do.

erratic Unpredictable, irregular, liable to do unexpected things. erratically.

error (errors) A mistake. *In error*, by mistake.

erupt (erupts, erupting, erupted) To burst out. *The volcano erupted*, it poured out smoke and molten lava. eruption.

escalate (escalates, escalating, escalated) To become steadily greater or more serious.

escalator (escalators) A moving staircase.

escapade (escapades) A reckless or foolish adventure.

escape [1] (escapes, escaping, escaped) 1. To get out, to become free. 2. To avoid something. *To escape capture*.

escape [2] (escapes) 1. The act of escaping. 2. A means of escaping. *A fire-escape*.

escort [1] (pronounced *es*cort) (escorts) 1. A group of armed guards. 2. A companion, protector, or guard.

escort [2] (pronounced es*cort*) (escorts, escorting, escorted) To act as an escort.

Eskimo (Eskimos) A member of a race living in the American polar regions.

especial Special. especially.

espionage Spying.

esplanade (esplanades) A promenade.

Esq. Short for Esquire, used in addressing letters to men. *John Smith, Esq.*

essay (essays) A short piece of writing on a subject.

essence (essences) 1. The essential part of something. 2. A concentrated flavouring.

essential Absolutely necessary. essentially.

establish (establishes, establishing, established) To set something up, to get something generally accepted.

establishment (establishments) 1. Establishing. 2. A shop, office, or other place where business is carried on.

estate (estates) 1. An area of land on which houses, flats, or factories are built. *A housing estate*. 2. An area of land owned by one person. 3. A person's total possessions. *When the old man died, he left his estate to his son*.

estate agent A person who arranges the buying and selling of houses and land.

estate car A car with a van-shaped body and a door at the back.

esteemed Highly valued.

estimate [1] (estimates, estimating, estimated) To guess, to calculate approximately. estimation.

estimate [2] (estimates) 1. A judgement. 2. A calculation.

estuary (estuaries) A wide mouth of a river into which the tide flows.

etcetera (often shortened to etc.) And so on, and other things.

eternal Never ending. eternally.

eternity Time without end.

ethereal 1. Airy, heavenly. 2. Light and delicate.

eucalyptus An Australian tree. It provides an oil which is used to treat colds.

Eurasian (Eurasians) A person with one European parent and one Asian parent.

European Of Europe.

evacuate (evacuates, evacuating, evacuated) To move people or things out of a place or area. **evacuation.**

evade (evades, evading, evaded) 1. To get out of the way of something. 2. To find a way of avoiding doing something. *He was fined for evading payment of his bus fare.* **evasion, evasive.**

evangelist (evangelists) A preacher of the Christian gospel. **evangelism.**

evaporate (evaporates, evaporating, evaporated) 1. To change from liquid into steam or vapour, to dry up. 2. *Evaporated milk*, thick unsweetened tinned milk. **evaporation.**

evasion, evasive *See* **evade.**

eve (eves) The day before a great day. *Christmas Eve.*

even[1] 1. A word used for adding special emphasis to what is being said in such expressions as: *He was rude even to the headmaster. She never even wrote me a letter. Even the teacher could not reach it.* 2. *Even if*, although. 3. *Even so*, nevertheless, in spite of this.

even[2] 1. Smooth, flat, regular. 2. Equal. 3. *An even number*, a number that can be divided exactly by two. **evenly, evenness.**

even[3] (evens, evening, evened) To make something smooth or equal.

evening (evenings) The time between the end of the afternoon and night.

event (events) 1. A happening, an occurrence of some importance. 2. A competition in an athletics programme.

ever 1. At any time. *Nothing ever happens in our street.* 2. At all times. 3. *For ever*, always. 4. This word is also used for emphasis in such expressions as: *He is ever so rich.*

evergreen Having green leaves all the year round. *An evergreen tree.*

everlasting Going on for a long time, lasting for ever.

evermore For all time.

every All, each. *Every child must go to school.* **everybody, everyone, everything.**

everyday Ordinary.

everywhere In all places.

evict (evicts, evicting, evicted) To make somebody move out of a house. **eviction.**

evidence 1. Anything that gives reason to believe something. 2. *To give evidence*, to say what one knows in a lawcourt.

evident Plain, clear, obvious. **evidently.**

evil[1] Wicked, sinful, bad. **evilly.**

evil[2] (evils) 1. A sin. *An evil-doer*, a sinner. 2. A bad thing, a disaster.

evolution The process by which animals and plants are believed to have developed over many millions of years from very simple forms of life. **evolutionary.**

evolve (evolves, evolving, evolved) To develop naturally and gradually.

ewe (ewes) A female sheep.

exact Perfectly correct, accurate. **exactly, exactness.**

exaggerate (exaggerates, exaggerating, exaggerated) To say that something is larger, better, worse, or in some other way more impressive than it really is. **exaggeration.**

exam (exams) (informal) An examination.

examination (examinations) 1. A test of someone's knowledge or skill. 2. A close inspection. *An examination of the wreckage revealed the cause of the crash.*

examine (examines, examining, examined) 1. To test, to set an examination. 2. To look closely at something. examiner.

example (examples) 1. Something which illustrates a general rule. 2. Something which shows what other similar things are like. *On Open Day we exhibit examples of our work.* 3. *To set a good example*, to behave in a way which others ought to copy. 4. *To make an example of someone*, to punish him as a warning to others.

exasperate (exasperates, exasperating, exasperated) To irritate someone, to make him angry. exasperation.

excavate (excavates, excavating, excavated) To dig out, to unearth. excavation, excavator.

exceed (exceeds, exceeding, exceeded) 1. To be greater than something. 2. To do more than is allowed or expected. *To exceed the speed limit.*

exceedingly Very much, extremely.

excel (excels, excelling, excelled) To be very good at something.

excellent Very good. excellently, excellence.

except Not including, with the exception of. *Everyone had a prize except me!*

exception (exceptions) 1. Someone or something that does not follow the general rule. 2. *To take exception to something*, to object to it.

exceptional Unusual. exceptionally.

excerpt (excerpts) A piece taken from a book, play, or film.

excess Extra, too much.

excessive Too great, more than necessary. excessively.

exchange¹ (exchanges, exchanging, exchanged) To give one thing and get another thing for it.

exchange² (exchanges) 1. The act of exchanging. 2. *A telephone exchange*, a central office or building where the telephone lines in a particular area are connected.

exchequer *The Chancellor of the Exchequer*, the minister in the British government who is responsible for the country's money affairs.

excite (excites, exciting, excited) To stir up somebody's feelings, to make somebody or something become lively and active. excitable, excitability, excitement.

exclaim (exclaims, exclaiming, exclaimed) To shout out. exclamation.

exclamation mark The punctuation mark ! .

exclude (excludes, excluding, excluded) To shut somebody or something out. exclusion.

excrete (excretes, excreting, excreted) To pass waste matter out of the body. excrement.

excruciating Very painful. excruciatingly.

excursion (excursions) An outing.

excuse¹ (excuses) A reason given to explain why something wrong has been done.

excuse² (excuses, excusing, excused) 1. To allow somebody not to do something. *He was excused from swimming because of his cold.* 2. To say that somebody is not to be blamed for something, to forgive him. excusable, excusably.

execute (executes, executing, executed) To kill somebody officially as a punishment. execution, executioner.

executive (executives) A manager or other senior person in a business firm.

exercise[1] (exercises) 1. Using one's body. *Exercise keeps one healthy.* 2. Something done for practice or training. *Piano exercises.*

exercise[2] (exercises, exercising, exercised) 1. To take exercise, to do exercises. 2. *To exercise an animal*, to make it do something active. 3. To use. *To exercise patience.*

exertion (exertions) Effort.

exhaust[1] 1. The stale, smelly fumes that are given out from an engine. 2. The pipe these fumes come out of.

exhaust[2] (exhausts, exhausting, exhausted) 1. To use something up completely. 2. To make somebody very tired. exhaustion.

exhaustive Thorough.

exhibit (exhibits, exhibiting, exhibited) To put something on show.

exhibition (exhibitions) A collection of things attractively arranged for people to look at.

exile[1] (exiles, exiling, exiled) To banish, to send someone away from his own country.

exile[2] (exiles) 1. A person who is exiled. 2. *In exile*, living away from one's own country.

exist (exists, existing, existed) 1. To be, to live, to be real. *Do ghosts exist?* 2. To keep going, to live. *You can't exist without food.* existence.

exit (exits) 1. A way out. 2. *Exit Hamlet*, Hamlet leaves the stage.

exorbitant Much too high. *Exorbitant prices.*

expand (expands, expanding, expanded) 1. To become larger. 2. To make something larger. expansion.

expanse (expanses) A wide area. expansive, expansively.

expect (expects, expecting, expected) 1. To think that something is likely to happen. *I expect it will rain later.* 2. To think that something ought to happen. *Our teacher expects us to work hard.* 3. To think that someone or something is likely to come. *We are expecting visitors for tea.* 4. To be expecting a baby, to be pregnant.

expectant 1. Expecting. 2. *An expectant mother*, a woman who is expecting a baby.

expedition (expeditions) A journey with a definite purpose.

expel (expels, expelling, expelled) To turn someone out, to send him out by force. expulsion.

expenditure Spending.

expense (expenses) Cost.

expensive Costly, high priced.

experience[1] (experiences) 1. Gaining knowledge or skill by doing and seeing things. 2. An event which has taught a person something.

experience[2] (experiences, experiencing, experienced) To feel, to suffer, to have experience of something.

experienced Skilled and knowledgeable.

experiment[1] (experiments) A test or trial made so that the results can be studied. experimental, experimentally.

experiment[2] (experiments, experimenting, experimented) To make an experiment.

expert[1] Skilful. expertly, expertness.

expert[2] (experts) A person with a special skill or training in something.

expire (expires, expiring, expired) 1. To come to an end. *His permit expires next month.* 2. To die.

explain (explains, explaining, explained) 1. To make something plain to someone else. 2. To account for something. explanation, explanatory.

explode (explodes, exploding, exploded) 1. To go off with a loud bang. 2. To set off a bomb.

exploit[1] (pronounced *ex*ploit) (exploits) A bold and exciting adventure.

exploit[2] (pronounced ex*ploit*) (exploits, exploiting, exploited) 1. To use something to the full. 2. To make selfish use of something or somebody.

explore (explores, exploring, explored) To go through unknown areas in order to make discoveries. explorer, exploration.

explosion (explosions) 1. A loud bang. 2. The setting off of an explosive.

explosive [1] (explosives) A substance that will explode.

explosive [2] Liable to explode. explosively.

export [1] (pronounced *ex*port) (exports) Something that is sent abroad to be sold.

export [2] (pronounced ex*port*) (exports, exporting, exported) To send goods abroad to be sold. exporter.

expose (exposes, exposing, exposed) To uncover, to display, to make known. exposure.

express [1] (expresses) A fast train.

express [2] (expresses, expressing, expressed) To make something known by speech, writing, or actions. *To express oneself*, to say what one means. expressive.

expression (expressions) 1. A look on someone's face. 2. A word or a phrase. 3. *To read with expression*, to read aloud in a way that shows the feeling and the meaning of the words. expressionless.

expulsion *See* expel.

exquisite Very beautiful, very well made, delicate. exquisitely.

extend (extends, extending, extended) 1. To make longer, to stretch out. 2. To stretch, to reach. 3. To offer. *We extend a warm welcome to our guests*. extension.

extensive Stretching for a long way. extensively.

extent 1. The distance something extends, its length or area. 2. *To some extent*, partly. *To a great extent*, mostly, largely.

exterior (exteriors) The outside of something.

exterminate (exterminates, exterminating, exterminated) To destroy completely. extermination.

external Outside. externally.

extinct 1. No longer in existence. *The dinosaur is extinct*. 2. *An extinct volcano*, one that is no longer active.

extinguish (extinguishes, extinguishing, extinguished) To put out a fire or a light. extinguisher.

extra Additional, more than usual.

extract [1] (pronounced ex*tract*) (extracts, extracting, extracted) To pull out, to take out. extraction.

extract [2] (pronounced *ex*tract) (extracts) A short piece taken from a book, play, or film.

extraordinary Remarkable, unusual. extraordinarily.

extravagant Foolishly expensive, wasteful. extravagantly.

extreme [1] 1. Farthest possible. *The extreme tip of the island*. 2. Not moderate, very strong, as much as possible. *Extreme enthusiasm*.

extreme [2] (extremes) 1. The furthest point of something. 2. *Extremes*, opposites. *The extremes of heat and cold*. 3. *In the extreme*, very much.

extremely Very.

exuberant In high spirits, overflowing with life. exuberantly, exuberance.

exult (exults, exulting, exulted) To rejoice, to triumph. exultant, exultantly, exultation.

eye [1] (eyes) 1. The organ of the body with which we see. eyeball, eyebrow, eyelash, eyelid. 2. A small hole. *The eye of a needle*.

eye [2] (eyes, eyeing, eyed) To view, to watch.

eye-shadow Make-up for the eyelids.

eyesight The power of seeing.

eyesore (eyesores) Something that is ugly to look at.

eye-witness (eye-witnesses) A person who actually saw the event he is describing.

eyrie (eyries) An eagle's nest.

Ff

fable (fables) A short story. The characters are usually animals. *Aesop's fables.*

fabric (fabrics) Cloth, material.

fabulous 1. Legendary, occurring in stories. *Fabulous monsters.* 2. (informal) Wonderful. fabulously.

face[1] (faces) 1. The front part of the head. 2. An expression. *A straight face,* a serious expression. 3. The front surface of anything. *The face of a cliff.*

face[2] (faces, facing, faced) 1. To look in a certain direction, to have the front in a certain direction. *Our house faces south.* 2. To look at something firmly or bravely. *To face danger.*

facetious Trying to be funny. facetiously.

fact (facts) Something that is known to be true. factual.

factory (factories) A building where things are made by machinery.

faddy Fussy about food.

fade (fades, fading, faded) 1. To lose colour or freshness. *Faded flowers.* 2. To disappear gradually.

fag (fags) (informal) A cigarette.

Fahrenheit A scale for measuring temperature with the freezing-point of water at 32 degrees and the boiling-point at 212 degrees.

fail (fails, failing, failed) 1. To be unsuccessful. 2. To come to an end, to become weak or useless. 3. To neglect to do something. *We failed to clean our windows.* failure.

failing (failings) A fault, a weakness.

faint[1] (fainter, faintest) 1. Weak, dim, not clear. *Faint sounds. Faint colours. Faint shapes.* 2. Nearly unconscious, exhausted. *Faint with hunger.* 3. *Faint-hearted,* timid, cowardly. faintly, faintness.

faint[2] (faints, fainting, fainted) To lose consciousness for a short time.

fair[1] (fairs) 1. A group of outdoor entertainments including roundabouts, stalls, and sideshows. *A fun-fair.* fair-ground. 2. A market, bazaar, or exhibition.

fair[2] (fairer, fairest) 1. Light in colour, blond. *Fair hair.* 2. Honest, keeping to the rules. *A fair referee.* 3. Moderate, quite good. *A fair number.* 4. Favourable. *A fair wind.* 5. *A fair copy,* a neat, clean copy. 6. (old-fashioned) Beautiful. *A fair maiden.*

fairly 1. Honestly, without cheating. 2. Moderately.

fairy (fairies) An imaginary creature who can do magic. fairyland, fairy-tale.

faith (faiths) 1. Trust, strong belief. 2. A religion. *The Christian faith.* 3. *In good faith,* sincerely, trustingly.

faithful Loyal, true, reliable. faithfully, faithfulness.

fake[1] (fakes, faking, faked) To make a copy of something valuable or interesting and pretend to others that it is real.

fake[2] (fakes) Something that is faked.

falcon (falcons) A kind of hawk. falconer, falconry.

fall[1] (falls, falling, fell, fallen) 1. To drop down, to come down. *Rain falls.* 2. To become lower. *The temperature falls at night.* 3. To be captured. *The city fell after a long siege.* 4. To die. *King Harold fell at the Battle of Hastings.* 5. To happen. *My birthday fell on a Sunday this year.* 6. To become. *To fall ill.* 7. *To fall back,* to retreat. 8. *To fall behind,* to fail to keep level. 9. *To fall out,* to quarrel. 10. *To fall through,* not to happen.

fall[2] (falls) 1. The act of falling. 2. (American) Autumn. 3. *Falls,* a waterfall.

fallacy (fallacies) A false idea.

fall-out Dangerous radioactive dust from a nuclear explosion.

false 1. Not true, wrong. 2. Deceitful, treacherous. 3. Not genuine, not real. falsely, falseness.

falsehood (falsehoods) A lie.

falter (falters, faltering, faltered) To move or speak in a hesitating manner.

fame 1. Reputation. 2. Being famous.

familiar 1. Well known. 2. Common. 3. Friendly. **familiarly, familiarity.**

family (families) 1. A mother, a father, and their children. 2. A group of people who are closely related. 3. Any group of things or creatures which are in some way similar or related. 4. *Family planning*, deciding how many babies to have and when to have them. 5. *A family tree*, a diagram showing how people in a family are related.

famine (famines) A severe shortage of food.

famished Very hungry.

famous Well known, known to a lot of people.

fan[1] (fans) 1. A device for fanning oneself. 2. A device for blowing air.

fan[2] (fans, fanning, fanned) 1. To send a draught of air on something. 2. *To fan out*, to spread out like an open fan.

fan[3] (fans) An enthusiastic supporter. *A football fan.*

fanatic (fanatics) A person who is violently enthusiastic about something. **fanatically.**

fancy[1] 1. Decorated. *A fancy handkerchief.* 2. *To wear fancy dress*, to dress up in unusual clothes for amusement.

fancy[2] (fancies, fancying, fancied) 1. To imagine. **fanciful.** 2. To have a desire for something. *I fancy chicken for dinner.* 3. (informal) *He fancies himself*, he has a high opinion of himself.

fancy[3] 1. Imagination. 2. *To take a fancy to something*, to become fond of it.

fanfare (fanfares) A short, loud burst of music on trumpets.

fang (fangs) A long sharp tooth.

fantastic 1. Strange, unreal. 2. (informal) Wonderful. **fantastically.**

fantasy (fantasies) Something imagined, something which is more like a dream than real life.

far (farther, farthest) 1. A long way. *Do you live far away?* 2. Much. *Robert is a far better batsman than I am.* 3. *Far and away*, by a large amount. 4. Distant, opposite. *The far side of the field.* 5. *The Far East*, the countries of eastern Asia.

far-away Distant, remote. *Far-away places.*

farce (farces) A ridiculous comedy. **farcical.**

fare (fares) The money paid by passengers who travel by public transport.

farewell Good-bye.

far-fetched Unlikely, hard to believe.

farm (farms) 1. An area of land used to grow crops or to produce meat, milk, or eggs. 2. The buildings on a farm. **farmer, farming, farmhouse, farmyard.**

farther, farthest *See* far.

farthing (farthings) A small old coin.

fascinate (fascinates, fascinating, fascinated) To charm, to be very attractive to someone. **fascination.**

fashion (fashions) 1. The way or style in which clothes or other things are made at a particular time. **fashionable, fashionably.** 2. A way of doing something. *Don't giggle in that silly fashion!*

fast[1] (faster, fastest) 1. Quick. *A fast train.* 2. Quickly. *Don't talk so fast!* 3. Ahead of time. *The clock is 5 minutes fast.* 4. Firm, fixed. *To make fast*, to fasten. 5. Firmly. *The ship was stuck fast on the rocks.*

fast[2] (fasts, fasting, fasted) To go without food.

fasten (fastens, fastening, fastened) To tie, to attach, to fix firmly. **fastener.**

fastidious Choosing with very great care. **fastidiously.**

fat[1] 1. The white, greasy substance in meat. 2. Any of the oily, greasy substances used in cooking, such as butter, margarine, and lard. **fatty.**

fat[2] (fatter, fattest) 1. Having too much flesh on the body. 2. Thick. 3. Oily, full of fat. **fatness.**

fatal Causing death or disaster. **fatally.**

fatality (fatalities) A disaster that causes someone's death.

fate 1. Something that is bound to happen. **fated.** 2. Death or disaster. *What a terrible fate!*

father (fathers) A male parent. **fatherly, fatherhood, fatherless.**

fathom (fathoms) A unit for measuring the depth of water, 6 feet or nearly two metres.

fatigue Tiredness, weariness.

fatten (fattens, fattening, fattened) 1. To make fat. 2. To become fat.

fault (faults) A mistake, something which is not as it should be. **faulty.**

favour (favours) 1. Goodwill, friendliness. 2. A kind deed. *To do someone a favour.* 3. *Out of favour*, unpopular. 4. *To be in favour of something*, to like it, to support it. 5. *In my favour*, to my advantage. **favourable, favourably.**

favourite Liked the best. **favouritism.**

fawn (fawns) 1. A young deer. 2. A light colour between yellow and brown.

fear[1] (fears) Being afraid or worried, the feeling of a person who is facing danger or pain. **fearful, fearfully, fearless, fearlessly, fearlessness.**

fear[2] (fears, fearing, feared) To be afraid or anxious.

fearsome Frightful, dreadful.

feasible Possible, able to be done.

feast (feasts) 1. A large meal for a number of people. 2. A religious anniversary.

feat (feats) A deed which requires courage, cleverness, or strength.

feather (feathers) One of the growths which cover a bird's skin.

feather-brained Silly.

feathery Light and soft.

feature (features) 1. Any of the parts of the face, such as the eyes, nose, or chin. 2. An important or noticeable part of something.

3. A special film, television programme, or newspaper article.

February The second month of the year.

fee (fees) A payment, charge, or subscription.

feeble (feebler, feeblest) Weak, not energetic. **feebly, feebleness.**

feed (feeds, feeding, fed) 1. To give food to someone. *To feed a baby.* **feeding-bottle, feeder.** 2. To eat.

feel (feels, feeling, felt) 1. To touch. 2. To explore with the hands or fingers. *He felt his way round the dark room.* 3. To seem to the touch. *The cat's coat feels warm and smooth.* 4. To experience something. *To feel pain.* 5. To think. *I feel that school holidays should be longer.* 6. *I feel happy*, I am aware of being happy. 7. *I feel like a cup of tea*, I should enjoy one.

feeler (feelers) A projecting part on the head of some insects, used for feeling with.

feeling (feelings) 1. Something felt in the mind or in the body. *A feeling of happiness. A feeling of hunger.* 2. *To hurt someone's feelings*, to offend him.

feet *See* **foot.**

feign (feigns, feigning, feigned) To pretend.

fell[1] *See* **fall**[1].

fell[2] (fells) Wild, hilly country in the north of England.

fell[3] (fells, felling, felled) To cut down, to knock down.

fellow (fellows) 1. (informal) A man, a boy. 2. A person who belongs to the same group. *He does not like his fellow pupils.*

fellowship 1. Friendliness. 2. Doing things together.

felt[1] *See* **feel.**

felt² 1. A kind of thick woollen material. 2. *A felt-tipped pen*, a pen with a fibre point instead of a nib.

female (females) 1. A woman, a girl. 2. Any creature which can give birth to babies or lay eggs.

feminine Belonging to women, suitable for women.

fen (fens) An area of low, marshy ground.

fence¹ (fences) A barrier round a garden or field, or along a roadside.

fence² (fences, fencing, fenced) 1. To put a fence round something. 2. To practise fighting with foils.

fend (fends, fending, fended) 1. *To fend something off*, to keep it away from oneself. 2. *To fend for oneself*, to look after oneself.

fender (fenders) A low guard round a fireplace.

ferment (ferments, fermenting, fermented) To give off many tiny bubbles because of the action of substances such as yeast.

fern (ferns) A kind of plant. Some ferns have feathery leaves.

ferocious Fierce, savage, cruel. ferociously, ferocity.

ferret (ferrets) A small animal used for hunting rats and rabbits.

ferry¹ (ferries, ferrying, ferried) To carry people or goods across a river or channel.

ferry² (ferries) 1. A ship or aircraft used for ferrying. 2. The place from which a ferry starts.

fertile Fruitful, producing good crops. fertility.

fertilize (fertilizes, fertilizing, fertilized) To make fertile. fertilizer.

fervent Very enthusiastic. fervently, fervour.

fester (festers, festering, festered) To fill with poisonous pus. *A festering wound.*

festival (festivals) 1. A time when some event is celebrated. 2. A time when special exhibitions and entertainments are put on. festive, festivity.

festooned Decorated with streamers or garlands.

fetch (fetches, fetching, fetched) 1. To go for something and bring it back. 2. To be sold for a price. *How much would my watch fetch?*

fetching Attractive, charming. fetchingly.

fête (fêtes) A festival with side-shows, competitions, and entertainments.

fetters Prisoners' chains.

feud (feuds) A long-lasting quarrel.

fever (fevers) An illness with a high temperature and restlessness. feverish, feverishly.

few (fewer, fewest) 1. Not many. 2. *A few*, some, a small number. 3. *A good few* or *quite a few*, a moderate number.

fiancé (fiancés) A man engaged to be married.

fiancée (fiancées) A woman engaged to be married.

fiasco (fiascos) A complete failure.

fib¹ (fibs) (informal) A lie.

fib² (fibs, fibbing, fibbed) (informal) To tell a lie. fibber.

fibre (fibres) 1. A tiny, fine thread. 2. A mass of fibres. fibrous, fibre-board, fibre-glass.

fickle Changeable.

fiction 1. Something imagined or made up. 2. Stories and novels. fictitious.

fiddle¹ (fiddles) A violin.

fiddle² (fiddles, fiddling, fiddled) 1. To play a fiddle. 2. To play with something with one's fingers, to fidget. 3. (informal) To cheat. fiddler.

fiddlesticks (informal) Nonsense.

fidelity Faithfulness.

fidget (fidgets, fidgeting, fidgeted) To move about nervously or restlessly.

field¹ (fields) 1. A piece of ground usually surrounded by a hedge or fence. *A corn field. A games field.* 2. A battlefield. 3. An area. 4. The runners in a race.

field² (fields, fielding, fielded) To catch or stop the ball in cricket and other games. fielder, fieldsman.

field-glasses Binoculars for use out of doors.

fiend (fiends) A devil, a very wicked person.

fierce (fiercer, fiercest) Violent, cruel, angry. fiercely, fierceness.

fiery 1. Blazing, very hot, very red. 2. Easily becoming angry.

fifteen 1. The number 15. fifteenth. 2. (fifteens) A Rugby Union football team.

fifth *See* five.

fifty (fifties) The number 50. fiftieth.

fifty-fifty (informal) 1. Half and half. 2. Shared equally.

fig (figs) A small pear-shaped fruit.

fight¹ (fights) A struggle, a battle, a fierce contest.

fight² (fights, fighting, fought) To have a fight.

figure¹ (figures) 1. One of the signs we use for numbers. 1, 2, 3, and so on are figures. 2. The shape of a person's body. 3. A diagram or illustration.

figure² (figures, figuring, figured) To work out, to calculate.

file (files) 1. A metal tool with a rough surface used for making things smooth. 2. A line of people one behind the other. *Single file.* 3. A box or folder to keep papers in.

fill (fills, filling, filled) 1. To make something full. *To fill a hole.* 2. To become full. *The bath slowly filled.* 3. To block up. *To fill a gap.* 4. *To fill in a form,* to write in all that is wanted. 5. *To fill out,* to become larger or fatter, to make larger or fatter.

fillet (fillets) A slice of meat or fish without bones.

filling (fillings) Something used to fill a hole or a gap.

filling station A place where petrol is sold.

film¹ (films) 1. A moving picture, such as those shown at cinemas. 2. The material used in a camera for taking photographs. 3. A very thin layer of something. *A film of oil on the water.* filmy.

film² (films, filming, filmed) To make a moving picture.

filter¹ (filters) A device that removes dirt or other substances from liquid or smoke which passes through it.

filter² (filters, filtering, filtered) 1. To pass something through a filter. 2. To merge with another line of traffic at a road junction.

filth Disgusting dirt. filthy, filthily, filthiness.

fin (fins) 1. One of the parts of a fish's body used for swimming and steering. 2. A device shaped like a fin on an aircraft, rocket, or other machine.

final¹ 1. At the end, coming last. *The final goal.* 2. Definite, unchangeable. *That's final!* finally, finality.

final² (finals) The last race or game in a series. *The Cup Final.* finalist.

finance (finances) Money affairs. financial.

finch (finches) A kind of small bird.

find (finds, finding, found) 1. To discover something, to come across it. 2. To know something from experience. *I find that peppermint humbugs are the best value for money.* 3. *To find out,* to learn. 4. *To find someone out,* to discover him doing wrong. 5. *To find someone guilty,* to declare him guilty. finder.

fine¹ (fines) Money which has to be paid as a punishment.

fine² (fines, fining, fined) To make someone pay a fine.

fine[3] (finer, finest) 1. *Fine weather*, bright weather without rain. 2. Very thin. *Fine wire*. 3. In very tiny pieces. *Fine sand*. 4. Delicate and beautiful. *Fine embroidery*. 5. Pure. *Fine gold*. 6. Good, pleasing. *We had a fine time*. 7. Smart. *Fine clothes*. finely.

finery A smart, showy set of clothes.

finger[1] (fingers) 1. A part of the body at the end of the hand. finger-nail, finger-tip, fingerprint. 2. A narrow piece of anything. *Fish fingers*.

finger[2] (fingers, fingering, fingered) To touch with the fingers.

finicky Making a lot of fuss about unimportant things.

finish[1] (finishes, finishing, finished) 1. To stop something, to bring it to an end. 2. To come to an end.

finish[2] The end, the final point.

Finn (Finns) A Finnish person.

Finnish Of Finland.

fiord (fiords) A narrow inlet of the sea between high cliffs.

fir (firs) A kind of evergreen tree. fir-cone, fir-tree.

fire[1] (fires) 1. A burning mass. *A forest fire*. fire-alarm, fire-engine, fire-escape, fire-extinguisher. 2. Coal or wood burning in a fire-place to keep people warm or to heat a boiler or an oven. *An electric fire, a gas fire*, similar devices using electricity or gas. firelight, fire-lighter, fire-place, fireside, firewood. 3. *On fire*, burning.

fire[2] (fires, firing, fired) 1. To set something on fire. 2. To bake clay in a kiln or oven. 3. *To fire a gun*, to shoot a bullet from a gun, to make it go off. 4. (informal) To dismiss someone from his job.

fire-arms Small guns, rifles, and revolvers.

fire-brigade (fire-brigades) A team of men organized to fight fires.

fireman (firemen) A member of a fire-brigade.

fire-proof 1. That does not catch fire. 2. That does not break if it is heated.

firework (fireworks) A device which burns attractively or noisily.

firm[1] (firmer, firmest) Solid, fixed, steady. firmly, firmness.

firm[2] (firms) A business. *My father works for a building firm*.

first[1] 1. Earliest, before all others. 2. The most important. *The First Eleven*. 3. *First aid*, help given to an injured person before the doctor comes. 4. *First-class* or *first-rate*, of the best quality, excellent. firstly.

first[2] Before something else, before everything else. *I'm coming out, but I must put my shoes on first*.

fish[1] (fishes *or* fish) A water animal which breathes with gills.

fish[2] (fishes, fishing, fished) To try to catch fish. fisherman, fish-hook, fishing-line, fishing-rod.

fishmonger (fishmongers) A shopkeeper who sells fish.

fist (fists) A tightly closed hand.

fit[1] (fitter, fittest) 1. Suitable, good enough. *Is this dress fit to wear?* 2. In good health, strong. *A sportsman must be fit*. fitness. 3. Ready. *I'm so tired I'm fit to drop*.

fit[2] (fits, fitting, fitted) 1. To be the right size and shape. 2. To put something into place. *To fit new tyres*.

fit[3] The way something fits. *This is a good fit*, it is the right shape and size.

fit[4] (fits) 1. A sudden attack of illness causing violent movements or making a person unconscious. 2. An outburst. *A fit of coughing*. 3. *By fits and starts*, irregularly.

fitting Suitable. fittingly.

five (fives) The number 5. fifth.

fiver (fivers) (informal) A five-pound note.

fix[1] (fixes, fixing, fixed) 1. To make something firm, to fasten it, to attach it. 2. To settle, to decide. *We've fixed a date for the party*. 3. *To fix one's eyes on something*, to look at it steadily. 4. *To fix up*, to arrange. 5. (informal) To mend. *Can the garage fix the car?*

fix[2] A great difficulty. *To be in a fix*.

fixture (fixtures) 1. Something which is fixed to a building and which is not movable.

2. A date fixed for a sports event such as a football match.

fizz (fizzes, fizzing, fizzed) To give off lots of little bubbles, to make a hissing, spluttering sound. **fizzy, fizzily, fizziness.**

fizzle (fizzles, fizzling, fizzled) 1. To fizz. 2. (informal) *To fizzle out*, to come to a feeble end.

flabby (flabbier, flabbiest) Soft and feeble, not firm. **flabbily, flabbiness.**

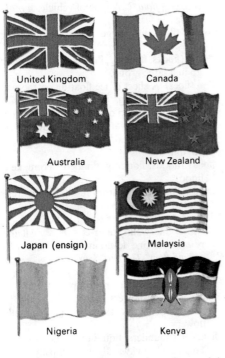

United Kingdom

Canada

Australia

New Zealand

Japan (ensign)

Malaysia

Nigeria

Kenya

flag¹ (flags) 1. A piece of coloured material used as a sign or signal. **flag pole, flagstaff.** 2. A little paper flag sold for charity. **flag-day.**

flag² (flags, flagging, flagged) 1. To signal with a flag. 2. To become tired or weak.

flagship (flagships) The chief ship of a fleet, the admiral's ship.

flagstone (flagstones) A paving-stone.

flake (flakes) A small, leaf-like piece of a substance. *Soap-flakes. Flakes of rust.* **flaky.**

flame¹ (flames) A tongue of fire, a jet of burning gas. **flame-thrower.**

flame² (flames, flaming, flamed) To give out flames, to burn.

flamingo (flamingos) A large, long-legged wading bird.

flan (flans) A kind of open tart.

flank (flanks) The side of something.

flannel (flannels) 1. A kind of soft cloth. 2. *Flannels*, trousers made of this. 3. *A face-flannel*, a piece of cloth used for washing oneself.

flap¹ (flaps, flapping, flapped) 1. To move a flat object up and down or from side to side. *The swan flapped his wings.* 2. To move like this. *The sail flapped in the breeze.*

flap² (flaps) A piece of material that hangs down from one edge, often to cover an opening. *The flap of an envelope.*

flare¹ (flares, flaring, flared) 1. To burn with a bright, unsteady flame. 2. *To flare up*, to become suddenly angry.

flare² (flares) A light or firework used as a signal.

flared Widening gradually. *A flared skirt*, one that is much wider at the lower edge than at the waist.

flash¹ (flashes) 1. A sudden short burst of flame or light. 2. *In a flash*, in an instant.

flash² (flashes, flashing, flashed) 1. To give out a flash or flashes. 2. To appear suddenly and disappear quickly. *The racing cars flashed past.*

flashy Bright and gaudy. *A flashy tie.*

flask (flasks) A kind of bottle.

flat¹ (flatter, flattest) 1. Level, spread out. *Flat on the ground.* 2. Smooth, without bumps. *A flat surface.* 3. Dull, uninteresting. *A flat voice.* 4. *To sing flat*, to sing below the proper note. 5. *A flat tyre*, a tyre with no air in it. 6. (informal) *Flat out*, at top speed.

flat² (flats) 1. A set of rooms for living in, usually on one floor of a building. 2. The sign ♭ in music.

flatten (flattens, flattening, flattened) 1. To make flat. 2. To become flat.

flatter (flatters, flattering, flattered) 1. To praise someone more than he deserves. 2. To make someone seem better or more attractive than he really is. **flattery.**

flavour[1] (flavours) The taste of something.

flavour[2] (flavours, flavouring, flavoured) To give something a flavour.

flaw (flaws) A weakness, a mistake, a crack.

flea (fleas) A small jumping insect that feeds on blood. **flea-bite.**

fledgeling (fledgelings) A young bird just ready to fly.

flee (flees, fleeing, fled) To run away.

fleece A sheep's woolly coat. **fleecy.**

fleet (fleets) A number of ships, aircraft, or vehicles.

flesh The soft substance between the skin and bones of animals.

flew *See* fly[1].

flex Insulated wire for electric current.

flexible 1. Easy to bend. 2. Easy to change. **flexibility.**

flick (flicks, flicking, flicked) To hit something lightly but sharply.

flicker (flickers, flickering, flickered) To burn or shine unsteadily.

flight (flights) 1. Flying. 2. A journey in an aircraft. 3. *A flight of stairs,* a set of stairs. 4. An escape, running away.

flimsy (flimsier, flimsiest) Thin, easily destroyed. **flimsily, flimsiness.**

flinch (flinches, flinching, flinched) To draw back, to wince.

fling (flings, flinging, flung) To throw something violently.

flint (flints) A very hard stone.

flip (flips, flipping, flipped) To flick.

flipper (flippers) 1. A limb used by water animals for swimming. 2. A device people can wear on their feet to help them to swim.

flit (flits, flitting, flitted) To move quickly but quietly.

float[1] (floats, floating, floated) 1. To stay on the surface of a liquid or in the air. *Wood floats on water.* 2. To make something float.

float[2] (floats) 1. An object designed to float. *A fishing float.* 2. A kind of vehicle. *A milk-float.*

flock[1] (flocks) A large group of sheep or birds.

flock[2] (flocks, flocking, flocked) To gather or go in a large group.

floe (floes) A sheet of ice floating on the sea.

flog (flogs, flogging, flogged) To beat violently with a whip or a stick.

flood[1] (floods) 1. Water spreading over what is usually dry land. 2. A large quantity of anything.

flood[2] (floods, flooding, flooded) To make a flood.

flood-lights Strong lamps used for lighting out of doors. **flood-lighting, flood-lit.**

floor (floors) 1. The part of a building on which one walks. **floor-boards.** 2. All the rooms on one level in a building. *The ground floor. The first floor.*

flop (flops, flopping, flopped) 1. To drop down suddenly. 2. To droop.

floral Made of flowers.

florist (florists) A shopkeeper who sells flowers.

flounder (flounders, floundering, floundered) To struggle awkwardly and clumsily.

flour A fine white powder made from wheat. It is used in cooking.

flourish (flourishes, flourishing, flourished) 1. To grow strongly, to be successful. 2. To wave something about. *He flourished his sword threateningly.*

flow (flows, flowing, flowed) 1. To move along in a stream. 2. To hang loosely. *Flowing hair.*

flower[1] (flowers) 1. The part of a plant which usually has colourful petals. 2. A flowering plant. flowery, flower-bed, flower-pot.

flower[2] (flowers, flowering, flowered) To produce flowers.

flown See fly[1].

flu Influenza.

fluent Flowing, skilful. fluently, fluency.

fluff Soft feathery or woolly stuff. fluffy.

fluid (fluids) A substance that flows easily, as liquids and gases do.

fluke (flukes) (informal) A lucky accident.

flung See fling.

fluorescent lighting Electric strip lighting.

fluoridation The addition of a chemical called fluoride to drinking water.

flush (flushes, flushing, flushed) 1. To blush. 2. To wash out a lavatory pan or a drain with a flood of water.

flustered Nervous and confused.

flute (flutes) A woodwind instrument.

flutter (flutters, fluttering, fluttered) To make quick flapping movements, to move restlessly.

fly[1] (flies, flying, flew, flown) 1. To go up in the air, to move along in the air, to be able to stay in the air. 2. To make something fly. *A pilot flies an aeroplane.* 3. To move very quickly. 4. To do something very suddenly. *To fly into a rage.* 5. To escape. flyer.

fly[2] (flies) A flying insect.

fly-over (fly-overs) A bridge carrying one road over another.

flywheel (flywheels) A type of heavy wheel used in machinery.

foal (foals) A young horse.

foam[1] Froth. foamy.

foam[2] (foams, foaming, foamed) To make foam, to bubble.

foam-rubber Spongy rubber.

fo'c'sle See forecastle.

focus (focuses, focusing, focused) 1. To adjust the lens of a camera, projector, telescope, or similar instrument in order to get a clear, sharp picture. 2. To concentrate on a single point.

fodder Food for cattle or horses.

foe (foes) An enemy.

foetus (foetuses) An embryo.

fog (fogs) Thick mist. foggy.

foil[1] (foils, foiling, foiled) To prevent.

foil[2] (foils) A thin sword used in fencing.

foil[3] A sheet of metal as thin as paper.

fold[1] (folds, folding, folded) 1. To double over, to bend part of a thing back on itself. 2. *To fold one's arms*, to cross one's arms in front of one's body.

fold[2] (folds) 1. A line where something is folded. 2. An enclosure for sheep.

folder (folders) A cover for loose papers.

foliage Leaves on trees and plants.

folk 1. People. 2. *Folk-dances, folk-songs, folk-tales*, dances, songs, and tales handed down from long ago, especially among country people.

follow (follows, following, followed) 1. To come or go after someone or something. follower. 2. To take someone or something as a guide. *Follow this road.* 3. To understand. *Did you follow what I said?* 4. To take an interest in something, to support. *Which team do you follow?* 5. *To follow something up*, to continue with it and go on to the next stage. follow-up.

folly Foolishness, stupidity.

fond Loving. *To be fond of someone*, to like him, to love him.

fondle (fondles, fondling, fondled) To touch lovingly.

fondly 1. Lovingly. 2. Foolishly.

font (fonts) A basin to hold water for baptism in a church.

food (foods) Anything which can be eaten, nourishment for people, animals, or plants.

fool[1] (fools) 1. A stupid person. 2. A jester.

fool[2] (fools, fooling, fooled) 1. To behave like a fool. 2. To trick or deceive someone.

foolhardy Rash, foolishly bold.

foolish Stupid, silly. foolishly.

foolproof So simple that even a fool cannot make a mistake.

foot (feet) 1. The part of the body on which people and animals walk. footprint, footstep, footpath. 2. The lowest part of anything. *The foot of a mountain.* 3. A measure of length, 12 inches or 30 centimetres.

football A game played with a large, air-filled ball. footballer.

footlights A row of lights across the front of the stage in a theatre.

footman (footmen) A man servant.

foot-plate (foot-plates) A platform for the driver and fireman on a steam locomotive.

for[1] 1. Intended to belong to. *This letter is for you.* 2. In place of. *I offer you new lamps for old!* 3. In defence of, in favour of. *He fought for his country.* 4. As far as, as long as. *We walked for five kilometres. They waited for two hours.* 5. Towards. *They sailed for the Pacific.* 6. Because of. *They could not see for smoke.* 7. At a cost of. *You can buy it for £1.*

for[2] Because, since.

forbid (forbids, forbidding, forbade, forbidden) 1. To tell someone not to do something. 2. Not to allow something.

forbidding Stern, threatening. forbiddingly.

force[1] (forces) 1. Strength, power, violence. forceful, forcefully. 2. A number of policemen or armed men. *The forces,* the army, navy, and air force.

force[2] (forces, forcing, forced) 1. To do something by strength or violence. 2. To compel.

forceps Special pincers used by a surgeon or dentist.

ford (fords) A shallow place where people can wade across a river.

fore *To the fore,* in front.

foreboding (forebodings) A feeling that trouble is coming.

forecast[1] (forecasts, forecasting, forecast) To say beforehand what is likely to happen.

forecast[2] (forecasts) Saying what is likely to happen. *The weather forecast.*

forecastle (forecastles) or fo'c'sle (fo'c'sles) 1. A raised deck at the bow of a ship. 2. The part of a ship near the bow, where the crew lives.

forefathers Ancestors.

foregone *A foregone conclusion,* an ending or result that can easily be foreseen.

foreground The part of a view nearest to the person who is looking at it.

forehead (foreheads) The part of one's face just above the eyebrows.

foreign 1. Belonging to another country. 2. Strange, not familiar.

foreigner (foreigners) A person from another country.

foreleg (forelegs) A front leg.

foreman (foremen) A man in charge of a group of workmen.

foremost Most important.

foresee (foresees, foreseeing, foresaw, foreseen) To see in advance that something will happen. foresight.

forest (forests) A large area of land covered with trees. forester, forestry.

foretaste A small taste of what something is going to be like.

foretell (foretells, foretelling, foretold) To say what will happen in the future.

forethought Careful planning.

forfeit[1] (forfeits, forfeiting, forfeited) To pay a penalty because of wrongdoing, or because of the rules of a game.

forfeit[2] (forfeits) Something forfeited as a penalty.

forgave *See* forgive.

forge[1] (forges) A blacksmith's workshop.

forge[2] (forges, forging, forged) 1. To shape metal by heating and hammering. 2. To make a copy of something to deceive people. forger, forgery. 3. *To forge ahead*, to get ahead by making great efforts.

forget (forgets, forgetting, forgot, forgotten) 1. To fail to remember something, to overlook it. 2. *To forget oneself*, to behave in a thoughtless and unworthy way. forgetful, forgetfully, forgetfulness.

forget-me-not (forget-me-nots) A small blue flower.

forgive (forgives, forgiving, forgave, forgiven) To cease to be angry with someone. forgiveness.

fork (forks) 1. A device with points or prongs used in eating. 2. An instrument with prongs used for digging, hay-making, and so on. 3. A place where something divides into branches. *A fork in the road*.

forked Divided into branches.

forlorn Unhappy, uncared for. forlornly.

form[1] (forms) 1. Shape, appearance. *The wicked witch appeared in the form of a toad.* 2. Kind, variety. *Caning is a painful form of punishment!* 3. A class in school. 4. A bench. 5. A printed paper with spaces to be filled in. 6. *In good form*, fit and successful.

form[2] (forms, forming, formed) 1. To give a shape to something, to make, to create. 2. To take shape, to develop.

formal Stiff and proper, keeping to certain rules and customs.

formality 1. Formal behaviour. 2. (formalities) Something which has to be done because of the rules.

formation 1. The forming of something. 2. A carefully arranged order or pattern. *Flying in formation.*

former 1. The first of two things just mentioned. 2. Of the past, earlier. *In former times.* formerly.

formless Shapeless.

formula (formulas) A way of writing mathematical or scientific information using letters, numbers, and signs.

forsake (forsakes, forsaking, forsook, forsaken) To abandon, to give up.

fort (forts) A fortified building.

forth Forwards, onwards.

forthcoming About to come, coming soon.

forthwith Immediately.

fortieth *See* forty.

fortify (fortifies, fortifying, fortified) To make stronger, to build defences. fortification.

fortitude Bravery.

fortnight (fortnights) A period of two weeks.

fortress (fortresses) A fort, a fortified town.

fortune (fortunes) 1. Chance, luck. fortunate, fortunately. 2. A large amount of money. 3. *To tell fortunes*, to tell people what is going to happen to them in the future. fortune-teller, fortune-telling.

forty (forties) The number 40. fortieth.

forward[1] 1. Towards the front, in the front. 2. Having made more than normal progress. *The crops are forward this year.* 3. Eager, too eager. forwardness.

forward[2] (forwards) A front-line player in football and other games.

forwards Onwards, towards the front.

fossil (fossils) The rock-like remains of a prehistoric animal or plant.

fossilized Turned into a fossil.

foster (fosters, fostering, fostered) To care for someone else's child as if he were a member of one's own family. foster-child, foster-mother, foster-home.

fought *See* fight [2].

foul [1] (fouler, foulest) 1. Filthy, disgusting.
2. Stormy, violent, rough. *Foul weather.*
3. *Foul play*, murder. foully, foulness.

foul [2] (fouls) A deliberate breaking of the
rules of a game.

found [1] *See* find.

found [2] (founds, founding, founded) 1. To
begin the building of something. *Romulus
and Remus are said to have founded Rome.*
founder. 2. *To be founded on something*, to
be based on it.

foundation (foundations) 1. Founding. 2. *The
foundations*, the strong base on which a
building is built.

foundry (foundries) A place where metal or
glass is melted and moulded.

fountain (fountains) A device which makes
jets of water.

fountain pen A pen which can be filled with a
supply of ink.

four (fours) The number 4. fourth, fourthly.

four-poster (four-posters) A bed with four
tall posts and curtains round it.

fourteen The number 14. fourteenth.

fowl (fowls) A bird, usually a farmyard cock
or hen.

fox (foxes) A wild animal of the dog family.

foxglove (foxgloves) A tall wild flower.

foxhound (foxhounds) A dog kept for fox-
hunting.

foyer (foyers) An entrance hall in a cinema
or some other large building.

fraction (fractions) 1. A small part of something. 2. In arithmetic, a number that is
not a whole unit, such as $\frac{1}{2}, \frac{2}{3}, \frac{7}{8}$. fractional,
fractionally.

fracture [1] (fractures) A break, a break in a
bone.

fracture [2] (fractures, fracturing, fractured) To
break, to crack.

fragile Easily broken. fragility.

fragment (fragments) A broken piece, a small
piece.

fragrant   Sweet-smelling. fragrantly, fra-
grance.

frail (frailer, frailest) Weak, fragile. frailty.

frame [1] (frames) 1. A firm, rigid structure
made of rods, bars, or girders. *The frame of
a tent.* framework. 2. An edging for a
picture. 3. *The human frame*, the body. 4. *A
frame of mind*, a state of mind.

frame [2] (frames, framing, framed) To put a
picture in a frame.

franc (francs) A unit of money in France and
other countries.

frank (franker, frankest) Honest, outspoken.
frankly, frankness.

franked Marked with a postmark.

frantic Wildly excited. frantically.

fraud (frauds) 1. Dishonesty. 2. (informal) A
cheat.

frayed Worn and ragged at the edge. fraying.

freak Not normal, very unusual. *A freak
storm.*

freckle (freckles) A small brown spot on the
skin. freckled.

free [1] (freer, freest) 1. Able to do what one
wants to do, able to move without hindrance. 2. To be had without paying. *A free
ride.* 3. Generous. *He's very free with his
money.* 4. Available, open. *Is the bathroom
free?* freely, freedom.

free [2] (frees, freeing, freed) To make free, to
set free.

free-wheel (free-wheels, free-wheeling, free-
wheeled) To ride along on a bicycle without turning the pedals.

freeze (freezes, freezing, froze, frozen) 1. To
change into ice, to become stiff and hard
with cold. 2. To be very cold, to feel very

cold. **3.** To make something very cold. **freezer.**

freezing-point (freezing-points) The temperature at which a liquid freezes.

freight Goods, cargo.

freighter (freighters) A cargo ship.

French Of France. **Frenchman, Frenchwoman.**

French window A long window which opens like a door.

frenzy Madness, wild excitement. **frenzied, frenziedly.**

frequent Happening often, numerous. **frequently, frequency.**

fresh (fresher, freshest) **1.** Newly made. *Fresh bread.* **2.** New or different. *Start a fresh page.* **3.** Not tinned or preserved. *Fresh fruit.* **4.** Cool and clean. *Fresh air.* **5.** Healthy-looking. *A fresh complexion.* **6.** *Fresh water*, water that is not salty. **freshly, freshness.**

freshen (freshens, freshening, freshened) To make something fresh, to become fresh.

fret (frets, fretting, fretted) To worry. **fretful, fretfully.**

fretsaw (fretsaws) A saw with a narrow blade for making fretwork.

fretwork Thin wood with patterns cut out of it.

friar (friars) A religious man who has vowed to live a life of poverty.

friction 1. Rubbing. **2.** Disagreement.

Friday (Fridays) The sixth day of the week.

fridge (fridges) (informal) A refrigerator.

friend (friends) **1.** A person whom one likes to talk to and go out with, a helpful, pleasant person. **2.** Someone who is not an enemy. *Who goes there, friend or foe?* **friendly, friendliness, friendship.**

frieze (friezes) A strip of pictures or designs along a wall.

frigate (frigates) A fast warship.

fright Sudden fear, terror.

frighten (frightens, frightening, frightened) To make someone afraid.

frightful (informal) **1.** Unpleasant. **2.** Very great. **frightfully.**

frill (frills) A decorative edging for clothes or curtains.

fringe (fringes) **1.** A decorative edging with many threads hanging loosely down. **2.** Front hair cut short and allowed to hang over the forehead. **3.** The edge of something. *The fringe of a crowd.*

fringed Having a fringe.

frisk (frisks, frisking, frisked) To move about playfully. **frisky, friskily, friskiness.**

fritter[1] (fritters) A slice of fruit or meat fried in batter.

fritter[2] (fritters, frittering, frittered) To waste something bit by bit.

frivolous Silly, not serious. **frivolously, frivolity.**

fro *To and fro*, backwards and forwards.

frock (frocks) A girl's or woman's dress.

frog (frogs) A small jumping animal which can live on land or in the water.

frogman (frogmen) A person with apparatus for under-water swimming.

frolic (frolics, frolicking, frolicked) To frisk, to play games.

from 1. Out of. *A traveller from Mars.* **2.** At a distance away. *We live one kilometre from the gasworks.* **3.** Since, ever since. *He has been a nuisance from the beginning of term.* **4.** Because of. *He's suffering from over-eating again!*

front (fronts) **1.** The most important side of a thing, the side which faces forwards. *The front of the house.* **2.** The part of a thing or place which is furthest forward. *It's cheaper* *in the cinema if you sit at the front.* 3. In a war, the place where the fighting is going on. 4. A road or promenade along the sea-shore.

frontier (frontiers) A boundary between two countries.

frost (frosts) 1. Freezing weather. 2. White, powdery ice which covers things in freezing weather. frosty, frostily, frostiness.

frostbite Injury done to a person's body by severe frost. frostbitten.

froth Masses of tiny bubbles. frothy.

frown (frowns, frowning, frowned)   To wrinkle one's forehead because one is angry or puzzled.

froze, frozen *See* freeze.

frugal Very economical, costing little. frugally.

fruit (fruit *or* fruits) 1. The part of a plant which contains the seeds and which is often used as food. 2. *A fruit cake*, a cake containing currants or other dried fruit. fruity.

fruitful 1. Bearing fruit. 2. Successful.

fruitless 1. Without fruit. 2. Unsuccessful.

frustrate (frustrates, frustrating, frustrated) To prevent someone from doing something. frustration.

fry (fries, frying, fried) To cook in hot fat. frying-pan, fryer.

fuddled Confused.

fudge A soft, sugary sweet.

fuel (fuels) Anything which is burnt to provide heat or power, such as coal, wood, or oil.

fug (informal) A stuffy atmosphere.

fugitive (fugitives) Someone who is running away.

fulfil (fulfils, fulfilling, fulfilled) 1. To carry something out successfully. *He fulfilled his promise.* 2. To satisfy. fulfilment.

full (fuller, fullest) 1. Holding as much or as many as possible. *The cinema was full.* 2. Containing a large number or amount. *The room was full of people I did not know.* 3. Complete, with nothing left out. *Give me the full facts.* 4. The maximum, the greatest possible. *Full speed ahead!* 5. *A full skirt*, a

skirt with lots of material hanging in folds. 6. *A full moon*, a moon that looks like a complete disc. fully, fullness.

full stop The punctuation mark . .

fumble (fumbles, fumbling, fumbled) To be clumsy with one's hands.

fume (fumes, fuming, fumed) 1. To give off fumes. 2. To be very angry.

fumes Strong-smelling gas or smoke.

fun 1. Amusement, enjoyment. 2. *To make fun of someone*, to make other people laugh at him.

function[1] (functions) 1. The special activity or purpose of something. *The function of a knife is to cut.* 2. A public event.

function[2] (functions, functioning, functioned) To work. *The telephone is not functioning.* functional.

fund (funds) A supply of money or other things, money to be used for a particular purpose.

fundamental Basic. fundamentally.

funeral (funerals) A ceremony held before a dead person is buried or cremated.

fungus (fungi) A kind of plant such as a mushroom or a toadstool.

funicular railway A cable railway.

funk (funks, funking, funked) (informal) To show fear, to try to avoid doing something because one is afraid.

funnel (funnels) 1. The chimney of a ship or steam-engine. 2. A device for pouring liquids into narrow openings.

funny (funnier, funniest) 1. Amusing, comical. 2. Strange, odd. funnily.

funny-bone (funny-bones) The sensitive part of a person's elbow.

fur[1] (furs) 1. The soft hair which covers certain animals. **furry.** 2. Skin from these animals used for clothing.

fur[2] 1. A chalky substance found inside kettles and water-pipes. 2. A rough coating on the tongue when a person is ill. **furred.**

furious Very angry. **furiously.**

furl (furls, furling, furled) To roll up a sail or umbrella.

furlong (furlongs) A measure of distance, 220 yards or 201 metres.

furnace (furnaces) A special fire-place for making a great heat.

furnish (furnishes, furnishing, furnished) To provide furniture.

furniture Tables, chairs, beds, cupboards, and other things needed in a house, school, or other building.

furrow (furrows) 1. A cut made in the ground by a plough. 2. A groove, a wrinkle.

further 1. To a greater distance, farther. 2. Also, in addition. 3. More, additional. *Can you give me any further information?*

furthermore Moreover, besides.

furthermost The most distant.

furthest To the greatest distance, farthest.

furtive Sly, stealthy. **furtively.**

fury Wild anger, rage. **furious, furiously.**

fuse[1] (fuses) 1. A safety device in an electric circuit. 2. A device for setting off an explosive.

fuse[2] (fuses, fusing, fused) To be put out of action because a fuse has melted.

fuselage (fuselages) The body of an aircraft.

fuss 1. Unnecessary excitement about unimportant things. 2. *To make a fuss of someone,* to do many kind things for him.

fussy (fussier, fussiest) 1. Making a fuss. 2. Having too many details. **fussily.**

futile Useless. **futility.**

future 1. The time to come. 2. What is going to happen in the time to come.

fuzzy (fuzzier, fuzziest) 1. Fluffy. 2. Blurred, indistinct.

Gg

gabble (gabbles, gabbling, gabbled) To talk quickly and indistinctly.

gable (gables) The triangular part of an outside wall between sloping roofs.

gadget (gadgets) A small useful tool or piece of machinery. *My pen-knife has a gadget for opening bottles.*

Gaelic An ancient language of Scotland and Ireland.

gag[1] (gags) Something used to gag someone.

gag[2] (gags, gagging, gagged) To stop up someone's mouth so that he cannot speak.

gaiety, gaily *See* gay.

gain[1] (gains, gaining, gained) 1. To obtain, to win, to get, to reach. 2. *To gain on someone,* to get nearer to him in a race.

gain[2] (gains) Something gained, profit.

gala (galas) A fête, a day of sports and entertainments.

galaxy (galaxies) A set or system of stars.

gale (gales) A very strong wind.

gallant 1. Brave, noble. 2. Polite to ladies. **gallantly, gallantry.**

galleon (galleons) A large ancient Spanish sailing ship.

gallery (galleries) 1. The highest balcony in a theatre. 2. A raised floor or platform over a part of a hall or church. 3. A long room or passageway. 4. *An art gallery,* a building used for displaying works of art.

galley (galleys) 1. A boat rowed by slaves or criminals in ancient times. **galley-slave.** 2. A ship's kitchen.

gallon (gallons) A unit of measure for liquids, 8 pints or 4·5 litres.

gallop[1] (gallops) 1. The fastest pace of a horse. 2. A fast ride on horseback.

gallop[2] (gallops, galloping, galloped) To go at a gallop.

gallows A wooden framework with a rope for hanging criminals.

galvanized iron Iron with a coating of zinc.

gamble (gambles, gambling, gambled) 1. To play a game for money. 2. To take great risks.

game[1] (games) 1. A form of playing, especially with rules, such as football and chess. 2. A scheme, a trick.

game[2] Wild animals or birds hunted for food or for sport. *Big game*, large animals such as tigers or elephants.

game[3] Brave, willing to go on.

gamekeeper (gamekeepers) A man employed to look after game animals or birds.

gammon A kind of ham or bacon.

gander (ganders) A male goose.

gang (gangs) A set of people who do things together. *A gang of robbers.*

gang-plank (gang-planks) A plank used for walking on or off a boat.

gangster (gangsters) A member of a gang of violent criminals.

gangway (gangways) 1. A way between rows of seats or people. 2. A movable bridge between a ship and the shore.

gaol (gaols) A prison. **gaoler.**

gap (gaps) An opening, a space, an interval of time.

gape (gapes, gaping, gaped) 1. To open one's mouth wide. 2. To stare in surprise.

garage (garages) 1. A building where a motor car is kept. 2. A place where cars may be serviced or repaired.

garbage Waste food, rubbish.

garbled Confused, misleading.

garden (gardens) A piece of ground for growing flowers, fruit, or vegetables. **gardener, gardening.**

gargle (gargles, gargling, gargled) To make a gurgling sound through liquid held in the back of the mouth.

gargoyle (gargoyles) A spout to carry water off the roof of a church. It is often carved like an ugly head.

garland (garlands) A wreath of flowers.

garlic An onion-like plant used for flavouring in cooking.

garment (garments) An article of clothing.

garrison (garrisons) Soldiers stationed in a town or fortress to defend it.

garter (garters) An elastic band used to keep a sock or stocking up.

gas[1] (gases) 1. Any air-like substance. 2. The inflammable gas which is used for heating and cooking. **gas-fire, gas-ring, gas-works.**

gas[2] (gases, gassing, gassed) To overcome someone with a poisonous gas.

gas[3] (American, informal) Gasoline, petrol.

gash (gashes) A long, deep cut.

gasoline (American) Petrol.

gasometer (gasometers) A large, round container storing gas for piping to houses and factories.

gasp[1] (gasps, gasping, gasped) To take short quick breaths, to breathe with difficulty.

gasp[2] (gasps) A gasping breath.

gastric Of the stomach. *Gastric flu.*

gate (gates) 1. A barrier on hinges used to close a gap in a wall or hedge. **gate-post.** 2. A way in or out of somewhere. **gateway.** 3. The number of people attending a football match.

gather (gathers, gathering, gathered) 1. To collect, to bring together. *To gather flowers*, to pick flowers. 2. To come together. *A crowd gathered.* 3. To understand, *I gather you have a birthday soon?*

gaudy (gaudier, gaudiest) Too bright and showy. **gaudily.**

gauge (gauges) 1. Size or measurement, especially the measurement between the two rails of a railway track. 2. An instrument for measuring size or strength.

gaunt Thin, lean.

gauntlet (gauntlets) A glove with a wide part that covers the wrist.

gauze Thin, transparent, net-like material.

gave See give.

gawky Awkward in manner. gawkily.

gay (gayer, gayest) Cheerful, light-hearted. gaily, gaiety.

gaze[1] (gazes, gazing, gazed) To look steadily at something for a long time.

gaze[2] A long, steady look.

gear[1] (gears) 1. A set of cog-wheels in a motor car by which the power of the engine is transmitted to the wheels. gear-box, gear-lever. 2. A similar device in other machines.

gear[2] Equipment, things needed for a particular purpose. Camping gear.

geese See goose.

Geiger counter An instrument which detects and measures radioactivity.

gelatine A tasteless substance which makes jelly when dissolved in water.

gelignite An explosive.

gem (gems) 1. A precious stone, a jewel. 2. Anything particularly beautiful or valuable.

general[1] 1. Belonging to everyone or everything, concerning everyone. General knowledge. A general election. 2. Not detailed. A general impression. 3. In general, generally.

general[2] (generals) An officer of high rank in the army.

generally Usually, on the whole.

generate (generates, generating, generated) To bring something into existence. To generate electricity. generator.

generation (generations) 1. Generating. 2. A single stage in a family. Three generations, children, parents, grandparents. 3. All people who are about the same age. My father's generation, the people who are about the same age as my father.

generous 1. Ready to give freely. A generous person. 2. Given freely. A generous present. generously, generosity.

genial Kindly, warm, cheerful. genially, geniality.

genius (geniuses) An exceptionally clever person.

gentile (gentiles) A person who is not a Jew.

gentle (gentler, gentlest) 1. Quiet and kind, not rough. 2. Moderate, not severe. gently, gentleness.

gentleman (gentlemen) 1. A polite word for a man. 2. A kind, well-mannered man. gentlemanly.

genuine True, not pretended or faked. Genuine feelings. genuinely, genuineness.

geography The scientific study of the earth, its lands and seas, its climate, its peoples, what they grow, what they produce, and how they live. geographical, geographer.

geology The scientific study of the rocks and other substances which make up the earth's crust. geological, geologist.

geometry A branch of mathematics which deals with lines, angles, and shapes. A geometry set, a case of drawing instruments. geometric, geometrical.

geranium (geraniums) A garden flower.

gerbil (gerbils) A small jumping animal.

germ (germs) A tiny living thing. Some germs cause diseases.

German Of Germany.

germinate (germinates, germinating, germinated) To start to develop or grow. germination.

gesture (gestures) A movement or an action which helps to show what one means or feels.

get (gets, getting, got) 1. To obtain, to earn, to win, to fetch, to receive. 2. To catch, to suffer. To get a cold. 3. To persuade. Get John to do it. 4. To prepare. I'll get tea now. 5. (informal) To understand. Do you get what I mean? 6. To manage to go somewhere, to arrive. Can you get here by tea-time? 7. To manage to put something somewhere. You won't get that big envelope in the post-box. 8. To put oneself somewhere, to move. Get on the bus quickly. 9. To get at something, to reach it. 10. To get away, to escape. 11. To get off, to be let off punishment. 12. To get on with someone, to be friendly with him. 13. To get on with *something*, to do it. **14.** *To get over an illness*, to recover.

getaway (getaways) An escape.

geyser (geysers) **1.** An apparatus for heating water. **2.** A natural spring which sends up a column of hot water.

ghastly (ghastlier, ghastliest) **1.** Horrible, shocking. **2.** Very pale, looking ill.

ghetto (ghettos) An area of a town where a group of people live crowded together.

ghost (ghosts) The spirit of a dead person appearing to someone living. **ghostly, ghostliness.**

giant (giants) **1.** A huge man. **giantess. 2.** Something much bigger than normal.

gibberish Nonsense, fast and meaningless talk.

giddy (giddier, giddiest) Having the feeling that everything is turning round, dizzy. **giddily, giddiness.**

gift (gifts) **1.** Something given to somebody, a present. **2.** An ability, a talent. *A gift for music.*

gifted Talented, clever.

gigantic Very large, giant-like. **gigantically.**

giggle¹ (giggles, giggling, giggled) To laugh in a silly way.

giggle² (giggles) A silly laugh.

gild (gilds, gilding, gilded) To cover something thinly with gold.

gill (gills) One of the parts of a fish's body with which it breathes.

gilt Covered thinly with gold.

gimmick (gimmicks) A clever or unusual way of attracting people's attention to something.

gin A strong alcoholic drink.

ginger 1. A hot-tasting flavouring. **ginger ale, ginger beer, gingerbread, ginger-nuts. 2.** A reddish-yellow colour. **gingery.**

gingerly Very carefully.

gipsy (gipsies) A member of a race of people who live in caravans and wander from place to place.

giraffe (giraffes) An African wild animal with a long neck and long legs.

girder (girders) A long, thick bar of wood, iron, or steel.

girdle (girdles) **1.** A belt tied round the waist. **2.** A corset.

girl (girls) **1.** A female child. **2.** A young woman. **3.** *A girl-friend*, a girl who is courted by a boy. **girlhood, girlish.**

girth (girths) **1.** A band fastened round the belly of a horse to keep its saddle in place. **2.** The measurement round something.

give (gives, giving, gave, given) **1.** To hand something over to someone to use or keep. **2.** To let someone have something, to provide. **3.** To pay. *How much did you give for those stamps?* **4.** To present, to show, to tell. *Give me the facts.* **5.** To collapse, to become less firm. *Will this branch give if I sit on it?* **6.** To do something suddenly. *He gave a shout.* **7.** *To give birth*, to have a baby. **8.** *To give chase*, to pursue. **9.** *To give in, to give up*, to stop trying to do something, to surrender. **10.** *To give way*, to break, to collapse. **11.** *To give way to traffic*, to let other traffic go first. **12.** *To give someone away*, to betray him. **13.** *To give a secret away*, to let it become known. **giver.**

glacial Of ice, icy.

glacier (glaciers) A slowly moving river of ice.

glad Pleased, joyful. **gladly, gladness.**

gladiator (gladiators) A man trained to fight at public entertainments in ancient Rome.

glamour Fascination, attractiveness, beauty. **glamorous.**

glance¹ (glances, glancing, glanced) **1.** To look briefly at something. **2.** To slip or slide off something. *The ball glanced off the edge of the bat.*

glance² (glances) A brief look.

gland (glands) An organ of the body that separates certain substances from the blood.

glare (glares, glaring, glared) **1.** To shine with a dazzling light. **2.** To look fiercely or angrily.

glass¹ The hard, clear substance used to make windows. **glassy.**

glass² (glasses) 1. A drinking cup made of glass. 2. A mirror, a looking-glass. 3. A telescope. 4. *A magnifying glass*, a lens that makes things look larger.

glasses A pair of spectacles or binoculars.

glass-house (glass-houses) A greenhouse.

glaze (glazes, glazing, glazed) 1. To fit glass into a window-frame. 2. *Glazed pottery*, pottery with a shiny surface.

glazier (glaziers) A man whose job is to fit glass into window-frames.

gleam¹ (gleams, gleaming, gleamed) To give a soft light which comes and goes.

gleam² (gleams) A ray of soft light.

glee Happiness, delight. gleeful, gleefully.

glen (glens) A narrow valley.

glide (glides, gliding, glided) To move smoothly and steadily.

glider (gliders) A kind of aeroplane without an engine.

gliding Flying in a glider.

glimmer (glimmers, glimmering, glimmered) To give a faint light.

glimpse¹ (glimpses, glimpsing, glimpsed) To see something very briefly.

glimpse² (glimpses) A brief view of something.

glint (glints, glinting, glinted) To flash, to glitter.

glisten (glistens, glistening, glistened) To shine like a wet surface.

glitter (glitters, glittering, glittered) To sparkle.

gloat (gloats, gloating, gloated) To be selfishly delighted about something.

global World-wide.

globe (globes) 1. Any object shaped like a ball or sphere. 2. A sphere with a map of the earth on it.

glockenspiel (glockenspiels) A musical instrument in which bells or bars are played with hammers.

gloom 1. Near darkness. 2. Sadness.

gloomy (gloomier, gloomiest) 1. Nearly dark. 2. Sad, depressed. gloomily.

glorious Splendid, magnificent, very beautiful. gloriously.

glory Fame, being glorious.

gloss A shiny surface. *Gloss paint*. glossy.

glove (gloves) A covering for the hand.

glow¹ (glows, glowing, glowed) 1. To send out brightness and warmth without flames. 2. To look or feel warm or excited. *Glowing with pride.*

glow² 1. Brightness. 2. Warmth.

glowering Frowning.

glow-worm (glow-worms) An insect which gives out a green light in the dark.

glucose A form of sugar.

glue¹ A substance used for sticking things together.

glue² (glues, gluing, glued) To stick with glue.

glum Dejected, gloomy. glumly.

glutton (gluttons) A greedy person. gluttonous, gluttony.

gnarled Twisted, rough, knobbly.

gnat (gnats) A small flying insect which bites.

gnaw (gnaws, gnawing, gnawed) To keep on biting something.

gnome (gnomes) A goblin or dwarf, living underground.

go¹ (goes, going, went, gone) 1. To start, to move. *Ready, steady, go!* 2. To travel. *To go on a journey*. 3. To stretch, to extend. *How far does this road go?* 4. To work, to be in working order. *Is your watch going?* 5. To disappear, to get lost, to die. *The light goes in the evening.* 6. To make one's way somewhere, to pay a visit. *To go to church.* 7. To become. *Milk goes sour in warm weather.* 8. To break. *Look out, that* branch is going! 9. To have a proper or usual place. *The butter goes in the fridge.* 10, To be given. *The prize goes to the first one home.* 11. To be sold. *The house went for a huge amount.* 12. To make a particular noise. *The gun went bang.* 13. *To go in for something,* to do it, to enjoy doing it. 14. *To go off,* to explode.

go² 1. Energy. *Full of go.* 2. (goes) An attempt. *To have a go,* to have a turn.

goal (goals) 1. The posts between which the ball has to be sent in football and other games. 2. The point scored when this is done. 3. A place one is trying to reach, a thing one is trying to achieve.

goal-keeper (goal-keepers) The player who guards the goal.

goat (goats) A small animal with horns.

gobble (gobbles, gobbling, gobbled) To eat quickly and greedily.

goblet (goblets) A kind of drinking-cup.

goblin (goblins) A mischievous demon.

God The creator of the Universe.

god (gods) Someone or something that is worshipped. goddess, godlike.

godparent (godparents) A person who promises when a child is baptized to see that it is brought up as a Christian. godfather, godmother, godchild, godson, god-daughter.

goggle (goggles, goggling, goggled) To stare.

goggles Large spectacles worn to protect the eyes.

go-kart (go-karts) A small simple racing car, often home-made.

gold 1. A precious metal. 2. Its yellowish colour. golden.

goldfinch (goldfinches) A small, brightly coloured bird.

goldfish (goldfish) A small yellowish-red fish.

goldsmith (goldsmiths) A craftsman who makes things of gold.

golf An outdoor game in which a small, hard ball is struck with clubs into a series of small holes. golfer, golf-club, golf-course, golf-links.

gollywog (gollywogs) A doll with a black face and fuzzy hair.

gondola (gondolas) A kind of boat used on the canals in Venice. gondolier.

gone *See* go¹.

gong (gongs) 1. A large metal disc which is struck with a stick as a signal. 2. A percussion instrument.

good¹ (better, best) 1. Of the kind that one wants, likes, or approves of. *Good friends. A good book.* 2. Well behaved, virtuous. *That's a good dog!* 3. Kind. *Would you be so good as to pass the salt?* 4. Quite large, considerable. *We've a good way to go yet.* 5. *It's a good five kilometres,* it's at least this. 6. *We shall be in good time,* we shall be early enough. 7. *Fresh milk is good for you,* it will make you healthy. 8. *We've as good as finished,* we've very nearly finished. 9. *Good morning, good-night, good-bye,* polite expressions used when meeting or leaving someone.

good² 1. Something that is good. *To do good.* 2. Advantage, benefit. *For the good of others.* 3. *It's no good!* it's no use! 4. *They've gone for good,* they've gone for ever.

good-humoured Cheerful. good-humouredly.

good-looking Handsome, attractive.

good-natured Kind, willing to help.

goodness 1. Kindness. 2. Any good quality. 3. *My goodness!* how surprising!

goods 1. Things which are bought or sold in a shop or warehouse. 2. Things which are carried on lorries or trains.

good-tempered Not easily made angry, gentle.

goodwill Friendliness.

goody-goody (goody-goodies) Someone who makes a great show of behaving well.

goose (geese) A large water-bird.

gooseberry (gooseberries) A small green fruit which grows on a prickly bush.

gooseflesh Skin covered with little bumps, called goosepimples, because of the cold or because of fear.

gore Blood. gory.

gored Wounded by the horns of an animal.

gorge ¹ (gorges, gorging, gorged) To eat greedily.

gorge ² (gorges) A narrow opening between hills or mountains.

gorgeous Colourful, beautiful, splendid. gorgeously.

gorilla (gorillas) A large kind of African ape.

gorse A prickly bush with yellow flowers.

gory 1. Covered with blood. 2. With much bloodshed.

gosling (goslings) A young goose.

gospel 1. The teachings of Jesus Christ. 2. The Gospels, the first four books of the New Testament, containing the story of the life and teaching of Jesus Christ.

gossip ¹ Gossiping chatter.

gossip ² (gossips, gossiping, gossiped) To chatter about other people.

got See get.

gouge (gouges, gouging, gouged) To gouge out, to scoop out.

govern (governs, governing, governed) To rule, to control, to manage. governor.

governess (governesses) A woman who is employed to teach children in their homes.

government (governments) The group of people who govern a country.

gown (gowns) 1. A woman's dress. 2. A loose, flowing garment.

grab (grabs, grabbing, grabbed) To seize suddenly and roughly, to snatch.

grace 1. Attractiveness, beauty of movement. graceful, gracefully. 2. With a good grace, without complaining. With a bad grace, reluctantly, unwillingly. 3. God's loving mercy. 4. A short prayer before or after a meal.

gracious 1. Kind, agreeable. 2. Merciful. graciously.

grade (grades) Quality, standard.

graded Sorted into grades.

gradient (gradients) A slope.

gradual Happening slowly but steadily. gradually.

graduated Marked off in units for measuring.

grain (grain or grains) 1. A seed of corn, wheat, rice, or similar plants. 2. A tiny piece of anything. A grain of sand. 3. The arrangement of lines which can be seen in a piece of wood.

gram (grams) A unit of weight in the metric system.

grammar 1. Rules for the use of words. Good grammar, using words properly. Bad grammar, not using words properly. grammatical. 2. A grammar school, a kind of secondary school.

gramophone (gramophones) A record-player, a machine for reproducing music or other sounds recorded on discs.

granary (granaries) A building for storing grain.

grand (grander, grandest) Great, splendid, important. grandly, grandeur.

grandchild (grandchildren) A child of one's son or daughter. grandson, granddaughter.

grandfather (grandfathers) 1. The father of one's mother or father. 2. A grandfather clock, a clock in a tall wooden case.

grandma (grandmas) Grandmother.

grandmother (grandmothers) The mother of one's mother or father.

grandpa (grandpas) Grandfather.

grandparent (grandparents) A grandfather or grandmother.

grandstand (grandstands) A stand with seats for spectators at a race-course or sports arena.

granite A hard, usually grey rock.

granny (grannies) 1. (informal) Grandmother. 2. A granny-knot, a wrongly-tied reef-knot.

grant (grants, granting, granted) 1. To give or allow what is asked for. *To grant a request.* 2. *To take something for granted,* to assume that it is true or certain.

granulated sugar Sugar in the form of white grains.

grape (grapes) A small green or purple fruit which grows in clusters on vines.

grapefruit (grapefruit *or* grapefruits) A citrus fruit, like a large yellow orange.

graph (graphs) A diagram for comparing numbers or amounts.

grapple (grapples, grappling, grappled) 1. To seize something, to wrestle with it. 2. To try to deal with something.

grasp[1] (grasps, grasping, grasped) To seize, to hold something firmly.

grasp[2] (grasps) The power to grasp.

grasping Selfish, greedy for money.

grass (grasses) A green plant with narrow, pointed leaves. grassy.

grasshopper (grasshoppers) A jumping, chirping insect.

grass-snake (grass-snakes) A kind of small, harmless snake.

grate[1] (grates) A metal frame for holding coal in a fire-place.

grate[2] (grates, grating, grated) 1. To shred into small pieces. *Grated cheese.* 2. To make an ugly, irritating noise.

grateful Thankful for a person's help or kindness. gratefully.

grating (gratings) A framework of criss-cross or parallel metal bars.

gratitude Thankfulness, being grateful.

grave[1] (graver, gravest) 1. Important, needing careful consideration. 2. Serious, solemn. gravely.

grave[2] (graves) A hole dug in the ground for a dead body. gravestone, graveyard.

gravel Small stones and coarse sand. gravelly.

gravity 1. The force which attracts things towards the earth. 2. Seriousness.

gravy A sauce made from meat juices.

graze (grazes, grazing, grazed) 1. To feed on growing grass. *Cows graze in the fields.*

2. To scrape something. *I grazed my knee when I fell.*

grease Soft, sticky fat or thick oil. greasy.

great (greater, greatest) 1. Big, large. 2. Important. 3. Unusually clever, exceptionally talented. *A great composer.* 4. *A great friend,* a very good friend. 5. (informal) Very good. 6. *Great-grandfather, great-grandmother,* the grandparents of one's mother or father.

greatcoat (greatcoats) An overcoat.

greed Wanting more food or money than is necessary. greedy, greedily, greediness.

Greek Of Greece.

green[1] A colour, the colour of grass.

green[2] (greener, greenest) Green in colour.

green[3] (greens) 1. An area of grass. *A village green.* 2. *Greens,* green vegetables.

greenery Green plants and leaves.

greengage (greengages) A kind of green plum.

greengrocer (greengrocers) A shopkeeper who sells fresh fruit and vegetables.

greenhouse (greenhouses) A building with a glass roof and walls for growing tender plants.

greenish Rather green.

greet (greets, greeting, greeted) To say words of welcome to someone.

greeting (greetings) 1. The first words used when meeting someone. 2. *Greetings,* good wishes.

grenade (grenades) A small bomb thrown by hand.

grew *See* grow.

grey[1] A colour between black and white, like clouds on a dull day.

grey[2] (greyer, greyest) Grey in colour.

greyhound (greyhounds) A kind of dog used for racing.

greyish Rather grey.

grid (grids) A grating.

grief 1. Great sadness. 2. *To come to grief*, to have an accident.

grievance (grievances) Something to complain about.

grieve (grieves, grieving, grieved) 1. To feel very sad. 2. To make someone very sad.

grill¹ (grills) 1. A device for grilling food. 2. A grating.

grill² (grills, grilling, grilled) To cook something under a flame or a glowing element.

grim (grimmer, grimmest) Stern, unfriendly, severe, cruel. grimly, grimness.

grimace¹ (grimaces) An ugly, twisted expression on the face.

grimace² (grimaces, grimacing, grimaced) To make a grimace.

grime A thick coating of dirt. grimy.

grin¹ (grins) A broad smile.

grin² (grins, grinning, grinned) To smile broadly.

grind (grinds, grinding, ground) 1. To make something into powder by crushing it. *To grind corn.* 2. To polish or sharpen something by rubbing it on a rough surface. *To grind scissors.* grinder, grindstone.

grip¹ (grips, gripping, gripped) To take firm hold of something.

grip² (grips) 1. A hold, a grasp. 2. A handle. 3. A traveller's bag.

grisly Horrible, frightful.

gristle Tough, uneatable lumps in meat. gristly.

grit¹ 1. Tiny pieces of stone or sand. 2. Courage. gritty, grittiness.

grit² (grits, gritting, gritted) 1. To put grit on something. *To grit the roads.* 2. *To grit one's teeth*, to clench the teeth.

grizzle (grizzles, grizzling, grizzled) (informal) To cry and whimper.

grizzly bear A large fierce North American bear.

groan¹ (groans, groaning, groaned) To make a deep sound of pain, sadness, or disapproval.

groan² (groans) A sound of groaning.

grocer (grocers) A shopkeeper who sells tea, sugar, jam, and other foods. grocery, groceries.

grog A drink of rum and water.

groom¹ (grooms) 1. Someone whose job is to look after horses. 2. A bridegroom.

groom² (grooms, grooming, groomed) To clean and brush a horse.

groove (grooves) A long, narrow cut in the surface of something.

grope (gropes, groping, groped) To feel about, to search blindly.

gross¹ (gross) Twelve dozen, 144.

gross² 1. Fat and ugly. 2. Coarse. 3. Obviously bad. *Gross carelessness.* grossly.

grotesque Absurd, ugly. grotesquely.

grotto (grottoes) A cave.

ground¹ (grounds) 1. The surface of the earth. 2. *The grounds of a house*, the gardens. 3. A piece of land used for sport. *A football ground.* groundsman. 4. *Grounds*, reasons. *What grounds have you for these suspicions?* groundless.

ground² *See* grind.

grounded Prevented from flying, kept on the ground.

groundsheet (groundsheets) A waterproof sheet which campers spread beneath them on the ground.

group¹ (groups) A number of people or things gathered together, people doing things together.

group² (groups, grouping, grouped) To make a group.

grouse¹ (grouse) A moorland bird.

grouse² (grouses, grousing, groused) To grumble, to complain. grouser.

grove (groves) A small wood.

grovel (grovels, grovelling, grovelled) To make oneself excessively humble.

grow (grows, growing, grew, grown) 1. To become bigger, taller, or longer. 2. To develop. 3. *To grow up*, to become an adult man or woman. 4. To cultivate. *To grow flowers.* 5. To become. *To grow older.* 6. *It grows on me*, I get to like it better and better. **grower, growth.**

growl[1] (growls, growling, growled) To make a rough noise in the throat as an angry dog does.

growl[2] (growls) A sound of growling.

grown-up (grown-ups) A fully grown person.

groyne (groynes) A breakwater.

grub (grubs) 1. A small wriggling creature, the larva of an insect. 2. (informal) Food.

grubby Rather dirty.

grudge[1] (grudges) *To have a grudge against someone*, to feel unkind or spiteful towards him.

grudge[2] (grudges, grudging, grudged) To be unwilling to let someone have something.

gruelling Exhausting.

gruesome Grisly, horrible, frightful. **gruesomely.**

gruff (gruffer, gruffest) With a rough, unfriendly voice or manner. **gruffly, gruffness.**

grumble (grumbles, grumbling, grumbled) To complain, to growl quietly.

grumpy (grumpier, grumpiest) Bad-tempered. **grumpily, grumpiness.**

grunt[1] (grunts, grunting, grunted) To make a noise like a pig.

grunt[2] (grunts) A sound of grunting.

guarantee[1] (guarantees) A promise to repair something if it goes wrong.

guarantee[2] (guarantees, guaranteeing, guaranteed) 1. To give a guarantee. 2. To make a solemn promise.

guard[1] (guards, guarding, guarded) 1. To protect someone or something. 2. *To guard a prisoner*, to prevent him from escaping. 3. *To guard against something*, to try to prevent it from happening.

guard[2] (guards) 1. *To be on guard*, to be on the look-out for danger. 2. A sentry, someone on guard. **guardsman, guardhouse.** 3. A group of soldiers or policemen on guard. 4. A device designed to protect people from injury. *A fire-guard.* 5. The man in charge of a train. *The guard's van.*

guarded Careful, cautious. **guardedly.**

guardian (guardians) 1. Someone who is legally in charge of a child whose parents cannot look after him. 2. A keeper, a protector.

guerrilla (guerrillas) A fighter who wages war by ambushes and surprise attacks.

guess[1] (guesses) An opinion which is not based on certain knowledge, an estimate. **guesswork.**

guess[2] (guesses, guessing, guessed) To make a guess.

guest (guests) 1. A person paying a visit to someone else's house. 2. A person staying in a hotel.

guest-house (guest-houses) A kind of small hotel.

guide[1] (guides) 1. A person or a thing that shows the way or gives advice. 2. *A guidebook*, a book that describes interesting sights for tourists. 3. *A Guide*, a member of the Girl Guides Association, an organization for girls.

guide[2] (guides, guiding, guided) To act as a guide. *A guided missile*, a rocket which can be controlled from the ground. **guidance.**

guile Craftiness. **guileful.**

guillotine (guillotines) 1. An instrument for cutting off people's heads. 2. An instrument for cutting paper.

guilt Responsibility for having committed a crime or done wrong.

guilty 1. Responsible for committing a crime. *The prisoner was found guilty.* 2. Aware of having done wrong. *A guilty conscience.* **guiltily.**

guinea (guineas) A former British unit of money worth 21 shillings.

guinea-pig (guinea-pigs) 1. A small, tailless animal often kept as a pet. 2. A person who is used in an experiment.

guitar (guitars) A musical instrument with strings which are plucked.

gulf (gulfs) A large bay. *The Gulf of Mexico.*

gull (gulls) A sea-gull.

gullet (gullets) The throat.

gully (gullies) 1. A ravine. 2. A deep gutter.

gulp (gulps, gulping, gulped) 1. To swallow hastily or greedily. 2. To gasp.

gum ¹ 1. A sticky substance used as glue. **gummy, gummed.** 2. *Chewing-gum*, a sweet for chewing.

gum ² (gums) The firm pink flesh round the teeth.

gumboot (gumboots) A long, rubber boot.

gum-tree (gum-trees) A eucalyptus tree.

gumption (informal) Practical common sense.

gun (guns) Any weapon which fires bullets, shells, or shot from a metal tube. **gunfire, gunshot.**

gunboat (gunboats) A small warship.

gunman (gunmen) An armed criminal.

gunner (gunners) A soldier in charge of a large gun. **gunnery.**

gunpowder Explosive powder.

gurgle (gurgles, gurgling, gurgled) To make a sound like bubbling water.

gush ¹ (gushes, gushing, gushed) To flow out in a rush. **gusher.**

gush ² (gushes) A rushing flow.

gust (gusts) A sudden rush of wind.

gut (guts, gutting, gutted) To take out the guts or inside of something.

guts 1. The insides of a person or animal. 2. (informal) Courage and determination.

gutter (gutters) A channel to carry away rain-water.

guy (guys) 1. The figure of Guy Fawkes burnt on 5th November. 2. (informal) A man. 3. *Guy ropes*, the ropes which hold a tent up.

guzzle (guzzles, guzzling, guzzled) To eat or drink greedily.

gym (informal) 1. (gyms) A gymnasium. 2. Gymnastics.

gymkhana (gymkhanas) A sports display with pony-riding or horse-riding.

gymnasium (gymnasiums) A building with apparatus for gymnastics.

gymnastics Exercises for strengthening one's body. **gymnast.**

gyroscope (gyroscopes) A rapidly spinning wheel fitted in a machine or a toy.

Hh

habit (habits) Something which a person does so often that he does it without thinking. **habitual, habitually.**

habitable Fit to be lived in.

habitat (habitats) The natural home of an animal or plant.

hack (hacks, hacking, hacked) To chop, to cut roughly.

hack-saw (hack-saws) A saw for cutting metal.

had *See* have.

haddock (haddock) A sea fish.

hadn't (informal) Had not.

hag (hags) An ugly old woman.

haggard Looking tired and worried.

haggis A traditional Scottish food.

haggle (haggles, haggling, haggled) To argue about the price of something.

hail ¹ Frozen raindrops. **hailstones, hailstorm.**

hail ² (hails, hailing, hailed) 1. *It is hailing*, hail is falling. 2. To greet someone, to call out to someone.

hair 1. The fine, thread-like growths on skin, especially on a person's head or an animal's body. 2. (hairs) One of these. **hairy, hairless, hairbrush, hairpin, hair-slide.**

hairdresser (hairdressers) A person who cuts, washes, and arranges people's hair. **haircut.**

hairpin bend A very sharp bend in a road.

hair-raising Terrifying.

hake (hake) A sea fish.

half¹ (halves) One of the two equal parts into which something is or can be divided. Half of 6 is 3. Half of 1 is ½.

half² Partly, not completely. *This meat is only half cooked.*

half-hearted Not very enthusiastic. half-heartedly.

halfpenny (halfpennies *or* halfpence) A coin worth half a penny.

half-time An interval between the two halves of a game.

half-way At a point half of the distance between two places.

half-wit (half-wits) A stupid person. half-witted.

halibut (halibut) A large flat fish.

hall (halls) 1. A large room for concerts, assemblies, meetings, or other purposes. 2. The first room or passage inside the front door of a house. 3. A large house like a palace.

hallelujah (hallelujahs) Alleluia.

hallo, hello, or hullo 1. A greeting. 2. A word used to attract someone's attention.

hallowed Holy, sacred.

Hallowe'en 31st October.

hallucination (hallucinations) Something which a person thinks he can see but which does not really exist.

halo (haloes) A circle of light. In paintings, a halo is often shown over the head of a holy person.

halt (halts, halting, halted) To stop.

halter (halters) A rope or strap with a noose.

halve (halves, halving, halved) 1. To divide something into halves. 2. To reduce something to half its size.

halves *See* half.

ham Meat from a pig's leg.

hamburger (hamburgers) A fried cake of chopped beef.

hamlet (hamlets) A tiny village.

hammer¹ (hammers) A hitting tool.

hammer² (hammers, hammering, hammered) 1. To hit with a hammer. 2. To hit hard. *To hammer on a door.*

hammock (hammocks) A hanging bed.

hamper¹ (hampers) A large basket with a lid.

hamper² (hampers, hampering, hampered) To hinder somebody, to make things difficult.

hamster (hamsters) A small animal often kept as a pet.

hand¹ (hands) 1. The part of the body at the end of the arm, below the wrist. 2. A worker. 3. A seaman. *All hands on deck!* 4. A pointer on a clock. 5. The cards dealt to a player in a card-game. 6. *At first hand,* directly from the person concerned. 7. *Out of hand,* out of control.

hand² (hands, handing, handed) To pass something with one's hands. *Please hand me my overcoat.*

handbag (handbags) A small bag carried by a woman.

handcuffs A device for locking a prisoner's wrists together.

handful (handfuls) 1. An amount that fills a person's hand. 2. A small number. *A handful of people.* 3. (informal) A troublesome person.

handicap (handicaps) A disadvantage.

handicapped 1. At a disadvantage. 2. Disabled.

handicraft (handicrafts) Skilful work done with the hands.

handiwork 1. Work done by the hands. 2. *Is this your handiwork?* did you do this?

handkerchief (handkerchiefs) A square piece of cloth or tissue for wiping one's nose.

handle¹ (handles) The part of a thing by which it is held. *The handle of a saucepan. A door handle.*

handle[2] (handles, handling, handled) 1. To touch something with the hands. 2. To deal with something, to manage it. *You won't enjoy your ride if you can't handle the horse!*

handlebars The bar with handles which a cyclist uses to steer a bicycle.

handrail (handrails) A rail for holding with the hand.

handsome 1. Attractive, good-looking. 2. Generous. *A handsome gift.* handsomely.

handwriting Writing done by hand. handwritten.

handy (handier, handiest) 1. Convenient, not far away. 2. Useful. 3. Clever with one's hands. *He's handy at carpentry.*

hang[1] (hangs, hanging, hung) 1. To fix something at the top and let it be free at the bottom. *We hung the picture on the wall.* 2. To float in the air. *A delicious smell of cooking hung about the house.* 3. *To hang wallpaper*, to paste it to the wall. 4. *To hang about*, to stand about doing nothing. 5. *To hang back*, to hesitate. 6. *To hang on to something*, to hold it, to keep it.

hang[2] (hangs, hanging, hanged) To put someone to death by hanging him with a noose tied round his neck.

hang[3] *To get the hang of something*, to understand it.

hangar (hangars) A large shed for aeroplanes.

hanger (hangers) A device on which to hang things.

hangman (hangmen) A man whose job is to put condemned persons to death by hanging them.

hanker (hankers, hankering, hankered) *To hanker after something*, to long for it.

haphazard Accidental, without planning.

happen (happens, happening, happened) 1. To occur, to take place. 2. *I happened to be there*, I was there by chance.

happening (happenings) An event, something which happens.

happy (happier, happiest) 1. Pleased, glad. 2. Lucky. happily, happiness.

harass (harasses, harassing, harassed) To trouble and worry someone. harassment.

harbour[1] (harbours) 1. A place where ships can shelter. 2. A place where ships unload.

harbour[2] (harbours, harbouring, harboured) To give shelter to someone or something.

hard (harder, hardest) 1. Firm, solid, not soft, not easily cut. *Hard rock.* 2. Difficult. *A hard problem.* 3. Severe, harsh, cruel. *A hard frost.* 4. Severely. *To freeze hard.* 5. With great effort. *To try hard.* 6. *Hard up*, poor, short of money. 7. *Hard of hearing*, rather deaf.

hardboard Board like very stiff, thick cardboard.

harden (hardens, hardening, hardened) To make hard, to become hard.

hard-hearted Cruel, unfeeling.

hardly 1. Only just, only with difficulty. 2. *Hardly any*, almost none.

hardship (hardships) Suffering.

hardware Tools and other goods sold by an ironmonger.

hard-wearing Not wearing out easily.

hardy (hardier, hardiest) Able to bear cold and hardship.

hare (hares) An animal like a large rabbit.

hare-lip (hare-lips) A deformed upper lip.

harem (harems) The women in a Muslim household.

hark Listen!

harm[1] (harms, harming, harmed) To damage.

harm[2] Damage, injury. harmful, harmfully, harmless, harmlessly.

harmonica (harmonicas) A mouth-organ.

harmonium (harmoniums) A kind of small organ.

harmony (harmonies) 1. Agreement. 2. A combination of musical notes sounding pleasantly together. **harmonious, harmoniously.**

harness[1] (harnesses) Straps and fittings worn by a horse.

harness[2] (harnesses, harnessing, harnessed) 1. To put a harness on a horse. 2. To control something and use it.

harp[1] (harps) A musical instrument with many strings. **harpist.**

harp[2] (harps, harping, harped) *To harp on something,* to keep on talking about it in a boring way.

harpoon (harpoons) A spear used in hunting whales.

harpsichord (harpsichords) A musical instrument with a keyboard like a piano.

harrow (harrows) A heavy frame with iron teeth towed behind a tractor for breaking up the soil.

harsh (harsher, harshest) Rough, unpleasant, stern, cruel. **harshly, harshness.**

harvest[1] (harvests) 1. The gathering in of the corn or other crops. 2. The crop that is gathered in.

harvest[2] (harvests, harvesting, harvested) To gather in the crops. **harvester.**

has *See* **have.**

hash (hashes) 1. A kind of stew. 2. (informal) *To make a hash of something,* to do it very badly.

hasn't (informal) Has not.

haste Hurry, being quick. **hasty, hastily, hastiness.**

hasten (hastens, hastening, hastened) To hurry.

hat (hats) A covering for the head.

hatch[1] (hatches) 1. An opening in a wall, especially between a kitchen and a dining-room. 2. An opening in the deck of a ship. **hatchway.**

hatch[2] (hatches, hatching, hatched) 1. To keep an egg warm until a baby bird breaks out of it. 2. To break out of an egg. 3. *To hatch a plot,* to plan it.

hatchet (hatchets) A small axe.

hate[1] (hates, hating, hated) To dislike someone or something very much.

hate[2] or hatred Very great dislike. **hateful.**

haughty (haughtier, haughtiest) Proud of oneself and looking down on other people. **haughtily, haughtiness.**

haul (hauls, hauling, hauled) To pull, to drag.

haunt (haunts, haunting, haunted) 1. To visit a place often. 2. *To be haunted,* to be inhabited or visited by a ghost.

have (has, having, had) 1. To possess, to own. *We have three cats.* 2. To contain. *This book has coloured pictures.* 3. To enjoy. *We had a marvellous time.* 4. To suffer. *I had mumps.* 5. To be compelled. *We had to do the washing-up.* 6. To cause something to be done. *Is it worth having this watch repaired?* 7. To receive, to obtain, to get. *Mary had six birthday cards.*

haven (havens) 1. A harbour. 2. A safe place.

haven't (informal) Have not.

haversack (haversacks) A bag worn on the back by soldiers and hikers.

havoc Great destruction.

hawk (hawks) A bird of prey.

hawser (hawsers) A thick rope, often made of steel.

hawthorn (hawthorns) A small thorny tree with red berries in winter.

hay Dried grass for feeding animals. **haymaking, hayrick, haystack.**

hay fever Irritation of the nose, throat, and eyes, caused by pollen.

hazard (hazards) Risk, danger. **hazardous, hazardously.**

haze A thin mist.

hazel (hazels) A small nut-tree.

hazy (hazier, haziest) 1. Misty. 2. Blurred, confused. **hazily.**

H-bomb A kind of nuclear bomb.

he (him, himself) The male person or animal being talked about.

head[1] (heads) 1. The part of the body containing the brains, eyes, and mouth. 2. Brains. *Don't be silly, use your head!* 3. A knob or swelling at the end of an object. *The head of a nail.* 4. The top of a thing, the highest part. *The head of the stairs.* 5. The front end of anything. *The head of a queue.* 6. The chief, the person in charge. 7. *A head wind*, a wind that blows directly in one's face. 8. *To come to a head*, to reach a crisis. 9. *Keep your head!* keep calm!

head[2] (heads, heading, headed) 1. To hit with the head. *John headed the ball into the net.* **header.** 2. To be in charge of something. 3. *To head for a place*, to go towards it.

headache (headaches) A pain in the head.

heading (headings) A headline, words written at the top of a piece of writing.

headlight (headlights) A powerful light on the front of a car or other vehicle.

headline (headlines) 1. Words in large print at the top of an article in a newspaper or magazine. 2. *The headlines*, the main points of the news.

headlong 1. Head first. 2. Thoughtlessly and hurriedly.

headmaster (headmasters) The person in charge of a school. **headmistress.**

head-on Front to front. *A head-on collision.*

head-phones A listening device which fits over one's head.

headquarters A central office from which orders are sent out, a base.

headway *To make headway*, to make progress.

heal (heals, healing, healed) 1. To become well again. *Has your wound healed?* 2. To make well again, to cure. **healer.**

health The condition of a person's body or mind. *Good health is a great blessing.*

healthy (healthier, healthiest) 1. Strong and well, free from illness. 2. Good for people's health. **healthily, healthiness.**

heap[1] (heaps) 1. A pile. 2. (informal) *Heaps*, plenty.

heap[2] (heaps, heaping, heaped) To put into a heap.

hear (hears, hearing, heard) 1. To receive sounds through the ears. 2. To receive news. *We haven't heard from John lately.*

hearse (hearses) A car for carrying a coffin to a funeral.

heart (hearts) 1. The organ that pumps the blood round the body. **heartbeat.** 2. *To have a soft heart*, to be kind. *To have a hard heart*, to be cruel. 3. *To lose heart*, to become discouraged. 4. *To learn something by heart*, to learn to say it from memory. 5. *To break someone's heart*, to make him very unhappy. **heart-breaking, heart-broken.** 6. The middle of something. *The children were lost in the heart of the forest.*

hearth (hearths) The floor of a fire-place.

heartless Cruel. **heartlessly.**

hearts A suit of playing-cards.

hearty (heartier, heartiest) 1. Sincere and enthusiastic. *Hearty congratulations!* 2. Big, strong, healthy. *A hearty appetite.* **heartily.**

heat[1] Warmth, the feeling received from the sun, a fire, or a radiator.

heat[2] (heats, heating, heated) 1. To make something hot. 2. To become hot.

heat[3] (heats) A trial race to decide which runners are to take part in the final.

heath (heaths) An area of waste land often covered with heather or bracken.

heathen[1] (heathen *or* heathens) A person who does not believe in God.

heathen[2] Not religious.

heather A low-growing bush with purple or white flowers.

heat-wave (heat-waves) A long period of hot weather.

heave (heaves, heaving, heaved) 1. To pull or lift something with great effort. 2. (informal) To lift and throw. 3. *To heave to*, to stop.

heaven 1. The home of God and the saints. 2. A happy place. 3. A feeling of happiness. 4. *The heavens*, the sky. 5. *Good heavens!* how surprising! heavenly.

heavy (heavier, heaviest) 1. Of great weight, hard to lift. 2. Serious, worse than usual. *Heavy rain*. 3. Hard, difficult. *Heavy work*. 4. Gloomy, dull. *A heavy sky*. heavily, heaviness.

Hebrew Jewish.

hectare (hectares) A measure of area of land, 10,000 square metres or about $2\frac{1}{2}$ acres.

hectic Excited and without rest.

hedge[1] (hedges) A row of bushes forming a kind of fence.

hedge[2] (hedges, hedging, hedged) 1. To make a hedge. 2. *To hedge in*, to surround. 3. To avoid giving a direct answer.

hedgehog (hedgehogs) A small animal covered with prickles.

hedgerow (hedgerows) A hedge.

heed[1] (heeds, heeding, heeded) To take notice of something.

heed[2] Care, attention. heedless.

heel[1] (heels) 1. The back part of the foot. 2. The part of a sock round the heel, the part of a shoe under the heel.

heel[2] (heels, heeling, heeled) 1. To repair the heel of a shoe. 2. To kick with the heel. 3. To lean over to one side.

hefty (heftier, heftiest) Big and strong.

heifer (heifers) A young cow.

height (heights) 1. The distance from the bottom of something to the top. 2. A high place. 3. *The storm was at its height*, it was at its greatest.

heir (heirs) The person who will inherit someone's title or belongings. *The heir to the throne*, the person who will become king or queen. heiress.

held *See* hold[1].

helicopter (helicopters) A kind of aircraft with a large horizontal propeller.

hell 1. A place of punishment after death. 2. A very unpleasant place. hellish.

he'll (informal) He will.

hello *See* hallo.

helm (helms) The handle or wheel used to steer a ship. helmsman.

helmet (helmets) A strengthened covering to protect the head. *A crash-helmet*.

help[1] (helps, helping, helped) 1. To aid, to assist, to do something which makes another person's work easier, or which makes his troubles less hard to bear. helper. 2. To avoid. *I can't help sneezing when I've got a cold*.

help[2] Aid, assistance. helpful, helpfully.

helping (helpings) A portion of food put on one's plate.

helpless Unable to look after oneself. helplessly.

hem[1] (hems) The edge of a piece of cloth, the border made by turning the edge over and sewing it down. hem-line.

hem[2] (hems, hemming, hemmed) 1. To make a hem. 2. *To hem in*, to surround.

hemisphere (hemispheres) Half the earth, half a globe.

hen (hens) 1. A female bird. 2. A farmyard chicken. hen-house.

hence From here, from this time.

henceforth From now onwards.

henchman (henchmen) A faithful, trusted follower.

her *See* she.

herald (heralds) In former times, an official who made public announcements.

heraldry The study of the badges and emblems of old families. heraldic.

herb (herbs) A plant used for flavouring or for making medicines. herbal.

herd¹ (herds) A number of cattle feeding or going about together.

herd² (herds, herding, herded) To crowd together.

here 1. In this place, at this place, to this place. *Stand here! Look here! Come here!* 2. At this point. *Here he stopped for us to ask questions.* 3. This place. *We live five kilometres from here.*

hereabouts Near here.

hereditary Passed on from parents to children. heredity.

heritage (heritages) Something that is inherited.

hermit (hermits) A man who lives quite alone.

hero (heroes) 1. A very brave and noble man. 2. The most important person in a play or story. *Jim Hawkins is the hero of 'Treasure Island'.* heroic, heroically, heroism.

heroin A very strong drug.

heroine (heroines) A female hero.

heron (herons) A long-legged wading bird.

herring (herring *or* herrings) A sea fish.

hers Belonging to her.

herself *See* she. This word is used in the same ways as himself.

he's (informal) 1. He is. 2. He has.

hesitate (hesitates, hesitating, hesitated) To pause uncertainly when doing something or when speaking. hesitant, hesitantly, hesitation.

hew (hews, hewing, hewed, hewn) To chop, to cut with an axe or sword.

hexagon (hexagons) A shape with six sides. hexagonal.

hibernate (hibernates, hibernating, hibernated) To stay sleepy and inactive through the winter. hibernation.

hiccup (hiccups, hiccupping, hiccupped) To make a sound like a sharp cough.

hide¹ (hides, hiding, hid, hidden) 1. To conceal something, to put it out of sight, to keep it secret. 2. To go to a place where one cannot be seen. hiding-place, hide-away, hide-out.

hide² (hides) An animal's skin, a skin used for making leather.

hide-and-seek A hiding game.

hideous Very ugly. hideously.

hiding *To give someone a hiding*, to thrash him.

hieroglyphics Picture-writing like that used by the ancient Egyptians.

hi-fi High-fidelity equipment.

higgledy-piggledy Mixed up, in complete confusion.

high (higher, highest) 1. Going up a long way. *High hills.* 2. Measuring from top to bottom. *Two metres high.* 3. Situated a long way above ground level or sea level. *High clouds.* 4. Above what is expected. *High prices.* 5. Very important. *A high rank in the army.* 6. Strong, intense, stormy. *A high wind.* 7. Favourable. *To have a high opinion of someone.* 8. *In high spirits*, cheerful, lively. 9. *The high seas*, the ocean. 10. *It's high time you went to bed*, it's past the proper time for bed. 11. Smelly, going bad. *This meat is high.* highness.

highbrow 1. Intellectual. 2. Complicated, hard to understand.

high-fidelity *High-fidelity equipment*, apparatus for reproducing sound very clearly.

Highlander (Highlanders) Someone who lives in the Highlands of Scotland.

highlands Hilly or mountainous country.

highlight (highlights) One of the most interesting or exciting parts of something.

highly 1. Very. 2. Favourably. *To think highly of someone.*

highly-strung Nervous, easily upset.

Highness A title used for a member of a royal family. *His Royal Highness.*

high school A kind of secondary school.

high tea An afternoon meal including cooked food.

highway (highways) A main road.

highwayman (highwaymen) A horseman who used to rob travellers on the highway.

hijack (hijacks, hijacking, hijacked) To seize control of a vehicle or aircraft during a journey. **hijacker.**

hike (hikes, hiking, hiked) To go for a long walk in the country. **hiker.**

hilarious Very funny, cheerful. **hilariously, hilarity.**

hill (hills) 1. A high piece of land with sloping sides. 2. A slope. **hilly, hillside, hilltop.**

hilt (hilts) The handle of a sword or dagger.

him *See* he.

himself *See* he. This word is used in various ways including: 1. *He hurt himself on the broken glass.* 2. *I heard the news from the headmaster himself.* 3. *John was by himself, he was alone.* 4. *Alan isn't himself today,* he's not very well.

hind At the back. *The hind legs of a horse.*

hinder (hinders, hindering, hindered) To delay, to get in someone's way when he wants to do something. **hindrance.**

Hindu (Hindus) A believer in Hinduism, one of the religions of India.

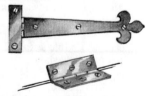

hinge (hinges) A device on which a door or gate swings when it opens. **hinged.**

hint¹ (hints) A suggestion, a slight indication.

hint² (hints, hinting, hinted) To give a hint.

hip (hips) 1. The bony part on each side of the body just above the top of the legs. 2. The fruit of the wild rose.

hippie (hippies) A person who refuses to live or behave or dress in the way that most people do. Hippies choose to live in what they regard as a 'natural' way.

hippopotamus (hippopotamuses) A large African river-animal.

hire (hires, hiring, hired) To borrow or lend something in return for payment. *We hired a boat for £15 a day.*

hire-purchase Buying something by paying in instalments.

his Belonging to him.

hiss (hisses, hissing, hissed) To make a sound like the sound of *s*.

historic Famous in history.

history (histories) 1. The study of things which happened in the past. 2. A book or story about past events. **historical, historically, historian.**

hit¹ (hits, hitting, hit) 1. To knock hard against something. 2. To strike in a particular place. *The bombs hit the target.* 3. To affect something badly. *The harvest was hit by the drought.*

hit² (hits) 1. A knock, a blow. 2. A success, a successful song.

hitch (hitches, hitching, hitched) 1. To pull up with a quick movement. *To hitch up one's trousers.* 2. To fasten with a hook or a loop. 3. (informal) To hitch-hike.

hitch-hike (hitch-hikes, hitch-hiking, hitch-hiked) To beg a lift in a car or other vehicle.

hither To this place. *Hither and thither,* in various directions.

hitherto Up to now.

hive (hives) A beehive.

hoard (hoards, hoarding, hoarded) To gather things together and store them, to keep things in a miserly way.

hoarding (hoardings) A tall wooden fence covered with advertisements.

hoar-frost A white frost.

hoarse (hoarser, hoarsest) Rough, husky, croaking. hoarsely, hoarseness.

hoax[1] (hoaxes) A deceitful trick played on someone for a joke.

hoax[2] (hoaxes, hoaxing, hoaxed) To deceive someone by a hoax.

hobble (hobbles, hobbling, hobbled) To walk with a limp.

hobby (hobbies) Something a person is fond of doing in his spare time.

hobnailed boots Boots with metal studs in the soles.

hockey 1. An outdoor game played with a ball and curved sticks. 2. In Canada, ice-hockey.

hoe (hoes) A tool for scraping up weeds.

hog (hogs) A male pig.

Hogmanay (Scottish) New Year's Eve.

hoist (hoists, hoisting, hoisted) To lift up by means of ropes, pulleys, or other equipment.

hold[1] (holds, holding, held) 1. To grasp something, to have it firmly in the hands. *Hold the ladder while I climb.* 2. To possess, to keep. *My father holds a driving licence.* 3. To contain. *How much does this bottle hold?* 4. To keep someone captive. *The suspect was held for questioning by the police.* 5. To keep oneself in a certain position. *Hold yourself up straight!* 6. To keep something back, not to let it go. *Hold your breath!* 7. *To hold a meeting*, to have a meeting. 8. To continue. *How long will this weather hold?* 9. Not to break. *Will that rope hold?* 10. *To hold back*, to hesitate. 11. *To hold out*, to last, to continue. 12. *To be held up*, to be delayed. 13. *To hold up*, to stop people and rob them. *The highwayman held up the travellers.*

hold[2] (holds) 1. A grasp. 2. A place to hold on to. 3. The part of a ship below decks where the cargo is stored.

hold-all (hold-alls) A traveller's bag.

holder (holders) A person or thing that holds something.

hold-up (hold-ups) 1. A delay. 2. An attack by an armed robber.

hole (holes) 1. An opening, a gap, a space. *A hole in a fence.* 2. An animal's burrow. *A rabbit-hole.*

holiday (holidays) 1. A day off from school or work. 2. *The holidays*, the time between terms when school is closed. 3. *To go on holiday*, to go away from home for a time to enjoy oneself. holiday-maker.

hollow[1] Not solid, having an empty space inside.

hollow[2] (hollows) 1. A hollow place. 2. A hole. 3. A small valley.

hollow[3] (hollows, hollowing, hollowed) To make something hollow.

holly An evergreen bush with prickly leaves.

hollyhock (hollyhocks) A very tall garden flower.

holster (holsters) A leather case for a pistol.

holy (holier, holiest) 1. Sacred, belonging to God. 2. Religious. holiness.

homage Great respect.

home[1] (homes) 1. The place where one lives with one's family. 2. A place where people live together and are cared for. *An old people's home.* 3. *To feel at home*, to feel comfortable and relaxed. homeless, homemade.

home[2] 1. At or to home. *When are you going home?* 2. *To bring something home to someone*, to make him realize it.

homesick Sad at being away from home. homesickness.

homestead (homesteads) A farmhouse.

homeward or homewards Towards home.

homework School work which has to be done at home.

homing 1. *A homing pigeon*, a pigeon trained to fly home. 2. *A homing missile*, one which can aim itself at its target.

honest Fair, true, not liable to steal or cheat or lie. honestly, honesty.

honey A sweet, sticky food made by bees.

honeycomb (honeycombs) A structure made out of wax by bees for storing their honey and eggs.

honeymoon (honeymoons) A holiday taken by a newly married couple.

honeysuckle A climbing plant with sweet-smelling flowers.

honour[1] 1. Great respect. 2. A reputation for being good, loyal, and noble. 3. A person or thing that brings honour. *You are an honour to the school.*

honour[2] (honours) A title, medal, certificate, or special reward given to a deserving person.

honour[3] (honours, honouring, honoured) 1. To feel or show great respect towards someone. 2. *To honour a promise*, to keep a promise.

honourable Good and noble. honourably.

hood[1] (hoods) 1. A covering for the head and neck like that on an anorak. 2. A folding roof or cover like that on a pram.

hood[2] (hoods, hooding, hooded) To cover with a hood.

hoodwink (hoodwinks, hoodwinking, hoodwinked) To deceive, to trick.

hoof (hoofs) The horny part of a horse's foot.

hook[1] (hooks) A bent or curved piece of metal or other material, such as a fish-hook or a cup-hook.

hook[2] (hooks, hooking, hooked) 1. To catch something by means of a hook. 2. To attach or fasten something by means of a hook.

hooligan (hooligans) A rowdy disorderly person, a member of a street gang. hooliganism.

hoop (hoops) A large ring.

hoop-la A fair-ground game in which rings are thrown over objects.

hoot (hoots, hooting, hooted) 1. To make a noise like the cry of an owl or the sound of a car horn. hooter. 2. To jeer.

Hoover[1] (Hoovers) The trade name of a kind of vacuum cleaner.

hoover[2] (hoovers, hoovering, hoovered) To use a vacuum cleaner.

hop[1] (hops) A climbing plant whose fruits are used to flavour beer.

hop[2] (hops, hopping, hopped) 1. To jump on one foot. 2. To move along by jumping. *The bird hopped across the lawn.*

hope[1] (hopes) 1. A feeling that something one wants is likely to happen. 2. A person or thing one hopes will be successful.

hope[2] (hopes, hoping, hoped) To have hope.

hopeful 1. Hoping. 2. Likely to turn out well. *The weather looks hopeful.* hopefully, hopefulness.

hopeless 1. Without hope. 2. Very bad. *I am hopeless at drawing.* hopelessly, hopelessness.

hopscotch A game played by hopping and kicking a stone into squares marked on the ground.

horde (hordes) A crowd, a gang.

horizon (horizons) The line in the distance where the earth and sky seem to meet.

horizontal Flat, level, parallel to the horizon. horizontally.

horn (horns) 1. One of the hard, pointed growths on the heads of cattle and some other animals. 2. A kind of musical instrument played by blowing. 3. A device for making warning sounds. *A fog-horn.*

hornet (hornets) A large kind of wasp.

hornpipe (hornpipes) A lively sailors' dance.

horny Made of horn, hard like horn.

horoscope (horoscopes) A forecast of future events by an astrologer.

horrible Horrifying, shocking, unpleasant. horribly.

horrid Horrible. horridly.

horrific Causing horror. horrifically.

horrify (horrifies, horrifying, horrified) To cause horror, to shock.

horror (horrors) 1. A feeling of great fear or dislike. 2. Something which causes this feeling.

horse (horses) 1. An animal used for riding or for pulling carts or other vehicles. **horseman, horsewoman, horsemanship, horseshoe.** 2. A wooden framework for jumping over in gymnastics. 3. *A clothes-horse*, a framework for drying clothes.

horseback *On horseback*, riding a horse.

horse-box (horse-boxes) A trailer for carrying horses.

horse-chestnut (horse-chestnuts) A large tree on which conkers grow.

horsepower A unit for measuring the power of engines.

hosanna A cry of praise to God.

hose (hoses) or hose-pipe (hose-pipes) A flexible tube through which water can pass.

hospitable Friendly and welcoming to strangers and guests. **hospitably, hospitality.**

hospital (hospitals) A place where doctors and nurses care for sick and injured people.

host (hosts) 1. A person who has guests and looks after them. **hostess.** 2. A crowd.

hostage (hostages) A person who is held captive and whose life is threatened unless certain demands are agreed to.

hostel (hostels) A building where certain people can get board and lodging. *A youth hostel.*

hostile Unfriendly, belonging to an enemy. **hostility.**

hostilities Fighting, warfare.

hot (hotter, hottest) 1. Very warm, giving off much heat. *A hot fire.* 2. Fiery, eager, angry. *A hot temper.* 3. Having a burning flavour like pepper or ginger. 4. *A hot dog*, a bread roll with a hot sausage in it **hotly.**

hotel (hotels) A building where meals and rooms are provided for travellers and for people on holiday.

hot-house (hot-houses) A heated greenhouse.

hot-pot A kind of stew.

hound[1] (hounds) A dog kept for hunting.

hound[2] (hounds, hounding, hounded) To chase, to pursue.

hour (hours) 1. A unit of time, 60 minutes. 2. A time of day. *Why are you up at this hour?*

hour-glass (hour-glasses) An old-fashioned device for measuring the time.

hourly Every hour, once an hour.

house[1] (houses) 1. A building for people to live in, usually for one family. 2. A building used by an official assembly, the assembly itself. *The Houses of Parliament.* 3. One of the divisions of children in a school, which compete against each other in games and so on.

house[2] (houses, housing, housed) To provide a house or shelter for someone or something.

house-boat (house-boats) A boat used as a home.

household (households) All the people who live in a house.

housekeeper (housekeepers) A woman employed to be in charge of the housework. **housekeeping.**

house-proud Very keen to keep the house clean and tidy.

house-trained Trained to behave properly in the house.

housewife (housewives) A woman who does the housework for her husband and family.

housework All the work that has to be done in the house, such as cleaning and cooking.

hovel (hovels) A small dirty house.

hover (hovers, hovering, hovered) 1. To hang still in the air, to stay in one place in the air. *The kestrel hovered above the cliff.* 2. To loiter, to hang about.

hovercraft (hovercraft) A vehicle that travels above the surface of land or water on a current of air fanned downwards by its engines.

how 1. In what way. *Show me how to do it.* 2. To what extent. *How certain are they?* 3. In what condition. *How are you? 4. How about a game of football?* shall we play football?

however 1. Nevertheless, in spite of this. 2. In whatever way, to whatever extent. *However hard she ran, she could not catch up.*

howl¹ (howls, howling, howled) To make a long, loud cry.

howl² (howls) A long, loud cry.

howler (howlers) A ridiculous mistake.

hub (hubs) The centre of a wheel.

hubbub A confused noise.

huddle (huddles, huddling, huddled) 1. To crowd together. 2. *Huddled up,* curled up.

hue¹ (hues) Colour.

hue² *Hue and cry,* a general cry of alarm.

huff *In a huff,* offended, in a bad mood.

hug¹ (hugs, hugging, hugged) 1. To clasp someone lovingly in one's arms. 2. To keep close to something. *The ship hugged the shore.*

hug² (hugs) A loving clasp with one's arms.

huge Very large, enormous. **hugely.**

hulking Large, clumsy.

hull (hulls) The body or frame of a ship.

hullabaloo Noise, uproar.

hullo *See* hallo.

hum¹ (hums, humming, hummed) 1. To sing with closed lips. 2. To make a gentle murmuring sound like bees.

hum² (hums) A humming sound.

human Belonging to man or mankind. *A human being,* a person.

humane Kind-hearted. **humanely.**

humanity 1. The human race. 2. Human nature. 3. Kind-heartedness.

humble¹ (humbler, humblest) Modest, meek. **humbly.**

humble² (humbles, humbling, humbled) To make someone less proud.

humbug¹ Dishonest talk or behaviour, nonsense.

humbug² (humbugs) A hard peppermint-flavoured sweet.

humid Moist, damp. **humidity.**

humiliate (humiliates, humiliating, humiliated) To make someone feel ashamed. **humiliation.**

humility Being humble.

humour¹ 1. Amusement, being funny. *A sense of humour.* **humorous, humorously, humorist.** 2. A mood. *In a good humour.*

humour² (humours, humouring, humoured) To try to please someone.

hump¹ (humps) A bump, a round lump.

hump² (humps, humping, humped) 1. To make a hump. 2. To carry something on one's back.

hunch¹ (hunches) *To have a hunch about something,* to believe one can guess what will happen.

hunch² (hunches, hunching, hunched) To bend, to make a hump.

hunchback (hunchbacks) Someone with a hump on his back. **hunchbacked.**

hundred (hundreds) The number 100. **hundredth.**

hundredweight (hundredweights) A unit of weight, 112 pounds or 50·8 kilograms.

hung *See* hang[1].

hunger The feeling of wanting food.

hungry (hungrier, hungriest) Feeling hunger. **hungrily.**

hunk (hunks) A large shapeless piece of something.

hunt[1] (hunts, hunting, hunted) 1. To chase wild animals and game, to try to kill them. **hunter, huntsman.** 2. To pursue something, to search for it.

hunt[2] (hunts) 1. A chase, a search, hunting. 2. A group of people hunting.

hurdle (hurdles) A framework for jumping over in hurdling.

hurdling A kind of racing in which competitors must jump over hurdles. **hurdler.**

hurl (hurls, hurling, hurled) To throw something as hard as possible.

hurrah or **hurray** A shout of happiness or approval.

hurricane (hurricanes) A very violent windy storm.

hurry[1] The wish to get something done quickly. *In a hurry*, hurrying.

hurry[2] (hurries, hurrying, hurried) 1. To move quickly, to do something quickly. 2. To try to make someone be quick. **hurriedly.**

hurt (hurts, hurting, hurt) To cause harm, pain, or distress.

hurtle (hurtles, hurtling, hurtled) To move along very quickly or violently.

husband (husbands) A married man.

hush (hushes, hushing, hushed) 1. To become silent. 2. To tell people to be silent. 3. *To hush something up*, to keep it secret.

husk (husks) The dry outer covering of a seed.

husky[1] (huskier, huskiest) 1. Dry, hoarse. 2. Big and strong.

husky[2] (huskies) An Eskimo dog.

hustle (hustles, hustling, hustled) 1. To push roughly, to jostle. 2. To hurry. **hustler.**

hut (huts) A small house or shelter.

hutch (hutches) A box for a pet rabbit to live in.

hyacinth (hyacinths) A sweet-smelling flower which grows from a bulb.

hydrant (hydrants) An outdoor water tap.

hydraulic Worked by water or other liquid. *Hydraulic brakes.*

hydroelectric Producing electricity by water-power.

hydrofoil (hydrofoils) A kind of boat which skims fast over the surface of the water.

hydrogen A very light inflammable gas.

hyena (hyenas) An animal like a wolf with a laugh-like cry.

hygiene Rules for keeping clean and healthy. **hygienic, hygienically.**

hymn (hymns) A song sung in a religious service. **hymn-book.**

hyphen (hyphens) The mark - . It is used in words like *wicket-keeper*, or when a word has to be divided at the end of a line.

hypnosis A condition like a deep sleep in which a person's actions may be controlled by someone else. **hypnotic.**

hypnotize (hypnotizes, hypnotizing, hypnotized) To put someone into a state of hypnosis. **hypnotist.**

hypocrite (hypocrites) A person who pretends to be more virtuous than he really is. **hypocritical, hypocritically, hypocrisy.**

hypodermic *A hypodermic syringe*, a device for giving injections.

hysteria Wild, uncontrollable excitement. **hysterical, hysterically, hysterics.**

Ii

I¹ One in Roman numerals.

I² (me, myself) A word used by a person when referring to himself.

ice¹ Frozen water.

ice² (ices) An ice-cream.

ice³ (ices, icing, iced) 1. To make something become very cold. 2. To cover something with ice or icing.

iceberg (icebergs) A large floating island of ice at sea.

ice-breaker (ice-breakers) A ship with strong bows for breaking through ice.

ice-cream (ice-creams) A creamy frozen food.

ice-hockey A kind of hockey played on ice by skaters.

icicle (icicles) A hanging piece of ice.

icing A sweet covering for a cake.

icy (icier, iciest) Very cold, like ice. icily.

idea (ideas) A thought, an opinion, an understanding of something, a plan.

ideal Just what is wanted, perfect. *Ideal weather for a swim.*

ideally 1. Perfectly. 2. Under perfect circumstances.

identical The very same, similar in every detail. *Identical twins.*

identify (identifies, identifying, identified) To discover who or what someone or something is. identification.

identity (identities) Who somebody is. *Can you prove your identity?* Can you prove who you are?

idiot (idiots) A stupid person, a fool. idiotic, idiotically, idiocy.

idle (idler, idlest) 1. Not working. 2. Lazy. 3. Worthless. *Idle gossip.* idly, idleness.

idol (idols) 1. A statue worshipped as a god. 2. Someone who is greatly loved or admired.

idolize (idolizes, idolizing, idolized) To love or admire very much.

if 1. On condition that, supposing that. *You can come if you pay your own fare.* 2. Whenever. *If I don't wear my glasses I get a headache.* 3. Even though. *I'll finish this job if it kills me!* 4. Whether. *Do you know if dinner is ready?*

igloo (igloos) An Eskimo's snow hut.

ignite (ignites, igniting, ignited) 1. To set on fire. 2. To catch fire. ignition.

ignition-key (ignition-keys) The key used to start a car or other vehicle.

ignoramus (ignoramuses) An ignorant person.

ignorant 1. Having no knowledge about something. 2. Uneducated, having little knowledge about anything. ignorantly, ignorance.

ignore (ignores, ignoring, ignored) To take no notice of someone or something.

ill 1. Sick, in bad health. illness. 2. Badly. *To ill-treat someone,* to treat him badly.

I'll (informal) 1. I will. 2. I shall.

illegal Against the law. illegally.

illegible Impossible to read. illegibly.

illegitimate *An illegitimate child,* a child whose parents were not married to each other when it was born.

illiterate Unable to read or write. illiteracy.

illogical Not logical. illogically.

illuminate (illuminates, illuminating, illuminated) To light something up, to decorate it with lights. illumination.

illusion (illusions) A false idea, a belief that something is real when it is not.

illustrate (illustrates, illustrating, illustrated) To explain or show something by the help of pictures or diagrams. illustration, illustrator.

I'm (informal) I am.

image (images) 1. A picture or a carving of something. 2. A copy, a likeness.

imaginary Not real, existing only in the mind.

imagination The power to imagine things.

imaginative Having a strong imagination. imaginatively.

imagine (imagines, imagining, imagined) To form pictures in the mind. *Can you imagine what it was like to live in Roman Britain?* imaginable.

imam (imams) A Muslim leader.

imbecile (imbeciles) A weak-minded person, a fool. imbecility.

imitate (imitates, imitating, imitated) To copy, to mimic. imitation, imitator.

immature Not mature, not fully grown.

immeasurable Very great, too big to measure. immeasurably.

immediate 1. Happening without delay. *I want an immediate answer.* 2. Next, nearest. *We talk to our immediate neighbours over the fence.*

immediately At once, without delay.

immense Very big, huge. immensely, immensity.

immerse (immerses, immersing, immersed) 1. To put something completely in water or other liquid. 2. *To be immersed in something*, to be very busy and interested with it.

immersion heater An electric water-heater in a hot-water tank.

immigrate (immigrates, immigrating, immigrated) To come into a country to settle there. immigrant, immigration.

imminent Likely to happen soon.

immobile Not movable, not moving.

immobilize (immobilizes, immobilizing, immobilized) To make something immobile and useless.

immoral Wicked, not moral. immorality.

immortal 1. Living for ever. 2. Famous for all time. immortality.

immovable Not movable.

immune Safe from the danger of catching a disease. immunity.

immunize (immunizes, immunizing, immunized) To make someone immune. immunization.

imp (imps) A small devil. impish, impishly.

impact (impacts) A collision, a violent coming together.

impale (impales, impaling, impaled) To stick a spear or spike through something or someone.

impartial Fair, not biased. impartially.

impassable Impossible to travel along or through.

impatient Not patient, restless. impatiently, impatience.

impede (impedes, impeding, impeded) To hinder.

impediment (impediments) Something that impedes or hinders.

impenetrable Unable to be penetrated.

imperative Urgent, essential.

imperceptible Very slight, not noticeable. imperceptibly.

imperfect Not perfect, not complete. imperfectly, imperfection.

imperial Of an empire or its rulers.

imperil (imperils, imperilling, imperilled) To bring somebody or something into danger.

impersonal 1. Not influenced by personal feelings. 2. Not referring to a particular person.

impersonate (impersonates, impersonating, impersonated) To pretend to be somebody else. impersonation.

impertinent Rude, not respectful. impertinently, impertinence.

imperturbable Calm, not excitable. imperturbably.

impetigo A skin disease.

impetuous Liable to act rapidly without thinking. impetuously.

impiety Lack of reverence. impious.

implement (implements) A tool, an instrument.

implore (implores, imploring, implored) To beg, to ask very earnestly.

imply (implies, implying, implied) To hint at something without actually saying it. implication.

impolite Rude, not polite. impolitely.

import[1] (pronounced im*port*) (imports, importing, imported) To bring goods into a country from abroad.

import[2] (pronounced *im*port) (imports) Something which is imported.

important 1. To be treated very seriously. *An important message.* 2. Well known and deserving respect. *An important visitor.* **importantly, importance.**

impose (imposes, imposing, imposed) 1. To fix a tax or penalty to be paid. 2. *To impose on someone*, to take unfair advantage of him. **imposition.**

imposing Important-looking. **imposingly.**

impossible 1. Not possible. 2. Outrageous, not to be put up with. **impossibly, impossibility.**

impostor (impostors) A person pretending to be someone else, a swindler. **imposture.**

impotent Lacking the strength to do something. **impotence.**

impoverished Poor.

impracticable Not able to be put into practice.

impractical Not practical, not easily done.

impregnable Not to be taken by force. *An impregnable castle.*

impress (impresses, impressing, impressed) 1. To have an influence on somebody. 2. To fix something in his mind. **impressive.**

impression (impressions) 1. An idea. *I have the impression that the weather is improving.* 2. *To make an impression on somebody*, to impress him.

imprison (imprisons, imprisoning, imprisoned) To put somebody into prison. **imprisonment.**

improbable Not likely. **improbably, improbability.**

impromptu Without preparation, without special rehearsal.

improper Not suitable, wrong, indecent. **improperly.**

improve (improves, improving, improved) 1. To make something better. 2. To become better. **improvement.**

improvise (improvises, improvising, improvised) 1. To make something up as one goes along. 2. To make do with what is there when the proper materials are lacking.

imprudent Rash, unwise. **imprudently.**

impudent Rude, openly lacking in respect. **impudently, impudence.**

impulse (impulses) 1. A push, a thrust forwards. 2. A sudden desire to do something without previous planning. **impulsive, impulsively.**

impunity Safety from harm or punishment.

impure Not pure. **impurity.**

in 1. At. *In London.* 2. Into. *He fell in the Thames.* 3. Inside, not outside. *The fish was in the bowl. You must stay in until the rain stops.* 4. During. *In October.* 5. Consisting of. *A serial in four episodes.*

inability Lack of ability.

inaccessible Not accessible, impossible to reach.

inaccurate Not accurate. **inaccurately, inaccuracy.**

inadequate Not adequate, not enough. **inadequately, inadequacy.**

inadvertent Unintentional, not deliberate. **inadvertently.**

inanimate Lifeless.

inappropriate Not appropriate, not suitable. **inappropriately.**

inarticulate Unable to speak confidently.

inattentive Not attentive, not taking proper notice. **inattentively, inattention.**

inaudible Not able to be heard. **inaudibly.**

incalculable Too great to be measured or calculated.

incapable Not able to do something.

incarnate In bodily form. **incarnation.**

incautious Not cautious, rash. **incautiously.**

incendiary bomb A bomb which starts a fire.

incense[1] (pronounced *in*cense) A substance which gives off a sweet spicy smell when burning.

incense[2] (pronounced in*cense*) (incenses, incensing, incensed) To make someone very angry.

incentive (incentives) An encouragement to do something.

incessant Continual, not stopping. **incessantly.**

inch (inches) A measure of length, 2·5 centimetres. Twelve inches make one foot.

incident (incidents) An event, a happening.

incidental 1. Not very important. 2. *Incidental music*, background music to a play. **incidentally.**

incinerator (incinerators) An apparatus for burning rubbish.

incite (incites, inciting, incited) To stir somebody up, to rouse him to action. **incitement.**

inclination (inclinations) A readiness to do something, a desire to do it.

incline¹ (inclines, inclining, inclined) 1. To have a feeling or idea. *I'm inclined to think he doesn't want to go.* 2. To be willing to do something. 3. To do something usually. *He is inclined to chatter.*

incline² (inclines) A slope.

include (includes, including, included) To consider or count something as part of the whole. *The trip will cost £1 including the train fare and meals.* **inclusion, inclusive.**

incoherent Muddled, rambling, **incoherently.**

income (incomes) Money which a person receives regularly for doing work or from his investments.

incompetent Unable to do a job properly. **incompetently, incompetence.**

incomplete Not complete. **incompletely, incompletion.**

incomprehensible Not able to be understood. **incomprehensibly, incomprehension.**

inconceivable Impossible to imagine, very hard to believe. **inconceivably.**

inconclusive 1. Not reaching a definite or satisfying end. 2. Not proving anything. **inconclusively.**

incongruous Out of place, absurd. **incongruously.**

inconsiderate Thoughtless, not caring about others. **inconsiderately.**

inconsistent Not consistent, contradictory. **inconsistently.**

inconspicuous Not easily noticed. **inconspicuously.**

inconvenient Not convenient, troublesome, awkward. **inconveniently, inconvenience.**

incorporate (incorporates, incorporating, incorporated) To include.

incorrect Not correct, wrong, mistaken. **incorrectly.**

increase¹ (increases, increasing, increased) 1. To make greater. 2. To become greater. **increasingly.**

increase² (increases) An increasing, the amount by which something increases.

incredible 1. Not credible, not to be believed. 2. (informal) Amazing. **incredibly.**

incredulous Not believing. *My father was incredulous when I said I'd won first prize.* **incredulously.**

incriminate (incriminates, incriminating, incriminated) To seem to prove that someone is guilty of wrongdoing.

incubate (incubates, incubating, incubated) To hatch eggs by sitting on them or by keeping them warm. **incubation, incubator.**

incurable Not able to be cured. **incurably.**

indebted Owing money or gratitude to somebody.

indecent Not decent, improper. **indecently, indecency.**

indecipherable Impossible to read.

indeed Really.

indefinite Vague, not clearly stated. **indefinitely.**

indelible Not easily rubbed out. **indelibly.**

independent Not controlled by anybody else, free of other people's orders or influence. **independently, independence.**

indescribable Not able to be described. **indescribably.**

indestructible Not able to be destroyed.

index (indexes) 1. A reference-list in alphabetical order at the end of a book. 2. *The index finger*, the first finger, the one used for pointing.

Indian 1. Of India. 2. Of American Indians.

indian ink Black drawing-ink.

indicate (indicates, indicating, indicated) 1. To point something out, to make it known. 2. To be a sign of something. *They say that a red sky at night indicates fine weather.* **indication, indicator.**

indifferent 1. Not interested, not caring. 2. Rather poor, not very good. *I'm an indifferent tennis-player.* **indifferently, indifference.**

indigestible Not easily digested.

indigestion 1. Difficulty in digesting food. 2. A pain caused by this.

indignant Angry and scornful. **indignantly, indignation.**

indignity (indignities) Shameful treatment.

indigo Deep blue.

indirect 1. Not going the straightest way. *An indirect route.* 2. Not going straight to the point. *An indirect answer.* **indirectly.**

indiscreet Not discreet. **indiscreetly, indiscretion.**

indispensible Necessary, essential.

indisposed Unwell, poorly. **indisposition.**

indisputable Not to be argued about, true. **indisputably.**

indistinct Not clear, confused, hazy. **indistinctly.**

indistinguishable Not to be distinguished, looking exactly alike. **indistinguishably.**

individual[1] 1. For one person. *An individual meat pie.* 2. Belonging to one person. *He has an individual style of bowling.* 3. Separate, on its own. *The judge considered each individual piece of evidence.* **individually.**

individual[2] (individuals) (informal) A person.

indivisible Not able to be divided. **indivisibly.**

indoor Happening or belonging inside a building.

indoors Inside a building.

induce (induces, inducing, induced) To persuade. **inducement.**

indulge (indulges, indulging, indulged) To let someone have his way. **indulgent, indulgence.**

industry[1] (industries) 1. The making of things in factories and workshops. 2. A trade, a business. **industrial.**

industry[2] Hard work. **industrious, industriously.**

inebriated Drunk.

inedible Not suitable for eating.

ineffective Useless, feeble. **ineffectively.**

inefficient Not capable of doing a job properly. **inefficiently, inefficiency.**

inequality (inequalities) A lack of equality.

inescapable Unavoidable, not to be escaped. **inescapably.**

inevitable Unavoidable, sure to happen. **inevitably, inevitability.**

inexcusable Very wrong, not to be excused. **inexcusably.**

inexhaustible Not able to be used up.

inexpensive Not expensive, cheap. **inexpensively.**

inexperienced Not experienced.

inexplicable Impossible to explain.

infallible Always right, never making a mistake, never failing. **infallibly, infallibility.**

infamous Wicked, with a bad reputation. **infamy.**

infant (infants) 1. A baby. 2. A young child. 3. *An infant school*, a school for children aged about 5 to 7. **infancy.**

infantile Babyish.

infantry Soldiers trained to fight on foot. **infantryman.**

infatuated Madly in love. **infatuation.**

infect (infects, infecting, infected) To give a disease to someone, to pass on something catching.

infection (infections) An infectious disease.

infectious 1. Catching, liable to be passed on from one person to another. 2. Suffering from an infectious disease.

inferior 1. Less important. 2. Of poor quality. **inferiority.**

inferno (infernos) A terrifying fire.

infidelity Unfaithfulness.

infiltrate (infiltrates, infiltrating, infiltrated) To move into a place gradually without being noticed. *The soldiers infiltrated into enemy territory.* **infiltration.**

infinite Endless, too big to be imagined or understood. **infinitely.**

infinity An infinite distance, an infinite number.

infirm Weak, ill. **infirmity.**

infirmary (infirmaries) A hospital.

inflame (inflames, inflaming, inflamed) 1. To become red, heated, or angry. 2. To make someone or something fiery or angry.

inflammable Easily set on fire.

inflammation (inflammations) A painful swelling or redness.

inflate (inflates, inflating, inflated) To fill something with air. **inflatable.**

inflation A general rise in prices. **inflationary.**

inflexible Not able to be bent or turned. **inflexibly.**

inflict (inflicts, inflicting, inflicted) To make somebody suffer something. *A severe punishment was inflicted on him.* **infliction.**

influence[1] (influences) 1. The power to affect something. *The weather has great influence upon the growth of crops.* 2. The power to persuade someone to think or do something.

influence[2] (influences, influencing, influenced) To have influence over something or somebody.

influential Having power and importance.

influenza An illness with fever and catarrh.

inform (informs, informing, informed) 1. To tell somebody something. 2. *To inform against somebody,* to report him to the police. **informer, informant.**

informal 1. Not formal, relaxed, free and easy. *An informal party.* 2. In this dictionary words marked 'informal' are normally used only in conversation. **informally, informality.**

information Something told to someone, news or knowledge.

informative Containing much information.

infrequent Not frequent, rare. **infrequently.**

infringe (infringes, infringing, infringed) *To infringe the rules,* to break the rules. **infringement.**

infuriate (infuriates, infuriating, infuriated) To make somebody very angry.

ingenious Clever, skilful. **ingeniously, ingenuity.**

ingle-nook (ingle-nooks) A corner by an old-fashioned fire-place.

ingot (ingots) A lump of metal.

ingrained Deeply fixed.

ingratitude Not being thankful.

ingredient (ingredients) One of the things in a mixture, one of the things used in a recipe for cooking.

ingrowing Growing inwards. *An ingrowing toenail.*

inhabit (inhabits, inhabiting, inhabited) *To inhabit a place,* to live in that place. **inhabitant, inhabitable.**

inhale (inhales, inhaling, inhaled) To breathe air, smoke, or gas deeply into one's lungs. **inhaler.**

inherit (inherits, inheriting, inherited) 1. To receive money, property, or a title from one's parents or ancestors when they are dead. *The young duke inherited a large fortune from his father.* 2. To get certain qualities or characteristics from one's parents or ancestors. *He has inherited his father's sense of humour.* inheritance, inheritor.

inhospitable Unwelcoming, unfriendly to visitors.

inhuman Cruel, without human feelings. inhumanly.

iniquitous Wicked. iniquitously, iniquity.

initial[1] Coming first, coming at the beginning. initially.

initial[2] (initials) The first letter of a person's name.

initiate (initiates, initiating, initiated) 1. To start a plan or scheme working. 2. To admit someone into a secret society or some similar group. initiation.

initiative 1. *To take the initiative*, to make the first move. 2. *To use one's initiative*, to do something without being told to do it.

inject (injects, injecting, injected) To put a medicine or drug into someone's body through a hollow needle. injection.

injure (injures, injuring, injured) To hurt, to damage, to do wrong to someone. injury.

injustice Unfairness.

ink (inks) A black or coloured liquid used with a pen for writing or drawing. ink-well, inky.

inkling A faint idea.

inland In the middle of a country, away from the coast.

inlet (inlets) A narrow strip of sea that penetrates for a short distance inland.

inmate (inmates) A person who lives in an institution with many other people.

inmost Furthest inside.

inn (inns) A public house, a small hotel. innkeeper.

inner Inside. *An inner tube*, the inflatable tube inside a tyre.

innings (innings) In cricket, the time during which a team or a player is batting.

innocent 1. Not guilty. 2. Harmless, knowing no evil. 3. *Innocent of*, without. innocently, innocence.

innocuous Harmless. innocuously.

innovation (innovations) Something recently invented or brought into use. innovator.

innumerable Too many to count.

inoculate (inoculates, inoculating, inoculated) To inject people so that they will be safe from a particular disease. *I have been inoculated against flu.* inoculation.

inoffensive Not offensive, not objectionable. inoffensively.

inquest (inquests) An official inquiry after a death to discover why the person died.

inquire (inquires, inquiring, inquired) To make an inquiry. inquirer.

inquiry (inquiries) An investigation, especially an official one.

inquisitive Curious, fond of asking questions. inquisitively, inquisitiveness.

insane (insaner, insanest) Mad. insanely, insanity.

insanitary Dirty and unhealthy.

inscribe (inscribes, inscribing, inscribed) To write or engrave words or letters on something. inscription.

inscrutable Mysterious, hard to understand. inscrutably.

insect (insects) A small six-legged animal with no backbone, such as a fly, an ant, or a bee.

insecticide (insecticides) A poison for killing unwanted insects.

insecure Not safe, not secure. insecurely, insecurity.

insensible Unconscious. insensibly, insensibility.

insensitive Not sensitive. insensitively.

inseparable Not to be separated. inseparably.

insert (inserts, inserting, inserted) To put something into something else. *To insert a coin in a slot machine.* insertion.

inside [1] (insides) 1. The inner part of something, the part nearest the middle. 2. The stomach and the other inner organs of the body.

inside [2] 1. Nearest the middle, in the middle. 2. On or in the inside of. *It is warmer inside the house.* 3. Indoors. *We'll stay inside if it rains.*

insignificant Unimportant. insignificance.

insincere Not sincere. insincerely, insincerity.

insipid Tasteless, dull. insipidly.

insist (insists, insisting, insisted) 1. To demand something very firmly, to say that something must happen. *I insist on coming with you.* 2. To say something very firmly or persuasively. *The accused man insisted that he was innocent.* insistent, insistence.

insolent Insulting, cheeky. insolently, insolence.

insoluble 1. Impossible to solve. 2. Impossible to dissolve.

insomnia Sleeplessness.

inspect (inspects, inspecting, inspected) To examine something, to look very carefully at it. inspection.

inspector (inspectors) 1. An official who inspects places or things. 2. An officer in the police.

inspire (inspires, inspiring, inspired) To fill someone with good and exciting thoughts or feelings. *The beautiful scenery inspired us to make up a poem.* inspiration.

install (installs, installing, installed) To put something into place ready for use. *They have installed a new heater in our classroom.* installation.

instalment (instalments) 1. *To pay by instalments,* to pay a small amount at a time. 2. An episode in a serial.

instance (instances) An example.

instant [1] 1. Happening at once. instantly. 2. *Instant coffee,* coffee that can be made very quickly.

instant [2] (instants) 1. A precise point of time. 2. A moment. *I'll be back in an instant.*

instantaneous In an instant. instantaneously.

instead 1. As an alternative. *If you haven't got a large loaf, I'll take two small loaves instead.* 2. *Instead of,* in place of.

instep (insteps) The top of the foot between the toes and the ankle.

instinct (instincts) 1. A natural tendency to behave in a certain way. 2. A feeling, an intuition. instinctive, instinctively.

institute (institutes) A society or organization, its offices or buildings.

institution (institutions) 1. A custom, a habit, a law. 2. A building where people can live or work together.

instruct (instructs, instructing, instructed) 1. To teach somebody. 2. To give orders to somebody. 3. To inform somebody of something. instruction, instructional, instructor.

instructive Giving instruction or information.

instrument (instruments) 1. A piece of apparatus, a tool. 2. *A musical instrument,* an object used to produce musical sounds. instrumental, instrumentalist.

insubordinate Disobedient, rebellious. insubordination.

insufficient Not sufficient. insufficiently.

insulate (insulates, insulating, insulated) 1. To cover something or wrap it up in order to prevent loss of heat. 2. To cover wires that carry electricity, in order to prevent them touching by mistake. *Insulating tape,* a sticky tape used for this purpose. insulation, insulator.

insult [1] (pronounced *in*sult) (insults) A piece of hurtful rudeness.

insult [2] (pronounced in*sult*) (insults, insulting, insulted) To be rude and unkind to someone.

insurance A system in which a person regularly pays money to a company which in return agrees to pay some back in case of sickness, loss or damage of property, or other emergencies. *An insurance policy*, an agreement to do this.

insure (insures, insuring, insured) To make an insurance agreement. insurer.

intact Untouched, undamaged.

integrate (integrates, integrating, integrated) To combine things or people into a complete whole or into a single group.

integration Getting different kinds of people to live happily together as equals.

integrity Honesty.

intellect A person's power of reasoning, his ability to understand things.

intellectual 1. With a good intellect, keen on studying and learning. 2. Needing a good intellect, requiring hard study.

intelligence 1. Cleverness, understanding. 2. Secret information, spying.

intelligent Clever. intelligently.

intelligible Understandable. intelligibly.

intend (intends, intending, intended) To have a particular plan in mind. *I intend to go camping next holidays.*

intense (intenser, intensest) Very great, violent. *Intense heat.* intensely, intensity.

intensive Thorough, concentrated. *An intensive search.*

intent Keen, eager. intently.

intention (intentions) A purpose, a plan.

intentional Deliberate, done on purpose. intentionally.

intercept (intercepts, intercepting, intercepted) To attack or stop someone or something on its way from one place to another. interception, interceptor.

interchange (interchanges) A place where people can change from one railway or motorway to another.

interchangeable Easily changed one for another. *A pen with interchangeable nibs.*

intercom (intercoms) (informal) A type of telephone communication system such as that used between the crew of an aircraft.

intercourse Communication or dealings between people.

interest[1] (interests) 1. A state of wanting to know about something. *I have a keen interest in astronomy.* 2. Something which concerns a person deeply, which is to his advantage or profit. *It is in your best interests to tell the police right away.* 3. Money which is paid regularly in return for a loan.

interest[2] (interests, interesting, interested) To make someone curious about something, to hold his attention. interestingly.

interfere (interferes, interfering, interfered) 1. To take part in something that is not one's concern. 2. To get in the way and prevent something from being done. interference.

interior (interiors) The inside.

interlude (interludes) An interval of time.

intermediate Coming between two stages, sizes, or times.

interminable Endless, seeming to go on for ever. interminably.

intermission (intermissions) An interval, a pause.

intermittent Stopping and starting at intervals. intermittently.

intern (interns, interning, interned) To put somebody into a prison camp, usually in time of war. internment, internee.

internal 1. Of or in the inside of something. 2. *An internal combustion engine*, a petrol engine like that used in a motor car.

international Between two or more nations, concerning two or more nations. *Interpol is an international police organization.* internationally.

interplanetary Between the planets.

interpret (interprets, interpreting, interpreted) 1. To make the meaning of something clear. 2. To translate from one language into another. interpreter, interpretation.

interrogate (interrogates, interrogating, interrogated) To question someone very closely. interrogation.

interrupt (interrupts, interrupting, interrupted) 1. To break in on something, to stop it for a time. *He's busy, don't interrupt his work.* 2. To speak to someone who is in the middle of saying something. interruption.

intersect (intersects, intersecting, intersected) To divide something by passing through it or by crossing it. intersection.

interstellar Between the stars.

interval (intervals) 1. A break, a gap. 2. A break between two parts of a concert, play, or film-show. 3. *At intervals*, from time to time, occasionally.

intervene (intervenes, intervening, intervened) To come between, to interrupt. intervention.

interview[1] (interviews) A meeting with someone to discuss a particular subject.

interview[2] (interviews, interviewing, interviewed) To be the person who asks the questions in an interview. interviewer.

intestines The tube-like organs of the body through which food passes after it has gone through the stomach.

intimate 1. Close and familiar, very friendly. 2. Private. *Intimate secrets.* intimately, intimacy.

intimidate (intimidates, intimidating, intimidated) To try to make a person do something by frightening him. intimidation.

into 1. To a place inside. *We ran into the garden.* 2. *To change into*, to become. *The frog changed into a handsome prince.*

intolerable Unbearable. intolerably.

intolerant Scornful of other people's views and opinions. intolerantly, intolerance.

intoxicate (intoxicates, intoxicating, intoxicated) To make someone drunk, to make him foolishly excited. intoxication.

intrepid Fearless, very brave. intrepidly.

intricate Complicated. intricately, intricacy.

intrigue[1] (intrigues) A secret plot or plan.

intrigue[2] (intrigues, intriguing, intrigued) 1. To arouse curiosity. *What an intriguing story! Is it really true?* 2. To plot.

introduce (introduces, introducing, introduced) 1. To make somebody known to someone else. 2. To make an announcement before a performance. 3. To bring something into use. *A new flavour of ice-cream has been introduced.* introductory.

introduction (introductions) 1. The act of introducing someone or something. 2. The opening or beginning of something. 3. A short section before the main part of a book, explaining and introducing it to the reader.

intrude (intrudes, intruding, intruded) To enter without being invited, to force a way in. intruder, intrusion.

intuition (intuitions) The power of suddenly understanding something without having to think it out in every detail. intuitive, intuitively.

inundate (inundates, inundating, inundated) To flood. inundation.

invade (invades, invading, invaded) 1. To attack and enter a country. 2. To enter anything by force.

invalid[1] (pronounced *in*valid) (invalids) Someone suffering from a long illness.

invalid[2] (pronounced in*va*lid) Not valid.

invaluable Very valuable, beyond price.

invariable Unchangeable. invariably.

invasion (invasions) 1. Invading. 2. Being invaded.

invent (invents, inventing, invented) 1. To plan and make something that has not been thought of before. 2. To make something up. invention, inventor, inventive.

invert (inverts, inverting, inverted) To turn something upside down. inversion.

invest (invests, investing, invested) *To invest money*, to put it into savings where it will gain interest, or to use it in some other profitable way. investment.

investigate (investigates, investigating, investigated) To look for information about something. investigation, investigator.

invigorating Strengthening, giving energy.

invincible Not able to be conquered. invincibly, invincibility.

invisible Not able to be seen. invisibly, invisibility.

invite (invites, inviting, invited) To ask someone politely to do something. invitation.

inviting Tempting, attractive. invitingly.

involuntary Done without thinking, not done deliberately. involuntarily.

involved 1. Complicated. 2. *To be involved in something*, to be mixed up in it. involvement.

inward 1. On the inside. 2. Going in. *The inward journey*.

inwardly In the mind, not speaking aloud.

inwards Towards the inside.

iodine A chemical sometimes used as an antiseptic.

IOU A written promise to pay some money.

irascible Easily made angry.

irate Angry. irately.

ire Anger.

iris (irises) 1. The coloured part of the eyeball. 2. A kind of flower.

Irish Of Ireland. Irishman, Irishwoman.

irksome Tiresome.

iron¹ (irons) 1. A metal used in making steel. 2. A tool made of iron. 3. A flat piece of metal with a handle used for smoothing clothes after washing. 4. *The Iron Age*, the period when the best tools and weapons were made of iron. 5. *Irons*, fetters.

iron² (irons, ironing, ironed) To smooth material with an iron. *An ironing board*, a special folding table used for this purpose.

ironmonger (ironmongers) A man who keeps a shop which sells tools. ironmongery.

irrational 1. Having no power of reasoning. 2. Unreasonable, absurd. irrationally.

irregular 1. Not usual, not regular. 2. Against the rules. 3. Uneven, rough in shape. irregularly, irregularity.

irrelevant Not to the point, not on the subject. irrelevantly, irrelevance.

irreparable Beyond repair. irreparably.

irrepressible Lively, impossible to discourage. irrepressibly.

irresistible Impossible to resist, very attractive. irresistibly.

irresponsible Stupid and careless, not showing a sense of responsibility. irresponsibly, irresponsibility.

irreverent Not respectful. irreverently, irreverence.

irrevocable Unalterable, gone beyond recall. irrevocably.

irrigate (irrigates, irrigating, irrigated) To supply dry land with water so that crops can grow. irrigation.

irritable Easily irritated. irritably.

irritate (irritates, irritating, irritated) 1. To annoy someone, to make him angry. 2. To cause an itch. irritation.

is *See* be.

Islam The religion of Muslims. Islamic.

island (islands) A piece of land surrounded by water.

isle (isles) An island.

isn't (informal) Is not.

isolated Lonely, separated. isolation.

Israeli Of Israel.

issue¹ (issues, issuing, issued) **1.** To come out, to flow out. *Smoke issued from the chimney.* **2.** To send out, to give out, to publish. *The police issued a warning that dangerous drugs were missing.*

issue² (issues) **1.** A matter for discussion. *We have several issues to talk about.* **2.** A result, an outcome. **3.** A magazine or other publication brought out at a particular time. *Have you seen this term's issue of the school magazine?* **4.** A set of stamps issued at a particular time. *A Christmas issue.*

isthmus (isthmuses) A narrow neck of land joining two larger areas of land.

it (itself) The thing being talked about.

Italian Of Italy.

italics Printing that slopes *like this.*

itch (itches, itching, itched) **1.** To have a feeling which makes one want to scratch. **2.** *To itch to do something*, to long to do it. itchy.

item (items) **1.** A single article in a list or collection. **2.** A single piece of news in a newspaper or broadcast.

itinerant Wandering.

itinerary (itineraries) A plan of a journey.

its Of it.

it's (informal) It is.

itself *See* it. This word is used in the same ways as himself.

ivory **1.** The substance of which elephants' tusks are made. **2.** Its pale cream colour.

ivy A creeping, climbing evergreen plant.

Jj

jab (jabs, jabbing, jabbed) To poke something roughly, to hit or stab it suddenly and sharply.

jabber (jabbers, jabbering, jabbered) To talk quickly in a confused way, to chatter.

jack¹ (jacks) A device for lifting a heavy object from the ground.

jack² (jacks, jacking, jacked) *To jack something up*, to lift it with a jack.

jack³ (jacks) The card in a suit of playing cards next in value above the ten. *The Jack of Hearts.*

jackal (jackals) A wild animal of the dog family.

jackdaw (jackdaws) A kind of black bird.

jacket (jackets) **1.** A coat which covers the top half of the body. **2.** An outer covering.

jackpot (jackpots) An amount of prize money which keeps on increasing until someone wins it.

jade A green stone used for making ornaments.

jaded Tired out, weary.

jagged With sharp, uneven edges.

jaguar (jaguars) A large fierce cat-like animal.

jam¹ (jams, jamming, jammed) **1.** To squeeze, to crush. *I jammed my fingers in the door.* **2.** To become wedged, to become stuck tight. *The surging crowd jammed in the doorway.*

jam² (jams) A tight and difficult situation. *A traffic jam*, traffic crowded so tightly together that it can move only very slowly.

jam³ A food made by boiling fruit with sugar.

jamboree (jamborees) **1.** A large gathering of Scouts. **2.** A celebration, merry-making.

jangle (jangles, jangling, jangled) To make an unpleasant ringing noise.

January The first month of the year.

Japanese Of Japan.

jar¹ (jars, jarring, jarred) **1.** To strike against something harshly. **2.** To have an unpleasant effect on someone's feelings.

jar² (jars) A kind of container, often made of glass. *A jam-jar.*

jaundice An illness which makes a person's skin turn yellow.

jaunt (jaunts) An outing.

jaunty (jauntier, jauntiest) Lively and perky. **jauntily.**

javelin (javelins) A kind of spear.

jaw (jaws) **1.** The bones of the mouth, in which the teeth are set. **jaw-bone. 2.** The lower part of the face.

jay (jays) A noisy, brightly-coloured bird.

jazz A kind of music first played and sung by Negroes in America. **jazzy.**

jealous **1.** Envious, unhappy because of someone else's good fortune. **2.** Afraid of losing something to someone else. **jealously, jealousy.**

jeans Trousers usually made of blue cotton cloth.

jeep (jeeps) A kind of motor vehicle for use on rough ground.

jeer (jeers, jeering, jeered) To laugh rudely at someone, to mock him.

jelly (jellies) **1.** A soft food which melts in one's mouth. **2.** Any substance like jelly.

jelly-fish (jelly-fish) A sea animal which looks rather like jelly.

jerk¹ (jerks, jerking, jerked) To make a sudden unexpected movement.

jerk² (jerks) A sudden pull or twist. **jerky, jerkily.**

jersey (jerseys) A close-fitting woollen garment worn on the top half of the body.

jest¹ (jests) A joke.

jest² (jests, jesting, jested) To make jokes.

jester (jesters) A professional entertainer at a king's court.

jet¹ A hard, black substance used for making ornaments. **jet-black.**

jet² (jets) **1.** A strong stream of gas, liquid, or flame forced out of a small opening. **2.** A small hole through which gas, liquid, or flame is forced. **3.** An aircraft with jet engines.

jet engine An engine which drives a vehicle or aircraft by sending out a powerful jet of gas.

jet-propelled Driven by jet engines. **jet-propulsion.**

jetty (jetties) A small pier or landing-place.

Jew (Jews) **1.** A member of the race descended from the ancient tribes of Israel. **2.** A believer in the Hebrew religion. **Jewish.**

jewel (jewels) **1.** A precious stone. **2.** An ornament made with precious stones.

jeweller (jewellers) A person who makes or sells jewellery.

jewellery Brooches, necklaces, and other ornaments made with jewels.

jig¹ (jigs) A lively dance.

jig² (jigs, jigging, jigged) **1.** To dance a jig. **2.** To move up and down quickly and jerkily.

jigsaw (jigsaws) **1.** A jigsaw puzzle. **2.** A kind of saw which can cut curved shapes.

jigsaw puzzle A picture on card or plywood cut into curved shapes. The shapes have to be fitted together to make the picture complete.

jingle (jingles, jingling, jingled) To make a tinkling sound like the noise of small bells.

jittery Nervous, jumpy.

job (jobs) **1.** Work which a person does regularly to earn his living. **2.** A particular task **3.** (informal) *That's a good job!* that's fortunate.

jockey (jockeys) A person who rides a horse in a race.

jodhpurs Special trousers worn for riding, fitting closely from knee to ankle.

jog (jogs, jogging, jogged) 1. To give something a slight knock. *I spilt my tea because someone jogged my elbow.* 2. *To jog someone's memory*, to help him remember. 3. *To jog along*, to move along steadily, to move along bouncing up and down.

join¹ (joins, joining, joined) 1. To put together, to come together, to fix together. 2. To become a member of a society or some other group. *He joined the Navy.*

join² (joins) A place where something is joined.

joiner (joiners) A person who makes things with wood.

joint¹ (joints) 1. A join. 2. The place where two bones fit together. 3. A piece of meat big enough to feed several people.

joint² Shared by two or more people. *A joint effort.*

joist (joists) One of the long beams in a building, to which the ceilings or floors are fixed.

joke¹ (jokes) Something done or said to make people laugh.

joke² (jokes, joking, joked) To make jokes.

joker (jokers) 1. A person who makes jokes. 2. A playing-card with a picture of a jester on it.

jolly¹ (jollier, jolliest) Joyful, gay. **jollity.**

jolly² (informal) Very. *These cakes are jolly good!*

jolt¹ (jolts, jolting, jolted) To jerk.

jolt² (jolts) A jerk.

jostle (jostles, jostling, jostled) To push roughly or rudely.

jot¹ (jots, jotting, jotted) To write quickly, to make notes.

jotter (jotters) (informal) A notebook.

journal (journals) 1. A newspaper or magazine. 2. A diary.

journalist (journalists) Someone who writes for a newspaper or magazine. **journalism.**

journey¹ (journeys) A distance travelled, an expedition.

journey² (journeys, journeying, journeyed) To make a journey, to travel.

joust (jousts, jousting, jousted) To fight on horseback with lances.

jovial Merry, cheerful. **jovially.**

joy Great happiness, great pleasure. **joyful, joyfully.**

jubilee (jubilees) A special anniversary celebration.

judge¹ (judges) 1. A person who tries accused people in a lawcourt. 2. A person who decides the result of a contest or competition. 3. A person who is able to give an opinion about whether something is good or bad. *Our headmistress is a good judge of character.*

judge² (judges, judging, judged) 1. To be a judge, to act as a judge. 2. To estimate, to make a guess about something. *The goalkeeper judged the speed of the ball perfectly.* **judgement.**

judo A Japanese way of wrestling.

jug (jugs) A container for liquids, with a handle and a lip. *A milk-jug.*

juggernaut (juggernauts) A huge vehicle.

juggle (juggles, juggling, juggled) To perform such tricks as throwing many balls into the air and catching them. **juggler.**

juice (juices) Liquid from fruit, vegetables, or other food. **juicy.**

juke-box (juke-boxes) A machine that plays a record when a coin is put in.

July The seventh month of the year.

jumble¹ (jumbles, jumbling, jumbled) To mix things up in confusion.

jumble² 1. A muddle. 2. *A jumble sale*, a sale of unwanted odds and ends and second-hand clothes.

jumbo (informal) Very large. *A jumbo jet*, a very large jet air-liner.

jump¹ (jumps, jumping, jumped) 1. To leap, to make oneself move through the air by pushing with the legs. *The wicket-keeper jumped sideways to catch the ball*. 2. To go over something by jumping. *The horse jumped the fence*. 3. To move suddenly and quickly. *He jumped out of his chair*. 4. (informal) *They jumped at our offer*, they accepted it eagerly.

jump² (jumps) The act of jumping.

jumper (jumpers) 1. A person or animal that jumps. 2. A jersey.

junction (junctions) A place where roads or railway lines join.

June The sixth month of the year.

jungle (jungles) A dense, steamy forest.

junior 1. Younger. *Junior to*, younger than. 2. *A junior school*, a school for young children, usually aged about 7 to 11.

junk¹ Old things of little or no value.

junk² (junks) A Chinese sailing-boat.

junket A food made from milk.

jury (juries) A group of 12 people who have to listen to all the evidence at a trial and then declare whether the accused person is guilty or not guilty. **juryman, juror.**

just¹ 1. Exactly. *It's just one o'clock*. 2. Hardly, barely. *I just caught the bus*. 3. Very recently. *He has just gone*. 4. Now, very soon. *They are just going*. 5. Only. *I just wanted a glass of water*.

just² 1. Fair, right. 2. Well-deserved. **justly.**

justice 1. Fairness. *To do someone justice*, to be fair to him. 2. The law. *To bring someone to justice*, to bring him to trial. 3. *A Justice of the Peace*, a magistrate.

justify (justifies, justifying, justified) To show that something done or said is right, reasonable, or proper. **justifiable, justification.**

jut (juts, jutting, jutted) To stick out.

juvenile Suitable for young people, to do with young people.

Kk

kale A green vegetable.

kaleidoscope (kaleidoscopes) A tube through which one can see colourful symmetrical patterns.

kangaroo (kangaroos) An Australian animal that jumps along.

kapok A substance used for stuffing cushions and toys.

karate A Japanese method of hitting with the sides of the hands and feet in self-defence.

kayak (kayaks) An Eskimo canoe.

keel (keels) The strip of wood or metal which runs along the middle of the bottom of a boat or ship.

keen (keener, keenest) 1. Eager, interested, enthusiastic. *A keen sportsman*. 2. Sharp. *A knife with a keen edge*. 3. Very cold. *A keen wind*. 4. *To be keen on something*, to be very fond of it. **keenly, keenness.**

keep¹ (keeps, keeping, kept) 1. To have something and not give it away, to hold on to something. *I don't want that pencil back, you can keep it*. 2. To look after something, to be in charge of it. *Will you keep my watch while I go swimming?* 3. To stay, to remain, to continue. *Keep still!* 4. To be faithful to something. *He kept his word*, he did what he had promised. 5. To provide a home, food, and clothing for someone or something. *It costs a lot to keep a large family*. 6. To make someone or something remain in a certain condition. *The fire will keep us warm.* 7. To remain good and usable. *Will the milk keep until tomorrow?* 8. To prevent. *Can't you keep your dog from barking?* 9. To hold, to detain. *He was kept in prison for 20 years.* 10. *To keep goal,* to defend the goal. 11. *To keep up with someone,* not to lag behind him. 12. *To keep watch,* to be on the look-out.

keep² (keeps) A strong tower in a castle.

keeper (keepers) A person who looks after someone or something.

keg (kegs) A small barrel.

kennel (kennels) A small hut for a dog to live in.

kept *See* keep¹.

kerb (kerbs) The stone edging of a path, pavement, or road. kerbstone.

kernel (kernels) The eatable part of a nut inside the shell.

kerosene Paraffin.

kestrel (kestrels) A kind of hawk.

ketchup A kind of sauce. *Tomato ketchup.*

kettle (kettles) A metal container with a spout, a lid, and a handle, used for boiling water.

kettle-drum (kettle-drums) A percussion instrument.

key (keys) 1. A device for working a lock. keyhole. 2. A device for winding up clockwork. 3. A lever which is pressed with the fingers. *The keys on a piano or a typewriter.* 4. A term used in music. *The key of C major.* 5. Something that provides a solution or an answer. *The key to a problem.*

keyboard (keyboards) The set of keys on a piano or similar instrument.

khaki Dull yellowish brown.

kick¹ (kicks, kicking, kicked) 1. To hit with one's foot. 2. To wave one's legs about vigorously. kicker.

kick² (kicks) 1. Kicking. 2. (informal) Excitement, a thrill.

kick-off The start of a football match.

kid¹ (kids) 1. A young goat. 2. (informal) A child.

kid² (kids, kidding, kidded) (informal) To deceive someone, to fool him.

kidnap (kidnaps, kidnapping, kidnapped) To take someone away by force illegally. kidnapper.

kidney (kidneys) One of the organs of the body.

kill (kills, killing, killed) 1. To cause the death of someone or something. killer. 2. To destroy something, to spoil it completely.

kiln (kilns) A kind of oven or furnace.

kilo (kilos) A kilogram.

kilogram (kilograms) A unit of weight, 1000 grams.

kilometre (kilometres) A unit of length, 1000 metres.

kilowatt (kilowatts) A unit of electrical power, 1000 watts.

kilt (kilts) A kind of skirt worn as part of the dress of men of the Scottish Highlands.

kin Family, relations. *Next of kin,* a person's closest relative. kinsman.

kind¹ (kinds) Sort, type. *What kind of sweet would you like?*

kind² (kinder, kindest) Friendly, gentle, concerned for others. kindness, kind-hearted.

kindergarten (kindergartens) A school or class for very young children.

kindle (kindles, kindling, kindled) 1. To set something on fire. 2. To catch fire.

kindling Small pieces of wood for starting a fire.

kindly 1. In a kind way. kindliness. 2. Please. *Kindly pass the salt.*

king (kings) 1. A man who is the crowned ruler of a country. 2. A piece in chess.

kingdom (kingdoms) A country ruled over by a king or queen.

kingfisher (kingfishers) A brightly-coloured bird which lives by rivers or streams.

kink (kinks) 1. A twist in a rope or wire. 2. A peculiar way of thinking or behaving. kinky.

kiosk (kiosks) 1. A telephone-box. 2. A small hut or stall where one can buy newspapers, sweets, ice-creams, and so on.

kipper (kippers) A smoked salted herring.

kiss¹ (kisses, kissing, kissed) To touch someone with one's lips as a sign of affection.

kiss² (kisses) Touching someone affectionately with one's lips.

kit (kits) 1. A set of tools, clothing or other equipment. *A soldier's kit.* kit-bag. 2. A set of all the things needed to make something. *A model aeroplane kit.*

kitchen (kitchens) A room where food is prepared and cooked.

kite (kites) A light framework covered with paper or cloth which can be made to fly at the end of a long string.

kitten (kittens) A young cat.

kiwi (kiwis) A New Zealand bird which does not fly.

knack (knacks) A clever way of doing something, a trick which needs practice.

knapsack (knapsacks) A canvas or leather bag carried on the back by soldiers or hikers.

knave (knaves) 1. A dishonest man. knavish, knavery. 2. The jack in a suit of playing-cards.

knead (kneads, kneading, kneaded) 1. To make dough ready for baking into bread by pressing, twisting, and turning it again and again. 2. To work at any other soft substance in a similar way.

knee (knees) The joint half way up a person's leg.

knee-cap (knee-caps) The bone at the front of a person's knee.

kneel (kneels, kneeling, knelt) 1. To go down on one's knees. 2. To be on one's knees.

knew *See* know.

knickers A woman's or girl's undergarment for the lower part of the body.

knife¹ (knives) A cutting instrument with a blade and a handle.

knife² (knifes, knifing, knifed) To stab with a knife.

knight (knights) 1. In the Middle Ages, a gentleman who fought on horseback for his lord or king, a brave and loyal warrior. 2. A man with the title 'Sir'. *Sir Winston Churchill.* knighthood. 3. A piece in chess.

knit (knits, knitting, knitted *or* knit) To make wool into clothing with long needles or special machines. knitting-machine, knitting-needles.

knob (knobs) 1. A round handle. *A door-knob.* 2. A lump or swelling. knobbly.

knock¹ (knocks, knocking, knocked) 1. To hit something, to strike it, to bump into it. 2. *To knock someone out,* to hit him so hard that he becomes unconscious.

knock² (knocks) 1. A hit, a blow. 2. The sound of knocking.

knocker (knockers) A device for knocking on a door.

knock-kneed Having knees that almost knock together when walking.

knock-out 1. *A knock-out punch,* a punch which makes someone unconscious. 2. *A knock-out competition,* a competition in which the competitors have to drop out one by one.

knot¹ (knots) 1. The twists and loops where two pieces of string, rope, or something similar are tied together. 2. A lumpy tangle of string or something similar. 3. A small group. *A knot of people.* 4. A dark round hard lump in wood. 5. A unit for measuring the speed of ships or aircraft.

knot² (knots, knotting, knotted) 1. To tie a knot. 2. To tangle.

knotty (knottier, knottiest) 1. Full of knots. 2. Puzzling. *A knotty problem.*

know (knows, knowing, knew, known) 1. To have in one's mind something which one has learnt. *We know the alphabet.* 2. To be able to recognize someone, to be acquainted with him. *How pleasant to know Mr. Lear!* 3. To have experience or understanding of something, to have ideas about something. *Terry knows all about cars.*

know-all (know-alls) A person who thinks he knows everything.

know-how The skill and ability needed for a particular job.

knowing Crafty, cunning.

knowingly Deliberately.

knowledge 1. Understanding. 2. Information, facts.

knowledgeable Having much knowledge. knowledgeably.

knuckle (knuckles) A joint in a finger.

koala (koalas) A small Australian animal.

Koran The holy book of Islam.

kosher food Food specially prepared according to Jewish laws.

kraal (kraals) A South African village surrounded by a fence.

Ll

L 50 in Roman numerals.

label¹ (labels) A piece of paper or card attached to something showing what the thing is, where it is going, or who owns it.

label² (labels, labelling, labelled) To attach a label.

laboratory (laboratories) A room or building for scientific experiments.

labour (labours) 1. Work, usually requiring strength and effort. laborious, laboriously. 2. *The Labour Party*, a political party.

labourer (labourers) A man who does heavy work, usually out of doors.

Labrador (Labradors) A breed of dog.

labyrinth (labyrinths) A maze, a place with confusing passages and turnings.

lace 1. A material with decorative patterns of holes. lacy. 2. (laces) A thin cord or string for tying up a shoe or a football.

lack¹ (lacks, lacking, lacked) To be without something.

lack² The absence of something, a shortage of something.

lacquer Varnish or paint that dries with a hard, shiny surface.

lad (lads) A boy.

ladder (ladders) 1. A climbing device of wood, metal, or rope with cross-pieces called rungs. 2. A line running up or down a stocking from a hole or flaw.

laden Carrying a large load.

ladle (ladles) A large spoon for serving soup or stew.

lady 1. (ladies) A polite word for a woman. 2. *Lady*, the title of a noblewoman or of the wife of a knight or baronet. *Sir John and Lady Smith.*

ladybird (ladybirds) A small beetle, usually red with black spots.

ladylike Behaving like a lady.

lag (lags, lagging, lagged) 1. To fall behind in a race or on a journey. 2. To wrap up pipes to protect them from frost or to prevent loss of heat.

lagoon (lagoons) A salt-water lake separated from the sea by coral, rocks, or sandbanks.

laid *See* lay[2].

lain *See* lie[3].

lair (lairs) The den or home of a wild beast.

laird (lairds) (Scottish) A landowner.

lake (lakes) A large area of water surrounded by land.

lamb (lambs) 1. A young sheep. 2. The meat from young sheep.

lame 1. Crippled, unable to walk properly. 2. Feeble. *What a lame excuse!* lamely, lameness.

lament (laments, lamenting, lamented) To express grief. lamentable, lamentation.

laminated Made of thin layers stuck tightly together.

lamp (lamps) A source of artificial light. *An oil lamp.* lamp-post, lamp-shade.

lance

lance (lances) A spear, as used by a warrior on horseback.

land[1] (lands) 1. A country. 2. Dry land, not the sea. 3. Ground for building or farming.

land[2] (lands, landing, landed) 1. To come to land from sea or air. 2. To put goods or passengers on land from a ship or aircraft.

landing (landings) The floor space at the top of a flight of stairs.

landing-stage (landing-stages) A platform where ships come to land goods or passengers.

landing-strip (landing-strips) A space cleared for aircraft to land.

landlady (landladies) 1. A woman who takes in lodgers. 2. A female landlord.

landlord (landlords) 1. A man who rents a house or land to someone else. 2. A keeper of a public house.

landmark (landmarks) An object in a landscape easily seen from a distance.

landscape (landscapes) A view or picture of the countryside.

landslide (landslides) The sliding down of earth or rock from a cliff or mountain.

lane (lanes) 1. A narrow country road. 2. A name given to some streets in towns. 3. A division of a road marked out to keep streams of traffic separate.

language (languages) Words spoken or written.

lanky (lankier, lankiest) Awkwardly tall and thin.

lantern (lanterns) A box with transparent sides through which a light shines.

lap[1] (laps) 1. The tops of the thighs of a person sitting down, or the clothes covering them. 2. Once round a race-track.

lap[2] (laps, lapping, lapped) 1. To drink by scooping with the tongue as a cat does. 2. To make a sound like lapping. *The little waves lapped gently on the shore.*

lapel (lapels) The folded-back part of the front of a coat.

lapse (lapses) 1. A fall from one's usual good behaviour. 2. Passing of time.

lapwing (lapwings) A bird of the plover family.

larch (larches) A kind of tree.

lard A kind of fat used in cooking.

larder (larders) A cool room or cupboard used for storing food.

large (larger, largest) Great in size, big. largeness.

largely Mostly.

lark (larks) A small songbird, in particular the skylark.

larva (larvae) The grub or caterpillar form of an insect.

lash[1] (lashes) 1. A whip. 2. An eyelash.

lash² (lashes, lashing, lashed) 1. To whip. 2. To make a sudden violent movement. 3. To bind tightly with cord or twine.

lass (lasses) A girl.

lasso (lassos) A rope with a noose used by cowboys for catching cattle.

last¹ 1. Coming after all others. *The last bus.* 2. Most recent. *The last time we played we won.* 3. *At last,* finally, in the end.

last² (lasts, lasting, lasted) To continue, to go on being used.

lastly Finally.

latch (latches) A type of fastening for a gate or door.

late (later, latest) 1. Coming after the proper time. *We'll be late for dinner.* 2. Near the end of a day or some other period of time. *It's getting late, so we ought to go to bed.* lateness. 3. *The late king,* the king who is now dead. 4. *The latest news,* the most recent news.

lately Recently, not long ago.

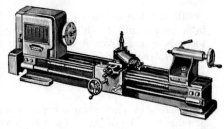

lathe (lathes) A machine for making rounded objects in wood or metal.

lather White froth, like that caused by soap and water in washing.

Latin The language of the ancient Romans.

latitude (latitudes) *Lines of latitude,* lines drawn from east to west on a map.

latter The second of two things or people just mentioned.

lattice window A window with small diamond-shaped panes of glass.

laugh¹ (laughs, laughing, laughed) To make the sound we make when we are amused or happy or scornful.

laugh² (laughs) or **laughter** The act or sound of laughing.

laughing-stock (laughing-stocks) A person other people laugh at.

launch¹ (launches) A motor boat.

launch² (launches, launching, launched) 1. To slide a ship into the water. 2. To fire off a rocket.

launderette (launderettes) A shop fitted with washing-machines where people can go to do their washing.

laundry 1. Clothes to be washed. 2. (laundries) A place where clothes are sent to be washed.

lava The fiery liquid that pours from a volcano and cools into rock.

lavatory (lavatories) 1. An apparatus which gets rid of the waste products from a person's body cleanly and hygienically. 2. A room containing this apparatus.

lavender 1. A sweet-smelling shrub. 2. The pale purple colour of its flowers.

law (laws) A general rule to be kept by everybody.

law-abiding Keeping to the laws.

lawcourt (lawcourts) A court where legal cases are tried.

lawful Legal, allowed by law. lawfully.

lawless Disorderly, not obeying the law. lawlessly, lawlessness.

lawyer (lawyers) A barrister or a solicitor, an expert in the laws of a country.

lawn (lawns) An area of mown grass in a garden or a park.

lay¹ *See* lie³.

lay² (lays, laying, laid) 1. To put something down in a particular place or in a particular way. 2. To make something lie down. *The crops were laid flat by the heavy rain.* 3. To arrange, to prepare. *Lay the table, please.* 4. To produce an egg. 5. *To lay off,* to stop. 6. *To lay on,* to supply.

lay-by (lay-bys) A space for vehicles to stop beside a main road.

layer (layers) A thickness of some material laid on or inside some other material. *A layer of icing on a cake.*

lazy (lazier, laziest) Not willing to work, idle. lazily, laziness.

L-driver (L-drivers) A person learning to drive a motor vehicle.

lead[1] 1. A heavy soft grey metal. leaden. 2. The black or grey substance in the middle of a pencil.

lead[2] (leads, leading, led) 1. To guide someone, especially by going in front of him. 2. To take someone away by force. *Lead the prisoner away!* 3. To go first, to be first. *To lead in a race.* 4. To be in charge of something, to be the most important person in a group. *To lead an expedition.* leader, leadership. 5. To stretch, to extend. *This road leads to the harbour.*

lead[3] (leads) 1. An example to be followed. 2. The first or most important position in something. 3. An electric wire. 4. A strap for leading a dog.

leaf (leaves) 1. One of the usually flat and green growths on a tree or other plant. leafy, leafless. 2. One of the sheets of paper in a book. 3. A flat sheet of something.

leaflet (leaflets) A printed paper with information or instructions.

league (leagues) 1. A group of sports clubs which play matches against each other. 2. *In league with,* working closely with.

leak[1] (leaks) A hole or crack through which water or gas can get in or out. leaky.

leak[2] (leaks, leaking, leaked) 1. To pass through a leak. 2. To have a leak.

lean[1] (leaner, leanest) 1. Thin. 2. Without fat. *Lean meat.*

lean[2] (leans, leaning, leaned, leant) 1. To be in a sloping position, to put something in a sloping position. *He leant the ladder against the wall.* 2. To support oneself on something. *He leant on the table.*

leaning (leanings) A tendency, an inclination.

lean-to A building supported against a wall of a larger building.

leap[1] (leaps, leaping, leaped, leapt) To jump, to jump over something.

leap[2] (leaps) An act of leaping.

leap-frog A game in which each player jumps with legs apart over the bended backs of the others.

leap year A year in which February has twenty-nine days.

learn (learns, learning, learnt, learned) To get knowledge and skill by studying or by practising or by being taught. learner.

leash (leashes) A dog's lead.

least 1. Smallest. 2. The smallest amount. 3. To the smallest extent.

leather A material made from animal skins. leathery.

leave[1] (leaves, leaving, left) 1. To go away from somewhere. 2. To put something somewhere and allow it to stay there. *I left my coat upstairs.* 3. To cause or allow something to remain. *Two from six leaves four.* 4. To give something to somebody in a will.

leave[2] (leaves) A time when a person has permission to be off duty. *On leave,* on holiday.

leaves *See* leaf.

lectern (lecterns) A stand for a reading book.

lecture[1] (lectures) A talk to an audience by a teacher or an expert.

lecture[2] (lectures, lecturing, lectured) To give a lecture. lecturer.

led *See* lead[2].

ledge (ledges) A shelf. *A window ledge.*

leek (leeks) An onion-like vegetable.

leer (leers, leering, leered) To look at someone unpleasantly and evilly.

leeward The side of a ship or island away from the wind.

left¹ Of or on the side opposite the right. *Most people write with the right hand but some write with the left hand.* left-handed.

left² The left-hand side. *In England we drive on the left.*

left³ *See* leave¹.

leg (legs) 1. One of the parts of the body used in standing, walking, and running. 2. One of the supports of a chair or other piece of furniture.

legacy (legacies) A piece of property or sum of money left to someone in a will.

legal 1. To do with the law. 2. Required or allowed by the law. legally, legality.

legalize (legalizes, legalizing, legalized) To make something legal.

legend (legends) An old story handed down from the past.

legendary 1. Known only in legends. 2. Famous.

legible Clearly written, easy to read. legibly, legibility.

legion (legions) 1. A division of the ancient Roman army. 2. *The Foreign Legion,* a unit of foreign volunteers in the French army.

legislate (legislates, legislating, legislated) To make laws. legislator, legislation.

legitimate Lawful. legitimately, legitimacy.

leisure Spare time.

leisurely Not hurried.

lemon (lemons) A yellow fruit with very sour juice.

lemonade A drink flavoured with lemons.

lend (lends, lending, lent) 1. To let someone have something for a certain time after which it is to be returned. 2. *To lend someone a hand,* to help him.

length (lengths) 1. The distance from one end of something to the other. 2. A piece of something which is normally measured by length. *A length of rope.* 3. *At length,* finally.

lengthen (lengthens, lengthening, lengthened) To make a thing longer.

lengthy (lengthier, lengthiest) Long.

lenient Not severe. leniently.

lens (lenses) A piece of glass with a slightly curved surface used to focus rays of light as in spectacles or a camera.

Lent The period from Ash Wednesday until Easter.

lent *See* lend.

leopard (leopards) A spotted wild animal.

leotard (leotards) A garment worn by acrobats and dancers.

leper (lepers) A person who has leprosy.

leprechaun (leprechauns) An Irish fairy.

leprosy A disease in which scales form on the skin and parts of the body waste away.

less (lesser, least) 1. Smaller. 2. A smaller amount. 3. To a smaller extent, not so much. 4. Minus. *One hundred less sixty leaves forty.*

lessen (lessens, lessening, lessened) 1. To make smaller. 2. To become smaller.

lesson (lessons) 1. A period of time during which something is taught. 2. Something to be learnt. 3. A passage from the Bible read in church.

lest For fear that. *They hid the baby Moses lest he should be killed.*

let (lets, letting, let) 1. To allow someone to do something, to allow something to happen. 2. *Let's go,* I suggest we go. 3. *To let somebody alone,* to stop teasing or disturbing him. 4. *To let someone down,* to disappoint him. 5. *To let off fireworks,* to fire them off. 6. *To let someone off,* to let him go free without being punished. 7. To hire something out. *Flat to let.*

lethal Deadly.

letter (letters) 1. One of the signs used to make up words in writing. 2. A written message, especially one sent by post.

letter-box (letter-boxes) A slot in a door for the postman to deliver letters.

lettuce (lettuces) A green vegetable used in salads.

level[1] **1.** Smooth, flat, horizontal. *You need a level field for playing cricket.* **2.** Even, equal. *The scores were level at half-time.*

level[2] (levels) **1.** Height. *At eye level,* at the same height as the eyes. **2.** (informal) *On the level,* honest.

level[3] (levels, levelling, levelled) To make something level.

level crossing A place where a road and a railway cross at the same level.

level-headed Sensible.

lever[1] (levers) **1.** A bar or other tool used to help lift a heavy weight or to force something open. **2.** A long handle which helps a person to work a machine. *A gear lever.*

lever[2] (levers, levering, levered) **1.** To use a lever. **2.** To move something with a lever.

levity Light-heartedness, not being serious.

liable 1. *Liable to,* likely to. **2.** *Liable for,* legally responsible for. **liability.**

liar (liars) Someone who tells lies.

liberal 1. Generous. **liberality. 2.** Broad-minded, not prejudiced, not too strict. **3.** *The Liberal Party,* a political party.

liberate (liberates, liberating, liberated) To set free. **liberator, liberation.**

liberty Freedom.

librarian (librarians) A person who looks after a library.

library (libraries) A place where books are kept and where people may go to read them or borrow them.

lice *See* **louse.**

licence (licences) An official document which shows that a person has been given permission to own or to use or to do something.

license (licenses, licensing, licensed) To grant a licence to someone.

lichen (lichens) A plant that grows on rocks and trees.

lick[1] (licks, licking, licked) **1.** To pass the tongue along something, to touch something with the tongue. **2.** (informal) To defeat somebody.

lick[2] (licks) The act of licking.

lid (lids) A cover, an opening top for something.

lie[1] (lies) A deliberately untrue statement.

lie[2] (lies, lying, lied) To tell a lie.

lie[3] (lies, lying, lay, lain) **1.** To be in a flat position. **2.** To remain in a certain place. *The ship was lying at anchor by the lighthouse.* **3.** *To lie low,* to keep oneself hidden.

lieu *In lieu of,* instead of.

lieutenant (lieutenants) An officer in the army or the navy.

life 1. Being alive, being able to breathe and grow as animals and plants do. **2.** (lives) The period between birth and death. **3.** *Many lives were lost,* many people were killed. **4.** *Full of life,* lively.

lifeboat (lifeboats) A boat for rescuing people at sea.

life-guard (life-guards) A person whose job it is to rescue swimmers.

life-jacket (life-jackets) A safety jacket to keep a person afloat in the water.

lifeless 1. Dead. **2.** Never alive. **3.** Dull. **lifelessly.**

lifelike Looking like the real thing.

lifelong Lasting a very long time.

lifetime The time during which a person is alive.

lift[1] (lifts, lifting, lifted) **1.** To raise something to a higher level. **2.** To rise, to go higher. *The plane lifted off the ground.* **3.** To pick something up.

lift[2] (lifts) **1.** An apparatus for taking people or goods from one floor to another.

2. *To give someone a lift,* to give him a ride in a car or other vehicle.

light[1] (lights) 1. That which makes it possible to see things, the opposite of darkness. *There was not enough light to read by.* 2. A thing which provides light or flame.

light[2] (lights, lighting, lit) 1. To cause something to shine or burn. *He lit the lamp with a match.* 2. To start shining or burning. *The camp fire would not light.* 3. To give light to someone or something. *The castle was lit by flood-lights.*

light[3] (lighter, lightest) 1. Having plenty of light. 2. Pale-coloured. **lightness.**

light[4] (lighter, lightest) 1. Not heavy, having little weight. *A light suitcase.* 2. Easy, not needing much effort. *Light work.* 3. Gentle, not violent. *A light wind.* 4. Lively, not serious. *Light music.* **lightly, lightness.**

lighten (lightens, lightening, lightened) 1. To make a thing lighter. 2. To become lighter.

lighter (lighters) A device for producing a flame. *A cigarette-lighter.*

light-hearted Gay, free from troubles. **light-heartedly, light-heartedness.**

lighthouse (lighthouses) A building with a bright flashing light to guide and warn ships.

lightning A flash of bright light in the sky during a thunderstorm.

lightning-conductor (lightning-conductors) A safety device to prevent buildings from being damaged by lightning.

lightship (lightships) An anchored ship with a bright flashing light to guide and warn other ships.

like[1] 1. Similar to, resembling. *He is like me.* 2. In the manner of. *We fought like tigers.*

like[2] (likes, liking, liked) 1. To be fond of someone or something. 2. To approve of something. 3. *I should like an ice-cream,* I wish to have one. **likeable.**

likely (likelier, likeliest) 1. Probable, to be expected. 2. Suitable. 3. *Very likely,* probably. **likelihood.**

likeness (likenesses) A similarity, a resemblance.

likewise Similarly.

lilac (lilacs) A shrub with purple or white flowers.

lily (lilies) A kind of flower that grows from a bulb.

limb (limbs) An arm or a leg. **limbless.**

lime[1] A fine white chalky powder.

lime[2] (limes) 1. A kind of tree. 2. A fruit rather like a lemon. **lime-juice.**

limelight *In the limelight,* receiving great publicity.

limerick (limericks) A light-hearted poem of five lines.

limestone A kind of rock.

limit[1] (limits) A line or point that marks the edge of something, a point that should not or cannot be passed.

limit[2] (limits, limiting, limited) To restrict something, to keep it within limits. **limitation.**

limp[1] (limps, limping, limped) To walk unevenly as when one leg or foot is injured.

limp[2] A limping movement.

limp[3] Not stiff, hanging loosely.

limpet (limpets) A shellfish that sticks itself firmly to rocks.

linctus Cough mixture.

line[1] (lines) 1. A length of thread, string, rope, or wire. 2. A long thin mark. 3. A row of people or things. 4. A railway, a length of railway track. 5. A transport system. *A shipping line.* 6. *On the right lines,* doing a thing the right way. 7. A military boundary, trenches. *The front line.*

line[2] (lines, lining, lined) 1. To mark something with a line or lines. 2. To form into lines. 3. To provide a border for something.

Cheering crowds lined the royal route. **4.** To provide a lining. *My boots are lined with fur.*

linen 1. A kind of cloth used to make sheets, tablecloths, and handkerchiefs. **2.** Articles made from this cloth.

liner (liners) A large passenger ship.

linesman (linesmen) In football or tennis, an official who helps the referee or umpire.

linger (lingers, lingering, lingered) **1.** To remain somewhere for a long time. **2.** To be slow to depart.

lingerie Women's underclothes.

linguist (linguists) An expert in foreign languages.

lining (linings) A layer of material on the inside of something.

link¹ (links) **1.** One ring in a chain. **2.** A person or thing which links people or things together.

link² (links, linking, linked) To connect, to join.

links A golf-course.

linnet (linnets) A small song-bird.

lino or **linoleum** A kind of floor-covering.

lint A soft material for covering wounds.

lion (lions) A large powerful wild animal. **lioness.**

lip (lips) **1.** One of the edges of the mouth. **2.** The edge of something hollow such as a cup or a crater.

lipstick A substance used for colouring the lips.

liquid (liquids) Any substance that can flow like water or oil.

liquor Alcoholic drink.

liquorice A strong-tasting black substance.

lisp¹ (lisps, lisping, lisped) To make the sound of *th* instead of *s* when speaking.

lisp² A lisping way of speaking.

list¹ (lists) A number of things or names written down.

list² (lists, listing, listed) To make a list.

list³ (lists, listing, listed) To lean over to one side in the water. *The ship listed severely after the collision.*

listen (listens, listening, listened) **1.** To hear something and pay attention to it. **2.** To try to hear something. **listener.**

listless Tired and not interested. **listlessly.**

lit *See* light².

literally 1. Word for word, exactly. **2.** (informal) Without exaggeration.

literate Able to read and write. **literacy.**

literature Novels, plays, poetry, and other writings.

lithe Twisting and moving freely, supple.

litre (litres) A unit of measure for liquids, about 1¾ pints.

litter¹ Untidy things left lying about.

litter² (litters, littering, littered) To scatter things untidily.

litter³ (litters) A family of baby animals born at one time.

little (less, least) **1.** Small. *A little baby.* **2.** Short. *A little while.* **3.** Some, a small quantity of something. *Have a little sugar.* **4.** Not much. *He got little thanks for all his hard work.*

live¹ Living.

live² (lives, living, lived) **1.** To have life, to remain alive. *Giant tortoises live to a great age.* **2.** *To live on something,* to have it as a food. **3.** To make one's home somewhere. *We live near London.* **4.** To pass one's life in a certain way. *He lived a life of luxury.*

lively (livelier, liveliest) Full of life, cheerful, bright, exciting. **liveliness.**

liver (livers) One of the organs of the body.

livery (liveries) A kind of uniform worn by a servant.

livestock Farm animals.

livid 1. Having a bluish colour like a bruise. 2. Very angry.

living 1. *See* live². 2. *To earn one's living*, to earn enough money for one's needs.

living-room (living-rooms) A sitting-room.

lizard (lizards) A reptile with four legs and a scaly skin.

llama (llamas) A South American animal like a camel without a hump.

load¹ (loads) 1. Something to be carried, a burden. 2. The amount usually carried by something. *A truck-load of coal.*

load² (loads, loading, loaded) 1. To put a load on something. 2. To add weight to something. 3. To give something in large quantities. *They loaded us with gifts.* 4. *To load a gun*, to put a shell or cartridge into it. 5. *To load a camera,* to put a film into it.

loaf¹ (loaves) A piece of bread as it comes from the oven before being cut into slices.

loaf² (loafs, loafing, loafed) To wait about doing nothing useful. **loafer.**

loam Good fertile soil.

loan¹ (loans) 1. Something which is lent to a person. 2. *To have the loan of something,* to borrow it.

loan² (loans, loaning, loaned) To lend.

loathe (loathes, loathing, loathed) To hate, to detest.

loathsome Disgusting, horrible.

lob (lobs, lobbing, lobbed) To throw or hit a ball slowly high in the air.

lobby (lobbies) An entrance hall.

lobster (lobsters) A large shellfish with feet and claws.

local¹ 1. Belonging to a particular place or area. *Local radio.* 2. Covering or affecting a small area. *Local showers.* **locally.**

local² (locals) (informal) A public house near one's home.

locality (localities) A place, a district.

locate (locates, locating, located) 1. To discover the exact position of something. 2. *Located,* situated.

location (locations) 1. The place where something is situated. 2. *To make a film on location*, to make it in natural surroundings, not in a studio.

loch (lochs) (Scottish) 1. A lake. 2. A creek.

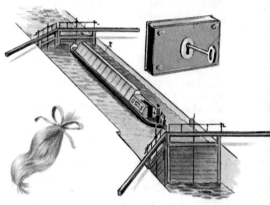

lock¹ (locks) 1. A mechanism to fasten a door so that it can be opened only with a key. 2. A section of a canal or river between gates where boats are raised or lowered to a different water level. 3. *A lock of hair,* hair that naturally hangs together.

lock² (locks, locking, locked) 1. To fasten with a lock. 2. To keep somebody or something in a certain place by means of a lock. 3. To become fixed in a certain position. *The front wheel locked when he put the brakes on too hard.*

locker (lockers) A small cupboard.

locket (lockets) A tiny case for a picture or a lock of hair worn round the neck on a chain.

locomotive (locomotives) A railway engine.

locust (locusts) An insect that flies in great swarms and destroys everything that grows.

lodge¹ (lodges) 1. A small house. 2. A room or house by the gate of a larger house.

lodge² (lodges, lodging, lodged) 1. To give someone a place to sleep. 2. To stay somewhere as a lodger. 3. To become fixed somewhere. *The ball lodged in the branches.*

lodger (lodgers) A person who pays to stay in someone else's house.

loft (lofts) 1. A room in the roof of a house. 2. *A pigeon loft*, a pigeon house.

lofty (loftier, loftiest) High. loftily.

log (logs) 1. A rough piece of a tree that has been cut down. 2. A log-book.

log-book (log-books) A record book.

logic Reasoning, sound thinking. logical, logically.

loiter (loiters, loitering, loitered) To linger, to hang about. loiterer.

lollipop (lollipops) A sweet on a stick.

lolly (lollies) Flavoured ice on a stick.

lonely (lonelier, loneliest) 1. Without friends or companions. 2. Sad because of being alone. 3. Isolated, a long way from towns or villages. *A lonely farmhouse.* loneliness.

long[1] (longer, longest) 1. Measuring a great distance. *A long road.* 2. Lasting a great time. *A long life.* 3. From one end to the other. *A cricket pitch is 22 yards long.* 4. From beginning to end. *The summer holidays are 6 weeks long.* 5. *To have a long face*, to look sad.

long[2] 1. For a long time. *Have you waited long?* 2. A long time. *It happened long ago.* 3. *As long as*, on condition that.

long[3] (longs, longing, longed) *To long for something*, to want it very much.

long-bow (long-bows) A powerful bow for shooting arrows.

longitude *Lines of longitude,* lines drawn from north to south on a map.

long-playing record A gramophone record which is to be played at 33⅓ revolutions a minute.

long-winded Using too many words, going on too long.

loo (loos) (informal) A lavatory.

look[1] (looks, looking, looked) 1. To turn the eyes towards something. 2. To face in a certain direction. *Our front windows look over the park.* 3. To seem. *It looks stormy.* 4. *To look after something*, to be in charge of it. 5. *To look down on someone*, to have a poor opinion of him. 6. *To look for something*, to search for it.

7. *To look forward to something*, to wait for it eagerly. 8. *Look out!* take care!

look[2] 1. The act of looking. 2. *Looks*, appearance, beauty.

looking-glass (looking-glasses) A mirror.

look-out (look-outs) 1. Someone whose job it is to keep watch. 2. A place from which a person can keep watch.

loom[1] (looms) A machine for weaving cloth.

loom[2] (looms, looming, loomed) To appear large and threatening.

loony (informal) Mad.

loop[1] (loops) 1. A shape made by a line curving round and crossing itself. 2. Anything formed into such a shape, like part of a knot.

loop[2] (loops, looping, looped) To make a loop.

loophole (loopholes) 1. A narrow gap, a small hole. 2. A way of avoiding a rule.

loose[1] (looser, loosest) 1. Not tight, not firm. *My tooth is loose.* 2. Free from captivity. *The lion is loose!* loosely.

loose[2] (looses, loosing, loosed) To make something become loose.

loosen (loosens, loosening, loosened) 1. To make something become loose. 2. To become loose.

loot[1] Things taken away by thieves.

loot[2] (loots, looting, looted) To take away loot.

lop (lops, lopping, lopped) To cut, to chop off.

lop-eared Having drooping ears.

lop-sided Unevenly balanced.

lord (lords) 1. A nobleman, a person allowed to use the title 'Lord' in front of his name. 2. A person in great authority. 3. *Our Lord,* Jesus Christ.

lordly Grand, proud, magnificent.

lorry (lorries) A truck, a goods vehicle.

lose (loses, losing, lost) 1. To have something taken away from one. 2. To be unable to find something. 3. *To lose one's way* or *to be lost,* not to know where one is. 4. *The ship was lost,* it was sunk. 5. *To lose a train,* to be too late to catch it. **6.** To be defeated. *We lost by six goals.* **7.** *This clock loses five minutes a day,* it gets five minutes slower every day. **loser.**

loss 1. Losing. **2.** *To be at a loss,* to be puzzled.

lot (lots) **1.** *A lot,* a large number, a large amount. **2.** *The lot,* everything, the whole number. **3.** *Lots,* plenty, a great amount. **4.** *To draw lots, to draw by lot,* to make a choice by some method which relies on chance.

lotion (lotions) A liquid to rub on the skin.

lottery (lotteries) A gambling game in which numbered tickets are sold and then drawn by lot.

lotto A gambling game like bingo.

loud (louder, loudest) Easily heard, noisy. **loudly, loudness.**

loud-speaker (loud-speakers) The device which produces the sound in a radio, record-player, or similar apparatus.

lounge¹ (lounges) A sitting-room.

lounge² (lounges, lounging, lounged) To stand about lazily, to do nothing in particular.

louse (lice) An insect, a pest.

lousy (lousier, lousiest) **1.** Full of lice. **2.** (informal) Very bad.

lout (louts) A clumsy bad-mannered person.

love¹ A strong warm feeling of liking someone or something. *To be in love with someone,* to love him or her very much.

love² (loves, loving, loved) To feel love for someone or something. **lovable, lover.**

love³ In tennis and other games, no score.

lovely (lovelier, loveliest) **1.** Beautiful. **2.** (informal) Pleasing, enjoyable. **loveliness.**

low¹ (lower, lowest) The opposite of high. **lowness.**

low² (lows, lowing, lowed) To make a noise like a cow.

lower (lowers, lowering, lowered) **1.** To let something down. *Lower the boats!* **2.** To make something less high. *Lower your heads.* **3.** To become less, to make something less. *Please lower your voice.*

lowly Humble. **lowliness.**

loyal True and faithful. **loyally, loyalty.**

lozenge (lozenges) A small medicine tablet to be sucked like a sweet.

lubricate (lubricates, lubricating, lubricated) To put oil or grease on something. **lubrication.**

lucid Clear, easily understood. **lucidly, lucidity.**

luck Chance, fortune. **luckless.**

lucky (luckier, luckiest) Having good luck, bringing good luck. **luckily.**

ludicrous Ridiculous.

ludo An indoor game played on a board with counters.

lug (lugs, lugging, lugged) To pull something, to drag it.

luggage Suitcases, trunks, bags, and boxes used for packing when making a journey. **luggage-rack.**

lugger (luggers) A small sailing-ship.

lugubrious Gloomy. **lugubriously.**

lukewarm Moderately warm.

lull¹ (lulls, lulling, lulled) To make someone quiet. *She lulled the baby to sleep.*

lull² (lulls) An interval of quiet in a storm.

lullaby (lullabies) A song for sending a baby to sleep.

lumbago A pain in the back.

lumber¹ (lumbers, lumbering, lumbered) To move along in a clumsy way.

lumber² **1.** Rough timber. **2.** Useless property stored untidily away.

luminous Shining in the dark.

lump[1] (lumps) 1. A shapeless mass. 2. A swelling. lumpy.

lump[2] (lumps, lumping, lumped) To put things together.

lunacy Madness.

lunar Belonging to the moon, to do with the moon.

lunatic (lunatics) A madman.

lunch (lunches) 1. The midday meal. 2. A snack eaten in the middle of the morning.

luncheon (luncheons) Lunch.

lung (lungs) One of the inner parts of the body used in breathing.

lunge (lunges, lunging, lunged) 1. To thrust forward with a sword. 2. To move forward suddenly.

lupin (lupins) A garden flower.

lurch[1] (lurches, lurching, lurched) To lean suddenly to one side.

lurch[2] To leave someone in the lurch, to desert him at a time when he needs help.

lure (lures, luring, lured) To tempt a person or an animal into a trap.

lurid 1. Unpleasantly bright. 2. Violent and shocking. luridly.

lurk (lurks, lurking, lurked) To stay hidden, to lie in wait.

luscious Rich and sweet in taste or smell.

lush (lusher, lushest) Growing plentifully.

lust (lusts) Strong or violent desire. lustful.

lustre Brilliance, glossiness.

lusty Strong and healthy. lustily.

lute (lutes) A stringed musical instrument. lutenist.

luxury (luxuries) 1. Something which a person enjoys but does not really need. 2. The enjoyment of luxuries. luxurious, luxuriously.

lying See lie[2,3].

lynch (lynches, lynching, lynched) To put someone to death without a proper trial by the action of a mob.

lyre (lyres) An ancient musical instrument like a small harp.

lyric (lyrics) Words for a song.

Mm

M 1,000 in Roman numerals.

mac (macs) (informal) A mackintosh.

macaroni A food made of flour paste formed into tubes.

machine (machines) 1. An apparatus designed to do a job. 2. Machine-gun, a gun that fires long bursts when the trigger is pulled.

machinery 1. Machines. 2. The moving parts of a machine.

Mach number A measurement of the speed of aircraft. Mach one is the speed of sound.

mackerel (mackerel) A sea fish.

mackintosh (mackintoshes) A rainproof coat.

mad (madder, maddest) 1. Mentally ill, insane. madman. 2. (informal) Excited, uncontrolled, angry. Like mad, furiously, with violent haste. madly, madness.

madam A respectful title used when speaking to a lady.

madden (maddens, maddening, maddened) To make mad. maddeningly.

made See make[1].

magazine (magazines) 1. A publication that comes out regularly. 2. Part of a gun where extra cartridges are kept. 3. A store for arms and ammunition.

maggot (maggots) The larva of some types of fly. maggoty.

magic 1. The pretended art of controlling nature or spirits, witchcraft. 2. Any unexplained power. 3. The art of doing conjuring tricks. magical, magically, magician.

magistrate (magistrates) A person who acts as a judge in local courts.

magnet (magnets) A piece of metal which has the power of attracting pieces of iron. magnetic, magnetism.

magnetize (magnetizes, magnetizing, magnetized) 1. To make a piece of metal into a magnet. 2. To attract like a magnet.

magnificent 1. Splendid, grand, important-looking. 2. (informal) Very good. magnificently, magnificence.

magnify (magnifies, magnifying, magnified) To make something seem larger or more important than it really is. magnification.

magnitude Greatness, size, importance.

magpie (magpies) A black and white bird.

mahogany A reddish-brown wood.

maid (maids) 1. (old-fashioned) A girl. 2. A female servant.

maiden¹ (maidens) (old-fashioned) A girl.

maiden² 1. Unmarried. 2. *A maiden over*, an over in cricket in which no runs are scored. 3. *A maiden voyage*, a ship's first voyage.

mail¹ Armour made of metal rings fastened together.

mail² Letters and other things sent by post.

mail³ (mails, mailing, mailed) To send something by post.

maim (maims, maiming, maimed) To cripple.

main¹ Most important, very important.

main² (mains) The main pipes and wires which carry water or gas or electricity to people's houses.

mainland The main area of a country or continent, not the islands around it.

mainly Chiefly, for the most part.

maintain (maintains, maintaining, maintained) 1. To keep something in good working order. maintenance. 2. *To maintain an opinion,* to stick to that opinion.

maize A type of corn with large seeds.

majesty Stateliness, royal appearance and authority. *Your majesty*, the polite way to speak to a king or a queen. majestic, majestically.

major¹ (majors) An officer in the army.

major² Greater, more important.

majority (majorities) The greater number, the larger part. *The majority voted to play rounders.*

make¹ (makes, making, made) 1. To construct or produce something, to bring it into existence. *To make bread.* 2. To cause something to take place. *The mouse made Ann scream.* 3. To cause someone or something to become something else. *They made him king.* 4. To earn. *He makes £2,000 a year.* 5. To become. *In time you will make a good cricketer.* 6. To behave in a certain way. *He made as if to steal the jewels.* 7. To reach. *The survivors were lucky to make the shore.* 8. To come to an answer about something. *What time do you make it?* 9. To score something in a game. *I made 20 runs today.* 10. *To make for*, to go towards. *He made for the door.* 11. *To make out:* (a) To see or hear clearly. *I can't make out which ship it is.* (b) To succeed in understanding. *I can't make out what this book is about.* (c) To suggest, to pretend. *He made out that he was ill.* 12. *To make a bed,* to tidy a bed after sleeping. 13. *To make up:* (a) *To make something up,* to invent it. (b) *To make up a fire,* to put fuel on it. (c) *To make up one's mind,* to decide. (d) *To make it up,* to end a quarrel. (e) *To make up to someone,* to try to win his favour. (f) To put make-up on. maker.

make² (makes) A sort, a brand. *What make of car is that?*

makeshift A thing used because nothing better is available.

make-up 1. Lipstick, face-powder, and other cosmetics. 2. Materials used by an actor to change his appearance.

malady (maladies) An illness.

malaria A fever spread by mosquitoes. malarial.

Malay or Malayan Of Malaya.

male (males) 1. A man, a boy. 2. Any creature of the sex that does not give birth to babies or lay eggs.

malefactor (malefactors) A criminal.

malevolent Spiteful, evilly inclined. malevolently, malevolence.

malice A desire to harm other people. malicious, maliciously.

malignant 1. Harmful. 2. Malicious. malignantly.

mallet (mallets) A wooden hammer.

malnutrition Lack of good food.

malt A food made from barley.

Maltese Of Malta.

mamma (mammas) (old-fashioned) Mother.

mammal (mammals) Any of those animals, including human beings, which feed their young with milk from the breast.

mammoth¹ (mammoths) A large extinct kind of elephant.

mammoth² Huge.

man¹ (men) 1. A human being. 2. Human beings in general. 3. A grown-up male human being. 4. A member of a team or crew. 5. A piece in a game of chess or draughts.

man² (mans, manning, manned) To supply something with the men needed to work it. *Man the guns!*

manage (manages, managing, managed) 1. To be in charge of something, to control it. 2. To be able to do something which is rather difficult. *Could you manage to carry this pile of books?* 3. To deal with something. *Can you manage a second helping?* manageable, management, manager.

mane (manes) The long hair on the back of the neck of a horse, lion, or other animal.

manger (mangers) A trough for horses or cattle to feed from.

mangle¹ (mangles) A device for squeezing water out of wet clothes.

mangle² (mangles, mangling, mangled) 1. To use a mangle. 2. To cut something up roughly or crush it.

mangy Dirty, nasty, and neglected.

manhandle (manhandles, manhandling, manhandled) To move something using human strength alone.

manhole (manholes) A hole through which a workman may go to inspect a drain or machinery.

manhood The state of being a grown-up man.

mania Madness.

maniac (maniacs) A raving madman.

manifest Obvious. manifestly.

manipulate (manipulates, manipulating, manipulated) To control something, to handle it skilfully. manipulator, manipulation.

mankind The human race.

manly Brave, strong. manliness.

mannequin (mannequins) A person whose job it is to wear and display new clothes.

manner The way a thing is done, how it happens.

manners Ways to behave among people. *It is bad manners to stare.*

manoeuvre¹ (manoeuvres) 1. A movement of troops, a rehearsal for warfare. 2. A movement made to deceive or outwit someone. 3. An awkward, complicated movement.

manoeuvre² (manoeuvres, manoeuvring, manoeuvred) To make a manoeuvre.

manor (manors) The main house in a village or small district.

manse (manses) The house where the minister of a church lives, especially in Scotland.

mansion (mansions) A grand house.

manslaughter Killing a person unlawfully but without intending to do so.

mantelpiece (mantelpieces) A shelf over a fire-place.

manual¹ Worked or done by hand.

manual² (manuals) A book of information or instructions.

manufacture (manufactures, manufacturing, manufactured) To make things by machine in a factory. manufacturer.

manure¹ Waste stuff or dung from animals used to fertilize the soil.

manure[2] (manures, manuring, manured) To put manure on the soil.

manuscript (manuscripts) Something written out by hand, not printed.

Manx Of the Isle of Man.

many (more, most) 1. Large in number, numerous. *Many people. Many times.* 2. *A good many*, a large number.

Maori (Maoris) A member of the brown-skinned race in New Zealand.

map[1] (maps) A drawing showing the shape of a continent, country, or area, often including marks for roads, rivers, hills, and other features.

map[2] (maps, mapping, mapped) 1. To make a map of a place. 2. *To map something out*, to plan it.

maple (maples) A kind of tree.

mar (mars, marring, marred) To spoil.

Marathon (Marathons) A very long running-race named after a place in Greece.

marauder (marauders) A person who makes raids in search of plunder. **marauding**.

marble (marbles) 1. A small glass ball used in various games. 2. A kind of stone used for buildings and sculptures.

March[1] The third month of the year.

march[2] (marches, marching, marched) 1. To walk as soldiers do, with regular steps. 2. To compel someone to walk somewhere. *They marched him off to prison.*

march[3] (marches) 1. A time spent marching. 2. A piece of music for marching.

mare (mares) A female horse or donkey.

margarine A food which can be used instead of butter.

margin (margins) 1. An edge, a border, a blank space round the edge of a page of writing. 2. An amount to spare. *He won by a narrow margin*, he only just won.

marigold (marigolds) A golden flower.

marijuana A kind of drug.

marina (marinas) A centre for pleasure boats.

marine[1] To do with the sea.

marine[2] (marines) A soldier trained to serve on a ship.

mariner (mariners) A seaman.

mark[1] (marks) 1. A spot, line, pattern, or design on something. 2. A number or letter put on a piece of work to indicate how good it is. *10 out of 10 is full marks.* 3. *Mark I*, the first version of a product, *Mark II*, the second version.

mark[2] (marks, marking, marked) 1. To put a mark on something. 2. *To be marked*, to have markings. *The zebra is marked with stripes.* 3. To give marks to a piece of work. 4. To pay attention to. *Mark my words!* 5. *To mark time*, to move the feet up and down without marching forward. **marker**.

mark[3] (marks) A unit of money in Germany.

market[1] (markets) A place where things are bought and sold. *A market town*, a town where a market is held. **market-day, market-place**.

market² (markets, marketing, marketed) 1. To buy or sell in a market. 2. To sell. **marketable.**

marking (markings) A mark.

marksman (marksmen) An expert in shooting at a target.

marmalade A kind of jam made from oranges or other citrus fruit.

maroon¹ Very dark red.

maroon² (maroons, marooning, marooned) To abandon somebody in a deserted place.

marquee (marquees) A large tent.

marriage (marriages) 1. The state of being married. 2. A wedding.

marrow (marrows) 1. A kind of vegetable. 2. The soft substance inside bones.

marry (marries, marrying, married) 1. To become someone's husband or wife. 2. To join two people together as husband and wife. *They were married in church.*

marsh (marshes) Wet, low-lying ground. **marshy.**

marshal (marshals) 1. An important officer or official. 2. In the U.S.A., an official responsible for keeping law and order in a particular place.

marsupial (marsupials) An animal such as a kangaroo with a pouch for carrying its young ones.

martial 1. Warlike. 2. *Martial law,* government controlled by the armed forces.

martyr¹ (martyrs) 1. A person put to death because of his religious beliefs. 2. Someone who suffers for the sake of a good cause. **martyrdom.**

martyr² (martyrs, martyring, martyred) To make someone a martyr.

marvel¹ (marvels) A wonderful or astonishing thing. **marvellous, marvellously.**

marvel² (marvels, marvelling, marvelled) To be filled with wonder or astonishment.

marzipan A sweet substance made with ground almonds.

mascot (mascots) An object which is supposed to bring good luck.

masculine Belonging to men, suitable for men. **masculinity.**

mash (mashes, mashing, mashed) To crush something up into a soft shapeless form. *Mashed potatoes.*

mask¹ (masks) 1. A covering for the face, a disguise. 2. A model of a face.

mask² (masks, masking, masked) 1. To cover the face with a mask. 2. To conceal something.

mason (masons) A stone-cutter, a builder in stone.

masonry Stonework, parts of a building made of stone.

mass¹ (masses) 1. A lump, a large quantity, a heap. 2. *Mass production,* manufacturing things in large quantities. 3. *A mass meeting,* a large meeting for discussion.

mass² (masses, massing, massed) To collect into a mass.

Mass³ (Masses) The Holy Communion service.

massacre (massacres) Cruel slaughter of large numbers of people.

massage¹ (massages, massaging, massaged) To rub and press the body to make it less stiff or painful.

massage² Massaging.

massive Large and heavy. **massively.**

mast (masts) An upright pole used to hold up sails, radio aerials, or flags.

master¹ (masters) 1. A male teacher in a

school. 2. A person in charge or command of something. 3. A great artist or composer. 4. *Master*, a word used before a boy's name when addressing a letter to him.

master[2] (masters, mastering, mastered) 1. To learn to do something perfectly. 2. To overcome something or somebody.

masterful Dominating.

masterly Most skilful.

masterpiece (masterpieces) Something done with the greatest skill.

mastery Full control and command of something.

mastiff (mastiffs) A kind of dog.

mastodon (mastodons) A large extinct animal like an elephant.

mat (mats) 1. A small piece of carpet or other floor covering. 2. A small piece of material used on tables to prevent damage when something is put down.

matador (matadors) The man who has to kill the bull in a bull-fight.

match[1] (matches) A small stick which bursts into flame when rubbed along a rough surface.

match[2] (matches) 1. A game or contest between two teams or players. 2. A marriage. 3. A person or thing which matches another person or thing.

match[3] (matches, matching, matched) To be equal or similar in some important way to another person or thing.

mate[1] (mates) 1. A friend, someone who works or plays with another person. 2. One of a pair of animals who have young ones. 3. One of the officers on a ship.

mate[2] (mates, mating, mated) To come together intending to have young ones.

material (materials) 1. Any substance from which something can be made. *Building materials.* 2. Cloth. *Sue has bought some material for a dress.*

materialize (materializes, materializing, materialized) To appear, to come into existence.

maternal Motherly.

maternity Motherhood. *A maternity hospital,* a hospital where mothers go when it is time for their babies to be born.

mathematics The science which deals with numbers, quantities, and shapes. **mathematical, mathematically, mathematician.**

maths (informal) Mathematics.

matinée (matinées) An afternoon performance of a play or film.

matrimony Marriage. **matrimonial.**

matron (matrons) 1. A former name for the woman in charge of nurses in a hospital. 2. A woman in charge of living arrangements in a boarding-school.

matt Not shiny. *Matt paint.*

matted Tangled.

matter[1] (matters) 1. A substance, anything which can be seen and touched. 2. A subject to be thought about or discussed or done. *John has several matters to deal with today.* 3. *What is the matter with Alan?* what is wrong with him?

matter[2] (matters, mattering, mattered) To be important.

matting A rough kind of floor covering.

mattress (mattresses) A large flat oblong cushion for sleeping on.

mature 1. Ripe, well-developed, ready for use. 2. Grown-up, like a grown-up person.

maul (mauls, mauling, mauled) To cause damage by rough or careless handling.

mauve Pale purple.

maximum[1] Greatest. *Maximum speed.*

maximum[2] The greatest number, the greatest amount. *10 out of 10 is the maximum.*

may[1] (might) This word is used in various ways: 1. To show possibility. *I may come tomorrow.* 2. To ask or give permission. *May I come in?* 3. To indicate a hope or wish. *Long may she reign.* 4. To express purpose. *He died that we might live.* 5. *We might as well go,* it would be sensible to go.

may[2] Hawthorn blossom.

May The fifth month of the year.

maybe Perhaps.

mayonnaise Salad cream.

mayor (mayors) The head of a town corporation. **mayoress.**

maypole (maypoles) A decorated pole used in folk dancing.

maze (mazes) A complicated and puzzling network of lines or paths.

me *See* I².

meadow (meadows) A field of grass.

meagre Poor, thin, scanty. **meagrely, meagreness.**

meal (meals) 1. An occasion when food is eaten. **mealtime.** 2. The food that is eaten. *A good meal of fish and chips.*

mean¹ (means, meaning, meant) 1. To indicate, to show, to signify. *A red light means stop. The word 'maybe' means 'perhaps'.* 2. To intend, to plan. *He means mischief.*

mean² (meaner, meanest) Not generous. **meanly, meanness.**

mean³ Average. *The mean temperature.*

meaning (meanings) What is meant. *The meaning is clear.*

means 1. A method, a way of doing something. 2. Income, money.

meantime *In the meantime,* meanwhile.

meanwhile During the same time.

measles An infectious disease causing red spots on the body.

measly (informal) Very small, worthless.

measure¹ (measures) 1. A unit used for measuring. 2. An instrument used for measuring. *A tape-measure.* 3. Size, quantity, amount. 4. A particular size. *Clothes made to measure.* 5. An action. *The police are taking stricter measures against shoplifting.*

measure² (measures, measuring, measured) 1. To find the size or amount of something. 2. To be a certain size. *A cricket pitch measures 22 yards.* 3. *To measure out,* to mark out a certain distance, to put aside a certain quantity. *We measured out the ingredients for a cake.* **measurable, measurably, measurement.**

meat Animal flesh used as food.

meaty (meatier, meatiest) Full of meat.

mechanic (mechanics) A person who operates or repairs machines.

mechanical 1. Of machines. 2. Done by machine. **mechanically.**

mechanism Machinery.

mechanize (mechanizes, mechanizing, mechanized) To bring machines into use for a particular job. **mechanization.**

medal (medals) A piece of metal shaped like a coin or a cross or a star, awarded for winning a race, for bravery, for good work, or for some other achievement.

medallist (medallists) A person who has been awarded a medal.

meddle (meddles, meddling, meddled) To interfere. **meddler.**

medical To do with the treatment of sick people. **medically.**

medicine (medicines) A liquid or tablet taken to improve one's health. **medicinal.**

medieval Connected with the Middle Ages.

mediocre Not very good, not very bad.

meditate (meditates, meditating, meditated) To think about things. **meditation.**

medium¹ Average. *Medium size,* middle size.

medium² (mediums) A person who claims to be able to receive messages from the dead.

medley (medleys) A mixture.

meek Obedient and gentle, not proud. **meekly, meekness.**

meet (meets, meeting, met) To come together with someone or something.

meeting (meetings) 1. A coming together. 2. A group of people gathered for a particular purpose.

megaphone (megaphones) A device to make a person's voice heard a long way away.

megaton (megatons) An explosive force equal to a million tons of standard explosive.

melancholy Sad.

mellow Soft, ripe, pleasant.

melodious Tuneful. **melodiously.**

melody (melodies) A tune.

melon (melons) A large, round, juicy fruit.

melt (melts, melting, melted, molten) 1. To change something into liquid by warming it. *The sun melted the snow.* 2. To become liquid by being warmed. *The snow melted in the sun.* 3. To go away slowly, to fade.

member (members) A person who belongs to a club or group. **membership.**

memorable Not to be forgotten. **memorably.**

memorial (memorials) Something to remind people of a person or an event. *A war memorial.*

memorize (memorizes, memorizing, memorized) To learn by heart.

memory (memories) 1. The ability to remember. *Elephants have good memories.* 2. Something that is remembered. *We have happy memories of last year's holiday.* 3. *In memory of,* as a memorial to.

men *See* **man**[1].

menace (menaces, menacing, menaced) To threaten. **menacingly.**

menagerie (menageries) A collection of wild animals, a small zoo.

mend (mends, mending, mended) 1. To repair something, to put it back into good condition. 2. To get better.

mending Clothes which are being mended.

mental 1. In the mind, to do with the mind. **mentally.** 2. *A mental hospital,* a hospital for people with mental illnesses. 3. (informal) Mad.

mentality (mentalities) 1. Mental powers. 2. An attitude of the mind.

mention (mentions, mentioning, mentioned) To speak about or refer to someone or something.

menu (menus) A list of the food to be served at a meal.

mercenary[1] Working only for money.

mercenary[2] (mercenaries) A soldier who will fight for any country that will pay him.

merchandise Goods to be bought and sold.

merchant (merchants) 1. A trader. *A coal-merchant.* 2. *Merchant ships,* ships which carry goods.

merciful Showing mercy. **mercifully.**

merciless Without mercy. **mercilessly.**

mercury A silver-coloured liquid metal.

mercy (mercies) 1. Not using one's power to hurt or punish somebody. *The king showed mercy and spared the traitor's life.* 2. A piece of good fortune. *Be thankful for small mercies.*

mere Not more than. *She's a mere baby,* she's only a baby.

merely Simply, only.

merge (merges, merging, merged) To become part of something else, to become joined together.

merger (mergers) A combination, merging.

meringue (meringues) A sweet brittle cake made from white of egg and sugar.

merit[1] (merits) 1. Something that deserves praise. 2. Something to be either praised or blamed. *We judge each case on its merits.*

merit[2] (merits, meriting, merited) To deserve.

mermaid (mermaids) A creature with the head and trunk of a woman and tail of a fish.

merry (merrier, merriest) Happy, cheerful, bright. **merrily, merriment.**

merry-go-round (merry-go-rounds) A fairground amusement.

mesh (meshes) One of the spaces in a net or a criss-cross screen.

mess¹ (messes) 1. An untidy or dirty state of things. messy, messily. 2. *To make a mess of something*, to spoil it, to do it badly. 3. A place where soldiers or sailors eat their meals.

mess² (messes, messing, messed) 1. *To mess something up*, to do it badly. 2. *To mess about*, to do things with no definite plan or purpose.

message (messages) A piece of information or a request sent from one person to another.

messenger (messengers) Someone who carries a message.

met *See* meet.

metal (metals) One of a type of substances such as iron, gold, silver, tin, copper, and lead. metallic.

meteor (meteors) A shooting star.

meteorite (meteorites) A meteor that has fallen to the earth.

meteorology The scientific study of the weather meteorological, meteorologist.

meter (meters) A measuring instrument. *A gas meter* or *an electricity meter*, instruments for measuring the amount of gas or electricity used.

method 1. (methods) A way or means of doing something. 2. Orderliness, a sensible way of doing something.

methodical Orderly, careful and systematic. methodically.

methylated spirits or meths A liquid fuel.

meticulous Very careful. meticulously.

metre (metres) The main unit of length in the metric system.

metric system A decimal measuring system.

miaow (miaows, miaowing, miaowed) To make a sound like a cat.

microbe (microbes) A microscopic living creature.

microphone (microphones) An instrument for picking up sound waves for recording, amplifying, or broadcasting.

microscope (microscopes) An instrument for magnifying tiny things.

microscopic Very small, invisible except through a microscope.

mid 1. The middle of something. *The engine failed in mid Atlantic.* 2. (old-fashioned) Among.

midday Twelve o'clock in the middle of the day.

middle 1. The point which is an equal distance from both ends or edges of something. 2. *A middle school*, a school for children aged about ten to fourteen. 3. *Middle-aged*, no longer young but not yet old. 4. *The Middle Ages*, the period in European history from about A.D. 1000 to about 1500.

middling Moderately good or well.

midge (midges) A small insect such as a gnat.

midget (midgets) An exceptionally short person.

midland Of the Midlands. *The Midlands*, the middle part of England.

midnight Twelve o'clock at night.

midshipman (midshipmen) A boy training to be a naval officer.

midst (old-fashioned) *In the midst*, in the middle.

midsummer In the northern hemisphere, the end of June. *Midsummer day*, 24th June.

midway Half-way.

midwife (midwives) A person who gives help when a baby is born.

might¹ *See* may.

might² Great power, great strength. mighty, mightily.

migraine (migraines) A very severe kind of headache.

migrate (migrates, migrating, migrated) To go to live in another country. *Swallows migrate every spring and autumn.* migration, migrant, migratory.

mild (milder, mildest) Gentle, not severe, not harsh. mildly, mildness.

mildew A stain or growth that forms in warm damp places.

mile (miles) A measure of distance, 1,760 yards or 1·61 kilometre.

mileage The number of miles travelled.

milestone (milestones) One of a series of stones placed along a road marking the miles between towns.

militant[1] Ready to fight. militancy.

militant[2] (militants) A militant person.

military Of soldiers.

milk[1] A white liquid food which comes from cows and other mammals.

milk[2] (milks, milking, milked) To get the milk from a cow or other animal. milking-machine.

milkmaid (milkmaids) A woman who milks cows.

milkman (milkmen) A man who delivers milk to people's houses.

milky (milkier, milkiest) White, like milk.

mill[1] (mills) 1. A building where corn is ground into flour. miller. 2. A factory or workshop. *A steel-mill.* 3. A grinding machine. *A coffee-mill.*

mill[2] (mills, milling, milled) 1. To grind something in a mill. miller. 2. *To mill about,* to move about in a confused crowd.

milligram (milligrams) One thousandth of a gram.

millilitre (millilitres) One thousandth of a litre.

millimetre (millimetres) One thousandth of a metre.

million (millions) The number 1,000,000. millionth.

millionaire (millionaires) An extremely rich person.

millstone (millstones) A heavy stone used to grind flour in a mill.

mime (mimes, miming, mimed) To tell a story by using gestures but no words.

mimic[1] (mimics) A person who is good at imitating other people. mimicry.

mimic[2] (mimics, mimicking, mimicked) To imitate someone or something.

minaret (minarets) A tall slender tower connected with a mosque.

mince[1] (minces, mincing, minced) To cut food into very small pieces.

mince[2] Minced meat.

mincemeat A mixture of various dried fruits used to fill tarts called mince-pies.

mind[1] (minds) 1. The power of thinking, feeling, and understanding. 2. An opinion, an intention. *To make up your mind,* to decide what to do. 3. Memory. *To call to mind,* to remember. 4. *Presence of mind,* ability to cope with emergencies.

mind[2] (minds, minding, minded) 1. To look after something or somebody. *Mind the baby for a moment, please.* minder. 2. To watch out for something. *Mind the step.* 3. To object to something, to dislike it. *Do you mind if I smoke?*

mine[1] Belonging to me.

mine[2] (mines) 1. A hole dug to get coal or other minerals from the ground. 2. An explosive hidden underground or in the sea to destroy enemies when they pass.

mine[3] (mines, mining, mined) 1. To dig mineral ore from a mine. miner. 2. To lay mines in land or in the sea.

mineral (minerals) 1. Any substance other than a vegetable substance which can be dug from the ground. Rocks, coal, and iron are minerals. 2. A fizzy soft drink.

mingle (mingles, mingling, mingled) To mix.

mingy (mingier, mingiest) (informal) Mean, stingy.

miniature Very small, made on a small scale.

minibus (minibuses) A small bus.

minim (minims) A note in music. It is written ♩ .

minimum[1] Smallest, least.

minimum[2] The smallest number, the smallest amount.

miniskirt (miniskirts) A very short skirt.

minister (ministers) 1. A clergyman. 2. A person in charge of a government department.

ministry (ministries) 1. The job done by a clergyman. 2. A government department.

mink (minks) 1. A small water animal. 2. Its fur.

minnow (minnows) A small freshwater fish.

minor 1. Smaller, less important. 2. Not very important.

minority (minorities) The smaller number, the smaller part.

minstrel (minstrels) A wandering musician.

mint[1] A plant with scented leaves used in cooking. *Mint sauce.*

mint[2] 1. A place where coins are made. 2. *In mint condition*, in perfect condition, unused.

minuet (minuets) A slow graceful dance.

minus Less. In arithmetic, the sign —. *Five minus three leaves two* $(5-3=2)$.

minute[1] (pronounced *min*ute) (minutes) 1. A unit of time. *There are 60 minutes in one hour.* 2. A short time. *Ready in a minute!*

minute[2] (pronounced mi*nute*) 1. Tiny. 2. Very detailed. **minutely.**

miracle (miracles) A wonderful happening which seems to be caused by supernatural or magical powers. **miraculous, miraculously.**

mirage (mirages) A trick of the light which in deserts makes pools of water seem to be present where there are none, or which makes distant objects appear close and sometimes upside-down.

mire Swampy ground, mud.

mirror (mirrors) A glass or metal surface which reflects things clearly.

mirth Happy laughter.

misadventure (misadventures) An unfortunate accident.

misapprehension (misapprehensions) A misunderstanding.

misbehave (misbehaves, misbehaving, misbehaved) To behave badly. **misbehaviour.**

miscalculate (miscalculates, miscalculating, miscalculated) To calculate wrongly. **miscalculation.**

miscellaneous Of mixed sorts.

mischance (mischances) A piece of bad luck.

mischief Naughtiness. **mischievous, mischievously.**

misconception (misconceptions) A misunderstanding.

misconduct Bad behaviour.

misdeed (misdeeds) A crime, a wicked act.

miser (misers) A person who stores up money and spends as little as possible. **miserly, miserliness.**

miserable Wretched and unhappy. **miserably.**

misery Suffering.

misfire (misfires, misfiring, misfired) To fail to fire. *The gun misfired.*

misfit (misfits) Something or someone that does not fit.

misfortune (misfortunes) 1. An unlucky event. 2. Bad luck.

misgiving (misgivings) A doubt.

misguided Mistaken, foolish. **misguidedly.**

mishandle (mishandles, mishandling, mishandled) To handle something roughly or clumsily.

mishap (mishaps) An unlucky accident.

misinformed Given the wrong information.

misjudge (misjudges, misjudging, misjudged) To judge someone or something wrongly.

mislay (mislays, mislaying, mislaid) To lose something for a time.

mislead (misleads, misleading, misled) To deceive someone.

misprint (misprints) A mistake made in the printing of a book.

miss[1] (misses, missing, missed) 1. To fail to hit, reach, meet, find, catch, or see something or someone. 2. To realize that something has gone. *I must have lost my pen on Friday, but I didn't miss it until Monday.* 3. To be sad because one is parted from someone or something. *I missed mother while she was away in hospital.*

Miss[2] A word used before the name of a girl or unmarried woman when speaking to her politely or addressing a letter. *Miss Muffet.*

missal (missals) A prayer-book.

mis-shapen Deformed, twisted.

missile (missiles) 1. A weapon or object which is thrown. 2. A weapon which is sent to its target in a rocket.

missing Lost, not in the proper place.

mission (missions) 1. A journey or expedition with a special purpose. 2. Special work which a person feels he ought to do. 3. A place or building where missionaries work.

missionary (missionaries) A person who goes to another country to preach his religion.

mist (mists) A cloud of very fine water drops floating in the air near the ground. **misty, mistily, mistiness.**

mistake[1] (mistakes) Something wrongly thought or done.

mistake[2] (mistakes, mistaking, mistook, mistaken) 1. To misunderstand. 2. *To be mistaken,* to be wrong. **mistakenly.**

mistletoe A plant that grows on oak trees.

mistook *See* **mistake**[2].

mistress (mistresses) 1. A woman schoolteacher. 2. A woman in charge of something.

mistrust (mistrusts, mistrusting, mistrusted) Not to trust somebody or something.

misunderstand (misunderstands, misunderstanding, misunderstood) To understand something wrongly.

misunderstanding (misunderstandings) A failure to understand something correctly.

misuse (misuses, misusing, misused) To use something wrongly, to treat it badly.

mite (mites) A tiny thing.

mitre (mitres) A bishop's hat.

mitten (mittens) A kind of glove.

mix (mixes, mixing, mixed) 1. To put things together and stir or shake them. 2. To get together in a single group. 3. *To mix things up,* to confuse them.

mixture (mixtures) 1. Mixing. 2. Something mixed.

moan[1] (moans, moaning, moaned) 1. To make a long low sound. 2. (informal) To complain.

moan[2] (moans) The sound of moaning.

moat (moats) A deep ditch round a castle.

mob[1] (mobs) An unruly and dangerous crowd.

mob[2] (mobs, mobbing, mobbed) To crowd round somebody.

mobile[1] Moving, movable. **mobility.**

mobile[2] (mobiles) A hanging work of art designed to move in the breeze.

mobilize (mobilizes, mobilizing, mobilized) To collect together to work or fight.

mock[1] (mocks, mocking, mocked) To make fun of someone or something. **mockery.**

mock[2] Not real, imitation. *Mock cream.*

model[1] (models) 1. A small-scale version of something. *A model aeroplane.* 2. A particular version of something. *We saw the latest models at the motor show.* 3. A thing or person to be copied. *Jane's handwriting is a model of neatness.* 4. A person who poses for an artist or photographer. 5. A person whose job it is to wear and display new clothes.

model² (models, modelling, modelled) 1. To make a model, especially with clay or plasticine. 2. To work as a model. 3. *To model yourself on someone,* to imitate him.

moderate Not too little and not too much, fairly good. moderately, moderation.

modern In the style used in present and recent times, not old.

modernize (modernizes, modernizing, modernized) To make a thing modern. modernization.

modest 1. Humble, not boastful. 2. Shy, bashful. 3. Moderate. modestly, modesty.

modify (modifies, modifying, modified) To alter something. modification.

Mohammedan (Mohammedans) A Muslim.

moist Slightly wet, damp. moisture.

moisten (moistens, moistening, moistened) 1. To make something moist. 2. To become moist.

mole (moles) 1. A small dark spot on a person's skin. 2. A small burrowing animal.

molehill (molehills) A small pile of earth thrown up by a mole.

molest (molests, molesting, molested) To interfere with someone, to annoy him.

mollusc (molluscs) A small animal with a soft body and usually a hard shell. Snails, oysters, and mussels are molluscs.

molten Melted.

moment (moments) 1. A very brief period of time. *Wait a moment.* 2. A particular point of time. *He arrived at the last moment.*

momentary Lasting only for a moment. momentarily.

momentous Serious, important.

monarch (monarchs) A king, queen, or emperor. monarchy.

monastery (monasteries) A house where monks live and work. monastic.

monaural Not stereophonic. *A monaural record.*

Monday (Mondays) The second day of the week.

money Metal coins or paper notes which have value for buying and selling. money-box.

mongol (mongols) A person born with a disease which makes him mentally defective.

mongoose (mongooses) A small animal that fights snakes.

mongrel (mongrels) A dog of mixed breeds.

monitor (monitors) A boy or girl given a particular job in a school, a prefect.

monk (monks) A man who is a member of a religious community.

monkey (monkeys) A kind of animal something like man.

mono (informal) Monaural.

monopolize (monopolizes, monopolizing, monopolized) To get control over so much of something that nobody else has a chance. monopoly.

monorail A railway using only one rail.

monotonous Dull, with no variation. monotonously, monotony.

monsoon (monsoons) A wind which blows in the region of the Indian Ocean and which brings heavy rains in the summer.

monster¹ (monsters) A large, horrible, frightening creature.

monster² Huge.

monstrous 1. Horrible. 2. Incredible. 3. Huge. monstrously, monstrosity.

month (months) 1. Any of the 12 parts into which the year is divided, such as January, February, and March. 2. A period of four weeks.

monthly Once a month, every month.

monument (monuments) A memorial.

monumental Large, massive.

moo (moos, mooing, mooed) To make a noise like a cow.

mood (moods) A state of mind. *To be in a good mood,* to feel cheerful.

moody (moodier, moodiest) 1. Gloomy, bad-tempered. 2. Liable to change mood without warning. moodily, moodiness.

moon The small planet which circles round the earth.

moonbeam (moonbeams) A beam of moon-light.

moonless With the moon not shining.

moonlight The light from the moon.

moor[1] (moors) An area of rough waste land often covered with heather.

moor[2] (moors, mooring, moored) To tie a boat to a quayside or buoy.

moorhen (moorhens) A black water-bird.

moorings 1. A place to moor a boat. 2. Things used to moor a boat.

moose (moose) A large North American deer.

mop[1] (mops) A bundle of strings or some other material fastened to the end of a stick for cleaning things.

mop[2] (mops, mopping, mopped) 1. To clean with a mop. 2. *To mop up,* to clear away the remains of something.

mope (mopes, moping, moped) To be in low spirits.

moped (mopeds) A bicycle with a small engine.

moral[1] 1. Concerned with right and wrong. 2. Virtuous, good. **morally, morality.**

moral[2] (morals) 1. The moral lesson taught by a story or event. 2. *Morals,* standards of behaviour.

morale Spirit. *Their morale was high,* they were cheerful.

morass (morasses) A marsh.

morbid 1. Thinking too much about sad things. 2. Unhealthy. **morbidly.**

more 1. *See* **many.** 2. *See* **much.** 3. Again. *Do it once more.* 4. *More or less,* approximately, almost.

moreover Besides.

morgue (morgues) A mortuary.

morning (mornings) The early part of the day, before noon.

moron (morons) A feeble-minded person.

morose Sullen, gloomy. **morosely.**

morphia A drug used to relieve pain.

Morse A code in which letters are represented by dots and dashes.

morsel (morsels) A small piece of some-thing, a mouthful.

mortal 1. Liable to die. *All men are mortal.* 2. Causing death. *A mortal wound.* **mortally, mortality.**

mortar[1] The cement mixture used to hold bricks or stones together in building.

mortar[2] (mortars) A short gun which shoots shells high in the air.

mortgage (mortgages) An arrangement to borrow money to buy a house.

mortuary (mortuaries) A place where dead bodies are kept for a time.

mosaic (mosaics) A picture or design made of many different coloured pieces of glass, stone, or other material.

Moslem (Moslems) A Muslim.

mosque (mosques) A building where Muslims worship.

mosquito (mosquitoes) A blood-sucking insect.

moss A plant which grows in damp places. **mossy.**

most 1. *See* **many.** 2. *See* **much.**

mostly Usually, chiefly.

motel (motels) A hotel for motorists.

moth (moths) 1. An insect which usually flies at night-time. 2. A clothes-moth, a small moth whose larvae feed on cloth.

moth-ball (moth-balls) A small ball of chemi-cal to keep moths out of clothes.

moth-eaten 1. Damaged by moths. 2. Old and untidy-looking.

mother[1] (mothers) A female parent. **motherly, motherhood, motherless.**

mother[2] (mothers, mothering, mothered) To act like a mother to someone.

motion (motions) Movement. **motionless.**

motive (motives) A reason for doing something.

motor[1] (motors) An engine.

motor[2] (motors, motoring, motored) To travel in a motor car. **motorist.**

motor bike (informal) A motor cycle.

motor boat A boat with a petrol engine.

motor car A vehicle with a petrol engine, usually for four or five passengers.

motor cycle A kind of bicycle with a petrol engine.

motorway (motorways) A modern road for fast long-distance traffic.

mottled Spotted.

motto (mottoes) 1. A short saying with a moral. 2. A short verse found in a Christmas cracker.

mould[1] A furry growth on something that has gone bad in the damp. **mouldy, mouldiness.**

mould[2] (moulds) A container in which some liquid is put to set to the required shape. *A jelly-mould.*

mould[3] (moulds, moulding, moulded) To give something its particular shape and character.

moult (moults, moulting, moulted) To lose feathers, to shed hair.

mound (mounds) A small hill.

mount[1] (mounts) 1. A mountain. 2. Something on which an object is mounted. 3. An animal on which someone is riding.

mount[2] (mounts, mounting, mounted) 1. To go up something, to get on to something. 2. To increase, to rise. *Tension mounted during the final minutes of the game.* 3. To put an object on something designed to display or carry it. *We mounted our photographs in an album.*

mountain (mountains) A high hill, a large mass of land rising to a peak. **mountainous.**

mountaineer (mountaineers) Someone who climbs mountains.

mountaineering Climbing mountains.

mourn (mourns, mourning, mourned) To feel sorrow because someone has died. **mourner.**

mournful Sad. **mournfully.**

mouse (mice) A small gnawing animal. **mouse-trap.**

mousse A flavoured cream, served cold.

moustache (moustaches) Hair growing on the upper lip.

mouth (mouths) 1. The opening in the face through which people and animals take in food. 2. An opening, an outlet. *The mouth of a river.*

mouthful (mouthfuls) As much as can be put in the mouth.

mouth-organ (mouth-organs) A musical instrument played by blowing and sucking.

move[1] (moves, moving, moved) 1. To go from one position to another. 2. To take something from one place and put it in another. **movable.** 3. To affect somebody's feelings. *We were moved to tears by their distress.*

move[2] (moves) 1. An action of moving. 2. A turn in a game. *Whose move is it next?*

movement (movements) 1. Moving or being moved. 2. A group of people organized for a particular cause. 3. A separate section of a piece of music. *The slow movement of a symphony.*

mow (mows, mowing, mowed, mown) 1. To cut grass. **mower, mowing-machine.** 2. *To mow down,* to knock down in large numbers.

Mr. The written form of a word used before a man's name when speaking to him politely or addressing a letter.

Mrs. The written form of a word used before a married woman's name when speaking to her politely or addressing a letter.

much (more, most) 1. A large amount of something. 2. *How much?* what quantity? what price? 3. To a large extent, by a great amount. 4. Greatly. 5. *I can't make much of this,* I can't understand it properly.

muck[1] 1. Dirt, filth. 2. Farmyard manure. **mucky.**

muck² (mucks, mucking, mucked) (informal) **1.** *To muck something up*, to make a mess of it. **2.** *To muck about*, to play about, to waste time.

mud Wet, soft soil. **muddy.**

muddle¹ Confusion, disorder, mess.

muddle² (muddles, muddling, muddled) **1.** To confuse, to bewilder. **2.** To mix things up. **3.** *To muddle through*, to complete a job in spite of muddle.

mudguard (mudguards) A device to stop mud splashing up from the wheels of a vehicle.

muffle (muffles, muffling, muffled) **1.** To wrap something up for warmth. **2.** To deaden the sound of something.

muffler (mufflers) A warm scarf.

mug (mugs) **1.** A kind of drinking cup. **2.** (informal) A face. **3.** (informal) A fool.

mugging (muggings) A violent attack on an innocent passer-by. **mugger.**

muggy (muggier, muggiest) Unpleasantly warm and damp.

Muhammadan (Muhammadans) A Muslim.

mule (mules) A cross between a horse and an ass.

multiple Having many parts.

multiply (multiplies, multiplying, multiplied) **1.** To find the answer when a certain number or quantity is taken a given number of times. *Three multiplied by four equals twelve* ($3 \times 4 = 12$). **multiplication.** **2.** To produce greater numbers. *Rabbits multiply rapidly*, they breed quickly.

multiracial Made up of many races or peoples.

multitude (multitudes) A great number, a crowd.

mum (mums) (informal) Mother.

mumble (mumbles, mumbling, mumbled) To speak indistinctly.

mummy¹ (mummies) (informal) Mother.

mummy² (mummies) The body of a person preserved after death as was the custom in ancient Egypt.

mumps A contagious disease with swellings in the neck.

munch (munches, munching, munched) To chew with much movement of the jaw.

municipal To do with a town or city.

munitions War supplies.

mural (murals) A painting on a wall.

murder¹ (murders) The crime of deliberately killing someone. **murderous, murderously.**

murder² (murders, murdering, murdered) To commit murder. **murderer.**

murky (murkier, murkiest) Dark and gloomy.

murmur¹ (murmurs, murmuring, murmured) To make a low monotonous sound.

murmur² (murmurs) A low monotonous sound.

muscle (muscles) One of the parts of the body used to produce movement.

muscular Having powerful muscles.

muse (muses, musing, mused) To think deeply or dreamily.

museum (museums) A building in which interesting and valuable objects are kept for display.

mushroom (mushrooms) An edible fungus.

music **1.** Pleasing or interesting sounds made by singing or playing various kinds of instruments. **2.** The signs representing these sounds on paper.

musical¹ **1.** Fond of music, good at music. **2.** Pleasant to listen to. **3.** To do with music, for use in music making. **musically.**

musical² (musicals) A play or film with much music and singing.

musician (musicians) A person who plays a musical instrument, an expert in music.

musket (muskets) A soldier's gun used before rifles were invented. **musketeer.**

Muslim (Muslims) A believer in Islam, a follower of Muhammad.

muslin A thin fine cotton cloth.

mussel (mussels) A kind of shellfish.

must 1. To be obliged to, to feel that one ought to. *I must go home soon.* 2. To be certain to. *You must be tired,* I am sure that you are tired.

mustang (mustangs) A wild horse.

mustard 1. A yellow powder or paste used to add a hot flavour to food. 2. *Mustard and cress,* small green plants eaten as salad.

muster (musters, mustering, mustered) To gather together.

musty (mustier, mustiest) Stale and damp and mouldy. **mustiness.**

mute Silent, dumb. **mutely.**

muted Muffled, made quieter.

mutilate (mutilates, mutilating, mutilated) To damage something by tearing or breaking or cutting off a part. **mutilation.**

mutineer (mutineers) Someone who takes part in a mutiny.

mutinous Rebellious. **mutinously.**

mutiny[1] (mutinies) An open rebellion, especially an attack by sailors against the captain of their ship.

mutiny[2] (mutinies, mutinying, mutinied) To take part in a mutiny.

mutter (mutters, muttering, muttered) To murmur, to speak in a low voice.

mutton The meat from sheep.

mutual Shared.

muzzle (muzzles) 1. An animal's nose and mouth. 2. A device put over an animal's muzzle to prevent it from biting. 3. The open end of a gun.

my Belonging to me.

myself *See* I[2]. This word is used in the same ways as **himself.**

mystery (mysteries) 1. Something that cannot be explained. 2. Secrecy. **mysterious, mysteriously.**

myth (myths) A tale about gods and goddesses handed down from ancient times.

mythical Happening in a myth, imaginary.

Nn

nab (nabs, nabbing, nabbed) (informal) To catch, to steal.

nag[1] (nags) (informal) A horse.

nag[2] (nags, nagging, nagged) To complain unceasingly, to scold.

nail[1] (nails) 1. A hard covering on part of the tip of a finger or a toe. **finger-nail, toe-nail, nail-brush, nail-scissors.** 2. A short metal spike used in carpentry to fasten pieces of wood together.

nail[2] (nails, nailing, nailed) To fasten with a nail.

naked Not wearing clothes. **nakedly, nakedness.**

name[1] (names) The word by which something or somebody is known.

name[2] (names, naming, named) 1. To give somebody a name. 2. To say the name of somebody or something.

nameless Having no name, not to be named.

namely That is to say.

nanny (nannies) (informal) 1. A children's nurse. 2. A grandmother.

nanny-goat (nanny-goats) A female goat.

nap (naps) A short sleep.

napalm Petrol jelly used as a weapon in fire bombs.

napkin (napkins) 1. A piece of cloth or paper used to keep oneself clean during a meal. 2. A piece of cloth or other material worn round a baby's bottom.

nappy (nappies) A baby's napkin.

narcotic (narcotics) A drug which produces sleep or unconsciousness.

narrate (narrates, narrating, narrated) To give an account of something, to tell a story. **narrator, narration.**

narrow (narrower, narrowest) 1. Thin, small. 2. *Narrow-minded,* not sympathetic towards other people's points of view.

narrowly Only just. *He narrowly escaped being run over.*

nasty (nastier, nastiest) 1. Unpleasant, disagreeable. 2. Dirty. 3. Ill-natured, spiteful. **nastily, nastiness.**

nation (nations) 1. A country and the people who live there. 2. A large number of people who have the same language and customs and history.

national Belonging to a nation.

nationalist (nationalists) An enthusiastic supporter of his nation.

nationality (nationalities) Being a member of a nation. *What is his nationality?* what nation does he belong to?

nationalize (nationalizes, nationalizing, nationalized) To make something the property of the nation. **nationalization.**

native[1] 1. Natural, possessed from birth. 2. Connected with a person's birth. *My native land*, the land where I was born.

native[2] (natives) 1. A person born in the place mentioned. *He is a native of Russia*, he was born in Russia. 2. One of the original inhabitants of a country.

Nativity The birth of Jesus. *A Nativity Play*, a play about the birth of Jesus.

natural[1] 1. Made by nature, to do with nature. 2. Normal, ordinary, to be expected. **naturally.**

natural[2] The sign ♮ in music.

naturalist (naturalists) A person who studies animals and plants.

nature[1] 1. The things in the universe that are not made by man, such as animals and plants, the sea and earth, the weather, and so on. 2. The powers that exist in these things. 3. *Nature study*, the study of animals and plants.

nature[2] (natures) 1. The general qualities or characteristics of a person or thing. *Angela has a kind nature*. 2. Sort, type. *Things of that nature*, things of that sort.

naughty (naughtier, naughtiest) 1. Badly behaved. 2. Shocking. **naughtily, naughtiness.**

nauseating Disgusting, sickening.

nautical To do with ships and sailors.

naval Belonging to the navy.

navel (navels) The small hollow in the middle of the surface of a person's stomach.

navigate (navigates, navigating, navigated) 1. To direct and control the course of a ship or plane. 2. To sail a ship. **navigable, navigator, navigation.**

navy[1] (navies) A fleet of ships and the men who sail in them.

navy[2] or **navy blue** Dark blue.

Nazi (Nazis) A member of the German National Socialist Party in Hitler's time.

near 1. Not far away. *The end is near*. 2. Close to. *Near the fire*.

nearly 1. Almost. *It's nearly dark*. 2. Closely. *Nearly related*. 3. *Not nearly*, far from. *There was not nearly enough food*.

neat (neater, neatest) 1. Tidy. 2. Cleverly done. 3. Small and attractive. **neatly, neatness.**

necessary Having to be done, essential, unavoidable. **necessarily, necessity.**

neck (necks) 1. The part of the body which joins the head and shoulders. 2. Something like a neck in shape. *The neck of a bottle*.

necklace (necklaces) An ornament worn round the neck.

nectar A sweet liquid collected by bees from plants.

need[1] (needs) 1. A want, a requirement. 2. An essential reason. *No need to go home yet*. 3. *In need*, in poverty and misfortune.

need[2] (needs, needing, needed) 1. To be without something which is necessary. *I need a handkerchief*. 2. To be obliged to do something, to have to do it. *You need not go*.

needle (needles) A thin, pointed instrument. *A knitting-needle*. **needlework**. 2. The pointer in a compass or a meter. **3.** The stylus point used to play a gramophone record.

needy (needier, neediest) Very poor.

ne'er (old-fashioned) Never.

negative (negatives) **1.** The word *no* or the word *not.* **2.** A sentence which denies or refuses something. **3.** In mathematics, a figure with a minus sign before it. **4.** In photography, a film for printing in which the colours or light and dark areas are reversed. **5.** In electricity, one of the terminals of a battery.

neglect (neglects, neglecting, neglected) **1.** To fail to care for something. *A neglected garden.* **2.** To fail to do something. *To neglect your duty.* **neglectful, neglectfully.**

negligent Careless. **negligently, negligence.**

negligible Not important, not worth considering.

negotiate (negotiates, negotiating, negotiated) **1.** To discuss and try to come to an agreement about something. **2.** To get past or over something. **negotiation, negotiator.**

Negro (Negroes) A black man. **Negress.**

neigh (neighs, neighing, neighed) To make a noise like a horse.

neighbour (neighbours) A person who lives near another.

neighbourhood The surrounding district.

neighbouring Near, close by.

neighbourly Friendly and helpful.

neither 1. Not either. **2.** *Neither this nor that,* not this and not that. **3.** Nor. *If mother doesn't go, neither shall I.*

nephew (nephews) The son of a person's brother or sister.

nerve (nerves) **1.** A thread-like organ of the body which carries messages between the brain and other parts of the body. **2.** *To suffer from nerves,* to get easily excited or upset. **3.** *To get on someone's nerves,* to annoy him. **4.** *To keep one's nerve,* to be calm and brave. **5.** (informal) *He's got a nerve!* he's cheeky!

nervous 1. Connected with the nerves. *A nervous disease.* **2.** Timid, fearful. *A nervous animal.* **nervously, nervousness.**

nervy (informal) Timid, easily upset.

nest[1] (nests) **1.** The place where a bird lays its eggs. **2.** The home of certain animals and insects.

nest[2] (nests, nesting, nested) To make a nest, to have a nest.

nestle (nestles, nestling, nestled) To cuddle, to get comfortably settled.

nestling (nestlings) A baby bird.

net[1] (nets) **1.** Material containing a large number of holes in a criss-cross pattern of strings, threads, or wires. **2.** Something made of this material. *A fishing net.*

net[2] (nets, netting, netted) To catch in a net.

netball A team game in which a ball has to be thrown into a high net.

netting Material for nets.

nettle (nettles) A wild plant. *A stinging nettle.*

network (networks) 1. A net. 2. A criss-cross pattern of lines. 3. A system consisting of many lines or parts. *A railway network.*

neuralgia Pain in the nerves of the face.

neurotic Suffering from a nervous illness.

neuter Neither masculine nor feminine.

neutral 1. Not taking sides. neutrality. 2. Having nothing distinctive about it. *The ship was painted a neutral shade of grey.* 3. A position of gears in which they do not transmit power from the engine.

never At no time.

nevermore Never again.

nevertheless In spite of that, however.

new (newer, newest) Appearing for the first time, just discovered, just bought or made, recent. newly, newness.

news 1. Information about recent events. 2. A broadcast of news.

newsagent (newsagents) A shopkeeper who sells newspapers and magazines.

newspaper (newspapers) A daily or weekly publication of news on large sheets of paper folded but not fixed together.

newt (newts) A small animal like a lizard.

next Closest, nearest, following immediately after.

nib (nibs) The pointed part of a pen which touches the paper in writing.

nibble (nibbles, nibbling, nibbled) To take tiny bites at something.

nice (nicer, nicest) 1. Pleasant, kind, friendly. 2. Precise, exact. nicely.

nick[1] (nicks, nicking, nicked) 1. To cut a notch in something. 2. (informal) To steal.

nick[2] (nicks) 1. A notch. 2. *In the nick of time,* at the last possible moment.

nickel A silver-coloured metal.

nickname (nicknames) A name used instead of someone's proper name.

nicotine A poisonous substance found in tobacco.

niece (nieces) The daughter of a person's brother or sister.

nigger (niggers) An impolite word for a Negro.

night (nights) The dark time between sunset and sunrise.

night-dress (night-dresses) A garment worn at night by a girl or woman.

nightfall The coming of night.

nightingale (nightingales) A small song-bird.

nightly Every night.

nightmare (nightmares) A frightening dream.

night-watchman (night-watchmen) A man employed to look after a place at night.

nil Nothing.

nimble (nimbler, nimblest) Quick, lively, agile. nimbly.

nincompoop (nincompoops) A silly person.

nine (nines) The number 9. ninth.

nineteen The number 19. nineteenth.

ninety (nineties) The number 90. ninetieth.

nip[1] (nips, nipping, nipped) 1. To pinch, to bite sharply. 2. (informal) To hurry along.

nip[2] (nips) 1. A small quick pinch or bite. 2. *A nip in the air,* a feeling of frost.

nipper (nippers) 1. (informal) A small boy. 2. *Nippers,* a tool for gripping or cutting.

nipple (nipples) The round, pinkish area or point in the centre of a person's breast.

nippy (nippier, nippiest) (informal) 1. Quick. 2. Cold.

nitrogen One of the gases in the air we breathe.

nitwit (nitwits) (informal) A stupid person.

no 1. Not one, not any. *We have no money.* 2. A word used when refusing, disagreeing, denying, or saying that something is not so.

noble[1] (nobler, noblest) 1. Of high rank. 2. Having a very good character. 3. Splendid. nobly, nobility.

noble[2] (nobles) or nobleman (noblemen) A man of high rank, such as a duke or a lord.

nobody No person, not anyone.

nocturnal 1. Active at night. 2. Of or in the night.

nod[1] (nods, nodding, nodded) 1. To bow the head to show agreement or to greet somebody. 2. To let the head fall forward in sleep.

nod[2] (nods) Nodding the head.

noise (noises) 1. A loud, unpleasant, and probably undesirable, sound. 2. A sound of any sort. *Did you hear a noise?* noisy, noisily, noisiness, noiseless, noiselessly.

nomad (nomads) A member of a wandering tribe.

no-man's-land The area between the camps of armies fighting each other.

nominate (nominates, nominating, nominated) To put forward somebody's name for an election. nomination.

nondescript Hard to describe.

none 1. Not one, not any. 2. Not at all. *After reading the instructions I'm none the wiser.*

non-existent Not existing.

nonplussed Amazed.

nonsense 1. Words that do not mean anything. 2. Foolish, pointless talk or behaviour. nonsensical.

non-stop Without stopping.

noodles A food rather like spaghetti.

nook (nooks) A quiet corner.

noon Twelve o'clock in the middle of the day.

no one No person, not anyone.

noose (nooses) A loop in a rope which becomes tighter when the rope is pulled.

nor And not.

normal Usual, typical, ordinary. normally, normality.

north 1. One of the points of the compass, the direction to the left of a person facing the sunrise. 2. From the north. *A north wind.* northerly. 3. In the north. *The north coast.* northern. 4. Towards the north. *We travelled north.* northward, northwards.

north-east Half-way between north and east.

northerner (northerners) A person who lives in the north.

north-west Half-way between north and west.

Norwegian Of Norway.

nose[1] (noses) 1. The part of the face which sticks out above the mouth. 2. The sense of smell. 3. The front end of a thing.

nose[2] (noses, nosing, nosed) 1. To push the nose into or against something. 2. To search, to pry.

nose dive The movement of falling or flying steeply downwards nose first.

nosey (nosier, nosiest) (informal) Inquisitive, prying. nosily.

nostalgia Homesickness, a longing for old times. nostalgic.

nostril (nostrils) One of the two openings in the nose.

not A word which alters the meaning of a statement to its opposite. *It is true, it is not true. Now you see me, now you do not.*

notable Remarkable.

notch (notches) A V-shaped cut in something.

note[1] (notes) 1. Something written down to help the memory. notebook. 2. A short letter. notepaper. 3. In music, a single sound of a particular pitch. 4. A quality, a sound, a tone. *There was a note of satisfaction in his voice.* 5. Notice. *Take note of what I say.* 6. Paper money. *A five-pound note.*

note[2] (notes, noting, noted) 1. To pay attention to something, to notice it. 2. To make a note of something.

nothing Not anything.

notice[1] (notices, noticing, noticed) To observe something.

notice[2] (notices) 1. A written announcement put up somewhere to be read by other people. 2. A warning. 3. Attention. *Take no notice*, pay no attention.

notice-board (notice-boards) A board for displaying notices.

notify (notifies, notifying, notified) To report something to somebody. notification.

notion (notions) An idea, an opinion.

notorious Widely known for bad reasons. notoriously, notoriety.

nougat A sweet made from nuts and sugar.

nought 1. Nothing. 2. (noughts) The figure 0.

noun (nouns) A naming word. *David, London, nursery*, and *zoo* are all nouns.

nourish (nourishes, nourishing, nourished)

To keep somebody alive and well by feeding him. **nourishment.**

novel[1] New and strange. **novelty.**

novel[2] (novels) A long story which fills a whole book.

novelist (novelists) A person who writes novels.

November The eleventh month of the year.

novice (novices) A beginner.

now 1. At this time. 2. By this time. 3. *Now that,* since. *Now that you mention it, I do remember.* 4. A word used to attract someone's attention. *Now, listen to me!*

nowadays In these days.

nowhere 1. No place. 2. In no place, to no place.

nozzle (nozzles) A spout, a piece fitted to the end of a hose-pipe.

nuclear To do with atomic energy, the great energy released when the nuclei of atoms are split or combined.

nucleus (nuclei) A centre round which other parts are grouped.

nude Naked. **nudity, nudist, nudism.**

nugget (nuggets) A lump of gold.

nuisance (nuisances) A thing or person that causes trouble.

numb[1] Without the power to feel or move. **numbly, numbness.**

numb[2] (numbs, numbing, numbed) To make numb.

number[1] (numbers) 1. A word or figure which shows how many. 1, 3, and 37 are all numbers. 2. A word or figure used to name things in a series. In most streets the houses are given numbers. 3. A quantity or amount. *A large number of people.* 4. A

song or dance performed as one item in a programme. 5. One issue of a newspaper or magazine.

number[2] (numbers, numbering, numbered) 1. To count. 2. To put a number on something.

numberless Too many to count.

numeral (numerals) A figure, a number.

numerous Many, consisting of a large number.

nun (nuns) A woman who is a member of a religious community.

nurse[1] (nurses) A person who is trained to look after sick people or young children.

nurse[2] (nurses, nursing, nursed) 1. To feed a baby, to look after a baby. 2. To look after sick people.

nursery (nurseries) 1. A room or building for young children. 2. A place where young plants and trees are grown.

nursery rhyme A song or poem popular with young children.

nursing home A small hospital.

nut (nuts) 1. A piece of metal designed to be screwed on a bolt. 2. A type of fruit with a hard shell. **nutty.**

nutcrackers An instrument for breaking the shell of a nut.

nutritious Nourishing.

nutshell (nutshells) The shell of a nut.

nuzzle (nuzzles, nuzzling, nuzzled) To press against something with the nose.

nylon A man-made substance used for making clothes and a wide variety of other things.

nymph (nymphs) A kind of goddess in ancient Greek stories.

Oo

oak (oaks) A large tree that produces acorns.

oar (oars) A pole with a flat blade used to row a boat. oarsman.

oasis (oases) A green and fertile place in a desert.

oath (oaths) 1. A solemn promise. 2. A swearword.

oats A kind of cereal crop. oatmeal.

obey (obeys, obeying, obeyed) To do what one is told to do. obedient, obediently, obedience.

object¹ (pronounced *ob*ject) (objects) 1. A thing that can be seen or touched. 2. A purpose. *What is the object of the expedition?*

object² (pronounced ob*ject*) (objects, objecting, objected) To say that one is not in favour of something. objection, objector.

objectionable Unpleasant.

objective (objectives) A place which a person is trying to reach, a thing which a person is trying to do.

obligation (obligations) A duty, something which ought to be done.

oblige (obliges, obliging, obliged) 1. *To be obliged to do something,* to have to do it. 2. To help someone, to do him a favour. *Will you oblige me by shutting the door?* 3. *To be obliged to someone,* to be grateful to him.

obliging Helpful. obligingly.

oblique Slanting. obliquely.

oblivious Not aware. obliviously.

oblong (oblongs) A rectangle, a shape like a door or the page of a book.

obnoxious Hateful, very unpleasant. obnoxiously.

oboe (oboes) A woodwind instrument.

obscene (obscener, obscenest) Indecent, repulsive. obscenely, obscenity.

obscure¹ (obscurer, obscurest) 1. Dim, not clear. 2. Hard to understand. 3. Not well known. obscurely, obscurity.

obscure² (obscures, obscuring, obscured) To make something obscure, to cover it up.

observant Quick at noticing things.

observation (observations) 1. A remark. 2. Observing, watching. *An observation post,* a place from which to keep watch.

observatory (observatories) A building from which the stars and planets are observed through telescopes.

observe (observes, observing, observed) 1. To see, to notice, to watch carefully. 2. To comment. 3. To obey a rule, to follow a custom. observer.

obsess (obsesses, obsessing, obsessed) To occupy the mind continually. obsession.

obsolete Out of date, not in use any more.

obstacle (obstacles) Something that gets in the way.

obstinate Difficult to persuade or deal with. obstinately, obstinacy.

obstreperous Noisy, rough and unruly. obstreperously.

obstruct (obstructs, obstructing, obstructed) To get in the way, to put something in the way. obstruction.

obtain (obtains, obtaining, obtained) To buy, to get, to be given something. obtainable.

obtuse 1. Stupid. 2. *An obtuse angle,* an angle greater than one right angle but less than two.

obvious Plain to see, understood at once. obviously.

occasion (occasions) 1. A particular or suitable time. 2. A special event, the time when this takes place.

occasional Happening from time to time, not continuous, not regular. *Some occasional showers.* occasionally.

occupation (occupations) 1. A job. 2. A pastime. 3. Occupying.

occupy (occupies, occupying, occupied) 1. To live in something. *To occupy a flat.* occupier, occupant. 2. To take up space. 3. To hold one's attention. *To occupy oneself,* to be busy with something. 4. To capture and keep territory in a war.

occur (occurs, occurring, occurred) 1. To happen, to take place. 2. To exist, to be found. 3. To come into one's mind. *A brilliant idea occurred to me.* occurrence.

ocean (oceans) 1. The sea. 2. A great area of sea, such as the Atlantic or Pacific Ocean.

o'clock By the clock. *School begins at nine o'clock.*

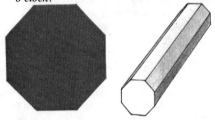

octagon (octagons) A shape with eight sides. octagonal.

octave (octaves) 1. A musical note together with the next note of the same name above or below it. 2. The interval between two notes of the same name.

October The tenth month of the year.

octopus (octopuses) A sea animal with eight arms.

oculist (oculists) A specialist in the treatment of eye diseases.

odd¹ (odder, oddest) Strange, queer. oddly, oddity.

odd² 1. *Odd numbers,* numbers which cannot be divided exactly by two, such as 1, 3, and 37. 2. Remaining, spare, left over. *An odd glove.* 3. Of various sorts. *Odd jobs.*

oddments Odds and ends.

odds 1. Chances, likelihood. *The odds are against it,* it is not likely. 2. *Odds and ends,* various bits and pieces.

ode (odes) A kind of poem.

odious Hateful, repulsive. odiously.

odour (odours) A smell.

of This word has many meanings including the following: 1. From. *A native of China.* 2. Concerning. *News of Granny.* 3. Belonging to. *The official residence of the Prime Minister.*

off This word has many meanings including the following: 1. Not on, no longer on. *Her glasses fell off.* 2. Away. *They ran off when the police arrived.* 3. Not working or operating. *The heating is off.* 4. Away or down from. *Keep off the grass! The cat jumped off the table.*

offence 1. (offences) A crime, the breaking of a law or rule or custom. 2. Hurt feelings. *To cause offence.*

offend (offends, offending, offended) 1. To commit an offence or crime. 2. To hurt someone's feelings.

offensive 1. Unpleasant, causing hurt feelings. 2. Used for attacking. *An offensive weapon.* offensively.

offer¹ (offers, offering, offered) 1. To hold something out to someone. 2. To say that one is willing to do something. 3. To suggest a price one is willing to pay for something.

offer² (offers) 1. A statement offering something. 2. *On offer,* offered for sale at a specially reduced price.

offering (offerings) Something offered, something given.

office (offices) 1. A room where clerks and secretaries work, a room where business is done. 2. A government department. *The Foreign and Commonwealth Office.* 3. *To hold office,* to have an important job.

officer (officers) 1. A person who commands others in the services. 2. A senior person in some other jobs. 3. One of the people responsible for running a club or society. 4. *A police officer,* a policeman.

official[1] **1.** Done or announced by someone with authority. **2.** To do with a position of trust or authority. **officially.**

official[2] (officials) A person who does an official job. *A government official.*

officious Too eager with advice and help.

offside In football, in a position where it is against the rules to play the ball.

offspring (offspring) A child or young animal.

often Frequently, many times.

ogre (ogres) A cruel giant.

oh A cry of surprise or some other sudden feeling.

oil[1] (oils) **1.** An inflammable liquid which does not mix with water. *Crude oil. Whale oil. Olive oil.* **2.** *Oils,* oil-colours.

oil[2] (oils, oiling, oiled) To put oil on something to make it run more smoothly.

oil-can (oil-cans) A can with a long spout used for oiling.

oil-colours Paints made with oil.

oil-field (oil-fields) An area where crude oil is found.

oil-painting (oil-paintings) A painting done in oil-colours.

oilskins A waterproof suit worn over other clothes.

oil-tanker (oil-tankers) A ship, or a large truck, used to transport oil.

oil-well (oil-wells) A well drilled for oil.

oily (oilier, oiliest) **1.** Like oil. **2.** Covered in oil.

ointment (ointments) A soft greasy substance used for healing cuts and sores.

O.K. (informal) **1.** All right, yes. **2.** Satisfactory. *Is everything O.K.?*

old (older, oldest) **1.** Having lived or existed for a long time. *The ruins of an old castle.*

2. Known for a long time. *An old friend.* **3.** *10 years old,* born or made ten years previously. **4.** Of the past. *In the old days.*

olden *In olden days,* in past times.

old-fashioned Out of date, not suitable for modern times.

olive (olives) **1.** A tree which bears a bitter-tasting fruit. **2.** Its fruit. *Olive oil,* oil obtained from this fruit.

Olympic Games   Olympics International athletic sports held once every four years.

omelette (omelettes) A food made of beaten eggs cooked in a frying-pan.

omen (omens) A sign of things to come.

ominous Threatening. **ominously.**

omit (omits, omitting, omitted) **1.** To leave something out. **2.** To fail to do something. **omission.**

omnibus (omnibuses) **1.** (old-fashioned) A bus. **2.** A collection of stories in a book.

omnipotent Having power over everything. **omnipotence.**

on This word has many meanings including the following: **1.** Situated at the top of, covering the top of. *Tea is on the table.* **2.** By, near. *On the right hand side of the road.* **3.** Attached to. *The picture is on the wall.* **4.** Concerning, about. *He gave us a lecture on how to behave.* **5.** Forwards. *We must move on to the next place.* **6.** Working, operating. *Is the heating on?* **7.** To a position on top of something. *The cat jumped on the table.*

once 1. A single time. *Once is enough.* **2.** On one occasion, at one time. *Once a week.*
    At some time in the past. *Once there was a king with three sons.* **4.** As soon as. *Once you read the instructions you will know how it works.* **5.** *At once,* immediately.

one[1] The number 1.

one[2] (oneself) **1.** A single person, any person. **2.** *One another,* each other.

oneself *See* **one**[2]. The word is used to refer to the person speaking or to people in general. *One should not be too proud of oneself.*

one-sided Favouring one side unfairly.

one-way street A street in which traffic may go only in one direction.

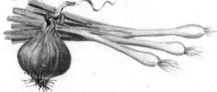

onion (onions) A strong-tasting vegetable.

onlooker (onlookers) A spectator.

only 1. Single, one. *The king was the only man able to tame the lion.* 2. No more than. *There are only five minutes left to play.* 3. *Only too,* very. *I'm only too happy to help.* 4. But then, however. *I would like to come, only I'm busy that night.*

onset (onsets) An attack, a vigorous beginning of something.

onslaught (onslaughts) A fierce attack.

onward or **onwards** Forward.

ooze (oozes, oozing, oozed) To leak slowly through narrow openings.

opal (opals) A precious stone.

opaque Not allowing light to pass through.

open¹ 1. Not closed, allowing people or things to pass through. *An open door.* 2. Not enclosed, not fenced in. *Open country. In the open air,* out of doors. 3. Not covered over. *An open boat.* 4. Spread out, unfolded. *Open arms.* 5. Ready for business. *The shop is open at 9.* 6. Honest, frank. *An open face.*

open² (opens, opening, opened) 1. To make a thing open. 2. To become open. 3. To start. *My story opens in a dark forest.* **opener.**

opening (openings) 1. A space. 2. A beginning.

openly Not secretly. **openness.**

opera (operas) A kind of play where most or all of the words are sung. **operatic.**

operate (operates, operating, operated) 1. To work, to act. *The lift is not operating today.* 2. To cause something to work. *Do you know how to operate this lift?* 3. To perform a surgical operation on someone.

operation (operations) 1. Operating. *In operation,* working. **operational.** 2. Treatment by a surgeon, involving the cutting of the patient's body. 3. A carefully planned movement of troops and equipment in a war. 4. Any carefully planned activity.

operator (operators) A person who works something. *A telephone operator.*

opinion (opinions) An idea which is not proved, a person's belief.

opium A kind of drug.

opponent (opponents) A person who is fighting or playing or arguing on the opposite side.

opportunity (opportunities) A good chance, a convenient occasion to do something.

oppose (opposes, opposing, opposed) To fight or play against someone or something, to be strongly against something. **opposition.**

opposite¹ 1. Facing. *The house opposite mine.* 2. Entirely different, as different as can be. *We hold opposite views.*

opposite² (opposites) One of two things which are entirely different. *Black is the opposite of white.*

oppress (oppresses, oppressing, oppressed) 1. To govern cruelly, to treat people unjustly. 2. To weigh down with worry or sorrow. **oppressive, oppressively, oppressor, oppression.**

opt (opts, opting, opted) To choose.

optical To do with the eyes or with seeing.

optician (opticians) A person who supplies spectacles.

optimist (optimists) A person who feels that all will turn out right in the end. **optimism.**

optimistic Cheerful, confident. **optimistically.**

option (options) A choice.

optional Not compulsory.

opulent Rich. **opulence.**

or A word which shows that a choice is available. *He offered her a bun or a sandwich.*

oral Spoken. **orally.**

orange¹ (oranges) A round, juicy fruit with reddish-yellow peel.

orange² Reddish-yellow.

orangeade A drink flavoured with oranges.

oratorio (oratorios) A musical composition on a religious subject for voices and orchestra.

orbit (orbits) The path followed by one planet or satellite moving round another in space.

orchard (orchards) A field of fruit trees.

orchestra (orchestras) A large number of musicians who play together. *A symphony orchestra.* **orchestral.**

orchid (orchids) A kind of flower.

ordeal (ordeals) A severe test of strength, character, or endurance.

order[1] (orders) 1. A command. *Obey the captain's orders.* 2. A request for something to be supplied. *An order for coal.* 3. Obedience to authority, good behaviour. *The police restored order.* 4. Condition. *In working order.* 5. Arrangement. *Alphabetical order.* 6. Tidiness. *Put the room in order,* tidy it up. 7. Kind, sort. *Bravery of the highest order.* 8. *In order to,* for the purpose of. 9. *In order that,* so that.

order[2] (orders, ordering, ordered) 1. To command. 2. To ask a supplier for something. *We must order some coal.*

orderly 1. Well arranged. 2. Well behaved.

ordinary Normal, usual, not exceptional. **ordinarily.**

ore (ores) A rock or mineral from which metal can be obtained. *Iron ore.*

organ (organs) 1. A part of an animal's body with a particular job to do. *The ears are the organs of hearing.* 2. A musical instrument with one or more keyboards.

organism (organisms) A living animal or plant.

organist (organists) A person who plays the organ.

organization (organizations) 1. Organizing. 2. A group of organized people.

organize (organizes, organizing, organized) 1. To make the arrangements for something. 2. To get people working together in an orderly way. **organizer.**

orgy (orgies) A wild, drunken party.

oriental Of the East, especially of China or Japan.

orienteering A sport involving cross-country running and map-reading.

origin (origins) The point where something began.

original 1. Earliest, first, existing from the beginning. **originally.** 2. Not a copy, not an imitation. *An original painting. An original idea.* 3. Able to produce new ideas. *An original thinker.* **originality.**

originate (originates, originating, originated) To begin. **originator.**

ornament (ornaments) An object or decoration intended to make something more beautiful. **ornamental.**

ornithology The scientific study of birds. **ornithologist.**

orphan (orphans) A child whose parents are dead.

orphanage (orphanages) A home for orphans.

orthodox 1. Generally accepted. *Orthodox opinion.* 2. *The Orthodox Church,* the Christian Churches of Eastern Europe.

ostentatious Showy. **ostentatiously.**

ostrich (ostriches) A large bird that runs swiftly but cannot fly.

other 1. Somebody or something different from the one just mentioned. *This egg is all right but the other was going bad.* 2. *The other day,* a few days ago.

otherwise 1. In another way, in a different way. 2. Or else. *Be careful, otherwise you'll fall.*

otter (otters) An animal that lives by rivers or streams.

ouch A cry of pain.

ought Should, must. *You ought to go now.*

oughtn't (informal) Ought not.

ounce (ounces) A unit of weight, 28·3 grams. 16 ounces make one pound.

our or **ours** Belonging to us. *Our house. This house is ours.*

ourselves *See* **we.**

out 1. Away from a place, not in it. *Out of bed.* 2. Not at home. *The doctor is out.* 3. In the open, published. *The secret is out.* 4. No longer in a game or a job. *The batsman is out.* 5. Finished. *The fire is out.* 6. Loudly. *He cried out in agony.* 7. *Out of,* (a) From. *Made out of straw.* (b) Without. *Out of breath.* (c) *Out of the way,* unusual. (d) *Six out of ten,* six from a possible total of ten.

out and out Thorough, thoroughly.

outback (Australian) The remote part of a country far from big towns and from the coast.

outboard motor An engine fitted on the stern of a small boat.

outbreak (outbreaks) The beginning of something unpleasant or violent. *The outbreak of war.*

outburst (outbursts) A sudden burst of something, an outbreak.

outcast (outcasts) A person disowned by his family and friends.

outcome (outcomes) A result.

outcry (outcries) A protest, an angry shout.

outdo (outdoes, outdoing, outdone) To do more, or to do better, than someone else.

outdoor Done outdoors, for outdoors.

outdoors Not inside any building or shelter, in the open air.

outer Near the outside, further from the centre.

outfit (outfits) All the clothes or equipment needed for a particular purpose.

outgrow (outgrows, outgrowing, outgrew, outgrown) 1. To grow too big or too old for something. 2. To grow larger than someone or something. *Susan has outgrown her brother.*

outhouse (outhouses) A shed or other small building attached to, or near, a larger building.

outing (outings) A pleasure trip.

outlandish Strange, odd, foreign-looking. **outlandishly.**

outlaw[1] (outlaws) In former times, a person who was punished by not being allowed to be protected by the laws of his country, a bandit.

outlaw[2] (outlaws, outlawing, outlawed) To declare a person to be an outlaw.

outlet (outlets) A way out.

outline[1] (outlines) 1. The shape of something. 2. A simple drawing which shows only the shape of a thing without any details or shading. 3. A summary.

outline[2] (outlines, outlining, outlined) To draw an outline, to give an outline.

outlive (outlives, outliving, outlived) To live longer than someone else.

outlook (outlooks) 1. A view. 2. A forecast.

outlying Distant, far from a town or city.

outnumber (outnumbers, outnumbering, outnumbered) To be greater in number than something else.

out-patient (out-patients) A person who visits a hospital for treatment but does not sleep there.

outpost (outposts) A distant settlement.

output The quantity of things produced.

outrage (outrages) A violent action, something that shocks public opinion. **outrageous, outrageously.**

outright Completely, altogether.

outside[1] 1. The outer part of something, the part furthest from the middle. 2. *At the outside,* at the most.

outside[2] 1. Furthest from the middle. 2. Of the outside, coming from the outside. 3. On the outer side, to the outer side. *Please go outside.* 4. Outdoors. *It's warm enough to play outside.*

outsider (outsiders) 1. A person who is not a member of a particular group. 2. A horse with no obvious chance of winning a race.

outsize Of larger than normal size.

outskirts The outer parts of an area, the suburbs of a town.

outspoken Frank in speech.

outstanding 1. Easily noticed, conspicuous. **outstandingly.** 2. Still requiring attention.

outstretched Stretched out, spread out.

outward 1. On the outside. **outwardly.** 2. Going out. *The outward journey.*

outwards Towards the outside.

outwit (outwits, outwitting, outwitted) To get the better of somebody by being clever.

outworn Worn out, used up.

oval Egg-shaped, shaped like an O.

oven (ovens) The part of a cooking stove into which food is put for baking or roasting.

over[1] 1. On, above, covering. *Fog lay over the city. All over*, in all parts. 2. To the other side of. *I climbed over the wall.* 3. On the other side of. *I live over the road.* 4. From an upright to a fallen position. *Don't fall over.* 5. From beginning to end. *Read your work over carefully.* 6. Remaining. *3 into 11 goes 3 and 2 over.* 7. Ended. *Their quarrel was soon over.* 8. More, more than. *The race is open to boys over ten.* 9. Too much. *Over-anxious. Over-enthusiastic.*

over[2] (overs) In cricket, a number of balls bowled in succession from one end.

overall (overalls) A loose-fitting garment worn over one's clothes to keep them clean.

overbalance (overbalances, overbalancing, overbalanced) 1. To fall over. 2. To make something fall over.

overboard Over the side of a ship into the water.

overcast Cloudy.

overcoat (overcoats) A warm outer coat.

overcome (overcomes, overcoming, overcame) 1. To defeat someone. 2. To get the better of something.

overcrowd (overcrowds, overcrowding, overcrowded) To crowd too many people or things together.

overdo (overdoes, overdoing, overdid, overdone) 1. To do something too much. 2. To cook something for too long.

overdose (overdoses) Too large a dose.

overdue Late, past the proper time.

overflow (overflows, overflowing, overflowed) To flood, to spill over.

overgrown Covered with unwanted plants.

overhang (overhangs, overhanging, overhung) To jut out over something as a shelf does.

overhaul (overhauls, overhauling, overhauled) 1. To examine something thoroughly and repair it if necessary. 2. To overtake.

overhead Above one's head, in the sky.

overhear (overhears, overhearing, overheard) To hear something accidentally.

overjoyed Delighted, very pleased.

overland Across the land.

overlap (overlaps, overlapping, overlapped) To lie partly covering another thing. *Overlapping tiles.*

overleaf On the other side of the paper.

overload (overloads, overloading, overloaded) To put too big a load on something.

overlook (overlooks, overlooking, overlooked) 1. To have a view of something from above. 2. To fail to notice something. 3. To let some wrong action pass without punishment.

overnight Through the night, for a night.

overpower (overpowers, overpowering, overpowered) To overcome someone.

overrated Valued too highly.

overrun (overruns, overrunning, overran, overrun) 1. To spread over an area and occupy it. 2. To use up more than the time allowed. 3. To go on too far.

overseas Beyond the sea, across the sea.

overseer (overseers) A foreman.

oversight (oversights) A mistake made because something was not noticed.

oversleep (oversleeps, oversleeping, overslept) To go on sleeping after the proper time for waking up.

overtake (overtakes, overtaking, overtook, overtaken) 1. To pass another moving vehicle and drive on in front of it. 2. To come upon somebody suddenly. *They were overtaken by a thunderstorm.*

overtime Time spent at work after the usual hours. *Overtime pay.*

overture (overtures) A piece of orchestral music, especially one performed at the beginning of a concert or opera.

overturn (overturns, overturning, overturned) To turn over, to upset.

overweight Too heavy.

overwhelm (overwhelms, overwhelming, overwhelmed) 1. To overcome completely. 2. To weigh down, to overload.

overwrought Worn out by work, worry, or excitement.

owe (owes, owing, owed) 1. To have a duty to pay money to someone. *I owe John £10.* 2. To have something as a result of someone's action or ability. *They owed their lives to the pilot's skill.*

owing to Because of, caused by.

owl (owls) A bird of prey which flies at night.

own¹ 1. A word used to emphasise who owns something. *This pen is my own*, it belongs to me and no one else. 2. *On one's own*, by oneself.

own² (owns, owning, owned) 1. To possess. 2. To admit. *To own up*, to confess.

owner (owners) The person who owns something. **ownership.**

ox (oxen) A male animal of the cow family.

oxygen One of the gases in the air. Animals and plants need it in order to live.

oyster (oysters) A kind of shellfish whose shell sometimes contains a pearl.

Pp

pace¹ (paces) 1. The distance a person covers when he takes a single step in walking. 2. Speed. *He walked at a brisk pace.*

pace² (paces, pacing, paced) 1. To walk with slow or regular steps. 2. To measure a distance in paces.

pacifist (pacifists) A person who believes that war could and should be abolished. **pacifism.**

pacify (pacifies, pacifying, pacified) To make peaceful, to make calm.

pack¹ (packs) 1. A bundle or box of things packed together. 2. A group of hounds or wolves. 3. A set of playing-cards.

pack² (packs, packing, packed) 1. To wrap things up or put them in containers. 2. To crowd together.

package (packages) A parcel or bundle.

packet (packets) A small parcel.

packing Material used to pack goods in.

pact (pacts) A solemn agreement.

pad¹ (pads) 1. A piece of padding. 2. A set of sheets of paper held together at one edge. *A writing pad.* 3. A protection for the batsman's legs in cricket.

pad² (pads, padding, padded) 1. To fill or cover with padding. 2. To walk softly.

padding Soft material used to make something more comfortable or to change its shape.

paddle¹ (paddles, paddling, paddled) 1. To move a boat along with a paddle. 2. To walk with bare feet in shallow water.

paddle² (paddles) 1. A short oar. 2. A time spent paddling.

paddle-steamer (paddle-steamers) A boat propelled by two large wheels at the sides.

paddock (paddocks) A small field.

paddy-field (paddy-fields) A rice-field.

padlock¹ (padlocks) A lock with a curved bar which forms a loop when closed.

padlock² (padlocks, padlocking, padlocked) To fasten something with a padlock.

pagan (pagans) A heathen.

page (pages) 1. One side of a sheet of paper in a book. 2. A boy servant.

pageant (pageants) 1. An entertainment based on historic events and people. 2. A grand procession. **pageantry.**

pagoda (pagodas) A sacred tower of the Far East.

paid *See* pay¹.

pail (pails) A bucket.

pain (pains) 1. Suffering. **painful, painfully, painless, painlessly.** 2. *To take pains,* to be careful and thorough.

paint¹ (paints) 1. A substance which is put on something to colour it. 2. *Paints,* a collection of tubes or small pans of paint. **paintbox, paintbrush.**

paint² (paints, painting, painted) 1. To put paint on something. 2. To make a picture with paints.

painter (painters) 1. Someone who paints. 2. A rope for tying up a boat.

painting (paintings) A painted picture.

pair¹ (pairs) 1. Two things of the same kind which go together. *A pair of shoes.* 2. A single thing with two similar parts. *A pair of trousers.*

pair² (pairs, pairing, paired) To form pairs.

Pakistani Of Pakistan.

pal (pals) (informal) A friend.

palace (palaces) 1. The official home of the ruler of a country, or of a bishop. 2. A large and splendid house.

pale (paler, palest) 1. Having little colour, whitish. 2. Dim, faint, not bright. **palely, paleness.**

palette (palettes) A board on which an artist mixes his colours.

paling (palings) A wooden fence.

palisade (palisades) A fence of pointed wooden sticks.

pall¹ (palls) A dark covering.

pall² (palls, palling, palled) To become tiresome.

pallid Pale, ill-looking. **pallor.**

palm¹ (palms) The inside part of a person's hand between the wrist and the fingers.

palm² (palms) A kind of tree with no branches and a mass of large leaves at the top, growing in hot countries. *A date-palm. A coconut-palm.*

Palm Sunday The Sunday before Easter.

paltry Worthless.

pampas-grass A tall feathery grass.

pamper (pampers, pampering, pampered) To take too much care of someone.

pamphlet (pamphlets) A thin paper-bound booklet.

pan (pans) 1. A flat dish, often without a cover. *A frying-pan.* 2. Anything dish-shaped.

pancake (pancakes) A food made from fried batter.

panda (pandas) *A giant panda,* a black and white animal from China.

panda car A police patrol car.

pandemonium A scene of confused uproar and disorder.

pane (panes) A sheet of glass in a window.

panel¹ (panels) 1. A flat piece of board, metal, or other substance forming part of a wall or other surface. 2. A group of people appointed to decide something.

panel² (panels, panelling, panelled) To cover something with panels. *A panelled wall.*

pang (pangs) A sudden feeling of sadness or pain.

panic¹ Sudden infectious fear. **panicky.**

panic² (panics, panicking, panicked) To give way to panic.

pannier (panniers) One of a pair of baskets or bags hung on each side of a horse or bicycle.

panorama (panoramas) A wide view.

pansy (pansies) A flowering plant.

pant (pants, panting, panted) To take many short quick breaths, to gasp.

panther (panthers) A leopard.

pantomime (pantomimes) A Christmas entertainment usually based on a fairy tale.

pantry (pantries) A room or cupboard where food is kept.

pants 1. Underclothing worn on the lower part of the body. 2. Trousers.

papa (papas) (old-fashioned) Father.

paper[1] (papers) 1. A substance made in thin flexible sheets. It is used to write on, to make books, to wrap things in, and so on. 2. A newspaper. 3. *Papers*, official documents.

paper[2] (papers, papering, papered) To paste wallpaper on a wall.

paperback (paperbacks) A book with paper covers.

papier-mâché Paper made into pulp and used for making models and other objects.

papyrus A kind of paper which was made out of reeds in ancient Egypt.

parable (parables) A story which teaches a moral.

parachute (parachutes) An umbrella-shaped apparatus used for dropping safely from an aircraft.

parade[1] (parades) 1. A procession. 2. A display of people moving past the spectators. 3. An assembly of soldiers for inspection and drill. parade-ground.

parade[2] (parades, parading, paraded) 1. To assemble for a parade. 2. To go in a parade.

paradise 1. The Garden of Eden. 2. Heaven. 3. Any place where people are perfectly happy.

paraffin An oil used as a fuel.

paragraph (paragraphs) A division of a piece of writing. Each paragraph starts on a new line.

parallel lines Lines which are always the same distance apart.

paralyse (paralyses, paralysing, paralysed) To make helpless, to afflict with paralysis.

paralysis A state of being unable to move or feel anything.

parapet (parapets) A low wall along a roof, along the side of a bridge, or along the front of a trench.

paraphernalia Numerous pieces of equipment or other possessions.

parasite (parasites) A small animal or plant that grows and feeds on another.

parasol (parasols) A kind of umbrella used as a sun-shade.

paratroops Troops trained to drop by parachute.

parcel (parcels) Something wrapped and tied up for carrying or posting. *Parcel post*.

parch (parches, parching, parched) To make something become hot and dry.

parchment A material for writing on, made from the skin of a goat or sheep.

pardon[1] (pardons) Forgiveness.

pardon[2] (pardons, pardoning, pardoned) To forgive, to excuse, to overlook. pardonable, pardonably.

parent (parents) A father or mother. parental.

parish (parishes) A small division of a county, an area served by its own church.

park[1] (parks) 1. A public garden, an area of ground for public use. 2. An area of grassland with trees round a large country house. 3. *A National Park*, a large area of beautiful countryside preserved by the government. 4. A place where cars or other vehicles may be left for a time. *A car park*.

park[2] (parks, parking, parked) To leave a vehicle for a time in a car park or other suitable place.

parking-meter (parking-meters) An instrument which measures the length of time a car is parked in a street.

parliament (parliaments) A gathering of people responsible for making the laws of their country. parliamentary.

parlour (parlours) A sitting-room.

parole A kind of promise. *A prisoner on parole*, a prisoner who has promised that he will not try to escape.

parquet floor A floor made of blocks of wood fitted together to make a pattern.

parrot (parrots) A tropical bird often kept as a pet.

parry (parries, parrying, parried) To turn aside a blow.

parsley A green herb.

parsnip (parsnips) A root vegetable.

parson (parsons) A clergyman.

part[1] (parts) 1. Some but not all. *We enjoyed parts of the film very much.* 2. A share in something. *He was put in prison for his part in the robbery.* 3. A piece of something. *Spare parts for the car.* 4. An area, a district. *I'm a stranger in these parts.* 5. The words to be spoken by a character in a play. 6. A character in a play.

part[2] (parts, parting, parted) 1. To separate or divide. 2. *To part with something,* to give it up, to give it away.

partial 1. Only in part, incomplete. **partially.** 2. *Partial to,* fond of.

participate (participates, participating, participated) To have a share in something, to take part in it. **participation.**

particle (particles) A tiny piece of something.

particular 1. Outstanding, special, important. *In particular,* specially. 2. *This particular example,* this one and no others. 3. Fussy, hard to please. **particularly.**

particulars Details.

parting (partings) 1. Separation. 2. The line where the hair is parted.

partisan (partisans) A keen supporter.

partition (partitions) A dividing wall.

partly In part, not completely.

partner (partners) One of a pair of people who share things or do things together. **partnership.**

partridge (partridges) A game bird.

party (parties) 1. A gathering of people for a happy occasion. *A birthday party.* 2. A group of people with the same political opinions. *The Liberal Party.* 3. A group of people. *We'll travel as a party.* 4. A person taking part in an action. *The guilty party.*

pass[1] (passes, passing, passed) 1. To go past. *We passed the palace but we didn't see the Queen.* 2. To move, to go, to travel. *They passed along a narrow lane.* 3. To give, to hand over. *Please pass the jam.* 4. To disappear. *The pain will soon pass.* 5. *To pass away,* to die. 6. To be successful. *Did Robert pass his test?* 7. To spend, to use. *How shall we pass the time?* 8. *To pass off,* to take place. *The concert passed off successfully.*

pass[2] (passes) 1. The act of passing. 2. A narrow way between hills or mountains. 3. A permit.

passable 1. Acceptable, satisfactory. 2. *The road is passable,* it can be travelled over.

passage (passages) 1. A long, narrow way between walls, a corridor. 2. A way through. *The police forced a passage through the crowd.* 3. A journey by sea or air. 4. A short extract from a piece of writing or music. 5. Passing. *The passage of time.*

passenger (passengers) 1. A person travelling by public transport. 2. A person being driven in a car.

passer-by (passers-by) A person who happens to be going past.

passion (passions) A strong feeling, an enthusiasm. **passionate, passionately.**

passive Not resisting, not active. **passively.**

Passover A Jewish religious festival.

passport (passports) An official document to be carried by a person travelling abroad.

password (passwords) A secret word which enables somebody to be recognized as a friend.

past[1] The time before the present.

past[2] Belonging to the past.

past[3] 1. After. *It is past midnight.* 2. Beyond. *You will find the shops just past the church.* 3. Up to and beyond. *James walked straight past me without saying hello.*

paste[1] (pastes) 1. A wet mixture used for sticking papers together or for hanging wallpaper. 2. Any soft wet mixture. *Fish-paste.*

paste² (pastes, pasting, pasted) To stick with paste.

pastel (pastels) A coloured chalk crayon.

pasteurize (pasteurizes, pasteurizing, pasteurized) To kill germs in milk by a heating process.

pastille (pastilles) A lozenge, a kind of sweet.

pastime (pastimes) A game, anything done for recreation.

pastor (pastors) A clergyman.

pastry (pastries) A mixture of flour, fat, and other ingredients baked in an oven.

pasture (pastures) Grassland for sheep or cattle.

pasty¹ (pastier, pastiest) Pale.

pasty² (pasties) A kind of pie.

pat¹ Without hesitation.

pat² (pats, patting, patted) To hit gently with the open hand or with something flat.

patch¹ (patches) 1. A piece of material put over a hole or damaged place. 2. A small area of ground. 3. Part of a surface different from the rest.

patch² (patches, patching, patched) 1. To put a patch on something. 2. *To patch something up*, to repair it roughly.

patchwork A piece of material made up of a variety of small pieces of cloth stitched together.

patchy Made up of odds and ends, uneven in quality. patchily, patchiness.

patent leather Leather with a shiny surface.

paternal Like a father, of a father.

path (paths) 1. A way to walk or ride along. 2. A line along which something moves.

pathetic Sad, causing pity. pathetically.

patience 1. The ability to endure pain or trouble or inconvenience without complaint. 2. A card game for a single player.

patient¹ Having patience. patiently.

patient² (patients) A person treated by a doctor or a nurse.

patio (patios) A paved area beside a house.

patriot (patriots) A person who loves his country and is ready to defend it. patriotic, patriotism.

patrol¹ (patrols, patrolling, patrolled) To go about to see that all is well.

patrol² (patrols) 1. *On patrol*, patrolling. 2. A group of men, ships, or aircraft on patrol. 3. *A patrol car,* a car used by police on patrol. 4. A group of Scouts.

patron saint A saint who is regarded as the special protector of a church or a group of people.

patter (patters, pattering, pattered) To make repeated light tapping sounds.

pattern (patterns) 1. Something which is to be copied, something which shows how a thing should be made. *A dress pattern.* 2. A decorative design such as that on a carpet or on wallpaper.

pauper (paupers) A very poor person.

pause¹ (pauses) A short stop or interval.

pause² (pauses, pausing, paused) To make a pause.

pave (paves, paving, paved) To cover an area with a surface of flat stones. paving-stone.

pavement (pavements) A path for pedestrians at the side of a street or road.

pavilion (pavilions) A building at a sports ground for the use of players or spectators.

paw¹ (paws) The foot of an animal with claws.

paw² (paws, pawing, pawed) To touch something with a paw, hoof, or hand.

pawn¹ (pawns) One of the small, least important pieces in chess.

pawn² (pawns, pawning, pawned) To leave something with a pawnbroker in order to borrow money from him.

pawnbroker (pawnbrokers) A shopkeeper who lends money to people who leave articles with him until they repay the loan.

pay¹ (pays, paying, paid) 1. To hand over to someone money which is due to him. *We pay the milkman on Saturdays.* 2. To be profitable. *It pays to be honest.* 3. To suffer for something one has done. *I'll make you pay for this!* 4. *To pay attention,* to give one's attention. 5. *To pay someone back,* to take revenge on him.

pay² Wages, money which has been earned.

payment (payments) 1. Paying. 2. Money which is to be paid.

pea (peas) A plant with pods containing round seeds which are used as a vegetable.

peace 1. Freedom from war, the absence of disorder or violence. peacemaker. 2. Quiet, calm, rest. peaceful, peacefully, peacefulness.

peach (peaches) A juicy round fruit with a large stone.

peacock (peacocks) A male bird with a splendid tail which it can spread. peahen.

peak (peaks) 1. The pointed tip of something, the highest point of something. 2. The front brim of a cap.

peal¹ (peals) 1. A loud ringing of bells. 2. An outburst of sound. *A peal of laughter.*

peal² (peals, pealing, pealed) To ring out loudly.

peanut (peanuts) A kind of nut.

pear (pears) A fruit which is narrower at the stalk end.

pearl (pearls) A small round silvery-white stone sometimes found in oyster shells and valued as a gem. *A pearl necklace.*

peasant (peasants) In some countries, a person who works on the land.

peat A substance dug from the ground. It is used as a fuel or in gardening.

pebble (pebbles) A small rounded stone.

peck (pecks, pecking, pecked) To strike at something with the beak.

peckish (informal) Hungry.

peculiar 1. Odd, unusual. 2. Particular, special. peculiarly, peculiarity.

pedal¹ (pedals) A part of a machine worked by the foot.

pedal² (pedals, pedalling, pedalled) To use a pedal, to move by the use of pedals. *Robert pedalled along on his bicycle.*

pedestrian (pedestrians) A person walking along the street. *A pedestrian crossing,* a place where pedestrians can cross a street.

pedigree (pedigrees) A list of a person's or animal's parents and ancestors. *A pedigree animal,* one bred from known parents and ancestors.

pedlar (pedlars) A man who travelled about with a pack of goods for sale.

peel¹ The skin or rind of a fruit or vegetable.

peel² (peels, peeling, peeled) 1. To take the skin or covering off something. 2. To lose a skin or covering. 3. To come off in thin layers.

peep (peeps, peeping, peeped) 1. To look through a narrow opening. 2. To take a short quick look.

peer¹ (peers, peering, peered) To look at something closely.

peer² (peers) A nobleman. peeress.

peevish Irritable, cross. peevishly.

peewit (peewits) A bird of the plover family.

peg¹ (pegs) 1. A clip for fixing washed clothes to a line. 2. A wooden or metal pin for fastening things or for hanging things on.

peg² (pegs, pegging, pegged) To fasten with pegs.

Pekingese (Pekingeses) A kind of small dog.

pelican (pelicans) A bird with a huge bill.

pellet (pellets) A tiny ball of something.

pelt (pelts, pelting, pelted) 1. To attack someone by throwing many things at him. 2. *Pelting rain,* very heavy rain.

pen¹ (pens) 1. An instrument for writing with ink. 2. *A pen-friend,* a person, often in a foreign country, to whom one writes letters regularly.

pen² (pens) An enclosed space for sheep or other animals.

penalize (penalizes, penalizing, penalized) 1. To punish. 2. In games, to give a penalty against someone. 3. To take away marks or points.

penalty (penalties) 1. A punishment. 2. In games, an advantage given to the other side when a player breaks a rule. 3. A goal scored as the result of a penalty.

pence *See* **penny.**

pencil¹ (pencils) An instrument containing a thin stick of lead for drawing or writing.

pencil² (pencils, pencilling, pencilled) To to write or draw with a pencil.

pendant (pendants) A hanging ornament.

pendulum (pendulums) A rod with a weight on the end, like the one in a pendulum clock.

penetrate (penetrates, penetrating, penetrated) To make or find a way into or through something, to pierce. **penetration.**

penguin (penguins) A bird of the Antarctic.

penicillin A substance valuable for curing certain infections.

peninsula (peninsulas) An area of land almost surrounded by water.

penitent Sorry, regretful. **penitence.**

penknife (penknives) A small folding pocket-knife.

penniless Very poor, without any money.

penny (pennies *or* pence) A bronze coin. In Great Britain, 100 pence equal one pound. Before 1971, 240 pence equalled one pound.

penny-farthing (penny-farthings) An early type of bicycle with a large front wheel and a small rear one.

pension (pensions) Regular payments made to somebody who is no longer working. *Old age pension.* **pensioner.**

pensive Deep in thought. **pensively.**

pentagon (pentagons) A shape with five sides.

peony (peonies) A garden plant with large flowers.

people 1. Men, women, and children. 2. (peoples) The inhabitants of a country, the members of a nation.

pepper (peppers) 1. A hot-tasting spice used for flavouring food. **peppery.** 2. A bright green or red vegetable.

peppermint 1. A kind of mint. 2. (peppermints) A sweet which tastes of peppermint.

per For each, in each. *Per cent*, in every hundred. *Thirty per cent* (30%), thirty in every hundred. *Per gallon,* for each gallon. *Per hour*, in each hour.

perceive (perceives, perceiving, perceived) To notice something, to become aware of it, to understand it. **perception.**

perceptible Noticeable, able to be perceived. **perceptibly.**

perceptive Quick to notice things. tively.

perch¹ (perch) A freshwater fish.

perch² (perches) A bird's resting place.

perch³ (perches, perching, perched) 1. To sit or rest on something. 2. To put something on a high place. *The house was perched on the edge of a cliff.*

percolator (percolators) An apparatus for making coffee.

percussion instrument A musical instrument played by hitting or shaking, such as a drum, a cymbal, or a tambourine.

perennial Lasting for many years.

perfect 1. Complete, without faults. Exact, precise. *A perfect fit.* **perfectly, perfection.**

perforate (perforates, perforating, perforated) To make a hole or holes through something. **perforation.**

perform (performs, performing, performed) 1. To do something, to carry it out. *To perform one's duty.* 2. To do something in front of an audience, such as acting in a play, singing, or playing a musical instrument. performer, performance.

perfume (perfumes) 1. A sweet smell. 2. A liquid with a beautiful smell.

perhaps Possibly, it may be.

peril (perils) Serious danger. perilous, perilously.

perimeter (perimeters) The boundary of something.

period (periods) A length of time.

periodical (periodicals) A magazine which is published at regular intervals.

periscope (periscopes) A device with mirrors for getting a view as if from a higher position.

perish (perishes, perishing, perished) 1. To die. 2. To rot. *The tyres are perished and must be changed.* 3. (informal) *I'm perished, I'm very cold.* perishable.

perky (perkier, perkiest) Lively. perkily, perkiness.

perm (perms) (informal) A permanent wave, a long-lasting way of curling the hair.

permanent Going on for a long time, intended to last for ever. permanently, permanence.

permissible Allowable.

permission A statement that something is allowed. *We had permission to go out.*

permissive Allowing, not objecting.

permit[1] (pronounced *per*mit) (permits) Written permission to go somewhere or to do something.

permit[2] (pronounced per*mit*) (permits, permitting, permitted) To allow, to say that something may be done. *Smoking is not permitted.*

permutation (permutations) One of the possible arrangements of a set of figures in various orders.

perpendicular Exactly upright, at right angles to the base. perpendicularly.

perpetual 1. Unending, going on for ever. 2. Frequently repeated. perpetually.

perplex (perplexes, perplexing, perplexed) To bewilder, to puzzle, to confuse. perplexity.

persecute (persecutes, persecuting, persecuted) To keep on worrying someone, to treat him cruelly. persecutor, persecution.

persevere (perseveres, persevering, persevered) To continue in spite of difficulties. perseverance.

Persian Of Persia.

persist (persists, persisting, persisted) To persevere, to last. persistent, persistently, persistence.

person (persons) A human being, an individual.

personal 1. Belonging to a particular person. *Personal property.* 2. Done or made by the person himself. *I got a personal letter from the headmaster.* personally. 3. About a person's looks or qualities. *You should not make personal remarks.*

personality (personalities) 1. The qualities that make up a person's character. *He has a friendly personality.* 2. A well-known person. *A television personality.*

personnel The people employed in a business or in the armed forces.

perspective 1. The art of drawing a picture so as to give an impression of depth and distance. 2. *To get something in perspective*, to give it its proper importance.

perspire (perspires, perspiring, perspired) To give off liquid through the pores of the skin, to sweat. perspiration.

persuade (persuades, persuading, persuaded) To cause someone to do something or to believe something. persuasion.

persuasive Able to persuade, convincing. persuasively.

pert Cheeky, not showing proper respect. pertly.

perturb (perturbs, perturbing, perturbed) To worry someone, to alarm him.

perverse 1. Tiresome, unreasonable. 2. Wilfully choosing to do wrong. perversely, perversity.

pervert (perverts, perverting, perverted) 1. To turn something to a wrong use. perversion. 2. To cause somebody to do wrong.

pessimist (pessimists) A person who expects the worst to happen. pessimism.

pessimistic Gloomy, expecting the worst. pessimistically.

pest (pests) 1. A troublesome or destructive animal or insect. 2. A nuisance.

pester (pesters, pestering, pestered) To bother somebody repeatedly, to trouble him.

pet¹ (pets) 1. An animal kept as a companion. 2. A person treated as a favourite.

pet² (pets, petting, petted) To fondle.

petal (petals) One of the coloured leaf-like parts of a flower. *A rose petal.*

petition (petitions) A request, especially a written one signed by many people.

petrel (petrels) A kind of sea bird.

petrify (petrifies, petrifying, petrified) To paralyse somebody with terror.

petrol A fuel used to drive motor-car engines.

petticoat (petticoats) A woman's garment worn under a dress.

petty Small, unimportant. pettiness.

petulant Peevish. petulantly.

pew (pews) A long bench with a back, used in churches.

pewter An alloy of lead and tin.

phantom (phantoms) A ghost, an apparition.

Pharaoh (Pharaohs) A ruler of ancient Egypt.

phase (phases) A particular stage in the development or progress of something.

pheasant (pheasants) A game bird.

phenomenal Remarkable, amazing. phenomenally.

phenomenon (phenomena) A thing or a happening, especially a remarkable or unusual thing or happening.

philately Stamp-collecting. philatelist.

philosophical 1. Connected with philosophy. 2. Calm, able to accept hardship without worrying. *John was very philosophical about his accident.* philosophically.

philosophy 1. The study of the meaning of existence. 2. (philosophies) A particular way of thinking about things. *James has an unusual philosophy of life.* philosopher.

phobia (phobias) A great fear of something.

phoenix (phoenixes) A mythical bird which was said to burn itself in a fire and be born again from the ashes.

phone¹ (phones, phoning, phoned) To telephone.

phone² (phones) A telephone.

phoney (informal) Not genuine.

phosphorescent Luminous, glowing. phosphorescence.

photo (photos) (informal) A photograph. *A photo-finish*, a finish so close that a photograph is necessary to be sure who has won.

photograph¹ (photographs) A picture made on film by the use of a camera and then printed on paper. photographic.

photograph² (photographs, photographing, photographed) To take photographs. photographer, photography.

phrase (phrases) 1. A small group of words. 2. A part of a tune.

physical 1. Able to be touched and seen. 2. Of the body. *Physical education.* physically.

physician (physicians) A doctor.

physics The branch of science which includes the study of heat, light, and sound.

physiotherapy Medical treatment by massage, heat, and exercises. physiotherapist.

pianist (pianists) A person who plays the piano.

piano (pianos) A musical instrument with a keyboard.

piccolo (piccolos) A small flute.

pick¹ (picks) A pickaxe.

pick² (picks, picking, picked) 1. To choose, to take, to gather. *Pick a partner.* 2. To take something out of a hole or cavity.

To pick someone's pocket. 3. *To pick fruit, to pick flowers,* to break them off from where they are growing and collect them. 4. *To pick a bone,* to take all the meat off it. 5. *To pick holes in something,* to find faults in it. 6. *To pick a lock,* to open it without using the key.

pickaxe (pickaxes) A heavy tool for breaking up hard ground.

picket (pickets) A group of strikers who try to prevent others from working.

pickle¹ (pickles) A strong-tasting food made mainly from vegetables and vinegar.

pickle² (pickles, pickling, pickled) To preserve something in vinegar or salt water. *Pickled onions.*

pickpocket (pickpockets) Someone who steals from people's pockets.

pick-up (pick-ups) 1. The part of a record-player holding the stylus. 2. An open truck for carrying small loads.

picnic¹ (picnics) A meal eaten out of doors.

picnic² (picnics, picnicking, picnicked) To have a picnic. picnicker.

pictorial Shown in pictures, with pictures. pictorially.

picture¹ (pictures) 1. A drawing, painting, or photograph of something. 2. A description of something. 3. (informal) *The pictures,* the cinema.

picture² (pictures, picturing, pictured) To imagine.

picturesque Attractive to look at. picturesquely.

pidgin English A simple version of the English language used in the Far East.

pie (pies) Meat or fruit covered with pastry and baked in a deep dish.

piebald Having light and dark patches.

piece (pieces) 1. A part or bit of something. *A piece of cake.* 2. An instance, an example. *An interesting piece of news.* 3. A single object, especially one of a set. *A chess piece.* 4. Something which has been composed or created. *A piece of poetry.*

piecemeal Piece by piece.

pier (piers) 1. A long structure built out into the sea. 2. One of the pillars that support a bridge.

pierce (pierces, piercing, pierced) To bore a hole in something, to go through it.

piety Devotion to God.

pig (pigs) 1. An animal kept by farmers for its meat. 2. (informal) A grubby, greedy, or unpleasant person.

pigeon (pigeons) A bird of the dove family.

pigmy (pigmies) A member of an African race of very small people.

pigsty (pigsties) A building for pigs.

pigtail (pigtails) A plait of hair.

pike (pikes) 1. A very long and heavy spear. 2. A large, fierce, freshwater fish.

pilchard (pilchards) A small sea-fish.

pile¹ (piles) 1. A number of things one on top of the other, a heap. 2. A heavy beam driven straight down into the ground as a support for a building or other structure.

pile² (piles, piling, piled) 1. To make into a pile. 2. To become a pile. *To pile up.*

pilfer (pilfers, pilfering, pilfered) To steal things in small amounts. pilferer.

pilgrim (pilgrims) A person who makes a journey to a holy place.

pilgrimage (pilgrimages) A pilgrim's journey.

pill (pills) A small pellet of medicine.

pillar (pillars) A tall, upright support for part of a building, a column.

pillar-box (pillar-boxes) A box, standing in a street, in which letters are posted.

pillion (pillions) A seat for a second person behind the rider of a motor cycle or horse.

pillow (pillows) A cushion for a person's head to rest on, especially in bed. pillow-case.

pilot¹ (pilots) 1. The person who controls an aircraft while it is flying. 2. A person who guides ships in and out of harbour. 3. A guide.

pilot² (pilots, piloting, piloted) To act as a pilot.

pilot-light (pilot-lights) A small flame in a gas cooker or heater which lights the main jets.

pimple (pimples) A small inflamed spot on the skin. **pimply.**

pin¹ (pins) 1. A piece of stiff wire with a round head at one end and a point at the other. It is used for fastening papers or pieces of material together. 2. Any other object with a similar shape or used for a similar purpose.

pin² (pins, pinning, pinned) To fasten with a pin.

pinafore (pinafores) A kind of apron.

pincers A tool for gripping things.

pinch¹ (pinches, pinching, pinched) 1. To squeeze between thumb and finger. 2. To squeeze painfully. *I pinched my fingers in the door.* 3. (informal) To steal.

pinch² (pinches) 1. A painful squeeze. 2. An amount which can be picked up with the thumb and finger. *A pinch of salt.*

pincushion (pincushions) A soft pad for sticking pins in to keep them ready for use.

pine¹ (pines) A kind of evergreen tree.

pine² (pines, pining, pined) To become ill with longing or regret.

pineapple (pineapples) A tropical fruit.

ping (pings) A sharp ringing sound.

ping-pong (informal) Table tennis.

pin-hole (pin-holes) A tiny round hole.

pink¹ (pinker, pinkest) Pale red.

pink² (pinks) A garden flower.

pinnacle (pinnacles) The highest peak of something.

pint (pints) A unit of measure for liquids, one eighth of a gallon or 0·57 litre.

pioneer¹ (pioneers) 1. A person who is the first to do something, an explorer. 2. A person who is among the first to settle in a new country.

pioneer² (pioneers, pioneering, pioneered) To be a pioneer.

pious Devoted to God. **piously.**

pip (pips) 1. A seed of certain fruit such as apples and oranges. 2. *The pips,* the sound of a time-signal on a radio or telephone,

pipe¹ (pipes) 1. A tube. *A water-pipe.* 2. A small tube with a bowl at one end, used for smoking tobacco. 3. A simple flute.

pipe² (pipes, piping, piped) 1. To pass something along pipes or wires. 2. To play a pipe.

pipeline (pipelines) A line of pipes to carry oil or other substances over long distances.

piper (pipers) 1. A person who plays a pipe. 2. A person who plays the bagpipe.

piping 1. Thin, high. *A piping voice.* 2. *Piping hot,* very hot.

pirate (pirates) A sea-robber. **piratical, piracy.**

pistol (pistols) A small gun for use with one hand.

piston (pistons) The part of an engine which moves inside the cylinder.

pit (pits) 1. A deep hole. 2. A coal-mine.

pitch¹ A black, sticky substance like tar. **pitch-black, pitch-dark.**

pitch² (pitches) 1. The lowness or highness of a musical note. 2. Intensity. *Excitement was at a high pitch.* 3. An area of ground marked out for playing a game. *A football pitch.*

pitch³ (pitches, pitching, pitched) 1. To put up a tent. 2. To throw. 3. To fall. *He pitched forward.* 4. To rise and fall as a ship does in a storm. 5. *To pitch a note,* to sing on the exact note. 6. *A pitched battle,* a battle in which the two sides are arranged in battle formation.

pitcher (pitchers) A large jug.

pitchfork (pitchforks) A long fork with two prongs for haymaking.

piteous Pitiful. piteously.

pitfall (pitfalls) An unsuspected danger.

pith A white spongy substance in stems of plants or in fruit peel.

pitiful 1. Causing pity. 2. Causing contempt. pitifully.

pitiless Showing no pity. pitilessly.

pitted Marked with small holes or scars.

pity[1] 1. A feeling of sorrow for someone's troubles or sufferings. 2. Something that makes a person feel sorrow or regret. *It is a pity you can't come.* 3. *To take pity on someone*, to help him when he is in trouble.

pity[2] (pities, pitying, pitied) To feel pity for someone.

pivot (pivots) A point on which something turns.

pixy (pixies) A small fairy.

placard (placards) A poster.

place[1] (places) 1. Any particular part of space, any particular area, any particular spot or position. 2. Somewhere to sit, a seat. *Are there any spare places?* 3. *To take place*, to happen. 4. *In place of*, as a substitute for.

place[2] (places, placing, placed) To put something in a certain place.

placid Peaceful, calm. placidly.

plague[1] (plagues) 1. A deadly, infectious disease. 2. Anything which causes great trouble by coming in large quantities. *A plague of locusts.*

plague[2] (plagues, plaguing, plagued) To pester, to worry continually.

plaice (plaice) A flat sea-fish.

plain[1] (plainer, plainest) 1. Easy to see, easy to understand. 2. Simple, not decorated. 3. Straightforward, frank, honest. *Plain-spoken.* 4. Not beautiful. plainly, plainness.

plain[2] (plains) A large flat area of country.

plaintive Sad-sounding. plaintively.

plait[1] (plaits) A rope-like length of hair or other material made by twisting three or more strands together.

plait[2] (plaits, plaiting, plaited) To twist into a plait.

plan[1] (plans) 1. An arrangement made in advance. *We have already made plans for our summer holidays.* 2. A map or diagram.

plan[2] (plans, planning, planned) To make a plan. planner.

plane[1] (planes) 1. An aeroplane. 2. A tool used for smoothing wood. 3. A kind of tree.

plane[2] (planes, planing, planed) To smooth wood with a plane.

planet (planets) A heavenly body which travels in orbit round a sun. Earth and Mars are planets.

plank (planks) A long flat piece of wood.

plant[1] (plants) 1. Any living thing which is not an animal. Trees, flowers, and vegetables are all plants. 2. Industrial machinery and buildings.

plant[2] (plants, planting, planted) 1. To set plants in the ground to grow. 2. To put something firmly into place. planter.

plantation (plantations) An area of land planted with trees or with a single crop such as tea, cotton, or sugar.

plaster[1] (plasters) **1.** A dressing for a wound. *Sticking-plaster.* **2.** A mixture of lime, sand, water or other minerals used to cover walls and ceilings. **3.** *Plaster of paris,* a white mixture that dries hard.

plaster[2] (plasters, plastering, plastered) **1.** To cover a surface with plaster. **plasterer.** **2.** To cover anything thickly.

plastic (plastics) An artificial substance made from chemicals.

plasticine A soft substance made in various colours and used for modelling.

plate[1] (plates) **1.** An almost flat dish. **2.** A flat, thin sheet of metal. **3.** The thin piece of plastic to which false teeth are fixed.

plate[2] (plates, plating, plated) To cover a metal with a thin coating of a more valuable metal.

plateau (plateaux) An area of high but level land.

plateful (platefuls) The amount that goes on a plate.

plate-glass Thick glass used for shop windows.

platform (platforms) **1.** The raised surface alongside the lines at a railway station. **2.** A stage in a hall. **3.** Any flat raised surface.

platinum A very valuable silver-coloured metal.

platoon (platoons) A group of soldiers, part of a company.

platypus (platypuses) An Australian animal which lays eggs.

plausible Seeming to be right or reasonable. **plausibly, plausibility.**

play[1] (plays, playing, played) **1.** To have fun, to move about in a lively, happy way. **2.** To take part in a game, to do something in a game. **3.** To perform something. *I played the part of Joseph in the Nativity play.* **4.** To perform on something. *John can play the piano.* **5.** *To play up,* to behave badly. **6.** *To play a fish,* to allow it to exhaust itself by pulling against the line. **player.**

play[2] (plays) A story performed by actors on a stage or on television.

play-back The playing of something recorded on a tape-recorder.

playful Lively, not serious. **playfully, playfulness.**

playground (playgrounds) An area of ground where children may play.

playing-card (playing-cards) One of a set of cards used in various games.

playing-field (playing-fields) A field for playing games.

playtime (playtimes) A time when schoolchildren may go out to play.

playwright (playwrights) A person who writes plays.

plea (pleas) **1.** A request. **2.** An excuse.

plead (pleads, pleading, pleaded) **1.** To ask earnestly. **2.** To offer something as an excuse. **3.** *To plead guilty,* to admit that one is guilty.

pleasant Agreeable, friendly, enjoyable. **pleasantly.**

please[1] A polite word used when making a request. *Please come in.*

please[2] (pleases, pleasing, pleased) **1.** To satisfy someone, to be agreeable to him. **pleasingly.** **2.** To choose. *Do as you please.*

pleasure **1.** A feeling of being pleased. **2.** Something that gives happiness. **pleasurable.**

pleat (pleats) A fold made in cloth.

pleated With many pleats. *A pleated skirt.*

pledge[1] (pledges) An agreement, a promise.

pledge[2] (pledges, pledging, pledged) To make a pledge.

plenty As much or more than is necessary, a large quantity. **plentiful, plentifully.**

pliable Bent easily, flexible.

pliers A tool for gripping things. *A pair of pliers.*

plight (plights) A serious condition.

plimsolls Light, rubber-soled shoes.

plod (plods, plodding, plodded) To walk slowly and heavily. **plodder.**

plop (plops) The sound of an object dropping into water.

plot[1] (plots) **1.** A secret plan. **2.** The outline of what happens in a story. 3. A piece of ground for a house or garden.

plot² (plots, plotting, plotted) To make a secret plan. **plotter.**

plough¹ (ploughs) A farming tool for turning over the soil.

plough² (ploughs, ploughing, ploughed) To use a plough **ploughman.**

plover (plovers) A kind of wading bird.

pluck¹ (informal) Courage. **plucky, pluckily.**

pluck² (plucks, plucking, plucked) 1. To pull the feathers off a bird. 2. To pick flowers or fruit. 3. To snatch.

plug¹ (plugs) 1. Something used to stop up a hole. 2. A device which fits into an electric socket.

plug² (plugs, plugging, plugged) 1. To stop up a hole. 2. *To plug in*, to put an electric plug into a socket. 3. (informal) To keep on mentioning something.

plum (plums) A soft juicy fruit with a stone in the middle.

plumage Feathers growing on a bird.

plumber (plumbers) A person who fits and repairs water-pipes in buildings.

plumbing 1. The job of a plumber. 2. The water-pipes and water-tanks in a building.

plume (plumes) A large feather.

plump (plumper, plumpest) Rounded, slightly fat. **plumpness.**

plunder¹ (plunders, plundering, plundered) To take away someone's property violently and dishonestly, especially in wartime.

plunder² Loot.

plunge (plunges, plunging, plunged) 1. To dip or dive suddenly or violently. 2. To thrust violently.

plural (plurals) The form of a word used when referring to more than one. *Men* is the plural of *man*. *Girls* is the plural of *girl*.

plus With the addition of. In arithmetic, the sign +. *2 plus 2 equals 4* (2+2=4).

plywood A sheet of wood made of thin layers glued together.

p.m. *Post meridiem*, after midday. *4 p.m.*

pneumatic 1. Filled with air. *Pneumatic tyres.*

2. Worked by compressed air. *A pneumatic drill.*

pneumonia A serious illness of the lungs.

poach (poaches, poaching, poached) 1. To cook something in gently boiling water. 2. To hunt illegally on somebody else's land. **poacher.**

pocket¹ (pockets) A bag-shaped part of a garment, designed for carrying things.

pocket² (pockets, pocketing, pocketed) To put things into one's pocket.

pocket-knife (pocket-knives) A small folding knife.

pocket-money Money given to a child to spend as he or she pleases.

pod (pods) A long seed container which grows on various plants.

podgy (podgier, podgiest) Short and fat.

poem (poems) A piece of poetry.

poet (poets) A person who writes poetry.

poetry Writing arranged in lines, usually with a regular rhythm and often with a pattern of rhymes. **poetic.**

poignant Very sad and distressing. **poignantly.**

point¹ (points) 1. The sharp end or tip of something. *The point of a pencil.* 2. A dot. *A decimal point.* 3. A mark on a scale, a mark on a dial. *The points of the compass.* 4. A position. *At this point we must turn and go back.* 5. A unit used in scoring in a game or competition. *A penalty point.* 6. The main idea of something, the purpose of it. *What is the point of doing that?* 7. *Points*, a device for changing a train from one track to another.

point² (points, pointing, pointed) 1. To make a sign towards something, especially with one finger. 2. To aim. 3. To sharpen something. 4. *To point something out*, to show it, to explain it. **pointer.**

point-blank At very close range.

pointless Without aim or purpose. **pointlessly.**

poise[1] (poises, poising, poised) To balance.

poise[2] An appearance of quiet self-confidence.

poison[1] (poisons) A substance causing death or serious illness. **poisonous, poisonously.**

poison[2] (poisons, poisoning, poisoned) To give poison to somebody, to put poison in something. **poisoner.**

poke (pokes, poking, poked) To push at or into something with a finger, stick, or other long thin object. **poker.**

poky (pokier, pokiest) Small and inconvenient.

polar To do with the North or South Pole.

polar bear A large white bear which lives in the Arctic.

pole[1] (poles) 1. *The North Pole, the South Pole*, the two points on the earth's surface furthest away from the equator. 2. One of the two ends of a magnet.

pole[2] (poles) A long piece of wood or metal, a tall post. *A telegraph pole.*

pole-vault (pole-vaults) A jump made with the help of a long pole.

police The organization which has the job of keeping order and of catching criminals. **policeman, police station.**

policy (policies) 1. A plan of action. 2. *An insurance policy*, an insurance agreement.

polio (informal) Poliomyelitis.

poliomyelitis A disease which can cause paralysis.

Polish Of Poland.

polish[1] 1. A substance used for polishing. 2. Smoothness, a shine.

polish[2] (polishes, polishing, polished) 1. To make something smooth and shiny. 2. (informal) *To polish something off*, to finish it. **polisher.**

polite (politer, politest) Having good manners. **politely, politeness.**

political To do with the governing of a country and the organizing of its affairs. **politically.**

politician (politicians) A person interested in, or employed in, politics.

politics Political matters.

poll (polls) 1. Voting at an election. 2. *An opinion poll*, an attempt to find out what the public thinks by putting questions to a number of people.

pollen A fine yellow powder found in flowers.

polling station A place where people vote in an election.

pollute (pollutes, polluting, polluted) To make a thing dirty or impure. **pollution.**

polo A game like hockey, played on horseback.

poltergeist (poltergeists) A mischievous and destructive ghost.

polygamy Having more than one wife at a time. **polygamous.**

polythene A plastic material. *Polythene bags.*

pomp Grand and dignified display.

pompom (pompoms) A ball-shaped decoration made of wool or other material.

pompous Self-important. **pompously, pomposity.**

poncho (ponchos) A square garment with a central hole for the head.

pond (ponds) An area of water, a small lake.

ponder (ponders, pondering, pondered) To consider something, to think it over.

ponderous Heavy, bulky. **ponderously.**

pontoon[1] A card game.

pontoon[2] (pontoons) A flat-bottomed boat. *A pontoon bridge*, a temporary bridge resting on a line of pontoons.

pony (ponies) A small breed of horse.

pony-trekking Touring on a horse.

poodle (poodles) A kind of dog.

pool (pools) A pond, a puddle.

pools A kind of gambling, usually on the results of football matches.

poop (poops) The raised deck at the stern of a ship.

poor (poorer, poorest) 1. Having very little

money. 2. Small in quantity. *A poor crop.* 3. Low in quality. *Poor workmanship.*

poorly 1. In a poor way. 2. (informal) Unwell.

pop[1] (pops) 1. A sharp explosive sound 2. A bottled fizzy drink. *Ginger pop.* 3. Popular music.

pop[2] (pops, popping, popped) 1. To make a sharp explosive sound. 2. To move or do something quickly.

Pope The head of the Roman Catholic Church.

poplar (poplars) A tall, straight tree.

poppy (poppies) A flower, usually with red petals.

popular Liked by many people. popularly, popularity.

populate (populates, populating, populated) 1. To inhabit. 2. To fill with people.

population (populations) The total number of people living in a particular place.

porcelain Fine china.

porch (porches) A small roofed area outside the entrance to a building.

porcupine (porcupines) A small animal covered with long prickles.

pore (pores) A tiny opening in the skin through which sweat passes.

pork Meat from a pig.

pornography Indecent books, magazines, or pictures. pornographic.

porous Full of tiny holes, allowing liquid to pass through very slowly.

porpoise (porpoises) A sea animal like a small whale.

porridge A food made from boiled oatmeal.

port[1] (ports) 1. A harbour. 2. A town with a harbour.

port[2] The left-hand side of a ship looking forward towards the bows.

port[3] A kind of wine.

portable Easy to carry.

portcullis (portcullises) An iron grating which could be lowered in a castle gateway to keep attackers out.

porter (porters) 1. A person whose job is to carry luggage. 2. A door-keeper.

porthole (portholes) A small round window in the side of a ship.

portion (portions) 1. A part or share of something. 2. An amount of food suitable for one person.

portly Stout, fat.

portrait (portraits) A painting, drawing, or photograph of a person.

portray (portrays, portraying, portrayed) To make a picture of somebody or something.

Portuguese Of Portugal.

pose (poses, posing, posed) 1. To get into position to be photographed or painted. 2. To behave in an unnatural way, to show off. 3. To put a question for discussion.

posh (informal) Smart, elegant.

position (positions) 1. A place where something is or should be. 2. A condition, or situation, or attitude. *I am in no position to blame him, it was all my fault.* 3. A regular job.

positive 1. Definite, sure. *I'm positive he was here this morning.* 2. *A positive answer*, an answer that says 'yes'. 3. In mathematics, a figure greater than zero. 4. In electricity, one of the terminals of a battery. positively, positiveness.

posse (posses) A band of men summoned to help a sheriff.

possess (possesses, possessing, possessed) 1. To have something, to own it, to control it. possessor. 2. *To be possessed,* to be mad.

possession 1. (possessions) Something owned. 2. The possessing of something. *To have possession of something,* to possess it.

possessive Keeping things for oneself. possessively.

possible Able to exist, able to happen, able to be done. possibility.

possibly 1. In a possible manner. 2. Perhaps.

post[1] (posts) 1. An upright piece of wood, metal, or concrete. 2. A job.

post[2] The collecting, conveying, and delivering of letters and parcels. postman, post office, postal.

post[3] (posts, posting, posted) 1. To send

something through the post. 2. To put up a notice.

postage The charge made for sending something by post. *A postage stamp.*

postcard (postcards) A card for sending by post. *A picture postcard.*

poster (posters) A large sheet of paper with pictures or printing for display on a wall.

posterity Descendants, people yet to be born.

posthumous Coming after the death of the person concerned. *Posthumous fame.* posthumously.

postmark (postmarks) An official mark stamped over the postage stamp on an envelope.

post-mortem (post-mortems) An examination of a dead person to find out why he died.

postpone (postpones, postponing, postponed) To put something off until another time. postponement.

postscript (postscripts) Something added to a letter or book after the main part has been finished.

posy (posies) A small bunch of flowers.

pot¹ (pots) A round container such as a jampot, a teapot, or a flower-pot.

pot² (pots, potting, potted) To put something into a pot.

potato (potatoes) A vegetable often eaten as part of a main course.

potent Powerful. potency.

potential Possible at some time in the future. potentially.

pothole (potholes) 1. A deep natural hole in the ground. 2. A hole in a road.

potholing The sport of exploring potholes. potholer.

potion (potions) A drink of medicine, or poison, or magical liquid.

potter (potters) A maker of pots or pottery.

pottery Pots or other articles made of baked clay.

pouch (pouches) A small bag for carrying things, a pocket.

pouffe (pouffes) A large cushion for sitting on.

poultice (poultices) A hot pad put on a sore part of the body.

poultry Hens, ducks, geese, and other farmyard birds.

pounce (pounces, pouncing, pounced) To swoop and attack something.

pound¹ (pounds) 1. A unit of weight, 16 ounces or 0·45 kilogram. 2. A unit of money, 100 pence.

pound² (pounds, pounding, pounded) 1. To thump repeatedly. 2. To crush in this way.

pour (pours, pouring, poured) 1. To make something flow. 2. To flow. 3. *It was pouring*, it was raining heavily.

pout (pouts, pouting, pouted) To push out one's lips when one is annoyed.

poverty The state of being poor. *Povertystricken,* extremely poor.

powder¹ Very small particles, anything crushed or ground into dust. powdery.

powder² (powders, powdering, powdered) 1. To make into powder. 2. To cover with powder.

powder-puff (powder-puffs) A pad used to powder the face.

power 1. The ability to do something. *The magician had the power to turn the frog back into a prince.* 2. The right, the authority. *The government has the power to increase taxes.* 3. Strength, force, energy. *Electric power.* 4. *A power point,* a socket for electricity. powerless, powerlessly.

powered 1. Fitted with an engine. 2. *Powered by,* driven by. 3. Having power. *Highpowered,* very powerful.

powerful Having or producing great power. powerfully.

practicable Capable of being done or used.

practical 1. Concerned with doing or making something. *Practical difficulties.* 2. Clever at doing or making things. 3. Useful, usable. *A practical gift.* 4. *A practical joke,* a trick played on someone.

practically 1. In a practical way. 2. Almost.

practice 1. Practising. 2. The doing of something. 3. (practices) A doctor's or lawyer's business.

practise (practises, practising, practised) 1. To do something repeatedly in order to become skilful at it. 2. To do something as a habit. 3. To work as a doctor or a lawyer.

prairie (prairies) A large area of flat grass-covered land in North America.

praise¹ (praises, praising, praised) To speak approvingly of someone or something.

praise² (praises) The act of praising.

praiseworthy Deserving praise.

pram (prams) A small four-wheeled vehicle to carry a baby.

prance (prances, prancing, pranced) To leap about happily.

prank (pranks) A practical joke.

prattle (prattles, prattling, prattled) To talk about unimportant things.

prawn (prawns) A kind of shellfish like a large shrimp.

pray (prays, praying, prayed) 1. To talk to God. 2. To ask earnestly.

prayer (prayers) The act of praying, what is said when praying. **prayer-book.**

preach (preaches, preaching, preached) To give a religious or moral talk. **preacher.**

precarious Not secure, liable to fall. **precariously.**

precaution (precautions) An action taken to avoid harm in the future. *Precautions against fire.*

precede (precedes, preceding, preceded) To come or go in front of someone or something.

precinct (precincts) 1. An area round a cathedral. 2. *A pedestrian precinct,* an area for pedestrians only.

precious Very valuable, much valued.

precipice (precipices) The steep face of a cliff or rocky mountain.

precipitous Very steep. **precipitously.**

precise Correct, exact. **precisely, precision.**

predator (predators) An animal that hunts prey. **predatory.**

predecessor (predecessors) *Your predecessors,* those who were there before you.

predicament (predicaments) A difficult, unpleasant, or dangerous situation.

predict (predicts, predicting, predicted) To foretell, to forecast, to prophesy. **predictable, predictably, prediction.**

predominantly Mostly.

preen (preens, preening, preened) To make the feathers clean and tidy with the beak.

prefab (prefabs) (informal) A prefabricated house.

prefabricated Made in sections and assembled later.

preface (prefaces) A piece at the beginning of a book written to introduce it to the reader.

prefect (prefects) A school pupil who is given certain duties to perform.

prefer (prefers, preferring, preferred) To like one thing better than another. **preferable, preferably, preference.**

prefix (prefixes) A word or syllable joined to the front of another word to alter its meaning, as in *un*happy, *re*play, and *dis*order.

pregnant Having an unborn baby growing inside the body. **pregnancy.**

prehistoric Belonging to the very early times before written records were kept.

prejudice (prejudices) A fixed opinion which is not based on a fair examination of the facts. **prejudiced.**

preliminary¹ Introductory, preparing for what follows.

preliminary² (preliminaries) The first stage in a series of events.

prelude (preludes) 1. An introduction. 2. A short piece of music.

premature Too early. prematurely.

premeditate (premeditates, premeditating, premeditated) To think something out beforehand. premeditation.

premier (premiers) A Prime Minister.

première (premières) A first performance.

premium (premiums) 1. An amount of money paid regularly to an insurance company. 2. *Premium Bond,* a kind of savings certificate which has a chance of winning a money prize.

premonition (premonitions) A feeling that something is going to happen.

preoccupied Completely absorbed in something. preoccupation.

prep (informal) School work to be done in the evening.

preparatory Preparing. *A preparatory school,* a school for children who will later go to Public Schools.

prepare (prepares, preparing, prepared) 1. To get ready, to make ready. 2. *Be prepared,* be ready, able, and willing. preparation, preparatory.

preposterous Ridiculous, unthinkable, impossible. preposterously.

prep school (informal) A preparatory school.

prescribe (prescribes, prescribing, prescribed) 1. To say what is to be done. 2. To give a prescription.

prescription (prescriptions) A doctor's order to a chemist to prepare a certain medicine.

presence Being present. *In the presence of someone,* in the place where he is.

present¹ 1. In a particular place, here, there. *Were you present at the scene of the crime?* 2. Existing at this moment. *This present government.*

present² The time now passing, the present time.

present³ (presents) A gift. *A birthday present.*

present⁴ (pronounced pre*sent*) (presents, presenting, presented) 1. To give, to offer. 2. To show, to reveal. 3. To put on a play or other entertainment. presentation.

presentable Fit to be seen. presentably.

presently Soon.

preservative (preservatives) A substance used for preserving things.

preserve (preserves, preserving, preserved) 1. To keep something safe. 2. To keep something in good condition. preservation, preserver.

president (presidents) 1. The head of a republic. *The President of the United States.* 2. The person in charge of a club, business, or other organization. presidential.

press¹ (presses, pressing, pressed) 1. To push, to squeeze, to squash. 2. To make something flat or smooth. 3. To urge, to persuade, to compel.

press² (presses) 1. The act of pressing. 2. A device for pressing things. 3. A printing machine, a printing business. *Oxford University Press.* 4. *The press,* the newspapers. *A press conference,* an interview with a group of reporters.

press gang A band of men who went about forcing others to join the navy or army.

pressing Urgent, needing attention.

pressure (pressures) 1. A force which presses or pushes. 2. Strong persuasion. *To put pressure on someone.* 3. Speed, urgency. *To work at high pressure.*

pressurized aircraft An aircraft which maintains a comfortable air pressure for the passengers however high it flies.

prestige Good reputation.

presume (presumes, presuming, presumed) 1. To suppose something to be true. *I presume you would like some cake?* presumably. 2. To dare. *I would not presume to contradict a professor!* presumption.

presumptuous Too confident, too bold.

pretend (pretends, pretending, pretended) 1. To behave as if things are not as they really are. *Let's pretend that you are a princess.* 2. To claim. *I don't pretend to be a good foot-baller.* **pretender, pretence.**

pretty[1] (prettier, prettiest) 1. Pleasant to see. 2. Pleasant to hear. **prettily, prettiness.**

pretty[2] (informal) Fairly, moderately. *We won pretty easily.*

prevailing Usual, normal.

prevalent Common, widespread.

prevent (prevents, preventing, prevented) To stop or hinder something. **prevention, preventive.**

preview (previews) A showing of something before it is generally available.

previous Earlier in time.

prey[1] 1. An animal hunted, killed, and eaten by another. 2. *A bird of prey*, a bird that lives by hunting.

prey[2] (preys, preying, preyed) *To prey on*, to hunt.

price[1] (prices) The sum of money for which something is to be bought.

price[2] (prices, pricing, priced) To fix a price on something.

priceless 1. Very valuable. 2. (informal) Very amusing.

prick (pricks, pricking, pricked) 1. To make a hole in something with a pointed instrument. 2. To cause sharp pain. 3. *To prick up one's ears*, to pay special attention.

prickle (prickles) A thorn, a spike. **prickly.**

pride[1] 1. A satisfied or conceited feeling because of what one is or what one has done. 2. Somebody or something which makes one feel pride. *Her baby was her pride and joy.* 3. *A pride of lions*, a group of lions.

pride[2] (prides, priding, prided) *To pride one-oneself on something*, to be pleased and satisfied about it.

priest (priests) 1. A clergyman. 2. A man who leads people in their religion. **priestess.**

prig (prigs) A person pleased with his own righteousness. **priggish, priggishly.**

prim (primmer, primmest) Disliking anything rough and rude. *Prim and proper.* **primly.**

primarily Chiefly, in the first place.

primary 1. First. 2. *A primary school,* a school for young children. 3. *Primary colours,* red, blue, and yellow.

prime[1] 1. Chief, most important. *The Prime Minister.* 2. The best stage of growth and development. *A man in the prime of life.*

prime[2] (primes, priming, primed) 1. To get something ready for use by filling it. *To prime a pump.* 2. To put on a first coat of paint. **primer.**

primitive 1. At an early stage of development. 2. Simple, not complicated.

primrose (primroses) A pale yellow spring flower.

prince (princes) 1. The son of a king or queen. 2. A male member of a royal family. **princess.**

principal[1] Chief, most important. **principally.**

principal[2] (principals) The head of a school or college.

principle (principles) A general rule about something.

print[1] (prints, printing, printed) 1. To put words or pictures on paper by means of a machine called a printing press or some other device which leaves a print. 2. To write in letters rather like those in a printed book. 3. To make a photograph on special paper from a negative. **printer.**

print[2] (prints) 1. A mark made by pressing or stamping. 2. A printed picture or photograph.

prior 1. Earlier. 2. *Prior to*, before.

priority The right to be first, the right to have or do something before others.

priory (priories) A building where monks or nuns live or lived.

prism (prisms) A block of glass that breaks up white light into the colours of the rainbow.

prison (prisons) A place where criminals are kept locked up. prisoner.

private¹ (privates) An ordinary soldier.

private² 1. Belonging to one person or one group of people. *A private road.* 2. Not to be known or talked about by everyone. *A private letter.* 3. Quiet, secluded. *We found a private place for a picnic.* privately, privacy.

privet An evergreen shrub used for garden hedges.

privilege (privileges) An advantage, or a right to do something, which only certain people have. privileged.

prize¹ (prizes) 1. Something given to the winner of a game or competition, something given as a reward. 2. Something captured from the enemy in war.

prize² (prizes, prizing, prized) 1. To value something very highly. 2. To lever something open.

probable Likely to be so, likely to happen. probably, probability.

probation 1. Testing a person's character or abilities. 2. *A probation officer,* a person appointed to supervise the behaviour of someone who has been found guilty of a crime. 3. *On probation,* being supervised by a probation officer.

probe¹ (probes, probing, probed) To penetrate into something, to examine it.

probe² (probes) A piece of equipment used for probing.

problem (problems) A question to be solved, a difficulty to be overcome.

procedure (procedures) The regular way of doing something.

proceed (pronounced pro*ceed*) (proceeds, proceeding, proceeded) To go on to something, to continue forwards.

proceedings Actions, happenings.

proceeds (pronounced *pro*ceeds) The profits from something.

process¹ (processes) A series of actions for a particular purpose, a method of manufacture.

process² (processes, processing, processed) To treat or change something by a series of actions. *Processed cheese.*

procession (processions) A line of people or vehicles moving steadily forwards.

proclaim (proclaims, proclaiming, proclaimed) To announce something publicly. proclamation.

procure (procures, procuring, procured) To obtain something. procurable.

prod (prods, prodding, prodded) To poke.

prodigal Wasteful, foolishly extravagant.

produce¹ (pronounced *pro*duce) Things produced. *Garden produce.*

produce² (pronounced pro*duce*) (produces, producing, produced) 1. To make something or bring it into existence. 2. To bring something into view. *He produced a handkerchief.* 3. To get a play ready for performance. producer, production.

product (products) Something produced.

productive Producing, able to produce.

profession (professions) An occupation for which a person must study for a long time, such as being a lawyer or a doctor.

professional¹ 1. Connected with a profession. 2. Doing something as a regular job, or for money. *A professional footballer.* sionally.

professional² (professionals) A professional sportsman.

professor (professors) One of the senior teachers in a university.

proficient Skilled. proficiently, proficiency.

profile (profiles) A side view of a face.

profit[1] (profits) 1. Money gained in doing business. 2. An advantage, a benefit, a gain.

profit[2] (profits, profiting, profited) To gain profit from something. profitable, profitably.

profound (profounder, profoundest) Very deep. profoundly.

profuse Plentiful. profusely, profusion.

programme (programmes) 1. A play, entertainment, or other item on radio or television. 2. A list of events which are to take place. 3. A printed leaflet giving details of a play, football match, or some other event.

progress[1] (pronounced *progress*) 1. A forward movement, an advance. 2. Development, improvement.

progress[2] (pronounced pro*gress*) (progresses, progressing, progressed) To make progress. progressive, progressively, progression.

prohibit (prohibits, prohibiting, prohibited) To forbid. prohibition.

project[1] (pronounced pro*ject*) (projects, projecting, projected) 1. To stick out, to jut out. 2. *To project a film or slide*, to make the picture shine on a screen. projector, projection.

project[2] (pronounced *pro*ject) (projects) 1. The task of studying a topic and discovering what one can about it. 2. A plan, a scheme, an undertaking.

projectile (projectiles) Something thrown or shot through the air.

prolific Producing a great quantity.

prologue (prologues) An introduction to something.

prolong (prolongs, prolonging, prolonged) To make something longer.

prom (proms) (informal) A promenade concert.

promenade (promenades) 1. An area set aside for walking or riding, especially by the seaside. 2. *A promenade concert*, a concert at which some of the audience stand.

prominent 1. Easily seen, jutting out. 2. Important. prominently, prominence.

promise[1] (promises) 1. A statement that one will undertake to do something, or not to do something. *In marriage, people make a promise not to leave each other.* 2. *To show promise*, to give evidence of being likely to succeed in the future.

promise[2] (promises, promising, promised) 1. To make a promise. 2. To show promise. promisingly.

promontory (promontories) A cliff jutting out into the sea.

promote (promotes, promoting, promoted) 1. To move somebody to a higher rank. 2. To encourage the growth of something. 3. To organize the selling of a new product. 4. To organize a public entertainment. promoter, promotion.

prompt[1] Without delay. promptly, promptness.

prompt[2] (prompts, prompting, prompted) 1. To urge or cause somebody to do something. *Greed prompted the knave to steal the tarts.* 2. To help an actor if he forgets his words. prompter.

prone 1. Lying stretched out with face downwards. 2. Liable to. *Accident-prone.*

prong (prongs) One of the spikes of a fork.

pronounce (pronounces, pronouncing, pronounced) 1. To speak a word in a particular way, to speak the sounds of a language. *Right* and *write* are pronounced the same. *Foreign people have difficulty in pronouncing English words correctly.* pronunciation. 2. To make a serious announcement, to declare something officially. pronouncement.

pronounced Obvious.

proof[1] (proofs) Evidence, especially evidence strong enough to be convincing.

proof[2] Safe against something. *Bullet-proof glass.*

prop[1] (props) A support.

prop[2] (props, propping, propped) To support something or somebody.

propaganda Spreading ideas and information in order to make people believe something.

propel (propels, propelling, propelled) To drive something forward. **propulsion.**

propeller (propellers) A device which turns rapidly to propel a ship or aircraft.

proper 1. Right, correct, suitable. 2. Respectable. *Prim and proper.* 3. (informal) Great, complete. *We got into a proper muddle!* **properly.**

property (properties) 1. A person's possessions. 2. Land or buildings belonging to someone. 3. A special quality belonging to something.

prophecy (prophecies) A prediction, a statement about what will happen in the future.

prophesy (prophesies, prophesying, prophesied) To make a prophecy.

prophet (prophets) 1. A great religious teacher. 2. A person who prophesies. **prophetic, prophetically.**

proportion (proportions) 1. The relationship of one thing to another in quantity or size or importance. 2. A part, a share. *If you work for us, we'll give you a proportion of our profits.* 3. *Proportions,* size, measurements.

propose (proposes, proposing, proposed) 1. To suggest a plan. *I propose we go fishing.* **proposition.** 2. *To propose to someone,* to ask her or him to become one's wife or husband. **proposal.**

proprietor (proprietors) An owner. **proprietress.**

propulsion *See* **propel.**

prose Any piece of writing which is not in the form of verse.

prosecute (prosecutes, prosecuting, prosecuted) To take legal action against somebody. **prosecutor, prosecution.**

prospect[1] (pronounced *pro*spect) (prospects) 1. A wide view. 2. Something looked forward to, a hope.

prospect[2] (pronounced pro*spect*) (prospects, prospecting, prospected) To search for gold or some other mineral. **prospector.**

prospectus (prospectuses) A brochure describing and advertising a school or a business company.

prosper (prospers, prospering, prospered) To do well, to succeed. **prosperous, prosperously, prosperity.**

prostrate Lying flat, overcome. **prostration.**

protect (protects, protecting, protected) To keep safe, to guard. **protective, protectively, protector, protection.**

protein (proteins) A substance in food which is necessary to build up the body.

protest[1] (pronounced *pro*test) (protests) An objection.

protest[2] (pronounced pro*test*) (protests, protesting, protested) To make a protest.

Protestant (Protestants) A Christian not of the Roman Catholic or Orthodox Churches.

prototype (prototypes) The first example made to test the design of a new thing.

protractor (protractors) An instrument for measuring angles.

protrude (protrudes, protruding, protruded) To stick out.

proud (prouder, proudest) 1. Having a proper pride or dignity. 2. Arrogant, conceited. **proudly.**

prove (proves, proving, proved) 1. To show that something is really true, to establish it beyond doubt. 2. To turn out to be, to be found to be. *My pen proved to be useless.*

proverb (proverbs) A short, well-known saying which gives general advice, such as '*Look before you leap*'. **proverbial.**

provide (provides, providing, provided) 1. To supply, to give. **provider.** 2. *To provide for* *something*, to make ready for it. 3. *Providing that* or *provided that*, on condition that.

Providence God's loving care. providential, providentially.

provident Providing for future needs.

province (provinces) 1. A part of a country. 2. *The provinces*, all the parts of a country away from the capital. provincial.

provisional Temporary. provisionally.

provisions Supplies of food and drink.

provoke (provokes, provoking, provoked) 1. To make someone angry. 2. To arouse someone or something. provocative, provocatively, provocation.

prow (prows) The front end of a boat or ship, the bows.

prowess Bravery, skill.

prowl (prowls, prowling, prowled) To go about stealthily. prowler.

proximity Nearness.

prudent Careful, wise. prudently, prudence.

prudish Too easily shocked by anything that is rude or improper. prudishly.

prune1 (prunes) A dried plum.

prune2 (prunes, pruning, pruned) To cut unwanted twigs or branches off a tree or shrub.

pry (pries, prying, pried) To look inquisitively into something.

psalm (psalms) One of the Hebrew hymns or songs collected in the Bible. psalmist.

psychiatry The treatment of mental illness. psychiatric, psychiatrist.

psychic Having the power to be aware of supernatural things.

psychology The study of the mind and how it works. psychologist, psychological.

pub (pubs) (informal) A public house.

puberty The stage at which a young person begins to become an adult.

public1 1. Belonging to people in general, for general use. 2. Generally known. publicly.

public2 1. *The public*, people in general. 2. *In public*, not in secret or in private.

publication 1. Publishing. 2. (publications) Something published.

public house A house with public rooms where alcoholic drinks are served.

publicity 1. Making a thing public, advertising. 2. Being made public.

Public School A kind of secondary school where fees are charged.

public-spirited Ready to do things for the general good of other people.

publish (publishes, publishing, published) 1. To have something printed and put it on sale. 2. To announce something publicly. publisher.

pucker (puckers, puckering, puckered) To wrinkle or crease.

pudding (puddings) 1. A food made in a soft mass. *Christmas pudding. Yorkshire pudding.* 2. The sweet course of a meal.

puddle (puddles) A small pool, usually of rain-water.

puff1 (puffs) 1. A short spurt of air, smoke, or steam. 2. A small cloud of something. 3. *Puff pastry*, a light flaky pastry. 4. Something made of puff pastry. *Cream puffs.*

puff2 (puffs, puffing, puffed) 1. To make puffs, to come out in puffs, to gasp. 2. To make something swell. *He puffed out his chest.*

puffin (puffins) A sea bird with a large bill.

pug (pugs) A small dog with a flat face.

pugnacious Fond of fighting. pugnaciously.

pull (pulls, pulling, pulled) 1. To take hold of something and try to move it towards oneself. 2. To make something move along behind one. *To pull a sledge.* 3. To move. *The train pulled out of the station.* 4. *To pull a face*, to make a funny face. 5. *To pull through*, to recover from an illness. 6. *To pull oneself together*, to get control of oneself. 7. *To pull up*, to stop. 8. *To pull someone's leg*, to play a joke on him.

pullet (pullets) A young hen.

pulley (pulleys) A wheel with a groove in the rim for a rope to run over, used for lifting things.

pullover (pullovers) A knitted garment which covers the top part of the body.

pulp1 A soft, wet mass of something.

pulp[2] (pulps, pulping, pulped) To make into pulp.

pulpit (pulpits) A small enclosed platform used by the preacher in church.

pulse (pulses) 1. The regular beat of a person's arteries as the blood is pumped through them. 2. A steady throbbing.

pumice-stone (pumice-stones) A piece of light stone, or lava, used for cleaning.

pump[1] (pumps) 1. A machine for forcing air or liquid into or out of something, or along pipes. 2. A soft, light shoe.

pump[2] (pumps, pumping, pumped) To use a pump.

pumpkin (pumpkins) A large, round, yellow fruit.

pun (puns) A witty use of words which sound alike but which have different meanings.

punch[1] A hot drink made from wine.

punch[2] (punches) 1. A blow with the fist. 2. An instrument for making holes in paper, leather, metal, or other substances.

punch[3] (punches, punching, punched) 1. To hit with the fist. 2. To make a hole with a punch.

punctual Exactly on time. punctually, punctuality.

punctuate (punctuates, punctuating, punctuated) To put full stops, commas, and other marks into a piece of writing.

punctuation mark A mark used in punctuating.

puncture[1] (punctures, puncturing, punctured) To make a hole in something with a sharp object.

puncture[2] (punctures) A hole in a pneumatic tyre.

punish (punishes, punishing, punished) To make somebody suffer because he has done something wrong. punishment.

punt[1] (punts) A small flat-bottomed boat moved along by a long pole.

punt[2] (punts, punting, punted) 1. To move a punt along with a pole, to go in a punt. 2. To drop a ball and kick it before it touches the ground.

puny (punier, puniest) Small and feeble.

pup (pups) A puppy.

pupil (pupils) 1. A person learning from a teacher. 2. The circular opening in the middle of the eye.

puppet (puppets) A kind of doll that can be made to move by wires or strings. *A glove-puppet*, a doll which fits over a person's hand so that his fingers can move it.

puppy (puppies) A young dog.

purchase[1] (purchases) 1. The buying of something. 2. Something bought.

purchase[2] (purchases, purchasing, purchased) To buy.

pure (purer, purest) Clean, clear, not mixed with anything else. purely, purity.

purge (purges, purging, purged) To get rid of an unwanted part or thing.

purify (purifies, purifying, purified) To make a thing pure. purification.

purple Deep reddish-blue.

purpose (purposes) Something that a person means to do, a plan, an intention. *On purpose*, deliberately, not accidentally. purposeful, purposeless.

purposely On purpose.

purr (purrs, purring, purred) To make a gentle murmuring sound as a contented cat does.

purse (purses) A small bag to keep money in.

pursue (pursues, pursuing, pursued) 1. To chase, to try to catch up with someone or something. 2. To work hard at something for a considerable time. *To pursue one's studies.* pursuer, pursuit.

pus A whitish liquid which forms in boils and septic wounds.

push (pushes, pushing, pushed) 1. To use force to try to move something away from oneself. 2. To make one's way by pushing. 3. To press something.

push-chair (push-chairs) A chair on wheels to carry a young child.

pussy (pussies) (informal) A cat or kitten.

put (puts, putting, put) 1. To place something in a certain position, to move something to a certain position. 2. To express something in words. *He put it very tactfully.* 3. *To put off a visit,* to postpone it. 4. *To put someone off his food,* to make him not want it. 5. *To put a fire out,* to make it stop burning. 6. *To put someone up,* to give him a place to sleep. 7. *To put up with something,* to suffer it patiently. 8. *To put an end to something,* to finish it. 9. *To put someone to death,* to execute him. 10. *To put up prices,* to make prices higher.

putrefy (putrefies, putrefying, putrefied) To become putrid.

putrid Rotten and smelly.

putt (putts, putting, putted) In golf, to strike a ball gently towards a hole. **putter.**

putty A substance used to set glass in window frames.

puzzle1 (puzzles) 1. A problem or question that is difficult to solve. 2. A kind of pastime or game which requires skill. *A jigsaw puzzle.*

puzzle2 (puzzles, puzzling, puzzled) 1. To make someone think deeply. 2. To think deeply.

pyjamas A thin coat and trousers for sleeping in.

pylon (pylons) A steel tower used to carry electric cables.

pyramid (pyramids) 1. A structure with a square base and four sloping sides which come to a point. 2. An ancient Egyptian monument shaped like this.

pyre (pyres) A large pile of wood for burning a corpse.

python (pythons) A large snake that crushes its prey.

Qq

quack1 (quacks, quacking, quacked) To make a noise like a duck.

quack2 (quacks) 1. The noise made by a duck. 2. (informal) A man pretending to be a doctor.

quad (quads) (informal) 1. A quadrangle. 2. A quadruplet.

quadrangle (quadrangles) A courtyard or lawn with buildings all round it.

quadruped (quadrupeds) A four-footed animal.

quadruple 1. Made up of four parts. 2. Multiplied by four.

quadruplet (quadruplets) One of four babies born to the same mother at one time.

quagmire (quagmires) A bog, a marsh.

quail1 (quails) A small bird of the partridge family.

quail2 (quails, quailing, quailed) To flinch, to show fear.

quaint (quainter, quaintest) Attractive in an old-fashioned or unusual way. **quaintly, quaintness.**

quake (quakes, quaking, quaked) To shake, to tremble.

qualify (qualifies, qualifying, qualified) 1. To reach an acceptable standard, usually by an examination or test. 2. *To be qualified to do something,* to be properly trained for it. **qualification.**

quality 1. The goodness or lack of goodness in something. *These shoes are of poor quality, they are letting water in already.* 2.

(qualities) A characteristic of someone or something, a feature of a person's character.

qualm (qualms) A feeling of doubt or uneasiness.

quandary (quandaries) A state of uncertainty.

quantity (quantities) An amount, a certain number of things, a certain measure of something.

quarantine A period when a person or animal is separated from others to prevent the spread of a disease.

quarrel[1] (quarrels) An angry argument, a violent disagreement. **quarrelsome.**

quarrel[2] (quarrels, quarrelling, quarrelled) To have a quarrel.

quarry (quarries) **1.** A place where stone or slate is dug out of the ground. **2.** A hunted animal or bird.

quart (quarts) A unit of measure for liquids, 2 pints or 1·14 litre.

quarter[1] (quarters) **1.** One of the four equal parts into which something is, or can be, divided. A quarter of 4 is 1. A quarter of 1 is ¼. **2.** A period of three months. **3.** *A quarter past four*, 15 minutes past four o'clock. **4.** A district in a town. **5.** *Quarters*, lodgings. **6.** *At close quarters*, close together.

quarter[2] (quarters, quartering, quartered) **1.** To divide into quarters. **2.** To place troops in lodgings.

quarter[3] Mercy. *The enemy gave no quarter.*

quarterly Once every three months.

quartet (quartets) A group of four musicians.

quaver[1] (quavers) A note in music. It is written ♪ .

quaver[2] (quavers, quavering, quavered) To shake, to tremble.

quay (quays) A harbour wall or pier against which ships tie up to unload.

queasy (queasier, queasiest) Feeling sick.

queen (queens) **1.** A woman who is the crowned ruler of a country. **2.** The wife of a king. **3.** A piece in chess.

queer (queerer, queerest) **1.** Strange, unusual. **2.** Unwell. *To feel queer.* **queerly, queerness.**

quell (quells, quelling, quelled) To suppress.

quench (quenches, quenching, quenched) **1.** To satisfy a thirst. **2.** To put out a fire.

querulous Cross and complaining. **querulously.**

query[1] (queries) **1.** A question. **2.** A question mark.

query[2] (queries, querying, queried) To question.

quest (quests) A long search for something.

question[1] (questions) **1.** Something which is asked, something which has to be decided. **2.** *In question*, being discussed. **3.** *Out of the question*, impossible. **4.** *Called in question*, doubted.

question[2] (questions, questioning, questioned) **1.** To ask a question of somebody, to examine him. *The suspect was questioned by the police.* **2.** To have doubts. *We questioned the skill of the guide when we knew we were lost.*

question mark The punctuation mark ? .

questionnaire (questionnaires) A list of questions to be answered.

queue[1] (queues) A line of people or vehicles waiting for something.

queue[2] (queues, queuing, queued) To stand in a queue.

quibble (quibbles, quibbling, quibbled) To avoid giving a straight answer to a question.

quick (quicker, quickest) **1.** Moving at speed. **2.** Soon done. **3.** Lively, bright, clever. *Quick-witted.* **4.** (old-fashioned) Alive. **quickly, quickness.**

quicken (quickens, quickening, quickened) To become quicker.

quicksand (quicksands) An area of sand which would swallow up anyone who walked on it.

quicksilver Mercury.

quid (quid) (informal) A pound (£1).

quiet (quieter, quietest) **1.** Without sound, silent. **2.** Without movement, peaceful. **3.** *To keep something quiet*, to keep it secret. **quietly, quietness.**

quieten (quietens, quietening, quietened) **1.** To make quiet. **2.** To become quiet.

quill (quills) A large feather, especially one used as a pen.

quilt (quilts) A bed-cover filled with feathers or other soft material.

quin (quins) (informal) A quintuplet.

quintet (quintets) A group of five musicians.

quintuplet (quintuplets) One of five babies born to the same mother at one time.

quit (quits, quitting, quitted or quit) To go away, to leave.

quite 1. Completely. **2.** Rather.

quits *To be quits with someone*, to be even with him.

quiver[1] (quivers) A case for holding arrows.

quiver[2] (quivers, quivering, quivered) To tremble, to shake.

quiz (quizzes) A set of questions which test people's knowledge.

quotation marks The punctuation marks " " or ' '.

quote (quotes, quoting, quoted) To repeat words which were first spoken or written by someone else. **quotation.**

Rr

rabbi (rabbis) A Jewish religious leader.

rabbit (rabbits) An animal which lives in a burrow. **rabbit-hole, rabbit-hutch.**

rabble (rabbles) A disorderly crowd.

rabies A disease which causes madness in dogs.

race[1] (races) **1.** A group of people with the same origin, the same characteristics, and the same colour of skin. **racial. 2.** *The human race*, human beings, people.

race[2] (races) A competition in which competitors try to be the first to reach a certain point. **race-track.**

race[3] (races, racing, raced) **1.** To have a race. **2.** To move very fast. **racer.**

race-course (race-courses) A ground set out for horse-racing.

race-horse (race-horses) A horse bred for racing.

rack (racks) **1.** A framework for supporting things. *A plate-rack.* **2.** An instrument of torture.

racket (rackets) **1.** An uproar, a wild noise. **2.** A light bat such as is used in playing tennis. **3.** (informal) A dishonest way of making money.

radar A radio system or apparatus that detects solid objects which come within its range, used in navigation.

radiant 1. Bright, shining. **2.** Joyful, happy. **radiantly, radiance.**

radiate (radiates, radiating, radiated) **1.** To send out rays of light or heat or other energy. **radiation. 2.** To be arranged like the spokes of a wheel.

radiator (radiators) **1.** An apparatus that radiates heat. **2.** An apparatus that keeps a car engine cool.

radio 1. Broadcasting, sending and receiving sound through the air by means of electrical waves. **2.** (radios) An apparatus for receiving radio transmissions or programmes.

radioactive Giving out atomic rays. **radio-activity.**

radiogram (radiograms) An apparatus consisting of a radio and a record player.

radiography X-ray photography. **radiographer.**

radish (radishes) A small vegetable eaten in salads.

radius (radii) A straight line from the centre of a circle to the circumference.

raffia Long fibres used to make baskets, mats, and other things.

raffle (raffles) A way of raising money by selling numbered tickets which may win prizes.

raft (rafts) A flat floating platform of logs or other materials.

rafter (rafters) One of the sloping beams of wood supporting a roof.

rag (rags) A torn piece of cloth.

ragamuffin (ragamuffins) A dirty, ragged person.

rag doll A cloth doll stuffed with rags or soft material.

rage[1] (rages) Violent anger.

rage[2] (rages, raging, raged) To be full of rage.

ragged 1. Badly torn. *Ragged clothes.* 2. Dressed in rags. *A ragged beggar.* 3. Rough, jagged. *Ragged rocks.*

raid[1] (raids) A sudden attack.

raid[2] (raids, raiding, raided) To make a raid. **raider.**

rail (rails) 1. A long bar or rod. *A towel rail.* 2. A steel bar forming part of a railway track. 3. *By rail*, by railway.

railings A fence made with rails.

railway (railways) A system of transport using tracks made of steel rails on which trains run.

rain[1] Water falling in drops from the sky. **rain-drop, rain-water, rainy.**

rain[2] (rains, raining, rained) 1. *It is raining*, rain is falling. 2. To come down or send down like rain.

rainbow (rainbows) The curve of many colours seen in the sky when the sun shines through rain.

raincoat (raincoats) A waterproof coat.

rainfall The amount of rain which falls at a certain place in a certain time.

raise (raises, raising, raised) 1. To lift something, to make it rise. 2. To bring up young children or animals. 3. To manage to get something. *To raise a loan.* 4. *To raise a siege*, to end it.

raisin (raisins) A dried grape.

raja (rajas) An Indian prince.

rake[1] (rakes) A tool with many teeth used in gardening.

rake[2] (rakes, raking, raked) 1. To use a rake. 2. To search through something.

rally[1] (rallies, rallying, rallied) To recover, to revive.

rally[2] (rallies) 1. A recovery. 2. In tennis, an exchange of several hits before a point is scored. 3. A large gathering of people for a particular purpose. 4. A competition to test skill in driving. *The Monte Carlo Rally.*

ram[1] (rams) **1.** A male sheep. **2.** A heavy beam for hammering with great force.

ram[2] (rams, ramming, rammed) To push forcefully, to strike heavily.

ramble (rambles, rambling, rambled) To walk for pleasure, to wander. **rambler.**

ramp (ramps) A slope joining two levels.

rampage (rampages, rampaging, rampaged) To rush wildly and violently about.

rampart (ramparts) A broad wall built as a defence.

ramshackle In a bad state of repair.

ran *See* **run**[1].

ranch (ranches) A large cattle farm in America. **rancher.**

rancid Stale, unpleasant-tasting.

random *At random*, without any particular aim or plan.

rang *See* **ring**[3].

range[1] (ranges) **1.** A line or series of things. *A range of mountains.* **2.** A varied collection of things. *This shop sells a wide range of goods.* **3.** The distance over which something can operate. *The range of a gun.* **4.** An area of ground with targets for shooting. *A rifle range.* **5.** A kitchen fire-place with ovens for cooking in.

range[2] (ranges, ranging, ranged) **1.** To vary between two limits. *Prices ranged from £2 to £5.* **2.** To wander. *Tigers ranged about the jungle.* **3.** To set in a line, to arrange.

Ranger Guide A senior Guide.

rank (ranks) **1.** A line of people or things. *A taxi-rank.* **2.** A person's position in the forces or in society. *To hold a high rank in the army*, to be a senior officer in the army.

ransack (ransacks, ransacking, ransacked) **1.** To search thoroughly. **2.** To rob, to plunder.

ransom[1] (ransoms) **1.** A sum of money demanded so that a captive may be set free. **2.** *To hold someone to ransom*, to keep him captive and demand a ransom.

ransom[2] (ransoms, ransoming, ransomed) **1.** To pay a ransom. **2.** To allow someone to go free in exchange for a ransom.

rap (raps, rapping, rapped) To knock sharply but lightly.

rapid Quick, speedy. **rapidly, rapidity.**

rapids A part of a river where the water flows rapidly over rocks.

rapier (rapiers) A long narrow sword.

rapture (raptures) Great delight. **rapturous, rapturously.**

rare (rarer, rarest) Unusual, uncommon. **rarely, rareness, rarity.**

rascal (rascals) A dishonest, naughty, or mischievous person.

rash[1] (rasher, rashest) Too hasty, reckless.

rash[2] (rashes) A number of tiny red spots on the skin.

rasher (rashers) A slice of bacon.

raspberry (raspberries) A small soft red fruit.

rasping Harsh.

rat (rats) An animal like a large mouse.

rate (rates) **1.** Speed. *He drove off at a great rate.* **2.** An amount of money charged for something. **3.** *At any rate*, whatever happens. **4.** Quality or standard. *First-rate. Second-rate.*

rates Charges paid by householders to a local authority to help to pay for public services such as education, water-supplies, and so on. **rate-payer.**

rather 1. Fairly, somewhat. **2.** (informal) *Yes rather*, yes indeed. **3.** More truly. *He ran, or rather staggered, to the finishing line.* **4.** Preferably. *I would rather not come.*

ratio (ratios) A relationship between two numbers or quantities.

ration[1] (rations) An amount of something allowed to a person in a time of shortage.

ration[2] (rations, rationing, rationed) To share something out in fixed quantities.

rational Reasonable, sensible, sane. **rationally.**

rattle[1] (rattles, rattling, rattled) To make a rapid series of short sharp sounds.

rattle[2] (rattles) 1. A rattling noise. 2. A baby's toy which rattles.

rattlesnake (rattlesnakes) A poisonous American snake which makes a rattling noise with its tail.

raucous Hoarse, harsh-sounding. **raucously.**

ravage (ravages, ravaging, ravaged) 1. To plunder. 2. To do widespread damage.

rave (raves, raving, raved) 1. To talk wildly. 2. To talk very enthusiastically.

raven (ravens) A large black bird like a crow.

ravenous Very hungry. **ravenously.**

ravine (ravines) A deep narrow valley.

raw (rawer, rawest) 1. Not cooked. *Raw food.* 2. In the natural state, not yet prepared for use. *Raw materials.* 3. Not experienced. *A raw recruit.* 4. Damp and cold. *A raw wind.* 5. Sore, with the skin rubbed off. *My new shoe has made a raw place on my heel.* **rawness.**

ray (rays) A narrow line of light, heat, or other form of energy.

rayon An artificial silky material.

raze (razes, razing, razed) To destroy something completely, to knock it to the ground.

razor (razors) A sharp instrument used for shaving.

reach[1] (reaches, reaching, reached) 1. To stretch out the hand. *He reached for another chocolate.* 2. To get to somewhere or something. *They reached home. We reached a decision.*

reach[2] (reaches) 1. The distance a person can reach with his arm. 2. A convenient distance for travelling. *My uncle lives within reach of the sea.* 3. A straight stretch of a river.

react (reacts, reacting, reacted) To have a reaction.

reaction (reactions) A feeling or action caused by some thing, person, or event.

reactor (reactors) An apparatus for producing atomic power.

read (reads, reading, read) To look at something which is written or printed and understand it. **readable.**

reader (readers) 1. A person who reads. 2. A school book used when learning to read.

ready (readier, readiest) 1. Prepared. *Ready for bed.* 2. Quick, prompt. *Ready answers.* 3. Handy, within easy reach. *Keep your weapons ready.* **readily, readiness.**

real 1. Actually existing, not imaginary. **reality.** 2. Genuine, not fake.

realistic Like the real thing. **realistically.**

realize (realizes, realizing, realized) To come to understand something. *I realize that the job will take a long time.* **realization.**

really Truly, without doubt.

realm (realms) A kingdom.

reap (reaps, reaping, reaped) To cut and gather grain crops. **reaper.**

reappear (reappears, reappearing, reappeared) To appear again. **reappearance.**

rear[1] The back of something, the part furthest from the front.

rear[2] (rears, rearing, reared) 1. To bring up young children or animals. 2. To rise up on the hind legs.

rear-guard (rear-guards) Soldiers protecting the rear of an army.

reason[1] (reasons) 1. An explanation or excuse. 2. A cause. *What is the reason for that?* 3. The ability to think things out. 4. Good sense. *It's against all reason to start in this weather.*

reason[2] (reasons, reasoning, reasoned) 1. To think. 2. To argue sensibly.

reasonable 1. Sensible. 2. Moderate, fair. *A reasonable price.* **reasonably.**

reassure (reassures, reassuring, reassured) To remove a person's doubts and fears. **reassurance.**

rebel[1] (pronounced re*bel*) (rebels, rebelling, rebelled) To refuse to obey someone in authority, especially the government. rebellious, rebelliously, rebellion.

rebel[2] (pronounced *reb*el) (rebels) Someone who rebels.

rebound (rebounds, rebounding, rebounded) To bounce back.

rebuild (rebuilds, rebuilding, rebuilt) To build again.

rebuke[1] (rebukes, rebuking, rebuked) To speak severely to someone for doing wrong.

rebuke[2] (rebukes) Words spoken in rebuking someone.

recall (recalls, recalling, recalled) 1. To call back. 2. To remember.

recapture (recaptures, recapturing, recaptured) To capture again.

recede (recedes, receding, receded) To go back. *When the flood had receded, the animals came out of the Ark.*

receipt (receipts) 1. The act of receiving something. 2. Written proof that a payment has been received.

receive (receives, receiving, received) 1. To accept or take in something which is given or sent. *To receive a letter.* 2. To welcome someone. *To receive a guest.* receiver.

recent Made a short time ago, having happened a short time ago. recently.

receptacle (receptacles) A container.

reception (receptions) 1. A welcome. 2. A party where people are given an official welcome. 3. An office in a garage, hotel, or other place where people are received when they arrive. receptionist.

receptive Quick to receive new ideas.

recess (recesses) An alcove.

recipe (recipes) Directions for cooking food.

recital (recitals) A concert given by a small number of performers.

recite (recites, reciting, recited) To speak aloud from memory. recitation.

reckless Doing things without thinking or caring about the consequences. recklessly, recklessness.

reckon (reckons, reckoning, reckoned) 1. To calculate. 2. To consider.

reclaim (reclaims, reclaiming, reclaimed) To bring something back into profitable use. *Reclaimed land.* reclamation.

recline (reclines, reclining, reclined) To lean or lie back.

recognize (recognizes, recognizing, recognized) 1. To realize that one knows somebody or something. 2. To acknowledge. *I do not recognize your authority.* recognizable, recognition.

recoil (recoils, recoiling, recoiled) To spring back, to move backwards.

recollect (recollects, recollecting, recollected) To remember. recollection.

recommend (recommends, recommending, recommended) 1. To suggest, to advise. 2. To speak well of someone or something. recommendation.

recompense (recompenses, recompensing, recompensed) To repay somebody for something.

reconcile (reconciles, reconciling, reconciled) 1. To make people become friends again, to settle a difference. 2. *To reconcile oneself to something*, to overcome one's objections to it. reconciliation.

recondition (reconditions, reconditioning, reconditioned) To put something into good working order again.

reconnaissance (reconnaissances) An advance into enemy territory to gather information.

reconsider (reconsiders, reconsidering, reconsidered) To think again about something.

reconstruct (reconstructs, reconstructing, reconstructed) To rebuild, to construct something again.

record[1] (pronounced re*cord*) (records, recording, recorded) 1. To write something down for future reference. 2. To put music or other sounds on a tape or disc.

record[2] (pronounced *rec*ord) (records) 1. A written account of things that have happened or things that have been done. 2. A disc on which music or other sound has been recorded. 3. The best performance or most remarkable event of its kind.

recorder (recorders) 1. Someone who writes down a record of events. 2. A tape-recorder. 3. A musical instrument played by blowing into one end.

recording (recordings) Music or other sounds recorded on a disc or tape.

record-player (record-players) An apparatus for playing gramophone records.

recount (recounts, recounting, recounted) To tell.

re-count (re-counts) A second counting of something.

recover (recovers, recovering, recovered) 1. To return to normal health and strength. 2. To get back something which was lost. recovery.

recreation (recreations) Games, hobbies, or other things which a person does in his leisure time. recreation ground.

recruit[1] (recruits) A person who has just joined the armed forces or some other organization.

recruit[2] (recruits, recruiting, recruited) To get recruits.

rectangle (rectangles) A shape with four straight sides and four right angles. rectangular.

rectify (rectifies, rectifying, rectified) To put something right.

rector (rectors) A clergyman in charge of a parish.

rectory (rectories) A rector's house.

recuperate (recuperates, recuperating, recuperated) To recover after an illness. recuperation.

recur (recurs, recurring, recurred) To happen again, to be repeated. recurrent, recurrence.

red[1] A colour, the colour of blood.

red[2] (redder, reddest) Red in colour.

Red Cross An international organization for the relief of suffering.

redden (reddens, reddening, reddened) 1. To become red. 2. To make something red.

reddish Rather red.

redeem (redeems, redeeming, redeemed) 1. To get something back by making a payment. 2. To save. *A redeeming feature*, a quality that compensates for someone's bad qualities. redemption.

red-handed In the act of committing a crime. *To catch someone red-handed*.

red-hot Glowing with heat.

Red Indian One of the original inhabitants of North America.

reduce (reduces, reducing, reduced) 1. To make something less or smaller. 2. To bring somebody or something into a different state. *The town was reduced to ashes*. reduction.

redundant More than is necessary, no longer useful. redundancy.

reed (reeds) A plant which grows in or near water. reedy.

reef (reefs) A line of rock or coral just below or just above the surface of the sea.

reef-knot (reef-knots) A kind of knot.

reek (reeks, reeking, reeked) To give off an unpleasant smell.

reel[1] (reels) 1. A cylinder or other device on which cotton, fishing-line, film, or other things may be wound. 2. A lively Scottish dance.

reel[2] (reels, reeling, reeled) 1. To stagger. 2. To be dizzy.

re-enter (re-enters, re-entering, re-entered) To come back into somewhere. re-entry.

refer (refers, referring, referred) *To refer to:* 1. To mention. 2. To be connected with. 3. To go to someone or something for information or help. *I often refer to my dictionary.* 4. To tell a person to go to someone or something for information or help. *When I ask my teacher how to spell a word he refers me to the dictionary.*

referee[1] (referees) A person whose job is to see that a game is played according to the rules.

referee[2] (referees, refereeing, refereed) To act as a referee.

reference (references) 1. Words referring to or mentioning something. 2. *With reference to*, concerning, about. 3. *A reference book*, a book to be referred to for information.

refill (refills, refilling, refilled) To fill something again.

refine (refines, refining, refined) To purify, to process a raw material such as oil or sugar to make it suitable for use. **refinery.**

refined With good manners. **refinement.**

refit (refits, refitting, refitted) To modernize and repair a ship.

reflect (reflects, reflecting, reflected) 1. To throw back light. *Sunlight was reflected off the windscreens.* **reflector.** 2. To show an image as in a mirror. *Her face was reflected by the surface of the pond.* 3. To consider, to think something over. **reflection.**

reflex (reflexes) 1. An action that a person does without any conscious thought. 2. *A reflex camera*, one in which the scene to be photographed is viewed through the lens.

reform (reforms, reforming, reformed) To improve by putting right what is wrong. **reformer, reformation.**

refrain[1] (refrains) The chorus of a song.

refrain[2] (refrains, refraining, refrained) To hold oneself back from doing something.

refresh (refreshes, refreshing, refreshed) To give new strength, to make fresh.

refreshments Something to eat or drink.

refrigerate (refrigerates, refrigerating, refrigerated) To make something cold or frozen.

refrigerator (refrigerators) An apparatus for keeping food cool and fresh.

refuel (refuels, refuelling, refuelled) To fill with fuel.

refuge (refuges) A place of shelter.

refugee (refugees) A person who has had to leave his home or country because of some emergency.

refund (refunds, refunding, refunded) To pay back money.

refuse[1] (pronounced re*fuse*) (refuses, refusing, refused) To say 'no' to something, not to do what one is asked to do. **refusal.**

refuse[2] (pronounced *refuse*) Rubbish.

regain (regains, regaining, regained) 1. To get something back. 2. To reach somewhere again.

regal To do with a king or queen, royal. **regally.**

regard[1] (regards, regarding, regarded) 1. To look closely at something. 2. To consider. *Janet was regarded as the best singer in the school.*

regard[2] (regards) 1. A look, a gaze. 2. Concern, care, attention, respect. 3. *Kind regards*, kind wishes.

regarding Concerning, about.

regardless Without paying attention, without caring.

regatta (regattas) A meeting for boat or yacht races.

regent (regents) A person who rules a country at a time when the king or queen cannot do so.

regiment (regiments) A unit in the army. **regimental.**

region (regions) An area, a part of a country, a part of the world. **regional.**

register[1] (registers) 1. A book in which information is recorded. *An attendance register.* 2. *A cash register*, a till which records the money put into it.

register[2] (registers, registering, registered) 1. To record information officially. *To register a new car.* 2. To show, to indicate. *The thermometer registered 100 °C.* 3. *To register a letter*, to have the details recorded at the post office for safety. **registration.**

registrar (registrars) The official in charge of a registry office.

registry office A place where births, marriages, and deaths are officially recorded.

regret[1] (regrets, regretting, regretted) To be sad or sorry about something. **regretful, regretfully, regrettable, regrettably.**

regret[2] (regrets) A sorrowful feeling.

regular 1. Evenly spaced, coming or happening at equal intervals. *The regular ticking of the clock.* 2. Normal, correct, proper. **regularly, regularity.**

regulate (regulates, regulating, regulated) 1. To control. 2. To adjust something to make it work at the right speed. **regulator.**

regulation (regulations) 1. The regulating of something. 2. A rule, a law.

rehearse (rehearses, rehearsing, rehearsed) To practise something which is to be performed. **rehearsal.**

rehouse (rehouses, rehousing, rehoused) To provide somebody with a new house.

reign[1] (reigns) The period during which a king or queen governs a country.

reign[2] (reigns, reigning, reigned) To be a king or queen, to rule.

rein (reins) A narrow strap used to guide a horse.

reindeer (reindeer) A kind of deer that lives in cold regions.

reinforce (reinforces, reinforcing, reinforced) To make something stronger. *Reinforced concrete*, concrete strengthened by iron rods or wires.

reinforcements Extra forces brought up when necessary.

reject (rejects, rejecting, rejected) 1. To throw something away. 2. To refuse to accept something. **rejection.**

rejoice (rejoices, rejoicing, rejoiced) To feel and show great happiness.

relapse[1] (relapses, relapsing, relapsed) To fall back into a former condition. *He said a few words, then relapsed into silence.*

relapse[2] (relapses) Relapsing. *To have a relapse*, to become ill again after improving.

relate (relates, relating, related) 1. To tell a story, to give an account of something. 2. To connect in some way, to have reference to something. 3. *To be related to somebody*, to belong to the same family. **relation.**

relationship (relationships) The connection between people or things.

relative[1] Comparative. **relatively.**

relative[2] (relatives) A person to whom one is related.

relax (relaxes, relaxing, relaxed) To become less stiff, less tense, or less strict. **relaxation.**

relay (relays, relaying, relayed) To pass on a message or a radio or television broadcast.

relay race A race in which teams of runners compete.

release (releases, releasing, released) To set free, to allow out, to unfasten.

relegate (relegates, relegating, relegated) To put a team down into a lower division of a league. **relegation.**

relent (relents, relenting, relented) To become less stern, to begin to show mercy.

relentless Without pity. **relentlessly.**

relevant Connected with the matter being discussed. **relevantly, relevance.**

reliable Trustworthy, to be relied on. **reliably, reliability.**

reliant Relying, trusting. **reliance.**

relic (relics) Something which has survived from a past age.

relief 1. The ending of pain, worry, or trouble. 2. Help, assistance, something which brings relief.

relief map A map which shows hills and valleys.

relieve (relieves, relieving, relieved) 1. To

bring relief. **2.** *To relieve someone of something*, to take it away from him.

religion (religions) A set of beliefs about God or about gods, the worship of God or gods. **religious, religiously.**

relish (relishes, relishing, relished) To enjoy.

reluctant Unwilling to do something. **reluctantly, reluctance.**

rely (relies, relying, relied) *To rely on*, to trust, to depend on.

remain (remains, remaining, remained) **1.** To be left over. **remainder. 2.** To stay, to continue.

remains 1. Something left over. **2.** Ruins. **3.** A dead body.

remark[1] (remarks, remarking, remarked) To observe, to make a comment.

remark[2] (remarks) A comment, something said.

remarkable Worth noticing, unusual. **remarkably.**

remedy[1] (remedies, remedying, remedied) To cure something, to put it right.

remedy[2] (remedies) A cure.

remember (remembers, remembering, remembered) To keep something in one's mind, to be able to bring something back to one's mind. **remembrance.**

remind (reminds, reminding, reminded) To help someone to remember something, to make him think of it. **reminder.**

remnant (remnants) A small amount left over.

remorse Deep regret for something that one has done wrong. **remorseful.**

remote (remoter, remotest) Far away. **remotely, remoteness.**

removal (removals) Removing. *A removal van*, a van for carrying furniture.

remove (removes, removing, removed) **1.** To move somebody or something from one place to another. **2.** To take off clothes or covers. **3.** To get rid of somebody or something. **remover, removable.**

remunerative Profitable.

rend (rends, rending, rent) To tear.

render (renders, rendering, rendered) **1.** To give something. **2.** To perform something. **3.** To change something into a new state or form. *She was rendered helpless by anger.*

rendezvous (rendezvous) **1.** A meeting place. **2.** An appointment to meet somebody somewhere.

renegade (renegades) A traitor.

renew (renews, renewing, renewed) To make new, to restore, to replace. **renewal.**

renounce (renounces, renouncing, renounced) To declare that one is giving something up. **renunciation.**

renovate (renovates, renovating, renovated) To restore something to good condition. **renovation.**

renown Fame.

renowned Famous.

rent[1] (rents) A regular payment for the use of a thing or a place.

rent[2] (rents, renting, rented) To pay rent for something.

rental (rentals) Rent.

repair[1] (repairs, repairing, repaired) To mend.

repair[2] (repairs) **1.** The act of repairing something. **2.** *In good repair*, well repaired.

repay (repays, repaying, repaid) To pay back. **repayment.**

repeat (repeats, repeating, repeated) **1.** To say or do something again. **2.** To happen again. **repeatable.**

repeatedly Again and again.

repel (repels, repelling, repelled) **1.** To drive someone or something away. **2.** To cause a feeling of dislike. **repellent.**

repent (repents, repenting, repented) To be sorry for what one has done. **repentant, repentance.**

repertory theatre A theatre with its own company of actors.

repetition 1. Repeating something. **2.** Something that is repeated.

replace (replaces, replacing, replaced) **1.** To put something back in its place. **2.** To take the place of someone or something. **3.** To put a new thing in the place of an old one. **replacement.**

replay (replays) **1.** A football match played again after a draw. **2.** The playing back of a recording.

replica (replicas) An exact copy.

reply[1] (replies) An answer.

reply[2] (replies, replying, replied) To answer.

report[1] (reports, reporting, reported) **1.** To give an account of something, to give information about something. **2.** To go to someone and say that one has come or that one is ready for work. *Competitors for the next race should report to the starter at once.*

report[2] (reports) **1.** An account of something that has happened. **2.** An explosion, a bang.

reporter (reporters) A person who collects news for a newspaper or radio or television.

repose Rest, peacefulness.

reprehensible Deserving blame or disapproval. **reprehensibly.**

represent (represents, representing, represented) **1.** To be a picture or model of something or somebody. **2.** To be an example of something. *This work represents the best I can do.* **3.** To act on somebody else's behalf. *We are here to represent the school.* **representation, representative.**

reprieve (reprieves, reprieving, reprieved) To postpone or cancel somebody's punishment.

reprimand[1] (reprimands, reprimanding, reprimanded) To speak severely to somebody for doing wrong.

reprimand[2] (reprimands) Words spoken in reprimanding someone.

reprisal (reprisals) An act of revenge.

reproach[1] (reproaches, reproaching, reproached) To find fault with someone, to scold him.

reproach[2] (reproaches) Words spoken in reproaching someone.

reproduce (reproduces, reproducing, reproduced) **1.** To cause something to happen again, to produce a copy of something.

2. To produce children or young animals. **reproduction, reproductive.**

reproof (reproofs) A reprimand.

reprove (reproves, reproving, reproved) To reprimand someone.

reptile (reptiles) An animal that creeps or crawls. Snakes and lizards are reptiles.

republic (republics) A country which has an elected government but no king or queen.

repugnance Strong dislike. **repugnant.**

repulse (repulses, repulsing, repulsed) To resist an attack, to drive back an enemy.

repulsive Disgusting. **repulsively.**

reputation (reputations) A widely-held opinion about somebody or something. *Billy Bunter has a reputation for greed.*

request[1] (requests, requesting, requested) To ask for something politely.

request[2] (requests) **1.** Requesting. **2.** Something requested.

requiem (requiems) A church service for the dead.

require (requires, requiring, required) **1.** To need. **2.** To order someone to do something. **requirement.**

rescue (rescues, rescuing, rescued) To get someone safely away from captivity or danger. **rescuer.**

research (researches) Careful searching for information, a scientific investigation.

resemble (resembles, resembling, resembled) To be like someone or something. **resemblance.**

resent (resents, resenting, resented) To feel bitter or angry about something. **resentful, resentfully, resentment.**

reserve[1] (reserves, reserving, reserved) **1.** To store for special use. **2.** To keep something for a particular person or purpose only. **reservation.**

reserve[2] (reserves) **1.** A person or thing kept back to be used later if necessary. **2.** An area which is set aside for certain people or animals to live in.

reserved Shy, not talkative.

reservoir (reservoirs) An artificial lake where water is stored.

reside (resides, residing, resided) *To reside somewhere*, to live there, to have one's home there. **resident, residence.**

resign (resigns, resigning, resigned) **1.** To give up one's job or position. **2.** *To resign oneself to something*, to decide to endure it patiently. **resignation.**

resist (resists, resisting, resisted) To oppose something, to try to stop it, to refuse to give in to it. **resistant, resistance.**

resolute Firm, determined. **resolutely, resolution.**

resolve (resolves, resolving, resolved) To make a decision about something.

resort (resorts) A place where people go for holidays.

resound (resounds, resounding, resounded) To echo.

resourceful Clever at finding ways of doing things. **resourcefully, resourcefulness.**

resources 1. Wealth. **2.** Useful materials, valuable supplies.

respect[1] **1.** An admiration for somebody's good qualities or important position. **2.** Serious consideration, care. *We should have respect for the needs of others.* **3.** A detail, a particular point or aspect. *It was a good game in some respects.* **respectful, respectfully.**

respect[2] (respects, respecting, respected) To have respect for somebody or something.

respectable Deserving respect or admiration. **respectfully, respectability.**

respite Rest, relief.

resplendent Splendid.

respond (responds, responding, responded) **1.** To answer, to reply. **2.** To react.

response (responses) **1.** A reply. **2.** A reaction.

responsible 1. Having the duty of looking after something. **2.** Deserving the praise or blame for something. **3.** Trustworthy. *A responsible boy.* **4.** *A responsible job*, one needing a trustworthy person. **responsibly, responsibility.**

rest[1] (rests) **1.** A period of quiet, freedom from work or other activities. **2.** A support. *An arm-rest.* **restful, restfully, restfulness.**

rest[2] (rests, resting, rested) **1.** To have a rest. **2.** To give a rest. *To rest the horses.* **3.** To support something on something. **4.** To be supported on something.

rest[3] The remainder, the others. *I must go on now. Will you follow with the rest?*

restaurant (restaurants) A place where meals can be bought and eaten.

restless Never still, fidgeting. **restlessly, restlessness.**

restore (restores, restoring, restored) **1.** To give or put something back. **2.** To repair something, to make it as it was before. **restoration.**

restrain (restrains, restraining, restrained) To hold back, to keep someone or something under control. **restraint.**

restrict (restricts, restricting, restricted) To keep someone or something within certain limits. **restriction.**

result[1] (results) **1.** Something which happens because of certain actions or events. **2.** The final score in a game, the final order of competitors in a competition. **3.** The answer to a sum or problem.

result[2] (results, resulting, resulted) **1.** To happen because of certain other actions or events. **2.** *To result in*, to have as a result.

resume (resumes, resuming, resumed) To begin again after stopping for a time. **resumption.**

Resurrection The rising of Jesus from the tomb.

retail (retails, retailing, retailed) To sell goods to the public. **retailer.**

(retains, retaining, retained) **1.** To keep something. **2.** To hold something in place.

retainer (retainers) (old-fashioned) A servant.

retaliate (retaliates, retaliating, retaliated) To pay someone back for an unkind action. **retaliation.**

reticent Not saying all that one knows or feels. **reticence.**

retinue (retinues) A number of servants or attendants belonging to an important person.

retire (retires, retiring, retired) **1.** To give up work, usually because of old age. **retirement. 2.** To move back, to withdraw. **3.** To go to bed.

retort[1] (retorts, retorting, retorted) To make a quick reply.

retort[2] (retorts) A quick reply.

retrace (retraces, retracing, retraced) To go back over something again.

retreat[1] (retreats, retreating, retreated) To move back after a defeat, to move away.

retreat[2] (retreats) **1.** Retreating. **2.** A quiet peaceful place.

retribution A punishment that has been deserved.

retrieve (retrieves, retrieving, retrieved) To bring back, to get back. **retrievable.**

retriever (retrievers) A kind of dog which can retrieve birds that have been shot.

retro-rocket (retro-rockets) A rocket used for manœuvring a spacecraft.

retrospect *In retrospect*, as one looks back in time. **retrospective.**

return[1] (returns, returning, returned) **1.** To come or go back somewhere. **2.** To send back, to give back. *Please return my book soon.* **returnable.**

return[2] (returns) **1.** Returning. **2.** *A return match*, a second match between two teams who have already played one match. **3.** *A return ticket*, a ticket to go somewhere and come back. **4.** *Many happy returns*, a birthday greeting.

reunion (reunions) A coming together again after a separation.

rev (revs, revving, revved) (informal) To speed up the engine of a motor vehicle.

Rev. or **Revd.** Reverend.

reveal (reveals, revealing, revealed) **1.** To allow something to be seen. **2.** To make something known. **revelation.**

revel (revels, revelling, revelled) **1.** To make merry. **reveller, revelry. 2.** *To revel in something*, to enjoy it greatly.

revenge[1] (revenges) An injury done to somebody in return for what he has done. *To have revenge, to take revenge*, to perform an action of revenge.

revenge[2] (revenges, revenging, revenged) *To be revenged on somebody*, to have revenge on him.

revenue (revenues) Income, especially the annual income of a state.

reverberation (reverberations) An echoing sound.

revere (reveres, revering, revered) To respect deeply, to honour. **reverent, reverently, reverence.**

Reverend The title of a clergyman. *The Reverend John Mark.*

reverie (reveries) A day-dream.

reverse[1] **1.** The opposite of something, the opposite side of something, the opposite way of doing something. **2.** *Reverse gear*, the gear used to drive backwards.

reverse[2] (reverses, reversing, reversed) **1.** To turn something the other way round. **2.** To go backwards, to drive a vehicle backwards. **reversal, reversible.**

review (reviews) 1. A survey, an inspection. 2. An account of what a person thinks about a book, or a play, or a concert. reviewer.

revise (revises, revising, revised) 1. To read something through and make alterations if necessary. 2. To get ready for a test or examination by going over one's work and learning it thoroughly. revision.

revive (revives, reviving, revived) 1. To come back to life, to become conscious again. 2. To bring someone or something back to life or consciousness. revival.

revolt (revolts, revolting, revolted) 1. To rebel. 2. To fill someone with disgust or horror.

revolution (revolutions) 1. A rebellion which overthrows the government. 2. A full turn of a wheel or other object. 3. A complete change.

revolutionary 1. Rebellious. 2. Causing or encouraging great changes.

revolve (revolves, revolving, revolved) To turn as a wheel does.

revolver (revolvers) A kind of pistol that can fire several shots without being reloaded.

revulsion A sudden feeling of disgust.

reward [1] (rewards) Something promised or given to someone for behaving well or for doing a good deed.

reward [2] (rewards, rewarding, rewarded) To give someone a reward.

rewrite (rewrites, rewriting, rewrote, re-written) To write something again.

rheumatism A disease causing pain and swollen joints. rheumatic.

rhinoceros (rhinoceroses) A large animal with either one or two horns on its nose.

rhododendron (rhododendrons) A flowering evergreen shrub.

rhubarb A plant whose stalks are used as fruit.

rhyme [1] (rhymes) 1. A similarity of sound in the endings of words, as in *wall* and *fall*, or *fix* and *tricks*. 2. A short rhyming poem.

rhyme [2] (rhymes, rhyming, rhymed) To have rhymes at the ends of words or lines.

rhythm (rhythms) 1. A regular pattern of sounds or movements, as in the ticking of a clock or the moving of a dancer's feet. 2. A regular beat or pattern in music or poetry. rhythmic, rhythmical, rhythmically.

rib (ribs) One of the curved bones round the upper part of the body.

ribbon (ribbons) A narrow length of silk or other material. *A hair ribbon.*

rice A white grain used as food.

rich (richer, richest) 1. Having much money or property. 2. Splendid, costly. 3. Specially full of goodness and colour. *Rich creamy milk.* richly, richness.

riches Wealth.

rick (ricks) A large neat stack of hay.

rickety Unsteady, liable to fall down.

rickshaw (rickshaws) A two-wheeled carriage pulled by a man.

ricochet (ricochets, ricocheting, ricocheted) To bounce off something. *The bullet ricocheted off the rocks.*

rid (rids, ridding, rid) 1. To make oneself free of something. 2. *To get rid of something*, to remove it. riddance.

riddle (riddles) 1. A puzzling question. 2. A sieve.

ride [1] (rides, riding, rode, ridden) 1. To sit on and be carried by a horse or a bicycle. 2. To travel in a vehicle. rider.

ride [2] (rides) Riding, a time spent in riding.

ridge (ridges) A raised line where two sloping surfaces meet. *The ridge of a roof.*

ridicule (ridicules, ridiculing, ridiculed) To make fun of somebody or something.

ridiculous Absurd, deserving to be laughed at. ridiculously.

rim (rims) The outer edge of a wheel or other round object.

rind (rinds) A hard outer skin or covering.

ring¹ (rings) 1. A circle. 2. Any object shaped like a circle. 3. The space where a circus performs. 4. A platform where boxing matches are fought.

ring² (rings, ringing, ringed) To put or make a ring round something.

ring³ (rings, ringing, rang, rung) 1. To cause a bell to sound. 2. To make a sound like a bell. 3. To make a telephone call.

ringleader (ringleaders) The leader of a gang, a person who encourages others to do mischief.

ring-road (ring-roads) A road which enables traffic to go round a town.

rink (rinks) A place made for ice-skating.

rinse (rinses, rinsing, rinsed) To wash something in clean water.

riot¹ (riots) Noisy, violent behaviour by a crowd.

riot² (riots, rioting, rioted) To take part in a riot. riotous, riotously, rioter.

rip (rips, ripping, ripped) To tear violently.

rip-cord (rip-cords) The cord which is pulled to make a parachute open.

ripe (riper, ripest) Ready for harvesting, ready for eating. *Ripe fruit.* ripeness.

ripen (ripens, ripening, ripened) 1. To become ripe. 2. To make ripe.

ripple (ripples, rippling, rippled) To make tiny waves. *The surface of the pond rippled in the breeze.*

rise¹ (rises, rising, rose, risen) 1. To get up. 2. To go upwards. 3. To rebel.

rise² (rises) 1. An upward slope. 2. An increase in a wage or a price.

rifle (rifles) A kind of gun fired from the shoulder.

rift (rifts) A split, a crack.

rig¹ (rigs, rigging, rigged) 1. To provide a ship with sails and rigging. 2. *To rig up,* to put something up, to make something out of available materials.

rig² (rigs) A framework of girders used to support drilling equipment. *An oil rig.*

rigging The ropes used to support a ship's masts and sails.

right¹ Of or on the same side as the right hand, which is the hand which most people use when writing.

right² The right-hand side. In this book, the odd numbered pages are on the right and the even numbered pages are on the left.

right³ 1. Good, proper, just. *It is not right to steal.* 2. Correct, true. *Is the clock right?* rightly.

right⁴ (rights) 1. That which is right. 2. Something a person is allowed to do or have by law or custom. 3. *To be in the right,* to have the law on one's side. rightful.

right⁵ 1. Straight, directly. *Go right on.* 2. Completely. *Turn right round.* 3. Exactly. *Stand right in the middle.* 4. *It serves him right,* it is what he deserves.

right angle An angle of 90 degrees, like any of the angles in a square.

righteous Law-abiding, virtuous. righteously, righteousness.

rigid 1. Stiff, not able to be bent. 2. Strict, harsh. rigidly.

rising (risings) A rebellion.

risk[1] (risks) The chance of meeting danger or of suffering injury or loss. **risky.**

risk[2] (risks, risking, risked) To take a risk.

rissole (rissoles) A fried ball of minced meat with other ingredients.

rite (rites) A ceremony.

ritual (rituals) A rite which is regularly repeated.

rival[1] (rivals) A competitor, a person who is competing with someone else. **rivalry.**

rival[2] (rivals, rivalling, rivalled) To be a rival.

river (rivers) A stream of water flowing into the sea or into a lake or into another river.

rivet (rivets) A stout metal pin for fastening metal plates.

road (roads) A hard level way made for the use of traffic.

roam (roams, roaming, roamed) To wander.

roar (roars, roaring, roared) 1. To make a loud deep sound, to shout noisily. 2. *A roaring trade*, a brisk, successful trade.

roast (roasts, roasting, roasted, roast) To cook in an oven or over a fire.

rob (robs, robbing, robbed) To steal something from somebody or somewhere. **robber, robbery.**

robin (robins) A small bird with a red breast.

robot (robots) A machine made to act like a man.

robust Strong and healthy. **robustly.**

rock[1] (rocks) 1. A large stone. 2. A large mass of stone. *The house is built on solid rock.* 3. A kind of hard sweet made in the shape of a stick.

rock[2] (rocks, rocking, rocked) 1. To move gently to and fro. 2. To sway, to shake.

rock[3] A kind of popular music.

rockery (rockeries) A part of a garden where plants grow between large stones.

rocket (rockets) 1. A firework or signal which shoots high into the air. 2. A tube-shaped device filled with fast-burning fuel which is used to launch a missile or a spacecraft.

rocking-chair (rocking-chairs) A chair which can be rocked by a person sitting in it.

rocking-horse (rocking-horses) A toy horse which can be rocked, for a child to sit on.

rocky (rockier, rockiest) 1. Full of rocks. 2. Unsteady.

rod (rods) A straight, slender stick or bar.

rode *See* ride[1].

rodent (rodents) An animal that gnaws things. Rats and squirrels are rodents.

rodeo (rodeos) A display by cowboys of horse-riding and rounding up cattle.

roe (roes) A mass of eggs from a fish.

rogue (rogues) A rascal. **roguish, roguishly, roguery.**

role (roles) An actor's part in a play.

roll[1] (rolls) 1. A piece of paper or other material curled into a tube shape. 2. A small bun-shaped loaf of bread. 3. A list of names, a register.

roll[2] (rolls, rolling, rolled) 1. To turn over and over like a ball or wheel running along the ground. 2. To turn something over and over to make a ball or a tube shape. 3. To make something flat and smooth by rolling a rounded object over it. *To roll out pastry.* **rolling-pin.** 4. To sway from side to side. 5. To make a long drawn out rumbling or rattling sound. *The drums rolled.*

roller (rollers) A cylinder-shaped tool or device for rolling.

roller-skate (roller-skates) A set of wheels to be fixed under a shoe for skating on a smooth surface.

rolling-stock Railway wagons and coaches.

Roman Of Rome.

Roman Catholic Belonging to the Church which has the Pope as its head.

romance (romances) A love story.

romantic 1. Like a romance. 2. Giving feelings of pleasure and wonder.

romp (romps, romping, romped) To play rather roughly and noisily.

roof (roofs) The top covering of a building, shelter, or vehicle.

rook (rooks) 1. A black bird like a crow. 2. A piece in chess, also called a castle.

room (rooms) 1. A division of a building with walls and a ceiling and a floor. *A dining-room.* 2. Space for somebody or something. *Is there room for me?*

roomy (roomier, roomiest) Having plenty of space.

roost (roosts) A bird's resting place.

rooster (roosters) A male farmyard fowl.

root (roots) 1. The part of a plant which grows into the ground. 2. A basis or source from which something grows. 3. *To take root*, to grow roots, to become established.

rope[1] (ropes) A thick cord made of twisted strands.

rope[2] (ropes, roping, roped) To tie something with a rope.

rope-ladder (rope-ladders) A ladder with sides made of rope.

rosary (rosaries) A string of beads used while saying prayers.

rose[1] *See* rise[1].

rose[2] (roses) A beautiful flower with a thorny stem.

rosette (rosettes) A large circular badge made of cloth.

rosewood A dark tropical timber.

rosy (rosier, rosiest) 1. Pink. 2. Cheerful. **rosily, rosiness.**

rot[1] 1. Decay, rottenness. 2. (informal) Nonsense.

rot[2] (rots, rotting, rotted) To become rotten, to go bad.

rotary Rotating.

rotate (rotates, rotating, rotated) 1. To turn round as a wheel does. 2. To come round again and again, to come round in turn. **rotation.**

rotor (rotors) The large horizontal propeller on a helicopter.

rotten 1. Having become unfit to eat. *Rotten eggs.* 2. Having become soft or crumbly and unfit for use. *Rotten wood.* 3. (informal) Bad, nasty. *A rotten trick.* **rottenness.**

rough (rougher, roughest) 1. Uneven, not smooth. *A rough road.* 2. Stormy, violent. *A rough wind.* 3. Harsh, unpleasant. *A rough voice.* 4. Done or made quickly and not exact. *A rough sketch. A rough guess.* **roughly, roughness.**

roughen (roughens, roughening, roughened) 1. To make something rougher. 2. To become rougher.

round[1] (rounder, roundest) Shaped like a circle or a ball. **roundness.**

round[2] (rounds) 1. One stage in a competition or contest. *The winners will go on to the next round.* 2. A series of visits made by a tradesman to his customers or a doctor to his patients. *A paper round.* 3. A whole slice. *A round of bread.* 4. A single bullet or shell.

round[3] 1. Surrounding. *There is a hedge round the garden.* 2. To every part of. *Show your friends round the garden.* 3. In a curve about. *I walked round the corner.* 4. In a new direction. *They all looked round.* 5. By a longer way. *The gate is locked so we must go round.* 6. To a place where someone or something is likely to be. *I went round to see if Angela was in.*

round[4] (rounds, rounding, rounded) 1. To go round something. 2. To make a thing round or curved. 3. *To round something off*, to finish it. 4. *To round up people or animals*, to gather them together.

roundabout[1] Not going the shortest way.

roundabout[2] (roundabouts) 1. A road junction where vehicles must go round a circle. 2. An amusement at a fun-fair.

rounders A team game played with a bat and ball.

Roundhead (Roundheads) An opponent of King Charles I.

roundish Nearly round.

round-shouldered With the shoulders permanently bent forwards.

rouse (rouses, rousing, roused) **1.** To wake. **2.** To make somebody more energetic or fierce.

rout (routs, routing, routed) To defeat the enemy and make them run away.

route (routes) A way between two places.

routine (routines) A settled and regular way of doing things.

rove (roves, roving, roved) To roam, to wander. **rover.**

row[1] (rows) A number of persons or things in a line.

row[2] (rows, rowing, rowed) To move a boat along by means of oars. **rower, rowing-boat.**

row[3] (rows) **1.** A tiresome and disturbing noise. **2.** A noisy or violent quarrel.

rowdy (rowdier, rowdiest) Rough and noisy. **rowdily.**

royal To do with a king or queen, fit for a king or queen. **royally, royalty.**

rub (rubs, rubbing, rubbed) **1.** To move something backwards and forwards on something else. *The cat rubbed her back against my legs.* **2.** *To rub something off, to rub something out,* to remove something by rubbing.

rubber (rubbers) **1.** A substance used to make tyres, bouncing balls, elastic bands, and other products. **2.** A piece of rubber for rubbing out pencil marks.

rubbish 1. Waste material. **2.** Nonsense.

rubble Broken bits of brick, stone, or rock.

ruby (rubies) A deep red jewel.

rucksack (rucksacks) A bag worn strapped on the back by walkers and climbers.

rudder (rudders) A flat hinged piece at the back of a ship or aircraft, used for steering.

ruddy (ruddier, ruddiest) Red and healthy-looking.

rude (ruder, rudest) **1.** Not polite, not respectful. **2.** Not decent, vulgar. **3.** Roughly made. **rudely, rudeness.**

rueful Sorrowful. **ruefully.**

ruffian (ruffians) A violent, brutal person.

ruffle[1] (ruffles, ruffling, ruffled) To disturb the smoothness of something.

ruffle[2] (ruffles) A frill.

rug (rugs) **1.** A thick blanket. **2.** A floor mat.

Rugby A kind of football in which the ball may be carried.

rugged Rough, uneven.

rugger (informal) Rugby football.

ruin[1] (ruins) **1.** Destruction, serious damage. **2.** The remains of an old building.

ruin[2] (ruins, ruining, ruined) To spoil something completely. **ruinous, ruinously.**

rule[1] (rules) **1.** A law, a regulation, a custom which ought to be followed. **2.** Government. **3.** *As a rule,* usually.

rule[2] (rules, ruling, ruled) **1.** To govern. **2.** To make a decision. *The referee ruled that the player was off-side.* **3.** *To rule a line,* to draw a straight line with the help of a ruler.

ruler (rulers) **1.** A person who governs. **2.** A strip of wood or metal, often marked with inches or centimetres, used for measuring or drawing straight lines.

rum A strong alcoholic drink.

rumble (rumbles, rumbling, rumbled) To make a deep continuous sound like distant thunder.

rummage (rummages, rummaging, rummaged) To turn things over and make them untidy while looking for something.

rummy A card game.

rumour (rumours) Something which is passed around as news but which may not be true.

rump (rumps) The tail end of an animal.

rumple (rumples, rumpling, rumpled) To crease, to crumple.

rumpus (informal) A noisy disturbance.

run[1] (runs, running, ran, run) **1.** To move with quick steps. **2.** To go, to travel. *The bus runs every hour.* **3.** To flow. *Blood ran down his face.* **4.** To manage something, to look after it. *Alan's uncle runs a grocery business.* **5.** *To run a risk,* to take a chance. **6.** *To run someone over,* to knock him down with a car or other moving vehicle. **7.** *To run out* *of something*, to have none left when one needs it.

run[2] (runs) **1.** A time spent running. *To go for a run.* **2.** An enclosure for animals. *A chicken run.* **3.** A series of events coming together. *A run of good luck.* **4.** A point scored in cricket when the batsmen run between the wickets. **5.** A line running up or down a stocking from a hole or flaw.

rung[1] *See* ring[3].

rung[2] (rungs) One of the cross-bars used as steps on a ladder.

runner (runners) **1.** A person or animal that runs, especially in a race. **2.** The part of a sledge that slides along the ground.

runny (runnier, runniest) Flowing like liquid.

runway (runways) A track which aircraft use when taking off or landing.

rural Belonging to the countryside.

ruse (ruses) A deceitful trick.

rush[1] (rushes, rushing, rushed) **1.** To move with force and speed. **2.** To capture something by rushing. **3.** To make somebody or something rush. *Don't rush me.*

rush[2] (rushes) The act of rushing. *The rush hour*, a busy time of day when people are travelling to or from work.

rush[3] (rushes) A plant which grows in or near water.

rusk (rusks) A kind of biscuit for a baby.

Russian Of Russia.

rust[1] The reddish-brown substance which forms on iron when it has been wet.

rust[2] (rusts, rusting, rusted) **1.** To become rusty. **2.** To make something become rusty.

rustic Rural.

rustle (rustles, rustling, rustled) **1.** To make a gentle sound such as that of a light wind through trees. **2.** To steal cattle or other animals. rustler.

rusty (rustier, rustiest) Covered with rust.

rut (ruts) A groove made by the passing of the wheels of vehicles over the ground.

ruthless Cruel, without pity. ruthlessly, ruthlessness.

rye A kind of cereal plant.

Ss

sabbath (sabbaths) A weekly day of rest and prayer, Saturday for Jews, Sunday for Christians.

sabotage Damage done on purpose to machinery or equipment.

sabre (sabres) A sword with a curved blade.

saccharine A sweet substance used instead of sugar.

sack[1] (sacks) **1.** A large oblong bag made of strong material. **2.** (informal) *To get the sack*, to be dismissed from one's job.

sack[2] (sacks, sacking, sacked) To dismiss someone from his job.

sacking Rough cloth from which sacks are made.

sacrament (sacraments) A solemn religious ceremony, such as Baptism and Holy Communion.

sacred Holy, religious, belonging to God. sacredness.

sacrifice[1] (sacrifices) **1.** The killing of a person or animal as an offering to a god. **2.** The giving up of something valuable or enjoyable for some special purpose. **3.** Something offered or given as a sacrifice.

sacrifice[2] (sacrifices, sacrificing, sacrificed) To offer or give something as a sacrifice.

sacrilege Disrespectful treatment of something sacred. sacrilegious.

sad (sadder, saddest) Unhappy, sorrowful. sadly, sadness.

sadden (saddens, saddening, saddened) To make someone sad.

saddle[1] (saddles) A seat for the rider of a horse or a bicycle.

saddle² (saddles, saddling, saddled) To put a saddle on a horse.

sadist (sadists) A person who enjoys being cruel. **sadistic, sadistically, sadism.**

safari (safaris) An expedition to see or hunt big game. *A safari park*, a park where big game animals are kept.

safe¹ (safer, safest) 1. Free from danger, protected, secure. 2. Not dangerous. **safely.**

safe² (safes) 1. A strong box or cupboard in which money and valuables can be locked for safety. 2. A ventilated food cupboard.

safeguard (safeguards, safeguarding, safeguarded) To protect.

safety Being safe, freedom from danger.

safety-pin (safety-pins) A pin looped over and fitted with a clip to guard the point.

safety-valve (safety-valves) A device for preventing pressure rising above danger level.

sag (sags, sagging, sagged) To curve down in the middle because of weight or pressure.

saga (sagas) 1. An old story of heroes. 2. A long story.

said *See* say.

sail¹ (sails) 1. A sheet of canvas or other material hung from the mast to catch the wind and move a boat forwards. 2. An arm of a windmill. 3. A trip in a boat.

sail² (sails, sailing, sailed) 1. To be moved along by a sail. **sailing-ship.** 2. To start a voyage, to make a voyage. *When does the ship sail?* 3. To control a boat.

sailor (sailors) A seaman, a member of the crew of a ship.

saint (saints) A holy person. **saintly, saintliness.**

sake *For the sake of*, because of.

salad (salads) A mixture of vegetables eaten raw or cold. *Fruit salad*, a mixture of fruit.

salary (salaries) Regular pay. *A salary of £2,500 a year.*

sale (sales) 1. The selling of something. 2. *On sale* or *for sale*, to be sold. 3. A time when goods are offered at lower prices. *Winter sales.*

salesman (salesmen) A person whose job it is to sell things. **salesmanship.**

saliva The liquid which is always present in a person's mouth.

salmon (salmon) A large fish with pink flesh.

saloon (saloons) 1. A car seating four or five people, with a fixed roof. 2. A place where drinks are served, a bar, a public room.

salt¹ (salts) The substance which gives sea water its taste and which is used for flavouring food.

salt² (salts, salting, salted) To use salt to flavour or preserve food.

salt-cellar (salt-cellars) A small dish or pot for salt.

salty (saltier, saltiest) Tasting of salt.

salute¹ (salutes, saluting, saluted) 1. To raise the hand to the forehead as a sign of respect. 2. To give a polite greeting to someone.

salute² (salutes) 1. The act of saluting. 2. Something done to welcome somebody or to show respect to him.

salvage (salvages, salvaging, salvaged) 1. To save waste or damaged material which can be used again. 2. To save a wrecked or damaged ship.

salvation The saving of someone or something.

salvo (salvoes) The firing of a number of guns at the same time.

same 1. Not different, alike. *Twins are exactly the same age.* 2. Not changed. *The old house was just the same as ever.* 3. *All the same*, in spite of that.

sameness Dullness, monotony.

sample (samples) A specimen, an example, a part of something used for testing.

sanatorium (sanatoriums) A kind of hospital.

sanctuary (sanctuaries) A place of safety. *A bird sanctuary.*

sand 1. Tiny grains of stone such as are found on the seashore or in deserts. 2. *The sands*, a sandy area.

sandal (sandals) A kind of shoe consisting of a sole and straps to go round the foot.

sand-bag (sand-bags) A sack filled with sand used as a defence.

sand-dune (sand-dunes) A hill of sand.

sandpaper Paper with a coating of sand or powdered glass, used for smoothing wood.

sand-storm (sand-storms) A storm in which clouds of sand are blown in the wind.

sandwich (sandwiches) Two slices of bread with meat, cheese, or some other filling between them.

sandy 1. Made of sand, covered with sand. 2. Coloured like sand, light brown. *Sandy hair.*

sane (saner, sanest) Healthy in the mind, not mad. sanely, sanity.

sang *See* sing.

sanitary Free from dirt and germs.

sanitation Drainage and other arrangements for making things sanitary.

sank *See* sink[1].

sap[1] The liquid that rises in a plant.

sap[2] (saps, sapping, sapped) To weaken someone's energy and strength.

sapling (saplings) A young tree.

sapphire (sapphires) A blue jewel.

sarcastic Amusing but hurtful. sarcastically, sarcasm.

sardine (sardines) A small fish, usually sold in tins.

sari (saris) A garment worn by Hindu women.

sash (sashes) A strip of cloth worn round the waist or over one shoulder.

sash window A window that slides up and down.

sat *See* sit.

Satan The Devil.

satchel (satchels) A bag which hangs from the shoulder for carrying books.

satellite (satellites) 1. A small planet which moves in orbit round a larger one. 2. A man-made object travelling in orbit round a planet.

satin A material with a silky, shiny front side and a dull back.

satire A piece of writing which ridicules someone or something. satirical, satirist.

satisfactory Adequate, good enough. satisfactorily.

satisfy (satisfies, satisfying, satisfied) 1. To make someone pleased or contented. 2. To be enough for someone's needs. 3. To convince someone, to get rid of his doubts. satisfaction.

saturate (saturates, saturating, saturated) To soak thoroughly. saturation.

Saturday (Saturdays) The last day of the week.

sauce 1. (sauces) A liquid flavouring for food. *Tomato sauce.* 2. (informal) Cheek, impertinence.

saucepan (saucepans) A metal cooking pan with a lid and a handle.

saucer (saucers) A small curved dish on which a cup is put.

saucy (saucier, sauciest) Cheeky, cheerfully rude. saucily, sauciness.

sauna bath A kind of steam bath.

saunter (saunters, sauntering, sauntered) To walk in a leisurely way.

sausage (sausages) Minced meat and other ingredients enclosed in a tube of skin. sausage-meat.

savage[1] Fierce, cruel. savagely, savagery.

savage[2] (savages) A member of a primitive tribe.

save (saves, saving, saved) 1. To make somebody or something safe, to keep somebody or something safe. 2. To keep money or things for use later. 3. To avoid wasting something. *You would save much time if you put things tidily away.* 4. To prevent a ball going into the goal. saver.

savings Money saved up. *A savings bank*.

saviour (saviours) A person who saves or rescues somebody or something.

savour Taste, flavour.

savoury Tasty but not sweet.

saw[1] *See* see.

saw[2] (saws) A cutting tool with a zigzag edge.

saw[3] (saws, sawing, sawed) To cut with a saw.

sawdust Wood dust produced when sawing.

saxophone (saxophones) A kind of wind instrument.

say (says, saying, said) 1. To produce words with the voice, to speak. 2. To give an opinion.

saying (sayings) A well-known remark, a proverb.

scab (scabs) A dry crust which forms over a wound or sore.

scabbard (scabbards) A sheath for a sword or dagger.

scaffold (scaffolds) A platform on which a criminal is executed.

scaffolding A structure of poles and planks for workmen to stand on.

scald (scalds, scalding, scalded) 1. To injure with hot liquid or steam. 2. To clean something with boiling water.

scale[1] (scales) 1. The series of marks used for measuring on a ruler, thermometer, or similar instrument. 2. A system of units for measuring. *The centigrade scale.* 3. A series of musical notes going up or down one step at a time. 4. Proportion, relative size. *The scale of the map is one centimetre to the kilometre*, one centimetre on the map represents one kilometre on the ground. 5. Size. *On a large scale*.

scale[2] (scales, scaling, scaled) To climb.

scale[3] (scales) One of the thin flakes covering the skin of fish and other creatures. **scaly**.

scales An instrument for weighing. *A pair of scales*.

scallywag (scallywags) A rascal.

scalp[1] (scalps) The skin on the top of the head where the hair grows.

scalp[2] (scalps, scalping, scalped) To cut off someone's scalp.

scalpel (scalpels) A surgeon's knife.

scamp (scamps) A rascal.

scamper (scampers, scampering, scampered) To run quickly like a frightened animal.

scampi A kind of sea food like large shrimps.

scan (scans, scanning, scanned) To look carefully at all parts of a thing.

scandal (scandals) 1. A shameful or disgraceful action. 2. Unkind gossip, talk that hurts someone's reputation. **scandalous, scandalously**.

Scandinavian Of Scandinavia, of Norway, Sweden, Finland, or Denmark.

scanty (scantier, scantiest) Barely enough, small. **scantily, scantiness**.

scapegoat (scapegoats) A person blamed for somebody else's wrongdoing.

scar[1] (scars) A mark that remains after injury or damage.

scar[2] (scars, scarring, scarred) To mark with a scar.

scarce (scarcer, scarcest) Rare, in short supply. **scarcity**.

scarcely Hardly, barely.

scare (scares, scaring, scared) To frighten.

scarecrow (scarecrows) A figure dressed in old clothes and set up in a field to scare birds off the crops.

scarf (scarves) A strip of material worn wrapped round the neck.

scarlet Bright red.

scarlet fever An infectious disease with a rash.

scathing Harsh and critical.

scatter (scatters, scattering, scattered) 1. To throw things in various directions, to distribute things in various places. 2. To move in various directions.

scavenger (scavengers) An animal or bird that feeds on refuse or dead creatures.

scene (scenes) 1. The place where something happens. 2. An exciting, noisy, or quarrelsome happening. 3. Part of a play or film. 4. A view.

scenery 1. A view of the countryside. 2. Things used to set a scene on a stage.

scent¹ (scents) 1. Smell. 2. A liquid with a beautiful smell, a perfume.

scent² (scents, scenting, scented) 1. To smell. 2. To give something a beautiful smell.

sceptical Not ready to believe things. sceptically, scepticism.

schedule (schedules) A timetable, a list of details.

scheme¹ (schemes) A plan.

scheme² (schemes, scheming, schemed) To make plans, to plot.

scholar (scholars) 1. A pupil. 2. A person who studies a great deal.

scholarship (scholarships) An award made to someone to help to pay his school or college fees.

school¹ (schools) 1. A place where children are educated. 2. All the children who attend a particular school. 3. The time during which children are being taught at school. *School begins at 9 o'clock.* schoolchild (schoolchildren), schoolboy, schoolgirl, schoolteacher, schoolmaster, schoolmistress.

school² (schools) A large number of whales or fish swimming together.

schooner (schooners) A kind of sailing ship.

science (sciences) 1. Knowledge which has been collected and arranged by people who observe things carefully and make experiments. 2. A particular branch of science such as biology or astronomy. scientist, scientific, scientifically.

science fiction Stories about space travel or other exciting scientific developments.

scissors A cutting instrument with two hinged blades. *A pair of scissors.*

scoff (scoffs, scoffing, scoffed) To mock or jeer at something.

scold (scolds, scolding, scolded) To blame somebody crossly, to find fault noisily.

scone (scones) A small bun.

scoop¹ (scoops) 1. A kind of shovel. *A coal scoop.* 2. A scooping movement.

scoop² (scoops, scooping, scooped) 1. To move something with a scoop. 2. To make a hole with a scoop or some other instrument.

scooter (scooters) 1. A child's toy with two wheels and a platform for the feet. 2. A kind of small motor cycle.

scope The opportunity or ability to do something.

scorch (scorches, scorching, scorched) To darken the surface of something by burning or heating it.

score¹ (scores) 1. The number of points made in a game. score-board, score-card. 2. Twenty.

score² (scores, scoring, scored) 1. To make a score. 2. To keep a record of a score. scorer. 3. To scratch the surface of something.

scorn¹ (scorns, scorning, scorned) 1. To treat something as worthless. 2. To ridicule somebody.

scorn² Despising or ridiculing someone or something. scornful, scornfully.

scorpion (scorpions) A kind of spider with a dangerous sting in the tail.

Scot (Scots) A person from Scotland.

Scotch or Scottish Of Scotland.

scoundrel (scoundrels) A wicked person.

scour (scours, scouring, scoured) 1. To rub a thing clean and bright. *To scour out a saucepan.* 2. To search every part of a place thoroughly for somebody or something.

scourge (scourges) 1. A heavy whip. 2. Something that causes severe suffering.

scout[1] (scouts) 1. A soldier sent out to get information about the enemy. 2. *A Scout,* a member of the Scout Association, an organization for boys founded by Baden-Powell.

scout[2] (scouts, scouting, scouted) To act as a scout.

scowl (scowls, scowling, scowled) To have a bad-tempered look on one's face.

scraggy Thin and bony.

scram (informal) Go away!

scramble[1] (scrambles, scrambling, scrambled) 1. To climb or crawl awkwardly. 2. To struggle with others who all want the same thing. 3. *Scrambled eggs,* eggs beaten with milk and cooked.

scramble[2] (scrambles) 1. The action of scrambling. 2. A motor-cycle race over rough country.

scrap[1] Rubbish, waste. *Scrap metal.*

scrap[2] (scraps) 1. A small piece of something. scrappy. 2. (informal) A fight.

scrap[3] (scraps, scrapping, scrapped) 1. To throw away useless things. 2. (informal) To fight.

scrap-book (scrap-books) A book with blank pages on which pictures, newspaper cuttings, and so on may be stuck.

scrape[1] (scrapes, scraping, scraped) 1. To rub with something hard or sharp. *I scraped the saucepan clean.* 2. To injure or damage something by scraping. *The gate-post scraped the car.* 3. To manage with difficulty to do something. *I scraped into the first team this week.* 4. *To scrape things together,* to collect them together with difficulty.

scrape[2] (scrapes) 1. The act or sound of scraping. 2. A place which has been scraped. 3. An awkward or dangerous situation.

scratch[1] (scratches, scratching, scratched) 1. To damage a surface with something sharp. 2. To rub one's skin to stop itching.

scratch[2] (scratches) 1. A mark or injury caused by scratching. 2. The act or sound of scratching. scratchy.

scratch[3] Hurriedly put together. *A scratch team.*

scrawl (scrawls, scrawling, scrawled) To write hurriedly and untidily.

scream[1] (screams) A loud, sharp cry or sound.

scream[2] (screams, screaming, screamed) To give a loud, sharp cry or sound.

scree Loose stones covering a mountain side.

screech (screeches, screeching, screeched) To make a harsh, piercing sound.

screen[1] (screens) 1. A framework covered with material used to protect people from draughts or heat, or to hide something from view. *A fire screen.* 2. Anything which gives shelter or protection. *A smoke screen.* 3. A smooth surface on which films or slides may be projected.

screen[2] (screens, screening, screened) 1. To shelter, to protect, to hide from view. 2. To project pictures on a screen.

screw[1] (screws) 1. A device like a nail with a spiral thread cut into it. 2. A twist, a turn. 3. A propeller.

screw[2] (screws, screwing, screwed) 1. To use a screw to fix something. 2. To twist.

screw-driver (screw-drivers) A tool for turning a screw.

scribble (scribbles, scribbling, scribbled) 1. To write hurriedly and carelessly. 2. To make meaningless marks with a pen or pencil.

script (scripts) The words of a play or a broadcast. script-writer.

scripture 1. *Holy Scripture,* the Bible. 2. The study of the Bible in schools.

scroll (scrolls) A roll of paper or parchment.

scrounge (scrounges, scrounging, scrounged) (informal) To get things one wants without paying for them. scrounger.

scrub (scrubs, scrubbing, scrubbed) To wash briskly with a stiff brush. **scrubbing-brush.**

scruffy (informal) Dirty, untidy.

scrum (scrums) A knot of players struggling for the ball in Rugby football.

scruple (scruples) Hesitation about whether it is right to do something.

scrupulous Careful, very attentive to small details. **scrupulously.**

scrutiny Thorough examination of something.

scuffle (scuffles, scuffling, scuffled) To have a rough and confused struggle.

scull (sculls) A kind of oar.

scullery (sculleries) A small room where the washing-up is done.

sculptor (sculptors) An artist who makes representations of things in stone, wood, or other materials.

sculpture The work of a sculptor.

scum Dirty-looking froth floating on a liquid. **scummy.**

scurvy A disease caused by lack of fresh fruit and vegetables.

scuttle (scuttles, scuttling, scuttled) 1. To sink one's own ship deliberately. 2. To run with short steps.

scythe (scythes) A tool with a long curved blade for cutting grass or corn.

sea (seas) 1. The salt water which covers most of the earth's surface. 2. A particular part of the sea, a large expanse of water. 3. A large area of something. *A sea of mud.*

seafaring Travelling on the sea. **seafarer.**

sea-going Suitable for crossing the sea. *A sea-going ship.*

sea-gull (sea-gulls) A sea bird.

seal¹ (seals) A sea animal often hunted for its fur. **sealskin.**

seal² (seals) 1. A design stamped on wax, lead, or other material to show that a thing is genuine. 2. A device for stamping a seal.

seal³ (seals, sealing, sealed) 1. To put a seal on something. 2. To close something and fasten it firmly. 3. To make a thing airtight.

sealing-wax A coloured wax used for sealing letters or parcels.

sea-lion (sea-lions) A sea animal, a kind of large seal.

seam (seams) 1. A line where two pieces of material are sewn together. 2. A layer of coal underground.

seaman (seamen) A sailor.

seamanship The skill needed to sail a ship.

seaplane (seaplanes) An aeroplane designed to land on water.

search¹ (searches, searching, searched) 1. To look carefully for something. 2. To examine a person or a place thoroughly in order to find something.

search² (searches) The act of searching.

searchlight (searchlights) A powerful spotlight for use out of doors.

search-warrant (search-warrants) An official document allowing the police to search a building.

seashell (seashells) The empty shell of a shellfish.

sea-shore The land at the edge of the sea.

sea-sick Sick because of the movement of a ship. **sea-sickness.**

seaside A place by the sea where people go for holidays.

season (seasons) 1. One of the four divisions of the year, namely spring, summer, autumn, and winter. 2. Any period during the year. *The cricket season.* 3. *A season ticket,* a ticket that can be used on several occasions during a certain period. **seasonal.**

seasoning Salt, pepper, and other things used for flavouring.

seat[1] (seats) Something for sitting on. *To take a seat*, to sit down.

seat[2] (seats, seating, seated) 1. *To seat oneself*, to sit. 2. To have seats for a certain number of people. *The coach seats 48 people.*

seaweed Plants which grow in the sea.

seaworthy In a suitable condition for a sea voyage. seaworthiness.

secateurs Clippers used for pruning. *A pair of secateurs.*

secluded Quiet, away from others.

second[1] 1. Next after the first. secondly. 2. Another like the first. 3. *Second-rate*, not of the highest quality.

second[2] (seconds) 1. A unit of time. Sixty seconds make one minute. 2. A moment.

second[3] (seconds) A helper for a fighter in a boxing-match or a duel.

second[4] (seconds, seconding, seconded) To support somebody in a fight or a debate.

secondary Coming second. *A secondary school*, a school for older children.

second-hand Not new, having already been owned by someone else.

secret[1] 1. Not to be made known. *Secret information.* 2. Hidden, not generally known. *A secret garden.* 3. *A secret agent*, a spy. secretly, secrecy.

secret[2] (secrets) 1. Something which is secret. 2. *In secret*, secretly.

secretary (secretaries) A person whose job is to write letters, to look after papers, and to make business arrangements for another person, or for some organization. secretarial.

secretive In the habit of keeping things secret.

section (sections) A part or division of something.

sector (sectors) A part of a town, country, or area.

secure[1] (securer, securest) 1. Safe, not in danger. 2. Firmly fixed. securely, security.

secure[2] (secures, securing, secured) To make a thing secure.

sedate Calm, serious. sedately.

sedative (sedatives) A drug intended to make a person calm or sleepy. sedation.

sediment Solid matter which settles at the bottom of a liquid.

seductive Irresistibly attractive. seductively.

see (sees, seeing, saw, seen) 1. To use the eyes in order to recognize or get to know things. 2. To understand. *Do you see what I mean?* 3. To experience something. *The old man had seen five reigns.* 4. To visit somebody, to meet somebody, to have an interview with him. *Come up and see me some time.* 5. To accompany. *You must let me see you home.* 6. To imagine. *I can't see myself living on the moon.* 7. *To see to something*, to attend to it. 8. *To see something through*, not to give it up until it is finished.

seed (seeds) A small part of a plant which can be sown to produce new plants.

seedling (seedlings) A young plant.

seedy (seedier, seediest) 1. Shabby. 2. (informal) Unwell.

seek (seeks, seeking, sought) To try to find something or somebody.

seem (seems, seeming, seemed) To give the impression of being, to appear to be. *You seem depressed.*

seen *See* see.

seep (seeps, seeping, seeped) To trickle, to ooze.

see-saw (see-saws) A plank balanced in the middle on which children can play by making the ends move up and down.

seethe (seethes, seething, seethed) To boil, to be agitated.

segregate (segregates, segregating, segregated) To cut off from other things or people. segregation.

seize (seizes, seizing, seized) 1. To take hold of something eagerly or violently. 2. *To seize up*, to become jammed. seizure.

seldom Rarely, not often.

select[1] (selects, selecting, selected) To choose. selective, selectively, selection, selector.

select[2] Carefully chosen. *A select group of friends.*

self(selves) A person's own nature or desires.

self-confident Believing in one's own ability to do things. **self-confidence.**

self-conscious Awkward in behaviour through thinking too much of the impression one is making on other people. **self-consciously, self-consciousness.**

self-control The ability to control one's own behaviour.

self-defence Defending oneself.

self-explanatory Not needing any explanation.

self-important Having too high an opinion of one's own importance.

selfish Not concerned about others, wanting things only for oneself. **selfishly, selfishness.**

self-portrait (self-portraits) An artist's portrait of himself.

self-possessed Calm, confident.

self-preservation The desire to stay alive and safe.

self-raising flour Flour which will make cakes rise during cooking.

self-respect A feeling of respect for oneself.

self-righteous Thinking too much of one's own good qualities. **self-righteously, self-righteousness.**

selfsame The very same.

self-satisfied Having too high an opinion of oneself. **self-satisfaction.**

self-service Having an arrangement for customers to serve themselves. *A self-service cafeteria.*

sell(sells, selling, sold) To hand over goods or property in exchange for money.

semaphore A kind of signalling using arms.

semibreve(semibreves) A note in music. It is written **o** .

semicircle (semicircles) A half circle. **semicircular.**

semicolon (semicolons) The punctuation mark *;* .

semi-detached house A house joined to one other house of similar design.

semi-final (semi-finals) A match played to decide who shall take part in the final.

semiquaver (semiquavers) A note in music. It is written ♪ .

semolina Hard round grains of wheat, used to make milk puddings.

send(sends, sending, sent) 1.To cause somebody or something to move somewhere. 2.*To send for somebody*, to ask him to come.

senile Sick and feeble because of being very old.

senior 1. Older. 2. More important in rank. **seniority.**

sensation (sensations) 1. Feeling. *A warm sensation.* 2. A very exciting happening. **sensational, sensationally.**

sense[1] (senses) 1. Any of the five ways by which a person can be aware of things, namely sight, hearing, smell, taste, and touch. 2. A feeling, an awareness. *A sense of humour.* 3.The power to think and make wise decisions. *If you have any sense you will go home before the rain starts.* 4. *Common sense*, the kind of sensible thinking to be expected of a normal person. 5.Meaning. *That doesn't make sense.* 6.*To be out of one's senses*, to be mad.

sense[2] (senses, sensing, sensed) To be vaguely aware of something. *We sensed that a storm was brewing.*

senseless 1. Foolish, pointless. 2. Unconscious. **senselessly, senselessness.**

sensible 1.Wise, able to make good decisions. 2. Practical, useful. *Sensible clothes.* **sensibly.**

sensitive 1. Easily hurt, delicate. *A sensitive skin.* 2. *To be sensitive to something*, to be quick to react to it. **sensitively, sensitivity.**

sent *See* send.

sentence[1] (sentences) 1. A group of words beginning with a capital letter and ending with a full stop or a question mark or an exclamation mark. 2. A punishment given to a criminal in a lawcourt.

sentence[2] (sentences, sentencing, sentenced) To announce a sentence in a lawcourt.

sentiment (sentiments) A thought or feeling.

sentimental 1. Showing one's feelings too easily, too soft-hearted. 2. Liable to make people sentimental. *A sentimental story.* sentimentally, sentimentality.

sentinel (sentinels) A sentry.

sentry (sentries) A soldier on guard.

sentry-box (sentry-boxes) A small shelter for a sentry.

separate[1] Divided from others, not joined to others. separately.

separate[2] (separates, separating, separated) 1. To make separate. 2. To become separate. separation.

September The ninth month of the year.

septic Infected, poisoned. *A septic wound.*

sequel (sequels) 1. Something that follows as a result of something else. 2. A book which continues the story of an earlier book.

sequence (sequences) A row of things or a number of events which follow one another in a particular order.

sequin (sequins) A tiny disc sewn on clothes to make them glitter.

serene Clear and peaceful, calm. serenely, serenity.

sergeant (sergeants) A rank in the army or police force.

serial (serials) A story told or presented in several episodes.

series (series) 1. A sequence. 2. A sequence of broadcasts. *A new television series.*

serious 1. Solemn. *A serious face.* 2. Very bad, severe. *A serious disaster.* 3. Keen and careful. *A serious worker.* seriously, seriousness.

sermon (sermons) A talk given by a preacher.

serpent (serpents) A snake.

servant (servants) 1. A person employed to do housework. 2. A person who serves others.

serve (serves, serving, served) 1. To do a particular job, to do one's duty. *To serve in the army.* 2. To place food on the table ready for a meal, to give food to someone at a meal. 3. To look after the needs of customers in a shop. 4. In tennis, to set the ball in play by hitting it towards the court beyond the net. 5. *It serves him right*, he deserves it. server.

service[1] (services) 1. Doing one's duty, working for others, acting as a servant. 2. *The Services*, the army, navy, and air force. 3. An arrangement to provide something regularly for people to use if they wish. *A bus service.* 4. A gathering for the worship of God. *A church service.* 5. A complete set of crockery for use at table. *A dinner service.* 6. Serving the ball in a game of tennis. 7. The servicing of a car or other machine.

service[2] (services, servicing, serviced) To examine a car or other machine and put it into good working order.

serviceable Useful, hard-wearing.

serviette (serviettes) A table-napkin.

session (sessions) A time spent at a particular activity.

set[1] (sets, setting, set) 1. To put, to lay, to arrange, to fix, to establish. 2. To become stiff or hard. *Put the jelly in a cool place to set.* 3. To go down below the horizon. *The sun sets.* 4. *To set about something*, to start doing it. 5. *To set off, to set out*, to begin a journey. 6. *To set something off*, to start it, to make it explode. 7. *To set upon someone*, to attack him. 8. *To set fire to something*, to cause it to start burning. 9. *To set sail*, to begin a voyage.

set[2] (sets) 1. A group of people or things of a similar kind. 2. A group of things that go together. *A train set.* 3. An apparatus for receiving radio or television programmes. 4. The scenery on a stage.

set-back (set-backs) Something which checks or hinders progress.

set-square (set-squares) A geometrical instrument in the shape of a triangle with one of the angles a right angle.

settee (settees) A kind of sofa.

settle (settles, settling, settled) 1. To go and live somewhere. 2. To rest somewhere for a time. 3. To make somebody or something steady or comfortable. 4. To become steady or comfortable. 5. To decide, to agree. *To settle a problem.* 6. To pay a bill. *To settle a debt.* settler, settlement.

set-up (set-ups) (informal) An arrangement, the organization of something.

seven (sevens) The number 7. seventh.

seventeen The number 17. seventeenth.

seventy (seventies) The number 70. seventieth.

sever (severs, severing, severed) To cut, to break.

several Three or more but not very many.

severe 1. Strict. *A severe father.* 2. Serious, violent. *A severe storm.* severely, severity.

sew (sews, sewing, sewed, sewn) To work with a needle and thread. sewing-machine.

sewage Waste liquid carried away in drains.

sewer (sewers) A drain for sewage.

sex 1. (sexes) Being male or female. *Can you tell the sex of my kitten?* 2. The instinct which causes male and female to be attracted to each other. sexual.

sextant (sextants) An instrument used in navigation.

sexy (informal) 1. Attractive to people of the opposite sex. 2. Much concerned with sex.

shabby (shabbier, shabbiest) 1. Nearly worn out. 2. Mean, unfair. *A shabby trick.* shabbily, shabbiness.

shack (shacks) A roughly-made hut.

shackles Fetters, chains.

shade¹ (shades) 1. An area sheltered from bright light. 2. Something that shuts out bright light, something that makes light less bright. 3. A colour, the quality or depth of a colour. *John has painted his door a nice shade of blue.* 4. A slight difference. *This word has several shades of meaning.*

shade² (shades, shading, shaded) 1. To keep strong light away from something. 2. To provide a shade for a light or lamp. 3. To make parts of a picture darker with many pencil or crayon marks.

shadow¹ (shadows) 1. An area of shade. 2. The dark shape that appears on the ground or on a wall when an object is between it and a light. shadowy.

shadow² (shadows, shadowing, shadowed) 1. To darken. 2. To follow someone secretly.

shady (shadier, shadiest) 1. Giving shade. 2. Situated in shade. 3. (informal) Not to be trusted. *A shady character.*

shaft (shafts) 1. A long, thin rod or pole. 2. A long, narrow space going straight up and down. *A lift-shaft.* 3. A ray of light.

shaggy (shaggier, shaggiest) Rough and hairy. shagginess.

shake¹ (shakes, shaking, shook, shaken) 1. To move something to and fro or up and down. *To shake hands.* 2. To tremble. *We were shaking with cold.* 3. To shock, to trouble severely. *They were shaken by the bad news.*

shake² (shakes) An act of shaking. shaky, shakily, shakiness.

shall A word used in sentences which refer to the future. *We shall arrive at tea-time tomorrow.*

shallow (shallower, shallowest) Not deep.

sham (shams, shamming, shammed) To pretend.

shamble (shambles, shambling, shambled) To walk in a tired and awkward way.

shambles A place of bloodshed or confusion.

shame 1. A guilty feeling caused by something foolish, awkward, or wrong. 2. Something to be regretted. *What a shame to cut down those trees!* shameful, shamefully, shameless, shamelessly.

shampoo (shampoos) A kind of soap for washing hair.

shamrock (shamrocks) A plant like clover.

shandy (shandies) A mixture of beer and lemonade or other soft drink.

shan't (informal) Shall not.

shanty (shanties) 1. A roughly-made hut. 2. A sailors' song.

shape¹ (shapes) The outline of something, its form. *Balls are round in shape.* shapeless.

shape² (shapes, shaping, shaped) To make something into a particular shape.

shapely (shapelier, shapeliest) Attractive in shape. shapeliness.

share¹ (shares) One of the parts into which something is divided among several people or things.

share² (shares, sharing, shared) 1. To divide something, to give part of it to others. 2. To use something which other people also use.

shark (sharks) A large fierce sea-fish.

sharp¹ (sharper, sharpest) 1. Having a thin cutting edge or piercing point. 2. Clever, bright. 3. Tasting slightly sour. 4. Sudden, severe. *A sharp bend.* 5. *To sing sharp*, to sing above the proper note. 6. *At six sharp*, at six o'clock exactly. sharply, sharpness.

sharp² (sharps) The sign ♯ in music.

sharpen (sharpens, sharpening, sharpened) To make something become sharp.

shatter (shatters, shattering, shattered) To break suddenly and violently in pieces.

shave (shaves, shaving, shaved) 1. To make the skin smooth by cutting off the hairs with a razor. shaver, shaving-brush. 2. To cut a thin slice off something.

shavings Thin curling slices shaved off wood.

shawl (shawls) A piece of cloth worn round the shoulders or wrapped round a baby.

she (her, herself) The female person or animal being talked about.

sheaf (sheaves) A bundle of corn stalks tied together after reaping.

shear (shears, shearing, sheared, shorn) 1. To cut the wool off a sheep. 2. To cut with shears or some other sharp tool.

shears A cutting tool like a large pair of scissors. *A pair of shears.*

sheath (sheathes) 1. A case for the blade of a sword or dagger. 2. Any similar close-fitting cover.

sheathe (sheathes, sheathing, sheathed) To put something into a sheath.

shed¹ (sheds) A small building used for storing things or for housing animals.

shed² (sheds, shedding, shed) To let something fall or flow.

sheen A shine on the surface of something.

sheep (sheep) An animal bred for wool and meat.

sheepdog (sheepdogs) A dog trained to help a shepherd look after sheep.

sheepish Shy and embarrassed. sheepishly.

sheer 1. Complete. *Sheer nonsense.* 2. Straight up and down. *A sheer precipice.*

sheet (sheets) 1. One of the pieces of smooth cloth between which a person sleeps in bed. 2. A flat, thin piece of something. *A sheet of paper.* 3. A flat area of something. *A sheet of water.*

sheikh (sheikhs) An Arab chieftain.

shelf (shelves) 1. A length of board attached to a wall or fitted in a piece of furniture so that things may be placed on it. 2. A flat, level surface that sticks out like a shelf.

shell[1] (shells) 1. A hard outer covering. Eggs, nuts, snails, crabs, and tortoises have shells. 2. The outer walls of a building. *After the fire only the shell of the building remained.* 3. A large hollow bullet filled with explosive.

shell[2] (shells, shelling, shelled) 1. To take something out of its shell. 2. To fire shells at something.

shellfish (shellfish) A sea animal with a shell.

shelter[1] (shelters) 1. Protection. 2. A small building that gives protection.

shelter[2] (shelters, sheltering, sheltered) To protect, or cover, or hide somebody or something.

shelve (shelves, shelving, shelved) 1. To put something on a shelf. 2. To slope.

shepherd (shepherds) A person who looks after sheep. shepherdess.

sheriff (sheriffs) A law officer.

sherry (sherries) A kind of wine.

shield[1] (shields) 1. A piece of armour carried to protect the body. 2. A protection.

shield[2] (shields, shielding, shielded) To guard, to protect.

shift[1] (shifts, shifting, shifted) To move.

shift[2] (shifts) 1. A change of position. 2. A group of workers who work together during a particular period of the day or the night.

shifty (shiftier, shiftiest) Tricky, deceitful. shiftily, shiftiness.

shilling (shillings) A former British coin. Twenty shillings equalled one pound.

shin (shins) The front of the leg below the knee.

shine (shines, shining, shone) To be bright, to give out light.

shingle Pebbles on the beach.

shiny (shinier, shinest) Shining, polished.

ship[1] (ships) A large boat, a sea-going vessel.

ship[2] (ships, shipping, shipped) To send something by ship.

shipping Ships.

shipshape Tidy, in good order.

shipwreck (shipwrecks) The wreck of a ship.

shipyard (shipyards) A place where ships are built.

shirt (shirts) A thin garment worn on the upper part of the body.

shiver (shivers, shivering, shivered) To tremble with cold or fear. shivery.

shoal (shoals) A large number of fish swimming together.

shock[1] (shocks) 1. A sudden unpleasant surprise. 2. A violent knock or jolt. 3. The pain caused by electricity passing through a person's body.

shock[2] (shocks, shocking, shocked) 1. To give someone a shock. 2. To fill someone with disgust. shockingly.

shoddy (shoddier, shoddiest) Of poor quality.

shoe (shoes) 1. An outer covering worn on the foot. shoelace, shoemaker. 2. A U-shaped piece of iron nailed to a horse's hoof.

shone *See* shine.

shook *See* shake[1].

shoot[1] (shoots, shooting, shot) 1. To fire a bullet or shell from a gun, to send off any kind of missile. 2. To wound or kill by shooting. 3. To move very quickly. 4. To grow quickly. 5. To take a photograph, to film. 6. To kick or hit the ball at the goal in football and other games.

shoot[2] (shoots) The young tip of a growing plant.

shooting star A heavenly body seen moving quickly across the sky.

shop[1] (shops) 1. A building where goods are sold to the public. shopkeeper. 2. A workshop.

shop[2] (shops, shopping, shopped) To go to buy things in a shop. shopper.

shoplifter (shoplifters) A person who steals things from a shop while pretending to be a customer. shoplifting.

shore (shores) The land at the edge of the sea or of a lake.

shorn *See* shear.

short (shorter, shortest) 1. Measuring a small distance, not long. *A short walk*. 2. Not tall. *A short person*. 3. Not lasting very long. *A short visit*. 4. Less than the amount or number or distance required. *Our team was two players short*. 5. Bad-tempered. *Your mother was a bit short this morning*. 6. Abruptly, suddenly. *He stopped short*.

shortage (shortages) A scarcity, a lack of sufficient supplies.

shortbread or shortcake A kind of rich, sweet biscuit.

shortcoming (shortcomings) A fault, a failure.

shorten (shortens, shortening, shortened) 1. To make a thing shorter. 2. To become shorter.

shorthand A way of writing very quickly by using special signs.

shorthanded Short of helpers or workers.

shortly 1. Soon. 2. Briefly.

shorts Short trousers.

short-sighted Unable to see distant objects clearly.

short-tempered Easily made angry.

shot¹ *See* shoot¹.

shot² (shots) 1. The firing of a gun. 2. Something fired from a gun. 3. *He is a good shot*, he is an expert in shooting. 4. A photograph or film scene taken from a particular place. 5. An attempt to do something.

shotgun (shotguns) A gun that fires many small lead balls.

should Ought to.

shouldn't (informal) Should not.

shoulder (shoulders) The part of a body where an arm or front leg joins the trunk.

shoulder-blade (shoulder-blades) A flat bone towards the top of the back.

shout¹ (shouts) A loud cry.

shout² (shouts, shouting, shouted) To speak very loudly, to cry out.

shove (shoves, shoving, shoved) To push.

shovel¹ (shovels) A tool like a spade. *A coal shovel*. shovelful.

shovel² (shovels, shovelling, shovelled) To use a shovel.

show¹ (shows, showing, showed, shown) 1. To allow something to be seen, to bring it into view, to point it out. 2. To appear, to be visible. *The damage won't show*. 3. To guide somebody somewhere. *Show him in*. 4. To make something clear. *This book will show you how to do it*. 5. *To show off*, to try to impress other people.

show² (shows) 1. A showing of something. 2. An exhibition, a display. 3. An entertainment.

shower¹ (showers) 1. A brief fall of rain or snow. showery. 2. Water falling like rain. *A shower-bath*. 3. A number of things coming down together.

shower² (showers, showering, showered) 1. To come down in a shower. 2. To send things down in a shower.

show-jumping A display of skilled riding in which horses have to jump over fences and other obstacles. show-jumper.

showy (showier, showiest) Likely to catch the attention, bright, gaudy. showily.

shrank *See* shrink.

shrapnel Pieces of metal scattered from an exploded shell.

shred[1] (shreds, shredding, shredded) To cut or tear into thin strips.

shred[2] (shreds) A thin strip.

shrew (shrews) A small mouse-like animal.

shrewd (shrewder, shrewdest) Wise, clever. shrewdly, shrewdness.

shriek[1] (shrieks, shrieking, shrieked) To scream.

shriek[2] (shrieks) A scream.

shrill (shriller, shrillest) Making a high, piercing sound. shrilly, shrillness.

shrimp (shrimps) A small shellfish.

shrink (shrinks, shrinking, shrank, shrunk, shrunken) 1. To become smaller. 2. To make a thing smaller. 3. To move back because of fear or embarrassment. shrinkage.

shrivel (shrivels, shrivelling, shrivelled) 1. To become dry and wrinkled. 2. To make something become dry and wrinkled.

shroud (shrouds, shrouding, shrouded) To cover, to hide.

shrub (shrubs) A bush, a plant like a small tree.

shrubbery (shrubberies) Part of a garden where shrubs grow.

shrug (shrugs, shrugging, shrugged) To lift the shoulders slightly.

shrunk, shrunken *See* shrink.

shudder (shudders, shuddering, shuddered) To shake.

shuffle (shuffles, shuffling, shuffled) 1. To walk without raising the feet properly. 2. To mix a pack of playing-cards before dealing them.

shunt (shunts, shunting, shunted) To move railway wagons from one track to another. shunter.

shut (shuts, shutting, shut) 1. To close something, to put the cover on something, to fill a gap with something. *Please shut the door.*

2. To become closed. *The door shut behind him.* 3. (informal) *To shut up,* to stop talking.

shutter (shutters) 1. A panel or screen which can be closed over a window. 2. A device for opening and closing the aperture in a camera.

shy (shyer, shyest) 1. Reluctant to meet other people. 2. Easily frightened. shyly, shyness.

sick 1. *To be sick,* to throw up food through the mouth. 2. Unwell, ill. 3. *Sick of,* tired of. sickness.

sicken (sickens, sickening, sickened) 1. To become ill. 2. To disgust.

sickly (sicklier, sickliest) Weak, pale, unhealthy.

side (sides) 1. One of the flat, or fairly flat, surfaces of something such as a box, a sheet of paper, or a hill. 2. An edge of something, an area near an edge. 3. One of the two sides of somebody or something which is not the front or the back. *The cars were parked side by side.* 4. One of two opposing teams of players.

sideboard (sideboards) A piece of dining-room furniture with drawers and cupboards.

side-car (side-cars) A small vehicle with one wheel, fixed beside a motor cycle.

sidelights Small lights at the front of a motor vehicle.

side-show (side-shows) An entertainment at a fair.

sideways 1. Towards the side. 2. From the side. 3. Edge first.

siding (sidings) A short length of railway track by the side of a main line.

siege (sieges) The besieging of a castle or a town.

sieve (sieves) A stiff network of wire or plastic set in a round frame.

sift (sifts, sifting, sifted) To shake through a sieve.

sigh[1] (sighs) A sad sound made by breathing out.

sigh[2] (sighs, sighing, sighed) To give a sigh.

sight¹ (sights) 1. The ability to see. *The sense of sight.* sightless. 2. The quality of a thing which can be seen. *The sight of blood makes Alan feel sick.* 3. An object or a view interesting or remarkable to see. sightseer, sightseeing. 4. The device on a gun used to aim it at something.

sight² (sights, sighting, sighted) To see something, to observe it.

sign¹ (signs) 1. A board which conveys information quickly by means of words, or a picture, or a design. *A road sign.* 2. A mark or object used to convey a meaning. 3. A gesture. 4. An indication. *A red sky at night is supposed to be a sign of good weather.*

sign² (signs, signing, signed) 1. To make a sign. 2. To write one's signature.

signal¹ (signals) 1. A sign. 2. A set of lights or a sign used to give instructions to train-drivers.

signal² (signals, signalling, signalled) To show something by means of a signal. signaller.

signal-box (signal-boxes) A building from which railway signals are controlled.

signalman (signalmen) A man who controls railway signals.

signature (signatures) A person's name written by himself in his normal handwriting.

signature tune A piece of music played at the beginning or end of a regular broadcast.

significance Importance, special meaning. significant, significantly.

signpost (signposts) A sign at a road junction showing directions and distances to places.

silencer (silencers) A device for making an engine or gun quieter.

silent Not talking, not making a sound, without sound. silently, silence.

silk A kind of fine thread used to make a smooth, delicate fabric. silky.

silkworm (silkworms) A kind of caterpillar which produces silk.

sill (sills) The shelf along the bottom of a window.

silly (sillier, silliest) Foolish, thoughtless. silliness.

silver 1. A valuable shiny white metal. silvery. 2. Coins made of silver-coloured metal.

silver-plated Covered with a thin coating of silver.

similar Of the same sort, alike.

similarity (similarities) A resemblance, a likeness.

similarly In the same way.

simmer (simmers, simmering, simmered) To keep a liquid just at boiling point.

simple (simpler, simplest) Plain, easy, not complicated. simply, simplicity.

simplify (simplifies, simplifying, simplified) To make a thing simpler.

simultaneous Taking place at the same time. simultaneously.

sin¹ (sins) The breaking of God's laws, the doing of something known to be wrong.

sin² (sins, sinning, sinned) To commit a sin, to do wrong.

since 1. After the time when. *I have not seen her since she married.* 2. Because. *Since I have no licence, I must not drive.*

sincere (sincerer, sincerest) Genuine, true, honest. sincerely, sincerity.

sinewy Strong, muscular.

sinful Wicked, wrong. sinfully, sinfulness.

sing (sings, singing, sang, sung) 1. To make music with the voice. 2. To make a pleasant continuous noise.

singe (singes, singeing, singed) To burn something slightly.

single 1. One only. singly. 2. Not married. 3. For the use of one person. *A single bed.* 4. *A single ticket*, a ticket for a journey to a place but not back again.

single-handed Without helpers, on one's own.

singlet (singlets) A garment like a vest.

singular 1. Referring to one person or thing. 2. Extraordinary.

sinister Evil-looking, frightening.

sink¹ (sinks, sinking, sank, sunk, sunken) 1. To go down, to go down into something. 2. To cause a thing to sink. 3. To become weaker.

sink² (sinks) A basin fitted with a drain to take away water, used for washing dishes.

sinner (sinners) A person who sins.

sip (sips, sipping, sipped) To drink by taking a tiny amount into the mouth at a time.

sir 1. A word sometimes used when talking politely to a man. 2. *Sir*, the title of a knight or baronet. *Sir Robert Peel.*

sire (old-fashioned) A word used when talking to a king.

siren (sirens) A device which makes a loud hooting sound.

sister (sisters) 1. A daughter of the same parents as the person speaking or being spoken about. 2. A senior nurse in a hospital. 3. A nun.

sit (sits, sitting, sat) 1. To take up a position in which the body rests on the buttocks. 2. To rest, to stay. 3. To put somebody in a sitting position. sitter.

site (sites) A place for a building.

sitting-room (sitting-rooms) A room with comfortable chairs for sitting in.

situated Placed.

situation (situations) A position.

six (sixes) The number 6. sixth.

sixpence (sixpences) A former British coin.

sixteen The number 16. sixteenth.

sixty (sixties) The number 60. sixtieth.

size (sizes) 1. The largeness or smallness of something. 2. A particular measurement. *A size seven shoe.*

sizeable Fairly large.

sizzle (sizzles, sizzling, sizzled) To make a hissing and crackling sound.

skate¹ (skates) 1. A steel blade fixed under a boot for sliding easily over ice. 2. A roller-skate.

skate² (skates, skating, skated) To move on skates. skater.

skeleton (skeletons) The framework of bones inside human beings and other animals.

skeleton key A key that will open several different locks.

sketch¹ (sketches) 1. A quickly-made drawing. sketch-book. 2. A short amusing play.

sketch² (sketches, sketching, sketched) To make a sketch.

skewer (skewers) A pointed stick used for holding meat for cooking.

ski¹ (skis) A long strip of wood fastened to the foot for sliding over snow.

ski² (skis, skiing, ski'd) To move on skis. skier.

skid (skids, skidding, skidded) To slip or slide accidentally.

skill (skills) The ability to do something well or expertly. skilful, skilfully.

skilled Trained, experienced.

skim (skims, skimming, skimmed) 1. To remove something from the surface of a liquid. 2. To move quickly and lightly over a surface.

skin¹ (skins) 1. The outer layer of the body of a person or animal. 2. The outer covering of a fruit or vegetable.

skin² (skins, skinning, skinned) To remove the skin from something.

skin-diving The sport of diving without a diving suit. skin-diver.

skinny (skinnier, skinniest) Very thin.

skip (skips, skipping, skipped) 1. To jump along lightly and quickly. 2. To jump over a rope which is being turned over the head and under the feet. skipping-rope. 3. *To skip something*, to leave it out.

skipper (skippers) The captain of a ship or team.

skirmish (skirmishes) An unplanned fight between small groups.

skirt¹ (skirts) A woman's garment that hangs from the waist.

skirt² (skirts, skirting, skirted) To go round the edge of something.

skittle (skittles) A bottle-shaped piece of wood to be knocked over by a ball in the game of skittles.

skull (skulls) The bony framework of the head.

skunk (skunks) A North American animal which sends out a bad-smelling liquid when attacked.

sky (skies) The space above our heads when we are in the open air.

sky-diving The sport of diving through the air from an aircraft. sky-diver.

skylark (skylarks) A small bird which sings as it hovers high in the air.

skylight (skylights) A window in a roof.

skyline (skylines) The shape of things seen on the horizon.

skyscraper (skyscrapers) A very tall building.

slab (slabs) A thick flat piece of something.

slack (slacker, slackest) 1. Lazy. 2. Loose. slackly, slackness.

slacken (slackens, slackening, slackened) 1. To make or become looser. 2. To make or become less. *To slacken speed.*

slacks Trousers.

slag heap A hill made of waste material from a coal-mine.

slain *See* slay.

slam (slams, slamming, slammed) 1. To shut violently. 2. To hit violently.

slang A type of language used in everyday speech but not normally used when writing or on important occasions.

slant (slants, slanting, slanted) To slope.

slap (slaps, slapping, slapped) To smack.

slapdash Careless.

slash (slashes, slashing, slashed) To make big cuts in something.

slat (slats) A thin strip of wood or other material.

slate (slates) A flat piece of a grey stone as used for roofs.

slaughter (slaughters, slaughtering, slaughtered) 1. To kill an animal for food. 2. To kill many animals or people on the same occasion.

slaughterhouse (slaughterhouses) A place where animals are killed for food.

slave¹ (slaves) A person who belongs to somebody else, a servant who cannot leave his master.

slave² (slaves, slaving, slaved) To work very hard.

slavery Being a slave. *Sold into slavery.*

slay (slays, slaying, slew, slain) To kill. slayer.

sledge (sledges) or sled (sleds) A vehicle running on strips instead of wheels.

sledge-hammer (sledge-hammers) A very large heavy hammer.

sleek (sleeker, sleekest) Soft, smooth, and glossy.

sleep¹ (sleeps) The state of complete rest and unconsciousness such as people normally enjoy each night in bed. sleepless, sleeplessly, sleeplessness.

sleep² (sleeps, sleeping, slept) To have a sleep.

sleeper (sleepers) 1. Someone who is sleeping. 2. One of the beams of wood or concrete on which railway lines are laid. 3. A sleeping-car.

sleeping-bag (sleeping-bags) A warm bag for sleeping in when camping.

sleeping-car (sleeping-cars) A railway carriage fitted with beds for passengers to sleep on.

sleepy (sleepier, sleepiest) Ready for sleep. sleepily.

sleet Half-melted falling snow or hail.

sleeve (sleeves) 1. Part of a garment to cover an arm. sleeveless. 2. A cover for a gramophone record.

sleigh (sleighs) A sledge.

slender Narrow, slim, thin.

slew See slay.

slice[1] (slices) A thin piece cut off something.

slice[2] (slices, slicing, sliced) 1. To cut into slices. 2. To cut cleanly or easily.

slick[1] Clever, quick, cunning.

slick[2] (slicks) A patch of oil floating on water.

slide[1] (slides, sliding, slid) To slip smoothly over the surface of something.

slide[2] (slides) 1. The act of sliding. 2. A slippery surface or a smooth slope on which people may slide. 3. A picture which can be projected on a screen. 4. *A hairslide*, a device for keeping the hair tidy.

slight Small, not important. slightly.

slim[1] (slimmer, slimmest) Thin, slender.

slim[2] (slims, slimming, slimmed) To try to make oneself slimmer.

slime Any unpleasant slippery substance. slimy.

sling[1] (slings) 1. A device for throwing stones. 2. A piece of material tied round the neck to support an injured arm.

sling[2] (slings, slinging, slung) 1. To throw something. 2. To hang something up.

slink (slinks, slinking, slunk) To move stealthily.

slip[1] (slips, slipping, slipped) 1. To slide accidentally, to fall. 2. To move without attracting attention. 3. To escape. 4. To do something with a smooth, easy motion. *To slip a coat on.*

slip[2] (slips) 1. A slide, a fall. 2. A mistake. 3. A cover for a pillow. 4. A garment worn under a dress. 5. A piece of paper.

slipper (slippers) A light shoe to wear indoors.

slippery Smooth, liable to cause slipping.

slipshod Careless.

slit[1] (slits) A long narrow opening in something.

slit[2] (slits, slitting, slit) To make a slit in something.

slither (slithers, slithering, slithered) To slide, to slip.

slithery Slippery.

slog (slogs, slogging, slogged) 1. To hit hard and wildly. 2. To work hard.

slogan (slogans) A motto, a memorable phrase used in advertising.

sloop (sloops) A kind of sailing ship.

slop (slops, slopping, slopped) To spill carelessly.

slope[1] (slopes) A line or surface which goes gradually upwards or downwards.

slope[2] (slopes, sloping, sloped) 1. To have a slope. 2. To make a slope.

sloppy (informal) 1. Wet, runny. 2. Careless. 3. Weak and foolish. sloppily, sloppiness.

slot (slots) A narrow opening to put things in.

sloth Laziness. slothful.

slouch (slouches, slouching, slouched) To sit, stand, or move in a lazy way.

slovenly Untidy, careless. slovenliness.

slow[1] (slower, slowest) 1. Taking a long time, not fast. 2. Behind the correct time. *The clock is five minutes slow.* slowly, slowness.

slow[2] (slows, slowing, slowed) *To slow up, to slow down*, to move less fast.

slug (slugs) A small slimy creature.

sluggish Slow, lazy. sluggishly, sluggishness.

slum (slums) An area of old, over-crowded houses.

slumber (slumbers, slumbering, slumbered) To sleep.

slump (slumps, slumping, slumped) To fall suddenly and heavily.

slung See sling[2].

slunk See slink.

slush Melting snow. slushy.

sly (slyer, slyest) Cunning, deceitful. slyly, slyness.

smack[1] (smacks, smacking, smacked) 1. To hit someone or something sharply with the palm of the hand. 2. To make a sound like smacking.

smack² (smacks) 1. The act or sound of smacking. 2. A kind of fishing boat.

small (smaller, smallest) 1. Little in size, not large. smallness. 2. *Small arms*, guns small enough to be carried in the hands.

smallpox A serious disease with disfiguring spots.

smart¹ (smarter, smartest) 1. Neat, well-dressed, fashionable. 2. Clever. 3. Fast. *A smart pace*. 4. Painful. *A smart blow*. smartly, smartness.

smart² (smarts, smarting, smarted) To feel a sharp pain.

smash¹ (smashes, smashing, smashed)   To break something into pieces, to break something in a violent or spectacular way. 2. To hit violently.

smash² (smashes) The act or sound of smashing.

smear¹ (smears) A sticky or dirty mark. smeary.

smear² (smears, smearing, smeared) To make a smear.

smell¹ (smells, smelling, smelt) 1. To use the nose in order to recognize or get to know things. 2. To give out a smell. *Bad eggs smell*.

smell² 1. The ability to smell. *The sense of smell*. 2. (smells) The quality of a thing which can be smelt. *This meat looks all right, but it has a funny smell*. smelly.

smile¹ (smiles) A pleased, happy, or amused expression on the face.

smile² (smiles, smiling, smiled) To make a smile.

smirk (smirks) A silly, smug smile.

smith (smiths) A person who works with metals. *A silversmith*.

smithereens Small fragments.

smock (smocks) A loose garment.

smoke¹ 1. The mixture of gas and sooty particles that goes up when something is burnt. 2. *To have a smoke*, to smoke tobacco. smoky, smokeless.

smoke² (smokes, smoking, smoked) 1. To give out smoke. 2. To suck in tobacco smoke through the mouth and breathe it out again. smoker.

smoke-screen (smoke-screens) A screen of dense smoke.

smooth¹ (smoother, smoothest) 1. Having a surface without any lumps, scratches, or other marks that can be felt. *A sheet of glass is very smooth*. 2. Not bumpy. *A smooth ride*. 3. Without lumps. *A smooth cake-mixture*. smoothly, smoothness.

smooth² (smoothes, smoothing, smoothed) To make a thing smooth.

smother (smothers, smothering, smothered) 1. To suffocate somebody or something. 2. To cover something thickly.

smoulder (smoulders, smouldering, smouldered) To burn slowly without a flame.

smudge (smudges) A dirty mark.

smug (smugger, smuggest) Thoroughly pleased with oneself. smugly, smugness.

smuggle (smuggles, smuggling, smuggled) To move goods illegally from one country to another. smuggler.

smut (smuts) A piece of dirt. smutty.

snack (snacks) A small meal. snack-bar.

snag (snags) A difficulty, an obstacle.

snail (snails) A kind of small soft creature with a shell.

snake (snakes) A long reptile without legs.

snaky Twisting, snake-like.

snap¹ (snaps, snapping, snapped) 1. To make a quick or sudden bite. 2. To say something quickly and angrily. snappy, snappily. 3. To break with a sudden sharp noise. 4. To take a snapshot of something.

snap[2] (snaps) 1. The act or sound of snapping.
2. A snapshot.

snap[3] A card game.

snapshot (shapshots) A photograph taken with a simple camera.

snare (snares) A trap.

snarl (snarls, snarling, snarled) 1. To growl and show the teeth as a fierce dog does.
2. *Snarled up*, confused, tangled.

snatch (snatches, snatching, snatched) To take hold of something quickly and un-expectedly.

sneak[1] (sneaks, sneaking, sneaked) 1. To move quietly and secretly. 2. (informal) To tell tales. sneaky, sneakily.

sneak[2] (sneaks) (informal) A person who tells tales.

sneer[1] (sneers, sneering, sneered) To make a scornful and contemptuous face at some-body, to say something scornful.

sneer[2] (sneers) A scornful expression or remark.

sneeze[1] (sneezes, sneezing, sneezed) To have an uncontrollable outburst of air through the mouth and nose as a person often does when he has a cold.

sneeze[2] (sneezes) The act or sound of sneez-ing.

sniff (sniffs, sniffing, sniffed) 1. To draw air in noisily through the nose. 2. To smell something by sniffing.

snigger (sniggers, sniggering, sniggered) To laugh quietly or slyly.

snip (snips, snipping, snipped) To cut with scissors or shears.

snipe (snipes, sniping, sniped) To shoot at someone from a hiding place. sniper.

snippet (snippets) A small piece of some-thing.

snivel (snivels, snivelling, snivelled) To weep and whine.

snob (snobs) A person who thinks it is important to have wealth or possessions or influence and who looks down on people without them. snobbish, snobbishly, snob-bishness, snobbery.

snoop (snoops, snooping, snooped) To pry into other people's affairs. snooper.

snooze (snoozes, snoozing, snoozed) To have a short sleep.

snore[1] (snores, snoring, snored) To breathe roughly and noisily while sleeping.

snore[2] (snores) The sound of snoring.

snorkel (snorkels) A tube which supplies air to someone swimming under water.

snort (snorts, snorting, snorted) To make a short loud noise by forcing air violently through the nose.

snout (snouts) The nose of an animal.

snow[1] Frozen drops of water falling from the air in white flakes. snowflake, snowstorm.

snow[2] (snows, snowing, snowed) *It is snow-ing*, snow is falling.

snowball (snowballs) A ball of snow pressed together.

snowdrift (snowdrifts) A bank of deep snow.

snowdrop (snowdrops) A small white flower.

snowman (snowmen) A figure modelled in snow.

snowplough (snowploughs) A device for pushing or throwing snow off roads or railways.

snowy 1. Covered with snow. 2. Very white.

snub (snubs, snubbing, snubbed) To behave or speak to someone with contempt.

snub-nosed Having a short nose.

snuff[1] Powdered tobacco sniffed up the nose.

snuff[2] (snuffs, snuffing, snuffed) To put out a candle by pinching the wick.

snug Warm and comfortable. snugly.

snuggle (snuggles, snuggling, snuggled) To cuddle up.

so 1. To such an extent. *He is not so ill that he can't see visitors.* 2. Therefore, for that reason. *And so I ran away.* 3. Also. *Peter is going and so am I.* 4. (informal) Very. *I'm so pleased you can come.* 5. *So far,* up till now. 6. *So that,* in order that. 7. *I told you so,* that is just what I told you. 8. *Or so,* about. *A dozen or so people.*

soak (soaks, soaking, soaked) 1. To make something thoroughly wet. 2. *To soak up,* to take up moisture into a material which has numerous tiny holes or spaces.

soap A substance used with water for washing. **soapy.**

soar (soars, soaring, soared) To rise in the air, to fly.

sob[1] (sobs, sobbing, sobbed) To gasp noisily while crying.

sob[2] (sobs) The act or sound of sobbing.

sober 1. Not drunk. 2. Calm, serious.

soccer (informal) Association football.

sociable Friendly, enjoying the company of others.

social 1. Living in groups or societies. 2. Concerned with society, for the benefit of people living in society. *Social welfare.* 3. Giving people an opportunity to meet others. *A social club. A social evening.*

socialism A set of political beliefs.

society (societies) 1. People living together in one group or one nation, a community. 2. Being together with others, company. *We enjoy the society of our friends.* 3. An organized group of people, a club. *A secret society.*

sock (socks) A garment which covers the foot and lower part of the leg.

socket (sockets) A hole into which something fits. *A socket for an electric light bulb.*

soda Whitish crystals sometimes used in cleaning.

soda-water A fizzy water used in cold drinks.

sodden Soaked, wet through.

sofa (sofas) A long comfortable seat with raised ends and back.

soft (softer, softest) 1. Easily pressed into a new shape, easily cut, not hard. *As soft as butter.* 2. Smooth, pleasant to touch. *As soft as fur.* 3. Gentle, mild. *A soft breeze.* **softly, softness.** 4. *Soft drinks,* cold drinks such as lemonade or ginger beer.

soften (softens, softening, softened) 1. To make softer. 2. To become softer. **softener.**

soft-hearted Kind, sympathetic.

soggy (soggier, soggiest) Very wet, soaked.

soil[1] The ground, the top layer of the earth in which plants grow.

soil[2] (soils, soiling, soiled) To stain with dirt.

solar Belonging to the sun.

sold *See* sell.

solder[1] An alloy which melts easily and is used for joining metals.

solder[2] (solders, soldering, soldered) To join metals with solder.

soldier (soldiers) A member of an army, a person paid to fight on land.

sole[1] Single, one and only. **solely.**

sole[2] (soles) 1. The bottom of a person's foot. 2. The bottom of a sock or shoe. 3. A kind of flat fish.

solemn Serious, thoughtful. **solemnly, solemnity.**

solicitor (solicitors) A kind of lawyer.

solid Not hollow, having no space inside. *A tennis ball is hollow but a cricket ball is solid.* **solidly, solidity.**

solitary 1. Alone, lonely. 2. One only.

solitude Being on one's own.

solo[1] On one's own. *To fly solo.*

solo[2] (solos) A piece of music performed by one person. **soloist.**

soluble 1. Able to be solved. 2. Able to be dissolved in a liquid.

solution (solutions) 1. An answer to a problem. 2. Something dissolved in a liquid.

solve (solves, solving, solved) To find the answer to a problem. solvable.

sombre Dark, gloomy, dismal. sombrely.

sombrero (sombreros) A hat with a wide brim.

some 1. One, a, an unknown. *Some person has taken my coat.* 2. An unknown number of people or things, an unknown quantity of something. *Have you taken some sweets?* 3. Approximately. *There were some ten people present.*

somebody Some person, any person.

somehow In some way.

someone Some person, any person.

somersault (somersaults) The action of jumping and turning heels over head before landing on the feet.

something Some thing, any thing.

sometimes At some times.

somewhat Rather, to some extent.

somewhere In some place, to some place.

son (sons) Someone's male child.

son-et-lumière A kind of entertainment given after dark with special sound and lighting effects.

song (songs) 1. A short piece of music for singing, something which is sung. 2. Words for a song.

song-bird (song-birds) A bird that sings.

sonic boom The bang heard when an aircraft goes faster than the speed of sound.

soon (sooner, soonest) 1. Not long after. 2. In a short time. 3. Early. *Have we come too soon?* 4. Willingly. *If there are no apples I would just as soon have a banana.*

soot The black powder left inside a chimney by smoke. sooty.

soothe (soothes, soothing, soothed) To make calm.

sopping Soaked, very wet.

soppy (soppier, soppiest) (informal) Foolish, silly.

soprano (sopranos) A female or boy singer with a high voice.

sorcerer (sorcerers) A wizard. sorceress, sorcery.

sordid Dirty, mean. sordidly, sordidness.

sore¹ (sorer, sorest) 1. Painful. 2. Annoyed. sorely, soreness.

sore² (sores) A painful or inflamed place on the body.

sorrow Sadness or unhappiness, regret. sorrowful, sorrowfully.

sorry (sorrier, sorriest) Feeling sorrow.

sort¹ (sorts) A group of things or people which are alike in some way, a kind, a type. *What sort of sweets do you like best? Rounders is a sort of baseball*, rounders is rather like baseball.

sort² (sorts, sorting, sorted) To arrange things into groups or sets. *Sort out some good apples.*

SOS An urgent request for help.

sought *See* seek.

soul (souls) The part of a human being that is believed to be immortal.

sound¹ (sounder, soundest) 1. Healthy, in good condition. 2. Reliable. 3. Reasonable. 4. Thorough. soundly, soundness.

sound² (sounds) Something that can be heard, any kind of noise. soundless, soundlessly.

sound³ (sounds, sounding, sounded) 1. To make a sound. 2. To give an impression by means of a sound. *He sounds angry.*

sound-barrier *To go through the sound-barrier*, to go faster than the speed of sound.

sound-effects Noises used in a play or film.

sound-proof Not allowing sound to pass through.

sound-track (sound-tracks) The sound recorded on a film.

soup (soups) A liquid food usually made from meat or vegetables.

sour (sourer, sourest) 1. Having a sharp taste like that of vinegar, lemons, or unripe apples. 2. *Sour milk*, bad milk. 3. Bad-tempered. **sourly, sourness.**

source (sources) The place from which something starts.

south 1. One of the points of the compass, the direction to the right of a person facing the sunrise. 2. From the south. *A south wind.* **southerly.** 3. In the south. *The south coast.* **southern.** 4. Towards the south. *We travelled south.* **southward, southwards.**

south-east Halfway between south and east.

southerner (southerners) A person who lives in the south.

south-west Half-way between south and west.

souvenir (souvenirs) A thing which reminds one of a person, place, or event.

sou'wester (sou'westers) A waterproof hat with a wide flap at the back.

sovereign (sovereigns) 1. A reigning king or queen. 2. An old coin once worth £1.

Soviet Of Russia.

sow[1] (sows, sowing, sowed, sown) To plant seeds.

sow[2] (sows) A female pig.

soya bean A kind of bean valuable as a food.

space[1] (spaces) 1. The immeasurable regions in which the planets and stars move. 2. A distance between two or more things. 3. An empty gap, an empty area. 4. A period of time.

space[2] (spaces, spacing, spaced) *To space things out*, to arrange them neatly with spaces between.

spacecraft (spacecraft) or **spaceship** (spaceships) A vehicle for travelling in space.

spacesuit (spacesuits) Special clothing worn in space.

spacious With plenty of space. **spaciously, spaciousness.**

spade (spades) A tool for digging.

spades A suit of playing-cards.

spaghetti A kind of macaroni.

span[1] *See* **spin.**

span[2] (spans) 1. The part of a bridge between supports. 2. A length of time. 3. The length across something. *The span of a bird's wing.*

span[3] (spans, spanning, spanned) To stretch from one side of something to the other.

Spaniard (Spaniards) A Spanish person.

spaniel (spaniels) A kind of dog with long ears.

Spanish Of Spain.

spank (spanks, spanking, spanked) To smack somebody as a punishment.

spanner (spanners) A tool for turning nuts.

spare[1] (spares, sparing, spared) 1. To allow something to go unharmed. 2. To be able to supply or provide something. *Have you a sandwich to spare?* 3. *To spare somebody the trouble of something*, to save him the trouble.

spare[2] In reserve for use when needed. *A spare tyre.*

sparing Making economical use of something. **sparingly.**

spark (sparks) A glowing speck, a small bright flash.

sparkle (sparkles, sparkling, sparkled) To send out sparks of light.

sparrow (sparrows) A common small bird.

sparse Thinly scattered. **sparsely.**

spasm (spasms) A sudden jerking movement which a person cannot help making.

spasmodic Occasional. **spasmodically.**

spastic (spastics) A person suffering from a disease which makes it difficult to control the body.

spat *See* **spit.**

spate A sudden rush.

spatter (spatters, spattering, spattered) To splash, to sprinkle.

spawn The eggs of fish, frogs, and other water animals.

speak (speaks, speaking, spoke, spoken) 1. To use the voice to produce words. 2. To know a language. *I speak French a little.* 3. *To speak the truth*, to say what is true. **speaker.**

spear (spears) A weapon with a metal point on a long pole.

special 1. Of a rare or unusual kind. **2.** Reserved for a particular person or occasion. **specially.**

specialist (specialists) An expert in a particular subject.

specialize (specializes, specializing, specialized) To give particular attention to one thing or subject, to become a specialist.

species (species) A number of animals or plants which are alike in certain ways.

specific Detailed, definite. **specifically.**

specimen (specimens) An example of something.

speck (specks) A small spot, a tiny piece.

speckled Covered with specks.

spectacle (spectacles) **1.** An exciting or impressive display. **spectacular. 2.** Something seen. *An odd spectacle*, an odd sight.

spectacles A pair of glass lenses in a frame to help a person to see more clearly. *A pair of spectacles.*

spectator (spectators) A person who watches something.

spectre (spectres) A ghost.

speech (speeches) **1.** Speaking. **2.** A talk given in public.

speechless Unable to speak. **speechlessly.**

speed¹ 1. Quickness, swiftness. *At speed*, in a comparatively short time, quickly. **speedy, speedily. 2.** The rate at which something moves. *A speed of fifty kilometres per hour.*

speed² (speeds, speeding, sped) To move at great speed.

speed-boat (speed-boats) A fast motor boat.

speeding Driving faster than the speed limit.

speedometer (speedometers) An instrument which measures a vehicle's speed.

speedway (speedways) A track for motor-cycle racing.

spell¹ (spells, spelling, spelled, spelt) To put letters into a certain order to make a word.

spell² (spells) A short time, a continuous period. *A spell of good weather.*

spell³ (spells) A saying supposed to have magic power, a magic charm.

spellbound Enchanted.

spend (spends, spending, spent) **1.** To pay out money. **2.** To use something up. *All our ammunition was spent.* **3.** To pass time. *We spent a day by the sea.*

sphere (spheres) A globe, something which appears round from every direction. **spherical.**

spice (spices) A substance, such as ginger or cloves, used to flavour food. **spicy.**

spick-and-span Bright and tidy.

spider (spiders) A creature with eight legs that spins webs.

spied *See* **spy².**

spike (spikes) A sharp point. **spiky.**

spill¹ (spills) A thin length of wood or folded paper used to light a fire.

spill² (spills, spilling, spilled, spilt) **1.** To flow over the side of a container. **2.** To cause something to do this.

spin (spins, spinning, span, spun) **1.** To twist something into a thread. **spinning-wheel. 2.** To make something by forming threads. *Spiders spin webs.* **3.** To turn round and round. *A spinning top.*

spinach A green vegetable.

spin-drier (spin-driers) A machine used for drying clothes after washing them.

spine (spines) **1.** The series of bones along the middle of the back of people and many animals, the backbone. **spinal. 2.** A sharp spike like a needle.

spineless Feeble, lacking in will-power. spine-
lessly.

spinster (spinsters) An unmarried woman.

spiral Winding round and round, like a
clockwork spring or the thread of a screw.

spire (spires) The pointed structure on a
church tower.

spirit (spirits) 1. The soul. 2. A ghost, a
supernatural being. 3. Courage, enthusiasm, liveliness. *The injured sportsman
showed great spirit.* 4. A state of mind. *In
high spirits,* cheerful, lively. 5. A liquid used
as a fuel or for cleaning. *Methylated spirit.*
6. *Spirits,* strong alcoholic drink.

spirited Brave, lively. spiritedly.

spiritual[1] To do with the soul, religious.
spiritually.

spiritual[2] (spirituals) A religious song of the
North American Negroes.

spit (spits, spitting, spat) To send liquid
forcefully out of the mouth.

spite 1. A desire to hurt someone. spiteful,
spitefully. 2. *In spite of something,* although
it has happened or is happening.

splash[1] (splashes, splashing, splashed) 1. To
make liquid fly through the air in drops.
Baby enjoys splashing in the bath. 2. To fly
through the air in drops. *The bath water
splashed on the floor.* 3. To make someone
or something wet by splashing. *The bus
splashed us as it went past.*

splash[2] (splashes) The act or sound of splashing.

splendid Magnificent, excellent, impressive.
splendidly, splendour.

splint (splints) A strip of wood or other
material used to keep a broken bone
straight while it heals.

splinter (splinters) A sharp broken piece of
wood or metal.

split[1] (splits, splitting, split) To divide something up, to cut or chop it.

split[2] (splits) A crack, a separation.

splutter (splutters, spluttering, spluttered) To
make quick repeated spitting sounds.

spoil (spoils, spoiling, spoiled, spoilt) 1. To

make a thing less valuable or useful or
pleasant. 2. To make a person selfish by
giving in to his wishes all the time.

spoke[1], spoken *See* speak.

spoke[2] (spokes) One of the wires or rods
joining the rim of a wheel to its hub.

sponge[1] (sponges) 1. A lump of absorbent
material used in washing. 2. A sea creature
that soaks up water. spongy. 3. A light soft
cake.

sponge[2] (sponges, sponging, sponged) To
wash with a sponge.

spontaneous Happening or done quite naturally. spontaneously.

spook (spooks) (informal) A ghost. spooky.

spool (spools) A reel or cylinder on which
something is wound. *A spool of film.*

spoon (spoons) An instrument used in serving
and eating food. *A soup-spoon.* spoonful.

spoor (spoors) The track of an animal.

sport (sports) An amusement or game, especially one done out of doors such as
football, athletics, or fishing. sportsman,
sportsmanship.

sporting 1. Connected with sport. 2. Fond of
sport.

sports car A fast car, usually for two people.

spot[1] (spots) 1. A small roundish mark. 2. A
pimple. 3. A drop of something, a small
quantity. 4. A place. *I know a good spot for
a picnic.*

spot[2] (spots, spotting, spotted) 1. To mark
with spots. 2. To see or recognize someone
or something. spotter.

spotless Perfectly clean. spotlessly.

spotlight (spotlights) A strong light which
can shine in a beam.

spotty (spottier, spottiest) Covered in spots.

spout[1] (spouts) 1. A pipe or mouth out of which liquid pours. 2. A jet of liquid.

spout[2] (spouts, spouting, spouted) 1. To send out a jet of liquid. 2. To come out in a jet.

sprain (sprains, spraining, sprained) To injure a joint by twisting it violently.

sprang *See* spring[2].

sprawl (sprawls, sprawling, sprawled) 1. To sit or lie with arms and legs carelessly spread out. 2. To spread out carelessly or irregularly.

spray[1] (sprays) 1. A shower of small drops of liquid. 2. A tool or device for spraying. 3. A small bunch of flowers.

spray[2] (sprays, spraying, sprayed) To scatter liquid on something in small drops.

spread (spreads, spreading, spread) 1. To lay something out flat, to stretch something out. 2. To make something cover a surface. *To spread butter.* 3. To make something move outwards over a wide area, to make something known. *To spread a disease. To spread a rumour.* 4. To move outwards over a wide area. *The rumour spread.*

sprightly Lively, brisk. **sprightliness.**

spring[1] The season between winter and summer. **springtime.**

spring[2] (springs, springing, sprang, sprung) 1. To jump suddenly, to move upwards suddenly. 2. To start something, to make something happen without warning. *To spring a surprise on someone.*

spring[3] (springs) 1. The act of springing. 2. A place where water flows out of the ground. 3. A springy device made of a coil of metal or wire.

spring-board (spring-boards) A board from which people spring when diving.

springy (springier, springiest) Able to bend and spring back, or to stretch like elastic.

sprinkle (sprinkles, sprinkling, sprinkled) To scatter drops or small particles. **sprinkler.**

sprint (sprints, sprinting, sprinted) To run a short distance very fast.

sprout (sprouts, sprouting, sprouted) To begin to grow, to develop, to put out leaves.

spruce[1] Neat and smart.

spruce[2] (spruces) A kind of fir-tree.

sprung *See* spring[2].

spud (spuds) (informal) A potato.

spun *See* spin.

spur[1] (spurs) A sharp device fixed to a rider's heel for urging a horse to go faster.

spur[2] (spurs, spurring, spurred) To urge on.

spurn (spurns, spurning, spurned) To reject or refuse rudely.

spurt (spurts, spurting, spurted) 1. To gush out. 2. To speed up suddenly.

spy[1] (spies) A person who tries to discover secret information.

spy[2] (spies, spying, spied) 1. To be a spy. 2. To see, to observe.

squabble (squabbles, squabbling, squabbled) To have a noisy little quarrel.

squad (squads) A small group of trained people.

squadron (squadrons) 1. Part of a fleet. 2. Part of an air force. 3. Part of a tank or cavalry regiment.

squall (squalls) A sudden wind. **squally.**

squalor Dirt, filth. **squalid.**

squander (squanders, squandering, squandered) To waste money or other resources.

square[1] (squares) 1. A shape with four equal sides and four right angles. 2. An open space in a town with buildings on all four sides.

square[2] 1. Square shaped. 2. Honest, fair. **squarely.** 3. *A square metre*, an area equal to that of a square with sides one metre long.

squash[1] (squashes, squashing, squashed) To crush, to squeeze.

squash[2] A fruit drink.

squat[1] (squatter, squattest) Short and thick.

squat[2] (squats, squatting, squatted) 1. To sit on one's heels. 2. To move in and live somewhere without permission. **squatter.**

squaw (squaws) An American Indian woman.

squawk (squawks, squawking, squawked) To make a loud harsh cry.

squeak[1] (squeaks) A high shrill noise. **squeaky, squeakily.**

squeak² (squeaks, squeaking, squeaked) To
make a squeak.

squeal¹ (squeals) A long shrill cry.

squeal² (squeals, squealing, squealed) To
make a long shrill cry.

squeamish Liable to feel sick. squeamishly.

squeeze (squeezes, squeezing, squeezed) 1. To
press something from opposite sides, to
crush it. 2. To get the liquid out of something by squeezing it. 3. To force something
into or through a gap. squeezer.

squib (squibs) A kind of firework.

squint (squints, squinting, squinted) 1. To
have eyes looking in different directions.
2. To peep at something, to look through
half-shut eyes.

squirm (squirms, squirming, squirmed) To
wriggle and twist.

squirrel (squirrels) A small animal which
lives in trees.

squirt (squirts, squirting, squirted) To send
out a jet of liquid.

St. 1. Saint. 2. Street.

stab (stabs, stabbing, stabbed) To push a
knife, dagger, or other sharp instrument
into somebody or something.

stabilize (stabilizes, stabilizing, stabilized)
To make something become steady or
stable. stabilizer.

stable¹ (stabler, stablest) Steady, firmly fixed,
not changeable. stability.

stable² (stables) A building in which horses
are kept.

stack¹ (stacks) 1. A pile, a heap. 2. The part
of a chimney which projects above the roof.

stack² (stacks, stacking, stacked) To pile
things up.

stadium (stadiums) A sports arena.

staff (staffs) The people who work somewhere. *The staff of a school*, the teachers.

stag (stags) A male deer.

stage (stages) 1. A raised platform for per-
formances in a hall or theatre. 2. A point or
step in the development of somebody or
something.

stage-coach (stage-coaches) A horse-drawn
vehicle which used to carry people and
goods on a regular route.

stagger (staggers, staggering, staggered) 1.
To walk unsteadily. 2. To shock and
confuse.

stagnant Not flowing.

stain¹ (stains, staining, stained) 1. To colour
something. 2. To spoil something with
dirty marks.

stain² (stains) A mark that stains something.

stainless steel Steel that does not rust easily.

stair (stairs) One of a series of steps going
from one floor of a building to another.

staircase (staircases) A series of stairs.

stake (stakes) 1. A strong pointed stick to be
driven into the ground. 2. A sum of money
bet on something.

stalactite (stalactites) A stony spike hanging
from the roof of a cave.

stalagmite (stalagmites) A stony spike rising
from the floor of a cave.

stale Old, dry, not fresh, worn out.

stalk[1] (stalks) A stem of a flower or other small plant.

stalk[2] (stalks, stalking, stalked) To hunt stealthily.

stall[1] (stalls) 1. A small open-fronted shop, a table or counter where things are sold in the open air. 2. *Stalls*, the seats on the ground floor of a theatre or cinema. 3. A part of a stable or cowshed.

stall[2] (stalls, stalling, stalled) To stop accidentally. *The engine stalled.*

stallion (stallions) A male horse.

stamina The power of endurance.

stammer (stammers, stammering, stammered) To hesitate and repeat sounds while talking.

stamp[1] (stamps, stamping, stamped) 1. To bring the foot heavily down on to the ground. 2. To print a mark with a stamp. 3. To put a postage stamp on to a letter or parcel.

stamp[2] (stamps) 1. The act of stamping. 2. A small device for printing words or marks on a paper or other things. *A date stamp.* 3. A mark made by printing with a stamp. 4. *A postage stamp*, a small piece of paper which must be stuck on a letter or parcel before it is posted. stamp-album, stamp-collector.

stampede (stampedes) A sudden rush of a herd of animals or a group of people.

stand[1] (stands, standing, stood) 1. To be upright on the feet, to be in an upright position. 2. To move to an upright position. 3. To put something down in an upright position. 4. To remain unchanged or unmoved. 5. To put up with something, to endure it. *I can't stand hot weather.* 6. *To stand for something*, to represent it, to be a sign for it. *What do your initials stand for?* 7. *To stand out*, to be easily seen, to stick out. 8. *To stand up to someone*, to be ready to oppose him. 9. *To stand up for someone*, to support or defend him.

stand[2] (stands) 1. A support to stand things in or on. *An umbrella stand.* 2. A stall where things are sold or displayed. 3. A structure with rows of seats for spectators at games or races.

standard[1] Of the usual kind, of the normal quality.

standard[2] (standards) 1. A flag, a banner. *The Royal Standard.* 2. A degree of skill or success. *The standard of work in this class is very high.* 3. Something used for comparison when making judgements. *That's not expensive by modern standards.*

standard lamp A tall lamp that stands on the floor.

stand-by Something ready to be used when needed.

stand-in (stand-ins) A person acting as a substitute.

stand-offish Not friendly.

standpoint (standpoints) A point of view.

standstill A halt, a stop.

stank *See* stink[2].

stanza (stanzas) A verse in a poem.

staple (staples) 1. A U-shaped nail sharpened at both ends. 2. A kind of wire clip for fastening through papers. stapler.

star[1] (stars) 1. One of the heavenly bodies seen at night as specks of light. starry, starless, starlight. 2. A pattern with five or six points. 3. A famous and popular entertainer.

star[2] (stars, starring, starred) 1. To take one of the chief parts in a show. 2. To have as a star. *A film starring Charlie Chaplin.*

starboard The right-hand side of a ship looking towards the bows.

starch A substance in foods such as bread and potatoes. starchy.

stare (stares, staring, stared) To look continuously at somebody or something.

starfish (starfishes *or* starfish) A sea animal shaped like a five-pointed star.

starling (starlings) A common European bird.

start[1] (starts, starting, started) 1. To begin, to make the first move, to take the first step. 2. To set something going. starter. 3. To move suddenly. *He started up in anger.*

start² (starts) 1. The act of starting. 2. An advantage which a person has at the beginning of something.

startle (startles, startling, startled) To surprise somebody, to make him jump. startlingly.

starve (starves, starving, starved) 1. To suffer or die because of lack of food. 2. To make someone starve. starvation.

state¹ (states) 1. A condition, the way in which someone or something is. *The playing-field was in a bad state after the rain.* 2. A country, a group of people under one government. 3. A part of a country which governs its own affairs. *The United States of America.*

state² To do with a country or its government or its ruler. *State secrets.*

state³ (states, stating, stated) To say something clearly or formally. statement.

stately Dignified, imposing. stateliness.

statesman (statesmen) A person who plays an important part in governing a country.

static Not moving.

station¹ (stations) 1. A stopping place for trains or buses with buildings for passengers and staff. 2. A place where firemen, policemen, soldiers, or others are stationed.

station² (stations, stationing, stationed) To put someone in a particular place to do a particular job.

stationary Not moving.

stationery Paper and all kinds of writing materials.

statistics Facts given in the form of figures.

statue (statues) A figure made of stone, metal, or other materials.

status A person's rank at work or in society.

staunch Trustworthy, loyal. staunchly.

stave (staves) One of the sets of five parallel lines for writing down music.

stay (stays, staying, stayed) 1. To remain, to keep still in the same place, to continue in the same condition. 2. To live somewhere as a visitor. *We stayed in a farmhouse for our holidays.*

steady¹ (steadier, steadiest) 1. Firm, not shaking. 2. Regular, continuous. steadily, steadiness.

steady² (steadies, steadying, steadied) To make something steady.

steak (steaks) A thick slice of meat or fish.

steal (steals, stealing, stole, stolen) 1. To take and keep something which belongs to somebody else. 2. To move stealthily. *He stole up to her.*

stealthy (stealthier, stealthiest) Quietly and secretly. stealthily.

steam¹ The vapour produced by boiling water. steamy.

steam² (steams, steaming, steamed) 1. To give out steam. 2. To move under steam power. 3. To cook in steam.

steam-engine (steam-engines) A locomotive driven by steam.

steamer (steamers) A ship driven by steam.

steam-roller (steam-rollers) A machine used to flatten the surface when making roads.

steed (steeds) A horse.

steel A metal made of iron and other minerals. steely.

steep (steeper, steepest) Rising or falling sharply. steeply, steepness.

steeple (steeples) A church spire and its tower.

steeplechase (steeplechases) 1. A race across country. 2. A long race over hurdles.

steeplejack (steeplejacks) A man who works on very high buildings.

steer¹ (steers) A young bull raised for beef.

steer² (steers, steering, steered) To control the direction in which something is to move. steering-wheel.

stem (stems) 1. The part of a plant growing up from the ground. 2. A part of a plant that joins a leaf, fruit, or flower to its stalk or branch.

stench (stenches) A bad smell.

stencil (stencils) A device used for duplicating or simple printing.

step¹ (steps) 1. A complete movement forward with one foot when walking. 2. The sound of a person putting down his foot when walking. 3. A flat place to put one's foot when walking from one level to another. 4. One of a series of actions in making or doing something.

step² (steps, stepping, stepped) 1. To make a step, to walk. 2. *To step something up*, to increase it.

stepbrother (stepbrothers) A son of one's stepfather or stepmother. stepsister.

stepfather (stepfathers) A man who is not one's real father but who is now married to one's mother. stepmother, stepson, stepdaughter.

step-ladder (step-ladders) A folding ladder with steps.

stepping-stone (stepping-stones) One of a series of flat stones placed to help people cross a stream.

stereo (informal) Stereophonic.

stereophonic Giving the impression that sound is coming from several different directions at the same time.

sterile Barren, not fertile.

sterilize (sterilizes, sterilizing, sterilized) 1. To make sterile. 2. To kill the germs in or on something. sterilizer, sterilization.

sterling British money.

stern¹ (sterner, sternest) 1. Strict, keen on discipline. 2. Unkind, grim. sternly, sternness.

stern² (sterns) The back end of a ship.

stethoscope (stethoscopes) An instrument used by doctors to listen to patients' heartbeats and breathing.

stew¹ (stews, stewing, stewed) To cook slowly in water or gravy or juice.

stew² (stews) Meat stewed with vegetables.

steward (stewards) 1. A person who attends to the needs of passengers on a ship or aircraft. stewardess. 2. An official who manages someone else's estate or property. 3. An official who manages a race-meeting or a show.

stick¹ (sticks) 1. A thin length of a branch of a tree. 2. A long thin piece of wood made for a particular purpose. *A walking-stick.* 3. A rod-shaped piece of anything. *A stick of chalk. A stick of rock.*

stick² (sticks, sticking, stuck) 1. To push a thing into something. 2. To be pushed into something. *A thorn stuck in my leg.* 3. To fasten one thing to another, to join things together. 4. To become fastened or joined. 5. To become jammed. *The lock is stuck.* 6. (informal) To put up with something, to endure it. 7. To stop, to hesitate, to remain. 8. *To stick out*, to come out from a surface roughly at right angles, to be easily noticed. 9. *To stick up*, to be upright, to be seen above the surrounding surface.

stickleback (sticklebacks) A small freshwater fish.

sticky (stickier, stickiest) Covered with glue or any substance that sticks to one's hands.

stiff (stiffer, stiffest) 1. Not easily bent, stirred, or moved. 2. Difficult. *A stiff test.* 3. Strong. *A stiff wind.* stiffly, stiffness.

stiffen (stiffens, stiffening, stiffened) 1. To make stiff. 2. To become stiff.

stifle (stifles, stifling, stifled) To suffocate.

stile (stiles) A step or steps for climbing over a fence.

still¹ 1. Without movement. 2. Silent. 3. Not fizzing. *Still lemonade.* stillness.

still² 1. Up to this time, up to that time. *Are you still there?* 2. Even. *I shall be still better at French next year.* 3. Nevertheless, on the other hand.

stilt (stilts) One of a pair of poles used to walk on as an amusement.

stimulate (stimulates, stimulating, stimulated) To arouse interest or excitement.

sting[1] (stings) 1. The part of the body which certain small creatures use to attack with. *A bee's sting.* 2. A painful wound caused by poison in the sting of certain creatures or plants.

sting[2] (stings, stinging, stung) 1. To use a sting to give a wound. 2. To feel pain as if from a sting.

stingy (stingier, stingiest) Mean, not generous. **stingily, stinginess.**

stink[1] (stinks) A bad smell.

stink[2] (stinks, stinking, stank, stunk) To have a bad smell.

stir (stirs, stirring, stirred) 1. To move a liquid or soft substance round and round. *To stir a cup of tea.* 2. To move slightly. *To stir in your sleep.* 3. To excite. *Stirring music.* **stirringly.**

stirrup (stirrups) A metal foot-rest hanging from a horse's saddle.

stitch[1] (stitches) 1. A loop of thread made in stitching or knitting. 2. A pain in the side caused by running.

stitch[2] (stitches, stitching, stitched) To move a threaded needle in and out of cloth in sewing.

stoat (stoats) An animal like a weasel.

stock[1] (stocks) 1. A number of things kept ready to be used or to be sold, a supply. 2. The animals kept on a farm, livestock. 3. A sweet-smelling garden flower.

stock[2] (stocks, stocking, stocked) To keep a stock of something.

stockade (stockades) A wall of upright stakes.

stock car An ordinary car used for racing.

stocking (stockings) A garment which covers a person's foot and leg.

stockist (stockists) A shopkeeper who keeps a stock of particular goods.

stocks A wooden framework in which criminals were once locked as a punishment.

stocky (stockier, stockiest) Short and strong. **stockily, stockiness.**

stodgy (stodgier, stodgiest) Dull, heavy.

stoke (stokes, stoking, stoked) To put fuel into a furnace. **stoker.**

stole, stolen *See* **steal.**

stomach (stomachs) 1. The organ of the body in which food is digested. 2. The middle of the front of a person's body.

stone[1] (stones) 1. Rock, solid mineral which is not metal. 2. A piece of stone or rock of any kind. 3. A jewel. 4. The large, hard seed of such fruits as the plum and apricot. 5. A unit of weight, fourteen pounds or 6·35 kilograms. 6. *The Stone Age*, the period when all tools and weapons were made of stone.

stone[2] (stones, stoning, stoned) 1. To throw stones at somebody or something. 2. To take the stones from fruit.

stone[3] Absolutely. **stone-cold, stone-dead, stone-deaf.**

stony (stonier, stoniest) 1. Full of stones. 2. Like stone. **stonily.**

stood *See* **stand**[1].

stool (stools) A seat without a back.

stoop (stoops, stooping, stooped) To bend forwards and downwards.

stop[1] (stops, stopping, stopped) 1. To come to an end, to cease. 2. To bring something to an end, to put an end to its movement or progress. **3.** To prevent, to hinder. **4.** To come to rest, to stay somewhere for a while. **5.** To fill a hole or crack.

stop[2] (stops) **1.** An action of stopping. **2.** A place to stop. *A bus-stop.*

stoppage (stoppages) The stopping of something.

stopper (stoppers) Something which fits into the top of a bottle to close it.

stop-watch (stop-watches) A kind of watch used for timing races and other activities.

storage The storing of goods.

store[1] (stores) **1.** A collection of things kept for future use. **2.** A place where things are stored. **store-room. 3.** A shop. **4.** *In store,* coming in the future. *A treat in store.*

store[2] (stores, storing, stored) To put something safely away for future use.

storey (storeys) All the rooms on one floor of a building.

stork (storks) A long-legged bird.

storm[1] (storms) **1.** A period of violent, windy weather. **2.** A sudden, violent attack. *To take a place by storm.* **stormy.**

storm[2] (storms, storming, stormed) To attack suddenly and violently.

story (stories) **1.** Words which tell of real or imaginary happenings, an account of something. *The story of Cinderella. The story of a person's life.* **story-teller. 2.** A lie. *Don't tell stories!*

stout (stouter, stoutest) **1.** Strong and thick. **2.** Rather fat. **3.** Brave. **stoutly, stoutness.**

stove (stoves) An apparatus used for heating or cooking.

stow (stows, stowing, stowed) To pack or store something away.

stowaway (stowaways) A person who hides in a ship or aircraft in order to travel without paying.

straggle (straggles, straggling, straggled) **1.** To fall behind, to lag. **straggler. 2.** To be spread out untidily. *A straggling village.*

straight (straighter, straightest) **1.** Not bending, not curving. *A straight road.* **2.** Correctly placed, tidy. *Put the room straight before tea.* **3.** Honest, direct. *A straight answer.* **straightness.**

straighten (straightens, straightening, straightened) **1.** To make straight. **2.** To become straight.

straightforward 1. Not complicated. **2.** Honest. **straightforwardly.**

strain[1] (strains, straining, strained) **1.** To stretch, to pull hard. *The dog strained at the leash.* **2.** To make the greatest possible effort with something. *We strained our ears to hear the faint cries.* **3.** To injure something by stretching it or making it work too hard. *To strain a muscle.* **4.** To put something into a sieve or other device to separate the liquid from the solid parts. **strainer.**

strain[2] (strains) **1.** Straining, stretching. *The rope broke under the strain.* **2.** An injury caused by straining. **3.** A severe test of a person's courage, strength, or endurance.

strait (straits) A narrow area of water joining two larger areas. *The Strait of Gibraltar.*

strand (strands) One of the threads or fibres twisted together to make rope or yarn.

stranded Left in a difficult, awkward, or dangerous position. *A stranded ship.*

strange (stranger, strangest) Unusual, queer, previously unknown. **strangely, strangeness.**

stranger (strangers) **1.** A person one does not know. **2.** A person in a place he does not know. *I'm a stranger here.*

strangle (strangles, strangling, strangled) To kill by squeezing the throat. **strangler, strangulation.**

strap[1] (straps) A strip of leather or other material with a buckle. *A watch strap.*

strap[2] (straps, strapping, strapped) To fasten with straps.

strategy (strategies) The art of planning large operations in war. **strategic, strategist.**

stratosphere A layer of air high above the earth's surface.

stratum (strata) A layer.

straw (straws) 1. Dry cut stalks of corn. 2. A thin tube for drinking through.

strawberry (strawberries) A juicy red fruit.

stray (strays, straying, strayed) To wander, to become lost.

streak (streaks) A long thin line. streaky.

stream[1] (streams) 1. Water which moves in a particular direction along a channel. 2. Anything which flows along like a stream.

stream[2] (streams, streaming, streamed) 1. To move or flow like a stream. 2. To send out a stream.

streamer (streamers) A long ribbon or strip of paper fixed at one end.

street (streets) A road in a town with houses along it.

strength 1. Being strong. 2. Power.

strengthen (strengthens, strengthening, strengthened) 1. To make stronger. 2. To become stronger.

strenuous Needing great effort. strenuously.

stress[1] (stresses) 1. Pressure, strain. 2. An emphasis.

stress[2] (stresses, stressing, stressed) To emphasize.

stretch[1] (stretches, stretching, stretched) 1. To make something wider or longer or tighter by pulling. 2. To become wider or longer when pulled. *Elastic stretches.* 3. To extend, to reach out.

stretch[2] (stretches) 1. The act of stretching. 2. A continuous length of time or space.

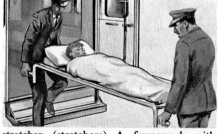

stretcher (stretchers) A framework with handles at each end for carrying a sick or injured person.

strewn Scattered.

strict (stricter, strictest) 1. Stern, keen on discipline. *A strict master.* 2. Exact. *The strict truth.* strictly, strictness.

stride[1] (strides, striding, strode) To walk with long steps.

stride[2] (strides) A long step in walking or running.

strife Fighting, conflict.

strike[1] (strikes, striking, struck) 1. To hit. 2. To attack suddenly. 3. To sound. *The clock struck 12.* 4. To find. *To strike gold.* 5. *To strike a match*, to light it. 6. *To strike a tent*, to take it down. 7. *To strike out*, to delete. 8. *To strike out for*, to go in a certain direction. 9. To refuse to work in order to protest about wages or conditions of work. striker.

strike[2] (strikes) 1. A hit. 2. Refusal to work, as a form of protest. 3. A sudden discovery of something. *An oil strike.*

striking Interesting and impressive.

string[1] (strings) 1. Fine cord used for tying things. 2. A length of stretched wire or thread used to sound a note in a musical instrument. *A guitar string. The strings*, stringed instruments. 3. A series of things in a line. *A string of buses.*

string[2] (strings, stringing, strung) 1. To put strings on something. 2. To put things on a string.

stringed *A stringed instrument*, a musical instrument with strings.

stringy Having tough fibres.

strip[1] (strips, stripping, stripped) 1. To undress. 2. To take the covering off something. 3. To deprive somebody of something.

strip[2] (strips) A long narrow piece of something.

stripe (stripes) A long narrow mark. *Zebras have black and white stripes.*

striped Having stripes.

strive (strives, striving, strove, striven) To struggle, to try very hard.

strode *See* stride[1].

stroke[1] (strokes) 1. A blow, a hit, a movement. 2. A kind of sudden serious illness.

stroke[2] (strokes, stroking, stroked) To pass the hand gently along something.

stroll (strolls, strolling, strolled) To walk at a comfortable pace.

strong (stronger, strongest) 1. Having great power, not easily broken or damaged, able to resist. 2. Very noticeable in flavour or smell. 3. *Strong drink*, alcoholic drink. **strongly.**

stronghold (strongholds) A fortress.

strove *See* **strive.**

struck *See* **strike**[1].

structure (structures) 1. A thing which has been built or put together. 2. The building of something, the way a thing is built or put together. **structural, structurally.**

struggle[1] (struggles, struggling, struggled) To make violent or strenuous efforts in fighting, or in trying to get free, or in doing something difficult.

struggle[2] (struggles) The act of struggling.

strung *See* **string**[2].

strut[1] (struts, strutting, strutted) To walk in a stiff, self-satisfied way.

strut[2] (struts) A bar of wood or metal used as part of a framework.

stub[1] (stubs, stubbing, stubbed) To hit or press a thing against something. *To stub one's toe.*

stub[2] (stubs) A short piece of something which remains when the rest has been used up. *A pencil stub.*

stubble 1. The short stalks left in the ground when corn has been cut. 2. Short hairs visible on a man's chin when he has not shaved recently. **stubbly.**

stubborn Obstinate. **stubbornly, stubbornness.**

stuck *See* **stick**[2].

stuck-up (informal) Conceited.

stud (studs) 1. A short nail with a thick head. 2. One of the knobs on the sole of a football boot. 3. A fastener for fixing a detachable collar to a shirt.

student (students) A person who studies.

studio (studios) 1. An artist's or photographer's work-room. 2. A place for making films, or radio or television broadcasts.

studious Keen on studying. **studiously.**

study[1] (studies, studying, studied) To give time regularly to learning about something.

study[2] (studies) 1. The studying of something. 2. A private room used for studying.

stuff[1] (stuffs) A material, a substance.

stuff[2] (stuffs, stuffing, stuffed) To fill something with some stuff packed tightly.

stuffing 1. Material used to stuff something. 2. A flavoured mixture put inside meat before cooking.

stuffy (stuffier, stuffiest) Badly ventilated.

stumble (stumbles, stumbling, stumbled) 1. To strike the foot against something and fall over. 2. To move or speak in a hesitating way.

stump[1] (stumps) 1. The bottom of the trunk that remains when a tree is cut down. 2. One of the three upright sticks used as a wicket in cricket.

stump[2] (stumps, stumping, stumped) 1. To get a batsman out in cricket by touching the stumps with the ball while he is out of his crease. 2. (informal) To be too difficult for somebody. *The question stumped me.*

stumpy (stumpier, stumpiest) Short and thick.

stun (stuns, stunning, stunned) 1. To knock somebody unconscious. 2. To amaze.

stung *See* **sting**[2].

stunk *See* **stink**[2].

stunt (stunts) Something done to attract people's attention.

stupendous Of amazing size. **stupendously.**

stupid Foolish, not intelligent. **stupidly, stupidity.**

sturdy (sturdier, sturdiest) Strong, healthy, vigorous. **sturdily, sturdiness.**

stutter (stutters, stuttering, stuttered) To stammer. **stutterer.**

sty (sties) **1.** A pigsty. **2.** An inflamed swelling on the edge of the eyelid.

style (styles) The way or manner in which something is done, or made, or written.

stylish Smart, fashionable. **stylishly.**

stylus (styluses) The diamond or sapphire point used in a pick-up to play gramophone records.

subdue (subdues, subduing, subdued) **1.** To overcome, to conquer. **2.** To make quieter.

subject[1] (pronounced *sub*ject) (subjects) **1.** A member of a particular state or country. *British subjects.* **2.** A person, or thing, or idea, being talked or written about. *What is the subject of that book?* **3.** Something studied in school. *History is my favourite subject.*

subject[2] (pronounced sub*ject*) (subjects, subjecting, subjected) *To subject someone to something,* to make him suffer it.

submarine (submarines) A kind of ship which can travel under the surface of the sea.

submerge (submerges, submerging, submerged) **1.** To go under water. **2.** To cause something to go under water. **submersion.**

submit (submits, submitting, submitted) **1.** To surrender. **2.** To put oneself under somebody else's control. **3.** To hand something in, to put something forward for consideration. **submission.**

subordinate Lower in rank, less important.

subscription (subscriptions) **1.** A regular contribution or payment to something. **2.** A membership fee.

subsequent Later, following, next. *The subsequent day.* **subsequently.**

subside (subsides, subsiding, subsided) **1.** To sink. **2.** To become quiet. **subsidence.**

substance (substances) Any kind of matter or material, anything which can be seen, or touched, or used in the making of something.

substantial **1.** Strongly made. *A substantial box.* **2.** Considerable, large. *A substantial improvement.*

substitute[1] (substitutes, substituting, substituted) **1.** To use something instead of the usual thing. **2.** To employ somebody instead of the usual person. **substitution.**

substitute[2] (substitutes) A person or thing which is or can be substituted for another.

subtle (subtler, subtlest) **1.** Clever, ingenious. *A subtle argument.* **2.** Faint but pleasing. *A subtle flavour.* **subtly, subtlety.**

subtract (subtracts, subtracting, subtracted) To take one number or amount away from another. **subtraction.**

suburb (suburbs) An area of houses on the edge of a town or city. **suburban.**

subway (subways) A tunnel for pedestrians.

succeed (succeeds, succeeding, succeeded) **1.** To do what one has set out to do. **2.** To do well. **3.** To come after, to take the place of another person. *When the Emperor dies, the Prince will succeed him.*

success (successes) **1.** Doing what one has set out to do, doing well. **2.** A person or event that does well. *Was your party a success?* **successful, successfully.**

succession (successions) A series, a number of things coming one after the other.

successor (successors) A person who comes after and takes the place of another person.

succumb (succumbs, succumbing, succumbed) To be overcome.

such **1.** Of this kind, of that kind, of the same kind. *I have never seen such beautiful roses.* **2.** So great. *The shock was such that he never fully recovered.* **3.** Truly, really. *He's such a nice man,* he's a very nice man.

suck (sucks, sucking, sucked) **1.** To draw in liquid or air. *To suck milk through a straw.* **2.** To keep something in the mouth and lick it and squeeze it with the tongue. *To suck a sweet.*

suction Sucking.

sudden Happening or done quickly and unexpectedly. **suddenly, suddenness.**

suds Froth on soapy water.

sue (sues, suing, sued) To claim compensation from somebody in a court of law.

suede A kind of soft leather.

suet A kind of hard fat used in cooking.

suffer (suffers, suffering, suffered) 1. To feel pain, to have a loss or other unpleasant experience. 2. To put up with something, to tolerate it.

sufficient Enough. sufficiently, sufficiency.

suffix (suffixes) A word or syllable joined to the end of another word to alter its meaning or use, as in sudden*ly*, sudden*ness*.

suffocate (suffocates, suffocating, suffocated) 1. To kill or choke somebody by stopping his breathing. 2. To have difficulty in breathing. suffocation.

sugar A sweet substance obtained from various plants. sugar-beet, sugar-cane, sugary.

suggest (suggests, suggesting, suggested) To put forward an idea, to give an impression of something. suggestion.

suicide Killing oneself. *To commit suicide.* suicidal.

suit[1] (suits) 1. A set of clothes of the same material and colour. 2. One of the four sets in a pack of playing-cards, namely diamonds, hearts, clubs, and spades.

suit[2] (suits, suiting, suited) To be convenient or appropriate for somebody or something. suitable, suitably, suitability.

suitcase (suitcases) A case for carrying clothes and other things.

suite (suites) 1. A set of furniture. 2. A set of rooms.

suitor (suitors) (old-fashioned) A man courting a woman.

sulk (sulks, sulking, sulked) To be silent and bad-tempered. sulky, sulkily, sulkiness.

sullen Gloomy, dismal, bad-tempered. sullenly, sullenness.

sulphur A yellow chemical.

sultan (sultans) A Muslim ruler.

sultana (sultanas) A kind of raisin.

sultry (sultrier, sultriest) Hot and damp.

sum[1] (sums) 1. The total obtained when numbers are added together. 2. A problem to be solved in arithmetic. 3. An amount of money.

sum[2] (sums, summing, summed) *To sum up*, to give a summary at the end of a talk or discussion.

summarize (summarizes, summarizing, summarized) To make a summary of something.

summary (summaries) A short version giving the main points of something said or written.

summer (summers) The warm season between spring and autumn. summery.

summit (summits) The top of something.

summon (summons, summoning, summoned) To command someone to appear.

summons (summonses) A command to appear in a lawcourt.

sumptuous Magnificent, splendid. sumptuously.

sun 1. The heavenly body from which the earth gets warmth and light. 2. The warmth or light from the sun. sunbeam, sunlight, sunshine.

sunbathe (sunbathes, sunbathing, sunbathed) To sit or lie in the sun.

sunburn A brown or red colour of the skin caused by the sun. sunburnt.

Sunday (Sundays) The first day of the week.

sundial (sundials) A device which shows the time by a shadow cast by the sun.

sunflower (sunflowers) A large yellow flower.

sung *See* sing.

sun-glasses Dark glasses which protect a person's eyes from the sun.

sunk, sunken *See* sink[1].

sunless Without sunshine.

sunny (sunnier, sunniest) With the sun shining.

sunrise Dawn, the rising of the sun.

sunset The going down of the sun.

sunstroke An illness caused by too much heat from the sun.

super (informal) Excellent, splendid.

superb Magnificent. superbly.

superficial Not thorough, not going deeply into something. superficially.

superfluous More than is needed or required. superfluity.

superhuman Having more than normal human power or ability.

superintend (superintends, superintending, superintended) To supervise. superintendent.

superior[1] 1. Greater, higher, better. 2. Proud of oneself, haughty. superiority.

superior[2] (superiors) A person senior in rank to another. *A Mother Superior*, a nun in charge of a convent.

supermarket (supermarkets) A large self-service shop which sells many kinds of food and other goods.

supernatural Not to be explained by natural laws, to do with gods, or ghosts, or fairies, or other mysterious beings.

supersonic Faster than the speed of sound.

superstition (superstitions) An idea or an action based on a belief in supernatural happenings. superstitious, superstitiously.

superstructure (superstructures) The parts of a ship built above the main deck.

supervise (supervises, supervising, supervised) To look after the organization of something. supervisor, supervision.

supper (suppers) An evening meal.

supple (suppler, supplest) Easy to bend, bending easily.

supplement (supplements) 1. A part added later to improve or complete something. *An up-to-date supplement to an encyclopedia.* supplementary. 2. A magazine, usually coloured, sometimes sold with a newspaper.

supply[1] (supplies, supplying, supplied) To give or provide what is wanted. supplier.

supply[2] (supplies) 1. The supplying of something. 2. Something which is supplied. 3. A stock of something, an amount which can be supplied when needed.

support[1] (supports, supporting, supported) 1. To hold something up, to keep it in place, to keep it going. 2. To give help to someone or something. 3. *To support a football team*, to go to watch it regularly, to encourage it. supporter.

support[2] (supports) 1. The act of supporting. 2. A person or thing which supports.

suppose (supposes, supposing, supposed) 1. To guess, to think. *Why do you suppose he would do a thing like that?* 2. *To be supposed to do something*, to be expected to do it, to have to do it. supposition.

suppress (suppresses, suppressing, suppressed) 1. To put an end to something. 2. To prevent something becoming generally known. suppression, suppressor.

supreme Highest in rank, greatest. supremely, supremacy.

sure (surer, surest) 1. Certain, having no doubts, confident. 2. Reliable. 3. (informal) Yes, certainly. *Sure, I'll be there.* surely.

surf White foaming waves breaking on the shore.

surface[1] (surfaces) 1. The outside of something. *The surface of the moon.* 2. One of the sides of something. *A cube has six surfaces.*

surface² (surfaces, surfacing, surfaced) To come to the surface.

surf-board (surf-boards) A board used to ride the surf in the sport of surf-riding.

surge (surges, surging, surged) To rush forwards or upwards.

surgeon (surgeons) A doctor who performs operations. surgical.

surgery (surgeries) 1. A doctor's or dentist's room where he sees his patients. 2. A time when this office is open.

surly (surlier, surliest) Bad-mannered and bad-tempered. surliness.

surname (surnames) A person's last name, the name which all members of his family have.

surpass (surpasses, surpassing, surpassed) To do better than others, to be better than others.

surplice (surplices) A white loose-fitting garment sometimes worn by priests or members of church choirs.

surplus (surpluses) An amount left over when the required amount has been taken or used.

surprise¹ (surprises) 1. Something which was not expected. 2. The feeling a person has at something which was not expected.

surprise² (surprises, surprising, surprised) 1. To give someone a surprise, to cause a surprise. surprisingly. 2. To attack or come upon someone suddenly and unexpectedly.

surrender (surrenders, surrendering, surrendered) 1. To give oneself up to the enemy, to give in. 2. To give something up to someone.

surround (surrounds, surrounding, surrounded) To be round someone or something on all sides.

surroundings The things and places which surround someone or something.

survey¹ (pronounced *sur*vey) (surveys) 1. A general look at something. 2. An examination of something, an investigation. *A traffic survey.*

survey² (pronounced sur*vey*) (surveys, surveying, surveyed) To make a survey. surveyor.

survive (survives, surviving, survived) To continue to live after the death of another person or after some serious danger. survival, survivor.

susceptible *To be susceptible to something*, to be easily influenced or affected by it.

suspect¹ (pronounced sus*pect*) (suspects, suspecting, suspected) 1. To have a feeling that something undesirable is happening or about to happen. *They suspected an ambush.* 2. To have a feeling that someone or something is not to be trusted. *I suspect his honesty.* 3. To have a feeling that someone is guilty of something. *They suspected him of murder.*

suspect² (pronounced *sus*pect) (suspects) A person who is suspected of something.

suspend (suspends, suspending, suspended) 1. To hang something up. 2. To put a stop to something for a time. 3. To deprive somebody for a time of his job or his place in a team. suspension.

suspense Uncertainty, strain.

suspension bridge A bridge supported by steel cables hanging from a framework.

suspicion (suspicions) **1.** A feeling that something is wrong. **2.** An uncertain feeling about somebody or something. **suspicious, suspiciously.**

swag[1] (informal) **1.** Stolen goods. **2.** (Australian) A swagman's bundle.

swagger (swaggers, swaggering, swaggered) To walk or behave in a self-satisfied way.

swagman (swagmen) (Australian) A tramp.

swallow[1] (swallows, swallowing, swallowed) **1.** To allow food to pass down the throat. **2.** To take something in. *The ship was swallowed up in the fog.*

swallow[2] (swallows) A kind of small bird with a forked tail.

swam *See* **swim**[1].

swamp[1] (swamps) A marsh. **swampy.**

swamp[2] (swamps, swamping, swamped) **1.** To flood something with water. **2.** To overwhelm, to overload.

swan (swans) A large water-bird.

swank (swanks, swanking, swanked) (informal) To boast.

swarm[1] (swarms) **1.** A large number of bees clustering together. **2.** A crowd.

swarm[2] (swarms, swarming, swarmed) **1.** To move in a swarm. **2.** To climb something by clinging with the arms and legs.

swarthy (swarthier, swarthiest) With a dark complexion.

swat (swats, swatting, swatted) To slap and crush something. *To swat a fly.* **swatter.**

sway (sways, swaying, swayed) To move from side to side.

swear (swears, swearing, swore, sworn) **1.** To make a solemn promise, to take an oath. *He swore to tell the truth.* **2.** To use curses or rude words. **swear-word.**

sweat[1] (sweats, sweating, sweated) To perspire.

sweat[2] Perspiration. **sweaty.**

sweater (sweaters) A woollen pullover or jumper.

swede[1] (swedes) A root vegetable.

Swede[2] (Swedes) A Swedish person.

Swedish Of Sweden.

sweep[1] (sweeps, sweeping, swept) **1.** To clean with a large brush or broom. **sweeper. 2.** To move something quickly and forcefully. *The wind swept Ann's hat away.* **3.** To move along quickly or importantly. *The king's carriage swept past.*

sweep[2] (sweeps) **1.** A sweeping movement. **2.** A chimney-sweep, a man who cleans chimneys.

sweet[1] (sweeter, sweetest) **1.** Having a taste like that of sugar. **2.** Pleasant, attractive, delightful. **sweetly, sweetness.**

sweet[2] (sweets) **1.** A small piece of something sweet made mainly from sugar or chocolate. **2.** A dish eaten after a meat course, such as a jelly, a tart, or a trifle.

sweet corn Maize.

sweetheart (sweethearts) A lover.

swell[1] (swells, swelling, swelled, swollen) To become bigger, or fuller, or louder.

swell[2] The slow rise and fall of the open sea.

sweltering Very hot.

swept *See* **sweep**[1].

swerve (swerves, swerving, swerved) To change direction suddenly in the course of a movement.

swift[1] (swifter, swiftest) Fast, speedy. **swiftly, swiftness.**

swift[2] (swifts) A bird like a swallow.

swig (swigs, swigging, swigged) (informal) To take a drink of something.

swill[1] (swills, swilling, swilled) To clean with water.

swill[2] Waste food given to pigs.

swim[1] (swims, swimming, swam, swum) **1.** To move oneself through the water. **swimming bath, swimming pool, swimmer. 2.** To cross something by swimming. *We swam the river easily.* **3.** To be covered in liquid. *Beans swimming in tomato sauce.* **4.** To feel dizzy. *My head's swimming.*

swim[2] (swims) A time spent swimming.

swindle (swindles, swindling, swindled) To cheat someone.

swine (swine) A pig.

swing[1] (swings, swinging, swung) **1.** To move

to and fro like a pendulum or a door blown by the wind. **2.** To turn suddenly. *He swung round to see what the noise was.*

swing² (swings) **1.** A swinging movement. **2.** A seat hung from a tree or framework for a child to swing on. **3.** *In full swing*, full of activity.

swipe (swipes, swiping, swiped) **1.** To hit hard. **2.** (informal) To steal.

swirl (swirls, swirling, swirled) To move with twists and turns. *The water swirled round.*

swish (swishes, swishing, swished) To make a rustling or hissing sound.

Swiss Of Switzerland.

switch¹ (switches) A device for turning electricity on or off.

switch² (switches, switching, switched) **1.** To turn an electric current on or off. **2.** To turn suddenly from one thing to another.

switchboard (switchboards) An apparatus for connecting telephone wires when calls are being made.

swivel (swivels, swivelling, swivelled) To turn, to twist, to swing right round.

swollen *See* swell¹.

swoop (swoops, swooping, swooped) **1.** To dive through the air. **2.** To make a sudden attack.

swop (swops, swopping, swopped) (informal) To exchange one thing for another.

sword (swords) A weapon with a long steel blade.

swore, sworn *See* swear.

swot (swots, swotting, swotted) (informal) To study hard.

swum *See* swim¹.

swung *See* swing¹.

sycamore (sycamores) A kind of tree.

syllable (syllables) A word or a part of a word containing only one vowel sound.

syllabus (syllabuses) An outline or summary of things to be studied.

symbol (symbols) A sign which has come to represent something.

symbolize (symbolizes, symbolizing, symbolized) To be a symbol of something.

symmetrical Having exactly corresponding shapes on each side of an imaginary dividing line. **symmetrically, symmetry.**

sympathize (sympathizes, sympathizing, sympathized) To have sympathy for others, to give them support and encouragement. **sympathizer.**

sympathy (sympathies) The ability to understand and share other people's feelings. **sympathetic, sympathetically.**

symphony (symphonies) A kind of composition for an orchestra.

symptom (symptoms) One of the things that a person notices is wrong with him when he is ill.

synagogue (synagogues) A place where Jews meet to worship.

synchronize (synchronizes, synchronizing, synchronized) **1.** To make things happen at the same time. **2.** To make two or more clocks or watches show the same time. **synchronization.**

synonym (synonyms) A word with the same meaning as another word. **synonymous.**

synthetic Artificial. **synthetically.**

syringe (syringes) An instrument for giving injections.

syrup A thick sweet liquid.

system (systems) **1.** A set of things which together make up one complex unit. *A railway system.* **2.** An organized set of ideas, a planned way of doing something. **systematic, systematically.**

Tt

tabby (tabbies) A cat with striped fur.

table (tables) 1. A piece of furniture, with legs and a wide, flat top. table-cloth. 2. A list, information arranged in an orderly way. *Multiplication tables.*

tablespoon (tablespoons) A large spoon used for serving food.

tablet (tablets) 1. A pill. 2. A piece of soap. 3. A flat slab of stone with carved writing.

table-tennis A kind of tennis played indoors on a table.

tack[1] (tacks) A small nail with a broad head.

tack[2] (tacks, tacking, tacked) 1. To fix something with tacks. 2. To sew something quickly with long stitches. 3. To sail a zig-zag course against the wind.

tackle[1] Equipment.

tackle[2] (tackles, tackling, tackled) 1. In football, to go for the player with the ball and try to get it from him. 2. *To tackle a job*, to try to deal with it.

tacky (tackier, tackiest) Sticky. tackiness.

tact Skill in not hurting somebody's feelings. tactful, tactfully, tactless, tactlessly.

tactics The art of organizing battles. tactical, tactically.

tadpole (tadpoles) A creature that grows up to become a frog or a toad.

taffeta A kind of silky fabric.

tag[1] (tags) 1. A label. 2. A chasing game.

tag[2] (tags, tagging, tagged) To follow somebody closely.

tail[1] (tails) 1. A projecting part at the end of the back of animals, birds, and fish. *Mice have long tails.* tailless. 2. The end part of something. *A tail light*, a light at the rear of a vehicle. 3. The side of a coin opposite the side with the head on it.

tail[2] (tails, tailing, tailed) 1. To follow somebody or something. 2. *To tail off*, to become smaller, to become less successful.

tailor (tailors) A man whose job is making clothes.

take (takes, taking, took, taken) 1. To get hold of something. *Take my hand.* 2. To capture. *They took many prisoners.* 3. To carry, to remove. *You can take your work home.* 4. To guide, to accompany. *I will take you home.* 5. To have, to use. *Do you take sugar?* 6. To get, to accept. *Take my advice!* 7. To need. *How long will the job take?* 8. To consider, to suppose, to understand. *Judging by your expression, I take it that you disapprove.* 9. To organize something, to be in charge of it. *Who is taking us for games tomorrow?* 10. *To take notes*, to write notes of what one hears or reads. 11. *To take a photograph*, to use a camera to make a photograph. 12. *To take someone in*, to deceive him. 13. *To take off*, to begin a flight. 14. *To take place*, to happen.

takings Money received.

talcum powder A soft, pleasant-smelling powder.

tale (tales) A story. *To tell tales*, to tell about someone's wrongdoing.

talent (talents) A special ability to do something.

talented Skilful at something, having talent.

talk[1] (talks, talking, talked) To speak, to say things. talker.

talk[2] (talks) 1. Conversation, discussion. 2. A lecture.

talkative Fond of talking.

tall (taller, tallest) 1. Of more than average height. *James is tall for his age.* 2. In height. *John is almost two metres tall.*

tallish Rather tall.

talon (talons) A claw.

tambourine (tambourines) A percussion instrument.

tame[1] (tamer, tamest) 1. Not wild or fierce, not dangerous to humans. *Tame animals.* 2. Dull, uninteresting. tamely, tameness.

tame² (tames, taming, tamed) To make an animal tame. **tamer.**

tamper (tampers, tampering, tampered) To meddle with something.

tan¹ Yellowish brown.

tan² (tans, tanning, tanned) 1. To make an animal's skin into leather. **tanner.** 2. *To be tanned by the sun*, to be made brown by the sun.

tandem (tandems) A bicycle for two people.

tang A sharp taste.

tangerine (tangerines) A kind of small orange.

tangible Able to be touched.

tangle (tangles, tangling, tangled) 1. To become confused and muddled. *Tangled string.* 2. To make something into a confused muddle.

tank (tanks) 1. A container for a liquid or a gas. *A petrol tank.* 2. An armoured fighting vehicle.

tankard (tankards) A kind of mug.

tanker (tankers) 1. A ship designed to carry oil. 2. A lorry with a large tank for carrying liquid. *A milk tanker.*

tantalize (tantalizes, tantalizing, tantalized) To torment somebody with the offer of something which he can never have. **tantalizingly.**

tantrum (tantrums) A fit of bad temper.

tap¹ (taps) 1. A device for controlling the flow of a liquid or a gas. *A water tap. A gas tap.* 2. A quick light hit.

tap² (taps, tapping, tapped) To hit something quickly and lightly.

tape¹ (tapes) 1. A narrow strip of cloth, paper, or plastic. *Sticky tape. Insulating tape.* 2. *Recording tape*, a plastic tape coated with a magnetic substance used to make sound recordings.

tape² (tapes, taping, taped) 1. To fasten or surround something with tape. 2. To record sound on tape.

tape-measure (tape-measures) A tape marked out in inches or centimetres.

taper (tapers, tapering, tapered) To become gradually narrower towards one end.

tape-recorder (tape-recorders) An apparatus for recording and playing back sound using magnetic tape. **tape-recording.**

tapestry (tapestries) A piece of cloth with pictures or patterns woven into the material.

tar¹ A black sticky substance used in road-making. **tarry.**

tar² (tars, tarring, tarred) To put tar on something.

tarantula (tarantulas) A kind of spider.

target (targets) Something to be aimed at.

Tarmac The trade name for a mixture of tar and crushed stone used for making roads, paths, and playgrounds.

tarnish (tarnishes, tarnishing, tarnished) To become dull or discoloured instead of shiny.

tarpaulin (tarpaulins) A large, thick, waterproof sheet.

tart¹ Sour, sharp-tasting. **tartly, tartness.**

tart² (tarts) 1. Pastry with jam or fruit on it. 2. A shallow fruit pie.

tartan A kind of cloth from the Scottish Highlands with a criss-cross pattern.

task (tasks) A piece of work to be done.

task-force (task-forces) A group of men with orders to carry out a particular operation.

tassel (tassels) A bunch of loose threads decorating the end of a cord.

taste¹ (tastes, tasting, tasted) 1. To use the tongue to recognize or get to know things. 2. To have a taste or flavour.

taste² (tastes) 1. The ability to taste. *The sense of taste.* 2. Flavour, the quality of a thing which a person can taste. *This fish looked all right, but it has a funny taste.* 3. The ability to appreciate beautiful things. *The colours you chose for your bedroom show that you have good taste.* **tasteful, tastefully, tasteless, tastelessly.**

tasty (tastier, tastiest) Pleasant to the taste.

tattered Torn, in rags.

tatters Rags.

tattoo¹ (tattoos) 1. Something tattooed on a person's skin. 2. A drum-beat. 3. A display given by troops for entertainment.

tattoo[2] (tattoos, tattooing, tattooed) To make
a design on a person's skin by pricking it
and putting in colouring.

tatty (informal) Shabby, ragged.

taught *See* teach.

taunt (taunts, taunting, taunted) To mock
someone with insults.

taut Tightly stretched.

tavern (taverns) An inn, a public house.

tawdry Showy but of no value.

tawny Yellowish brown.

tax[1] (taxes) Money which people have to pay
to the government in order to run the
affairs of the country.

tax[2] (taxes, taxing, taxed) To put a tax on
somebody or something. taxable.

taxi[1] (taxis) A car with a driver which may
be hired for short journeys.

taxi[2] (taxies, taxiing, taxied) To move along
the ground before or after flying. *The plane
taxied across the aerodrome.*

tea[1] 1. A kind of hot drink. 2. The dried
leaves of an Asian shrub from which this
drink is made. teapot, tea-leaves, tea-bag.

tea[2] (teas) An afternoon meal at which tea is
usually drunk. tea-time, tea-tray.

teach (teaches, teaching, taught) 1. To pass
on knowledge or skill to somebody. *Ethel
taught me how to stand on my head.* 2. To
give instruction in a particular subject.
Miss Bishop teaches the piano. teacher.

teachable Able to be taught.

tea-cloth (tea-cloths) A cloth used to dry
dishes.

teak A hard wood from the Far East.

team (teams) 1. A set of people playing on
the same side in a game. 2. A group working
together. *Team-work*, a combined effort.

tear[1] (tears, tearing, tore, torn) 1. To pull
apart, to pull into pieces, to pull away from
the proper place. 2. To rush. *He tore down
the road with the police after him.*

tear[2] (tears) 1. A drop of salty water coming
from somebody's eye. tear-drop, tearful,
tearfully. 2. *Tear gas*, a gas that makes
people's eyes water painfully.

tease (teases, teasing, teased) To make fun
by bothering somebody or by making
joking remarks.

teaspoon (teaspoons) A small spoon used for
stirring tea.

teat (teats) 1. A nipple through which milk is
sucked by the young. 2. The rubber cap on
a baby's feeding bottle.

technical Concerned with machinery or with
the way things work.

technician (technicians) A mechanic.

technique (techniques) A skilled way of doing
something.

teddy-bear (teddy-bears) A stuffed toy bear.

tedious Long and boring. tediously.

teem (teems, teeming, teemed) 1. To swarm,
to be present in large numbers. 2. To rain
hard.

teenage Connected with teenagers.

teenager (teenagers) A person aged from 13
to 19.

teens The period of a person's life from 13
to 19 years of age.

teeny (teenier, teeniest) Tiny.

teeth *See* tooth.

teething Beginning to grow teeth.

teetotaller (teetotallers) A person who never
drinks alcoholic drink.

telegram (telegrams) A short message to be
delivered quickly by the post office.

telegraph pole A pole carrying telephone
wires.

telepathy The ability to understand what is
in the mind of someone else without the
help of speaking, writing, or other signs.
telepathic.

telephone[1] (telephones) An instrument connected by wires to other apparatus which
enables one person to speak to another a
long distance away.

telephone[2] (telephones, telephoning, tele-
phoned) To speak by telephone.

telephoto lens A camera lens which makes
distant objects appear nearer.

telescope[1] (telescopes) An instrument for
seeing distant objects more clearly.

telescope[2] (telescopes, telescoping, telescoped) To make something shorter by sliding one section inside another like the tubes of a portable telescope.

televise (televises, televising, televised) To send out by television.

television 1. Sending out and receiving pictures through the air by means of radio waves. 2. An apparatus for receiving such pictures. 3. Televised programmes.

tell (tells, telling, told) 1. To pass on a story or information or instructions by speaking. **teller.** 2. To distinguish, to decide. *Can you tell the difference between the twins?* 3. (informal) *To tell someone off,* to tell him that one is angry with him.

temper 1. A condition of the mind and feelings. *To be in a good temper.* 2. *To lose one's temper,* to become uncontrollably angry.

temperament A person's nature or character.

temperamental Liable to quick changes of mood.

temperance Moderation, self control.

temperature (temperatures) 1. The hotness or coldness of something. 2. *To have a temperature,* to be ill and have a body temperature higher than normal.

tempest (tempests) A violent storm. **tempestuous.**

temple (temples) 1. A building used for worship. 2. The part of the head between the forehead and the ear.

tempo (tempos) The speed or pace of something, especially of a piece of music.

temporary For a short time only. **temporarily.**

tempt (tempts, tempting, tempted) To try to persuade somebody to do something which he ought not to do, or which he would not do of his own accord. **tempter, temptation.**

ten (tens) The number 10. **tenth.**

tenant (tenants) A person who rents somewhere to live or work.

tend (tends, tending, tended) 1. To take care of something. 2. To have a tendency.

tendency (tendencies) An inclination.

tender[1] (tenderer, tenderest) 1. Soft, delicate, easily damaged. *Tender plants.* 2. Easily cut, easily chewed. *Tender meat.* 3. Loving. *A tender kiss.* **tenderly, tenderness.**

tender[2] (tenders) A truck attached to a steam locomotive to carry coal and water.

tennis A game played with rackets and a ball.

tenor (tenors) A male singer with a high voice.

tense Stretched tight, strained, excited. **tensely, tension.**

tent (tents) A kind of shelter made of canvas.

tentacle (tentacles) A thin, snake-like part of certain animals. *The tentacles of an octopus.*

tepee (tepees) A wigwam.

tepid Slightly warm.

term (terms) 1. A period of time during which a school or college is open. 2. An expression. *Technical terms.* 3. A condition of an agreement. *Terms of peace.* 4. *Terms,* charges. *The terms at this hotel are reasonable.* 5. *On good terms,* friendly with one another.

terminal (terminals) 1. One of the two places on a battery for wires to be attached. 2. A terminus, the end of a transport route.

terminate (terminates, terminating, terminated) To stop, to end.

terminus (termini) The end of a railway line or bus route.

terrace (terraces) 1. A raised level place in front of a building. 2. A levelled area in a garden or on a hillside. 3. A row of houses all joined together.

terrestrial Belonging to the planet earth.

terrible Frightening, dreadful. **terribly.**

terrier (terriers) A kind of small dog.

terrific (informal) 1. Very great. 2. Excellent. terrifically.

terrify (terrifies, terrifying, terrified) To fill somebody with fear.

territory (territories) 1. An area of land. 2. An area of land belonging to an individual or nation. territorial.

terror (terrors) Great fear.

terrorist (terrorists) A person who commits acts of violence for political reasons. terrorism.

terrorize (terrorizes, terrorizing, terrorized) To fill people with terror.

terse Brief. tersely.

test¹ (tests) 1. An examination or trial of something or somebody. 2. A test-match.

test² (tests, testing, tested) To make a test.

testament (testaments) 1. A written statement. 2. *The Old Testament, the New Testament*, the two main parts of the Bible.

testify (testifies, testifying, testified) To give evidence.

testimony Evidence.

test-match (test-matches) An international match in cricket and some other games.

test pilot A pilot who flies aircraft to test them.

test-tube (test-tubes) A glass tube used for experiments in chemistry.

testy (testier, testiest) Cross, irritable. testily.

tether¹ (tethers) A rope for tying up an animal.

tether² (tethers, tethering, tethered) To tie up with a tether.

text (texts) 1. The words in a book. 2. A sentence from the Bible.

text-book (text-books) A book intended to teach the basic facts about a subject.

textile (textiles) Cloth.

texture (textures) The way the surface of a thing feels. *Silk has a smooth texture.*

than A word used when making comparisons. *Robert is older than Jane.*

thank (thanks, thanking, thanked) 1. To tell a person that one appreciates something he has done or something he has given.

thankful, thankfully, thankfulness. 2. *Thank you* or *thanks*, a polite way of thanking someone. 3. *Thanks to*, because of.

that¹ (those) The one there, the one indicated. *I am enjoying this book, but that one on the table was boring.*

that² This word is used in several kinds of sentence including the following: 1. *Have you opened the letter that came this morning?* 2. *I hope that you are well.* 3. *Alan slept so soundly that he didn't hear the alarm.* 4. *Speak louder so that we can all hear.*

thatch¹ (thatches, thatching, thatched) To make a roof out of straw or reeds. thatcher.

thatch² Straw or reeds used to make a roof.

thaw¹ (thaws, thawing, thawed) 1. To become unfrozen. 2. To unfreeze something.

thaw² (thaws) The melting of snow or ice.

the 1. A particular one, this or that, these or those. *Shut the window and draw the curtains.* 2. *The rich, the poor*, all rich people, all poor people.

theatre (theatres) 1. A building designed for the performance of plays to an audience. 2. *An operating theatre*, a room where a surgeon performs operations.

theatrical Of acting or plays.

thee *See* thou.

theft (thefts) Stealing.

their or theirs Belonging to them.

them *See* they.

theme (themes) A subject.

themselves *See* they. This word is used in the same ways as himself.

then 1. At that time. *There were giants then.*

2. That time. *Since then, until then.* 3. Next, afterwards. *Then there were nine.* 4. In that case. *If you did it, then you should own up.*

theology The study of religion.

theory (theories) 1. An idea suggested to explain something. 2. The general principles of something. *The theory of music.* **theoretical.**

there 1. In that place, at that place, to that place. *Cheer up, we'll soon be there.* 2. This word is also used to call attention to something, or for emphasis. *There she goes! There, what did I tell you?*

therefore And so, for that reason.

thermometer (thermometers) An instrument for measuring temperature.

Thermos (Thermoses) The trade name for a container which keeps hot drinks hot.

thermostat (thermostats) An automatic device for keeping a steady temperature. **thermostatic, thermostatically.**

these *See* this.

they (them, themselves) The people or things being talked about.

thick (thicker, thickest) 1. Measuring a comparatively long distance through from one surface to the opposite one, not thin. *A thick slice of bread.* 2. Measuring from one surface through to the opposite one, measuring from the top surface down to the bottom. *The snow was ten centimetres thick.* 3. Consisting of a great number of people or things crowded together. *A thick crowd.* 4. Dense, hard to see through. *Thick mist.* 5. Not able to flow as quickly as water. *Thick gravy.* **thickly, thickness.**

thicken (thickens, thickening, thickened) 1. To make thicker. 2. To become thicker.

thief (thieves) A person who steals.

thigh (thighs) The part of the leg above the knee.

thimble (thimbles) A small cap to protect the end of one's finger when sewing.

thin[1] (thinner, thinnest) 1. Not fat. *A thin person.* 2. Not thick. *A thin slice of bread. Thin hair. Thin gravy.* **thinly, thinness.**

thin[2] (thins, thinning, thinned) 1. To make thin. 2. To become thin.

thine (old-fashioned) Your, yours.

thing (things) 1. Anything which can be touched or seen, any object, any person, any animal. *What's that thing floating in the water?* 2. An action, a happening. *An odd thing happened to me today.* 3. An idea, a thought. *I have several things on my mind.* 4. *Things,* circumstances. *Things are getting worse and worse.*

think (thinks, thinking, thought) To use the mind, to have an idea, to have an opinion. **thinker.**

third[1] 1. Next after the second. **thirdly.** 2. *Third degree,* cruel questioning.

third[2] (thirds) One of the three equal parts into which something is or can be divided.

thirst (thirsts) A strong desire for something to drink. **thirsty, thirstily, thirstiness.**

thirteen The number 13. **thirteenth.**

thirty (thirties) The number 30. **thirtieth.**

this (these) The one near here, the one being considered. *This dictionary is printed in black and red.*

thistle (thistles) A wild plant with prickly leaves.

thong (thongs) A narrow strip of leather.

thorn (thorns) A sharp pointed growth on the stem of a plant. **thorny.**

thorough Complete, without leaving anything out.

thoroughfare (thoroughfares) A road, a busy road.

those *See* that.

thou (thee, thyself) (old-fashioned) You.

though 1. In spite of the fact that. *I shall go even though you tell me not to.* 2. However. *He never did come back in the end, though, in spite of his promises.*

thought[1] *See* think.

thought[2] (thoughts) 1. Thinking, consideration. 2. An idea, an opinion. **thoughtful, thoughtfully, thoughtfulness.**

thoughtless Lacking in consideration. **thoughtlessly, thoughtlessness.**

thousand (thousands) The number 1000. **thousandth.**

thrash (thrashes, thrashing, thrashed) **1.** To hit repeatedly, to beat someone with a stick or whip. **2.** To move the limbs about violently. **3.** To defeat someone.

thread[1] (threads) **1.** A length of cotton, wool, nylon, or other substance which can be used for sewing or for making cloth. **2.** A long thin length of any other substance. **3.** The raised line which goes round and round a screw.

thread[2] (threads, threading, threaded) **1.** To pass thread through the eye of a needle. **2.** To put things on a thread. *To thread beads.*

threadbare Shabby, badly worn.

threat (threats) **1.** A warning, a sign of coming trouble or danger. **2.** Something or someone likely to cause trouble or danger.

threaten (threatens, threatening, threatened) **1.** To make threats. **2.** To be a threat. **threateningly.**

three (threes) The number 3. **third.**

three-dimensional Having depth as well as breadth and height.

thresh (threshes, threshing, threshed) To separate the grain from the husks of corn.

threw *See* **throw**[1].

thrift Being thrifty.

thrifty (thriftier, thriftiest) Careful with money. **thriftily.**

thrill[1] (thrills) **1.** A feeling of great excitement. **2.** Something which causes great excitement.

thrill[2] (thrills, thrilling, thrilled) To cause a feeling of great excitement. **thrillingly.**

thriller (thrillers) An exciting story about crime.

thriving Successful, growing strongly.

throat (throats) **1.** The front of the neck. **2.** The tube in the neck through which food and air pass into the body.

throb[1] (throbs, throbbing, throbbed) To beat with a steady rhythm, to vibrate.

throb[2] (throbs) A throbbing sound or movement.

throne (thrones) A chair used by a king or queen in official ceremonies.

throng[1] (throngs, thronging, thronged) To crowd.

throng[2] (throngs) A crowd.

throttle[1] (throttles, throttling, throttled) To strangle.

throttle[2] (throttles) A device to control the flow of petrol to an engine, an accelerator.

through **1.** Into something and out at the other end or side. *The train went through the tunnel.* **2.** From one end or side to the other. *Is the meat cooked right through?* **3.** From beginning to end of something. *All through the night.* **4.** By means of. *We arranged our holiday through a travel agent.* **5.** Because of. *Accidents happened through Alan's stupidity.* **6.** All the way. *Does this train go through to London?* **7.** *To see something through*, to finish it. **8.** *To get through an exam*, to pass it.

throughout All through, right through.

throw[1] (throws, throwing, threw, thrown) **1.** To make something move through the air by a jerk of the arm. **2.** To make somebody or something move suddenly through the air. **3.** To move the arms or other parts of the body violently about. **4.** To form clay into a pot on a wheel. **thrower.**

throw[2] (throws) An action of throwing.

thrush (thrushes) A kind of song-bird.

thrust (thrusts, thrusting, thrust) **1.** To push suddenly or violently. **2.** To stab with a sword.

thud (thuds) The sound of a hard object hitting something softer.

thug (thugs) A murderous criminal.

thumb (thumbs) The short thick finger growing separately from the others.

thump (thumps, thumping, thumped) 1. To hit something heavily. 2. To make a thud.

thunder[1] 1. The loud sound that follows lightning. thundery, thunder-storm. 2. A loud rumbling sound. thunderous.

thunder[2] (thunders, thundering, thundered) To make the sound of thunder.

thunderstruck Amazed.

Thursday (Thursdays) The fifth day of the week.

thus In this way.

thy (old-fashioned) Your.

thyself *See* thou. This word is used in the same ways as himself.

tick[1] (ticks) 1. A light regular sound. *Tick-tock*, the sound of a clock. 2. The mark √.

tick[2] (ticks, ticking, ticked) 1. To make a tick. 2. *To tick somebody off*, (informal) to tell him that one is angry with him.

ticket (tickets) A small piece of paper or card such as one buys to travel on a bus or train.

tickle (tickles, tickling, tickled) 1. To touch a person's skin lightly so as to make him laugh or feel irritated. 2. To itch, to have a tickling feeling.

ticklish 1. Liable to laugh when tickled. 2. Needing care and skill. *A ticklish problem.*

tidal wave A very large wave in the sea.

tiddler (tiddlers) (informal) Any tiny fish.

tiddlywinks A game played with small coloured counters.

tide (tides) The rising and falling of the sea which happens twice a day. tidal.

tidings (old-fashioned) News.

tidy[1] (tidier, tidiest) Neat, carefully arranged. tidily, tidiness.

tidy[2] (tidies, tidying, tidied) To make tidy.

tie[1] (ties, tying, tied) 1. To make a knot. 2. To fasten with string or cord. 3. To finish a game or competition with an equal score or in an equal position.

tie[2] (ties) 1. A strip of material worn under the collar of a shirt and tied in a knot in front. 2. An equal result in a game or competition.

tiger (tigers) A large fierce animal of the cat family. tigress.

tight (tighter, tightest) 1. Firmly fastened. 2. Closely fitting. 3. Fully stretched. 4. Crowded close together. *Tight as sardines.* 5. (informal) Drunk. tightly, tightness.

tighten (tightens, tightening, tightened) 1. To make tighter. 2. To become tighter.

tight-fisted Mean, miserly.

tight-rope (tight-ropes) A tightly stretched rope for acrobats to perform on.

tights A garment which fits tightly over the legs and lower part of the body.

tile (tiles) A thin piece of baked clay or other material for covering roofs, walls, or floors. tiled Covered with tiles.

till[1] Until.

till[2] (tills) A box or drawer for money on the counter of a shop.

tiller (tillers) A lever used to turn a rudder.

tilt (tilts, tilting, tilted) To lean.

timber (timbers) Wood for building or carpentry.

time[1] (times) 1. The passing by of minutes, hours, days, or years. *You don't notice time when you are busy.* 2. A particular moment in time. *The time is just one o'clock.* 3. A length of time. *Is there time for another cup of tea?* 4. A period of history. *In the time of King John.* 5. The speed and rhythm of a piece of music. *If you are playing in a group you must keep time with the others.* 6. *Times*, multiplied by. *4 times 2 is 8* ($4 \times 2 = 8$).

time[2] (times, timing, timed) 1. To measure the time taken to do something. 2. To note the time at which something is done.

time bomb A bomb designed to explode at a particular time.

timely Happening at the right time.

timetable (timetables) 1. A table showing when buses, trains, or other forms of transport depart and arrive. 2. A table showing when various lessons take place in school.

timid Not very brave. **timidly, timidity.**

timorous Timid. **timorously.**

timpani Kettle-drums.

tin[1] A soft silvery metal.

tin[2] (tins) A container made of thin sheet iron coated with tin. **tin-opener.**

tin[3] (tins, tinning, tinned) To pack something into tins. *Tinned fruit.*

tin-foil A thin silvery sheet used in packing food, tobacco, and other products.

tinge (tinges, tingeing, tinged) To colour slightly.

tingle (tingles, tingling, tingled) To have a slight stinging feeling under the skin.

tinker[1] (tinkers) A travelling repairer of pots and pans.

tinker[2] (tinkers, tinkering, tinkered) To try to adjust or repair something without the proper knowledge and skill.

tinkle (tinkles, tinkling, tinkled) To make a number of light ringing sounds.

tinny (tinnier, tinniest) 1. Like tin. 2. Thin and of poor quality.

tinsel A shiny material used in decoration.

tint (tints) A pale shade, a kind of colour. *A light yellow tint.*

tinted Slightly coloured.

tiny (tinier, tiniest) Very small.

tip[1] (tips) 1. The thin end of something. 2. A piece fitted to the end of something. 3. A small present of money given to somebody who has done one a service. *Don't forget to give the waiter a tip.* 4. A piece of advice. 5. A place where rubbish is tipped.

tip[2] (tips, tipping, tipped) 1. To move on to one edge, to overturn. 2. To empty a container thus. 3. To give someone a tip.

tiptoe *On tiptoe,* on the toes.

tire (tires, tiring, tired) 1. To become tired. 2. To make a person tired.

tired Feeling that one needs to rest or sleep. **tiredness.**

tiresome Annoying. **tiresomely.**

tissue (tissues) A piece of soft paper used for cleaning or for blowing one's nose.

tissue-paper Very thin paper.

tit (tits) A small bird.

titbit (titbits) A small piece of something good to eat.

title (titles) 1. The name of a story, or a picture, or a piece of music. 2. A word which shows a person's profession or position, such as *Dr., Lord, Sir, Mrs.*

titter (titters, tittering, tittered) To give a silly laugh.

to 1. In the direction of, towards. *Travelling to the moon.* 2. As far as. *They got to their destination.* 3. Rather than, compared with. *Susan prefers dogs to cats.*

to and fro Backwards and forwards.

toad (toads) A creature like a large frog.

toadstool (toadstools) A kind of fungus.

toast[1] (toasts, toasting, toasted) To make something crisp and brown by heating it. **toaster.**

toast[2] 1. Toasted bread. 2. *To drink a toast,* to wish someone happiness or success while drinking a glass of wine.

tobacco The dried leaves of certain plants prepared for smoking in pipes, or cigarettes, or cigars.

tobacconist (tobacconists) A shopkeeper who sells tobacco.

toboggan (toboggans) A long, narrow sledge. **tobogganing.**

today This present day.

toddler (toddlers) A young child just learning to walk.

to-do A fuss, much excitement.

toe (toes) 1. A part of the body at the end of the foot. **toe-nail**. 2. Part of a shoe or sock covering the toes.

toffee (toffees) A kind of sweet.

together 1. In company, side by side. 2. Brought into contact, joined one to the other.

toil¹ (toils, toiling, toiled) 1. To work hard. 2. To make slow and difficult progress.

toil² Hard work.

toilet (toilets) A lavatory. **toilet-paper, toilet-roll**.

token (tokens) 1. A sign of something. 2. A counter, a voucher. *A book token.*

told *See* tell.

tolerate (tolerates, tolerating, tolerated) To put up with something, to endure it, not to protest about it. **tolerable, tolerance, toleration**.

toll¹ (tolls, tolling, tolled) To ring a bell slowly.

toll² (tolls) A payment, a charge made for using some bridges or roads.

toll-bridge (toll-bridges) A bridge where a toll is charged.

tomahawk (tomahawks) An American Indian axe.

tomato (tomatoes) A soft juicy fruit.

tomb (tombs) A place where dead bodies are buried or placed. **tomb-stone**.

tomcat (tomcats) A male cat.

tommy-gun (tommy-guns) A kind of small machine-gun.

tomorrow The day after today.

tom-tom (tom-toms) A kind of drum.

ton¹ (tons) A unit of weight, 2,240 pounds or about 1,020 kilograms.

ton² (informal) 100 miles per hour.

tone¹ (tones) 1. A musical sound. 2. A quality which indicates the character of something. *There was an angry tone in his voice.* 3. A shade of a colour.

tone² (tones, toning, toned) *To tone something down*, to make it quieter or less violent.

tongs A tool for picking things up. *Coal tongs.*

tongue (tongues) 1. The long soft movable part of the mouth used in talking, tasting, and licking. 2. A language.

tongue-tied Unable to speak because of shyness.

tongue-twister (tongue-twisters) Something which is difficult to say.

tonic (tonics) Something which makes a person stronger and healthier.

tonight This night, the night which follows today.

tonne (tonnes) A metric unit of weight, 1000 kilograms.

tonsillitis A disease of the tonsils.

tonsils The two soft, small organs in the throat.

too 1. Also, in addition. *Jamie can come too.* 2. More than is wanted. *The tea is too hot.*

took *See* take.

tool (tools) An instrument or device which a person uses to do a certain job.

tooth (teeth) 1. One of the hard, white parts growing in rows in the mouth which are used for biting and chewing. **toothache, toothbrush, toothpaste**. 2. One of a row of pointed parts of something. *The teeth of a saw.*

toothless Without teeth.

top¹ (tops) 1. The highest part or point of a thing. 2. The upper surface of a thing. 3. The person, or thing, or team in the highest position. 4. A toy which spins on its point.

top² Highest. *The top floor.*

top³ (tops, topping, topped) 1. To put a top on something. 2. To be the top of something.

top-heavy Too heavy at the top.

topic (topics) A subject for discussion or study.

topical In the news.

topple (topples, toppling, toppled) To overturn.

topsy-turvy Upside down, muddled.

torch (torches) A portable electric light.

tore *See* tear[1].

toreador (toreadors) A bullfighter.

torment (torments, tormenting, tormented) To cause severe suffering, to torture. **tormentor.**

torn *See* tear[1].

tornado (tornadoes) A violent storm.

torpedo[1] (torpedoes) A weapon which travels under its own power just below the surface of the water to its target.

torpedo[2] (torpedoes, torpedoing, torpedoed) To attack with torpedoes.

torrent (torrents) A violent rushing stream.

torrential Rushing like a torrent.

tortoise (tortoises) A kind of slow animal with a hard shell. **tortoiseshell.**

torture[1] (tortures, torturing, tortured) To cause somebody great pain. **torturer.**

torture[2] (tortures) Cruel treatment that causes great pain.

Tory (Tories) A supporter of the Conservative Party.

toss (tosses, tossing, tossed) 1. To throw. 2. To move about restlessly in bed.

total[1] Complete. *A total eclipse.* **totally.**

total[2] (totals) The amount to which something adds up.

total[3] (totals, totalling, totalled) To add up to something. *The bills totalled over £20.*

totem pole A post carved by American Indians.

totter (totters, tottering, tottered) To walk unsteadily, to wobble. **tottery.**

touch[1] (touches, touching, touched) 1. To feel something, to put the hand or fingers on something. 2. To come into contact with something, to hit it lightly. *The car touched the kerb.* 3. To be in contact, not to be separated. 4. To affect a person's feelings. *Mother was touched by the gift of flowers.* 5. To come up to a certain level briefly. *The temperature touched 23 °C.* 6. *To touch down,* to land. 7. *To touch up,* to improve something by small changes.

touch[2] (touches) 1. The act of touching something. 2. The sense which enables a person to feel things. *The sense of touch.* 3. A very small amount of something. *There is a touch of frost this morning.* 4. *To kick a ball into touch,* to kick it across the touch-line. 5. *To get in touch with someone,* to communicate with him.

touch-down (touch-downs) 1. The landing of an aircraft. 2. In Rugby football, the pressing of the ball on the ground behind the goal-line.

touch-line (touch-lines) A line along the side of a football pitch.

touchy (touchier, touchiest) Easily offended. **touchily, touchiness.**

tough (tougher, toughest) 1. Strong, not easily broken. 2. Hard to cut, hard to chew. *Tough meat.* 3. Rough, violent. *A tough criminal.* 4. Difficult. *A tough problem.* **toughly, toughness.**

toughen (toughens, toughening, toughened) 1. To make tougher. 2. To become tougher.

tour[1] (tours) A journey which passes through various places and ends where it began.

tour[2] (tours, touring, toured) To make a tour, to travel about on holiday. **tourist.**

tournament (tournaments) A series of games or contests.

tow (tows, towing, towed) To pull a vehicle or boat along. **tow-bar, tow-rope.**

toward or **towards** 1. In the direction of something. 2. As a contribution to. *Put this towards a new bicycle.* 3. In relation to. *Good will towards men.*

towel (towels) A cloth for drying things.

tower[1] (towers) 1. A kind of tall building. 2. A tall part of a building. *A church tower.*

tower[2] (towers, towering, towered) To rise to a great height.

town (towns) A place where there are many houses with shops, schools, places to work, and so on. **townspeople.**

towpath (towpaths) A path beside a canal or river.

toxic Poisonous.

toy (toys) Something to play with. toyshop.

trace[1] (traces, tracing, traced) 1. To copy something by drawing over it on transparent paper. tracing-paper. 2. To follow up traces of something or somebody.

trace[2] (traces) A mark, a sign, a piece of evidence. *The criminals left no traces.*

tracer (tracers) A bullet or shell which leaves a visible trail.

track[1] (tracks) 1. A path made by regular use. 2. A trace left by a moving person, animal, or vehicle. 3. A set of rails for trains or other vehicles. 4. A road or path for racing. 5. A metal belt used instead of wheels to drive tanks and some types of tractor. 6. *To keep track of somebody*, to know where he is.

track[2] (tracks, tracking, tracked) To follow the tracks left by something or somebody. tracker.

traction engine A steam engine once used on the roads.

tractor (tractors) A motor vehicle designed for farm use.

trade[1] (trades) 1. The buying, or selling, or exchanging of goods. 2. An occupation, a job. *I worked at the weaver's trade.*

trade[2] (trades, trading, traded) 1. To take part in trade. trader, tradesman. 2. *To trade something in*, to hand in an old thing as part of the payment for a new one.

trade-mark (trade-marks) A special sign used by one manufacturer.

trade union An organized group of workers.

tradition (traditions) 1. The passing on of ideas, or customs, or stories, or tunes from one generation to another. 2. Something passed on in this way. traditional, traditionally.

traffic 1. Moving vehicles. 2. Trading.

traffic lights Signals for controlling traffic.

traffic warden A person who controls the movement and parking of vehicles in a town.

tragedy (tragedies) 1. A very sad event. 2. A serious story which tells of terrible events and ends sadly. tragic, tragically.

trail[1] (trails) A track, a trace.

trail[2] (trails, trailing, trailed) 1. To pull something along behind. 2. To go along behind someone or something. 3. To hang loosely downwards.

trailer (trailers) 1. A vehicle designed to be towed by another vehicle. 2. A series of short extracts from a film shown in advance to advertise it.

train[1] (trains) 1. A number of railway coaches or wagons joined together. 2. A number of people or animals making a journey together. *A camel train.* 3. Part of a dress or robe that trails along the ground. 4. A series of events or ideas. *A train of thought.*

train[2] (trains, training, trained) 1. To give someone instruction and practice in doing something. trainer. 2. To prepare oneself by practising.

traitor (traitors) A person who betrays his country or his friends.

tram (trams) A passenger vehicle which runs along lines set in the road. tramlines, tramway.

tramp[1] (tramps) 1. A homeless person who walks from place to place. 2. The sound of tramping. 3. A long walk.

tramp[2] (tramps, tramping, tramped) 1. To walk with heavy footsteps. 2. To walk for a long distance.

trample (tramples, trampling, trampled) To tread heavily on something.

trampoline (trampolines) A large piece of canvas attached by springs to a square metal frame for use in gymnastics.

tramp steamer A small cargo ship.

trance (trances) A sleep-like condition.

tranquil Calm, peaceful. tranquilly, tranquillity.

tranquillizer (tranquillizers) A drug used to make a person calmer.

transaction (transactions) A piece of business.

transatlantic Across the Atlantic Ocean.

transfer[1] (pronounced trans*fer*) (transfers, transferring, transferred) To move something or somebody from one place to another.

transfer[2] (pronounced *trans*fer) (transfers) 1. A picture or design that can be transferred from one surface to another. 2. The act of transferring something or somebody.

transform (transforms, transforming, transformed) To change. transformation.

transformer (transformers) A device which changes electrical voltage.

transient Brief, soon past. transience.

transistor (transistors) 1. A very small electronic device used in radio sets and other equipment instead of a valve. 2. A radio made with transistors.

transistorized Made with transistors instead of valves.

transit *In transit*, while being transported.

translate (translates, translating, translated) To give the meaning of something said or written in another language. translator, translation.

translucent Allowing light to pass through. *Very thin china is translucent.*

transmit (transmits, transmitting, transmitted) 1. To pass something on. 2. To send out radio communications or television programmes. transmitter, transmission.

transparency (transparencies) A transparent photograph for projecting on a screen.

transparent Clear enough to see through.

transplant (transplants, transplanting, transplanted) To take a living thing from one place and put it to grow somewhere else.

transport[1] (pronounced trans*port*) (transports, transporting, transported) To take people or goods from one place to another in a vehicle, ship, or plane.

transport[2] (pronounced *trans*port) 1. Transporting people or goods. 2. Vehicles, ships, or planes used for transport.

trap[1] (traps) 1. A device for catching animals or people. 2. A small vehicle pulled by a pony.

trap[2] (traps, trapping, trapped) To catch in a trap. trapper.

trap-door (trap-doors) A kind of door in a floor or ceiling.

trapeze A pair of long, hanging ropes with a cross-bar for an acrobat to perform on.

trash Rubbish.

travel (travels, travelling, travelled) To make a journey, to move from place to place. traveller.

trawler (trawlers) A kind of fishing-boat.

tray (trays) A flat board with raised edges, used for carrying things.

treacherous False, disloyal, not to be trusted. treacherously, treachery.

treacle A thick sticky liquid made from sugar. treacly.

tread¹ (treads) 1. A sound of walking. 2. The part of a tyre with the pattern cut into it that touches the road.

tread² (treads, treading, trod, trodden) To walk, to put one's foot on the ground somewhere. *Who has trodden on my best geraniums?*

treason Treachery towards one's own country. treasonable.

treasure¹ (treasures) 1. A store of money or valuable things. 2. Something or somebody that is highly valued.

treasure² (treasures, treasuring, treasured) 1. To value highly. 2. To store.

treasury (treasuries) A storehouse for valuables.

treat¹ (treats, treating, treated) 1. To behave in a certain way towards somebody or something. *He treats his dog cruelly.* 2. To give medical attention to somebody. 3. To deal with something in a particular way. *This bicycle should be treated for rust.* 4. To pay for food and drink for somebody. *I'll treat you all to ices.* treatment.

treat² (treats) 1. Something that gives unusual pleasure. 2. An entertainment or outing that gives someone pleasure.

treaty (treaties) An agreement between nations. *A peace treaty.*

treble¹ Three times as much, three times as many.

treble² (trebles) 1. A boy with a high singing voice. 2. *A treble recorder*, a medium-sized recorder.

tree (trees) A large plant with a single wooden trunk. treeless.

trek¹ (treks, trekking, trekked) To make a long and exhausting journey.

trek² (treks) A long and exhausting journey.

trellis (trellises) A criss-cross structure used to support climbing plants.

tremble (trembles, trembling, trembled) To shake, to shudder.

tremendous Enormous, great. tremendously.

tremor (tremors) A shaking, a vibrating.

trench (trenches) A long, narrow hole in the ground, a ditch.

trend (trends) The general direction in which something is going.

trendy (trendier, trendiest) (informal) Following the trend of fashion, fashionable. trendily.

trepidation Anxiety, alarm.

trespass¹ (trespasses) (old-fashioned) A sin.

trespass² (trespasses, trespassing, trespassed) To go into another person's property without permission. trespasser.

tress (tresses) A lock of hair.

trestle table A table consisting of boards laid on movable supports called trestles.

trial (trials) 1. The trying of someone or something. 2. *On trial*, being tried.

triangle (triangles) 1. A shape with three straight sides and three angles. triangular. 2. A percussion instrument.

tribe (tribes) A society of people living together ruled by a chief. tribal, tribesman.

tribulation (tribulations) A trouble, a difficulty.

tributary (tributaries) A river which flows into another river.

tribute (tributes) Something which is said, or done, or given, to show respect or admiration.

trick¹ (tricks) 1. Something done in order to deceive someone or make him look foolish. 2. A clever way of doing something. 3. The cards played in a round of whist or other games. trickery.

trick² (tricks, tricking, tricked) To deceive someone with a trick.

trickle (trickles, trickling, trickled) To flow slowly or thinly.

tricky (trickier, trickiest) 1. Cunning. 2. Skilful. 3. Difficult. trickily.

tricycle (tricycles) A three-wheeled vehicle worked by pedals.

tried, trier *See* try[1].

trifle (trifles) 1. A sweet dish of custard, cream, pieces of cake, jam, and other ingredients. 2. Something of almost no importance. 3. A small amount.

trifling Unimportant.

trigger (triggers) The lever which fires a gun.

trim[1] Neat and tidy.

trim[2] (trims, trimming, trimmed) 1. To make something trim by cutting away what is unwanted. 2. To decorate. *A hat trimmed with feathers.* 3. To balance the weight of the contents of a boat or aircraft.

Trinity *The Holy Trinity*, God regarded as Father, Son, and Holy Spirit.

trio (trios) A group of three.

trip[1] (trips, tripping, tripped) 1. To stumble. 2. To move with light steps.

trip[2] (trips) 1. A fall. 2. A journey, an excursion. tripper.

tripe 1. Part of the stomach of an ox used as food. 2. (informal) Nonsense.

triple Having three parts.

triplet (triplets) One of three children born to the same mother at one time.

tripod (tripods) A stand or support with three legs.

triumph[1] (triumphs) 1. A victory, a great success. 2. Triumphing. triumphal, triumphant, triumphantly.

triumph[2] (triumphs, triumphing, triumphed) 1. To have a triumph. 2. To celebrate a triumph.

trivial Not important. trivially, triviality.

trod, trodden *See* tread[2].

troll (trolls) An unpleasant supernatural creature in folk tales.

trolley (trolleys) 1. A small vehicle to be pushed or pulled by hand. 2. A small table on wheels.

trolley-bus (trolley-buses) An electric bus which gets its power from overhead wires.

trombone (trombones) A large brass instrument. trombonist.

troop[1] (troops) 1. A group of people. 2. A company of scouts. 3. *Troops*, soldiers.

troop[2] (troops, trooping, trooped) To move along in large numbers.

trophy (trophies) 1. A prize. 2. A souvenir of a victory or success.

tropics The hot regions of the world on either side of the equator. tropical.

trot (trots, trotting, trotted) To move along at a pace between a walk and a gallop.

trouble[1] (troubles) 1. Difficulty, grief, worry. 2. Disturbance, discontent. 3. Illness. *Heart trouble.* 4. *To take trouble*, to take great care over something.

trouble[2] (troubles, troubling, troubled) 1. To cause trouble. 2. To take trouble.

troublesome Causing trouble.

trough (troughs) A long, narrow box for animals to feed or drink from.

trousers A garment with two legs, worn over the lower part of the body. *A pair of trousers.*

trousseau (trousseaux) A collection of clothing for a bride.

trout (trout) A freshwater fish.

trowel (trowels) 1. A tool for digging small holes. 2. A tool for laying mortar in building.

truant (truants) A child who stays away from school without a proper excuse. *To play truant*, to be a truant. truancy.

truce (truces) An agreement to stop fighting for a time.

truck (trucks) 1. A lorry, a goods vehicle. 2. A railway wagon. 3. A barrow, a trolley.

trudge (trudges, trudging, trudged) To walk with tired, heavy steps.

true (truer, truest) 1. Correct, in agreement with the facts. *A true story.* 2. Loyal, honourable, faithful. *A true friend.* 3. Real, proper, normal, genuine. **4.** Exact, accurate, perfectly adjusted. **truly.**

trumpet[1] (trumpets) A brass instrument. **trumpeter.**

trumpet[2] (trumpets, trumpeting, trumpeted) To make a sound like a trumpet.

truncheon (truncheons) A short club as carried by policemen.

trundle (trundles, trundling, trundled) To roll along noisily or awkwardly.

trunk (trunks) **1.** The main stem of a tree. **2.** The main part of a human body. **3.** A large case for use when travelling. **4.** An elephant's long nose. **5.** *Trunks*, shorts. **6.** *A trunk call*, a long-distance telephone call. **7.** *A trunk road*, a main road.

trust[1] (trusts, trusting, trusted) **1.** To believe in the goodness, or strength, or truth of someone or something. **2.** *To trust someone with something*, to allow him to look after it. **3.** To hope. *I trust you are well?* **ingly.**

trust[2] **1.** The feeling that someone or something can be trusted. **2.** Responsibility. *To be in a position of trust.* **3.** *To take something on trust*, to believe it without having proof. **trustful, trustfully, trustfulness.**

trustworthy Reliable, deserving to be trusted.

trusty (old-fashioned) Trustworthy.

truth (truths) Whatever is true, something that is true. **truthful, truthfully, truthfulness.**

try[1] (tries, trying, tried) **1.** To attempt something, to make an effort to do it. **2.** To test something, to use something in order to find out what it is like. **3.** To examine the case against an accused person in a law-court. **4.** To annoy. **trier.**

try[2] (tries) **1.** An attempt. **2.** In Rugby football, a touch-down which scores points.

T-shirt (T-shirts) A garment like a vest with short sleeves.

tub (tubs) A round container.

tuba (tubas) A large, deep-sounding brass instrument.

tubby (tubbier, tubbiest) Short and fat.

tube (tubes) **1.** A hollow length of metal, rubber, plastic, or other material, such as is used to carry water or gas. **2.** A container for such things as toothpaste. **3.** An underground railway in London.

tubular bells A musical instrument with tube-shaped bells.

tuberculosis A serious disease of the lungs or other parts of the body.

tuck (tucks, tucking, tucked) **1.** To push the loose end of something into a secure or tidy position. *Jamie tucked his shirt into his trousers.* **2.** *To tuck someone up*, to tuck the bed-clothes round him comfortably. **3.** (informal) *To tuck in*, to eat heartily.

Tuesday (Tuesdays) The third day of the week.

tuft (tufts) A bunch of things growing together.

tug[1] (tugs) **1.** A sudden pull. **2.** A vessel designed for towing ships.

tug[2] (tugs, tugging, tugged) To pull hard.

tuition Teaching.

tulip (tulips) A kind of flower which grows from a bulb.

tumble (tumbles, tumbling, tumbled) To fall.

tumble-down Almost in ruins.

tumbler (tumblers) A flat-bottomed drinking glass.

tummy (tummies) (informal) The stomach.

tumult (tumults) An uproar, a confused disturbance. **tumultuous.**

tuna (tuna *or* tunas) A large sea-fish.

tune[1] (tunes) **1.** A series of notes which make a pleasant and memorable pattern of sound. **tuneful, tunefully. 2.** *In tune*, at the correct pitch. *Out of tune*, not in tune.

tune[2] (tunes, tuning, tuned) **1.** To put an

instrument in tune. **tuner.** 2. To adjust a radio for the best reception of a particular programme.

tuning-fork (tuning-forks) A forked piece of metal which when struck sounds a particular note.

tunic (tunics) 1. A kind of jacket like those worn by policemen and members of the armed services. 2. A loose garment hanging from the shoulders to below the waist.

tunnel[1] (tunnels) An underground passage.

tunnel[2] (tunnels, tunnelling, tunnelled) To make a tunnel.

turban (turbans) A covering for the head made by wrapping a length of cloth round it.

turbine (turbines) A kind of engine which is operated by a jet of gas, or steam, or water.

turbot (turbot *or* turbots) A sea fish.

turbulent Violent, disorderly. **turbulently, turbulence.**

turf (turves) A layer of earth with grass growing on it.

Turk (Turks) A Turkish person.

turkey (turkeys) A large bird kept for eating.

Turkish Of Turkey.

turmoil Confusion, commotion.

turn[1] (turns, turning, turned) 1. To move round as a wheel does. 2. To go round a corner. 3. To move and face a new direction. 4. To become. *She turned pale. The frog turned into a handsome prince.* 5. To cause something to turn. 6. To control something by means of a switch, knob, or tap. *Please turn the radio on.* 7. *To turn something down,* to refuse it. 8. *To turn out,* to happen, to be. *How did it all turn out in the end?* 9. *To turn someone out,* to send him away, to expel him. 10. *To turn out one's pockets,* to empty them. 11. *To turn up,* to come, to arrive.

turn[2] (turns) 1. Turning, the act of turning. 2. The proper time for one person in a group to do something. *It's Robert's turn to bowl next, then John's, then Alan's.* 3. (informal) An unpleasant surprise. 4. An

attack of an illness. 5. *A good turn,* a helpful action.

turnip (turnips) A kind of root vegetable.

turnstile (turnstiles) A kind of gate which turns and allows one person through at a time.

turntable (turntables) The part of a record-player on which the record turns.

turpentine or **turps** A liquid used for thinning paint.

turquoise Greenish-blue.

turret (turrets) 1. A small tower. 2. A revolving shelter for guns.

turtle (turtles) 1. A sea animal with a hard shell. 2. *To turn turtle,* to capsize.

tusk (tusks) A long pointed tooth such as those of the elephant or walrus.

tussle (tussles) A fight.

tutor (tutors) A teacher.

twaddle (informal) Nonsense.

twang (twangs, twanging, twanged) To make the sound as of a tight string being pulled and suddenly released.

tweed (tweeds) A woven woollen cloth.

tweezers A tool for picking up or gripping small objects. *A pair of tweezers.*

twelve (twelves) The number 12. **twelfth.**

twenty (twenties) The number 20. **twentieth.**

twerp (twerps) (informal) A silly fool.

twice Two times.

twiddle (twiddles, twiddling, twiddled) To turn something aimlessly in the hand.

twig (twigs) A small piece of a branch of a tree.

twilight The dim light between day and night.

twin (twins) 1. One of two children born to the same mother at one time. 2. One of two things exactly alike. *Twin beds.*

twine Thin strong string.

twinge (twinges) A sudden sharp pain.

twinkle (twinkles, twinkling, twinkled) To sparkle.

twirl (twirls, twirling, twirled) To turn round and round.

twist[1] (twists, twisting, twisted) 1. To turn something round. *He twisted her arm behind her back.* 2. To turn things round each other. *To twist wires together.* 3. To turn and curve. *The road twisted up the mountain.* 4. To change something into an unnatural or abnormal shape. *The twisted wreckage of his bicycle.*

twist[2] (twists) A twisting, a turning round.

twitch[1] (twitches, twitching, twitched) To jerk.

twitch[2] (twitches) A jerk.

twitter (twitters, twittering, twittered) To chirp continuously.

two (twos) The number 2.

tying *See* tie[1].

type[1] (types) 1. An example of something, one of a group of people or things with certain characteristics in common. *A peppermint is a type of sweet.* 2. A set or class of people or things with certain characteristics in common.

type[2] (types, typing, typed) To write with a typewriter. typist.

typewriter (typewriters) A machine with a keyboard for printing letters on paper.

typhoid A fever which affects the intestines.

typhoon (typhoons) A violent windy storm.

typhus A serious kind of fever.

typical Belonging to a certain type, normal, usual. typically.

tyrannical Cruel, like a tyrant.

tyrant (tyrants) A harsh or cruel ruler who has absolute power.

tyre (tyres) 1. An air-filled rubber tube round a wheel. 2. A rim of steel or rubber round a wheel.

Uu

ubiquitous Found everywhere.

udder (udders) The part of a cow or goat from which milk is drawn.

ugly (uglier, ugliest) 1. Unpleasant to look at. 2. Threatening. ugliness.

ulcer (ulcers) A kind of sore.

ultimate Last, final. ultimately.

ultimatum (ultimatums) A final demand, a last warning.

ultramarine Bright blue.

umbrage *To take umbrage,* to be offended.

umbrella (umbrellas) A folding framework covered with fabric, used to keep the rain off the person who carries it.

umpire (umpires) A referee in certain games.

unable Not able.

unaccountable Not able to be explained.

unaccustomed Not accustomed, unusual.

unanimous With everyone completely in agreement. unanimously, unanimity.

unannounced 1. Without being announced. 2. Without warning.

unanswerable Not able to be answered.

unarmed Without weapons.

unassuming Modest.

unattended Not being looked after.

unauthorized Not authorized.

unavoidable Not able to be avoided.

unaware Not aware.

unawares Unexpectedly.

unbalanced 1. Not balanced. 2. Not sane.

unbearable Not endurable. unbearably.

unbeaten Not defeated.

unbecoming Not attractive, not suitable.

unbend (unbends, unbending, unbent) 1. To straighten. 2. To relax.

unbending Firm, not yielding.

unbiased Not biased.

unbounded Not limited.

uncalled-for Not needed, not wanted.

uncanny Unnatural, mysterious. uncannily.

unceasing Continuous. unceasingly.

uncertain 1. Changeable, not reliable. 2. Not certain. uncertainly, uncertainty.

unchangeable Not able to be changed.

uncharitable Severe, harsh. uncharitably.

uncharted Not explored, not mapped.

uncivilized Not civilized, primitive.

uncle (uncles) 1. A brother of one's father or mother. 2. The husband of one's aunt.

unclean Not clean, dirty.

unclothed Naked.

unclouded 1. Not clouded. 2. Not gloomy.

uncomfortable Not comfortable.

uncommon Rare, unusual, remarkable. uncommonly.

uncomplimentary Not complimentary, not flattering.

unconcerned Not concerned, not worried, not caring.

unconditional Without conditions. unconditionally.

unconfirmed Not confirmed, not proved.

unconscious 1. Not conscious. 2. Not aware. unconsciously, unconsciousness.

uncouth Awkward, rough, bad-mannered.

uncover (uncovers, uncovering, uncovered) To take the cover off something, to reveal it.

uncut Not cut, not trimmed.

undamaged Not damaged.

undaunted Not discouraged, not dismayed.

undecided Not decided, not certain.

undeniable Not to be denied. undeniably.

under This word has many meanings including the following: 1. Beneath, lower than. *Under the table.* 2. Covered by. *Under water.* 3. Less than. *Children under 5 years old.* 4. In the process of, during. *Road under construction.* 5. Possessing, using. *He went under the name of Sanders.* 6. Subject to, obeying. *The troops were under the command of Wellington.*

underarm *To bowl underarm,* to bowl without raising the arm above the shoulder.

undercarriage (undercarriages) The wheels and landing gear of an aeroplane.

underclothes or underclothing Clothing worn under dresses, skirts, trousers, or other outer garments.

under-developed Not yet fully developed.

underdog (underdogs) A poor and helpless person, somebody who is oppressed.

underdone Not cooked thoroughly.

underestimate (underestimates, underestimating, underestimated) To form too low an estimate of somebody or something.

underfed Having had too little food.

underfoot On the ground, where one is going to walk.

undergarment (undergarments) An article of underclothing.

undergo (undergoes, undergoing, underwent, undergone) To experience something, to suffer it.

undergraduate (undergraduates) A student at a university who has not yet taken a degree.

underground[1] 1. Below the ground. 2. Secret.

underground[2] (undergrounds) An underground railway.

undergrowth Shrubs and bushes growing beneath tall trees.

underhand Secret, deceitful.

underline (underlines, underlining, underlined) 1. To draw a line under a word. 2. To emphasize.

undermine (undermines, undermining, undermined) To dig away at the bottom of something, to weaken it gradually.

underneath Under.

underpaid Not paid enough.

underpass (underpasses) A place where one road passes under another.

underrate (underrates, underrating, underrated) To underestimate.

underside (undersides) The lower side of something.

undersized Of less than the normal size.

understand (understands, understanding, understood) 1. To know the meaning of something, to know what it is or how it works. 2. To learn something, to get an impression from what is said or done. *I understand the field is too wet for games today.* understandable, understandably.

understanding[1] 1. The power to think clearly, intelligence. 2. An agreement. 3. Consideration, sympathy.

understanding[2] Sympathetic.

understudy (understudies) An actor who learns another actor's part so that he can take his place if necessary.

undertake (undertakes, undertaking, undertook, undertaken) To make oneself responsible for something, to start to do it.

undertaker (undertakers) A person whose business it is to arrange funerals.

undertone (undertones) A quiet tone.

underwear Underclothes.

underwent *See* undergo.

underworld 1. The place of the dead in legends. 2. The world of criminals.

undesirable Unwelcome, not wanted.

undeveloped Not developed.

undid *See* undo.

undistinguished Not special in any way.

undo (undoes, undoing, undid, undone) 1. To untie or unfasten something. 2. To get rid of the results of something.

undone 1. Not done. 2. Unfastened.

undoubted Certain. undoubtedly.

undress (undresses, undressing, undressed) To take off the clothes.

undue More than is right and proper. unduly.

undying Everlasting.

unearned 1. Not earned. 2. Not deserved.

unearth (unearths, unearthing, unearthed) 1. To dig up something buried. 2. To discover something, to bring it into view.

unearthly 1. Supernatural. 2. Very strange.

uneasy Anxious, uncomfortable. uneasily, uneasiness.

unemployed Not having a job, not working. unemployment.

unequal Not equal. unequally.

unerring Absolutely accurate. unerringly.

uneven Not even, not level, not regular. unevenly.

unexpected Not expected, surprising. unexpectedly.

unfailing Never failing, always reliable. unfailingly.

unfair Not fair, unjust. unfairly, unfairness.

unfaithful Not faithful. unfaithfully, unfaithfulness.

unfamiliar 1. Not well known. *Unfamiliar surroundings.* 2. Not having knowledge about something. *I am unfamiliar with this district.*

unfasten (unfastens, unfastening, unfastened) To open fastenings, to unlock.

unfeeling Hard-hearted. unfeelingly.

unfinished Not finished.

unfit Not fit, not suitable.

unflagging Not becoming tired.

unfold (unfolds, unfolding, unfolded) To open out.

unforeseen Unexpected.

unforgettable Not able to be forgotten.

unforgiveable Not to be forgiven.

unfortunate Not fortunate, unhappy, unlucky. unfortunately.

unfreeze (unfreezes, unfreezing, unfroze, unfrozen) To change back into a normal condition after being frozen.

unfurl (unfurls, unfurling, unfurled) To unroll, to spread out.

ungainly Clumsy, not graceful.

ungrateful Not grateful. ungratefully.

ungrudging Not grudging, generous. ungrudgingly.

unguarded 1. Not guarded. 2. Not discreet.

unhappy (unhappier, unhappiest) Not happy, sad. unhappily, unhappiness.

unharmed Not harmed, safe.

unhealthy (unhealthier, unhealthiest) Not healthy. unhealthily, unhealthiness.

unheard-of Extraordinary, not known before.

unicorn (unicorns) A mythical creature rather like a horse with a long straight horn.

uniform[1] The same. uniformly, uniformity.

uniform[2] (uniforms) An official style of clothes worn by members of an organization or pupils of a school.

unify (unifies, unifying, unified) To make into one. unification.

unimportant Not important.

unintelligible Not able to be understood. unintelligibly.

uninterrupted Without interruptions.

uninvited Without being invited.

union (unions) 1. Uniting or being united. 2. An association of workers. *A trade union.*

Union Jack The British flag.

unique Being the only one of its kind.

unison *In unison*, exactly together.

unit (units) 1. A single thing. 2. A group of things that belong together. *A kitchen unit.* 3. A quantity or amount used as a basis for measuring or counting. A metre is a unit of length, a dollar a unit of money. 4. An organized group of people and their equipment. *An army unit.*

unite (unites, uniting, united) To join together, to make one or to become one.

unity 1. Being united, being one. 2. Harmony, agreement.

universal Concerning everything and everybody, general. universally.

universe Everything that exists, the whole of space and everything in it.

university (universities) A college or group of colleges where people study for degrees.

unjust Not fair, not just. unjustly.

unkempt Untidy.

unkind Not kind, rather cruel. unkindly.

unless If not.

unlike Not like, different from. unlikely.

unload (unloads, unloading, unloaded) To remove a load from something.

unlock (unlocks, unlocking, unlocked) To open a lock.

unlucky (unluckier, unluckiest) Not lucky, unfortunate. unluckily.

unmentionable Not to be mentioned.

unmistakable Clear, free from doubt. unmistakably.

unnatural Not natural, artificial. unnaturally.

unnecessary Not necessary. unnecessarily.

unoccupied Not occupied.

unpack (unpacks, unpacking, unpacked) To take out things which have been packed.

unpleasant Not pleasant, disagreeable. unpleasantly, unpleasantness.

unpopular Not popular, disliked. unpopularity.

unpromising Not showing promise.

unqualified Not qualified.

unquestionable Beyond doubt. unquestionably.

unravel (unravels, unravelling, unravelled) To disentangle.

unreadable Not able to be read.

unreal Imaginary, not like real life. unreality.

unreasonable Not reasonable. unreasonably.

unrest Disturbance, discontent.

unrestricted Not restricted.

unrivalled Without close rivals.

unroll (unrolls, unrolling, unrolled) To undo something that has been rolled up.

unruly Not easily controlled, badly behaved.

unsaid Not spoken, not expressed.

unsavoury Disgusting.

unscathed Not injured, not harmed.

unscrew (unscrews, unscrewing, unscrewed)

To undo something that has been screwed up.

unscrupulous Not having a conscience, wicked. **unscrupulously.**

unseal (unseals, unsealing, unsealed) To undo something that has been sealed.

unseemly Not proper, not decent.

unseen Not seen, invisible.

unselfish Not selfish. **unselfishly.**

unsettle (unsettles, unsettling, unsettled) To make somebody troubled or uncertain.

unsightly Ugly.

unsound Not in good condition, not reliable.

unsteady Not steady. **unsteadily.**

unstuck Not stuck, not fastened.

unsuspected Not suspected.

unthinkable Not to be considered.

untidy Not tidy. **untidily.**

untie (unties, untying, untied) To undo something which has been tied.

until Up to the time when.

untimely Happening at an unsuitable time.

untiring Without tiring.

untold Not able to be counted.

untouched Not touched.

untrue Not true.

untruth (untruths) A lie.

untwist (untwists, untwisting, untwisted) To straighten something twisted.

unusual Not usual, rare. **unusually.**

unutterable Not able to be described. **unutterably.**

unwanted Not wanted.

unwary Not cautious. **unwarily.**

unwelcome Not welcome. **unwelcoming.**

unwell Ill.

unwieldy Awkward to handle.

unwilling Not willing. **unwillingly, unwillingness.**

unwind (unwinds, unwinding, unwound) To unroll.

unwise Not wise, foolish. **unwisely.**

unwonted Unusual.

unworthy Not worthy. **unworthiness.**

unwrap (unwraps, unwrapping, unwrapped) To take something out of its wrapping.

unwritten Not written.

unyielding Not yielding.

unzip (unzips, unzipping, unzipped) To undo a zip-fastener.

up This word has many uses including the following: **1.** To a vertical or standing position, in a vertical or standing position. *To stand up.* **2.** To a higher place or condition. *To climb up.* **3.** In a high place. *We live up in the hills.* **4.** Thoroughly, completely. *Eat your potatoes up.* **5.** More energetically. *Play up!* **6.** Out of bed, dressed and ready. *He isn't up yet.* **7.** *Your time is up!* your time is finished. **8.** *Up to,* until. *We have up to the end of the month to finish our work.* **9.** *Not up to much,* not worth much, not very good. **10.** *It is up to us,* we are the people who must do it. **11.** (informal) *What's up?* what is happening? **12.** *What have you been up to?* what have you been doing?

upheaval (upheavals) A violent change or disturbance.

uphill 1. Up a slope. **2.** Difficult. *We shall have an uphill task.*

uphold (upholds, upholding, upheld) To support.

upholstery The padding and covers of chairs and other furniture.

upkeep The cost of keeping something in good repair.

upland (uplands) An area of country high above sea-level.

upon On.

upper Higher.

uppermost Highest.

upright 1. Vertical, erect. **2.** Honest.

uproar (uproars) A noisy disturbance. **uproarious, uproariously.**

uproot (uproots, uprooting, uprooted) To pull something up by the roots.

upset (upsets, upsetting, upset) **1.** To overturn, to tip over. **2.** To trouble, to disturb, to offend.

upside-down 1. With the bottom at the top. **2.** Untidily arranged.

upstairs 1. To a higher floor in a building.
2. On a higher floor.

up-to-date Modern.

upward or **upwards** Towards a higher position.

uranium A valuable metal used as a source of atomic energy.

urban Belonging to a city or large town.

urchin (urchins) A rough boy.

urge[1] (urges, urging, urged) 1. To drive someone or something onwards. 2. To persuade or ask vigorously.

urge[2] (urges) A strong desire.

urgent To be done at once, needing immediate attention. **urgently, urgency.**

urine The waste liquid passed from the body.

urn (urns) 1. A metal container with a tap, used for hot drinks. 2. A kind of vase.

us *See* **we.**

usable Able to be used.

use[1] (uses, using, used) 1. To employ something for some purpose, to do something with it. *I used my new pen to write the letter.* 2. *To use up*, to consume. *We may soon use up our stock of fuel.* 3. *To be used to something*, to know it well, to experience it regularly. **user.**

use[2] (uses) 1. Using, being used. *Out of use*, not being used. 2. The purpose or value of something. *What use is that strange tool?*

useful Helpful, capable, producing good results. **usefully, usefulness.**

useless Not useful. **uselessly, uselessness.**

usher (ushers) A person who shows people to their seats in a theatre or other public place.

usherette (usherettes) A female usher, especially in a cinema.

usual Normal, customary, such as happens frequently or repeatedly. **usually.**

utensil (utensils) A tool, an instrument, a dish or pan. *Kitchen utensils.*

utilize (utilizes, utilizing, utilized) To make use of something.

utmost Farthest, greatest.

utter[1] Complete, total. *Utter darkness.*

utter[2] (utters, uttering, uttered) To speak. **utterance.**

Vv

V 5 in Roman numerals.

vacant Empty, unoccupied. **vacantly, vacancy.**

vacation (vacations) 1. A holiday. 2. A period between terms at a university or college.

vaccinate (vaccinates, vaccinating, vaccinated) To inoculate someone against smallpox. **vaccination.**

vaccine (vaccines) A substance used for inoculations.

vacuum An absolutely empty space, a space without any air in it.

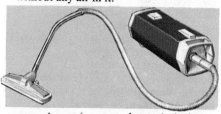

vacuum-cleaner (vacuum-cleaners) A cleaner which sucks up dirt and dust.

vacuum-flask (vacuum-flasks) A flask used to keep hot liquids hot and cold ones cold.

vagabond (vagabonds) A tramp.

vagrant (vagrants) A tramp, a wanderer.

vague (vaguer, vaguest) Not clear, not certain. **vaguely, vagueness.**

vain (vainer, vainest) 1. Proud and conceited. 2. Unsuccessful, useless. *In vain*, without useful result. **vainly.**

vale (vales) (old-fashioned) A valley.

Valentine card A card sent to one's sweetheart on St. Valentine's Day, 14th February.

valiant Brave. **valiantly.**

valid Legally acceptable, usable. *This ticket is valid for three months.*

valley (valleys) A stretch of lower land between hills.

valour Bravery.

valuable Of great value.

valuables Valuable things.

value[1] 1. The amount of money that would or should be given for something. 2. The importance, or usefulness, or worth of something. valueless.

value[2] (values, valuing, valued) To regard something highly, to think of it as very good.

valve (valves) 1. An electronic device used in radios and other equipment. 2. A device for controlling the flow of liquid or gas.

vampire (vampires) In legends, a spirit or creature that sucks blood.

van (vans) A vehicle for carrying goods. *A baker's van.*

vandal (vandals) A person who deliberately destroys or spoils things. vandalism.

vanguard (vanguards) The troops at the front of an advancing army.

vanilla A flavouring used for ice-cream and other foods.

vanish (vanishes, vanishing, vanished) To disappear.

vanity Conceit, pride in oneself.

vanquish (vanquishes, vanquishing, vanquished) To defeat, to conquer.

vaporize (vaporizes, vaporizing, vaporized) To turn into vapour.

vapour (vapours) Steam, mist, or some other gas-like substance into which a liquid is changed by heat.

variable Varying, changeable. variably, variability.

variation (variations) 1. Varying. 2. Something that has been altered.

varied Of various sorts.

variety (varieties) 1. Change, absence of sameness. *A dull life has no variety.* 2. A number of different things. *There was a variety to choose from.* 3. A different kind of something. *There are many rare varieties of butterflies on the island.* 4. *A variety show*, a kind of entertainment including short musical and comic items.

various 1. Different. 2. Several.

varnish (varnishes) A clear liquid used like paint to give a hard, shiny surface.

vary (varies, varying, varied) To be different, to alter, to change.

vase (vases) A jar or vessel used as an ornament or to hold cut flowers.

vast Very large. vastly, vastness.

vat (vats) A very large container for liquids.

vault[1] (vaults) 1. An arched roof. 2. An underground room. 3. A jump made by vaulting.

vault[2] (vaults, vaulting, vaulted) To jump over something with the help of the hands or a pole.

veal Meat from a calf.

veer (veers, veering, veered) To turn, to change direction.

vegetable (vegetables) A plant, especially a plant used as a food.

vegetarian (vegetarians) A person who does not eat meat.

vegetation Plants of all kinds.

vehement Strong, eager, violent. vehemently, vehemence.

vehicle (vehicles) A device for carrying people or things. Cars, lorries, carts, and sledges are vehicles.

veil (veils) A thin cloth used to cover something.

vein (veins) 1. One of the tubes in the body through which the blood flows back to the heart. 2. A line in a leaf, or in a piece of rock, or in the wing of an insect.

velocity Speed.

velvet A kind of thick soft material used for curtains and dresses. velvety.

vendetta (vendettas) A quarrel between families in which murders are committed in revenge for other murders.

veneer (veneers) A thin layer of valuable wood used to cover cheaper wood.

venerable Old, worthy of respect.

vengeance 1. Revenge. 2. *With a vengeance,* strongly, thoroughly.

venison Meat from deer.

venom The poison from snakes and other poisonous animals.

venomous Deadly, poisonous. venomously.

vent (vents) A hole or slit in something.

ventilate (ventilates, ventilating, ventilated) To allow air freely in and out. ventilator, ventilation.

ventriloquist (ventriloquists) An entertainer who seems to be able to make a dummy speak. ventriloquism.

venture[1] (ventures) An adventurous undertaking.

venture[2] (ventures, venturing, ventured) To risk, to dare.

veranda (verandas) An open space with a floor and a roof along one side of a house.

verb (verbs) A word which indicates what someone or something does or experiences. Jane *ran* to school. James *feels* tired. The medicine *made* John better.

verdict (verdicts) The decision reached by a jury at the end of a trial.

verge (verges) An edge, a border.

verger (vergers) A caretaker of a church.

verify (verifies, verifying, verified) To show the truth of something.

vermilion Bright red.

vermin 1. Harmful wild creatures such as rats and mice. 2. Creatures such as fleas and lice which live on people or animals.

verruca (verrucas) A kind of wart.

versatile Skilful in many ways. versatility.

verse (verses) 1. A piece of writing consisting of rhymed lines, poetry. 2. A group of rhymed lines in a song or poem. 3. One of the numbered parts of a chapter of the Bible.

version (versions) 1. A particular account of something. *John's version of the quarrel is different from Timothy's.* 2. A particular translation of something. *The Authorized Version of the Bible.* 3. A particular way in which something is made.

versus Against.

vertebra (vertebrae) One of the bones which make up the backbone.

vertical Straight up and down, upright. vertically.

very 1. Most, extremely. *Very small.* 2. That one and no other. *That's the very thing!*

vessel (vessels) 1. A receptacle, a container. Cups, bottles, and basins are vessels. 2. A ship, a boat.

vest (vests) An undergarment worn on the upper part of the body.

vestige A small trace of something.

vestry (vestries) The room in a church where the clergyman or choir prepare for services.

vet (vets) A person trained to look after the health of animals.

veteran (veterans) A person who has had long experience in something.

veto[1] (vetoes) A statement forbidding something.

veto[2] (vetoes, vetoing, vetoed) To forbid.

vex (vexes, vexing, vexed) To annoy, to trouble. vexation.

via By way of.

viaduct (viaducts) A long bridge with many arches carrying a road or railway.

vibrate (vibrates, vibrating, vibrated) To move rapidly to and fro, to throb, to quiver. **vibration.**

vicar (vicars) A clergyman in charge of a parish.

vicarage (vicarages) A vicar's house.

vice[1] (vices) 1. Evil, wickedness. 2. A fault, a wicked habit.

vice[2] (vices) An apparatus attached to a workbench for holding things steady.

vice-captain (vice-captains) A person who may do the job of the captain when necessary.

vice-president (vice-presidents) The man next in authority under the president.

vice versa The other way round. *We hate them and vice versa*, we hate them and they hate us.

vicinity The surrounding area, the neighbourhood.

vicious Spiteful, evil, wicked. **viciously, viciousness.**

victim (victims) A person who suffers death, injury, hardship, or loss.

victimize (victimizes, victimizing, victimized) To treat someone unjustly. **victimization.**

victor (victors) The winner.

Victorian Belonging to the reign of Queen Victoria.

victory (victories) Success in a battle or competition. **victorious, victoriously.**

video tape Tape used to record television programmes.

view[1] (views) 1. A scene, something to be looked at. *What a lovely view of the mountains!* 2. A sight, a look. *We had a good view*, we were able to see clearly. 3. *In view, on view*, able to be seen. 4. An opinion. *What is your view on this problem?* 5. An intention. *With a view to*, in order to.

view[2] (views, viewing, viewed) To look at something, to consider it. **viewer.**

vigilant Watchful. **vigilantly, vigilance.**

vigour Strength, energy. **vigorous, vigorously.**

Viking (Vikings) A Scandinavian seafarer of the early Middle Ages.

vile Shameful, disgusting.

villa (villas) 1. A kind of house. 2. A country house in Roman times.

village (villages) A group of houses and other buildings in a country area. A village is smaller than a town. **villager.**

villain (villains) A wrongdoer, a scoundrel. **villainous, villainously, villainy.**

vindictive Spiteful, determined on revenge. **vindictively.**

vine (vines) A climbing plant that bears grapes.

vinegar A sour liquid used to flavour food.

vineyard (vineyards) An area of land planted with vines.

vinyl A kind of plastic.

viola (violas) A stringed instrument slightly larger than a violin.

violate (violates, violating, violated) 1. To break a law or a promise. 2. To break in upon something. *To violate someone's privacy.* **violation.**

violent Having great force, intense, causing harm. **violently, violence.**

violet[1] Purple.

violet[2] (violets) A small purple or white flower.

violin (violins) A stringed instrument played with a bow. **violinist.**

viper (vipers) A kind of poisonous snake, an adder.

virgin[1] (virgins) A maiden, a person who has not mated.

virgin[2] Pure, untouched, unused.

virile Manly.

virtually (informal) As good as, almost. *This coat is virtually new.*

virtue (virtues) 1. Goodness. 2. Any particular kind of goodness such as honesty, kindness, or justice. **virtuous, virtuously.**

virtuoso (virtuosi) A highly skilled musician. **virtuosity.**

virus (viruses) A living thing, too small to be seen even through a microscope, which can cause disease.

visa (visas) An official mark on a passport

giving permission for a person to enter or leave a certain country.

visible Able to be seen. **visibly, visibility.**

vision (visions) 1. Sight. 2. Imagination, understanding. 3. A dream.

visit[1] (visits, visiting, visited) 1. To go to see some person or place. 2. To stay somewhere for a while. **visitor.**

visit[2] (visits) 1. The act of visiting. 2. Time spent visiting.

visor (visors) The part of a helmet that closes over the face.

vista (vistas) A view.

visual To do with seeing. *Visual aids*, pictures and diagrams used by teachers.

visualize (visualizes, visualizing, visualized) To imagine.

vital Essential to life, extremely important. *It is vital to get food quickly to the flooded areas.* **vitally.**

vitality Energy.

vitamin (vitamins) A chemical substance present in certain types of food. Vitamins are essential to health.

vivacious Lively, gay. **vivaciously, vivacity.**

vivid Bright, lively, clear. **vividly.**

vivisection The performing of scientific experiments on living animals.

vixen (vixens) A female fox.

vocabulary (vocabularies) 1. A list of words. 2. *A person's vocabulary*, all the words he knows.

vocal To do with the voice, spoken or sung.

vocalist (vocalists) A singer.

vodka A strong alcoholic drink.

vogue Fashion, popularity.

voice (voices) 1. The sound of speaking or singing. *I heard her voice in the next room.* 2. The power to speak or sing. *He lost his voice when he was ill.* **voiceless.**

void[1] Empty. *Void of*, without.

void[2] (voids) An empty space, a vacuum.

volcano (volcanoes) A mountain with an opening through which molten lava, gases, and ash sometimes flow.

vole (voles) An animal like a small rat.

volley (volleys) 1. A shower of missiles. 2. In tennis, the hitting back of a ball before it bounces.

volley-ball A game in which a large ball is thrown over a net.

volt (volts) A unit for measuring electricity. **voltage.**

volume (volumes) 1. The amount of space occupied by a substance, a liquid, or a gas. 2. A quantity or amount of something. *Volumes of smoke poured from the chimney.* 3. The amount of sound produced by a radio set or other apparatus. *Turn up the volume.* 4. A book.

voluntary Done willingly. **voluntarily.**

volunteer[1] (volunteers) A person who offers to do something of his own free will.

volunteer[2] (volunteers, volunteering, volunteered) 1. To offer oneself as a volunteer. 2. To offer something voluntarily.

vomit (vomits, vomiting, vomited) To be sick.

vote[1] (votes, voting, voted) To show one's preference for someone or something by putting a mark on paper, by raising one's hand, or by making some other sign. **voter.**

vote[2] (votes) The act of voting.

voucher (vouchers) A kind of ticket or receipt.

vow[1] (vows) A solemn promise.

vow[2] (vows, vowing, vowed) To make a vow.

vowel (vowels) Any of the letters, a, e, i, o, u.

voyage (voyages) A journey in a ship.

vulgar Rude, ill-mannered. **vulgarly, vulgarity.**

vulnerable Easily attacked, easily wounded, easily damaged.

vulture (vultures) A large bird that feeds on dead animals.

Ww

wad (wads) A pad of soft material.

waddle (waddles, waddling, waddled) To walk like a duck.

wade (wades, wading, waded) To walk through water.

wafer (wafers) A kind of light biscuit sometimes eaten with ice-cream.

wag (wags, wagging, wagged) To move briskly from side to side or up and down.

wage¹ (wages) Money received regularly for doing work. wage-earner.

wage² (wages, waging, waged) *To wage war*, to fight a war.

wager (wagers) A bet.

waggle (waggles, waggling, waggled) To wag.

wagon (wagons) 1. An open railway truck. 2. A four-wheeled vehicle pulled by horses or oxen.

wagtail (wagtails) A kind of bird with a long tail.

wail¹ (wails, wailing, wailed) To cry, to howl, to complain loudly.

wail² (wails) A wailing cry, a complaint.

waist (waists) The part of the body between the hips and the ribs.

waistcoat (waistcoats) A thin sleeveless coat worn under a jacket.

wait¹ (waits, waiting, waited) 1. To remain in a place or to delay doing something until an expected event happens. 2. To act as a waiter.

wait² (waits) 1. A time spent waiting. 2. *To lie in wait*, to hide ready to attack.

waiter (waiters) A person who brings food to the tables in a restaurant. waitress.

waiting-room (waiting-rooms) A room for people to wait in.

wake¹ (wakes, waking, woke, waked, woken) 1. To cease sleeping. 2. To arouse somebody from sleep.

wake² (wakes) The track left by a ship in the water.

wakeful Unable to sleep.

walk¹ (walks, walking, walked) To move on foot at an ordinary speed. walker.

walk² (walks) 1. A journey on foot. 2. A way of walking. 3. *A walk of life*, a job, a profession.

walkie-talkie (walkie-talkies) (informal) A portable radio telephone.

walking-stick (walking-sticks) A stick used by a person when walking.

walk-over (informal) An easy victory.

wall¹ (walls) An upright structure of brick, stone, or other material such as that which forms the side of a house.

wall² (walls, walling, walled) To surround something with a wall. *A walled garden.*

wallaby (wallabies) A kind of small kangaroo.

wallet (wallets) A pocket case for money and papers.

wallflower (wallflowers) A sweet-smelling garden plant.

wallow (wallows, wallowing, wallowed) To roll about in mud or water.

wallpaper (wallpapers) Paper used to cover the walls of rooms.

walnut (walnuts) A kind of nut.

walrus (walruses) A large sea animal with two long tusks.

waltz (waltzes) A kind of dance.

wan Sad, pale, ill-looking. wanly.

wand (wands) A thin rod. *A magic wand.*

wander (wanders, wandering, wandered) 1. To go about with no particular purpose in mind. 2. To stray from one's proper route. wanderer.

wane (wanes, waning, waned) To become less.

wangle (wangles, wangling, wangled) (informal) To get something by tricks or special persuasion.

want¹ (wants, wanting, wanted) 1. To need something, to require it. 2. To wish for something, to desire it. 3. To be without, to lack.

want² (wants) 1. A lack, a shortage. 2. A need. *In want of money.*

wanton 1. Playful. 2. Irresponsible, done without reason. *Wanton damage.*

war (wars) 1. Fighting between armies or nations. 2. Any serious struggle.

warble (warbles, warbling, warbled) To sing.

warbler (warblers) A kind of small bird.

war-cry (war-cries) A shout made before and during battle.

ward[1] (wards) 1. A room for patients in a hospital. 2. A child under the protection of a guardian.

ward[2] (wards, warding, warded) *To ward something off*, to keep it away.

warden (wardens) 1. A person in charge of a hostel or other institution. 2. A person with certain kinds of official duties. *A traffic warden.*

warder (warders) A guard in a prison, a gaoler.

wardrobe (wardrobes) A cupboard to hang clothes in.

warehouse (warehouses) A large building used for storing goods.

wares Goods for sale.

warfare Making war, fighting.

war-head (war-heads) The explosive end of a torpedo or missile.

warily, wariness *See* wary.

warlike Ready for war, fond of war.

warm[1] (warmer, warmest) 1. Fairly hot. 2. Enthusiastic, affectionate. warmly, warmth.

warm[2] (warms, warming, warmed) 1. To make something warm. 2. To become warm.

warm-hearted Loving, kind.

warn (warns, warning, warned) To tell somebody about a danger, to give advance notice about something.

warning (warnings) Something that warns.

warp (warps, warping, warped) To bend or twist out of the proper shape.

war-path *On the war-path*, ready and eager to fight.

warrant (warrants) An official document giving someone the right to do something.

warren (warrens) A place where there are many rabbit burrows.

warring At war, fighting.

warrior (warriors) A soldier, a fighting man.

warship (warships) A ship for use in war.

wart (warts) A small hard growth on the skin.

wary (warier, wariest) Watchful, cautious. warily, wariness.

was *See* be.

wash[1] (washes, washing, washed) 1. To make a thing clean in water. 2. *To wash up*, to wash the dishes after a meal. 3. To be carried along by moving water. *The sailor was washed overboard.* 4. To flow against or over something. *The waves washed against the pier.*

wash[2] 1. The act of washing. 2. Things to be washed, washing. 3. The waves which spread out behind a moving ship.

washable Able to be washed safely.

washer (washers) A ring of rubber, fibre, or metal.

washing Clothes to be washed, or being washed, or which have just been washed.

wasn't (informal) Was not.

wasp (wasps) A kind of flying insect with a sting.

wastage (wastages) An amount wasted or lost.

waste[1] 1. Thrown away, used up. *Waste paper.* 2. Not cultivated, not in use. *Waste land.* 3. *To lay waste*, to destroy buildings or crops.

waste[2] Anything waste or wasted. wasteful, wastefully.

waste[3] (wastes, wasting, wasted) 1. To use something up with no result, to use too much of something, to let something become valueless by not using it. 2. To lose strength. *To waste away*, to become weaker.

watch[1] (watches, watching, watched) 1. To look at something carefully for some time. 2. To look out for something, to be on guard. watcher.

watch[2] (watches) 1. The act of watching. 2. A period of duty on a ship. watchful, watchfully, watchfulness.

watch[3] (watches) An instrument worn on the wrist or carried in the pocket for telling the time.

watchman (watchmen) A person employed as a guard at night.

water[1] The transparent, colourless liquid found in rivers and seas.

water[2] (waters, watering, watered) 1. To sprinkle water on seeds or growing plants. **watering-can.** 2. To give water to an animal to drink. 3. To fill with water. *My eyes are watering.*

water-closet (water-closets) A lavatory flushed by water.

water-colour (water-colours) A kind of paint for mixing with water.

watercress A plant used in salads.

waterfall (waterfalls) A fall of water where a stream or river flows over a cliff or big rock.

water-lily (water-lilies) A kind of flowering plant with broad leaves floating on the surface of water.

waterlogged Thoroughly soaked or filled with water.

water-main (water-mains) A thick pipe supplying water.

water-polo A ball game played by swimmers.

waterproof Not allowing water to pass through.

watertight Waterproof.

waterway (waterways) A channel along which ships or boats may pass.

waterworks The machinery and buildings by which water is supplied to a town.

watery Wet, full of water, containing too much water.

watt (watts) A unit of electrical power.

wave[1] (waves, waving, waved) 1. To move one's hand up and down, or to and fro. 2. To move up and down, or to and fro. *Trees waving in the breeze.* 3. To put waves or curls into hair.

wave[2] (waves) 1. A ridge of water, especially

one in the sea that curls and breaks on the shore. 2. Something curved like a wave. 3. The act of waving.

waver (wavers, wavering, wavered) 1. To move unsteadily. 2. To be undecided. **waverer.**

wavy (wavier, waviest) Having waves or curves.

wax A substance which melts easily into an oily liquid. It is used for making candles and various kinds of polish.

waxworks An exhibition of lifelike models of people in wax.

way (ways) 1. A road, street, lane, path, or passage. 2. A route, a direction, a journey. 3. Progress. *Under way,* moving. 4. A method, a series of actions leading to a particular result. *That's not the way to tie a reef-knot.* 5. Normal behaviour. *It's Susan's way to be generous.* 6. A state, a condition. *Things are in a bad way.*

wayfarer (wayfarers) A traveller.

waylay (waylays, waylaying, waylaid) 1. To stop somebody and rob him. 2. To stop somebody and speak to him.

wayside (waysides) The side of a road.

we (us, ourselves) A word used by a person when referring to himself and the others with him.

weak (weaker, weakest) Feeble, fragile, not strong. **weakly, weakness.**

weaken (weakens, weakening, weakened) 1. To become weaker. 2. To make weaker.

weakling (weaklings) A feeble person.

wealth Riches.

wealthy (wealthier, wealthiest) Rich. **wealthiness.**

weapon (weapons) An instrument used in fighting.

wear[1] (wears, wearing, wore, worn) 1. To have something on one's body, to be dressed in it. 2. To have something attached to one's clothes. *She wore a brooch on her dress.* 3. To cause damage by constant use or rubbing. *My penknife has worn a hole in my pocket.* 4. To last. *Good clothes wear* *well.* **5.** *To wear out,* to become useless after use. **6.** *To wear someone out,* to make him exhausted. **7.** *To wear off,* to become less. *The pain will soon wear off.*

wear[2] Damage from continued use. *Fair wear and tear,* normal damage from use.

weary (wearier, weariest) Tired. **wearily, weariness.**

weasel (weasels) A small fierce animal with a long, slender body.

weather[1] The conditions of sunshine, temperature, wind, and rain at a particular time. *Stormy weather. Fine weather.*

weather[2] (weathers, weathering, weathered) **1.** To come through some difficulty successfully. *To weather the storm.* **2.** *Weathered,* worn by exposure to the weather.

weather-beaten Worn or tanned by exposure to the weather.

weave (weaves, weaving, wove, woven) **1.** To make threads into cloth on a loom. **weaver.** **2.** To move with many twists and turns.

web (webs) A net of fine threads spun by a spider.

web-footed Having the toes joined by pieces of skin.

wed (weds, wedding, wed, wedded) To marry.

we'd (informal) **1.** We would. **2.** We had.

wedding (weddings) A marriage ceremony. **wedding-cake, wedding-ring.**

wedge[1] (wedges) A V-shaped object.

wedge[2] (wedges, wedging, wedged) **1.** To fix something with a wedge. **2.** To push something into position so that it remains firm.

Wednesday (Wednesdays) The fourth day of the week.

wee (Scottish) Small.

weed[1] (weeds) A wild plant growing where it is not wanted. **weed-killer.**

weed[2] (weeds, weeding, weeded) To remove weeds.

weedy (weedier, weediest) **1.** Full of weeds. **2.** Thin, feeble, weak.

week (weeks) **1.** Seven days from Sunday to Saturday. **2.** Any period of seven days.

week-day (week-days) Any day except Sunday.

week-end (week-ends) Saturday and Sunday.

weekly 1. Once a week. **2.** Lasting a week.

weep (weeps, weeping, wept) To cry, to shed tears.

weevil (weevils) A kind of small beetle.

weigh (weighs, weighing, weighed) **1.** To measure the heaviness of something by the use of scales or some other means. **weighing-machine. 2.** To have a certain heaviness. *Your parcel weighed three kilograms.* **3.** *To weigh anchor,* to lift the anchor and sail away. **4.** *To weigh something up,* to consider it. **5.** *To weigh something down,* to keep it down with weights. **6.** *To weigh somebody down,* to make him distressed, troubled, or anxious.

weight (weights) **1.** The heaviness of something, the amount it weighs. **2.** A piece of metal of exactly measured heaviness used on scales. **3.** A heavy object. **weightless.**

weighty (weightier, weightiest) **1.** Heavy. **2.** Important.

weir (weirs) A dam or barrier across a river to control the flow of water.

weird (weirder, weirdest) Unnatural, strange. **weirdly.**

welcome[1] **1.** Received with pleasure, giving pleasure. *A welcome visit.* **2.** *Welcome to,* allowed to, free to. *You are welcome to borrow my bicycle.*

welcome[2] (welcomes) A greeting.

welcome[3] (welcomes, welcoming, welcomed) To show pleasure at the arrival of somebody or something.

weld (welds, welding, welded) To join two pieces of metal together by heat and pressure.

welfare People's health and happiness. *A welfare officer,* an official concerned with people's welfare.

well[1] (wells) A deep hole dug or drilled to obtain water or oil from under ground.

well[2] (better, best) **1.** In a good, right, or satisfactory manner. **2.** In good health.

3. Indeed. *You may well be surprised.* **4.** *To wish someone well*, to wish him good luck. **5.** *Well-being*, health and happiness. **6.** *Well-bred*, well brought up. **7.** *Well off*, rich, fortunate. **8.** *Well-to-do*, rich.

we'll (informal) **1.** We shall. **2.** We will.

wellingtons Knee-length rubber boots.

Welsh Of Wales.

went *See* **go.**

wept *See* **weep.**

were *See* **be.**

we're (informal) We are.

weren't (informal) Were not.

west 1. One of the points of the compass, the direction in which the sun sets. **2.** From the west. *The west wind.* **westerly. 3.** In the west. *The west coast.* **western. 4.** Towards the west. *Sailing west.* **westward, westwards.**

western (westerns) A cowboy film.

wet[1] (wetter, wettest) **1.** Covered or soaked in water or other liquid. **2.** *Wet weather*, rainy weather. **3.** *Wet paint*, paint not yet dry. **wetness.**

wet[2] (wets, wetting, wet, wetted) To make something become wet.

whack (whacks, whacking, whacked) To hit something with a stick.

whale (whales) A kind of large sea animal.

whaler (whalers) A ship or person that hunts whales.

wharf (wharfs) A platform at the edge of the water where ships are loaded or unloaded.

what This word is used in several kinds of sentence including the following: **1.** In questions. *What is the time, please?* **2.** In exclamations. *What a lovely day!* **3.** In pointing something out. *Show me what you have done.*

whatever 1. No matter what. *Whatever happens, don't speak a word.* **2.** Anything that. *Do whatever you like.*

wheat 1. A cereal plant. **2.** Its seed, used for making flour.

wheel[1] (wheels) A circular framework or disc which turns on an axle. *A bicycle wheel.*

wheel[2] (wheels, wheeling, wheeled) **1.** To move something on wheels. **2.** To move in a curve.

wheelbarrow (wheelbarrows) A small cart with one wheel and a pair of handles.

wheel-chair (wheel-chairs) An invalid's chair on wheels.

wheeze[1] (wheezes, wheezing, wheezed) To make a gasping, whistling noise while breathing.

wheeze[2] A sound of wheezing. **wheezy.**

whelk (whelks) A kind of shellfish.

when 1. At what time or times. *When can you come?* **2.** What time. *Since when have you been able to speak French?* **3.** Since, considering that. *How can we perform well when no one comes to rehearsals?*

whenever At whatever time, every time. *Come and see us whenever you are passing. Whenever it rains, the water comes in.*

where 1. What place, in what place, to what place. *Where are they? Tell me where they are.* **2.** In the place in which. *My spectacles were just where I left them.*

whereabouts In or near what place.

whereupon After which.

wherever In or to whatever place.

whether If.

whey The watery part of sour milk.

which This word is used in several kinds of sentence including the following: **1.** In questions. *Which way did he go?* **2.** In pointing something out. *I don't know which to choose. This is the one which I like best.*

whichever 1. The one which. *Take whichever you like.* **2.** No matter which. *Whichever you choose, you will be happy.*

whiff (whiffs) A slight smell of something.

while[1] 1. During the time that. *I finished my tea while you were getting ready.* 2. Although, but.

while[2] (whiles) A period of time. *A long while ago.*

while[3] (whiles, whiling, whiled) To pass time. *We whiled away the time on the river.*

whilst While.

whim (whims) A sudden impulse to do something.

whimper (whimpers, whimpering, whimpered) To make weak crying sounds.

whine[1] (whines) A long complaining cry, a continuous high-pitched sound.

whine[2] (whines, whining, whined) To make a whine.

whinny (whinnies, whinnying, whinnied) To make a noise like a horse.

whip[1] (whips) A cord or strip of leather attached to a handle.

whip[2] (whips, whipping, whipped) 1. To beat with a whip. 2. To beat cream until it is stiff. 3. To move or do something suddenly. *James whipped out his pistol.*

whippet (whippets) A kind of small greyhound.

whirl[1] (whirls, whirling, whirled) To move rapidly round and round, to turn quickly.

whirl[2] (whirls) A whirling movement.

whirlpool (whirlpools) A place in a sea or river where the water whirls round.

whirlwind (whirlwinds) A violent wind that blows in a spiral.

whisk[1] (whisks) A device for beating eggs or other foods.

whisk[2] (whisks, whisking, whisked) 1. To beat eggs or other foods. 2. To move briskly.

whisker (whiskers) Hair or bristles growing on the face.

whisky A strong alcoholic drink.

whisper[1] (whispers, whispering, whispered) To speak in a special quiet way, to talk secretly.

whisper[2] (whispers) A whispering voice.

whist A card game.

whistle[1] (whistles, whistling, whistled) 1. To make a musical or shrill sound by blowing air through the lips. 2. To make a similar sound by some other means.

whistle[2] (whistles) 1. The sound of whistling. 2. An instrument which makes the sound of whistling.

white[1] A colour, the colour of fresh snow.

white[2] (whiter, whitest) White in colour. *White-hot*, intensely hot. whiteness.

whiten (whitens, whitening, whitened) 1. To make white. 2. To become white.

whitewash A liquid used to whiten walls and ceilings.

whiting (whitings) A sea fish.

whitish Rather white.

Whit Sunday or Whitsun The seventh Sunday after Easter.

whiz (whizzes, whizzing, whizzed) 1. To make a noise like something rushing through the air. 2. To rush noisily.

who (whom) Which person. *Who did that? It was the man whom I saw yesterday.*

whoever Whatever person.

whole[1] 1. Complete, entire. *Rowland ate the whole cake.* 2. In one piece, unbroken. *The snake swallowed the rabbit whole.*

whole[2] (wholes) 1. A complete thing. *Two halves make a whole.* 2. *On the whole,* considering everything, in general. wholly.

wholemeal Flour from which no part of the grain has been removed.

wholesale 1. The selling of goods in large quantities to shopkeepers who then sell them in much smaller quantities to customers. 2. On a large scale, extensive. *Wholesale destruction.*

wholesome Favourable to health.

who'll (informal) Who will.

whom *See* who.

whoop (whoops) A loud cry.

whooping-cough A disease accompanied by a gasping cough.

who's (informal) Who is. *Who's coming out?*

whose Of whom, of which. *Whose coat is this?*

why For what reason. *Why did you do that? Tell me why you did that.*

wick (wicks) The thread or strip of material which one lights in a candle or oil-lamp.

wicked Bad, spiteful, naughty. **wickedly, wickedness.**

wickerwork Things made from woven reeds or canes.

wicket (wickets) 1. The three stumps at which the ball is bowled in cricket. 2. The strip of grass between the two wickets.

wicket-keeper (wicket-keepers) The fielder who stands behind the wicket.

wide (wider, widest) 1. Measuring from side to side. *The road is 9 metres wide.* 2. Broad. *A wide river.* 3. Fully. *Wide awake.* 4. Away from the target. *My shot went wide.* **widely.**

widen (widens, widening, widened) 1. To make wider. 2. To become wider.

widespread Found in many places, common.

widow (widows) A woman whose husband has died.

widower (widowers) A man whose wife has died.

width (widths) Breadth, the distance from one side of something to the opposite side.

wield (wields, wielding, wielded) To hold and use something.

wife (wives) A married woman.

wig (wigs) A head-covering of false hair.

wiggle (wiggles, wiggling, wiggled) To move with quick side-to-side movements.

wigwam (wigwams) An American Indian hut or tent.

wild (wilder, wildest) 1. Living in the free and natural way, not tamed. *Wild animals.* 2. Not cultivated, not inhabited. *Wild country.* 3. Violent. *A wild storm.* 4. Reckless, excited. *Wild behaviour.* **wildly, wildness.**

wilderness (wildernesses) A desert, a stretch of wild country.

wile (wiles) A cunning trick. **wily, wiliness.**

wilful 1. Obstinate. 2. Intentional, deliberate. **wilfully.**

will[1] (would) A word used in sentences which refer to the future. *They will arrive at tea-time tomorrow. They said they would come.*

will[2] 1. The power of a person's mind, the strength of his determination. **will-power.** 2. A desire or determination.

will[3] (wills) A document stating what a person wishes to be done with his property after his death.

will[4] (wills, willing, willed) 1. To desire. 2. To try to control something by will-power.

willing Ready to help, ready to do what is needed. **willingly, willingness.**

willow (willows) A kind of tree with thin, easily-bent branches.

wilt (wilts, wilting, wilted) To droop, to become limp.

wily (wilier, wiliest) Crafty, cunning.

win[1] (wins, winning, won) 1. To come first in a race, game, or competition. 2. To be victorious in a war or battle. 3. To be successful in gaining something. **winner.**

win[2] (wins) A victory.

wince (winces, wincing, winced) To make a movement or expression of pain.

winch (winches) A device for pulling or lifting things by means of a rope wound on a cylinder.

wind[1] (winds) 1. A steady movement of air, a current of air. **windless.** 2. Gas in the stomach. *Baby has got wind.*

wind[2] (winds, winding, wound) 1. To move or go in twists or curves. *The road wound up the mountain.* 2. To twist something round and round to make a ball or a coil. *The cotton is wound on a reel.* 3. To turn a handle or key round and round. *Don't forget to wind your watch.*

wind[3] (winds) A turn, a twist.

wind-cheater (wind-cheaters) A jacket which keeps the wind out.

winded Out of breath.

windfall (windfalls) 1. A fruit blown down from a tree. 2. A piece of unexpected good fortune.

wind instrument A musical instrument in which the sounds are produced by blowing.

windjammer (windjammers) A large sailing-ship.

windmill (windmills) A mill whose power comes from the wind.

window (windows) An opening in a wall, usually filled with a pane of glass.

window-box (window-boxes) A box on a window-sill to grow flowers in.

window-sill (window-sills) The shelf along the bottom of a window.

windpipe (windpipes) A tube in the body from the mouth to the lungs.

windscreen (windscreens) The window in front of the driver of a car or other vehicle.

windward The side of a ship or island towards the wind.

windy (windier, windiest) 1. With a strong wind. *Windy weather.* 2. Exposed to the wind. *A windy place.* windily.

wine (wines) An alcoholic drink made from grapes or other fruits. wine-glass.

wing (wings) 1. One of the parts of the body by which a bird or insect flies. *On the wing*, flying. 2. One of the flat surfaces which support an aircraft in the air. 3. A part of a building, not the main part. *The north wing.* 4. One of the parts of a motor car which cover the wheels. 5. A player in football or other games whose position is at one side of the pitch.

wink¹ (winks, winking, winked) 1. To close and open an eye. 2. To shine unsteadily, to flash on and off. winker.

wink² (winks) The act of winking.

winkle (winkles) A kind of shellfish.

winnings Money won by gambling.

winter (winters) The cold season between autumn and spring. wintry.

wipe (wipes, wiping, wiped) 1. To clean or dry something by rubbing it. wiper. 2. *To wipe out*, to destroy completely.

wire¹ (wires) 1. Metal drawn out into a long thin rod or thread. 2. A telegram.

wire² (wires, wiring, wired) 1. To fasten with wire. 2. To fit electrical wiring to something.

wireless (wirelesses) Radio.

wiring A system of wires carrying electricity.

wiry (wirier, wiriest) 1. Like wire. 2. Lean and strong.

wisdom The quality of being wise.

wise (wiser, wisest) Having understanding, good judgment, and much knowledge. wisely.

wish¹ (wishes, wishing, wished) 1. To desire, to want, to long for something. 2. To say that one hopes something for somebody. *We wish you a merry Christmas.* 3. To say or think what one would like to happen.

wish² (wishes) 1. A desire, a longing. 2. The act of wishing.

wish-bone (wish-bones) A V-shaped bone from a chicken.

wishful thinking Unreal thinking based on wishes, not on facts.

wisp (wisps) A thin, untidy bundle or piece. *A wisp of hair.* wispy.

wistful Rather sad, as if longing for something. wistfully.

wit (wits) 1. Intelligence, quickness, cleverness. 2. Witty talk. 3. A witty person.

witch (witches) A woman who uses magic for evil purposes.

witchcraft Sorcery, the arts of the witch and the wizard.

witch-doctor (witch-doctors) A male witch among primitive peoples.

with This word has many meanings including

the following: **1.** Having. *A house with tall chimneys.* **2.** Accompanied by. *Come with me.* **3.** Against. *St. George fought with the dragon.* **4.** By means of. *He wrote it with a pen.* **5.** Because of. *I was stiff with cold.* **6.** Concerning. *Be patient with us.*

withdraw (withdraws, withdrawing, withdrew, withdrawn) **1.** To take away something or somebody. **2.** To move back from somewhere, to retreat. **withdrawal.**

wither (withers, withering, withered) To become dry and shrivelled.

withhold (withholds, withholding, withheld) To keep something back.

within Inside.

without Free from, not having. *I like my chips without vinegar.*

withstand (withstands, withstanding, withstood) To resist.

witness[1] (witnesses) **1.** A person who sees something happen. **2.** A person who gives evidence in a court of law.

witness[2] (witnesses, witnessing, witnessed) To see something happen.

witty (wittier, wittiest) Clever and amusing. **wittily.**

wizard (wizards) A magician, a male witch. **wizardry.**

wizened Dried up, shrivelled.

woad A kind of blue dye.

wobble (wobbles, wobbling, wobbled) To move unsteadily from side to side.

woe (woes) Sorrow, grief, distress. **woeful, woefully.**

woke, woken *See* **wake**[1].

wolf (wolves) A fierce wild animal of the dog family.

woman (women) A grown-up female human being.

womb (wombs) The organ in a female body where a baby develops before it is born.

won *See* **win**[1].

wonder[1] (wonders) **1.** A feeling of surprise and admiration. **2.** Something that causes a feeling of surprise and admiration. **wonderful, wonderfully.**

wonder[2] (wonders, wondering, wondered) **1.** To be filled with wonder. **2.** To be curious, to ask oneself. *I wonder what that means.*

won't (informal) Will not.

woo (woos, wooing, wooed) To try to win the love of somebody. **wooer.**

wood (woods) **1.** The hard substance of a tree under the bark. **2.** An area of land where trees grow.

wooded Covered with trees.

wooden 1. Made of wood. **2.** Stiff. **woodenly.**

woodland Wooded country.

wood-louse (wood-lice) A small insect-like creature.

woodman (woodmen) A man who works in a forest.

woodpecker (woodpeckers) A bird that taps trees with its beak to find food.

woodshed (woodsheds) A shed for storing wood cut for fuel.

woodwind Those wind instruments of an orchestra which can be made of wood.

woodwork 1. Carpentry, making things with wood. **2.** Things made of wood.

woodworm (woodworms) A kind of beetle that bores into wood.

woody (woodier, woodiest) **1.** Covered with trees. **2.** Like wood.

wool 1. The soft hair of sheep and some other animals. **2.** Thread or cloth made from this hair.

woollen Made of wool.

woollens Clothes made of wool.

woolly (woollier, woolliest) **1.** Covered in wool. **2.** Made of wool. **3.** Like wool. **4.** Vague, confused. **woolliness.**

word[1] (words) **1.** One of the units that make up language. This sentence contains five words. **2.** Something that is said. *Don't say a word to your mother about this.* **3.** A promise. *I give you my word it won't happen again.* **4.** An order. *Fire when I give the word.*

word[2] (words, wording, worded) To put something into words.

wordy (wordier, wordiest) Using too many words.

wore *See* wear[1].

work[1] (works) 1. An action which needs effort or energy. *Digging the garden is hard work.* 2. Something that has to be done, a person's employment. *Mum has work to do in the house. Has Dad gone to work yet?* 3. Something produced by work. *Teacher wants to see our work when we have finished.* 4. *Works,* the moving parts of a machine.

work[2] (works, working, worked) 1. To do work. worker. 2. To act or operate in the intended way. *Is the lift working?* 3. To succeed. *Will the idea work?* 4. To make somebody or something work. *Our new teacher works us very hard. Do you know how to work the lift?* 5. *To work loose,* to become loose gradually. 6. *To work out,* to calculate.

workable Practicable.

workbench (workbenches) A bench where people do carpentry or other jobs.

working (workings) 1. The way something works. 2. A mine or quarry.

workman (workmen) A working man.

workmanship A person's skill in doing his work.

workshop (workshops) A place where things are made or repaired.

world (worlds) 1. The earth, its countries and peoples. 2. Some part of the earth or its peoples. *The English-speaking world.* 3. The universe.

worldly Concerned with money or status.

worm[1] (worms) A kind of long, thin wriggling creature which lives in the soil.

worm[2] (worms, worming, wormed) To move by crawling or wriggling.

worm-eaten Eaten by worms or grubs.

worn *See* wear[1].

worry[1] (worries, worrying, worried) 1. To trouble someone, to cause anxiety. 2. To be uneasy, to be anxious. 3. To seize and shake something with the teeth. *The dog was worrying his bone.*

worry[2] (worries) 1. Being worried. 2. Something that worries somebody.

worse *See* bad.

worsen (worsens, worsening, worsened) 1. To become worse. 2. To make worse.

worship[1] 1. Reverence, honour and respect to God. 2. Great respect and admiration paid to someone or something.

worship[2] (worships, worshipping, worshipped) To give worship. worshipper.

worst *See* bad.

worsted A kind of woollen cloth.

worth 1. Having a certain value. *This diamond is worth £200.* 2. The amount bought for a certain sum. *A pound's worth of flowers.* 3. Worthy of. *The castle is worth visiting.*

worthless Valueless.

worthwhile Important enough to do.

worthy 1. *Worthy of,* good enough for, deserving. *Worthy of praise.* 2. Respectable. *A worthy old woman.* worthily, worthiness.

would *See* will[1].

wound[1] *See* wind[2].

wound[2] (wounds) An injury to the body.

wound[3] (wounds, wounding, wounded) To give a wound to somebody.

wove, woven *See* weave.

wrangle (wrangles, wrangling, wrangled) To have a noisy argument.

wrap (wraps, wrapping, wrapped) To put a covering round something.

wrapper (wrappers) Something used for wrapping.

wrath Anger. wrathful, wrathfully.

wreath (weathes) Flowers or leaves woven into a ring.

wreck[1] (wrecks) 1. Ruin, destruction. 2. A wrecked ship, anything that has suffered ruin or destruction.

wreck[2] (wrecks, wrecking, wrecked) To cause the ruin or destruction of something. wrecker.

wreckage Pieces of a wreck.

wren (wrens) A small brown bird.

wrench[1] (wrenches) 1. A sudden or painful pull. 2. A tool for twisting nuts and pipes.

wrench[2] (wrenches, wrenching, wrenched) To pull or twist violently.

wrestle (wrestles, wrestling, wrestled) To fight by struggling and trying to throw an opponent down without hitting him. wrestler.

wretch (wretches) 1. An unfortunate or miserable person. 2. A rogue.

wretched 1. Feeling very uncomfortable or ill. 2. Poor in quality. wretchedly, wretchedness.

wriggle (wriggles, wriggling, wriggled) To move the body about with quick twists.

wring (wrings, wringing, wrung) 1. To twist something and squeeze it tightly. 2. To get the water out of something by wringing it. 3. *Wringing wet*, so wet that water may be wrung out.

wringer (wringers) A mangle.

wrinkle[1] (wrinkles) A small crease or line in the skin or in the surface of something.

wrinkle[2] (wrinkles, wrinkling, wrinkled) To form wrinkles.

wrist (wrists) The joint between the arm and the hand.

write (writes, writing, wrote, written) 1. To make letters and words on paper or some other surface. 2. To be the author or composer of something. 3. *To write to somebody*, to send a letter to him. writer.

writhe (writhes, writhing, writhed) To twist or roll about.

writing 1. The action of someone who writes. 2. Something written. 3. *Writings*, the works of an author.

wrong[1] 1. Not right, not just, not fair. *It is wrong to hurt animals*. 2. Not correct. *That answer is wrong*. 3. Not working properly. *My watch has gone wrong*. wrongly.

wrong[2] (wrongs) 1. Something that is wrong. wrongdoing, wrongdoer. 2. *To be in the wrong*, to be guilty of some fault.

wrong[3] (wrongs, wronging, wronged) To be unfair or unjust to somebody.

wrongful Illegal, not justified. wrongfully.

wrote *See* write.

wrung *See* wring.

wry Twisted out of shape. wryly.

Xx

X 10 in Roman numerals.

Xmas Christmas.

X-ray[1] (X-rays) A ray which can penetrate solid things.

X-ray[2] (X-rays, X-raying, X-rayed) To photograph the inside of someone or something by means of X-rays.

xylophone (xylophones) A percussion instrument.

Yy

yacht (yachts) 1. A sailing boat built for racing or cruising. 2. A private ship. yachtsman.

yachting Sailing in a yacht.

yap (yaps, yapping, yapped) To make short sharp barking sounds.

yard (yards) 1. A measure of length, 36 inches or about 91 centimetres. 2. An open space with a hard surface, surrounded by buildings and walls.

yarn (yarns) 1. Thread. 2. (informal) A story.

yawn[1] (yawns, yawning, yawned) 1. To open the mouth widely and breathe in deeply when tired or bored. 2. To be wide open.

yawn[2] (yawns) The act of yawning.

ye (old-fashioned) You.

year (years) A unit of time, twelve months. It takes one year for the earth to travel round the sun.

yearly Every year, once a year.

yearn (yearns, yearning, yearned) To long for something.

yeast A substance used in making bread, beer, and wine.

yell[1] (yells) A loud cry.

yell[2] (yells, yelling, yelled) To give a yell.

yellow[1] A colour, the colour of buttercups or lemons.

yellow[2] (yellower, yellowest) 1. Yellow in colour. 2. Cowardly.

yellowhammer (yellowhammers) A small bird with a yellow head and throat.

yellowish Rather yellow.

yelp (yelps, yelping, yelped) To make a shrill bark or cry.

Yeoman (Yeomen) *A Yeoman of the Guard*, a guard at the Tower of London.

yes A word used to show agreement or consent.

yesterday The day before today.

yet This word has many meanings including the following: 1. Up to this time. *Has the ice-cream man come yet?* 2. At some time in the future. *The gipsy said there were more dangers yet to come.* 3. Ever, still, again. *Jack found that the beanstalk had grown yet taller.* 4. Nevertheless. *He was in great pain, yet he played on.*

yew (yews) A kind of evergreen tree.

yield (yields, yielding, yielded) 1. To give in, to surrender. 2. To produce a crop. *These trees yield excellent pears.*

yodel (yodels, yodelling, yodelled) To produce a musical high-pitched call.

yoga A method of meditation and self control.

yogurt A type of food made from milk.

yoke (yokes) A curved bar put across the shoulders of oxen pulling a cart.

yokel (yokels) A simple-minded person from the country.

yolk (yolks) The yellow part of an egg.

yonder Over there.

you (yourself, yourselves) 1. The person or people being spoken to or written to. 2. Any person. *People say that you should not walk under ladders.*

young[1] (younger, youngest) Having lived or been in existence for a comparatively short time, not old.

young[2] Young people or young animals.

youngster (youngsters) A young person.

your or yours Belonging to you.

yourself, yourselves *See* you. These words are used in the same ways as himself.

youth[1] 1. Being young. 2. The early part of one's life. youthful.

youth[2] (youths) A young person. *A youth club*, a club for young people.

yule or yuletide Christmas.

Zz

zeal Enthusiasm, eagerness. zealous, zealously.

zebra (zebras) An animal like a horse with black and white stripes.

zebra crossing A place marked with black and white stripes for pedestrians to cross the road.

zero (zeros) 1. Nought, the figure 0. 2. *Zero hour*, the exact time at which a military operation is to begin.

zest Great enthusiasm.

zigzag[1] (zigzags) A line with many sharp turns like this ∧∧∧∧∧ .

zigzag[2] (zigzags, zigzagging, zigzagged) To move in a zigzag.

zinc A white metal.

zip (zips, zipping, zipped) To close something with a zip-fastener.

zip-fastener (zip-fasteners) A device with rows of small teeth for fastening two edges together.

zither (zithers) A stringed instrument played by plucking.

zodiac *The signs of the zodiac*, twelve areas of the sky frequently referred to in astrology.

zone (zones) An area.

zoo (zoos) A place where wild animals are kept for people to look at.

zoology The scientific study of animals. zoological, zoologist.

zoom (zooms, zooming, zoomed) 1. To fly suddenly upwards. 2. (informal) To move quickly.